The Diplomats

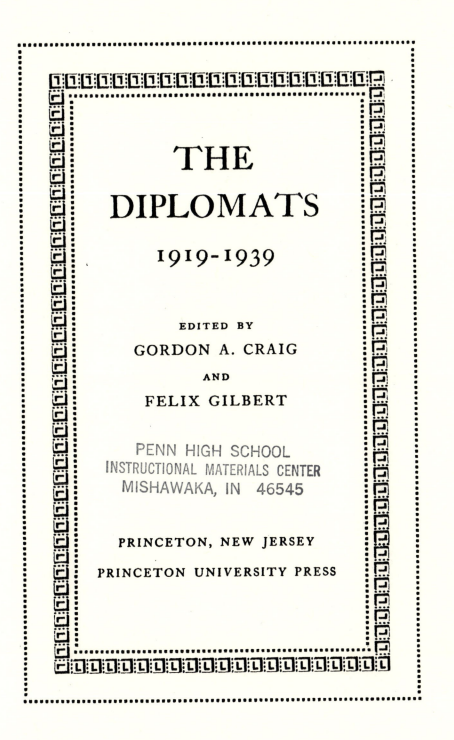

THE
DIPLOMATS

1919-1939

EDITED BY

GORDON A. CRAIG

AND

FELIX GILBERT

PRINCETON, NEW JERSEY

PRINCETON UNIVERSITY PRESS

Published by Princeton University Press, Princeton, New Jersey
In the United Kingdom by Princeton University Press, Chichester, West Sussex
Copyright © 1953 by Princeton University Press; copyright © 1981
renewed by Princeton University Press
All Rights Reserved

Library of Congress Card No. 53-6378

Princeton University Press books are printed
on acid-free paper and meet the guidelines
for permanence and durability of the Committee
on Production Guidelines for Book Longevity
of the Council on Library Resources

First Princeton Paperback printing, 1994

Printed in the United States of America

1   3   5   7   9   10   8   6   4   2

88131

To

Theodor Ernst Mommsen
and to the memory of
Frank Mansfield Craig, 1882-1952

ACKNOWLEDGMENTS

THE EDITORS and contributors wish to express their gratitude to:

Theodor Ernst Mommsen, for having first suggested to the editors the usefulness of a symposium on interwar diplomacy, and Datus C. Smith and Joseph R. Strayer for having seconded the suggestion so enthusiastically;

the Research Committee of Princeton University, the Rutgers University Research Council, the Board of Directors of the American Philosophical Society, and Edward F. D'Arms and the Board of Directors of the Rockefeller Foundation for grants in aid of research and assistance in meeting necessary travel and conference expenses;

Bernard C. Noble and Bernadotte Schmitt of the Division of Historical Policy Research, the Department of State, for permitting the use of certain papers bearing on the Japanese problem; the Swedish Foreign Office for allowing one of the contributors to have access to its files; and Herman Kahn, Director of the Franklin D. Roosevelt Library, Hyde Park, N.Y., for assistance and advice to several of the contributors;

Alexis Saint-Léger Léger and Joseph Clark Grew for their interest and counsel; and Walter Johnson and the Directors of Houghton Mifflin Company for having made available to the editors the proofs of Mr. Grew's *Turbulent Era: A Diplomatic Record of Forty Years*, which has now been published under the editorship of Professor Johnson;

Allen Macy Dulles, for information included in his unpublished Princeton B.A. thesis on the British Foreign Office; and Robert B. Glynn, for permitting the use of his unpublished Harvard honors thesis on Nevile Henderson;

Fred Aandahl, Gerald Aylmer, Cyril E. Black, Percy Corbett, Edward Mead Earle, Carl Hillger, Leonard Krieger, Philip Noel Buxton, E. S. Passant, Raymond J. Sontag, Jacob Viner, John W. Wheeler-Bennett and Sir Llewellyn Woodward for information and advice; and

Elizabeth D'Arcy and Mrs. Benton Schrader of Princeton, N.J., Joan Connolly of Bryn Mawr College, and Patricia and Gordon Decato of Keene, N.H. for typing, and retyping, the manuscript; and Harriet Anderson for seeing it through the press.

For the shortcomings of the book, none of the individuals or institutions mentioned above can be held accountable; but, if this volume makes any contribution to our knowledge of the recent past, they deserve much of the credit.

CONTENTS

Book One: The Twenties

CONTENTS
Book Two: The Thirties

ILLUSTRATIONS

In a 16-page inset, at the beginning of Book Two, the following diplomats and statesmen are represented:

The Diplomats

INTRODUCTION

THERE are few extended discussions of diplomacy in which the author does not, sooner or later, get around to quoting Sir Henry Wotton's definition of the diplomat as "an honest man sent to lie abroad for the good of his country," and it would be a pity to violate a tradition so firmly established. However hackneyed by use, this seventeenth century conceit does at least convey a sense of the atmosphere of suspicion which has always surrounded the diplomatic profession. It is not surprising that diplomats are the object of some distrust in the countries to which they are accredited. They are, after all, aliens, representing the interests and ambitions of their own nations, seeking information which will be of advantage to their own governments, and protected—as they pursue their not necessarily friendly activities—by international codes and conventions that transcend local law. But diplomats are apt also to encounter suspicion in their native lands and to discover that, among their fellow citizens, there are many who disapprove of men who spend most of their life abroad, or dwelling on affairs abroad, and who believe that facility in strange tongues and intimacy with foreign statesmen must lead inevitably to "secret deals" at the expense of the nation. In this atmosphere, the diplomat becomes a kind of wanderer between two worlds, in neither of which he is wholly accepted.

The intensity of the suspicion with which the diplomat is customarily regarded might be understandable if his role in the international politics of our time were more decisive than it obviously is. But the fact of the matter is that the age in which diplomats held the fate of nations in their hands lies definitely in the past; and, for the last century and more, their influence has been subject to a process of marked diminution.

I

Diplomacy, as we know it, had its origins in the period in which the modern sovereign state emerged in Europe—that is, the period from the sixteenth to the eighteenth century—and its forms and conventions still reflect the social and economic conditions of that age. The characteristic feature of the period in which diplomacy arose was the absolute state—the state which was governed by a ruler with virtually unlimited powers and which was, moreover, completely identified with the personality, the ambitions, and even the whims of that ruler. In the age

[3]

of absolutism, the men who were sent on missions abroad were in a real sense personal representatives of their prince and, during their tours of duty, they consorted exclusively with other princes or with royal representatives whose positions corresponded to their own. As trusted agents of their sovereign, they were given a high degree of freedom of action —a privilege which was in any case made necessary by the primitive state of long-distance communication—and they were expected to display judgment and initiative in the conduct of their sovereign's affairs. Their duties in this respect, however, were facilitated by the fact that the European states of this period were autarchical entities and that the factors that determined their international behavior and their intercourse with their neighbors—such things as political ambition, economic power, and military resources—were, or seemed to be, easily calculable. With the essential facts at their disposal, and provided further with such time-honored rules of thumb as *ragione di stato* and balance of power, the diplomats possessed a conceptual framework within which they could move with confidence.

The diplomatic practices and conventions which emerged in this situation persisted in the subsequent period, although the conditions that shaped them were profoundly altered. If the eighteenth century was the classical age of diplomacy, the nineteenth century marked the beginning of the process by which the diplomat's freedom was restricted and his functions transformed. Technical invention made communication between foreign capitals both easier and more rapid. The ambassador's long summary reports to his sovereign, carried by courier over dangerous routes and often arriving long after the described conditions had changed or the projected actions had been executed, were replaced by telegraphic dispatches and, eventually, by telephone conversations. When this happened, the age of the "great ambassadors," who were perforce policy-makers in their own right, was over. Only in the most remote regions was independent action along the line of eighteenth century diplomacy possible or necessary. The policies of the Great Powers were now closely controlled by the administrative agencies of the home governments, and the Foreign Offices in particular began to play an important role as the protectors of system and continuity in the conduct of foreign policy.

At the same time, the position of the diplomat was affected by the remarkable economic changes which were ushered in by the industrial revolution and the era of free trade. As intercourse between nations expanded in the private economic sphere, the number of people who could claim to be well-informed about conditions in countries other than their own increased; the monopolistic position of the diplomat was broken, and he became much more exposed to competition and criticism. Simultaneously, the nature of his functions changed and their scope was enlarged, for he was now expected to provide information on economic and military questions of the most highly technical nature. His staff grew in numbers and was divided into functional departments; he became increasingly dependent upon his experts; and, although he was still apt to regard diplomacy as an art which could, and should, be professed by a chosen few, this contention was patently contradicted by the facts of his daily existence.

But the most important change in the position of the diplomat was brought about by developments in the constitutional sphere, and, specifically, by the collapse of absolutism and the rise of democratic institutions. The spread of democracy and the growing belief in the necessity of democratic control of foreign policy challenged one of the characteristic features of traditional diplomacy: its secrecy. The secret character of diplomatic negotiation could not, of course, be lightly abandoned in deference to democratic sentiment, for all nations do not enjoy the same degree of political enlightenment, and practices which seem reprehensible to some are considered indispensable by others. Since negotiation is a process in which—if success is desired—some regard must be given to the conditions imposed by the opposite party, secret diplomacy did not disappear with the speed demanded by advocates of democratic control; and this fact in itself enhanced, in some countries, the suspicion with which diplomats were regarded. Nor was this the only respect in which the impact of democracy was felt. As governments became more dependent on the expressed wishes of the electorate, the whole concept of rational power calculation was jeopardized. What might seem to the diplomat's mind as a shrewd stroke of policy—a Hoare-Laval Pact, for instance—could be abruptly and indignantly rejected by an aroused public opinion; and, in consequence, the most difficult problem confronting the diplomat in the new age was that of reconciling reason of state with popular desire.

Finally, the emergence of democratic government undermined a basic assumption of the diplomatic profession: the idea, namely, that the diplomat was the personal representative of the sovereign. In large part, the prestige and the effective action of the diplomat depends upon the maintenance of this fiction; but the fact that it has been maintained, and with it the ceremonial, the punctilio, and the observance of social hierarchy and custom which the role involves, has strengthened

[5]

the popular impression that the diplomat is something of an anachronism, forming part of a social tradition that belongs to the past. In a world of ordinary citizens and forthright and industrious businessmen and workers, the diplomat seems to stand out as the man with top hat and monocle—as indeed he is, or was until recently, portrayed in neon tubing over a restaurant in the shadow of the old State Department building in Washington.

The contrast between the traditions of the diplomatic profession and the world of modern industrialism and democracy developed slowly throughout the nineteenth century. The first great climax in the conflict came with the outbreak of the first world war. By many people in the Western states in particular, this catastrophe was laid at the door of the professional diplomat; and "secret diplomacy" was widely regarded as one of its primary causes. The demand for a New Diplomacy, as a first step toward attaining a better and more peaceful world, was now heard on every hand.

The new techniques and methods which were introduced into diplomatic practice in the attempt to satisfy this demand, and the resultant strains and confusion of purpose which ensued, will be discussed in the pages below. But the search for New Diplomacy was not the only, or even the most important, development in the period which followed the war. From the turmoil engendered by the conflict, new forms of political organization emerged, and the democratic states found themselves confronted with totalitarian powers—the Soviet Union, Fascist Italy, and Nazi Germany—which denied the laws and the values which they themselves recognized. When this happened, the anomalies of the diplomat's position were further heightened. If sent to represent his country's interests in a totalitarian society, he found himself, curiously enough, in a situation not dissimilar to that which faced the diplomat of the eighteenth century when he was accredited to another country; that is, if he was to be successful, he had to ignore the political, economic, and social strata which democratic opinion insisted were important and to concentrate his energies upon the task of establishing a personal relationship with the despot and his immediate aides. In his relations with his own government, on the other hand, he was forced to adjust his methods to the requirements of democratic sentiment or suffer the consequences. With the totalitarian states professing a newer— or older—diplomacy than the New Diplomacy demanded in the democracies, the position of the professional diplomat was, to say the least, uncomfortable.

II

This book is concerned with the diplomacy of the period between the two world wars, and its pattern is necessarily determined by the events of the period. Thus, it deals successively with the reorganization of the European system which took place at the end of the first world war; the first stirrings of dissatisfaction with the Peace Settlement, and the beginnings in the 1920's of the movement known as revisionism; the totalitarian onslaught against the Peace Settlement which was inaugurated in the 1930's; and the weak and hesitant response which this challenge met among the founders and guardians of the existing order. The focus throughout is primarily European, since Europe was still clearly the decisive area in world politics; but, in the concluding chapters of the book, an attempt is made to describe the shift to non-European forces which terminated this period of world history.

But, although this book deals with the development of foreign affairs from 1919 to 1939, it does not pretend to provide a complete chronological account of the period. This is a book about diplomats—the envoys in the field and the officials in the Foreign Offices—and the events of the period are considered from their point of view, rather than from a more general perspective. As the events of the period are described, the reader is invited to concern himself, neither with the figures whose names appeared most frequently in the headlines—Stresemann and Briand, Hitler and Mussolini—nor with such forces for historical change as economic potential, demographic tendencies, or ideological zeal, but rather with the actions and the problems of the diplomats who helped to formulate national policies and who conducted the negotiations by which they were implemented. To be more concrete, the basic problem with which this book is concerned is that of the significance which traditional diplomacy possessed in a period in which its institutions were assailed from the democratic, as well as from the totalitarian, side but during which—and this must be emphasized—it continued to be employed by all Powers as an instrument for attaining national objectives.

These remarks may serve to explain the selection of the individual diplomats whose work is discussed in these pages. Here again the pattern has been influenced by the events of the period, and an attempt has been made to choose, for extended treatment, men whose influence or actions were important at decisive moments in the history of these years. Three other considerations have also, however, been taken into account here. In the first place, diplomats, like other people, have personalities of their own, and their reactions to problems are influenced by individual attitudes and idiosyncrasies. An effort has been made, then, to illustrate this personal element in diplomacy, and to show how some of the diplomats, like Rumbold and Schulenburg, responded instinctively to new problems by invoking the traditional canons of their profession, while others, like Dirksen and Nevile Henderson, sought desperately to launch themselves upon what they believed to be the wave of the future.

In the second place, in discussing an age in which the tenets of traditional diplomacy were being questioned, it would be unwise to neglect the role of the Foreign Offices of the various Powers. It was, after all, the permanent officials of these establishments who stood as the custodians of diplomatic system and propriety; and it has consequently seemed advisable here to discuss the typical problems which they experienced as their methods and principles were challenged, in the democratic societies, by the champions of open diplomacy and, in the totalitarian, by arrogant amateurs like Ribbentrop and Ciano.

Finally, the struggle between the old and the new diplomacy assumed new and interesting forms in those countries which, because they were new creations, possessed no diplomatic tradition or, because they were aggressively revolutionary, recognized none. Thus, a Benes, who created a tradition for his country, and a Chicherin, who succeeded in convincing the Bolshevists that the aristocratic diplomatic tradition had at least defensive uses, have a place in a book of this kind also.

Granted all this, the choice of the men who have been included in this volume will probably seem arbitrary to some readers. Why, after all, when such permanent officials as Berthelot and Bernhard von Bülow are treated at length, is there no fuller discussion of Vansittart, whose influence was as great as, and perhaps more protracted than, theirs? Why, when Undén and Arthur Henderson and Beck have chapters of their own, are Titulescu and Nansen omitted? Why are Franco's diplomats neglected, and why the short but noisy career of Curtius? The answer to these questions must be twofold. If all those who justly deserve a place in a discussion of the diplomacy of the interwar years were included here, this book would become an unmanageable dictionary, rather than an admittedly selective treatment. Furthermore, in the case of the most notable omission here—Vansittart—it was thought wiser to defer an appraisal of his diplomacy until the documents bearing on the period of his greatest influence have been published, as they will be, presumably, in the near future.

A further word should perhaps be spoken on the question of availability of material. The publication of the files of the British, German, and Italian Foreign Offices is now under way, although it has not yet advanced far enough to give more than fragmentary coverage of the period as a whole. The volumes which have appeared are of essential importance to the diplomatic historian, but it need hardly be pointed out that he cannot afford to rely upon them solely. In general, the dispatches published do not reflect the factors that shaped the policies set forth in them; and the British editors have warned their readers that they have not tried to present "a complete record of the processes of formulation of policy as distinct from execution," since reasons of constitutional propriety forbid the publication of "discussion and divergencies of view in the Cabinet and between Departments and individuals." In other countries as well, much that went on behind the scenes does not appear in the published correspondence. To discover the details of the discussions and conflicts which preceded policy decisions, the historian is forced to rely upon other materials, and particularly upon memoirs and diaries written by participants. The existence or nonexistence of such materials has not been the least important of the factors which have determined the organization of this volume.

III

This is a book without a hero. In it, there appear honest men and evil men, fighters for lost causes and enthusiastic gravediggers, fools and knaves, men with whom we sympathize and men whom it is difficult to regard without contempt, men who lived according to the values and traditions in which they were educated and men who lost or abandoned their principles and their faith—but few men, if any, who are likely to be regarded by future generations as great historical figures.

This point is made lest the reader of these pages conclude that we have intended to make a hero, if not of any individual official or envoy, then of the professional diplomat as a type. This impression may, indeed, seem to be borne out by the fact that the different chapters of this book, however much they vary in content and approach, do stress certain problems in which the professional point of view is treated sympathetically. Again and again in the chapters that follow, there will be references to the tendency of the political leaders of the state to prefer "diplomacy by conference" to the technique of negotiation by note and official exchange of views—a preference which had unfortunate results on many occasions. Again and again, the reader will find the professionals excluded from important discussions and the advice of trained observers in the missions abroad neglected in favor of the intuitive judgments or chance impressions of tourists who possess the ear of the political ministers. He will notice also frequent references to the custom in this period of entrusting matters which could have been performed perfectly well by embassy staffs to special and extraordinary missions, headed by politicians with dubious qualifications and negligible experience in foreign affairs. And he will certainly detect a note of criticism in the accounts of the growing tendency of home governments to give attention, and preferment, to those diplomats who reported what their superiors wanted to hear rather than to those whose analyses of the developing situation have been justified by history.

Despite the emphasis placed upon these aspects of interwar diplomacy, it should not be concluded that this book is intended as a defense of the professional diplomat or, further, that it seeks to advance the view that the world would have become a happier and more peaceful place if only the professionals had been given their heads and permitted to arrange matters in their own way. It has no such thesis. It is quite apparent that the professional diplomats would not have lost their former privileges and prerogatives if they had not, in fact, been somewhat out of step with the prevailing forces of the day and if, indeed, there had not been a good deal of truth in the frequently reiterated charge that they had failed adequately to adjust their thinking and their methods to the requirements of modern society.

Nevertheless—and if the book must have a thesis, this is it—it is dangerous to carry distrust of professional diplomacy to the point where you always insist upon doing what the professionals say must not be done and always refuse to do what they describe as necessary. Too many of the interwar political leaders succumbed to this kind of perverseness, with odd, and sometimes fateful, results. Surely they would have been better advised to make the necessary reforms in the machinery of diplomacy, so that it might, while becoming once more an effective means of promoting the national interest, have also been able to operate again—in the words of Sir Robert Peel—as "the great engine used by civilized society for the purpose of maintaining peace."

It need hardly be added that the problem of adjusting the machinery and the methods of diplomacy to the needs of contemporary society is still of importance, not least of all to the United States of America. This nation has been projected into a dominant role in world affairs with a suddenness and finality which has still not been fully appreciated by many of its citizens. In addition, it approaches its new problems and responsibilities with a tradition that is deeply opposed to that of international diplomacy. In the circumstances, a book which shows how dangerous suspicion of the conventions and practices of diplomacy can be, if it is not modified by an earnest desire to make use of those aspects of the diplomatic art which have been proven by time and experience, may serve a useful purpose.

Nelson, N. H.   G.A.C.
    August, 1952   F.G.

Book One: The Twenties

A NOTE ON ABBREVIATIONS

The most frequently cited collections of printed diplomatic correspondence and other documents are consistently referred to in the footnotes by short titles. For the convenience of the reader, the abbreviated title employed and the full titles of the collections follow.

BRITISH DOCUMENTS. *Documents on British Foreign Policy, 1919-1939*, edited by E. L. Woodward and Rohan Butler (London, H. M. Stationery Office, 1949 and continuing).

CONSPIRACY AND AGGRESSION. *Nazi Conspiracy and Aggression* (8 vols. and 2 supplements, Washington, Government Printing Office, 1946-1949).

DEGRAS. Jane Degras, ed., *Soviet Documents on Foreign Policy*, Volume I, 1917-24 (Oxford, 1951); Volume II, 1925-32 (Oxford, 1952).

DIRKSEN PAPERS. Ministry of Foreign Affairs of the USSR, *Documents and Materials Relating to the Eve of the Second World War*. Volume II, Dirksen Papers, 1938-1939 (Moscow, 1949).

DOCUMENTS AND MATERIALS. Ministry of Foreign Affairs of the USSR, *Documents and Materials Relating to the Eve of the Second World War*. Volume I, November 1937-1938 (Moscow, 1949).

DOCUMENTI ITALIANI. Ministero degli Affari Esteri, *I Documenti Diplomatici Italiani* (Rome, La Libreria dello Stato, 1952 and continuing).

FOREIGN RELATIONS. *Foreign Relations of the United States* (Department of State, Washington).

GERMAN DOCUMENTS. *Documents on German Foreign Policy, 1918-1945: From the Archives of the German Foreign Ministry* (Washington, Government Printing Office, 1949 and continuing).

NAZI-SOVIET RELATIONS. *Nazi-Soviet Relations 1939-1941: Documents from the Archives of the German Foreign Office*, edited by R. J. Sontag and J. S. Beddie (Washington, 1948).

POLISH WHITE BOOK. Republic of Poland, Ministry for Foreign Affairs, *Official Documents concerning Polish-German and Polish-Soviet Relations, 1933-1939* (London, 1940).

TRIAL OF MAJOR CRIMINALS. *The Trial of the Major War Criminals* (42 vols., Nuremberg, 1947-1949).

TRIALS OF WAR CRIMINALS. *Trials of War Criminals before the Nuernberg Military Tribunals under Control Council Law No. 10* (14 volumes, Nuremberg, 1946-1949).

VORGESCHICHTE. *Dokumente zur Vorgeschichte des Krieges*, herausgegeben vom Auswärtigen Amt der deutschen Regierung (Basel, 1940).

All other works are cited by their full title on the first reference in any chapter. Thereafter, short—but, it is to be hoped, easily recognizable—titles are used.

1

....

The British Foreign Office from
Grey to Austen Chamberlain

BY GORDON A. CRAIG

"THE FOREIGN OFFICE," said the Marquess of Londonderry in the House of Lords in March 1944, "is the pivot of the Government, and the Foreign Secretary should be the most dominant personality in the Cabinet after the Prime Minister. . . . It may be a harsh thing to say that the Foreign Office has not existed since the days of Sir Edward Grey."[1]

It was, indeed, a harsh thing to say in a chamber whose membership included three men who had served as Secretaries of State for Foreign Affairs, as well as three former Permanent Under-Secretaries for Foreign Affairs;[2] but there was more than a modicum of truth in Londonderry's statement. There can be little doubt that the prestige and authority of the Foreign Office during the postwar period was much less than that which it enjoyed in the period before 1914; and it is not difficult to demonstrate that, on numerous occasions, its influence on British policy was so negligible that its existence as the agency constitutionally charged with the conduct of British foreign relations seemed to have become more formal than real.

In the years before 1914, the formulation of British foreign policy in its broadest outlines was the responsibility of the Cabinet, as it was also their responsibility to explain and defend it before Parliament. Within the Cabinet itself, however, the Foreign Secretary was "the most important person who shape[d] the policy of [the] country."[3] He, after

---

[1] Parliamentary Debates: Lords, 5th series, CXXXI (1943-1944), 363.

[2] The Lord Chancellor, Viscount Simon, had been Foreign Secretary from 1931 to 1935, Viscount Templewood (Sir Samuel Hoare) in 1935, and the Earl of Halifax from 1938 to 1940. Lord Hardinge of Penshurst had served as Permanent Under-Secretary in the Foreign Office from 1905 to 1910 and from 1916 to 1920, Lord Tyrrell from 1925 to 1928, and Lord Vansittart from 1930 to 1938.

[3] Earl Grey of Falloden at the first annual dinner of the Royal Institute of Inter-

all, was in the best position to be informed of the plans and ambitions of other governments, thanks to the reports of his agents abroad and his conversations with foreign representatives in London; and he alone had, in the Foreign Office, an expert staff which made systematic and continuous studies of the foreign situation and—especially after the Foreign Office reforms of 1906[4]—advised him concerning the course Britain should take in given contingencies. The Cabinet itself was too cumbersome and too busy to devote much time to the details of policy. When pressing matters were brought before them, they were generally inclined to follow the Foreign Secretary's lead, and, for the rest—the normal day-by-day policy decisions—to trust to his discretion. It was realized, as J. A. Spender has written, that the ever pressing domestic concerns of the Cabinet, as well as the normal business of the Foreign Office, would be hopelessly disrupted if the Foreign Secretary found it "necessary to consult the Cabinet on more than a few urgent questions; and needlessly to multiply these was one of the sure signs of a bad Foreign Secretary."[5]

Before 1914, then, the right of the Foreign Secretary and the permanent officials in the Foreign Office to consider themselves as the chief advisors of the Cabinet in matters of foreign policy was never seriously questioned; and, although there were occasions when their advice was rejected by the Cabinet, such action was never taken lightly or without careful consideration of the Foreign Office point of view. Similarly, it was generally recognized that the *execution* of foreign policy decisions—discussion with foreign Powers and the varied tasks of negotiation— was the prerogative of the Foreign Secretary, his aides in the Foreign Office and the diplomats in the field; and necessary departures from this rule were made only after the Foreign Office had been informed and consulted.[6]

After the first world war, this state of affairs changed radically. In

---

national Affairs, July 16, 1930. See *Journal of the Royal Institute of International Affairs* (later *International Affairs*), IX (1930), 579.

[4] On these reforms, which strengthened the advisory functions of the staff of the Foreign Office, see Sir John Tilley and Stephen Gaselee, *The Foreign Office* (London, 1933), pp. 156ff.; Sir John Tilley, *London to Tokyo* (London, 1942), pp. 69-70; F. Ashton-Gwatkin, "Foreign Service Reorganization," *International Affairs*, XXII (1946), 58ff.

[5] J. A. Spender, *The Public Life* (2 vols., New York, 1925), II, 42. Mr. L. Amery in *The Observer* (London) of April 18, 1934 pointed out that, in the unwieldy Cabinet, "there is very little Cabinet policy on any subject."

[6] This applied even to the visits of foreign envoys to the sovereign. Canning had successfully insisted that "constitutional" doctrine made it the duty of the Foreign Secretary to be present at such meetings. See Algernon Cecil, "The Foreign Office," *Cambridge History of British Foreign Policy* (3 vols., Cambridge, 1923), III, 556.

matters of policy, Foreign Office advice was frequently ignored and often shrugged aside with an indifference which the Cabinet would not have dared to evince toward the views, let us say, of the Admiralty or the War Office.[7] Not only were policies adopted by the Prime Minister which ran counter to those advocated by the Foreign Secretary and his staff, but, on numerous occasions, the nature of these policies and the reasons for adopting them were not communicated—or were communicated belatedly and imperfectly—to the Foreign Office. Meanwhile, in the sphere of diplomacy proper, functions formerly reserved to the professional diplomats were farmed out to other departments of the government, while important tasks of negotiation were taken over by political leaders whose new-found enthusiasm for foreign affairs was generally unguided either by training or experience. In consequence, postwar British diplomacy came to be characterized by dangerous defects of coordination, as well as by a high degree of amateurishness, imprecision, and feckless opportunism. These faults of technique were directly related to the inadequacies of British policy in the interbellum period, a period which, it need hardly be added, is in little danger of being regarded by future historians as one in which British statesmanship distinguished itself.

The flouting of the Foreign Office, the dislocation of the processes of policy administration, and the supersession of the diplomatic corps by the political leaders and their private agents reached their height in the 1930's, and there will be occasion to revert later in this book to their consequences in the Munich period. But even in the days when the chief beneficiary of Munich was still an obscure German politician, these tendencies were manifesting themselves in Great Britain, and precedents were being established for the kind of diplomacy which was to guarantee his victory in 1938. It is of some importance, then, to consider the position and the problems of the British foreign service in the first decade of the postwar period.

I

The decline of the authority of the Foreign Office began with the coming of war in 1914. It was inevitable that, with the outbreak of the conflict, the Prime Minister and the Cabinet as a whole should have assumed a greater degree of responsibility for the daily decisions of policy. This development need not, however, have deprived the Foreign Office of its position as technical adviser to the government on international relations; and the fact that it tended to do so is probably due to

[7] See Harold Nicolson in *The Spectator*, December 29, 1944.

the character and methods of Sir Edward Grey and Mr. Asquith. The Foreign Secretary was inclined to believe—as his autobiography demonstrates[8]—that diplomacy did not count for much in wartime, and he was, in addition, temperamentally unfitted to fight for the prerogatives of his office against such confident and aggressive personalities as Churchill, Kitchener, and Lloyd George. Mr. Asquith, whose last years in office were marked by a fatal habit of indecision and a willingness to allow administrative problems to solve themselves, raised no objections as Grey abdicated his functions to the War Office and the Admiralty, and showed a similar degree of unconcern when those departments performed the assumed tasks spasmodically and with indifferent success. The resultant lack of system and direction did not contribute to the success of the war effort, although it did have a sensible effect in the chain of events which led to the fall of the Asquith government in December 1916.[9]

The substitution of Lloyd George for Asquith did not, however, improve the position of the Foreign Office. The new Prime Minister sought to increase the efficiency of the war effort by abolishing the old cabinet system and establishing a War Cabinet of six members who were relieved of all departmental duties so that they might devote their entire energies to the direction of the war. The new Foreign Secretary, Lord Balfour, was not a member of this body, but he was permitted to attend when he wished to do so, as was the Permanent Under-Secretary, Sir Charles Hardinge.[10] Theoretically, this should have assured the Foreign Office of a proper degree of influence in all policy matters. In actuality, the Foreign Office representatives were, with increasing frequency, placed in the position of approving decisions which had already been made by other agencies. The War Cabinet was, for instance, provided with a Secretariat under the direction of Sir Maurice Hankey, which was designed originally to prepare memoranda and perform liaison duties for the Cabinet, but which became, over the course of the years, an official general staff for the Prime Minister and a means by which—as one critic wrote—he could "conduct foreign policy without the inconveniences of Foreign Office intervention."[11] Lloyd George furthermore established a private

[8] Viscount Grey of Falloden, *Twenty-Five Years, 1892-1916* (New York, 1925), pp. 157ff. and especially p. 159.

[9] On these developments, see Eustace Percy, "Foreign Office Reform," *The New Europe*, XI (1919), 53ff.

[10] Hardinge of Penshurst, *Old Diplomacy* (London, 1947), p. 205; Blanche E. C. Dugdale, *Arthur James Balfour, First Earl of Balfour* (2 vols., New York, 1937), II, 176.

[11] *The Nation* (London) October 14, 1922. See also Sir Maurice Hankey, *Diplomacy by Conference, Studies in Public Affairs, 1920-1946* (London, 1946), pp. 61-82.

Secretariat which, under the leadership of Philip Kerr (later Lord Lothian), took up quarters in temporary huts erected in the garden of 10 Downing Street. This "Garden Suburb," or "Downing Street Kindergarten," also cultivated a taste for dabbling in matters of high policy, for its members tended to be contemptuous of the Foreign Office mind and Kerr himself once expressed the conviction that that department "had no conception of policy in its wider sense."[12]

Lord Balfour's biographer has denied that these developments disturbed the Foreign Secretary,[13] and this is probably true, since Balfour, as was perhaps befitting a philosopher, was not accustomed to resist things which he felt were inevitable and since, in any event, he subscribed to a policy of "a free hand for the Little Man." Her further statement, however, that no important steps in foreign policy were taken without Balfour's knowledge[14] is largely meaningless. The Foreign Secretary was always informed, but often too late for him to be able to influence decisions; and his acquiescence in this state of affairs could not help but have a deleterious effect upon Foreign Office morale and efficiency. With the two Secretariats arrogating to themselves more and more advisory and executive functions in foreign policy, the Foreign Office—as a contemporary critic noted—"came increasingly to feel that it had no adequate channels of communication with the War Cabinet; that it was at any given moment imperfectly acquainted with the Prime Minister's intentions, and that it could never be certain that any advice which it might have to tender on any matter would reach the Cabinet in the proper form. It relapsed more and more into the position of a rubber stamp."[15] Nor was this all. The Prime Minister soon began to interfere in an irresponsible manner with diplomatic appointments, and usually without consulting the Foreign Secretary or his staff in advance. In 1917, he attempted to recall Sir George Buchanan from St. Petersburg and to replace him with Arthur Henderson, a plan which was checked only by Henderson's realization, once he had reached Russia, that the change would be ill-advised;[16] and his attempt in the same year to force Lord Bertie out of the Paris Embassy—a scheme which Hardinge believed was hatched in the private Secretariat and never communicated to Balfour—would prob-

---

[12] Lord Riddell, *Intimate Diary of the Peace Conference and After* (London, 1933), p. 219. For an eye-witness account of the "Garden Suburb," see Joseph Davies, *The Prime Minister's Secretariat, 1916-1920* (Newport, 1952).

[13] Dugdale, *Balfour*, II, 175.

[14] *ibid.*

[15] Eustace Percy in *The New Europe*, XI (1919), 53ff.

[16] Mary Agnes Hamilton, *Arthur Henderson: A Biography* (London, 1938), pp. 125-128.

ably have succeeded if it had not been for spirited protests in *The Times*.[17]

More evidence of the declining influence of the Foreign Office was provided when the war drew to an end and the nations prepared to go to the Peace Conference at Paris. It had been assumed in the Foreign Office that, during the peace negotiations, the professional diplomats and official advisors of the government would be brought back to the center of the stage; and plans had been made to provide expert studies of the principal questions at issue and to select a qualified staff of negotiators, well-briefed and able to carry on discussions in French. But, as Balfour's Permanent Under-Secretary has written, Lloyd George "insisted on employing a staff of his own unofficial creation, who had no knowledge of French and none of diplomacy, and the Foreign Office organization was consequently stillborn." In the British delegation that went to Paris, the Foreign Office had only eighteen members, while the contingents from the War Office, the Admiralty, the Board of Trade and the Colonial Office numbered some 200, with an additional clerical staff of 200 more.[18] These figures are perhaps unimportant, since, in the last analysis, Lloyd George became wearied of the advice of experts from whatever department they might be drawn and, closeting himself with Wilson, Clemenceau, and Orlando, undertook to solve the problems of the conference by his own intuition. It is worth noting, however, that, while the Foreign Office experts were relegated to tedious and unrewarding labors on the various territorial committees,[19] Lloyd George's private aides were often permitted to indulge themselves with the exciting tasks of high-level negotiation and policy formulation. This was true, for instance, of the Prime Minister's private secretary, Philip Kerr, who on one occasion at least was empowered to engage in delicate negotiations with French and American representatives concerning the possibility of British participation in the postwar occupation of the Rhineland;[20] and who was furthermore reported to have been the sole author of the Allied reply to the German objections to the Peace Treaty.[21]

[17] Hardinge, *Old Diplomacy*, p. 214. Bertie was, however, replaced in April 1918 by Lord Derby after protests by Hardinge and some expressions of surprise and disagreement by the French ambassador in London, Paul Cambon. *Ibid.*, p. 226.

[18] *ibid.*, pp. 229-230. For other expressions of concern over the composition of the British delegation, see *The History of "The Times"*, IV (London, 1952), Part I, 463.

[19] On the frustrations suffered by those who served on the territorial committees, see especially Harold Nicolson, *Peacemaking 1919* (New York, 1939), pp. 124-131.

[20] House of Commons Sessional Papers, 1924, XXVI: Cmd. 2169, "France No. 1 (1924). Papers Respecting Negotiations for an Anglo-French Pact," pp. 59-69.

[21] A. L. Kennedy, *Old Diplomacy and New* (London, 1922), p. 307.

The degree of authority which Kerr was permitted to exert seems finally to have ruffled even the usually imperturbable Foreign Secretary. On one occasion, when Balfour asked Kerr whether Lloyd George had read a certain memorandum, the private secretary answered, "I don't think so, but I have." "Not quite the same thing is it, Philip—yet?," Balfour remarked.[22] The Foreign Secretary might have been excused a much stronger expression of irritation than this, for, before the conference was over, he had occasion to discover that Kerr was privy to secrets not disclosed to him. Even in such an important matter as the treaty in which Great Britain and the United States guaranteed to come to France's aid in the event of future German aggression, Balfour was not consulted; and he was informed of its contents by Kerr only after it had been drafted in accordance with the Prime Minister's personal instructions and had been approved by Wilson and Clemenceau.[23]

Even before the end of the Peace Conference, Lloyd George's cavalier treatment of the Foreign Office and the Diplomatic Service had begun to arouse some alarm among responsible observers. In a series of articles written in 1919, *The New Europe*, the well-informed journal of international affairs which was edited by R. W. Seton-Watson and George Glasgow, drew attention to the dangers implicit in the Prime Minister's policy, and it continued to revert to the subject until its unfortunate demise in 1920. Pointing out that foreign policy should not be allowed to grow "like Topsy in the sanctities of No. 10 Downing Street, out of the brains of miscellaneous informants and secretaries," it insisted that the Foreign Office must once more be made "capable of bearing the full responsibility for the formulation of advice on foreign policy through the Foreign Secretary to the Prime Minister" and must once more become the "recognized and accredited center into which all kinds of information about foreign countries shall flow." It recognized that the first step toward the restoration of the department's lost authority must be a thoroughgoing reform of the foreign service as a whole. Early in 1919, as a result of recommendations made earlier by the Royal Commission on the Civil Service, certain reforms had been carried through. The artificial separation of the Foreign Office and the Diplomatic Service had been abolished, and the two services had been amalgamated. The property qualification for candidature for the foreign service had also been eliminated, a step which presumably would open the career to the talents.[24] What was needed now, *The New Europe* insisted, was further

---

[22] Dugdale, *Balfour*, II, 199.   [23] Hardinge, *Old Diplomacy*, p. 241.
[24] On the partial reforms of 1919, see "Changes in the Organisation of the Foreign and

progress in the same direction: a greater systematization of promotion to bring talent to the fore; administrative improvements capable of encouraging initiative and extirpating the "vagueness" and "hand-to-mouth opportunism" which had often been apparent in the department; a more careful system of diplomatic appointments, which would assure the sending of the right men to the right places;[25] and, finally, careful coordination of the work of the foreign service with that of the newly established League of Nations. But such reforms would be useless unless the usurpation of the functions of the foreign service by irresponsible agencies and institutions was stopped. The journal cited in particular one wartime development—the establishment of a Commercial Diplomatic Service, administered by the Department of Overseas Trade which, in its turn, was responsible to the Foreign Office and the Board of Trade conjointly. In practice, this arrangement had led to the progressive absorption of commercial intelligence by the latter department, and the Foreign Office had much less influence in the economic and commercial aspects of diplomacy than it had before the war. If this, and similar developments caused by "departmental jealousy," were not checked, the administration of British foreign affairs would become increasingly chaotic and ineffective.[26]

These were reasonable views, but they elicited very little response in 1919. Even in normal times Foreign Offices do not enjoy much popularity in democratic states, where foreign affairs seem to be a dangerous distraction from the true business of the nation and where the officials who make a career of dealing with foreign affairs are apt to be viewed with grave suspicion. "On n'aime pas," Jules Cambon has written, "ces porteurs de secrets que sont les ambassadeurs."[27] And in 1919 the unpopularity of the British foreign service was at its height. Recent revelations concerning the nature and methods of prewar statesmanship had convinced large sections of the public that "secret diplomacy" had been the principal cause of the war and that, in consequence, the professional diplomats were among the major war criminals. This belief conditioned the thinking of several highly vocal groups which advocated the shack-

Diplomatic Service," *British Year Book of International Law* (1920-21), pp. 97-108. The Consular Service was not included in the amalgamation.

[25] *The New Europe* was generally critical of diplomatic appointments made in this period. See XII (July-October 1919), 209ff.

[26] *The New Europe*, XI (1919), 77ff., 102ff., 128ff., 147ff. See also the article by E. J. Davis, *ibid.*, XIV (Jan.-Apr. 1920), 73ff.

[27] Jules Cambon, *Le Diplomate* (Paris, 1926), pp. 10-11.

ling, if not the outright abolition, of the diplomatic agencies of the government.

Typical of these groups was the Union of Democratic Control, which had been founded in 1914 by E. D. Morel, whose *Morocco in Diplomacy* (1912) was one of the first revelations of the nature of prewar diplomacy,[28] Ramsay MacDonald, the leader of the Labor party, Norman Angell, the author of the widely read book *The Great Illusion*,[29] and Arthur Ponsonby, Charles Trevelyan, and Philip Snowden, who were to become leading lights in the Labor party.[30] The U.D.C. called for an end to "balance of power" politics and secret diplomacy and demanded, among other things, that, in the postwar world, there should be open and frequent declarations of policy by the government, submission of all treaties and engagements to Parliament, periodic revision of treaties, the forbidding of military conversations with other Powers except with parliamentary sanction and the establishment of a parliamentary committee on foreign affairs to keep the Foreign Secretary in touch with public opinion and to prevent the country from being confronted with *faits accomplis*.[31]

For this program there was doubtless much to be said, but members of the U.D.C., and of other Labor and Liberal groups, often went beyond it and expressed the belief that the professional diplomats as a class were socially and temperamentally unfitted to conduct Britain's foreign relations in the postwar world. It would be a mistake, one writer warned, to leave " 'the whole of that industry of protocolling, diplomatising, remonstrating, admonishing and having the honour to be' in the hands of the British Junkers."[32] The professional caste, said another, is discredited by "its methods, its archaic outlook upon life, its complacent self-sufficiency in face of shattering exposures of ignorance and incompetence" and by the patent fact that it is "a conscious aristocratic instrument . . . the last barrier interposed by Providence between the English governing

---

[28] On Morel, see F. Seymour Cocks, *E. D. Morel, The Man and His Work* (London, 1920) and his own numerous articles in *Foreign Affairs*, the journal of the Union of Democratic Control.

[29] On Angell's role in the movement, see *After All: The Autobiography of Norman Angell* (London, 1951), pp. 191-193.

[30] Trevelyan and Ponsonby were among the Labor party's "experts" on foreign affairs. Ponsonby served as Under-Secretary for Foreign Affairs in the first MacDonald government. Snowden was Chancellor of the Exchequer in both Labor Ministries.

[31] See, for instance, Arthur Ponsonby, "The Democratic Control of Foreign Affairs" in Organisation Centrale pour une Paix Durable, *Recueil de Rapports sur les différents points du Programme-Minimum*, deuxième partie (La Haye, 1916), pp. 252-261.

[32] J. H. Hudson, "Labour's Greatest Menace: The Foreign Office," *Foreign Affairs*, January 1920.

classes and the rising tide of world democracy."³³ "What can Labour do?" asked a third. "It is pledged, when it comes to power, to sweep the Foreign Office clean."³⁴

This atmosphere of suspicion of, and social antagonism toward, the Foreign Office and the Diplomatic Service was reinforced by the muddled optimism of the many people who, regardless of party affiliation, seemed to believe that, in the postwar world, there would be no need for the traditional agencies and techniques of foreign affairs, which would presumably be replaced by new methods and organizations. This type of thinking was doubtless encouraged by the exhortations of the President of the United States, who had promised a world in which "diplomacy shall proceed always frankly and in the public view." It was conditioned also by the fervent hopes entertained for the new League of Nations. And it was probably not uninfluenced by flights of oratory in the House of Commons, like that of the member who declared in 1918: "After the war, the old diplomacy of Court and upper classes will be, in the eyes of most people, obsolete and inadequate. In fact, what is the whole idea of the League of Nations except the substitution of open and popular diplomacy for the old system? The idea is that difficulties between nations should no longer be settled in conclaves of Ambassadors, but by public, international discussion, and by arbitration of a public kind."³⁵

In this situation, few people were receptive to the idea of making the Foreign Office once more an organization "capable of bearing the full responsibility for the formulation of advice on foreign policy" and fewer still became very interested in proposals of constructive reform for that office and the Diplomatic Service. As a result, none of the administrative reforms suggested by the writers of *The New Europe* or by men like Sir Robert Cecil were put into effect. There was no systematization of promotion; there were no real attempts to improve coordination between departments engaged in foreign policy functions. Even the awkward arrangement concerning the Department of Overseas Trade, which had tended to deprive the Foreign Office of its commercial and financial functions, was allowed to continue. This, as Sir William Tyrrell said during the second world war, "was a great weakening of that Office, [and] it also had a psychological effect. . . . It had, perhaps subconsciously the effect of leaving the members of the Foreign Office more and more disinterested in any of those questions"; and, apart from this, it succeeded

³³ Harold Grenfell, "Behind the Veil in Diplomacy," *ibid.*, May 1920.
³⁴ A. E. Mander, "Secret Diplomacy," *ibid.*, January 1921.
³⁵ Parliamentary Debates: Commons, 5th series, CIV (1918), 846.

ultimately in removing from the domain of the Foreign Office one of the most important problems of the 1920's, the problem of reparations, which was as much a political as a financial question, but which was handled for the most part by other departments.[36]

In addition, the unpopularity of the diplomatic agencies—which continued with some variations of intensity throughout the interwar period[37] —doubtless had an unfortunate influence on the quality of the personnel recruited by those agencies. Despite the amalgamation of the services and the abolition of the property qualification in 1919, the idea persisted that talent and initiative were less valuable to aspirants to a diplomatic career than aristocratic birth and private means;[38] and this idea was strengthened by contemporary studies of the services.[39] It seems likely that many promising candidates for the Civil Service preferred to find their way in the Treasury or other departments rather than to risk frustration and disappointment in diplomacy. The extent of this is difficult to estimate, but it was probably a not unimportant factor in reducing the over-all effectiveness of the diplomatic corps in this period.

Finally, the unpopularity of the Foreign Office and the Diplomatic Service was admirably designed to remove any hesitation which Lloyd George may have felt about continuing the course which he had set during the war and at the Peace Conference. The Prime Minister yielded to no man in his contempt for the professionals; and he was now encouraged to follow his natural bent and to provide the British people with a new type of diplomacy, which they apparently expected and desired.

II

In the summer of 1919, when the Peace Conference finally finished its labors, Lord Balfour resigned as Foreign Secretary and was replaced by the Marquess Curzon of Kedleston. This change was welcomed by those who were most critical of Lloyd George's methods. Curzon had held offices which were among the most exalted which the state had to offer;

[36] Parliamentary Debates: Lords, 5th series, CXXVI (1942-1943), 970. See also the speech of the Earl of Perth, *ibid.*, CXXXIV (1944-1945), 287-288; the remarks of Sir Walford Selby at a discussion at Chatham House on October 11, 1945, *International Affairs*, XXII (1946), 170; and his article on "The Foreign Office," in *The Nineteenth Century*, July 1945.

[37] The criticisms of the Diplomatic Service made after the second world war, for instance, are a mere repetition of those made in 1919. See House of Commons Sessional Papers 1942-1943, XI: Cmd. 6420, "Misc. No. 2 (1943). Proposals for the Reform of the Foreign Service," p. 2.

[38] Tilley and Gaselee, *The Foreign Office*, p. 195.

[39] See, for instance, George Young, *Diplomacy Old and New* (London, 1921), Chapter I, "Diplomacy and Personnel."

he had been Viceroy of India from 1898 to 1905 and a member of the Cabinet since 1915. He was a man of great abilities, strong convictions, and intense personal pride; and it was difficult to believe that he would "play the part of a mere figurehead or allow the effacement of the Foreign Office to continue."[40] He was no stranger to that organization, for he had served as Lord Salisbury's Under-Secretary in the years from 1895 to 1898; he had a proper appreciation of the role assigned to it in the business of the nation; and he respected the ability of the men who were to be his chief aides in the Foreign Office and the Diplomatic Service.[41]

With regard to the last point, it may be added that he had reason for this respect. Despite the critical tone of contemporary writing concerning it, the British foreign service in 1919 compared favorably with that of any other country in Europe. In the Foreign Office itself, the post of Permanent Under-Secretary was filled—after Sir Charles Hardinge went to the Paris Embassy at the end of the year[42]—by Sir Eyre Crowe, who was to continue in office until his death in 1925. Crowe has been described by Harold Nicolson as "the perfect type of British civil servant—industrious, loyal, expert, accurate, beloved, obedient and courageous."[43] He had served in the Foreign Office since 1885, had been the leading spirit in the administrative reforms of 1905-1906 and had, as chief of the Western Department, written that well-known memorandum of January 1, 1907, which, perhaps for the first time, laid bare the true nature of the German threat to British interests.[44] Since 1912 he had been Assistant Under-Secretary of State, had done notable work on the Ministry of Blockade during the war and had been a member, with the rank of Minister Plenipotentiary, of the British delegation to the Paris Conference. People meeting Crowe for the first time were sometimes repelled by his

[40] *The New Europe*, XIII (October 1919-January 1920), 59-60.

[41] On Curzon, see especially Harold Nicolson, *Curzon: The Last Phase, 1919-1925* (new ed., New York, 1939) and Earl of Ronaldshay, *The Life of Lord Curzon, being the Authorized Biography of George Nathaniel Marquess Curzon of Kedleston, K.G.* (3 vols., London, 1921). For shorter, but perceptive, accounts see Viscount d'Abernon, *An Ambassador of Peace* (3 vols., London, 1929-1930), I, 48-52; Winston Churchill, *Great Contemporaries* (rev. ed., London, 1938), pp. 273-288; J. D. Gregory, *On the Edge of Diplomacy* (London, 1928), pp. 245-255; Harold Nicolson, *Some People* (Boston, 1927), pp. 187-213; and Tilley, *London to Tokyo*, pp. 91-92.

[42] Hardinge had also been Viceroy of India, a circumstance which promised to create awkwardness, and there had also been differences between Curzon and him during the war. He was due for retirement but Curzon refused to take advantage of this and offered him the Paris post. See Hardinge, *Old Diplomacy*, pp. 243-244.

[43] Harold Nicolson, *Portrait of a Diplomatist* (New York, 1930), p. 239.

[44] The memorandum is printed in G. P. Gooch and Harold Temperley, eds., *British Documents on the Origins of the War, 1898-1914* (London, 1926-36), III, 397-420.

rigidity and the punctilio of his official manner, but there were few, on closer acquaintance, who did not admire his industry and his breadth of view.[45]

Crowe was assisted by a staff of more than ordinary talents. Sir William Tyrrell, who had been Grey's Private Secretary, a man who was "intuitive, conciliatory, elastic and possessed [of] a remarkable instinct for avoiding diplomatic difficulties,"[46] was Assistant Under-Secretary; the Assistant Secretaries included Sir John Tilley, Eric Phipps, and Victor Wellesley; while among the Senior Clerks were R. G. Vansittart and Alexander Cadogan, who were in time, like Tyrrell, to become Permanent Under-Secretaries. That the chief posts in the Diplomatic Service were also in good hands was admitted even by journals normally critical of diplomatic appointments.[47] Hardinge was at Paris; Sir George Buchanan, after years of distinguished service in St. Petersburg, was at Rome; Sir Auckland Geddes was on his way to Washington. The new and possibly crucial posts at Prague and Warsaw had been filled by Sir George Clerk and Sir Horace Rumbold, who quickly justified their appointments; and, when relations with the former enemy countries were resumed, the Berlin Embassy was occupied by Viscount d'Abernon, one of the most adroit and perspicacious British diplomats of the interwar period.[48]

But, if the competence of his subordinates was gratifying to the new Foreign Secretary, it did not weigh very heavily with the Prime Minister. For the professional diplomats Lloyd George had—as has already been indicated—very little respect; and his disregard extended even to their methods, especially to their penchant for exchanges of views by means of formal correspondence and carefully drafted notes. "I wish the French and ourselves never wrote letters to each other," Lloyd George said in 1920. "Letters are the very devil. They ought to be abolished altogether. . . . If you want to settle a thing you see your opponent and talk it over with him. The last thing you do is write him a letter."[49] Moreover, the Prime Minister was firmly convinced that it did no good to leave the

---

[45] *The Times*, April 29, 1925. See also Gregory, *On the Edge of Diplomacy*, pp. 255-261.

[46] Nicolson, *Portrait of a Diplomatist*, p. 239.

[47] See, for instance, *The New Europe*, XII (July-October 1919), 209ff.

[48] D'Abernon was not of the career service, having formerly been president of the Ottoman Bank in Constantinople, and initially there was some opposition in the Foreign Office to his appointment. See Hardinge, *Old Diplomacy*, p. 249, and the speech of Lord Vansittart in Parliamentary Debates: Lords, 5th series, CXXXIV (1944-1945), 295.

[49] Riddell, *Intimate Diary*, p. 206. For a very similar opinion, expressed by Aristide Briand, see below Chapter 10, § IV.

talking-over to the professional diplomats. "Diplomats were invented simply to waste time," he said during the war. "It is simply a waste of time to let [important matters] be discussed by men who are not authorized to speak for their countries."[50]

These last words were not idly spoken. Lloyd George believed—and his belief was doubtless strengthened by his awareness of the popular distrust of "old diplomacy"—that the great questions of foreign policy should be negotiated, not by career diplomats, but by men who possessed mandates from the people; and his was the strongest influence in carrying the methods which had been inaugurated at the Paris Conference over into the years that followed and in making the period subsequent to 1919 a period in which "diplomacy by conference" took precedence over the techniques of traditional diplomacy.[51] Thanks to him, the first years of peace were filled with elaborate confabulations between the political leaders of Great Britain, France, Italy, Germany, and other countries, conferences at which the problems created at the Paris meetings—reparations, security, the economic plight of Europe, relations with Soviet Russia, and the like—were debated in a white glare of publicity. These conferences were held in charming and unconventional places, far from the beaten paths used by orthodox diplomacy—at Cannes and San Remo and Spa and Genoa—but, even when they found their locations in national capitals, the professional diplomats did not bulk large in their councils, if, indeed, they were invited at all. Diplomacy by conference was Lloyd George's response to the popular demand for a "new diplomacy," and he was not inclined to have the effect spoiled by the obtrusive presence of members of the suspected caste. Even the Foreign Secretary, who came in time to detest these *omnium gatherums*, was often ignored in the selection of the British delegations. This was true, for instance, at the time of the Genoa Conference of 1922, of which Curzon wrote: "When I reflect that the P.M. is alone at Genoa, with no F.O. to guide him . . . I can feel no certainty that we may not find ourselves committed to something pregnant with political disaster here."[52]

This deliberate neglect of the resources and the experience of the British foreign service was reflected immediately in the paucity of results

---

[50] Kennedy, *Old Diplomacy*, pp. 364-365.

[51] "The French Prime Minister, Millerand, looked forward . . . early in 1920 to the resumption of normal diplomatic methods of negotiation, but the multiplicity of issues and the personal aptitudes of the British Prime Minister combined to compel the continuance of the conference method." W. M. Jordan, *Great Britain, France and the German Problem, 1918-1939* (London, 1943), p. 58.

[52] Nicolson, *Curzon*, p. 245.

attained by Lloyd Georgian diplomacy in the years from 1919 to 1922. The record of the Prime Minister's peripatetic activities, indeed, does much to justify Nicolson's statement that diplomacy by conference is "perhaps the most unfortunate diplomatic method ever conceived."[53] Because Lloyd George disliked writing letters, the conferences often assembled without any prior agreement concerning agenda and procedure and generally without any precise formulation of the issues which could be expected to arise for discussion. Because Lloyd George and his foreign colleagues could not, as the political leaders of their countries, remain long absent from their capitals, the conferences were apt to be seriously restricted in time, a fact which, in view of the absence of preliminary agreement and consultation, made it virtually impossible to achieve positive results. Finally, because it was important to Lloyd George and his colleagues to *seem* to have achieved positive results, since they had generally aroused a high degree of public expectation, they became adept at concluding their most inconclusive meetings with the publication of eloquent formulas, which hinted at agreement and progress but which in actuality disguised genuine and acute differences of opinion among the Powers.[54] It can scarcely be argued, for instance, that the twelve international conferences which were held on the reparations question made any progress toward achieving a reasonable solution of that troublesome problem. It would be more accurate to say that their principal result was a series of public clashes between British and French policy, awkwardly smoothed over by compromises which satisfied no one and which finally produced, in England, an unreasoning suspicion of France and, in France, a degree of exasperation which found its ultimate expression in the fateful occupation of the Ruhr in 1923.[55]

Some of the conferences got completely out of hand and produced unforeseen results which embarrassed the British and French participants. This was notably the case at the Genoa Conference of 1922, a meeting convoked, despite French reluctance, as a result of Lloyd George's insistence that it was time to face up to the Russian problem and that, by doing so, the Powers would be able to solve all of Europe's outstanding

---

[53] *ibid.*, p. 397.

[54] Lloyd George's latest biographer speaks almost approvingly of this aspect of the Prime Minister's diplomacy. "Failure to reach agreement or to do no more than expose divergencies to the world could, as a rule and for the moment, be veiled in intentional obscurity by drafting a dextrous formula, an art in which his secretaries became proficient." Thomas Jones, *Lloyd George* (Cambridge, Mass., 1951), p. 180. For a contemporary criticism of this practice, however, see "Is There a New Diplomacy?" *Fortnightly Review*, CXI (1922), 709-725. See also d'Abernon, *An Ambassador of Peace*, I, 163.

[55] See Jordan, *Great Britain, France and the German Question*, p. 59.

economic problems.[56] The conference failed signally to live up to its advance publicity, and its only tangible result was the dramatic rapprochement of Germany and Soviet Russia at Rapallo.[57] Nor was this event—which foreshadowed a significant shift in the European balance and which, at the same time, widened the rift in the Entente—uninfluenced by the deficiencies of Lloyd George's diplomatic methods. There had been much talk of "open diplomacy" and "the mobilization of world opinion" before the conference opened; and provision was made to keep the international public fully informed of the discussions of the various commissions into which the conference was divided. But after this concession to democracy had been made, the political commissions in particular found that they had very little to do, while secret talks, from which many of the participating states were excluded, were conducted between an intimate group in Lloyd George's villa on the one hand and—through various devious channels—the Russians on the other. The Germans were not admitted to these talks and, since they feared a Russian arrangement with the Entente at their expense, they were amenable to the suggestions made to them by Chicherin.[58] The resultant *débacle* justified Lord Grey's gibe, earlier in the year, that there was "both too much limelight and too much secrecy" in Lloyd George's diplomacy.[59]

But it was not only in his attempt to supplant the professional diplomats in the field of negotiation, that Lloyd George's methods had unfortunate results. Even more serious was his willingness to make important decisions on policy and far-reaching commitments to foreign governments without prior consultation with the Foreign Office or with its chief. This became apparent as early as 1920, at the time of the war between Poland and Russia. The dramatic reversal of Polish fortunes in that conflict and the beginning of the Russian advance upon Warsaw coincided with the assembling of the Spa Conference of July to consider

[56] On the Genoa Conference, see *inter alia*, J. Saxon Mills, *The Genoa Conference* (New York, 1922); Viscount Swinton, *I Remember* (London, 1946), pp. 17-25; A. J. Sylvester, *The Real Lloyd George* (London, 1947), pp. 80-98; Amedeo Giannini, *Saggi di storia diplomatica, 1920-1940* (Firenze, 1940), pp. 27-50; Degras, I, 287-318; Louis Fischer, *The Soviets in World Affairs* (new ed., 2 vols., Princeton, 1951), I, 318-354; Harry Kessler, *Walter Rathenau, His Life and Work* (New York, 1930), pp. 304-340; and *The History of "The Times"*, IV, Part II, 662-677.

[57] On the eve of the conference, Lloyd George gave the British press copies of a memorandum circulated at Paris in 1919, warning of the dangers of driving Germany into the arms of Russia. Fischer, *Soviets*, I, 323. This was, however, part of his attempt to induce the French to treat with the Soviets rather than an expression of a belief that a Russo-German treaty was imminent.

[58] See Kessler, *Rathenau*, pp. 319-20, 322-23.

[59] *The Times*, January 28, 1922.

the question of German coal deliveries; and it was at Spa that the Polish minister Grabski approached Lloyd George and pleaded for aid. The Prime Minister upbraided Grabski for the follies of his government and insisted that Polish forces must be withdrawn to positions 125 miles behind those they presently occupied; but, having done that, he went on to promise that, if the Poles retired and if the Russians then crossed the new line which he had sanctioned, "the British Government and their Allies would be bound to help Poland with all the means at their disposal." In any circumstances, this would have been an extraordinary commitment for a British Prime Minister to make; but its most remarkable feature was that it was made without the authorization of the Cabinet and without any attempt to consult the Foreign Office. Indeed, the Foreign Office was not informed of the nature of the Prime Minister's declaration until after he had returned to London, a fact which placed Sir Horace Rumbold, Britain's minister in Warsaw, in the humiliating position of being unable for three days to verify or deny press accounts of the Spa declaration.[60]

Worse was to follow, for the Russians did cross the line approved by Lloyd George, and the validity of his promises was immediately put to the test. He responded to this, not with the kind of determined action pledged at Spa, but with a series of equivocal public speeches in which he said that only "the most imperative call of national honour, national safety and national freedom can justify war." When the Poles, finding no comfort in this sort of thing, sued for an armistice, and when the Russians offered terms, Lloyd George seized upon these eagerly and, characteristically, approved them at once without asking the opinions of the men trained to analyze documents of this kind. It would be difficult to find a more revealing description of the haphazard nature of Lloyd George's diplomacy than the note concerning this episode which appears in the diary of his confidant Lord Riddell, the press magnate. "Golf with L. G. at St. George's Hill. . . . Before we left, a message arrived announcing that the Russian Government were prepared to grant the Poles an armistice and that instructions had been sent to the military commander to make the necessary arrangements. L. G. in a high state of glee. When we arrived at the golf-club he sat down in the dressing room and wrote out a message to his secretary at Downing Street, instructing him what documents to issue to the press. A very precise little document."[61] It was not until considerably later that the Prime Minister

[60] On these events, see especially Nicolson, *Curzon*, pp. 202-208 and Kennedy, *Old Diplomacy*, pp. 314-338.
[61] Riddell, *Intimate Diary*, p. 225.

was convinced, and persuaded to announce publicly, that his enthusiasm had been premature and that the Russian terms were, in fact, incompatible with the independence of Poland. By that time, however, it was too late to repair the damage which these vacillations had inflicted upon British prestige in Central Europe; and the Poles, who had meanwhile been saved by vigorous French measures before Warsaw, were left feeling that Britain was an unreliable friend in time of trouble.

To Lord Curzon, who regarded British prestige as an asset which must be maintained at all costs, this episode was a painful one. Even more painful was the accumulating evidence that it was not an exceptional case, that the Prime Minister was in fact incorrigible, that he would go on making policy at his breakfast table and neglecting to inform the Foreign Secretary of his decisions, that he would go on preferring the advice of his secretaries to that of the Foreign Office (and sometimes even permitting them, rather than the Foreign Office staff, to draft important notes to foreign governments),[62] and that he would continue to avoid the orderly channels of diplomatic communication in favor of casual conversations, or even sly intimations to foreign representatives, of which no written record was kept. Curzon could not help but be aware that the department over which he presided was being deprived of its constitutional functions and that the process by which this was being effected was making his country's policy seem confused and unreliable. Why, then, did he submit to these practices?

This problem has been considered by both of Curzon's biographers and they are generally agreed in their conclusions. Curzon's only weapon against the Prime Minister was the threat of resignation. It was a weapon which could easily be turned against him, for Lloyd George, after all, might be disposed to accept an offer of resignation. It was precisely that possibility that deterred Curzon. He knew that he was not a popular figure, but he hoped that he was a respected one; and he was "morbidly sensitive to the effect which his resignation might have upon the estimation in which the public held him,"[63] especially if (as was quite possible) they did not understand the principles which prompted his action. Resignation, moreover, would probably mean the end of his public career. Curzon remembered too clearly the long years in which his talents had been neglected by the party leaders after his retirement as Viceroy of India in 1905 to hope that he would be allowed to return to

[62] Sir Valentine Chirol, "Four Years of Lloyd-Georgian Foreign Policy," *Edinburgh Review* (January 1923), p. 4.
[63] Ronaldshay, *Curzon*, III, 255.

high office if he retired voluntarily again;[64] and that, of course, would mean sacrificing his last chance to become Prime Minister. Nor was he deterred only—or even primarily—by these personal factors. In all fairness to the Foreign Secretary, it must be emphasized that he was convinced that his resignation would remove the last restraints upon Lloyd George and deliver the country over to a personal diplomacy which would be disastrous.[65] And it should be added that many of his friends and professional colleagues shared this view and urged him to remain at his post, even at the cost of personal humiliation.[66]

In these circumstances, the hope entertained by the friends of the Foreign Office when Curzon first became Foreign Secretary—namely, that he would stop the decline of that department—was bound to be disappointed. His attitude made inevitable the continuation of the system which he himself described in October 1922, in a letter drafted for, but not sent to, the Prime Minister:[67] "a system under which there are in reality two Foreign Offices, the one for which I am for the time being responsible, and the other at No. 10—with the essential difference between them that, whereas I report not only to you but to all my colleagues everything that I say or do, every telegram that I receive or send, every communication of importance that reaches me, it is often only by accident that I hear what is being done by the other Foreign Office. . . . This condition of affairs has reached such a pitch that not only is it a subject of common knowledge . . . but it is known to every journalist in London . . . the Foreign Office and myself in particular having been held up to contempt for having abdicated our functions, or allowed them to be stolen away."

Neither the accuracy of this picture, nor the dangers implicit in the situation described, were realized by the general public. This was again due to the continued unpopularity of the diplomatic caste, but certainly also to the peculiar character of the House of Commons which had emerged from the Khaki Elections of 1918, a body which contained only a handful of men who had any understanding of foreign affairs or any critical standards concerning the way in which they should be administered.[68] As a result, it was not until the autumn of 1922, when Lloyd George's methods had brought the country uncomfortably close to war

[64] Nicolson, *Curzon*, pp. 24, 28-31.
[65] He wrote on one occasion that he stayed on "in the certain knowledge that if I were to go my place would be taken by the ———— combination, which I regarded as a great national peril." Ronaldshay, *Curzon*, III, 256.
[66] Nicolson, *Curzon*, p. 23.
[67] Ronaldshay, *Curzon*, III, 316-317.
[68] See the comments in "A Farewell Survey," *The New Europe*, XVII (1920), 50.

in the Near East, that anything in the nature of a public awakening was achieved.

The chain of events which led to the Near Eastern crisis of 1922 will be discussed later in this book.[69] Here it need only be said that the crisis was the result of Turkish opposition to the terms of the Treaty of Sèvres and of the disunity of the Entente Powers in face of that opposition. The deterioration of Anglo-French cooperation, in turn, had been caused in large part by Lloyd George's great admiration for the Greeks and his firm conviction that, in return for territorial advantages in Asia Minor, they would assume the chief burden of enforcing the Sèvres provisions upon the Kemal government. This belief was weakened neither by the remonstrances of his Foreign Secretary, who believed that the Greek government was incapable of preserving order five miles outside the gates of Salonika, nor by the obvious dissatisfaction of the French and Italian governments with the tendencies of his eastern policy; and it was persisted in even after it had become clear that those governments were entering into private arrangements with Kemal and moderating their previous objections to his ambitions. The importance of this defection became clear at the same moment that Curzon's doubts were justified. In August and September Kemal's armies drove the Greek forces headlong into the sea; and the British people made the unpleasant discovery that an isolated British force at Chanak was all that stood in the way of a Turkish surge across the Straits and into the lost Turkish provinces beyond. And when, on September 15, a group within the Cabinet—including Lloyd George and Winston Churchill, but not including Curzon—issued an appeal to the Dominions for aid, war seemed a very real possibility.

In the end it did not come to that, thanks to Kemal's realization that war might compromise a victory already virtually won and thanks to Curzon's success, in a series of hurried talks in Paris, in effecting a renewed semblance of Anglo-French cooperation. But the crisis did bring down Lloyd George. The convolutions of his policy since 1919 were attacked in the press of the right and of the left. *The Nation* described his methods as having "all the faults of the old [diplomacy] and none of its superficial virtues";[70] *The Times* declared roundly that his government had "made a treaty and departed from it . . . dallied with Bolshevism and supported campaigns against it . . . coquetted with Germany and played fast and loose with France . . . dragged from Conference to Conference their failure to face the reparations issue . . . [and

---

[69] See Chapter 6, §§ 11, III below.   [70] *The Nation*, October 7, 1922.

finally come] to the verge of an armed conflict in the Near East, the course and outcome of which no man could foretell. As a result of their inconsistencies, the word of England lost currency throughout a great part of the world as the word of an upright land."[71] Attacked by the Liberals for indulging in "the improvisations of an intermittent and incalculable dictatorship"[72] and repudiated by the Conservatives upon whose support his retention of office depended, Lloyd George yielded his place in the center of the political stage to the less dynamic personalities of Bonar Law, Stanley Baldwin, and Ramsay MacDonald.

III

The crisis of 1922 freed the foreign service of the eccentricities of Lloyd George; but this did not mean that the conditions under which the Foreign Office and the Diplomatic Service had operated before 1914 were in any sense restored. If anything, the war scare tightened the restrictions imposed upon those agencies and increased the difficulties under which the professional advisers on policy and the representatives abroad had to work. For one thing, it revitalized the old campaign against "secret diplomacy." The elections of November 1922, which were strongly influenced by the events in the Near East, brought back into the House of Commons some of the most inveterate opponents of the Foreign Office. Among the increased Labor representation, for instance, were seventeen members of the Executive and General Council of the Union of Democratic Control, including such stalwarts as Morel, Trevelyan, Ponsonby, and MacDonald. To this group the Chanak crisis was proof, not only of Lloyd George's deficiencies as a diplomat, but also of the dangers of orthodox diplomacy as such. They began almost at once to gather support for a Parliamentary resolution stipulating that no act of war against a foreign state should be committed, no treaty ratified, no diplomatic arrangement or written or verbal agreement involving military obligations concluded, and no military or naval staff talks held, without express authorization of Parliament—a bill of particulars so all-embracing and yet so ill-defined that, if passed, it would seriously have handicapped intercourse with other Powers.[73] At the same

[71] *The Times,* October 30, 1922.
[72] Asquith at Dumfries, October 6, 1922. See Ronaldshay, *Curzon,* III, 318.
[73] In the summer of 1923 a draft resolution of this kind was sent, together with a letter signed by 100 Labor and Liberal members of Parliament, to members of the Dominions Parliaments, who were asked for advice and support. See *Foreign Affairs,* v (1923-1924), 23-24. During the first MacDonald government, when the Lausanne Treaty was laid before Parliament, the government announced that henceforth all treaties would be laid

time, they entertained, and publicly expressed, the strongest possible suspicion even of the normal processes of diplomacy. As early as December 1922, Ronald McNeill, the Under-Secretary for Foreign Affairs, was forced to answer so many questions concerning recent visits of Lord Curzon and Sir William Tyrrell to Paris that he complained that the Opposition was always talking of "sinister rumours" and was apparently wholly convinced that secret deals and dark conspiracies were being hatched on all sides by their officials.[74]

This in itself need not have been a matter of much consequence. But the Chanak crisis had helped to reinforce in public opinion generally an atmosphere which Sir Alfred Zimmern has described as being compounded of "dull anxiety, of feverish suspicion, of reckless inquisitiveness."[75] Tired of war and troubled by grave economic problems, the English people were in no mood for foreign adventures; they were more interested in disarmament than in prestige; and they were fearful of commitments which might lead to more dangerous Chanaks. This popular temper had a perceptible, and not altogether fortunate, effect upon the policy of the governments that ruled England in the years that followed. The Bonar Law-Baldwin government of 1922-1924, the Mac-Donald government of 1924, and the Baldwin government of 1924-1929 all tended to follow rather than to lead public opinion in foreign affairs, to satisfy the immediate desires of the electorate rather than the ultimate interests of the nation,[76] to make foreign policy the prisoner of domestic politics rather than to seek to pursue a farsighted independent course and to carry the public with them step by step.[77] This preoccupation with public opinion made it seem necessary for the Prime Minister and the Cabinet as a whole to intervene in the details of policy to a greater extent than in the past and to exercise a stricter supervision over

---

before the House of Commons for a period of 21 days before ratification. Arthur Ponsonby declared at the same time that the government would enter no secret agreements and that it favored Parliamentary discussion of all agreements and understandings with foreign Powers. *Ibid.*, 216. The U. D. C. resolution was submitted to Commons during the second Baldwin Ministry but failed of passage, after a debate in which Charles Trevelyan warned that the Labor party would recognize as binding no agreement which had not been sanctioned by Parliament. *Ibid.*, VI (1924-1925), 233. On July 1927, however, Sir Austen Chamberlain declared in Commons that "there is nothing secret about British policy. There are no engagements or undertakings that are not known to the House of Commons and [the Government will] undertake no future engagements on behalf of our country without submitting those engagements to Parliament and having the approval of Parliament for them." Parliamentary Debates: Commons, 5th series, CCVIII (1927), 1775.

[74] Parliamentary Debates: Commons, 5th series, CLIX (1922), 3343.

[75] Sir Alfred Zimmern, *The League of Nations and the Rule of Law* (London, 1936), p. 485.

[76] See Nicolson, *Curzon*, p. 185.   [77] Zimmern, *League of Nations*, p. 485.

the executants of policy; and, not infrequently, it led them, because of shifts in the popular temper, to indulge in abrupt and awkward reversals of policy, even in the course of delicate negotiations for objectives previously agreed upon.

All of this made the tasks of the professional diplomats infinitely more difficult. Lord Curzon, who continued to serve as Foreign Secretary until 1924, discovered this during the conference which met at Lausanne in January and February 1923 to arrange a definitive treaty with the Turks. With an adroitness and an authority which won the admiration of his foreign colleagues, Curzon dominated the conference and succeeded, not only in winning all his principal objectives—although this achievement was not confirmed until after he had retired from office—but in laying the basis for the reestablishment of friendly relations between Turkey and Great Britain. His successes, however, were won in the face of a fearful, and at times bitterly critical, public opinion, and of a Cabinet which on more than one occasion threatened to withdraw its support. "I found Bonar," Curzon wrote at the beginning of the conference, "longing to clear out of Mosul, the Straits and Constantinople, willing to give up anything and everything rather than have a row, astonished at the responsibility I have assumed at Lausanne and prepared for me to back down everywhere."[78]

Another instance of the same sort of thing—but with a less happy result—came during the Corfu crisis later in the year. In face of this first attack by Mussolini upon the public law of Europe, Sir Robert Cecil in Geneva was originally instructed to mobilize the forces of the League of Nations. At the critical moment, however, this policy was reversed, and he was ordered to refer the dispute to the Conference of Ambassadors in Paris, which promptly gave in to the Duce's terms. The reasons for this change of front are not entirely clear, but it was probably not uninfluenced by the campaign being currently conducted by the *Daily Mail* and other newspapers, which were accusing Curzon, Cecil, and the Foreign Office of "war-mongering."[79]

Deference to public opinion was, during Ramsay MacDonald's first ministry, coupled with deference to party opinion; and, on at least one

[78] Ronaldshay, *Curzon*, III, 332. After Baldwin had become Prime Minister, Curzon wrote to him: "I must confess I am almost in despair as to the way in which Foreign Policy is carried on in this Cabinet. . . . We must act together and the P.M. must see his F.S. through." G. M. Young, *Stanley Baldwin* (London, 1952), p. 50.

[79] On this, see G. P. Pink, *The Conference of Ambassadors* (Geneva Research Center: Geneva Studies, XII, Nos. 4-5, 1942), pp. 207-246; Viscount Cecil, *A Great Experiment* (London, 1941), pp. 150-151; Nicolson, *Curzon*, pp. 368-371. See also Chapter 7, § IV, below.

occasion, MacDonald's obedience to his party's demands led him to overrule the Foreign Office and indulge in what might almost be described as diplomatic chicanery. The conspicuous example of this was during the negotiations for an Anglo-Russian agreement in 1924. These negotiations were held in London, and they stretched over a period of four months before it became clear that the Russians had not the slightest intention of making any compensation for the debts repudiated, and the British property confiscated, by them during the revolution. Since this was the chief issue of the talks, the Foreign Office announced that the negotiations would be broken off. At this point, however, a deputation from the Labor party, which had been conducting parallel talks with the Russian delegation—in itself a rather dubious procedure—protested to Arthur Ponsonby, MacDonald's Under-Secretary for Foreign Affairs. They argued that it would be fatal to the reputation of the Labor party if the conference disbanded without a result; and they submitted a compromise which they felt would be satisfactory to both parties. This was a formula quite as vague as those which Lloyd George's Secretariats had been so adept at producing; it covered irreconcilable differences between the parties with a veil of amicable platitudes; but the government nevertheless accepted it and gravely announced the conclusion of a treaty. Coming from a party which talked so much about the way in which the old diplomacy had deceived the British people, the conclusion of this bogus agreement was a curious procedure; and it was promptly turned against its authors, becoming one of the most important issues in the elections of October 1924 which turned Labor out of office.[80]

To the pressure of national and party opinion must be added that of public opinion in the Dominions. Before the war this had been an inconsiderable factor in the conduct of British foreign relations. This was no longer true. Curzon had explained to the French ambassador in December 1921 that "British foreign policy was now not the policy of the Cabinet in Downing Street alone, but was the policy of the Empire, and the points of view of the Prime Ministers of our distant Dominions had also to be seriously considered."[81] If there was any doubt about the importance of this, it was removed by the effects of the Chanak crisis of 1922 upon the Dominion governments. The famous telegram of September 15, which had asked whether the Dominions would send contingents

---

[80] On the Russian agreement, see especially Philip Viscount Snowden, *An Autobiography* (2 vols., London, 1934), II, 680-686.

[81] Cmd. 2169 (1924), p. 111.

to the Near East, had been the first intimation made to them of trouble in that quarter; and it was received with surprise and, especially on the part of Australia and Canada, with resentment.[82] From this time on, the Dominions were increasingly vigilant concerning steps taken by the British government which might involve them in troubles in Europe or in other areas in which they were not vitally interested, and British cabinets tended to become increasingly attentive to Dominion opinion. From the very beginning of his term as Foreign Secretary in the second Baldwin government, Austen Chamberlain stressed the importance of this factor in the conduct of British foreign relations. "The first thoughts of any Englishman on appointment to the office of Foreign Secretary," he said in his first public address after taking office, "must be that he speaks in the name, not of Great Britain only, but of the British Dominions beyond the seas, and that it is his imperative duty to preserve in word and act the diplomatic unity of the British Empire. Our interests are one. Our intercourse must be intimate and constant, and we must speak with one voice in the councils of the world."[83]

The difficulty here was that intimate and constant intercourse with the Dominions was virtually impossible to maintain, given the state of communications in the 1920's. Interchange of views was possible at Imperial Conferences, but these were held infrequently, and in the seven years ending in December 1926 there were only three plenary meetings of the Imperial Prime Ministers. Problems arose and solutions were demanded too suddenly for the British government always to consult the Dominions;[84] yet none of the governments of this period was willing to take a firm line in European affairs which might be repudiated by members of the Empire at a subsequent date. Their natural inclination, therefore, was to be tentative and hesitant in matters of crucial European importance, a fact which increased the difficulties of British negotiators abroad and which, in some European quarters, led to criticisms of British indecision and unreliability.

[82] See A. J. Toynbee, *The Conduct of British Empire Foreign Relations since the Peace Settlement* (London, 1928), pp. 47ff.; Gwendolen M. Carter, *The British Commonwealth and International Security: The Role of the Dominions, 1919-1939* (Toronto, 1947), pp. 84-90; *The History of "The Times"*, IV, Part II, 734; and Bruce Hutchison, *The Incredible Canadian: a candid portrait of Mackenzie King* (Toronto, 1952), pp. 89-97.

[83] Sir Austen Chamberlain, *Peace in Our Time: Addresses on Europe and the Empire* (London, 1928), pp. 1-2. See also his speech at Chatham House on February 4, 1930 in which he spoke of the "new distribution of executive power in the Empire [which] must profoundly affect the conduct of foreign affairs." *International Affairs*, IX (1930), 182.

[84] On attempts to solve this problem, see Toynbee, *British Empire Foreign Relations*, pp. 72-74.

The combined impact of national and Dominions public opinion upon the formulation of British foreign policy is seen perhaps most clearly in the question of European security in general and Britain's relations with the League of Nations in particular. Enthusiasm for the League of Nations was widespread in Great Britain and, to a somewhat lesser degree, in the Dominions, and no British government would have dared to ignore that organization in the conduct of its policy. Faith in the League was not, however, generally combined with an understanding of its machinery, or of the obligations which Britain had assumed in adhering to the Covenant; nor was the enthusiasm for the League as a moral cause matched by equal enthusiasm for efforts to strengthen League machinery so that it could, by compulsory arbitration or military sanctions, enforce the cause of peace against potential aggressors. As one historian has written, the notion of collective security "remained an alien on English soil throughout the decade which followed the war";[85] and many people believed that even to think seriously about the question of sanctions was unwholesome and possibly destructive of peace. For their part, the Dominions were disinclined to become involved in responsibilities in Europe and were, consequently, opposed to Britain's assuming new obligations under a strengthened Covenant.

In these circumstances, the governments which ruled Britain from 1923 to 1929 elected to follow a dual course, proclaiming on the one hand that their "whole policy" rested on the League but resisting, on the other, attempts to solve the security question by strengthening the Covenant. The two constructive efforts made to repair the gaps in the Covenant were rejected—the Draft Treaty of Mutual Assistance by the MacDonald government, the Geneva Protocol by the Baldwin government that succeeded it.[86] The reasons given in the two cases were similar: the plans were subversive of the true purpose of the League and would promote rather than prevent war; they would discourage disarmament and hence weaken the best assurance of peace; they were too complicated and, conversely, too logical for the British temperament; and they would not be supported by the Dominions. Britain preferred to confine her contribution to a solution of the security question to a regional pact in that part of Europe in which she had vital interests and did so by accepting the Locarno Treaties in 1925.

It is not possible to state with any degree of assurance what the attitude of the expert advisers in the Foreign Office was to these developments.

[85] Jordan, *Great Britain, France and the German Question*, p. 206.
[86] See Chapter 4, § III and Chapter 10, § I below.

In the case of the Draft Treaty, it seems likely that Foreign Office opinion was not very important. Mr. MacDonald was his own Foreign Secretary, a circumstance which seems at times to have persuaded him that it was unnecessary for him to keep in close touch with his department.[87] Moreover, the Prime Minister's views at this time carefully reflected those of the pacifist wing of his party; he was irreconcilably opposed to the Draft Treaty and was almost temperamentally incapable of discussing it rationally.[88]

In the case of the Geneva Protocol, the only Foreign Office memorandum which is available is one written in February 1925 by the Historical Adviser, Sir James Headlam-Morley.[89] This is a document which raises grave doubts as to the advisability of adopting an attitude of blank negation towards continental attempts to repair the gaps in the Covenant. Headlam-Morley argues that Britain cannot separate herself from the troubles of Europe; that the contention that the Dominions do not desire involvement in European affairs should not determine Britain's position; that the danger point in Europe is not the Rhine but the Vistula; and that, consequently, no security pact will be effective if it is not European, rather than regional, in scope. The author intimates further that, for the above reasons, the Geneva Protocol should not be rejected but revised.

To what extent this represented Foreign Office opinion in general is not known. Headlam-Morley's arguments may have had some influence on Austen Chamberlain, for at the outset at least he was not unalterably opposed to the Protocol.[90] But speculation on this point is neither helpful nor important. In the event, the decision on the Geneva Protocol was made by the Cabinet as a whole, which deferred to what it considered to be public opinion and—perhaps unnecessarily—to the desires of the Dominions[91] and which, after deciding on outright rejection of the

---

[87] Certainly the confusion during the affair of the Zinoviev letter betrays a lack of any effective liaison between MacDonald and the Foreign Office. There is, moreover, other evidence. MacDonald's Under-Secretary was at times so out of touch with his chief that he employed Norman Angell to communicate his views to MacDonald (Angell, *After All*, p. 239); and the Foreign Office, and everyone else, seems to have been excluded from the conversations between MacDonald and Herriot at Checquers, with resultant confusion. Snowden, *Autobiography*, II, 667.

[88] See the damaging account of Angell's discussion of this matter with MacDonald and H. M. Swanwick of the Union of Democratic Control. Angell, *After All*, pp. 240ff.

[89] Sir James Headlam-Morley, *Studies in Diplomatic History* (London, 1930), pp. 171ff., 187.

[90] Wickham Steed, *The Real Stanley Baldwin* (London, 1930), pp. 114-115. See, however, Sir C. Petrie, *Life and Letters of the Right Hon. Sir Austen Chamberlain* (2 vols., London, 1939-1940), II, 258.

[91] Carter (*British Commonwealth*, p. 121) believes that the objections of the Dominions were not insuperable.

Protocol, entrusted the drafting of the note explaining the British position, not to the Foreign Office or even to the Foreign Secretary, but to Lord Balfour.[92] And this step, once taken, was irrevocable, for, after the Baldwin Cabinet had, with some misgivings,[93] sanctioned the negotiations which led to the Locarno Treaties, and after those treaties had been signed, it steadfastly refused to countenance any further consideration of the security question.

IV

"The art of diplomacy," declares a British White Paper of 1943, "consists in making the policy of His Majesty's Government, whatever it may be, understood and, if possible, accepted by other countries."[94] To have made the British attitude on security explicable and palatable to other members of the League in the years after 1925 would have required a British representative possessed of great gifts of persuasion, understanding, and tact. Austen Chamberlain undertook to serve as that representative himself.

There is a story to the effect that Chamberlain was once, earlier in his life, considered as a possible candidate for the Paris Embassy; and that Paul Cambon, asked about this, said: "Ce cher Austen! Quel brave homme! Ce n'est pourtant pas un article d'exportation!"[95] The observation, if it is not apocryphal, was shrewd. For the direction of a difficult set of negotiations, Chamberlain possessed all the requisite qualities, as he demonstrated by the skillful manner in which he conducted the Locarno negotiations—working in close cooperation with his ambassadors in Paris and Berlin, clearing away misunderstandings and narrowing the issues by the exchange of written notes, and holding the crucial meetings only after a firm basis for agreement had been reached.[96] He was less well equipped, however, with those gifts which a representative of his country abroad should always possess—balance, perspective, humor and personal charm, the ability to state his country's position without alienating his hearers, the willingness to give a fair hearing to their point of view and to indicate that he understands the reasoning that informs it even when he cannot accept it.

---

[92] Sir Alfred Zimmern has described the argument against unhealthy preoccupation with sanctions, which Balfour wrote and Chamberlain read to the League Council in March 1925, as a "cheerful recommendation to adopt a policy of Couéism." *League of Nations*, p. 358.

[93] See Petrie, *Chamberlain*, II, 264. [94] Cmd. 6420 (1943), p. 2.

[95] Steed, *Stanley Baldwin*, p. 110.

[96] See Petrie, *Chamberlain*, II, 260, 264, 272, 281, 286-88; and Sir Victor Wellesley, *Diplomacy in Fetters* (London, 1944), p. 31.

Chamberlain began by impressing and ended by irritating his fellow members in the League. His attempts to convince them that they must, in approaching European problems, abjure the use of reason and logic, since these would only render their efforts suspect in English eyes, succeeded only in bewildering them—while causing extreme discomfort to those Englishmen who had also to listen to these arguments.[97] His manner before the Assembly was never entirely free from the faintest suggestion of condescension, and occasionally he was betrayed into verbal lapses in which he spoke of "your League" as if Britain was not willing to admit her membership.[98] When British policy was criticized, he was apt to grow shriller and to indulge in astonishing philippics against his foreign colleagues; and one such performance on his part was paraphrased by a British observer to read: "We are perfect. We are British. And yet you, you dagoes, dare to come here and criticize US!"[99] Nor is it to be imagined that his frequent argument that Great Britain had entire faith in the League but believed that its progress must be slow, like the imperceptible evolution of the British constitution, aroused much enthusiasm among continental statesmen or much confidence in Britain's willingness to aid in the solution of European problems.[100]

Chamberlain also attracted a certain amount of criticism because of a development which was probably unavoidable. The conclusion of the Locarno Pact foreshadowed the entrance of Germany into the League of Nations. In the interval before that could be effected, however, collaboration among the Locarno Powers had already become so close that there was a good deal of resentment in the corridors at Geneva over what was termed "the Locarno cabal."[101] These feelings were not allayed by the tactics pursued by Briand and Chamberlain during the Special Assembly of March 1926, tactics which seemed designed to settle the future composition of the League Council by private conversations and secret deals carried on behind the Assembly's back and which succeeded only in creating a major crisis which did not help the League's international reputation.[102] Moreover, even after Germany had made good her claim to a

---

[97] "No intelligently patriotic Briton can feel anything but shame at being guyed by the Foreign Secretary before the whole world as a man who will not think or plan, who scorns logic and relies on muddling through." *Foreign Affairs*, VII (1925-1926), 93.

[98] See, for instance, the account of his speech at the Eighth Assembly in F. P. Walters, *A History of the League of Nations* (2 vols., London, 1952), I, 346.

[99] Steed, *Baldwin*, p. 129.

[100] On this see Cecil, *A Great Experiment*, pp. 190-191.

[101] Jordan, *Great Britain, France and the German Question*, pp. 98-100.

[102] On this crisis, see G. Scelle, *Une Crise de la Société des Nations* (Paris, 1927); Cecil, *A Great Experiment*, pp. 177-178; Walters, *History of the League*, I, 316-325; and Chapter 3 below.

permanent seat on the Council, the "cabal" did not dissolve. There was doubtless good reason for this, for the Locarno Powers were forced to discuss among themselves questions which were not of immediate interest to the League. Unfortunately, however, they often arrogated to themselves other matters which did belong properly within the competence of the Council; and it sometimes appeared that their intention was to extend this practice further, leaving to the Council only "such weighty matters as the appointment of the governing body of the International Cinematographic Institute at Rome."[103] All things considered, Chamberlain's role as a charter member of the "cabal" did not improve his personal stature, or his country's reputation, at the seat of the League.

But quite apart from all this, it is doubtful whether Chamberlain's decision to represent his country at Geneva was a wise one. He was Foreign Secretary of a large country, a position which imposes a crushing burden upon its incumbent at any time. His position as Britain's representative on the Council not only greatly increased his labors but necessitated frequent absences from London, for, after Germany's entrance into the League, the Council met four times a year. He was left little time to supervise the administration of his department and none to institute reforms, the need for which had been recognized since 1919. And, inevitably, the added weight of work sapped his energies and reduced his overall efficiency, and was probably responsible for actions for which he was much criticized during his last three years of office.

Certainly much of the prestige which he had won by his careful management of the Locarno negotiations was dissipated by what appeared to be his bungling of the Geneva Naval Conference of 1927. That meeting, between representatives of Great Britain, Japan, and the United States, was reminiscent of the conferences of the Lloyd George period. It was convened without adequate diplomatic preparation; it began with a public meeting at which delegates hurled widely divergent plans at each other's heads; and it ended—after weeks of futile wrangling, and after an attempt at compromise had been indignantly repudiated by the British Cabinet under the inspiration of Mr. Winston Churchill—in total failure.[104] A year later, Chamberlain's reputation was damaged by an even more serious diplomatic *gaffe*. On July 30, 1928, the Foreign Secretary announced in the House of Commons that a compromise in regard to the

---

[103] Felix Morley, *The Society of Nations* (Washington, 1932), p. 385.

[104] The most succinct and penetrating discussion of the technical deficiencies of this conference is that of Sir Arthur Salter, "The Technique of Open Diplomacy," *Political Quarterly*, III (1932), 64-65.

limitation of naval armaments had been reached with France, that it had been communicated confidentially to the United States government, but that it could not yet be made public. This public avowal of the existence of a secret was a curious procedure;[105] and it aroused a good deal of irritable speculation. In the end, it transpired that Britain and France had agreed on a plan similar to one already rejected by the United States; and their rather feeble attempt to bring pressure on that country succeeded only in antagonizing American public opinion. But it appeared further—as the *Manchester Guardian* deduced from inspired articles in the French press—that, in order to reach agreement with France, concessions had been made to her in the pending question of land armaments, and there was evidence that the government was now inclined to accept the French point of view that trained reserves should not be included in estimates of national military strength which would be used in future schemes for disarmament. "If [this] principle . . . has been abandoned," declared *The Guardian,* "it is more than a concession: it is a betrayal!"[106] British public opinion, which was firmly wedded to the idea of disarmament, agreed, and a howl of criticism went up in which all of the old charges of "secret diplomacy" and "conspiracy with France" were revived.

These examples of diplomatic maladroitness—and they are recognized as such even by Chamberlain's biographer[107]—had repercussions in the general elections of 1929 which brought the Labor party back to power. Their wider significance, perhaps, is that, because of them, the first postwar decade ended, as it had begun, with a good proportion of the British public entertaining grave suspicions of British diplomacy and, inevitably, of the diplomatic establishment—that is, the Foreign Office and the Diplomatic Service. Had Chamberlain's personal prestige remained undiminished, it might have had some effect in enhancing the popular reputation of the Foreign Office. This was not the case.

The British foreign service was still regarded, at the end of this decade, as a last stronghold of aristocratic privilege and a preserve for Etonians and Harrovians who were inadequately prepared to meet the problems of modern democratic society.[108] The complete failure of the Conservative governments to entertain any suggestions of internal reform served only to reinforce this idea. In addition, there was a strong suspicion in

---

[105] See Salter's comments, *ibid.,* p. 66.

[106] *Manchester Guardian,* August 3, 1928.

[107] Petrie, *Chamberlain,* II, 324-325.

[108] See, for instance, R. Nightingale, *Personnel of the British Foreign Office and Diplomatic Service* (Fabian Tract No. 232), (London, 1930).

the ranks of Labor that the Foreign Office was a center of political reaction and that it had, in fact, been primarily responsible for the fall of the Labor government in 1924. This belief was based on the rather shaky thesis that the Foreign Office publication of the famous Zinoviev letter, which figured so largely in the 1924 elections, had been designed deliberately to embarrass the Prime Minister,[109] whereas the step seems to have been taken to anticipate publication in the press.[110] Still, the belief was a stubborn one and, in 1928, it was strengthened, when a Foreign Office official whose name had figured in the Zinoviev affair became involved in a Treasury inquiry into speculation in foreign exchange by civil servants, a circumstance which led the press to revive popular memory of the "Red letter plot."[111]

To this atmosphere of awakened distrust, the failures of Austen Chamberlain's diplomacy made their contribution. One of the by-products of the breakdown of the Geneva Naval Conference, for instance, was the resignation from the Cabinet of Lord Robert Cecil, who had served as one of the British negotiators in the naval talks. Cecil's action was the end result of a series of disagreements with his colleagues which dated back to the days of the Draft Treaty;[112] and his differences with Chamberlain at the time of the Special Assembly of 1926 had come close to precipitating a break at that time. His resignation now caused a public sensation, during which it was rumored that he had fallen prey to reactionary officials in the Foreign Office.[113] With the ground thus prepared, it was very easy, during the disclosures of the abortive arrangement with France in the following year, for critics on the left to assume that those reactionary officials were now firmly in the saddle and that "secret diplomacy" was again to be the order of the day unless the people—as

---

[109] In a speech at Dundee on October 25, 1924, E. D. Morel said: "The whole thing has an ugly look. . . . The work of world pacification which Labour has taken in hand must not be allowed to be jeopardized by certain highly-placed permanent officials in the Foreign Office. . . . If there has been a plot—and I am inclined to think there has—that plot has been hatched in the interests of the Tory Party, and its instigators will be found in the triangle of Fleet Street, the City and the Foreign Office." *Foreign Affairs*, VI (1924-1925), 129.

[110] On this affair, see, *inter alia*, Fischer, *Soviets*, II, 493-498; Snowden, *Autobiography*, II, 714-715; Gregory, *On the Edge of Diplomacy*, pp. 215-231; Young, *Baldwin*, pp. 85-88.

[111] Parliamentary Debates: Commons, 5th series, CCXV (1928), 47-106.

[112] Cecil, *A Great Experiment*, pp. 358-363.

[113] Cecil himself shared the belief in the influence of such officials on Chamberlain. See *ibid.*, p. 163. Later when he became one of Britain's representatives to Geneva during the second MacDonald government, he was given an office in the Foreign Office. Of that period, he has written: "I will say nothing of the permanent officials of the Foreign Office and the Cabinet Offices except that they were all very competent and some of them helpful." *Ibid.*, p. 201.

Norman Angell wrote in October 1928—took the control of foreign affairs away from "the expert, which means too often the Foreign Offices, the old-time diplomats, the devisers of secret treaties."[114]

V

If, in the above pages, emphasis has been placed on the question of the popularity of the Foreign Office and the Diplomatic Service, this has been done deliberately. Administrative and executive agencies which enjoy the respect, or at least the confidence, of Parliament, press, and public do not generally have to concern themselves about the protection of their powers and prerogatives. In democracies, however, this happy state is rarely attained by the Foreign Offices, and this fact is probably the chief reason why unwise and disruptive invasions of their legitimate sphere of activity are so frequent.

In an interesting book on the conduct of foreign relations in the inter-war period, Sir Victor Wellesley has declared that "British diplomacy is no longer master in its own house," and he has listed the "fetters" which in recent years have bound British diplomacy and prevented it from performing effectively the functions for which its personnel are trained: tighter parliamentary control over foreign affairs; the complication of consulting the Dominions; the pressure of an inquisitive, demanding, but often ill-informed public opinion; the failure of proper coordination between the work of political, military, and economic agencies of the government; and others.[115] Reference has been made to these factors above. But certainly the gravest disadvantage under which the British diplomatic establishment had to operate in these years was the persistent suspicion in which it was held by large sections of the British public. It was essentially this, for instance, which made possible Lloyd George's carefree, but always dangerous, flouting of the normal processes of diplomacy and the introduction, into the administration of British policy, of faults of coordination which were never entirely corrected before 1939.

The most flagrant abuses of the Lloyd George period were, of course, discontinued in the years which followed his dismissal from office; and Austen Chamberlain was never forced to feel the humiliation and the impotence which had been the experience of Lord Curzon. But as long as the public attitude toward the Foreign Office and the Diplomatic Service remained unchanged—and it did remain substantially unchanged

---

[114] *Foreign Affairs*, XI (1928-1929), issue of October.
[115] Wellesley, *Diplomacy in Fetters*, p. 7 and *passim*.

throughout the decade discussed—there was no assurance that Lloyd George's methods might not be employed in the future by other political leaders as confident and as self-willed as he. The precedents had been established. In the 1930's—with no apparent objections from a public which was bewildered by the sudden deterioration of the international situation—they were to be improved upon, first by Ramsay MacDonald and later, and more disastrously, by Neville Chamberlain.

The French Foreign Office:
The Era of Philippe Berthelot

BY RICHARD D. CHALLENER

THE FRENCH FOREIGN OFFICE, though not without its faults or its critics, emerged from the first world war and the Peace Conference with its prestige undimmed. There were, to be sure, not a few Frenchmen who were dissatisfied with the final terms of Versailles or who regretted such results as Clemenceau's decision to abandon French claims for a Rhineland buffer zone in favor of an Anglo-American treaty of guarantee which never materialized. But at the same time the Quai d'Orsay did not become the target for the attacks of well-meaning dilettantes who regarded the professional diplomat as an expendable luxury and the Foreign Office as an institution of questionable merit.

There was, after all, no nation more conscious than France of the fact that both her European and her international position depended upon a viable foreign policy. The British might once again come to look upon many phases of Continental politics with characteristic, pre-1914 aloofness, and the Americans could believe it sound policy to retire behind the Atlantic, but no Frenchman could approach international affairs with a similar spirit of quixotic detachment. As a people the French were acutely conscious of their geographic exposure to invasion, of their limited population and of their industrial backwardness. They all knew, though at times some French leaders might act as if they had forgotten, that their recent military triumph had been possible only because they had been members of a grand alliance. Nor were the French sure of the permanence of their victory—to a Poincaré, ever fearful of a revival of German military power, it was a truism that "Time, in passing, has already worked against us." Hence, if the fruits of victory were not to wither on the vine, the Quai d'Orsay would have to develop a foreign policy which would guarantee the French triumph and maintain the security of the nation.[1]

Nor did the French, unlike the Americans or the British, have many regrets about their prewar diplomacy. To a small minority their wartime President became known as "Poincaré la Guerre," but on the whole Frenchmen believed passionately and virtually unanimously in German war guilt. Because the French knew they could not have avoided defeat without their allies, they considered the diplomacy by which the Entente of 1914 had been formed as a necessary and brilliant policy which had saved their country; it was by no means a heinous "secret" diplomacy which had committed the French people to a war which could have been averted. And, above all, as a result of their victory the French had regained Alsace-Lorraine, the two "lost provinces" whose recovery had been the basic objective of French diplomacy since the war of 1870-1871. Small wonder, then, that the historical movement known as "revisionism" found in France the slimmest foothold of all. Typical was the verdict of Joseph Barthélmy, noted jurist and for many years a member of the Chamber Committee on Foreign Affairs: "It was thanks to secret diplomacy that France recovered from the state of isolation and weakness in which the disasters of 1870 had left her, by means of the Franco-Russian alliance, the Entente Cordiale, and the friendly attitude of Italy."[2]

As a result, the Foreign Office, though not without its critics, survived the first decade of the postwar period with surprisingly few changes. Indicative of the French temper was the fact that, at a time when the professional diplomat was regarded with suspicion in most democratic countries, the French immediately after the war moved not to attack but to strengthen the position of the professional element in the Quai d'Orsay. "May our diplomats, better recruited, better selected, better known and better loved, be worthy of our soldiers—our soldiers of yesterday, our soldiers of tomorrow," was the conclusion of a Chamber of Deputies report in 1920. Significantly, too, the only major change in Foreign Office organization in the 1920's was the creation in January 1920 of the post of permanent Secretary General. It was to be his function to direct all phases of French diplomacy and to coordinate all of the many activities of the Quai d'Orsay.[3] Back of this reform was the idea—

---

[1] For evidence of the awareness among French political leaders of the need for a successful foreign policy see, in particular, the reports of the Chamber of Deputies committees which examined the Quai d'Orsay budgets in 1920 and 1921. *Journal officiel, Chambre des Députés, Documents*, 1920, No. 802, pp. 855ff. and 1921, No. 2020, pp. 309ff.

[2] Joseph Barthélmy, *Le Gouvernement de France* (Paris, ed. of 1919), p. 119.

[3] Emmanuel de Levis-Mirepoix, *Le Ministère des affaires étrangères* (Angers, 1934), pp. 132-133.

concurred in although never formally approved by the Chamber of Deputies—that the frequent changes in French cabinets made it mandatory to have a permanent official of the highest rank, serving directly under the responsible minister, whose presence would assure the continuity of French foreign policy. It was also felt that the tendency for the Premier to hold the post of Minister of Foreign Affairs made it all the more necessary to have such a permanent official at the Quai d'Orsay. Hence, although a Foreign Minister might be in office for only a few months and, in addition, might be unable to give full-time attention to foreign affairs, the Secretary General would preserve the traditions of French diplomacy and prevent French policies from fluctuating with each passing ministry.[4]

The possibility of preserving continuity in French diplomatic policies was further enhanced by the fact that in the immediate years after Versailles many of the career personnel of the prewar era retained their positions and much of their authority. Paul Cambon, who as ambassador to Great Britain had been so influential in building the Entente of 1904, remained in London until the end of 1920, while his equally famous brother Jules presided over the Paris meetings of the Council of Ambassadors for some years after that. Camille Barrère, whose diplomatic talents had smoothed Franco-Italian relations, retained his post in Rome until 1924, and Jules Jusserand, once the confidant of Theodore Roosevelt, continued to represent the Third Republic at Washington until the same year. To be sure, the advice of these older diplomats was not always followed. Paul Cambon, for instance, resigned his post in part because he felt that the postwar French political leaders had an incomplete understanding of the need for close ties with Britain and seemed willing to disregard the traditions established in the years after 1871.[5] But at the same time the presence of these pre-1914 diplomats, many of whom had been the associates of Delcassé in the building of the French alliance system, helped to prevent any sharp break with the past, and these men

[4] *Journal officiel*, 1921, No. 2020, p. 317 and 1920, No. 802, p. 870. The *rapporteur*, M. Noblemaire, insisted upon the need for such a permanent official but at the same time expressed his preference for the British system of a permanent Under-Secretary of State. What Noblemaire hoped for was an official, not subject to removal with each ministerial change, who would act as liaison agent between the Foreign Office and the legislature rather than as director of the Quai d'Orsay itself. No action was ever taken to comply with his views.

[5] Paul Cambon, *Correspondance, 1870-1924* (Paris, 1946), III, 387. The attitude of the new French leaders would, Cambon felt, produce a new Fashoda and a new set of diplomatic disasters.

could be counted upon to represent the traditional attitudes and practices of the Foreign Office.[6]

The development of French political life in the decade of the 1920's was in itself another factor which helped to preserve the prestige of the Quai d'Orsay and to prevent frequent deviations in foreign policy. In the latter stages of the war and during the Peace Conference the figure of Georges Clemenceau had, of course, been dominant in French affairs. His Foreign Minister, Stephen Pichon, had occupied a purely subordinate position and had possessed a minimum of authority or independence; however, his willingness to accept Clemenceau's leadership had averted friction and disagreement.[7] But from the end of the Clemenceau ministry early in 1920 until April of 1925, the Premier always assumed for himself the office of Minister of Foreign Affairs. While this political development had the disadvantages already noted, it was also a clear indication of the importance which French leaders attached to foreign policy and, furthermore, served to preserve the stature of the Foreign Office itself. Above all, in direct contrast to the unhappy British experience with Lloyd George and Curzon, this tendency to unite the two offices in the hands of one man effectively prevented competition and jealousy from arising between the chief of the Cabinet and the minister responsible for the conduct of foreign relations.

Moreover, whereas France had between 1920 and 1930 no less than fifteen different ministries and ten different Premiers, there were only six individuals who served at the Quai d'Orsay. Of these six, Millerand and Leygues were in office only in 1920, and du Prey was a transient who held his post for a mere five days in June 1924. Actually, despite the chronic French ministerial instability, from January 1921 until March 1932—with the exception of two short interludes when Herriot was at the Foreign Office—French foreign policy was in the hands of but two men, those inveterate rivals, Raymond Poincaré and Aristide Briand.[8]

Raymond Poincaré, whose ministry was characterized by an attempt to give France an independent foreign policy, was a man of strong convictions and a legalistic outlook who took his stand upon the letter and the

[6] See, for example, the familiar article by Jules Cambon, "The Permanent Bases of French Foreign Policy," reprinted in Hamilton Fish Armstrong, *The Foreign Affairs Reader* (New York, 1947), pp. 103ff. Jules Cambon argued that, regardless of changes in forms of government, public opinion or the conduct of diplomacy, the principal foreign policy objectives of any great nation remained constant.

[7] Paul Cambon, *Correspondance*, III, 297, 303, 367.

[8] These statistics based upon the charts in F. L. Schuman, *War and Diplomacy in the French Republic* (New York, 1931), Appendix B.

law of the Versailles Treaty. His favorite device was to go into the French countryside on Sunday afternoons and, usually while dedicating a memorial to the war dead, deliver a long oration in which he insisted that Germany could and must pay every franc of her reparations obligations. Well before 1914 Poincaré, a representative spokesman of the Conservative-Nationalist tradition in French politics, had been convinced of Germany's aggressive intentions; after the war he continued to typify all those Frenchmen who believed that the "hereditary enemy" across the Rhine must be "kept down" by a program of treaty enforcement, military alliances with the new states of Central Europe, and a strong army. He deeply resented any and all Anglo-American attempts to conciliate the Weimar Republic as well as any diplomatic gesture by his own country which appeared to endanger any of France's treaty rights. When, at the Cannes conference in 1922, Briand appeared willing to concede on reparations in order to work more harmoniously with Britain, Poincaré participated in the campaign which drove Briand from the Foreign Office and shortly afterwards replaced him as Premier and Foreign Minister. During the next two and a half years, despite Anglo-American pressure, he went ahead with his policy of strict treaty enforcement, a program highlighted by the controversial occupation of the Ruhr. Although Poincaré frequently spoke of the need for close alliance with England and even continued negotiations begun by Briand, his policy, in reality, was an attempt to show the rest of the world that France could conduct an independent foreign policy.

Aristide Briand, on the other hand, was a man of more flexible disposition who was deeply devoted to the preservation of European peace. An orator rather than a thinker, a pre-1914 Socialist who had gradually abandoned most of the tenets of the left, Briand had his greatest successes on the platform and seemed to possess an uncanny ability to grasp the mood of his audience. His speeches at the League of Nations, particularly the one heralding the entry of Germany into the Geneva councils in which he proclaimed, "Arrière les canons, arrière les mitrailleuses," made him the spokesman of the French moderates and the Left as well as of the international peace movement. Though Briand was actually as "security-conscious" as Poincaré and never as idealistic as his enemies charged, the policies which he put into practice were diametrically opposed to those of his rival on many fundamentals. After the experiences of the first world war, Briand came to feel that French security depended upon cooperation with the League of Nations, closer ties with Great Britain and, ultimately, upon Franco-German rapprochement. His greatest days came after 1924 and after the failure of the Poincaré experiment. Then, through the Locarno pacts and the close collaboration in the League Council between Austen Chamberlain, Gustav Streseman, and himself, it seemed that Europe was about to enter a new era of peace and good will in which the "spirit of Geneva" would infuse international relations.

The rivalry between these two schools of thought on French foreign policy—the "côté Briand" and the "côté Poincaré"—lasted until the mid-1920's. From early 1922 until the elections of 1924, a period of two and a half years, Poincaré was in control; he enjoyed the support of public and parliament and, although there were dissidents, opposition was in large measure over his tactics rather than his aims. Then came the electoral victory of the Cartel des gauches in 1924, a dramatic reversal of French political fortunes which accurately reflected popular dissatisfaction with the economic disorders resulting from the Ruhr occupation and with Poincaré's policy of "going it alone." Shortly thereafter Briand began a "reign" at the Quai d'Orsay which lasted for seven consecutive years from 1925 until 1932. His unprecedented tenure of office was interrupted only once and then for a mere twenty-four hours. During this time Briand enjoyed a popularity with both the Chambers and with the public which was unmatched by any Foreign Minister since the era of Delcassé. Although his appointment in 1925 was a direct result of the recent electoral victory of the Left, he continued to be the only acceptable Foreign Minister long after the Cartel des gauches, broken on the rack of monetary problems, was but a faint political memory.

Indeed, from 1926 to 1929 Briand served as Minister of Foreign Affairs in a centrist ministry headed by Poincaré. The combination of these two former rivals was a necessary consequence of the facts of French political life after the abandonment of the Ruhr occupation and the failure of the Cartel to solve the financial difficulties of the Republic. After the "fall of the franc" both the public and the Chambers demanded a domestic program of conservative economics—this meant Poincaré. But at the same time, after the failure of the policy of strict and unilateral treaty enforcement, they also demanded a foreign policy based upon more liberal lines—and this meant Briand. Thus, although Poincaré had not changed his own views on French foreign relations, he and his followers could no longer hope to make their opinions prevail and had no choice but to accept Briand as head of the Quai d'Orsay and also to follow his policies. Popular and parliamentary support for the Briand program— strikingly confirmed by the next elections of 1928—meant that in the long run he remained at the French Foreign Office while a succession of ministries tried with varying success to cope with domestic problems.[9] And, regardless of the specific political complexion of these cabinets, Briand was to have a relatively free hand in carrying out his policies, at least until the depression began to produce its disrupting effect upon European relations at the end of the decade.

Although both Briand and Poincaré were able to put their respective policies into effect with popular and parliamentary support and though "secret diplomacy" was never the issue in France that it was in Anglo-Saxon countries, nonetheless there was a noticeable increase of interest on the part of both legislative houses and of the public to supervise the work of the Quai d'Orsay in the years after the war. In pre-1914 France there had been rather general agreement upon the orientation of French diplomacy and little parliamentary interest in restricting the Foreign Office. During the years when Delcassé was transforming the bases of French diplomacy, his policies had provoked almost no discussion in the Chamber of Deputies.[10] It was an aphorism of French politics that a ministry did not fall over an issue of foreign policy, a belief which, while exaggerated, contained more than a modicum of truth.[11] However, after Versailles the French legislature was no longer content to remain indifferent on foreign policy issues and expected that its views would be given some consideration by the Foreign Minister and his staff of permanent officials.

Early in 1921, for instance, the Chamber gave a strong indication of its outlook when a ministry fell from power over a question of foreign policy. In January of that year the Leygues Cabinet was overthrown when the Deputies refused to grant the Premier immunity from questions about the course which he intended to follow at the forthcoming London Conference. Similarly, eight years later, Briand, then serving as both Premier and Foreign Minister, fell after interpellations concerning French policies at the international conference to be held at The Hague. In both instances it was quite clear that the Deputies desired information in advance about the policies which their government would pursue at these conferences. Yet, despite these signs of a parliamentary willingness to enforce its views on the Quai d'Orsay, the examples of Leygues and Briand were unique in the 1920's. Moreover, both Cabinets were already

[9] For an exceptionally interesting contemporary analysis, see Charles Seignobos, "La signification historique des élections françaises de 1928," *L'Année politique*, III (July, 1928), 257-282.

[10] Bertha R. Leaman, "The Influence of Domestic Policy on Foreign Affairs in France, 1898-1905," *Journal of Modern History*, XIV (December, 1942), pp. 449-451.

[11] A. Soulier, *L'Instabilité ministérielle sous la Troisième République* (Paris, 1939), p. 203.

in dire difficulties over domestic and other questions; it is not inconceivable that the Chamber majority seized upon an issue of foreign policy as a means of disposing of an unpopular cabinet. Furthermore, what was denied to Briand and to Leygues was conceded to others on at least a half dozen occasions when the Chamber flatly admitted the right of the government to pursue its own foreign policies without being bound to any specific legislative program.[12] When, for instance, in 1919 a resolution was introduced into the Chamber calling upon the government to insist at the Peace Conference that Germany should have no military organization whatsoever, the presiding officer ruled that the proposal was an unwarranted and illegal interference with the freedom of the executive to conduct diplomatic negotiations.[13]

More famous was the sudden and dramatic resignation of Briand in 1922 during the negotiations at Cannes. Finding Millerand, the President of the Republic, Poincaré, at that time leader of the Senate Committee on Foreign Affairs, and even members of his own Cabinet opposed to his attitude on reparations and an Anglo-French alliance, Briand returned abruptly from the meetings with Lloyd George. After outlining his policies to the Chamber, he unexpectedly resigned without bothering to request a formal vote of confidence. Whether Briand could have secured a favorable response on such a vote remains an unanswered question although it is certain that his parliamentary majority was fast decreasing in the face of mounting criticism of his foreign policies. His opponents felt that he was becoming a pawn for Lloyd George. Among the evidence cited by Briand's critics was a widely-publicized newspaper photograph in which the British Prime Minister appeared to be giving him golf lessons. Here, his enemies charged, was proof that Briand not only engaged in frivolous activities when serious problems were at stake but also was completely under the influence of the Englishman. Parisian newspapers used the opportunity to launch bitter attacks against Briand and his policies.[14] Yet even though Briand's parliamentary position was decidedly

---

[12] John E. Howard, *Parliament and Foreign Policy in France* (London, 1948), pp. 57, 65-73, a complete analysis of these two situations. The earlier chapters contain a useful summary of the constitutional position of the Foreign Minister and the pre-1914 precedents.

[13] Henry Kittredge Norton, *Foreign Office Organization* (Philadelphia, 1929), p. 3. (Supplement to Volume CXLIII of the *Annals of the American Academy of Political and Social Science.*)

[14] There are a number of interesting accounts of this disastrous golf game. Among the more readable is A. J. Sylvester, *The Real Lloyd George* (London, 1947), pp. 71-74. It appears also that Briand was in real need of instruction in golf. Having never held a club in his hands before, he had great difficulty hitting the ball and spent a good portion of the afternoon in the rough. Though he wandered from the fairway, his precise location

unfavorable, the political complexities and personal animosities involved were such that, at least in retrospect, Briand's resignation appears a highly particularized incident rather than a point of new departure in legislative control of foreign policy.[15]

These examples of ministries forced from office over issues in which foreign affairs were a basic point of contention indicate that during the 1920's the French legislature exhibited a new found interest in maintaining checks upon the conduct of the Quai d'Orsay. However, as a general rule, the extent and effectiveness of this parliamentary control was and remained somewhat limited. In the first place, the examples already cited were not always clear-cut instances. Moreover, neither the Chamber nor the Senate ever succeeded in controlling the details of policy formulation. During the period from 1919 to 1924 the legislature was successful in establishing certain broad boundaries beyond which no Foreign Minister could go. For instance, the Chambers made it impossible for any ministry to remain in power if it did not insist upon complete fulfillment of German reparations. But how this was to be accomplished remained, in general, for the Foreign Minister to decide.[16] And after 1925, with the popularity of Briand and the altered composition of the Chamber, even this broad legislative control was less effective than during the earlier period. An indication of the relative weakness of the Chambers was, for instance, the fact that although the postwar governments submitted far more treaties to the Chambers for ratification than had been the rule prior to 1914, nevertheless such important agreements as the 1924 treaty with Czechoslovakia or the Franco-Belgian military convention were neither placed before the legislature nor, for that matter, even adequately described to the Deputies and Senators.

In the 1920's neither the Chamber nor Senate Committees on Foreign Affairs emerged as the masters of the Quai d'Orsay. They remained, in the words of an English historian, "channels for information about foreign policy rather than agents in the making of it."[17] Neither commit-

---

could always be charted by the flow of Gallic profanity emerging from the sand traps and other obstacles.

[15] See the complete analysis in Soulier, *L'Instabilité ministérielle*, pp. 203-204, 271-274. It is worth noting that the British ambassador in Paris, Lord Hardinge, reported to London during the Cannes negotiations that Briand was in grave danger of being overthrown by the Chamber of Deputies. House of Commons Sessional Papers, 1924, XXVI. Cmd. 2169, "France No. 1 (1924). Papers Respecting Negotiations for an Anglo-French Pact," p. 126.

[16] Howard, *Parliament and Foreign Policy*, pp. 144ff.

[17] David Thomson, *French Foreign Policy* (Oxford Pamphlets on World Affairs, No. 67, 1944), p. 11.

tee ever sought or obtained the power to alter or amend the terms of treaties submitted for ratification and, in this respect, fell far short of the achievement of the similar body in the United States Senate. As Louis Barthou somewhat ruefully observed when the Versailles Treaty came before his committee, the members were virtually compelled, whatever their personal opinions, to ratify a *fait accompli*. And although the principal powers of the legislative committees related to their authority to interrogate the Foreign Minister, it was a standard complaint of the members that both Poincaré and Briand neglected to keep them informed of their policies.[18] Moreover, throughout the 1920's members of parliamentary committees constantly felt that there was an incomplete liaison between themselves and the Quai d'Orsay particularly on matters which interested the legislators, a complaint which, like the others, was another indication of the relative weakness of the legislative branch as an effective controlling agent.[19]

It appears, then, that despite the interest of postwar Deputies and Senators in supervising the Quai d'Orsay, the agents of French diplomacy nonetheless continued to enjoy a wider latitude in carrying out their policies than their confrères across either the Channel or the Atlantic.

The Quai d'Orsay was itself an organization in which the highest positions, both in Paris and abroad, were staffed by professional members of the foreign service and in which consular and diplomatic services had been at least partially assimilated into a unified organization.[20] A decree of 1916 had, moreover, specifically reserved the top positions in the central administration to men who had worked in foreign service posts outside France. Henceforth a successful career in the field was to be virtually a *sine qua non* for promotion to a policy-making position in Paris. Since 1907 diplomatic and commercial affairs had been channeled through the same Paris divisions. Although fusion between the two services was not as effective in posts abroad as at the Quai d'Orsay, the French appear to have minimized competition between the two branches of their

[18] See the excellent discussion of the problems and powers of the Chamber committee by Joseph Barthélmy, himself a member during the 1920's. *Essai sur le travail parlementaire et le système des commissions* (Paris, 1934), pp. 257-266. Also useful is R. K. Gooch, *The French Parliamentary Committee System* (New York, 1935), pp. 241-247.

[19] *Journal officiel, Sénat, Documents*, 1933, No. 264, p. 327, report of the committee which examined the Foreign Office budget for 1933.

[20] Discussions of the structure of the Foreign Office in the 1920's are at best incomplete and sketchy, and there is a particular dearth of memoir material. Best are the two parliamentary reports already cited, Nos. 802 of 1920 and 2020 of 1921. Competent though brief surveys are to be found in Schuman, *War and Diplomacy*, pp. 28-45 and Norton, *Foreign Office Organization, passim*. An unreliable and journalistic work is Paul Allard, *Le Quai d'Orsay* (Paris, 1938) which does, however, contain some interesting material.

foreign service.[21] Throughout both services, in Paris and outside France, the major posts were held by career officials. There were, of course, occasional exceptions. The Foreign Minister was free to make political appointments at the ambassadorial level, and in 1924, for instance, the Cartel des gauches rewarded Jean Hennessy, a member of the Chamber of Deputies, with the post of ambassador to Switzerland. But although there were such incidents, by far the vast majority of the top diplomatic positions in the French foreign service were held by career men.[22]

The dominance of professionals even extended to the special corps of assistants appointed to serve the Foreign Minister as his own cabinet. These men, personally chosen by the minister, were to form a staff of advisers unconnected with the professional bureaucracy. In theory they were to provide the politically responsible Minister of Foreign Affairs with the opportunity to have as his immediate associates a group of men whose opinions would not reflect the opinions of the professional diplomats. But, in fact, the ministerial cabinet was normally composed of foreign service officers chosen from the diplomatic corps. With a change in ministry they simply returned to their former positions in the Foreign Office. It would seem also that, instead of representing a separate advisory staff, this group by and large reflected the attitudes and opinions of the career officialdom.

Although during the 1920's there was a minimum of discussion of possible defects or deficiencies in the Quai d'Orsay and no effective pressure for organizational reform, later criticisms suggest that even at this time the French Foreign Office was operating under a number of handicaps. There was, in the first place, a wide range of problems which were financial in character. The permanent personnel, like the vast majority of the *fonctionnaires*, were hard hit by the decline in value of the franc. In the long run only those who enjoyed a private income or who came from well-to-do families could afford the luxury of a diplomatic career. And, although the Foreign Office, unlike the other bureaus of the French government, was able to maintain its prestige and its attractiveness, never-

---

[21] The question of fusion of diplomatic and consular services had been an issue in France since at least 1876. It was at least partially resolved by the creation of tables of equivalent grades, the possibility of transfer from one service to the other, and by the merger, at the Paris level, of the highest positions. See Schuman, *War and Diplomacy*, pp. 43-45.

[22] Walter Sharp, *The French Civil Service: Bureaucracy in Transition* (New York, 1931), pp. 326-327. The high degree of professionalism in the French diplomatic corps particularly, and for good reason, impressed American observers. Norton, making his study in 1930, claimed that there was but one noncareer man then occupying a major post in the French foreign service. Norton, *Foreign Office Organization*, p. 43.

theless the recruitment of new personnel was adversely affected.[23] The system whereby officers in the foreign service were recalled to positions at the Quai d'Orsay did not work out as well in practice as in theory. For, while such personnel assigned to work in Paris retained their previous status with regard to rank and promotion, their salaries depended upon the jobs to which they were assigned in the central administration. It thus happened that recall to Paris and a more responsible position frequently involved a net loss in income. This situation, noted by parliamentary critics as early as 1921, was still only partially remedied by the first reforms of the Quai d'Orsay undertaken in 1932.[24]

It was also claimed, probably not without considerable justification, that the Foreign Office continued throughout the 1920's to function in the style and manner of prewar years and that its horizons were limited by traditional practices. In its daily routine the Quai d'Orsay frequently seemed to regard the typewriter as a new-fangled instrument and the telephone and telegraph as gadgets whose usefulness had not as yet been fully demonstrated. Diplomatic personnel abroad, it was said, all too often learned of decisions taken in Paris not through regular channels but rather through the medium of the press in the country in which they were stationed. Nor was the documentation or information furnished by the Quai d'Orsay always sufficient. Particularly galling to those who felt that the Foreign Office still lived in a pre-1914 world was the minimum budget and minimum attention devoted to overseas information and propaganda services.[25] Moreover, within the central administration itself, the system of departmental organization—in which items of major im-

---

[23] Sharp, *French Civil Service*, p. 145. See also Schuman, *War and Diplomacy*, pp. 44-45.

[24] For more than perfunctory criticism of the Foreign Office one must refer to documents of the Senate and Chamber published in 1933 when the question of departmental reorganization had at last become a live issue and an interministerial council was working on the problem. This and following paragraphs rely heavily upon the abundant materials in *Chambre des Députés, Documents*, 1933, No. 1535, pp. 494ff. and particularly pp. 510-511 and *Sénat, Documents*, 1933, No. 264, pp. 326ff. These reports, incidentally, placed considerable credence upon articles written for *Le Temps* and *Le Figaro* by the political and diplomatic commentator, Wladimir d'Ormesson. It is interesting and also somewhat disconcerting to compare the parliamentary reports of 1933 with those of 1920-1921 and to observe how many problems mentioned at the earlier date remained still unsolved in the 1930's.

[25] Both of the parliamentary reports of 1933, already cited, devoted by far the bulk of their criticisms to the insufficiency of the French propaganda services. The Chamber reporter even appended a long and useful bibliography on the subject. Joseph Paul-Boncour, who as Minister of Foreign Affairs in the early 1930's had much to do with the reorganization of the Quai d'Orsay, mentioned only the reform of these propaganda and information services when he discussed this period in his memoirs. Joseph Paul-Boncour, *Entre deux guerres* (Paris, 1945), II, 398ff.

portance were handled by various desks representing geographical areas of the world—not infrequently led to duplication of effort and to inefficiency.

Later critics contended that the Quai d'Orsay devoted insufficient attention to the economic aspects of foreign policy and to the affairs of the League of Nations. The parliamentary reports of the early 1930's, reflecting these sentiments, stressed the idea that modern diplomacy, like modern war, had become "total"—or, to put it another way, that the Foreign Office, to achieve success, would have to be concerned with the whole range of human activities and not merely with the traditional legal-political relationships between states. To be sure, in the postwar decade much of what these observers desired had already been accomplished. A functioning French embassy, like that in Berlin, had a special section devoted to financial questions and a whole battery of experts who studied and reported the conditions of the German economy; François-Poncet, the ambassador after 1931, had been selected for the post because of his knowledge of business and finance, and the director of the political section of the Berlin embassy was a career diplomat who had previously spent eight years in the economic and commercial services of the Paris administration.[26] Similarly, the French Foreign Office had always taken the League of Nations seriously. The councils of Geneva, even during the heyday of Poincaré and the nationalists, had always included as representatives of the Third Republic men who were not only important figures in French diplomacy but also firm friends of the League itself: Léon Bourgeois, even in pre-1914 years an advocate of international organization, Joseph Avenol, for more than a decade second in command to Secretary General Drummond, and, of course, Joseph Paul-Boncour and Aristide Briand. Moreover, although it was the French Left which showed the most devotion to Geneva, conservatives and nationalists, despite considerable skepticism about the capabilities of the existing organization, were always interested in transforming the League into an agency capable of providing a thorough and rigorous system of collective security.[27] Nevertheless, despite these signs of the broadening activi-

[26] See the interesting account of the Berlin embassy at work, reprinted from the newspaper *Petit Parisien*, in Alfred Zimmern, *The League of Nations and the Rule of Law, 1918-1935* (London, 1936), pp. 488-491.

[27] There is no need to elaborate upon the many projects, such as the Treaty of Mutual Assistance or the Geneva Protocol, which engaged the attention of the Quai d'Orsay in the 1920's and which were seriously sponsored by the French. For a convenient summary of the French attitude, see Zimmern, *League of Nations*, pp. 324-326, and for an estimate of the interest of French conservatives in the Geneva organization, Arnold Wolfers, *Britain and France between Two Wars* (New York, 1940), pp. 157-160.

ties of the French Foreign Office, the officials who directed French commercial relations and League of Nations affairs tended to occupy a subordinate position in the central administration. Their work, until the reforms of the 1930's, was improperly coordinated with that of the all-important *Direction politique*. Thus, although the Quai d'Orsay was expanding its functions and interests, it was less successful in integrating these newer concerns with economic affairs and the League with the familiar political services.[28]

If the continuation of certain "traditional practices" hampered French diplomacy after Versailles, mention should also be made of the perpetuation of what might be called "traditional prejudices" which arose from the social and educational background of the men in the French foreign service. Prior to 1914 many French diplomats had been recruited from the ranks of the aristocracy—for while most aspects of the Third Republic were anathema to these families, the foreign service, like the army, had continued to be an "acceptable" career for those descended from the aristocracy. After the war, however, one of the notable changes in the composition of the French foreign service was its infiltration by the sons of the upper middle class.[29] The foreign service, in a very real sense, became a blend of the old aristocracy with the newer representatives of big business and finance. Thus, for instance, while the French ambassador in Great Britain in the early 1920's bore the distinguished name of the Comte de Saint-Aulaire, the change was symbolized by the fact that such representatives of the business-financial world as André François-Poncet and Jean Herbette went to the embassies in Berlin and Moscow. Moreover, as noted earlier, both the low salary scales and the need for an advanced and costly education tended to prevent any influx of new foreign service personnel from the other strata of French society.

But whatever the social background of the French diplomats, by far the majority of them were the product of at least one common mold— the *École libre des sciences politiques*, a specialized school founded shortly after the Franco-Prussian war to provide the young Republic with a corps of trained administrators. The extent to which this "school of diplomats" had an educational monopoly is shown by the fact that of

[28] The reorganization of 1932-1933 suggested that the *fonctionnaires* directing commercial and League affairs should be put on a par with the officials who were in charge of the various "area desks" organized on a geographical basis within the *Direction politique*. It was suggested that they be given the status of assistant directors of the political section as a means of improving policy coordination. *Journal officiel, Chambre*, 1933, No. 1535, p. 510.

[29] Norton, *Foreign Office Organization*, p. 32.

the 192 men appointed to diplomatic or consular vacancies between 1907 and 1927, a total of 153 held diplomas from the *École libre*.[30] Instruction was admittedly less specialized than that in the law faculties of the various French universities, and, in addition to the standard courses in history and international relations, students could take courses in a wide variety of fields—economics, administration, public law, geography. Indeed, in the 1920's one of the more noticeable trends in the education and selection of new foreign service personnel was the extent to which the *École libre* taught and the Quai d'Orsay expected candidates to be informed about the economic and geographical aspects of international relations instead of the purely legal or diplomatic factors.[31] However, despite the new emphases in education, it seems quite possible—though documentation of this point is fragmentary—that the training of French diplomatic personnel remained somewhat narrow and academic. The *École libre*, in the words of Bertrand de Jouvenal, "fashioned minds which were not only specialized in their knowledge *mais presque dans leurs âmes*."[32] And as Jules Cambon—himself a great ambassador who distrusted the tendency to select the future members of the diplomatic corps on the basis of formal education and examinations—cautioned, the art of diplomacy required many skills and sensitivities which "aren't learned in school."[33]

Another aspect of French diplomacy which close observers began to notice in the postwar decade was the ever-increasing tendency for major decisions to be made in Paris and, in particular, by the officials who formed the permanent staff of the Quai d'Orsay. This development, which had its serious consequences in the 1930's, had several facets. In the first place, the French diplomats abroad were frequently neither consulted nor heeded, and they themselves played an ever-decreasing role in both the formulation and execution of policies. Secondly, it was the professional element in Paris which tended to become the masters of policy. Moreover, these career officials began to become more and more a "closed corporation," a self-perpetuating body of advisers which surrounded the politically responsible Foreign Minister. These officials, it might be added, had not only long since completed their own period of

---

[30] Sharp, *French Civil Service*, p. 112.

[31] *ibid.*, pp. 111-112, 147-148. Another brief but not too helpful discussion of the education of foreign service personnel is to be found in Louis Eisenmann, "The Study of International Relations in France," League of Nations, *Educational Survey*, III (March, 1932), 44-52.

[32] Bertrand de Jouvenal, *Après la défaite* (Paris, 1941), p. 50.

[33] Jules Cambon, *Le Diplomate* (Paris, 1926), p. 63.

service abroad but also had no desire to abandon the Quai d'Orsay for an embassy outside France.[34] In the words of a parliamentary investigating commission, established after the second world war to discover the reasons for the French defeat of 1940: "Our foreign policy thus became almost exclusively the work of the central administration of the Quai d'Orsay. . . . All too frequently the (foreign) ministers were informed of events occurring abroad only through the medium of the *fonctionnaires trop sédentaires* of their cabinet or of the various services. There existed, in fact, in the midst of our diplomatic personnel a group of bureaucrats who made their careers almost exclusively within the offices of the Quai d'Orsay and who came between our ministers and their diplomats abroad."[35]

Although these tendencies were certainly present, their extent and seriousness, at least during the 1920's, can be exaggerated. Joseph Paul-Boncour, himself prominent in French foreign affairs between the wars, has cautioned against the prevalent tendency to blame most of the ills of French diplomacy on the permanent staff of the Quai d'Orsay and to overlook the responsibility of the various Foreign Ministers.[36] Moreover, the process by which diplomatic decisions were focused in Paris—in part simply the result of improved communications—was not without its advantages. Paris, able if it so desired to gain information from a foreign capital at a moment's notice, was frequently better equipped

[34] See the pertinent discussion by Senator Bérenger, chairman of the foreign affairs commission of the French Senate in his report on the Foreign Office budget for 1933, *Journal officiel, Sénat* (1933), No. 264, p. 327. Both he and the Chamber *rapporteur* felt that the Quai d'Orsay did not sufficiently consult or rely upon its ambassadors in foreign countries. The report recommended the institution of regularly-scheduled meetings between the Minister of Foreign Affairs and all of his top-ranking ambassadors. The tendency for promising young officials to be recalled to Paris early in their careers and kept there indefinitely was noted by Sharp, *French Civil Service*, p. 331. For some interesting comments on the declining importance of the ambassador, see Jules Cambon, *Le Diplomate*, pp. 118ff. After the second world war all of these questions were raised once again in the course of a monumental parliamentary investigation into the causes of the French disaster of 1940. See, in particular, the testimony of Jean Dobler, from 1931 to 1937 the French consul-general in Cologne. *Assemblée nationale, 1946, Commission d'enquête parlementaire. Les événements survenus en France de 1933 à 1945 Témoignages et documents* (Paris, 1951), II, 469ff. Dobler was a witness with an ax to grind and, although the great bulk of his testimony pertained to events after 1933, it is clear that he believed that many of the failings which he observed at that time had been prevalent a decade earlier. He complained bitterly that the central administration had paid scant attention to the reports of French agents abroad and that the career officials in Paris were responsible for this. Unfortunately, when the investigating commission questioned other prominent diplomats, like François-Poncet or Coulondre, these issues were not pursued further. However, Dobler's testimony did make considerable impression upon the investigating commission and was specially noted in the final report written by the Deputy, Charles Serre.

[35] *Commission d'enquête, Rapport*, I, 86-87.
[36] Paul-Boncour, *Entre deux guerres*, II, 125.

to formulate policies. And with decisions centered at the level of the central administration, there was also a better chance to assure continuity and consistency in foreign policy. However, as would become more evident in the years after Hitler's rise to power, there was also the distinct disadvantage that the advice and reports of the diplomats on the spot would be ignored, that the decisions of the Paris career officials would be based upon inaccurate appraisals, and that French foreign policy would be the loser.

II

Although Briand and Poincaré were the political figures who dominated French foreign affairs in the first postwar decade, the Secretary General of the Quai d'Orsay, Philippe Berthelot, quite possibly left a more indelible mark upon French foreign policies and the conduct of French diplomacy. Although twenty years have passed since his retirement, one does not yet write with great confidence about the specific influence of Berthelot. He remains, at best, something of an enigma. Furthermore, since Berthelot destroyed his personal papers and published no memoirs—something as unique among French public officials as among contemporary American generals—it seems unlikely that the full and true measure of his role will ever be known.[37]

Philippe Berthelot prided himself on being the discreet *fonctionnaire*, the inscrutable civil servant whose own personality would never appear as part of the diplomatic record. Even the documents already published by the French and British Foreign Offices shed but little light upon his ideas, his character, or his influence. His name appears high on the list of French personnel at nearly every important international conference in the 1920's, but only rarely did he take part in the discussions or, from

[37] To date there is but one biography of Berthelot, that of his lifelong friend and admirer, Auguste Bréal: *Philippe Berthelot* (Paris, 1937). It is, however, noncritical and, though valuable, largely a series of anecdotes. Perhaps the best estimate of the Secretary General is to be found in Georges Suarez, *Briand, sa vie . . . son œuvre* (Paris, 1941), Vol. v, *passim*. It carries the story only through 1923 and, because of the death of Suarez, remains uncompleted. Of the greatest value are three short sketches by another of his friends, the poet-ambassador, Paul Claudel. These essays, originally written in 1937, are reprinted in Paul Claudel, *Accompagnements* (Paris, 1949), pp. 182-209. There is also some information of value in Allard, *Quai d'Orsay*, pp. 52ff. and a useful sketch, largely distilled from Bréal, in Robert Lengerle, *Nos grands chefs* (Paris, 1945), pp. 162ff. Periodical literature on Berthelot is also limited, but see Louis Dumont-Wilden, "Une grande figure de la diplomatie française," *Revue Bleue*, LXXV (October, 1937), 618-623 and "Philippe Berthelot" in *L'Asie nouvelle*, XXXV (December, 1934), 318ff. London and Paris dailies carried extensive death notices in their editions of November 22 and 23, 1934; of these the most valuable is the appraisal of Berthelot by Wladimir d'Ormesson in the November 23, 1934, issue of *Le Figaro*. See also Charles de Chambrun, *Traditions et souvenirs* (Paris, 1952), pp. 117-118.

the record, appear to have influenced the decisions which were reached. Furthermore, in the biographies and memoirs of the various European statesmen of the postwar decade—whether those of Paul-Boncour, Stresemann, or Austen Chamberlain—Berthelot is never a central figure and not infrequently is only casually mentioned as if he were a person of incidental importance.

To his admirers, however, Berthelot was the animator of French diplomacy, the one official who assured the continuity of French foreign policy and a man of such competence and broad vision that his advice, if followed at all times, would have spared his country most of its postwar diplomatic errors. Jean Giraudoux, the playwright-novelist who himself pursued an active career in the press and information services of the Quai d'Orsay, once made Philippe Berthelot the hero and Raymond Poincaré the villain of a particularly successful political novel, *Bella*. In the Giraudoux novel, Berthelot was ". . . the only plenipotentiary at Versailles, except Wilson, who would have reconstructed Europe generously, and the only one, without exception, who would have done it competently."[38] To the author of *Bella*, one of Berthelot's few lifelong friends, the Secretary General was not only the diplomat who had set Central Europe on its feet but also a statesman whose particular strength was his knowledge of man as a political animal: "Men, it may be, he did not know, but great men he knew to perfection. He knew the habits, the strength and weakness of the international tribe which spends its life, if not above, at any rate just outside the law. He even knew their special anatomy. He knew how to fatten and how to thin them down, and what food and drink raised their political genius to its highest point."[39]

Others, less inclined to worshipful praise, found something sinister in the regime of Berthelot at the Quai d'Orsay. In their eyes he was an all-powerful and irremovable permanent official who manipulated the political heads of the Foreign Office as if they were but puppets. "Some individuals," a French journalist observed, "go so far as to claim that the Minister of Foreign Affairs is only the *nominal* chief of the Quai d'Orsay and that, even if the man who holds the portfolio is Briand, the true minister is Philippe Berthelot."[40]

Midway between these extremes was the opinion that whatever his merits or failings, the Secretary General was simply unfathomable. André Géraud, political commentator for *L'Echo de Paris*, was a prolific writer

[38] Jean Giraudoux, *Bella* (Paris, 1926), p. 7.   [39] *ibid.*, p. 13.
[40] Allard, *Quai d'Orsay*, pp. 48-49.

who, as Pertinax, could fill two thick volumes with detailed accounts of the gravediggers of France, but despite his best efforts, he could never find a satisfactory answer to the riddle of Berthelot. The Secretary General, wrote Géraud, "was a strange man. He boasted that while paying tribute to the Geneva institution in high-sounding words, he knew how to safeguard the long-tested concepts and precedents of French foreign relations. That man has always baffled me. Whether he was more than an exhibitionist addicted to perpetual paradoxes, an opportunist, and a questionable connoisseur of exotic antiquities remains a riddle."[41]

The reign of Berthelot, from 1914 until the end of 1932, coincided with the years in which France exerted her greatest influence in European affairs since the time of the first Napoleon. Paradoxically, it terminated just at the date at which French diplomacy was beginning its abrupt slide into the trough of futility and French influence was falling toward its nadir. Philippe Berthelot, whose principal concern had been to find a viable solution to the German problem, retired at the very moment when Adolf Hitler came to power and initiated the series of diplomatic and military maneuvers which quickly put an end to the years of French hegemony in Europe.

The future Secretary General entered the foreign service in the closing years of the nineteenth century, but although his rise in the Paris administration had been rapid, he did not achieve prominence until the summer of 1914. During the crisis which preceded the outbreak of war he enjoyed a rare and unexpected opportunity to influence the course of events, and his conduct and initiative during those critical days were such that he immediately achieved a commanding position in the Quai d'Orsay. When the threat of a general European war suddenly arose in late July, the French President, Poincaré, the Premier and Foreign Minister, Viviani, and the foremost permanent official of the Quai d'Orsay, de Margerie, were all absent from Paris on their famous mission to Russia. Bienvenu-Martin, Minister of Justice in the Viviani Cabinet, had been chosen to serve as acting Premier and acting Foreign Minister, but he was a complete novice in the handling of foreign affairs. Berthelot, then the assistant director of European political affairs, was the only official of high rank and experience remaining on duty at the Quai d'Orsay and had been temporarily placed in charge of the political affairs division. Thus, until the French government returned to Paris, it was Berthelot who, as Bienvenu-Martin's principal adviser, had a

---

[41] André Géraud, "Diplomacy Old and New," reprinted from *Foreign Affairs* in Armstrong, *Foreign Affairs Reader*, p. 404.

large share in formulating French policies and in determining the initial replies of the Quai d'Orsay when Austria and Germany attempted to persuade France to keep hands off the pending Austro-Serbian conflict.[42]

Berthelot, it appears, was from the outset of the crisis suspicious of Austro-German intentions and felt that the two Powers, while not desiring war at any price, would certainly at the last instance not shrink from fighting. He believed that both Germany and Austria sought a brilliant diplomatic victory and hoped to frighten France into putting pressure on Russia to remain quiet while the Dual Monarchy disposed of the Serbs on its own terms. Determined to avoid what he regarded as a German trap, Berthelot therefore would not agree that his country should intervene at St. Petersburg to restrain the Russians unless Germany would exert similar pressure upon Vienna, and at the same time he studiously avoided giving any impression to the public, as the German ambassador desired, that France and Germany were working in close harmony to maintain Europe peace.[43] In addition to his refusal to put pressure on Russia, Berthelot advised the Serbians to play for time by conceding to Austria on all points which did not compromise their sovereignty and by making an appeal to the Great Powers to mediate the dispute. And, since the Serbian reply to the famous Austrian ultimatum hewed close to the line suggested by Berthelot, it was later claimed—though the charge is baseless—that the entire note was "inspired" by the French diplomatist.[44] This, incidentally, was the first but not the last time that he was accused of exercising secret influences far beyond the confines of the Quai d'Orsay. But, in any event, it was Berthelot's handling of these initial phases of the crisis which won for him the commanding position in the Foreign Office which, with but two brief exceptions, he was to hold for almost thirty years afterwards.

Throughout the course of the war Berthelot was considered by foreign diplomats as the official who was best-informed about French policies and the man to know if one desired to discover the objectives of French diplomacy. Though he was an important figure in most inter-Allied con-

[42] On the situation in the French Foreign Office, see Bienvenu-Martin's own account, "Mon intérim de chef de gouvernement," *La Revue de France*, XIII (August, 1933), 639-652. In this article Bienvenu-Martin expressly stated that Berthelot's advice had been of the greatest assistance to him.

[43] On Berthelot's general views, see Sidney B. Fay, *The Origins of the World War* (New York, ed. of 1931), II, 388. On his reaction to the initial Austro-German *démarches* designed to persuade France to remain on the sidelines, see, particularly, Pierre Renouvin, *The Immediate Origins of the War* (Eng. ed., New Haven, 1928), pp. 84-86, 102-104.

[44] Renouvin, *Immediate Origins*, pp. 93-94.

ferences, his influence remained unobtrusive. Only the initiated knew of it, and Berthelot himself remained virtually unknown to the French public.

Berthelot had expected that in recognition of his wartime services he would be named to head the French delegation at the Paris Peace Conference. He was, however, disappointed. For reasons which still appear uncertain Clemenceau passed over him and appointed instead an obscure diplomat, Dutasta, then the French ambassador at Berne, to be the principal French negotiator. Apparently "the Tiger" never fully trusted or admired Berthelot, and, as he always preferred to run his own show, wanted as chief of the French delegation some one who would be willing to accept a subordinate status.[45] Berthelot, however, was not a negligible figure at the Peace Conference. He represented France in the commission which concerned itself with the establishment of the new states of Central Europe that emerged from the debris of the now defunct Austro-Hungarian Empire. At the same time within the hierarchy of the Quai d'Orsay his importance continued to increase; when de Margerie accepted the Brussels embassy, Berthelot succeeded him as director of the Foreign Office's all-important division of political and commercial affairs. Furthermore, although there is again no direct evidence, it seems clear that Berthelot, who enjoyed close personal relations with Dutasta, was consulted on all major issues of the Peace Conference and shared at least indirectly in all of the territorial decisions made by the French representatives. At any rate Berthelot himself apparently believed that he had played a part in writing the Versailles Treaty which was larger than the one to which he had been officially assigned. For when Lloyd George asked him to explain just exactly what his role in the French delegation had been, Berthelot replied with a smile, "Everything . . . and nothing."[46]

Within a short period after the Peace Conference, however, Berthelot had become the most important of the permanent officials at the Quai

---

[45] Bréal, *Berthelot*, pp. 188-189. To Bréal the nomination of Dutasta appeared "incredible" and, unable to find a logical reason for Clemenceau's action, he concluded, "Let's not even try to explain it." Claudel, *Accompagnements*, pp. 198-199 could find no reason other than the caprice of Clemenceau. Poincaré, however, in his wartime diary indicated in an entry of December 29, 1918, that at this time there was considerable intrigue among the officials of the Quai d'Orsay, some of it involving Berthelot. His somewhat cryptic entry in his diary does not add much to the above account except to indicate that Berthelot was very disappointed and may possibly have been involved thereafter in efforts to have de Margerie removed from his position as director of the political affairs division. Raymond Poincaré, *Au Service de la France* (Paris, 1932), X, 459.
[46] Bréal, *Berthelot*, p. 195.

d'Orsay. As early as the autumn of 1919 he had unofficially reached the top; at that time Paul Cambon, the French ambassador in London, noted that as a result of the lethargy and illness of Pichon it was Berthelot who was "the real Minister of Foreign Affairs."[47] His career was officially climaxed when in September 1920 he was appointed to direct all phases of the Foreign Office's activities as its permanent Secretary General. In December of the same year he was given the rank of ambassador. From then until his retirement at the end of 1932, with the exception of a three-year interlude, Berthelot was the ranking permanent official at the Quai d'Orsay and considered by all observers as the animator or "motor" of French diplomacy.

But from 1922 to 1925 Berthelot was out of office and in disgrace. A special disciplinary council, over which Premier Poincaré had personally presided, suspended him from the foreign service for ten years and had, for all practical purposes, read him out of the Quai d'Orsay forever. Berthelot was accused of using the influence of the Foreign Office to try to avert the collapse of the Banque Industrielle de Chine, a personal intervention which appeared particularly culpable since his own brother was the managing director of the bank. As in most cases of this nature, there was certainly more involved than the official charges. Berthelot himself admitted that he had intervened in the bank crisis without bothering to notify Briand, then the Foreign Minister, but he also felt that Poincaré had for both personal and political reasons desired to have him removed from office. There is, indeed, some substantiation for his view. Poincaré was committed to the policy of forcing Germany to fulfill her treaty obligations, while Berthelot—as will shortly be noted—was even at this time of the opinion that France should reach some accommodation with the Weimar Republic. Furthermore, Poincaré, like Clemenceau, was a man of strong and forceful temperament who wanted to run his own diplomatic show without interference from a career official of independent mind; significantly, during the thirty months which Poincaré held the Foreign Ministry, he never bothered to fill the vacant post of Secretary General. At any rate, Berthelot was restored to his former position in 1925 when Herriot rescinded the verdict of the disciplinary council and, in the presence of Berthelot, had all of the records pertaining to the "case Berthelot" destroyed.[48] His restoration at this time was of course a logical result of

---

[47] Paul Cambon, *Correspondance*, III, 365.
[48] The best account of the whole scandal is to be found in Suarez, *Briand*, V, 108ff. Both Bréal and Claudel are inclined to minimize the affair and charge it up to Poincaré's

the fact that the Cartel des gauches now controlled the political destinies of France. It was widely believed that Berthelot had suffered primarily because of his political differences with Poincaré; to reverse the earlier verdict was considered an act of political justice. But more important was the fact that Berthelot returned to his post as permanent director of the Quai d'Orsay just at the moment when the French were in the process of making an abrupt switch from a policy of coercing Germany to one of trying to conciliate her.

If Philippe Berthelot appears difficult to understand, it is in large part because of his personality. Through rigorous self-discipline he appeared always imperturbable, always the master of his emotions. His wit was barbed and pointed, and, as Géraud noted, he rejoiced in cynicism and paradox. Human beings, he once wrote, preferred to fight in civil wars rather than in foreign wars because "they know the people they are killing."[49] The Polish leader Pilsudski he once described as a man with a furtive expression who looked as if he always expected something unpleasant to happen to him.[50] Intellectually brilliant, Berthelot had few close friends and was one of those men who are feared rather than respected. That he should not dominate and rule was, to Berthelot, obviously unthinkable. He was, after all, both by birth and accomplishment one of the intellectual elite of the Third Republic. Son of Marcellin Berthelot, one of the founders of modern chemistry, Philippe had from his earliest years lived on terms of easy familiarity with the small group of republican intellectuals and political leaders who had made the Republic in the years after 1871. Social position and the influence of his noted father had in his youth opened all doors to him—in particular, the door of the Quai d'Orsay—and all of this he had considered as but his due. Small wonder, then, that Berthelot impressed others as dominating, if not domineering.

Though Philippe Berthelot gained his entrée into the foreign service through the influence of his father, he was far more than a mere dilettante. Indeed, it seems that almost from the moment he entered the Quai d'Orsay he deliberately set out to reach the top by making himself indispensable. He drove himself at top speed and showed an ability

---

vindictiveness. Most interesting is the fictionalized account of the Berthelot-Poincaré feud which is in Giraudoux' *Bella* and serves as the central theme of the novel. Giraudoux stresses the personal aspects also: Poincaré appears as a narrow-minded legalist determined to have his own way whatever the cost, while Berthelot is pictured as a man of flexible, generous disposition and breadth of vision whose superior talents naturally stirred up the resentment of his opponent.

[49] Bréal, *Berthelot*, p. 103.
[50] Hardinge of Penshurst, *Old Diplomacy* (London, 1947), p. 256.

to work endless hours without rest; like the hero of the typical success story, he was the first to enter the Quai d'Orsay in the morning and the last to leave at night. Berthelot made it his business to see every bit of correspondence, every document which went through the Foreign Office and to know everything that happened. Moreover, he remembered virtually all that he read or heard, for he was gifted with an almost encyclopedic memory. Thus over the years he gradually and intentionally drew all the many threads of French diplomacy to his own person. And though in later years there were not a few in French political life who would have liked to have him replaced, it was not as easy to find another man capable of performing his functions as it was to keep him in office—he had become, in fact, the "indispensable man" he had set out to be. These traits and this desire to reach the top, incidentally, suggest that Berthelot's disagreements with men like Poincaré and Clemenceau were not one-sided. These two "strong men" of twentieth century French politics must have sensed that they were in the presence of a man whose ambition to rule and control was not only as fierce as their own but also a threat to their own supremacy.

Berthelot's long period of ascendancy at the Quai d'Orsay was quite probably not without its disadvantages. He was frequently accused of "empire building" and, in particular, of filling the press and information services of the Foreign Office with his own favorites until that organization became a sort of Noah's ark in which men of first-rate talents worked alongside those of "the seventeenth order."[51] It is certain that he had a natural affinity for diplomats with literary or artistic skills. Both Jean Giraudoux and Paul Claudel were particular favorites whose careers Berthelot fostered; it was the Secretary General who put the former in charge of the French overseas information service after the Armistice and who in 1924 secured the latter's appointment as ambassador to the United States.[52]

More serious is the fact that it was during Berthelot's reign that, as earlier noted, there was an increasing tendency for Paris to make most

---

[51] Suarez, *Briand*, v, 125-126.

[52] Berthelot had become Giraudoux's "protector" even before 1914 and thereafter watched over his career; *Bella* was, in a very real sense, Giraudoux's revenge against Poincaré for firing his friend and, incidentally, the novel provoked the Foreign Minister into assigning Giraudoux to a job which kept him so busy he had almost no time to write. Paul Morand, *Adieu à Giraudoux* (Paris, 1944), pp. 25-34. On Berthelot's long interest in Claudel, see Charles Benoist, *Souvenirs* (Paris, 1934), III, 278-279 and Paul-Boncour, *Entre deux guerres*, II, 376, as well as the frequent references to Berthelot in *The Correspondence between Paul Claudel and André Gide, 1899-1926*, edited by Robert Mallet (London, 1952).

of the basic diplomatic decisions. Indeed, throughout the 1920's the power and importance of the office of Secretary General steadily grew, frequently at the expense of good administration. Since Berthelot sought and assumed responsibilities far beyond those which any man should have attempted, there was a noticeable failure during his years in office to delegate responsibility throughout the various echelons of the Foreign Office.[53] Likewise it was during these years also that the career personnel who never left Paris began to exercise increasing authority at the expense of French representatives abroad—Berthelot himself, it might be noted, had not served outside the walls of the Quai d'Orsay since the early years of the century. It is quite possible, however, that the Secretary General, himself gifted with a sense of detachment from his immediate surroundings, realized what was happening. Shortly after his retirement he was visited by Jean Dobler, French consul-general at Cologne, who complained that no one in the Quai d'Orsay bothered to read his dispatches warning of the growing strength of Hitler. Berthelot told his visitor that he should go directly to the Foreign Minister and tell his story to him in person. When Dobler protested that this was impossible, Berthelot replied with his usual bland smile, "His cabinet chief isn't a career man ... You have a chance."[54]

Philippe Berthelot, though essentially a man of the Left, always distrusted politicians and throughout his long career avoided political life. Presented with a chance to run for election to the Chamber, he spurned the opportunity. Briand supposedly offered to back his candidacy and argued that within a short time after election as a Deputy Berthelot could himself become the Foreign Minister. But Berthelot was not interested. In part this was because he was a poor speaker, ill at ease before large groups, and, by contrast, fully effective only around the conference table. But his scorn for politics was more likely a question of temperament. Aware of his own talents and abilities, Berthelot simply felt that the conflicts and compromises of political life were beneath a man of his stature. Typically, when he testified before the foreign affairs commission of the Chamber, he impressed the Deputies with the wealth of his knowledge and his mastery of detail, but at the same time he made them feel not only that he did not like to appear before the commission

[53] Wladimir d'Ormesson in *Le Figaro*, November 23, 1934.
[54] *Commission d'enquête, Témoignages et documents*, II, 501. Dobler, despite his bitter criticisms of most Paris career officials, was quite moderate in discussing Berthelot. Though Dobler thought that Berthelot had probably not been immune to the usual ailments of the sedentary bureaucrat, at the same time he felt that Berthelot's judgment had always been saved by his "incomparable intelligence."

but also that he had come "only because the Minister had told him to do so."[55] Furthermore, Berthelot avoided political life because he preferred to remain the civil servant who worked behind the scenes and who would not lose his office with a shift in ministries. As a permanent *fonctionnaire* he felt no doubt that he actually possessed more power and authority than the responsible minister. As a hostile yet discerning critic observed, Berthelot preferred the substance of power to its semblance.

It is, unfortunately, still not possible to say with finality where Berthelot stood on all of the great and troubled diplomatic issues of the 1920's. André Géraud appears to have come closest to the mark when he pointed out that the Secretary General believed that his own contribution was to try to bridge the gap between the old and the new diplomacy. That is, Berthelot felt that he succeeded in enabling France to adjust to the new era of diplomacy by conference and through the League of Nations without at the same time sacrificing any of the traditions or methods of the pre-1914 era. It is indeed certain that he had a deep sense of the history and of the traditions of his country and that these sentiments possessed a living reality for him.[56] Certainly, too, he was always a bit skeptical of the League of Nations. Even though he worked in close association with Briand and was "his man," Berthelot was never able to place quite as much faith in Geneva as his chief. The Secretary General, from 1919 until his retirement—and even during the heyday of the League in the mid-1920's—always doubted if the League could produce effective results, for he felt that a system of alliances, like that of pre-1914 Europe, was more in accord with the unchanging nature of man.[57] Likewise, the idea of "diplomacy by conference" was not pleasing to the Secretary General. Diplomacy, he felt, was a job for specialists. He preferred the meetings of experts behind closed doors, meetings carefully prepared by advance negotiations and conducted without fanfare or publicity. And the tendency for the public figures of the day to try to settle complicated international problems during informal chats while they played golf or sat on the banks of a river struck Berthelot as the negation of diplomacy.

Although Poincaré began the process of building alliances with the new states of Central Europe, it was Philippe Berthelot who was responsible for much of France's postwar interest in these countries. Indeed, it appears that Berthelot was throughout the 1920's "the most

---

[55] Barthélmy, *Essai sur . . . le système des commissions*, pp. 266-267.
[56] Suarez, *Briand*, v, 127.   [57] Bréal, *Berthelot*, pp. 214-215.

consistent artisan" of the new alliance system which bound France to the states which had been created from the wreckage of the Hapsburg Monarchy.[58] His interest in Central and Eastern Europe, moreover, antedated the Peace Conference. During the war he had become convinced that the survival of the Austro-Hungarian Empire was a political impossibility and he had entered into negotiations with Central European statesmen, like Benes, who were trying to obtain political independence for their peoples. Thus, as early as January of 1917, when Woodrow Wilson asked the Allies to clarify their war aims, it was Berthelot who edited the reply which stated that one of France's major objectives was to secure the liberation of the Czechs.[59] At the Peace Conference Berthelot, as the sole French representative on the subcommission which considered the problem of the new states, worked assiduously in behalf of the Poles, the Czechs, and the Yugoslavs as well as of the other peoples who had claims against the defeated Powers. It was the French diplomat, for instance, who was largely responsible for the fact that the Poles were able to keep many of the portions of Upper Silesia which were still in dispute after the famous plebiscite, for he drew up the partition scheme which was eventually accepted by Lloyd George and the British Foreign Office. His work during the war and at the Conference in behalf of the Czechs was, it might be noted, always remembered by the leaders of that country. When in 1927 Berthelot paid a visit to Prague, he was given a particularly warm welcome by Czech officials, and, at a banquet in his honor, Benes paid glowing tribute to him for the assistance which he had given the Czechoslovakian cause before and after the Armistice.

Berthelot's interest in the new Central European states was, however, not simply the result of any passionate devotion to the Wilsonian principle of nationalities. Indeed, according to Paul Claudel, Berthelot always felt that the old Austro-Hungarian Empire, whatever its faults, had at least provided Central Europe with an economic and geographic unity which was sorely missed when the new states were created in its stead.[60] But at the same time he believed that these countries could and should be won as the friends of France because they would be valuable partners in the job of holding Germany in check. In other words, Berthelot, as a diplomat who believed in France's traditional policy of

---

[58] Bertrand de Jouvenal, *D'Une guerre à l'autre* (Paris, 1940), I, 213. For an extended though superficial discussion of Berthelot's interest in the new European states, see Allard, *Quai d'Orsay*, pp. 44 ff.

[59] Bréal, *Berthelot*, p. 218; Claudel, *Accompagnements*, pp. 199-200.

[60] Claudel, *Accompagnements*, p. 200.

having allies to the east of Germany and who hesitated to put full faith in the League, prized these new states as potential military allies who would help to keep Germany from attempting to rupture the Versailles settlement. Significantly, when in 1925 France came to an agreement with the Weimar Republic which supposedly settled the Franco-German frontier for all time, it was Berthelot who persuaded Briand that a French treaty of mutual assistance with Czechoslovakia should be made an integral part of the Locarno pacts.[61] Thus, even when he was engaged in promoting a Western European settlement, Berthelot thought also in terms of France's allies to the east and wished to include them as partners in the agreement.

Berthelot was not, of course, at the Quai d'Orsay during the occupation of the Ruhr. He was, however, opposed to Poincaré's scheme to collect reparations at the point of a bayonet. To his friend, Auguste Bréal, he wrote early in 1924 that ". . . the new year is not pleasant because it is always raining and the government remains strong. It is true that the franc is steadily declining, but the public believes that this is the result of the jealousy of the rest of the world and of a conspiracy by our former allies and not the consequence of the policies being followed. Everything is thus for the best."[62] In Berthelot's case there is no doubt that his views were colored by his personal dislike of Poincaré. It was, after all, the Minister of Foreign Affairs who had presided over the council which had suspended him, and as long as the Lorrainer remained as head of the government, there was no possible chance for Berthelot to return to the Quai d'Orsay.

However, Berthelot's opposition to the Ruhr occupation was not founded solely upon personal pique. Even at this early date he had decided that, somehow or other, Germany and France must manage to live together in the same European system. His ideas were not based upon any love for the German or upon the belief that reparations were wrong. He continued to be suspicious of German intentions even though he advocated reaching an understanding with the Weimar Republic—indeed, it was at Berthelot's instigation that in the late 1920's the successive French consul-generals at Cologne were specifically instructed to act not merely as commercial agents but also as political observers and to report their findings to the Quai d'Orsay.[63] Berthelot's desire for a Franco-German rapprochement was based rather upon what he believed was a realistic estimate of the situation. Germany, he felt, could not forever

[61] Allard, *Quai d'Orsay*, p. 46. [62] Bréal, *Berthelot*, p. 205.
[63] *Commission d'enquête, Témoignages et documents*, II, 470.

be maintained in a position of inferiority; furthermore, when the defeated nation recovered, her political and military potential would far outweigh that of France. Would it not then be more intelligent, thought Berthelot, to attempt a rapprochement rather than to continue a policy of coercion?

Equally important in Berthelot's dislike for the Poincaré policy of the *main au collet* was the fact that he was convinced that France had been a victor in 1918 only because she had possessed allies at her side. As a matter of principle he opposed any policy, which like that of Poincaré, threatened to disrupt the Anglo-French entente and to place his country in the position of taking unilateral action which none of the other major powers would support. It was a basic point of Berthelot's diplomacy to maintain France's ties with England—during the war he had done much to improve relations with Great Britain, shortly afterwards he supported Briand's attempt to secure a Franco-British military and political alliance, and in 1934, just a few days before his death, he made a special trip to England to deliver a speech at a banquet promoting Anglo-French friendship. Thus, because the Poincaré program threatened the maintenance of the entente with England, Berthelot strongly disapproved of the occupation of the Ruhr and the attempt to keep Germany down by force.

As early as January of 1922, soon after his own removal from office, Berthelot wrote a letter to Briand in which he supported the policy of Briand, himself shortly to fall from power, to seek an alliance with England even to the extent of modifying the French stand on reparations. "Your logic remains intact," Berthelot wrote, "and the facts will soon show that without a firm Anglo-French entente we will encounter the gravest difficulties not only in our foreign policies but also in our domestic affairs as well."[64] Twelve months later, just two weeks after French troops had occupied the Ruhr, he again sent Briand a summary of his views on French foreign policy, and the opinions expressed in this letter contained the germ of Locarno two years before the event:

"It cannot be forgotten that if we are today the strongest and will remain so for another dozen years, in a period of from twenty to fifty years the weight of seventy million organized, hard-working men will end up by being heavier than that of thirty-eight million Frenchmen.

"If, then, we don't try to create a German republic hostile to war, we are doomed. So far, instead of gaining ground with German democratic opinion, we haven't ceased to stir up hatred of ourselves.

[64] Suarez, *Briand*, v, 408.

"Even admitting that we will succeed in making Germany yield by our pressure on the Ruhr, the policy which immediately follows should be very generous and should very possibly even sacrifice the very objectives of our action. However, I don't believe that any German government can yield now that the Anglo-Saxon world is more separated from us than it appears and that Italy is only waiting for the chance to declare herself against us."[65]

Aristide Briand shared many of these views. He, too, believed it necessary to try to work with Germany rather than against her and hoped to make the Weimar Republic a viable government. Like Berthelot he believed that, in pursuing this goal, France could not afford to disregard the attitude of Great Britain. It was upon such assumptions that Locarno was founded. And it was also upon these same assumptions that Briand and Berthelot began to work together in 1925.

Despite certain differences of approach and of opinion the combination of Briand and Berthelot appears to have been a successful working arrangement in the years from 1925 to 1932. To be sure, the Foreign Minister probably never shared his deepest thoughts with his Secretary General. What went on at Thoiry, when Briand and Stresemann dreamed beautiful dreams of future Franco-German cooperation, was apparently never fully revealed to Berthelot.[66] And the latter, as noted, had less confidence than his chief in the League. But on the whole their seven-year collaboration seems to have been successful. Unlike the 1930's, when Alexis Léger assumed Berthelot's position, the Briand-Berthelot period was not a time during which the Secretary General felt that he was being called upon to execute policies with which he was in fundamental disagreement. And parenthetically, it might be noted—as the chapter on Léger will indicate[67]—that Léger himself, then serving as Briand's *chef du cabinet*, regarded his years at the Quai d'Orsay immediately after Locarno as the happiest of his career and felt that during this period the views of the responsible political leaders harmonized with his own.

Berthelot regarded his own association with Briand as a partnership in which he provided the essential facts and wrote many of the basic state papers, while the Foreign Minister, with his ease and facility as a speaker, won the support of the Chambers and of the public. The two men, in a real sense, complemented each other—it was Berthelot, for instance, who conducted the intricate diplomatic preliminaries which led

[65] *ibid.*, p. 429.   [66] Géraud, "Diplomacy Old and New," p. 410.
[67] See below, Chapter 12, §1.

to Locarno,[68] while it was Briand who gained the approval of the French public with his speeches. Berthelot never ceased to marvel at the way his chief, even though unprepared, could grasp the essentials of any given problem within a matter of moments and then deliver a speech in which he appeared to possess knowledge that resulted from years of study. The difference between Poincaré and Briand, he is supposed to have remarked with his customary cynicism, was that "The one knows everything but understands nothing; the other knows nothing but understands everything."[69]

III

It is not yet possible, on the basis of the evidence available, to write more than a tentative estimate of Philippe Berthelot as a diplomat. What makes the task difficult is the fact that for the crucial years after 1925 there is but little information at hand. It is at least possible to trace the main lines of Berthelot's thought up to that point: his faith in established diplomatic practices, his belief in the Anglo-French entente, his desire for Franco-German rapprochement and his insistence upon Continental alliances. But, paradoxically, we know the least about Berthelot in the years after Locarno when he was acting as Briand's collaborator and when many of the policies which he had himself previously advocated were now the policies of the French government. To be sure, since he returned to the Quai d'Orsay just at the moment when the French were making an abrupt switch to the line which he had recommended and since he was essentially "Briand's man," it is logical to assume that he agreed with the program that Briand put into effect during his long stay at the Foreign Ministry. But any final estimate of Berthelot will have to wait until we know in some detail how he reacted to the specific events and policies of those years—was he, for instance, a convinced believer in the Briand approach or was he perhaps a traditional diplomatist who followed Briand hoping only that the Foreign Minister's policies would achieve a part of his goals? And since the Secretary General destroyed his personal papers and left no memoirs, the answers, unfortunately, may always be tentative.

There is, however, almost unanimous agreement on one point: that Berthelot was particularly adept and successful in conducting diplomatic negotiations whatever their difficulty or complexity. His grasp of detail and his encyclopedic memory made him an exceptionally able negotiator.

[68] Paul-Boncour, *Entre deux guerres*, II, 161.
[69] There are many versions of this remark, see Suarez, *Briand*, V, 128.

He once surprised Lord Curzon by conducting an entire meeting without either notes or aides while the British Foreign Secretary, himself no mean diplomatist, had felt it necessary to come well supplied with both documents and assistants. Nearly all of Berthelot's contemporaries— even those who personally disliked him—were agreed on his competence. Lord Hardinge, who regarded Berthelot as no friend of Britain, was of the opinion when Berthelot was removed from office in 1922 that "France could not long dispense with the services of such a very able and remarkable man."[70] And even Poincaré, when he heard that Dutasta and not Berthelot was to be the chief French negotiator at the Peace Conference, noted in his diary that the latter would certainly have fulfilled the assignment with greater competence.[71] Similarly a friend like Paul-Boncour, himself a Foreign Minister in the interwar years, wrote of Berthelot's "unequaled mastery" of the art of diplomacy; Harold Nicolson, whose familiar criticism of the Peace Conference emphasized the lack of organization, maintained that the negotiations would have proceeded far more smoothly had Berthelot been in charge; and Lloyd George, with whom it was never easy to associate, indicated that the French Secretary General ". . . was a good man to do business with because he understood that agreement meant a comprehension of what the other side were after and a readiness to concede to their point of view details which did not give away the substance of one's own objective."[72]

But was Berthelot more than just a skilled negotiator? Even his lifelong friend, Paul Claudel, wrote that there was little point in examining his general ideas or his guiding theories, for the Secretary General's real forte was in the conduct of the everyday, practical details of diplomacy. And Claudel went on to observe that throughout his life Berthelot had loved to gamble, first at cards, later at dominoes. His patience, his attention, and his skills, Claudel thought, may well have been the result, at least in part, of these interests: "Who knows if these games didn't serve as the veritable *Kriegsspiel* of the diplomat?"[73] But Claudel's estimate leaves the faint suspicion that Berthelot, who loved to operate behind the scenes, was perhaps a skillful manipulator who may well at times have played the diplomatic game for its own sake, *pour le sport* as it were, without sufficient realization of the con-

---

[70] Hardinge, *Old Diplomacy*, pp. 251-252.
[71] Poincaré, *Au Service*, X, 459.
[72] Paul-Boncour, *Entre deux guerres*, II, 339; Harold Nicolson, *Peacemaking, 1919* (New York, 1939), pp. 119-120; David Lloyd George, *The Truth about the Peace Treaties* (London, 1938), II, 1104.
[73] Claudel, *Accompagnements*, pp. 186-187.

sequences. Such a verdict, of course, without documentation cannot be proven, but whoever attempts a final estimate of Berthelot will at least have to consider this facet of his make-up.

In estimating the worth of Berthelot's policies it is important to remember that he resumed his post at the Foreign Office just at the point when French foreign policy was switching from one tactic to another. In the preceding three years the French under Poincaré had tried to conduct an independent policy—that is, to handle Germany on their own terms without regard for the views of their wartime allies. This program had, for a variety of reasons, become impossible and the French had caved in. At home there was rising discontent because the Ruhr occupation had led to the famous and disastrous "fall of the franc," and Poincaré's political opponents, though for some time slow to make use of this situation, eventually claimed that his foreign policies had provoked the French financial plight. At the same time both Great Britain and the United States exerted tremendous pressure upon France to come to a final and viable settlement with Germany, above all to put an end to the Ruhr occupation and to settle the troubled reparations question. Even Poincaré, although he had forced Germany to agree to full compliance with his policy and, literally, had the Germans on the run, had felt it necessary to yield to this pressure; considerably before the elections of 1924 he agreed to the meeting of what became the Dawes commission. It was, of course, the electoral victory of the left in 1924— ultimately bringing Berthelot and Briand to the Quai d'Orsay—which made it thenceforth impossible to continue the Poincaré foreign policy. And it was under these circumstances and after these events that the Locarno accords were reached and the opportunity presented to carry out the policy of Franco-German rapprochement and Anglo-French cooperation that Berthelot had advocated since at least 1922.

Locarno, however, whatever the insights of its creators, no longer appears the brightest page in the diplomatic history of the 1920's. Some if not all of the bloom is off the rose. Before the second world war, writers frequently referred to the Locarno era as the "years of hope"; today they seem more likely to have been "years of illusion." For—and there are innumerable reasons, ranging from the premature death of Stresemann to the coming of the world depression, which we cannot pause to explore—Locarno never led to a permanent settlement of Franco-German difficulties or established the bases of a lasting reconciliation. If Locarno and the various decisions which followed it left many Frenchmen dissatisfied, there were also on the other side of the Rhine, as the memoirs of Dirksen and Weizsäcker bear more than adequate testimony, many more Germans who likewise remained unconvinced.

More important, however, is the fact that Locarno, in essence, meant that France had knuckled under to Great Britain. She had, by yielding to the British demand to evacuate the Ruhr and by bringing in the British as guarantors of the Franco-German frontier, completely abandoned any hope of an independent policy or of any return to it. Furthermore, immediately afterwards the British, as well as the supposedly isolationist Americans, began to exert full pressure on the French to agree to disarmament conferences. The British argued at great length that, since the French now had the security pact which they had been clamoring for since Versailles, the time had now come to investigate the chances of reducing armaments, in particular, French armaments. All of this, in the setting of the 1920's, appeared to be Anglo-French cooperation or collaboration, but it really boiled down to French subservience to the wishes of England. The fact is that, after the end of the Ruhr experiment and after the signing of the Locarno pacts, the French never again would act alone; they had, indeed, lost a large part of their nerve, had caved in before English pressure and thereafter followed closely behind a British lion whose roar was frequently not very loud. Thus Berthelot's program of close Anglo-French cooperation, in other times and in other circumstances, was to make French policy a prisoner of the British. It was, indeed, a first and important step on the road to Munich.

It can, of course, be argued that Berthelot and other French diplomats tried to avoid this pitfall by keeping France's eastern alliances as the other theme of their foreign policy. But here again a number of difficulties were involved. In the first place, the British would never associate themselves with this program. They would never agree to an "Eastern Locarno" or permit themselves to be drawn in as even silent partners in France's continental alliance system. In Austen Chamberlain's paraphrase of Bismarck, "For the Polish Corridor, no British government ever will or ever can risk the bones of a British grenadier." England's idea of European—and French—security stopped with the Rhine, and what happened in Central or Eastern Europe involved faraway countries with which Britain was little concerned. Furthermore, and this is of course a story in itself, France's Eastern alliances were themselves insufficient. Individually the nations were weak, and they never learned, despite French prompting, to work together; no military implementation of the French alliances was ever worked out, and the defensively-oriented French army, after the mid-1920's, would have been of little value to these allies. Above all, the French alliance system had been built up in an era which assumed not only German disarmament but also the demilitarization of the Rhineland. When Hitler built up his armed forces and moved into the Rhineland, France's Eastern system almost overnight became valueless.

Perhaps, though, no French foreign policy could have been long successful. Many of France's difficulties in the 1920's appear in retrospect to have been almost inevitable. French power after the first world war was after all essentially artificial; it depended not only upon the continuing weakness of Germany but also upon the exclusion of Russia from European affairs. Certainly French hegemony could not long withstand the recovery of those states. Moreover, any attempt to conciliate Germany was fraught with unknown perils and imponderables almost beyond measure. It was impossible for France to enlist Britain as an ally in the East; on the other hand it was impossible to get along without England. But to follow her meant that French ties with Central Europe were increasingly worthless, while to rely on continental allies alone was to have no real strength. French foreign policy, in short, whether following the strategy of a Poincaré, a Briand or a Berthelot was throughout the 1920's caught on the horns of a dilemma for which there was no simple solution, and for which, quite possibly, there was none at all.

Perhaps the virtue of Philippe Berthelot was simply that he was always conscious of this dilemma and that he was not merely a doctrinaire advocate of Anglo-French collaboration or rapprochement with Germany. He was, it seems, not merely another Holstein who failed to realize that the policies which he had long advocated would, in turn, create new difficulties when they were put into operation. The clue to this—and it is admittedly only a clue—is furnished by the testimony of Paul Claudel. If Claudel is correct, Philippe Berthelot put the Locarno program into effect and between 1925 and 1932 went along with Briand not so much because he believed in the policy but simply because he could envisage no alternatives. Though he had himself recommended the course which led to Locarno and had strongly believed in working closely with Britain and in trying to conciliate Germany, he very quickly realized, once this strategy was attempted, that it was no panacea and that it led to new and grave difficulties for which no solution was in sight. Thus, although Berthelot implemented the policies which followed Locarno, he did so with no confidence and solely because his own analysis indicated that there were no alternatives. Moreover, under the impact of this bitter realization—and here we have an indication of why it is so difficult to learn much about the Berthelot of these later years—he isolated himself more and more in the accomplishment of his purely routine, administrative tasks.[74] Thus, after nearly thirty years of guiding French foreign policy, Berthelot recognized the impasse which confronted his nation, and, finding that the program which he himself had recommended was far from a complete success, took refuge in the routine of the Quai d'Orsay.

IV

Philippe Berthelot, after his retirement, lived long enough to witness the first signs of the collapse of the security system which he had tried to construct. With an increasingly bitter awareness, he understood that the structure of the postwar world was coming apart at the seams. And he feared that no one could solve the deepening crisis.

During the first world war Berthelot had been famous for his optimism. Even in the darkest days of 1917 he had never been without hope. Foreign diplomats, in need of consolation, frequently sought him out when they wanted a cheering word. But in the 1930's Berthelot was unnerved. Declining health may have deepened his natural skepticism. Possibly, too, the man who believed himself indispensable naturally felt that those who succeeded him were incapable of continuing the diplomatic struggle. But, in any event, those who had known him all their lives and who saw him in the months before his death in November of 1934 were struck by the pessimism with which Berthelot regarded the future.

Wladimir d'Ormesson, himself a one-time diplomat and writer for Parisian dailies, remembered that in his last interview with Berthelot, the former Secretary General's face was grave as he spoke cruel words about the pettiness of the politicians who were throwing away French security. d'Ormesson felt that Berthelot actually suffered to see what he regarded as his life's achievements being compromised amid the domestic turmoil in France.[75] Upon hearing of the assassination of Alexander of Yugoslavia, Berthelot wrote to a lifelong friend, "Destiny is against France. The death of the king of Yugoslavia annuls the only really good card in our game." And a little later: "Life more and more imitates the movies, and the law of the gangsters is being imposed everywhere. The

---

[74] On Berthelot's loss of faith in Locarno and his increasing tendency to turn inwards the only reference is Claudel, *Accompagnements*, p. 203.

[75] d'Ormesson in *Le Figaro*, November 23, 1934.

brigands have more energy than the honest men. Meanness, idiocy and dishonesty are rampant."[76]

Events after 1934 were to prove Berthelot was right—the gangsters and brigands did have more energy than the honest men. Thus Philippe Berthelot, in his last days, joined the ranks of the many clairvoyant European diplomats who sensed the gathering of the storm but who knew themselves powerless to avert its course.

[76] Both cited in Dumont-Wilden, in *Revue Bleue*, LXXV, 618.

3

....

Sweden: The Diplomacy of Östen Undén

BY ERIK LÖNNROTH

[THE CONGRESS OF VIENNA was the first international body to distinguish formally between Great Powers and lesser powers. The distinction was sharply challenged at the time and has been frequently debated since;* but, however insecure its legal basis may be, it has without a doubt been validated by international practice over the course of the years. One of the most notable—and, in the eyes of many thoughtful students, most fateful—developments of the nineteenth century was the increasing domination of European politics by the five states which were generally recognized as Great Powers: Great Britain, France, Germany, Austria-Hungary, and Russia; and it was clear, even before the coming of the first world war had helped to prove it, that the lesser states had lost that ability to exert a moderating and balancing influence in international affairs which they had possessed and exerted in earlier centuries.

For a brief period after the first world war, it appeared that this development might be checked, or even reversed. At the Peace Conference at Paris, a large number of new states were created which were not, perhaps, Powers of the first rank, but some of which—Poland, for instance, or Czechoslovakia—did not seem to be markedly inferior in strength to self-styled Great Powers like Italy or doubtful quantities like revolutionary Russia.[1] Moreover, the principle of equality of all states was now vigorously asserted, and a new international body, the League of Nations, was established to give it effective expression. In the decade that followed, the newly created states, and the lesser Powers

---

* At Vienna, the representative of Holland remarked that "of this newly invented term, 'the Great Powers,' he understood neither the precise meaning nor the intention." C. H. Hazen, "Le Congrès de Vienne," *Revue des études napoléoniennes*, xv (1919), 69. See also Federico Chabod, *Storia della politica estera italiana dal 1870 al 1896: I. Le premesse* (Bari, 1951), 154 and notes.

[1] See Arnold Toynbee, *The World after the Peace Conference* (London, 1925); and, as an introduction to the problems of the Scandinavian countries, *Survey of International Affairs, 1939-1946: The World in March 1939* (London, 1952), pp. 157-162.

in general, had a natural interest in the organization and development of the League, for it seemed to offer them both an assurance that their voices would not be unheard when questions of European importance were being determined and a possible means of restraining the dangerous ambitions, and appeasing the dangerous passions, of their greater neighbors.

The hopes entertained with regard to the League were not, in the end, realized; it succumbed to the domination of the Great Powers, and its activities and purposes were shaped in accordance with their desires. It would be misleading, however, to see the story of the League as a tragedy in which the vices of the Great Powers triumphed over the virtues of the lesser. For the small Powers too had special interests which restricted and determined their actions at Geneva. They could no more follow a course of pure idealism or internationalism than could the Great Powers. They too, in formulating policy, had to yield to the dictates of their national tradition and the requirements of their national security.

One of the most instructive examples of the conflict between internationalism and national interest, as it affected the smaller Powers, is the so-called League crisis of 1926,[2] a crisis which arose when the question of Germany's entry into the League precipitated a general scramble for seats on the Council and released animosities which threatened to rip the Covenant asunder. The decision of the Swedish government to sacrifice Sweden's seat in the interests of general pacification seems to offer one of the most shining examples of an altruistic policy which can be found in the 1920's.[3] As this chapter reveals, closer analysis indicates that Sweden's conduct in this affair was always guided by a careful regard for the requirements of national interest, and provides an instructive illustration of the limits within which the lesser Powers were confined in their support of the new world organization. *The Editors.*]

I

During the first world war, Sweden was transformed from a constitutional monarchy to a full parliamentary democracy. The change had

[2] A brief account will be found in F. P. Walters, *A History of the League of Nations* (2 volumes, London, 1952), I, 316-327. See also G. Scelle, *Une crise de la Société des Nations* (Paris, 1927); and Chapter 1, §IV above.

[3] An English journalist wrote in 1926: "It is important to understand that Sweden's concern was for the League only and that, not for the first time, she set aside all claims of separate interests for the sake of that concern." H. M. Swanwick, "Anarchy at Geneva," *Foreign Affairs* (London), VII (1925-1926), 286.

an immediate impact on the course of Swedish foreign policy, and was reflected in the abandonment of a policy which, while officially neutral, had been somewhat pro-German in tendency, in favor of a policy based upon the League of Nations.

The reality behind the constitutional transformation was an electoral reform which took place in 1918 and which completely changed the character of the first chamber or Senate of the Swedish *Riksdag*. In contrast to the second chamber, which was elected by universal and equal suffrage, the Senate had before 1918 been elected by a voting system in which the right to vote was dependent on the voter's economic status. The Conservatives, who had a large minority in the second chamber, could, under this system, always be sure of a majority in the first chamber and were thus able to check their Liberal and Social Democratic opponents. After the reform of the first chamber in 1918, however, the Conservatives could form no government without the support of the Liberals; and it became impossible to carry out a foreign policy that was not in accord with public opinion as expressed in the *Riksdag*.

The interwar years represent the highpoint of parliamentary power in Swedish history. During the second world war, a renewed concentration of power in the hands of the Executive was to take place and was, especially in the sphere of foreign policy, to limit public debate and parliamentary influence again. But this development was not foreseen, and would have seemed quite unlikely, during the 1920's and early 1930's when Sweden was generally ruled by weak minority governments which had no strong control over parliament as a whole. It is symptomatic of the influence of the parliament on foreign policy that, in 1921, a committee of the *Riksdag* was created for the purpose of discussing foreign affairs with the King and the government. Though this committee never seriously interfered with the actions of the government, its existence clearly demonstrated the claim of the *Riksdag* to control over Sweden's foreign policy. Between 1919 and 1939, no Swedish Foreign Minister dared to disregard the views of the parliamentary majority—with one exception. In 1923, the Conservative Foreign Minister Hederstierna made a speech recommending an alliance with Finland, but the newspapers expressed such strong opposition to the suggestion that he was forced to resign a few days later.

In the period between 1919 and 1932, there was little stability in Swedish politics; governments changed every two years and sometimes at shorter intervals. Alternating coalitions of Liberals, Conservatives, and Social Democrats succeeded each other and it was not until after 1932, when the Social Democrats began their cooperation with the Farmer's party, that there was greater stability. Nevertheless, even in the 1920's, during the period of greatest instability in domestic policy, Sweden's foreign policy kept a steady course. This can partly be explained by the fact that no strong partisan feelings were aroused by the issues of foreign policy once the conservative line of policy had been abandoned; although it might have been expected that the ideological differences of the parties would find some reflection in foreign policy, this was very seldom the case. During the interwar years, most of the Swedish Foreign Ministers were prominent lawyers, and party divergences were overbalanced by professional conformity in their approach to foreign affairs. Moreover, the departmental tradition in the Foreign Office seems to have been very strong.

The Swedish diplomats of the 1920's were professionally trained officials recruited from upper-class families; and the key posts in Paris, London, Berlin, Moscow, and Rome were still held by members of the nobility. Some of the diplomatic representatives had risen to prominence in party politics. Baron Palmstierna, the Minister in London, had been Minister of Foreign Affairs in the first Social Democratic cabinet; Count Ehrensvaerd in Paris had held the same post in a prewar Liberal cabinet; and Baron Ramel in Berlin was to serve as Foreign Minister for the Liberals in the early 1930's. But even if they owed their positions to their connections with political parties, they were aristocrats and had the same background as the other Swedish representatives abroad. The diplomats in the field and the staff of the Foreign Office in Stockholm formed a close unit, with the Cabinet Secretary—i.e. the permanent secretary of the Foreign Office—and the head of the Political Bureau as key figures. The diplomats were responsible for gathering the news about political developments in the outside world which touched on Sweden's interests and for its analysis and interpretation. In the conduct of Swedish foreign policy, therefore, the Foreign Minister and the government could rely on the work done by men who were all guided by the same professional "esprit de corps"; and the Foreign Office, with its officials at home and abroad, thus constituted a collective power of considerable importance. Its influence was not much mentioned in the political discussions of the day, but it can be seen in the continuity of Swedish foreign policy in this period, and, occasionally, in differences of opinion between the Foreign Minister on the one hand and his Cabinet colleagues on the other.

II

The most outstanding figure among the Swedish Foreign Ministers of the interwar period was Östen Undén. Born in 1886, he had been appointed to the chair of Civil Law at the University of Uppsala in 1917. When he had been an undergraduate at Lund University, he had joined the Social Democratic party. In 1917, when for the first time, the Social Democrats entered the government in a coalition with the Liberals, the young professor became a member of this coalition Cabinet. In 1920 when the first purely Social Democratic government was formed, Undén became Minister of Justice; and, in the Cabinets of 1924-1926, he served as Minister of Foreign Affairs, first under Prime Minister Hjalmar Branting and, after Branting's death in 1925, under Richard Sandler.

Undén had worked for the Foreign Office as an expert on international law from 1921 to 1924, and consequently was more the specialist than the politician when he became Foreign Minister. He had, indeed, never been a member of the *Riksdag* before he appeared there as a member of the Cabinet. He was a respected, but not a very popular, political personality; his way of thinking, his speech and general behavior were precise and rather formal. His legal education, combined with a certain natural stiffness and shyness, tended to keep others at a distance. On the other hand, his ability and will power enabled him to become a strong head of his department and to assert his influence within the government as the expert on foreign policy. By the parties and press of the opposition who tended to think of him as a rigid, somewhat ineffectual doctrinaire, he was on the whole underestimated.

In the 1920's, the activity of a Swedish Foreign Minister centered on the League of Nations which Sweden had joined in 1920. Two years later, Sweden had been elected member of the Council of the League, where she was given an opportunity to act in her natural role as the leading member of a group of small states, chiefly ex-neutrals, who worked to form a counterweight against the dominating influence of the Great Powers. Within this group, the three Scandinavian countries constituted a natural inner circle by virtue of their geographical proximity, their close cultural relations and linguistic kinship, and their common interest in peace and in moderating European tensions. There was close cooperation among them. They held common views on the chief issues discussed at Geneva; and Sweden, in her position as member of the Council, acted as their spokesman.

From the outset, the Scandinavian countries opposed the use of military sanctions by the League. In the early 1920's, the Swedish government stated frequently that, considering the weakness of the League structure, the employment of military sanctions would be a risky adventure. In the Swedish view, the victors of the first world war were now the leading Powers in the League, and the use of military sanctions would involve sacrifices for a system of security that these Powers had established but that Sweden regarded as by no means perfect. The Swedish alternative to sanctions was compulsory arbitration in international conflicts, an alternative that reflected a belief that arbitration alone could guarantee real impartiality in international conflicts, and which corresponded to that faith in the paramount importance of law which was deeply rooted in the Swedish national tradition. Undén, the former law professor, was a born champion of this cause; and during the League Assembly of 1925, he formally proposed that compulsory arbitration be accepted as a basic principle of League activity. The failure of the Geneva Protocol had stimulated search for other means to strengthen the efficiency of the League, and the committee in which Undén's suggestion was discussed showed great interest in his proposal, although the Assembly, in its resolution of September 25, 1925, confined itself to a recommendation in its favor.

The Swedish prescription for the solution of international disputes obtained a significant success in the Mosul question.[4] In the solution of this problem, Sweden played a leading role; and the Swedish member of the Council acted as *rapporteur* during the hearings. The actual issue here was the drawing of a frontier between Iraq and Turkey, but since Great Britain championed Iraq's cause, Britain and Turkey were the real antagonists. Branting, the Swedish delegate, was responsible for the proposal to invite Turkey to participate in the meetings of the Council in which the Mosul question was to be discussed, and his motion, which was accepted, can be regarded as providing the basis for the successful solution of the conflict. Branting also drew the provisional demarcation line, the so-called Brussels line, which was accepted by both parties and prevented military clashes during the negotiations.

After Branting's death, Undén succeeded him as *rapporteur*. Experts, meanwhile, had worked out a solution stipulating that all territory south of the Brussels line should go to Iraq, provided that Iraq, for the purpose of protection of the minorities, would remain a British mandate. Britain and Iraq agreed to this solution, but Turkey refused and declared that the Council of the League was not competent to make

[4] On this problem see Walters, *History of the League*, I, 305-310.

a decision. The Swedish Foreign Ministry, where the issue had been thoroughly discussed, recommended a solution *ex aequo et bono*. After Undén's attempts to persuade the Turks to accept the mediation of the Council had failed, he asked the Permanent Court to rule on the nature of the powers which the Council could exercise. The ruling of the Court established the competence of the Council and the Council subsequently gave a decision in agreement with the recommendation of the experts. The caution and precision with which Undén established the legal rights of the Council in this case was an important factor in the peaceful outcome of the conflict and in the strengthening of the idea of arbitration.

III

The final months of the Mosul conflict saw the emergence of another issue, which was of much more vital importance to the League and in which all the great European Powers and the entire European balance of power was involved. Germany's entry into the League and her claim to a seat on the Council inaugurated a thoroughgoing discussion of the whole problem of Council membership and reorganization. Here again Sweden played a prominent role; and it may be said that Undén's handling of this problem represents his main achievement as Foreign Minister. Under his direction, Sweden appeared as a star performer in the Geneva theatre. In the action which Sweden undertook, idealistic internationalism and national interest worked hand in hand and spurred each other to action.

On October 16, 1925, the Treaty of Locarno was signed. Germany was accepted as a member of the European family of states, in return for which she renounced all claims to a revision of her western boundary as laid down in the Treaty of Versailles. Germany, however, did not guarantee her eastern boundaries; her claims to a revision of the Polish frontier, especially with respect to the so-called Polish corridor between Eastern Prussia and the Reich, remained. In recognition of this, France tried to compensate her Polish ally by means of a guarantee against German aggression, but the British government gave no promises to the eastern allies of France, and, because of this, Poland especially could be regarded as the injured party in what was otherwise regarded as a notable peace settlement.

Locarno was only the first step on Germany's way to the full recognition of her title as Great Power. She had now to enter the League of Nations and to receive a permanent seat on the League Council. There could be no doubt that this second move would accentuate Poland's embarrassment. Could Poland and her powerful ally France permit these developments without making a countermove to offset Germany's growing influence? And, if they made such a countermove, would it not weaken Germany's willingness to adopt a policy of international collaboration? In the German *Reichstag*, the Nationalists, the Nazis, and the Communists had voted against the ratification of the Locarno Treaty, and there was considerable popular opposition to it. Any serious blow to Stresemann's policy of understanding with the West might well give the upper hand to the opposition parties.[5]

Sweden had one central interest in the developments on the international scene: pacification of the Baltic. The tension between Germany and France reached into this area: Poland was the ally of France, and had in the early 1920's sought to extend its influence to the north by trying to conclude an alliance with Finland, a development most unattractive to the Swedes. Germany and the Soviet Union, on the other hand, were linked by the Treaty of Rapallo. Together with Denmark, Sweden controlled the entrance to the Baltic, but in a war between the contending Powers in which one of them claimed passage through Öresund, Sweden and Denmark might become involved in a major conflict. If, on the other hand, Germany entered the League of Nations and could be won for peaceful cooperation with the Western Powers, the Rapallo front would be split, and the tension in the Baltic area considerably relieved. In the fall of 1925, things seemed to hang in the balance; the Swedish Foreign Office was receiving indications that Russia, dissatisfied with Germany's moves towards the Western Powers, was doing her best to stir up German opposition. The democratic Weimar Republic was popular in Sweden, and the restoration of Germany's international position was regarded as a question of justice and common sense. But the calculations of the Swedish Foreign Office were not determined by sentimental considerations. The line which Swedish foreign policy pursued was dictated by her position as a small neutral Power in the Baltic area, and by the wish to strengthen the true spirit of peace and collaboration in the League of Nations.

On November 4, 1925, the Polish plenipotentiary in Stockholm asked for Undén's views concerning an eventual Polish claim to a seat on the League Council. A permanent seat, Undén answered, was hardly possible. He even doubted the desirability of a nonpermanent seat; this would be in the interest neither of Poland nor of other countries, because

[5] See Gustav Stresemann, *His Diaries, Letters and Papers*, edited and translated by Eric Sutton (New York, 1937), II, 505-507.

a simultaneous entry of Germany and Poland into the Council would involve the risk of serious friction between these two Powers.

Two weeks later, on November 21, the German plenipotentiary came to Undén and expressed his concern about rumors of a Spanish claim to a permanent seat, and referred to reports that the Spanish government would make this a condition of her consent to Germany's membership in the Council. Undén was seriously disturbed by this information and, in December, decided to discuss the matter with the British Foreign Secretary, Austen Chamberlain.[6] Chamberlain informed him that the British government had decided to support the Spanish claim, but had not yet made up its mind how to handle the Polish case. Chamberlain's words, however, seemed to suggest that he personally had no objections to the Polish aspirations. Undén was so anxious to change Chamberlain's views about the Polish case that he expressed exaggerated hopes of Polish moderation, but he did not convince Chamberlain, who remained skeptical.

Undén seemed to be working wholeheartedly in the German interest, with the idea of giving Germany a seat on the League Council and refusing entry to that body to any other Power. The line of policy which he pursued in this regard had been previously formulated in agreement with all the Scandinavian Powers and was based on the principle that only really Great Powers should have permanent seats, the temporary seats circulating among the other nations. This program was inspired by the idea of making impossible the formation of permanent combinations of satellite Powers within the Council. But, in this fight for principle, Undén was spurred on by interests of a more concrete nature; the entire Locarno policy seemed to him endangered and he wanted to keep Germany on the course of cooperation with the West. To gain these aims, Undén mobilized all the resources of Swedish diplomacy.

On January 21, 1926, the Swedish Foreign Minister directed an appeal to the governments of Norway, Denmark, the Netherlands, Finland, Switzerland, and Belgium. Undén explained that probably Spain, and possibly Poland, would claim permanent seats on the League Council; and that Spain had already been assured of British support. Compliance with the aspirations of these states would, however, endanger the fundamental principles which determined the distribution of permanent and nonpermanent seats on the Council. The Swedish view was that, in addition to those Great Powers who already held permanent seats, there were only three Powers who could justly claim permanent seats, namely Ger-

---

[6] For Chamberlain's attitude, see Walters, *History of the League*, I, 317.

many, Russia, and the United States. At the coming meeting of the Council, therefore, Sweden was inclined to oppose claims from any other Power. Undén asked whether the governments to which he addressed his appeal could be counted upon to join Sweden in this attitude.

The various governments had answered by February 8. Norway, Finland, and Switzerland expressed agreement with the Swedish position without reservation. Denmark also accepted the Swedish point of view, but was skeptical about the outcome of the projected action; these doubts were influenced by the fact that Denmark possessed information about additional claims: namely, claims of Brazil to a permanent seat. The Belgian government was willing to join Sweden, but Paul Hymans, the Belgian delegate at Geneva, had little hope that the small Powers could hold out if the Great Powers agreed on a definite line of policy. The Dutch government shared Sweden's views about the undesirability of enlarging the Council, but had not yet decided whether to take a stand or to declare itself "disinterested."

As a result of Undén's appeal, therefore, he was in a position, in presenting the Swedish view on the organization of the Council, to act as spokesman for the group of small Powers. But because he acted on the basis of principle, he was forced to deal with the politically innocuous claims of Spain and Brazil on the same level as with the highly significant and explosive claim of Poland. Nevertheless, from now on, Sweden was bound by the principle which Undén had enunciated.

The outcome of the question depended essentially on Great Britain, who held the key position; and Sweden made her main diplomatic efforts in London. The task of dissuading Austen Chamberlain from supporting the Polish claim was given to Baron Palmstierna, the Minister in London. Palmstierna had a personal interest in this question because he was in full sympathy with Undén, who had succeeded him as Foreign Minister in a Social Democratic government, and he went about his task with commendable energy. Palmstierna was in close touch with those groups in England who shared the Swedish opposition to an enlargement of the Council; in particular, he sought the advice of Ramsay MacDonald. The minister was fully aware that opposition against Chamberlain in this question was strong in Britain, and was shared even by members of the Baldwin Cabinet. Palmstierna set his hopes on the combination of the two Social Democratic Foreign Ministers, Undén of Sweden and Vandervelde of Belgium, with the Labor party leader MacDonald. Joint action by Belgium and Sweden, he believed, might stop the project which had by now been submitted to the League Council; and his reports to Stockholm encouraged the Swedish government to put up a fight in the Council. Throughout the League crisis, Palmstierna exerted great influence on the course of Swedish policy, particularly when, in February 1926, a change in Chamberlain's formerly announced position seemed to justify his earlier optimistic evaluation of the situation. At that time Chamberlain seemed willing to delay decision over the Spanish claim and stated that the British government had made no commitments with regard to the claims of Poland and Brazil. It thus appeared, temporarily, that the Swedish attitude corresponded to Britain's real intentions.

This view was shared by the German Foreign Minister, Stresemann, who was in constant contact with Undén, whom he tried to make a wholehearted champion of Germany's interests within the League and on the Council. Stresemann actually claimed that the British government desired Sweden to take responsibility for opposing all claims for additional seats on the Council, with the exception of that of Germany. This argument may have affected Undén, although he tried to keep somewhat aloof from Germany and emphasized the independence of Swedish policy. It was not easy to do this, given the nature of Undén's instructions. For these directed him unequivocally to support the German claim to a seat, while opposing any further enlargement of the Council. In drawing up these instructions, the Swedish government seem not to have realized how far they were sticking their necks out and how exposed Sweden's position was really to be.

Their main error of judgment lay in their analysis of Chamberlain's attitude. In moderating his previous position, the British Foreign Secretary seems to have been motivated by a desire to counter any German threat to abandon the League of Nations and the Locarno policy. He apparently feared that, if Germany made out of this issue a question of prestige, any compromise between the German and the Franco-Polish interests would become impossible. He was perfectly willing, therefore, that Sweden should come forth as the chief opponent of the Polish claim, for the dispute then became one of principle, rather than an issue of national prestige and political rivalry; and it was in Britain's interest to keep the discussion on a somewhat abstract level. But, in taking an uncompromising line of opposition to the Polish claim, Sweden seemed to be acting for Germany, which threw doubts upon her true motives.

In the first days of March 1926, therefore, rumors began to spread that Chamberlain had changed front again and was now preparing a compromise. Simultaneously, the Polish government, which had been very critical of Sweden's position, suddenly adopted a different tone and expressed understanding and sympathy for the Swedish attitude.

Undén found himself in Geneva in a very difficult situation. His first task was to explain that Sweden was not acting on behalf of Germany but was following an independent line. But Undén was isolated. Vandervelde informed him that, if the question of the enlargement of the Council led to a showdown, Belgium could not vote against France and Britain. With the exception of Germany, which was still debarred from the League, no other Power shared Sweden's flat refusal to consider any compromise.

When Brazil and Spain presented their claims for permanent seats on the Council, Undén resisted strongly and remained firm even when Chamberlain attempted to influence him to take a less uncompromising line. Then Spain gave way, and the Brazilian delegate consented to ask for new instructions from home. On March 12, then, Undén seemed to have won out and to have prevented the enlargement of the Council. The true crisis came, however, when Vandervelde proposed the establishment of a new, temporary seat for Poland. This suggestion could not be reconciled with Unden's instructions or with the German point of view; but Sweden and Germany had now been placed in a most awkward position. If they remained adamant, they would appear to be the only obstacles to an agreement, for all the other Powers were willing to make concessions. Under the influence of representations by Vandervelde, Undén began to search for a way out of the dilemma. He asked Prime Minister Richard Sandler about the possibility of new instructions; he suggested a plan, which he had already mentioned in January to the Polish Minister in Stockholm. Sweden would resign her own nonpermanent seat in favor of Poland, thus appeasing Polish sensibilities without permitting an alteration of the constitution of the Council. Undén found little understanding in Stockholm. The Swedish press was strongly in favor of Germany's entry into the League, but was equally convinced of the correctness of the attitude of the small Powers in objecting to an enlargement of the Council. Public opinion in Sweden had no understanding of the change in atmosphere to which Vandervelde's compromise proposal had led; and the government refused to amend Undén's instructions.

Meanwhile, the clouds had darkened in Geneva. The Swiss Foreign Minister Motta recommended that the Swedish delegation make concessions. At the same time, in a secret meeting of the Council, Aristide Briand declared that France could not permit Germany to impose conditions for entering the League. If, as a result of German maneuvers, Poland was refused a Council seat, Briand declared, he would return to Paris and resign as Foreign Minister; and the Locarno policy would be at an end.

Under this pressure, Undén gave way as much as his instructions permitted. He promised to consult the German delegation about the situation, a suggestion which was eagerly accepted by the other members. It was clear that, if Germany too could be persuaded to favor a compromise, Sweden would appear to be more papal than the Pope in resisting any possible arrangement; and the Swedish government might in these circumstances agree to a change of Undén's instructions.

Undén had thus to work along two different lines. He had, in the first place, to get the permission of the Swedish Cabinet to resign the Swedish seat in the Council, so that Poland could enter the Council without enlargement of this body. For two days, telegrams of a truly dramatic character went back and forth between Geneva and Stockholm. But, in addition to his difficulties with his own government, Undén had to secure the German agreement. On March 15 the Germans expressed their willingness to accept Undén's suggestion on the condition that either Belgium or Czechoslovakia would join Sweden in resigning from the Council. Since Benes of Czechoslovakia was prepared to cooperate in order to save the situation, Undén, in reporting to Stockholm, informed his government that he now took it for granted that all obstacles to Sweden's abandonment of her Council seat were removed. The Cabinet gave way. The crisis was over, but it was followed by an anticlimax. Brazil declared her intention of insisting upon receiving a permanent seat in the Council; and the German entry into the League had after all to be postponed until the fall of 1926. But there was no longer any doubt that the real issue had been solved and that Germany would be able to take her seat. The question had been freed from those aspects which were politically explosive and had been reduced to the technical question of the constitutional structure of the League.[7]

Swedish public opinion had still not grasped the twofold aspect of the issue and did not realize that, if Undén had not achieved full victory, he had made an important contribution to European pacification. Swedish public opinion had been interested chiefly in the principle of maintaining the present size of the Council, and Brazil's stubbornness had won out over this principle at the last moment. Sweden's sacrifice of her Council seat seemed therefore to have been made in vain; Undén had diffi-

[7] On the negotiations, see Walters, *History of the League*, I, 323-325.

culty in defending himself against the Conservative opposition in the *Riksdag*; and, when the Cabinet resigned in May 1926, his personal popularity had quite obviously been diminished.

Undén's policy in the League of Nations crisis of 1926 can be correctly evaluated only if it is seen as an attempt to relieve the tension among the Great European Powers and to make Locarno a success. It can probably be said that the memory of the events of 1926, when he worked for an understanding among the Great Powers, had its influence in shaping the line which Undén has taken during recent years in the United Nations.

But it is important to note that, in his policy of 1926, Undén was not a starry-eyed idealist. He pursued a subtle policy, perhaps too subtle to be understood in all its implications by the Swedish people and the Cabinet. He was constantly aware of the relationship between European peace and Sweden's national interest in peace in the Baltic area. He did not embark on a new course, but continued the traditional line worked out by the professionals of his department. If Undén's performance seemed new and startling, the reason may be sought more in the personal qualities of this resolute, stubborn, and courageous man than in the contrast between a foreign policy of parliamentarism and a foreign policy of professionals.

4

∷∷

Czechoslovakia: The Diplomacy of Eduard Benes

BY PAUL E. ZINNER

IN THE ANNALS OF DIPLOMACY covering the period between the two world wars, Eduard Benes is likely to command a fair amount of attention. He belonged to a small group of statesmen who represented the lesser Powers of the Continent and who left an imprint on the European political scene—a group which also includes Nicolas Politis, Take Ionescu, and Nicolae Titulescu. But of all of these men Benes perhaps stands out as the one who was most often and most intimately involved in events of European significance, and the one on whom world attention was focused at crucial junctions in the post-Versailles period of Europe. The creation of Czechoslovakia, in which Benes shared top honors with Thomas G. Masaryk and Milan R. Stefanik, was symbolic of the introduction of a new, more democratic international order in Europe. The destruction of Czechoslovakia in 1938 in turn symbolized the breakdown of this order and the bankruptcy of Allied diplomacy.

Just how history will evaluate the diplomatic achievements and failures of Eduard Benes, remains to be seen. It is almost certain, however, that he will be recorded as one of the more controversial statesmen of his era. Indeed, no man who was as close to so many of the diplomatic skirmishes of the interwar period and who, in the last analysis, was responsible for such portentous decisions as Benes could possibly avoid being controversial. His judgments and decisions and the policies he advocated and tried to implement were often questioned and frequently censured by his contemporaries. Few people remained indifferent to him or to his policies, and he was either admired or hated by those who knew him. To date no unbiased biography of Benes exists.[1] In fact, there is no penetrating and

[1] The following, however, are useful: P. Crabites, *Benes, Statesman of Central Europe* (London, 1935); Radim N. Foustka, *Zivot, dilo a priklad Dr. Edvarda Benese* (*The Life, the Accomplishments and the Example of Dr. Eduard Benes*) (Praha, 1946);

reliable analysis and evaluation of his real significance in, and influence on, European politics. One of the difficulties in penetrating beyond the façade of his activities stems from his own secretiveness. He left nothing approaching an intimate journal of his daily doings and personal reflections on the affairs of the world.

With the exception of T. G. Masaryk, Benes never had any really intimate associates. Those who worked closely with him might have gleaned what they thought to be his intimate thoughts. It is questionable, however, if Benes ever directly confirmed their assumptions. But even those who worked closely with him and could possibly throw some light on his activities have thus far remained silent. In his own published statements, of which there are many, the subjective element is masterfully concealed. He intended, or so he said, eventually to publish his account of the events preceding the Munich debacle. It was to be an integral part, the first volume in fact, of his memoirs, which he began publishing in 1947.[2] But with characteristic taciturnity, he first published the second volume of reminiscences, which dealt with a less controversial period. The Communist coup, of course, intervened and disrupted whatever plans he might have had for additional volumes. His death in September 1948 postponed perhaps indefinitely the publication of such of his "intimate papers" as might have been preserved. The sketch presented here, therefore, does not purport to be an exhaustive and authoritative account of Benes' long diplomatic career. It will limit itself to a treatment in broad outline of the salient features of Benes' career as Foreign Minister of Czechoslovakia and statesman of international renown.

It is perhaps appropriate to open a discussion of Benes' diplomatic career by stating that it was in almost every respect *sui generis*. Few men, whatever their official position in the government of their particular country, were as intimately connected with the very existence of their native land as was Benes. Moreover, few representatives of small nations tried as assiduously and consistently to play the "great game" of inter-

---

Edward B. Hitchcock, *Benes, the Man and Statesman* (London, 1940); Godfrey Lias, *Benes of Czechoslovakia* (London, 1940); Compton Mackenzie, *Dr. Benes* (London, 1946); Jan Opocensky, ed. *Eduard Benes: Essays and Reflections Presented on the Occasion of his Sixtieth Birthday* (London, 1945); Jan Papousek, *Dr. Edvard Benes: Sein Leben* (Praha, 1937); J. Werstadt and others, *Dr. Edvard Benes, Sbornik Stati* (Dr. Eduard Benes: A Collection of Essays) (Praha, 1924) and *Edvard Benes, Filosof a Statnik* (Eduard Benes, Philosopher and Statesman) (Praha, 1937). Benes' own contributions to our knowledge of his life are cited in the notes below. His major speeches from 1924 to 1933 are collected in a mammoth volume of some 800 pages under the title *Boj o Mir a bezpecnost statu* (The Struggle for Peace and Security of the State) (Praha, 1934).

[2] Edvard Benes, *Pameti* (Memoirs) (Praha, 1947).

national politics traditionally reserved for the major Powers. Benes was imbued with a compelling sense of national and international mission. In his mind, as in that of his mentor and friend T. G. Masaryk, nationalism and internationalism were not competing but complementary doctrines and beliefs and the fulfillment of Czech national aspirations was equated with the attainment of the exalted aims of pan-humanism.[3] More concretely, Benes clearly saw that the welfare of a democratic Czechoslovakia coincided with the maintenance of a stable and peaceful Europe. In Benes, as in Masaryk, high moral purpose and the recognition of obvious national self-interest blended to such an extent that it was difficult if not impossible to determine the primacy of one or another as the underlying motive for policies they advocated. Both high moral purpose and national self-interest, however, required a "European" or internationalist orientation of Czechoslovak foreign policy and the confluence of two such powerful motivating elements must be held responsible for the presumptuous prerogative which Benes often exercised in meddling in the affairs of the Great Powers with an intent to steer them to the adoption of policies frequently unacceptable and sometimes distasteful to them.

Benes' heterodoxy is poignantly demonstrated by his education in the art of diplomacy and the unfolding of his career as a diplomat and statesman. He was certainly no "professional diplomat" in the full and traditional sense of the word. He was not "born" to be a diplomat, nor did he learn his *métier* by slow and easy stages in the service of a tradition-laden Foreign Office. He entered on a diplomatic career fortuitously at the somewhat advanced age of 31 years, and the first position he held was that of *de facto* Foreign Minister without, of course, a ministry to command or even a country to represent. His first "diplomatic mission" was to "sell" the Allied Powers on the desirability of establishing an independent Czechoslovak state.[4] It was a self-imposed task which he discharged with admirable skill and eminent success.

His greatest accomplishment was to extract from French, British, and Italian statesmen recognition of Czechoslovakia as a state even before the conclusion of an armistice with Austria-Hungary. The fact that Benes was invited to attend the plenary meeting of the Supreme War

---

[3] For a recent essay on Masaryk which stresses this aspect of his thinking, see "Thomas Masaryk, Maker of Czechoslovakia," *The Times Literary Supplement*, March 3, 1950.
[4] For an exhaustive account of Benes' activities during the first world war see his *Svetova valka a nase revoluce* (The World War and Our Revolution) (3 vols., Praha, 1927 and 1928). A much abbreviated English version is *My War Memoirs* (London, 1928).

Council on November 4, 1918, and was able to participate in the armistice negotiations was a triumph of incalculable moral and material benefit to him. None other of the so-called "succession states" could boast a similar achievement. The significance of the commitment the Allies had undertaken vis-à-vis Czechoslovakia particularly strengthened Benes' hand in setting forth the political and territorial demands of his country at the ensuing Peace Conference.[5] With this, his first diplomatic mission, Benes was launched on a lifelong career as Foreign Minister and it is not an exaggeration to call him Foreign Minister by profession. He held the portfolio of foreign affairs in the Czechoslovak government for seventeen years without interruption. When he relinquished it, it was only to step up to a higher office, the Presidency of the Republic. But even as President, Benes retained firm control over the conduct of his country's foreign affairs.

Benes combined some of the talents, prerogatives, and propensities of professional diplomat, statesman, and scholar. Obviously he was neither a professional diplomat in the traditional sense of the word, nor could he be identified with the type of "amateur" diplomat-statesman frequently encountered on the political scene of post-Versailles Europe. He shared the professional diplomat's expert knowledge derived from continual exposure to international affairs, and he also showed a marked inclination for secret negotiations and that most effective weapon of international diplomacy, the *fait accompli*. However, he was not unalterably opposed to "open diplomacy" which he found an effective means to plead the cause of a small country. What he had in common with the "amateur" diplomat-statesman of his era was a general disdain for expert advice and a penchant for informal diplomacy.

It is possible, in fact, to identify Benes as the exponent and practitioner *par excellence* of that personal diplomacy which became so popular in the 1920's and 1930's. Disregard for expert advice was in his case perhaps less disastrous than in the case of men like Lloyd George or Neville Chamberlain. Moreover, the circumstances of Benes' early career clearly imposed on him the practice of personal diplomacy. While working to promote the independence of Czechoslovakia in Paris during the first world war, he had no public opinion to consult. He could not even be identified with a known geographic or historical entity. Czechoslovakia at that time existed only as a projection of the personality and ideas of

[5] The reader may refer to the thoughts of a not altogether favorably inclined critic on this matter by consulting David Lloyd George, *Memoirs of the Peace Conference* (New Haven, 1939), pp. 601ff. For Benes' evaluation of the significance of his success see his *Problemy Nove Evropy* (Problems of the New Europe) (Praha, 1924), p. 10.

Masaryk and Benes. But, in subsequent years the habit of working alone without benefit of consultation, of making decisions on his own and assuming full responsibility for them, persisted; and Benes continued to practice personal diplomacy when it was perhaps no longer imperative and, possibly, had even become detrimental to him and to his country. Nevertheless, if Benes shared the "amateur" diplomat-statesman's passion for personal diplomacy, he did not share the "allures" and pretensions of the "great" European statesmen. His general mannerism was that of a permanent under-secretary of state. His speeches lacked lustre and were devoid of emotional overtones. They were dry, dull, painfully long, and full of facts and closely reasoned argumentation. Finally, he retained the true scholar's method of work. He was an avid student of international affairs who kept himself informed on every possible political development the world over. He sought to project pragmatic problems against a well-defined and unalterable philosophical frame of reference. To him the practice of politics, especially of international politics, without a firm philosophical foundation was unimaginable.

Benes' prerogative to run Czechoslovakia's foreign affairs virtually at will was never seriously challenged. Immediately after the foundation of the Republic, of course, there was no one else with sufficient ability and necessary familiarity with international affairs to plead the Czechoslovak cause abroad. So complete was Benes' sway in foreign affairs that he did not bother to return to Prague for consultation with the government and the "Revolutionary National Assembly," although to most of the Czechoslovak political leaders he was at that time not personally known. He had left Prague in 1915 as a little-known university lecturer who had not cut a swath in politics at all. Nevertheless, Benes remained at Paris where his headquarters had been during the war and made policy on the spot without benefit of advice from his government. He did not return to Prague until September 1919. Meanwhile, the Cabinet and the National Assembly at Prague refrained from any action on foreign affairs. The fate of the newborn Republic was in Benes' hands.[6] His influence in foreign affairs was only slightly modified as time went by. Strictly speaking, he was free from the formal constitutional controls governing Cabinet members and was also largely free from the rigid party controls which shackled every other Cabinet member and parliamentary deputy. This is not to say that Benes openly circumvented his constitutional

---

[6] See Ferdinand Peroutka, *Budovani Statu* (Building the State) (Praha, 1934), II, 1308ff. This is a monumental work totaling four volumes and giving an excellent documented account of the formative years of the Republic.

responsibility or flouted the consensus of the more powerful political leaders on crucial issues. In the case of Russia, he repeatedly postponed recognition of the Soviet regime because of the opposition of his conservative critics.[7] However, Benes guided public opinion rather than being led by it. His views found ready acceptance among the people, and even the political leaders usually deferred to his judgment, although his ideas were not always popular with them.

Benes reported to the foreign affairs committee of the House and Senate and to the full assembly of both Chambers often and at great length. As exposés of the unfolding international scene, his parliamentary speeches were masterly for the manner in which individual events were put into their historical perspective. But they seldom revealed anything of importance concerning the inner secrets of international diplomacy; and because the approach was often abstract, the dramatic immediacy of specific problems facing Czechoslovakia was obscured. Finally, Benes' speeches acquainted the National Assembly only with past events and actions. Rare was the occasion on which he consulted with members of the House or Senate in advance of diplomatic moves which he contemplated, and the same can be said of his relationship with members of the Cabinet and the chairmen of the political parties. His decisions were made alone or in consultation and agreement with Masaryk.

Benes' autocratic direction of Czechoslovakia's foreign policy had ad-

[7] Conservative elder statesmen were nettled by Benes' obviously privileged position in the Republic as one of the founders of the state and as T. G. Masaryk's closest friend, protégé and heir-apparent to the Presidency. Despite his undeniable merits in forging Czechoslovakia's independence, Benes was considered by the "elders" of Czechoslovak politics as an upstart on whom they did not want to bestow the same honors and privileges they had accorded to Masaryk. Benes' efforts to stay out of party politics, as Masaryk had done, and thus to groom himself for the role of the charismatic, benevolent philosopher-king (President) so perfectly played by Masaryk did not meet with the approval of the party chiefs who sought to exercise overriding influence in the country. It is safe to say that only Masaryk's staunch support saved Benes from being dismissed on a number of occasions, and only Masaryk's stubborn insistence brought about Benes' election to the Presidency in 1935. Political and personal opposition to Benes centered in the Agrarian party, which was the most powerful Czechoslovak party from the early 1920's until 1938, and which exercised overwhelming influence in domestic affairs. Benes was also bitterly opposed by Karel Kramar and Jiri Stribrny. The former was an archconservative Russophile, who had originally hoped to install a Russian prince as monarch in Czechoslovakia and whose hatred of the Soviet regime bordered on the pathological. The latter was a disgruntled member of the National Socialist party (a non-Marxist reform socialist party), which Benes finally joined and which was not big enough to contain the opposing views of these two men. Stribrny's career culminated in his leadership of a small but noisy "fascist league." The reader will find reference to Benes' difficulties with his domestic opponents in several of the biographic studies about him. See especially Mackenzie, *Dr. Benes*, *passim* and Hitchcock, *Benes*, pp. 200ff. For his own account of these difficulties see *Pameti*, *passim*, and his *Sest let exilu a svetove valky* (Six Years of Exile and World War) (Praha, 1946), pp. 22ff.

vantages as well as disadvantages. His long and uninterrupted tenure in office and his integrated approach to international affairs imparted both a stability and a unity and purpose to Czechoslovakia's foreign policy which it otherwise would certainly have lacked. Judging by the nature of the Czechoslovak government coalition, which never consisted of less than five political parties representing fundamentally opposing views, it is difficult to see how the Cabinet as a body, or for that matter any individual not enjoying Benes' unique status, could have devised and carried out a clear-cut policy. Compromise was the essence of Czechoslovak politics, and each party outdid the other in shirking responsibility. For this reason, the rougher the going, the more willing was Parliament to defer to Benes and to let him shoulder the heavy responsibilities of policy making. However, Benes' failure to take political leaders into his confidence left him relatively isolated. Consequently, domestic and foreign policies were not always as closely coordinated as they might, and indeed should, have been, for in the case of Czechoslovakia domestic and foreign problems were inextricably linked.[8]

Benes' reluctance to draw people into his confidence was also reflected in his relations with the staff of the Ministry of Foreign Affairs.[9] He showed little concern with the organization and personnel of the Ministry and made no serious effort to pack it with people carefully chosen because of their ability and their loyalty to him. He had a small coterie of loyal underlings, some of whom served as his personal secretaries at one time or another and then were rewarded with more exalted posts in the foreign service. His closest collaborator was Kamil Krofta, who succeeded Benes as Foreign Minister in 1935, and who, like Benes, was university professor by vocation.

The Ministry under Benes did not become a training school for capable diplomats, and since the country possessed no hereditary aristocracy with a "corner" on diplomatic assignments, Czechoslovakia's career diplomats were essentially run-of-the-mill civil servants with limited responsibilities and corresponding ability. Top diplomatic posts were originally occupied by individuals who had in one way or another

---

[8] Benes did, of course, take a much more active hand in the direction of domestic affairs after he became President.

[9] For a general survey of Czechoslovak foreign policy and the organization and functioning of the Ministry of Foreign Affairs, see Ministerstvo Zahranicnich Veci (Ministry of Foreign Affairs), *Deset let ceskoslovenske zahranicni politiky* (Ten Years of Czechoslovak Foreign Policy) (Praha, 1928). With the exception of this authoritative but somewhat arid source, details of Benes' relations with his staff and his direction of the Ministry can be gleaned only from personal conversation with his former associates.

collaborated in the Czechoslovak liberation movement abroad. Changes in top personnel were extremely rare. For example, Stefan Osusky held the post of minister at Paris from 1920 to 1939. There is no evidence that Czechoslovak representatives abroad, whatever their status, were entrusted with truly weighty matters. Nor is there any indication that their reports, judgments, and opinions were particularly heeded by Benes. Some of them substituted for Benes at international conferences (Osusky at Geneva, Veverka at Geneva and at meetings of the Little Entente, Fierlinger at Stresa), but all gatherings of importance were attended by Benes himself. He rarely delegated authority to any one, and while correspondence between the Ministry and the "field" was lively, it seemed for the most part limited to routine matters. Benes was not only Foreign Minister but served as a sort of roving ambassador of his country, traveling from one European capital to another, in an attempt to deal with the responsible European statesmen personally on the scene of action whenever possible. He became known as peripatetic journeyman and especially during the 1920's spent as much time away from as in Prague. Geneva was virtually an alternate seat of the Czechoslovak Foreign Ministry.

II

The foreign policy which Benes pursued with singular consistency reflected an immutable conviction concerning the interrelatedness between the continued welfare of Czechoslovakia and the maintenance of the Versailles *status quo*. Not that Benes unalterably opposed the readmission of the defeated Powers to the international community. But he resolutely combated "revisionism" under any guise and fought against upsetting the balance of power created at Versailles. He realized that if the defeated Powers were permitted to challenge the Versailles order rather than being gradually absorbed into it, a new contest for supremacy in Europe would develop in which Czechoslovakia, having been carved out of the Habsburg Monarchy and embodying sizable national minorities, would be a primary target for attack. He also realized, more keenly than his contemporaries, that an attack on Czechoslovakia would not be an end in itself but would be the start of a far broader revision of the European balance of power. As he put it: "Our state is the key to the whole postwar structure of Central Europe. If it is touched . . . the peace of Europe [is] seriously infringed. . . . It is for that reason that . . . our international position and our internal stability are a matter of great interest equally to France and the Soviet Union, equally to England

and Italy and to the Little Entente, as they ought to be to Germany, and Poland."[10] In the last analysis his view of European politics was correct, for the resurgence of the defeated Powers, notably Germany, coupled with the growth of aggressive fascism in several European countries, resulted in the gradual whittling away both of the form and substance of the Versailles peace settlement, causing not only the destruction of Czechoslovakia but terminating the hegemony on the continent of the great democracies who first yielded to the onslaught of the dictatorships of the Right and then, as a consequence of the second world war, receded before the Soviet Union.

The interrelationship between Czechoslovakia's welfare and the maintenance of the Versailles *status quo* provided a convenient platform for an integrated approach to the specific problems facing Czechoslovakia and the general problems of the international community. Essentially, Benes' foreign policy can be summed up as a continual search for security through complementary systems of bilateral and regional agreements, on the one hand, and a general scheme of arbitration and pacific settlement of disputes on the other. The chosen instrument for the latter was the League of Nations whose moral and political prestige Benes tried assiduously to increase.[11]

The system of regional and bilateral security agreements engineered by Benes suffered from an obvious weakness. It rested solely on solemn treaties with "third" Powers, i.e. states that were either geographically remote or were not directly exposed to the same immediate threats as was Czechoslovakia.[12] Benes was unable to settle on a permanent basis the differences between Czechoslovakia and its potential enemies Germany, Hungary, and Poland, all of which coveted Czechoslovak territory. Benes' inability to conclude lasting agreements with any or all of Czechoslovakia's predatory neighbors was often held against him by his domestic critics—notably the Agrarian leadership—who would have favored a less "cosmopolitan" and more "utilitarian" foreign orientation, including a rapprochement with Germany at the expense of solidarity

---

[10] Edouard Benes, *La lutte pour la sécurité collective en Europe et la guerre Italo-Abyssine. Sources et documents Tchecoslovaques* No. 29 (Praha, 1935), p. 59.

[11] It was perhaps Benes' efforts in this respect which led a distinguished historian of the League to describe him as "the cleverest, the best-informed, and for many years the most successful of European ministers." F. P. Walters, *A History of the League of Nations* (London, 1952), II, 116.

[12] The cornerstone of Czechoslovakia's bilateral security system was its mutual defense treaty with France, signed in January 1924. The other pillars of its defense system were treaties with Rumania and Yugoslavia within the framework of the Little Entente, and an assistance treaty with the Soviet Union signed in May 1935.

with France. The failure to come to terms with any of its potential ene-mies, of course, left Czechoslovakia in a precarious political and military position in which defense against aggression without considerable out-side help was at best a tenuous proposition, and, as is generally known, Czechoslovakia's paper alliances were of little tangible benefit to it at the time of greatest need. It is questionable, however, if an alternate course of action by Benes, for instance, a settlement with one or more of the neighboring states, would have been crowned with greater success. It seems highly unlikely that a settlement in good faith could have been effected without forswearing the birthright of the Republic.

The dispute over Czechoslovakia's frontiers and the sizable ethnic minorities incorporated in the country was one of a number of perennial fundamental issues which apparently could not be solved rationally. Lest Czechoslovakia's relations with its neighbors be misunderstood, it should be said explicitly that they were not uniformly bad. Only with Hungary was there virtually constant tension[13]—the result of many factors of historical as well as contemporary origin. Outstanding among them were the obstinate refusal of the Hungarian regime to acquiesce in the out-come of the first world war and to relent from continual revisionist agita-tion, and the genuine fear of the Czechoslovak government that a Hun-garian assault—diplomatic or military—against the "soft underbelly" of the Republic might be crowned with success. In the case of Germany and Poland, acute friction was preceded by a period of quiescence and nor-malcy. It was only in the 1930's, when Nazism triumphed in Germany and when Poland showed a marked shift toward totalitarianism, that Czechoslovakia's relations with these countries entered the crisis stage. By then, of course, opposing philosophies of state further obstructed the possibility of reaching an understanding between Czechoslovakia, on the one hand, and either Germany or Poland on the other.

The system of collective security envisaged by Benes was no less "un-realistic" than were the regional and bilateral agreements he concluded. It seemed to take too little cognizance of the very real possibility of a breakdown as a result of clashing interests and interpretations of the good of the international community, and it was devoid of precautions against the eventuality of a crisis. Of course, the ultimate aim of his system of collective security was to obviate international crises; as he put it, "European peace and collective security" were indivisible.[14] Benes

---

[13] For a fuller treatment of Czechoslovakia's difficulties with Hungary see, *inter alia*, Felix J. Vondracek, *The Foreign Policy of Czechoslovakia 1918-1935* (New York, 1937).

[14] Benes, *La Lutte*, p. 11.

readily admitted that a workable system of collective security could not be reached overnight but only step by step. Nevertheless, he often appeared to act as if that distant goal had already been achieved.

Benes was inclined to vest too much authority in the League of Nations, which he regarded all too obviously as a democratic forum where differences between great and small nations—based primarily on power—would be minimized. Conversely he was resolutely opposed to a European directorate of Great Powers. Following up on the premise of the small Powers' prerogative to take an active part in determining the good of the international community, the Czechoslovakian statesman sometimes went to considerable length to induce the Great Powers to subscribe to his concept of balance of power in Europe and to undertake commitments which they were not necessarily willing to risk. Fundamentally, he attempted to preserve the wartime alliance between France and England and sought to obtain a British guarantee of the security of Germany's eastern neighbors. He also strongly advocated bringing Soviet Russia into the European community as an antidote to resurgent German power and an "indispensable factor of peace in Europe." He attempted, in short, to achieve a synthesis of East and West, with Czechoslovakia—not only because of its geographic position but because of its racial, cultural, social and political heritage—as a bridge or unifying factor between them. The role he thus assigned to his country and to himself was an ambitious one, for it entailed navigating extremely hazardous waters and, indeed, spanning unbridgeable chasms. In his endeavor to reconcile basically irreconcilable points of view, Benes developed into an exponent of the middle course or "solution moyenne" as he called it.[15] In principle, the middle course is always a commendable one, for it presumably embodies the virtues of democratic parliamentarism. In practice, the middle course is more often than not difficult to maintain. Benes' efforts to play both ends against the middle were not successful for the simple reason that few if any of the European nations were willing to desist from playing power politics; and the inevitable result of the assiduous practice of power politics was the polarization of European political forces. Czechoslovakia, caught in the middle of this process, was one of its early victims.

Benes' propensity for "making" international policy was not always graciously received by the exponents of Great Power supremacy, although his critics were by no means limited to this quarter. Various aspects of

---

[15] For an excellent essay on Benes' "solution moyenne" or "midway philosophy" see Felix Weltsch, "A critical optimist," in Opocensky, *Eduard Benes*, pp. 118-156.

his concept of collective security and of his *modus operandi* at one time or another irritated virtually all of the Great Powers. His unorthodox views, coupled with his efforts to play the "great game" of international diplomacy traditionally thought to be reserved for the major Powers, contributed to his unpopularity in British conservative circles.[16] But the Soviet regime also found cause to be critical of him. For, despite his professed friendship for the Soviet Union, he lagged cautiously behind the Western European countries in extending *de jure* recognition to the Communist regime.[17]

III

Benes' long career in the field of diplomacy was at its height in the early 1920's when the lofty ideals bandied about at the Peace Conference had not yet completely vanished and the new international order created at Versailles had not yet been seriously challenged. At the Peace Conference itself, Benes was not a central, nor even an important figure. He concentrated on staking out Czechoslovakia's territorial and political claims and in this endeavor was singularly successful. He pleaded his cause earnestly with ant-like diligence, flooding the delegations of the Great Powers with elaborately detailed memoranda and statistics properly garnished with professions of adherence to the noblest democratic principles. The impression he created was that of an interminable and perhaps somewhat irritating speaker. Harold Nicolson, a junior member of the British delegation at the time, described him as a "competent, plausible little man."[18]

By concluding a series of commercial treaties and making political

[16] His unpopularity in the 1930's hardly needs comment. However, even in the 1920's, when Benes was generally acclaimed for his work at Geneva, acid overtones of criticism could be detected from the direction of London. Without assailing him directly, Conservative spokesmen warned incessantly against the dangers of the kind of "visionary efforts" in which he indulged. In September 1924, for instance, at a time when the Draft Treaty of Mutual Assistance and the Geneva Protocol were still very live issues, the *Times* declared: "The League and its best friends have . . . grounds for some uneasiness as to the course of its present deliberations. The extravagant oratory with which the League was exalted at its birth, and before its birth, has misled many of the lesser States and the masses in some of the larger States as to its real authority. . . . It is to be hoped, in the interest of the League itself, and of the principles for which it stands, that no illusions on this head will be entertained in the present session. The League, it seems, feels constrained to apply itself to the vast political problems of security and disarmament instead of confining its labors to the less ambitious subjects of a practical and administrative order, for which it has shown itself to be particularly well fitted. . . . *The lesser states may exercise, and do exercise, in the League a very great moral influence, but it is vain for them to aspire to more.* . . ." *The Times,* September 2, 1924. Italics mine.

[17] *De jure* recognition was extended to the Soviet Union on June 9, 1934. See Max Beloff, *The Foreign Policy of Soviet Russia* (2 vols., London, 1947-1948), I, 131.

[18] Harold Nicolson, *Peacemaking 1919* (London, 1933), p. 240.

alliances designed to reopen the clogged channels of diplomatic intercourse and to strengthen the newly created international order, Benes
successfully placed Czechoslovakia on firm footing in the international
community and quickly turned to broader issues. Under his guidance
the new state soon became a pillar of stability and strength in Central
Europe. Benes himself rapidly became established as a veteran statesman, although his tenure in office had hardly begun and his experience was still meager. However, he learned fast and indeed comported
himself as one of the charter members of the European diplomatic community. His understanding of international problems and the scope of
his vision clearly distinguished him from the run-of-the-mill representative of a small country.

His efforts during the first four or five years after the Peace Conference centered on consolidating Central Europe. He was the spiritual
father of the Little Entente, a coalition of Czechoslovakia, Rumania, and
Yugoslavia, dedicated originally and primarily to the containment of
Hungarian revisionist aspirations.[19] The Little Entente, however, was
not an exclusively defensive alliance. Its positive aims centered on political and economic integration in Central and Southeastern Europe, although the idea of a confederation was not on Benes' agenda. Progress
along constructive international lines at any rate was slow and halting.
In Benes' conception, the Little Entente served essentially as an instrument for dominating Central Europe. It was a safeguard against en-
croachments on the independence of action of the small victorious Powers
in this area. It not only guarded against the resurgence of Hungarian
power, or the restoration of the Habsburg Monarchy in one form or another, but was also intended to keep the Great Powers—both friendly
and unfriendly—at a respectable distance from the Central European
domain. Finally, through the medium of the Little Entente, its individual members could magnify their influence in international deliberations,
for when speaking and voting *en bloc* they came close to equaling the
status of a "Great Power." The most striking demonstration of the possibilities inherent in joint action was at the Genoa Conference in 1922,

[19] On the Little Entente, see especially Florin Codresco, *La Petite Entente* (Paris,
1930), a doctoral dissertation which is the most meticulous factual account on the
activities of the Little Entente in the 1920's; Aurel Cosman, *La Petite Entente* (Paris,
1926); J. O. Crane, *The Little Entente* (New York, 1931); Robert Machray, *The
Little Entente* (London, 1929) and *The Struggle for the Danube and the Little Entente,
1929-1938* (London, 1938); Albert Mousset, *La Petite Entente* (Paris, 1923); and
Bojidar Sarich, *La Petite Entente, Facteur de Paix en Europe* (Paris, 1933), another
doctoral dissertation.

where the Little Entente as such was asked to designate representatives to the various committees deliberating on the fate of Europe.

While Benes was busily laying the foundations of the Little Entente, he also tried to regulate his country's relations with its immediate neighbors. He showed considerable astuteness in establishing good relations with Austria, for the prevention of an *Anschluss* was as much a matter of concern to him then as it was in 1938. The assumption underlying his policy toward Austria was that, by preventing its economic collapse, which was indeed imminent in the early 1920's, the political independence of that country could also be saved and the integrity of Central Europe preserved. Benes approached the economic rescue of Austria both directly and through the good offices of the League of Nations. Direct negotiations with Karl Renner, the Austrian Chancellor in 1920, resulted in the conclusion of a commercial treaty and the extension of a Czech loan to Austria the following year. In December 1921 a treaty was negotiated between the two states establishing the bases of general cooperation and arbitration of disputes. In 1922, when Austria was again in dire financial straits, Benes was approached with a request for help. He took the matter to the League of Nations as the agency best designed to help Austria and simultaneously to request from her government a guarantee of her continued will to independent political existence. A general guarantee of the political independence of Austria was, of course, much more to Benes' liking than any direct deals he could have made with that country, for he realized that by taking a direct hand in settling Austria's affairs he was bound to evoke the jealousy, fear, and antagonism not only of the Central European countries but also of Italy, who followed Austria's development with considerable attention and not unselfish interest. In October 1922 a treaty was signed by Great Britain, France, Italy, Czechoslovakia, and Austria under League auspices, whereby the signatory Powers undertook to respect the political independence and territorial integrity of Austria and to refrain from compromising its sovereignty by imposing undue and unusual economic or financial burdens on it. A new loan to Austria negotiated through the League in 1923 was underwritten by several states, including Czechoslovakia who, along with Great Britain and France, guaranteed 24.5 per cent of the loan. By assisting Austria in overcoming her economic difficulties Benes undoubtedly made a major contribution to the stability of the Central European area in the 1920's.

In sharp contrast with the trend of Czechoslovak-Austrian relations was the air of tension that constantly hung over Benes' dealings with

Hungary. No sooner had Czechoslovakia ceased to fight off an armed invasion by Hungarian troops of the territory she had claimed and received at the Paris Peace Conference than the first threat of Habsburg restoration was raised at Budapest. The fall of Bela Kun's Red regime in the summer of 1919 was followed by the rise of Archduke Joseph to a commanding post in the country. This, in Benes' view, foreshadowed the possibility of Habsburg restoration, and he requested the Supreme Council of the Allies to intercede in order to exclude the Archduke from political activity, a request which was acted upon satisfactorily. In March 1921, the ex-Emperor-King Charles made an attempt to seize power at Budapest. His effort, although only halfheartedly supported by the regime of Admiral Horthy, elicited a frantic response from Benes. The Czech statesman considered the incident a *casus belli* and sent an ultimatum to the Hungarian government, demanding the immediate departure of the ex-ruler—an action taken, incidentally, before Benes had received replies to the requests for aid which he had simultaneously sent to the Western Powers and his allies in the Little Entente. A further attempt by Charles in October 1921 evoked an even sharper reaction from Benes, who served the Hungarian government with another ultimatum threatening armed intervention unless his conditions concerning the definitive settlement of the Habsburg question, and the adherence of Hungary to the terms of the Trianon Peace Treaty, were met. Charles was duly removed from the scene; but the rest of Benes' demands were not fulfilled and relations with Hungary remained strained. The revival of Hungarian revisionist agitation in 1927, the subsequent rapprochement between Hungary and Italy, and a number of incidents, such as the large scale counterfeiting of Czechoslovak (and French) banknotes in Hungary allegedly for the purpose of financing subversive activities in Czechoslovakia, kept the two countries at loggerheads.

As to Germany, the conclusion of a commercial treaty with that country in 1920 was considered something of a "coup" for Benes. Although the treaty did nothing more than to regulate trade between the two countries and specify certain questions pertaining to transportation and transit traffic of goods in and out of Czechoslovakia, it was an important symbolic step toward the restoration of "normalcy" in Central Europe. Among other things, the clarification of her transit rights through Germany was essential for Czechoslovakia in order to avoid virtual economic strangulation, for the bulk of her trade with Western Europe and with overseas areas had to be transported on German railroads or rivers.

Turning to broader European issues, Benes soon found himself mediating fundamental differences of opinion between France and Great Britain. The unsettled state of European economy gave considerable cause for worry to Great and small Powers alike. By 1921, Great Britain, hard hit by the general slump, showed particular interest in improving the general economic situation and took the initiative in convoking a general economic conference for that purpose. The British plan called for restoring equality at least in the commercial field between victor and vanquished on the Continent, and for inviting Soviet Russia to participate in the deliberations as a prelude to the resumption of normal trade relations with that country. The French government was somewhat balky at the suggestion, for it was still preoccupied with problems relating to its security and was trying—unsuccessfully—to draw Great Britain into a close military alliance. France was less worried about European trade than she was over the resurgence of German military and industrial power, over the possibility of a German-Russian rapprochement, and over attempts to revise the provisions of the peace treaties which might arise if equal status were granted to the defeated Powers. Preliminary conferences held between French and British statesmen at Cannes at the beginning of 1922, however, paved the way for a joint approach to the problem and set the stage for an international economic conference at Genoa.

The distant rumblings of a possible rapprochement with Russia naturally aroused Benes' keen interest, for he had long advocated such a course of action. He immediately initiated a meeting of the Little Entente which convened at Belgrade. There, a joint plan of action was decided on by the three Central European countries. Benes then proceeded to Paris and London, not only to make his and the Little Entente's views known, but also to iron out serious differences of opinion that had arisen anew between Great Britain and France as a result of the fall of Briand, who had been responsible for the Cannes commitments, and the succession of Poincaré as Premier.[20] Poincaré disliked conferences as a matter of principle, and he now posed again many of France's original doubts as to the wisdom of a European-wide conclave. Moreover, he also resisted *de jure* recognition of Communist Russia.

This is where Benes stepped in. He succeeded in associating himself both with the British position, championed by Lloyd George, and with France's reservations concerning treaty revision and a possible alteration of the European power balance. Having consulted with both the French and British governments, he produced a compromise plan which in-

[20] On the change-over from Briand to Poincaré, see Chapter 2, §1, above.

corporated Poincaré's proviso that neither reparations nor the peace treaties should be discussed at the conference and that participation of the Russian delegation should not imply *de jure* recognition of the Soviet government. He then went on to satisfy Lloyd George's views on the resumption of trade with Russia and the desirability of concluding a nonaggression convention. His efforts at mediation brought about a meeting between Poincaré and Lloyd George at the end of February at Boulogne, where the Genoa Conference was agreed upon.

The conference itself, as is known, ended in fiasco, not only because six days after its opening, on April 16, 1922, the Germans and Russians surprised the world by announcing the conclusion of a bilateral treaty (the Rapallo treaty), but because the Russian delegation, headed by Chicherin, was immovable in its refusal to acknowledge the responsibility of its government for prewar debts and for compensating foreign owners of nationalized property in Russia, a particularly hard blow at France. But although the conference failed, Benes utilized the opportunity afforded by its sessions to contact Chicherin and succeeded in negotiating a trade treaty with the Russian delegate. As a matter of diplomatic discretion, the treaty was not signed until June 5 at Prague. The terms of the treaty were not altogether favorable to Czechoslovakia, since she received no compensation for property previously held in Russia. On the other hand, the Soviet government gave up its previous *conditio sine qua non* concerning *de jure* recognition and the extension of credits, and agreed furthermore to respect the safety and freedom of Czechoslovak citizens and to cease propaganda in Czechoslovakia. The treaty also included a pledge of neutrality in the event of an attack on either one of the two countries by a third Power, and contained a diplomatic and consular agreement.[21]

Meanwhile, Benes also began to make his influence felt at Geneva. He embarked on what turned out to be a long and generally fruitless struggle to strengthen the League Covenant, to enlarge the scope of the League's jurisdiction over international disputes, and to extend the moral sanction of the League to regional and bilateral treaties. It was with the last mentioned of these projects that Benes opened his campaign to strengthen the peace in Europe. He proposed the amendment of Article 21 of the Covenant in order to "encourage regional conferences or conventions as an essential complement to universal agreements

---

[21] On the Genoa Conference, see the works cited above in Chapter 1, note 56. A text of the Soviet-Czechoslovak commercial treaty will be found in Papousek, *Dr. Benes*, p. 231.

which must necessarily be very general and ill defined in scope." Soon afterwards he plunged headlong into a far greater endeavor, that of elaborating a comprehensive system of arbitration, security, and disarmament.

The impulse for a general treaty of mutual guarantee had resulted from negotiations relating to the possibility of achieving European disarmament. In 1923, Lord Robert Cecil had prepared a draft treaty in line with a previous resolution of the League Assembly, which had expressed the view that disarmament must be conditional upon a defensive treaty of mutual guarantee, open to all, and ensuring that its signatories would receive prompt assistance from their cosignatories in the event of aggression. From the Cecil draft, amended in discussion with other Powers, arose the famous Draft Treaty of Mutual Assistance which the League considered in 1923 and 1924.[22]

To the idea of such a treaty Benes responded warmly, although he was at the same time one of the Draft Treaty's most thoughtful critics. He was concerned over the provision which required unanimity in the Council of the League before sanctions could be taken against an aggressor, recommending that a majority vote should suffice. He also objected to the procedural steps which must precede any action, for he felt that, in any instance involving sanctions, prompt action would be of paramount importance and that this was not sufficiently provided for. Moreover, he felt that the success or failure of any general security pact depended on the degree of perfection of a compulsory mechanism for the pacific settlement of disputes: without such mechanism, disarmament and a security pact would not eliminate the possibility of aggression. "To endeavor to prevent wars by the reduction or limitation of armaments is to mistake the means for the end, thus committing a fundamental error. The employment of the means—even with a large measure of success—in no way implies that the goal has been attained."[23] Nevertheless, although Benes did not consider the treaty an effective enough instrument, he guided its passage through the League, for then as on subsequent occasions, schemes advancing the concept of collective security, no matter how imperfect they might have seemed to him, received his enthusiastic support.

Benes' biggest hour came in 1924, when, after the Draft Treaty had

[22] Walters, *History of the League*, I, 223-228.
[23] Benes' reply to the League concerning the draft of the Treaty of Mutual Assistance circulated for comment among the members. See League of Nations, Official Journal, Supplement No. 26 (Geneva, 1924), pp. 247ff.

failed to secure the assent of the major Powers,[24] a fresh start was made to effect a system of "Arbitration, Security and Reduction of Armament." Benes, who had been elected to the League Council the year before, was rapporteur for the so-called Third (Armament) Committee. The introduction of the Protocol for the Pacific Settlement of International Disputes (better known as the Geneva Protocol) at the Fifth Assembly of the League in 1924 and the reception which was accorded to it was in a sense a personal triumph, for Benes had worked untiringly to satisfy as many divergent views as possible without sacrificing the general principle he aimed to achieve, the prohibition of aggressive war. Work on the Protocol was started as a result of a joint resolution submitted by Mac-Donald and Herriot. However, as a chronicler of the League puts it, the origins of the idea "could be traced to the skillful hands of Benes— Benes, of whom more than of any other European Minister it could be said that he knew exactly what he wanted and that what he wanted was in full harmony with the purposes of the League."[25]

The Geneva Protocol went further than the Draft Treaty, and satisfied Benes' objections to that instrument, by providing definitely for the pacific arbitration of disputes and by making refusal on the part of any Power to submit to such arbitration an offense punishable by the general application of sanctions against it. This ambitious scheme was greeted with enthusiasm, not only by Benes and Politis, who shared honors in its preparation, but by the entire Assembly. In the midst of the festive atmosphere accompanying the presentation of the Geneva Protocol, Benes declared that the Assembly was "in the presence of a system the adoption of which may entirely modify our present political life."[26] His hopes were quickly dashed, for a change in government in Great Britain brought the Conservative party back to power and it, presumably yielding to Commonwealth interests, torpedoed the Protocol.[27]

After this failure, Benes had to satisfy himself with the far less comprehensive system of security guarantees which was embodied in the Locarno treaties. The arbitration treaty signed by Czechoslovakia and Germany at this time was a far cry from the security system for which Benes had worked so hard, and the comfort Czechoslovakia could derive from strengthening its mutual security treaty with France was only partial compensation for the loss of general guarantees. Nevertheless,

[24] See Chapter 1, §III above.
[25] Walters, *History of the League*, I, 271-272.
[26] League of Nations, Official Journal, Supplement No. 26, p. 207.
[27] See Chapter 1, §III above.

Benes was able to go before the Czechoslovak National Assembly with words of praise for the Locarno treaties and encouragement for the prospect of international peace. At the same time, he expressed hope that, before long, "another Locarno might be achieved where Europe would come to terms with Russia," thereby contributing to the welfare of both Russia and Europe.

In the late 1920's Benes continued to work unceasingly on his favorite project of general security and arbitration. His standing in the League of Nations was unimpaired. He was repeatedly elected to the Council and was its rapporteur for security matters. In 1926 Germany's imminent entry into the League, combined with bids by Spain, Brazil, and Poland for permanent tenure of the League Council, caused a considerable scramble for Council seats. The Special Assembly of March 1926 failed to resolve the controversy. In order to help untie the Gordian knot that apparently hindered the unraveling of this delicate situation, Benes—like his Swedish counterpart Undén[28]—placed his seat at the disposal of any or all seekers. His magnanimous gesture, while not of immediate effect, contributed to the final solution and certainly raised his reputation at Geneva and in Europe generally. In September 1926, when new elections to the enlarged Council took place, Benes was restored to the seat he had vacated. In the following year, he won a further success when the League adopted two of his proposals making it obligatory for League members to facilitate meetings of the Council and improve and expedite the functioning of the organs of the League in time of emergency. Simultaneously, an Arbitration and Security Committee was formed with Benes as chairman; and in 1928, he presided over a session of a sub-commission of this committee which worked out sample types of arbitration and guarantee treaties. These were approved by the Assembly as a means for calming areas in Europe where disputes were still in progress and which were not included in the Locarno treaties. As Benes' stature increased, so did that of his country, or at least his claims with regard to it. Thus, in 1928, when the Kellogg-Briand Pact was being prepared for signature, Benes could claim special consideration for Czechoslovakia, arguing, not only that it was a signatory of the Locarno Treaties, but that it was a state which necessarily had an interest in all matters pertaining to European security.

IV

Although his efforts were only partially successful, Benes' diplomatic

[28] See Chapter 3 above.

labors in the 1920's, and especially his work at Geneva between 1924 and 1929, earned him widespread, if not unreserved, respect and recognition. With the turn of the decade, international developments took a definitely disadvantageous turn as far as he was concerned. Geneva now ceased to be, if it ever had been, the center in which the great decisions were made. When the long awaited Conference on Disarmament was finally convoked in 1932, it was overshadowed by impending events in Germany. At that Conference, Benes played his customary energetic role and, as rapporteur of the General Commission, was largely instrumental in formulating the draft resolution which was accepted by the majority of the delegations in July 1932. This resolution was, however, decisively rejected by Germany and by the Soviet Union, and subsequent events were to prove that it, and the work of the Conference as a whole, had no real significance.[29] Benes continued to seek compromises which would reconcile the divergent interests of the participating Powers, but it was clear now that his old gifts had little relation to the realities of the new age of power politics which was opening.

Necessarily, therefore, Benes was forced to return to the more traditional methods of diplomacy.[30] In the first years after Hitler's rise to power, he had two principal objectives: first, to prevent the establishment of a Great Power directorate which might reduce Czechoslovakia's European role; and, second, to strengthen his country's existing treaty system and, in particular, to improve the cohesion and power of the Little Entente. In pursuance of the first of these, he was a bitter opponent of the Four Power Pact which Mussolini had initiated in the spring of 1933. Before Ramsay MacDonald went to Rome to discuss the Pact in March 1933, Benes warned him against it; and his subsequent agitations in Warsaw and Paris, supported as they were by the Little Entente as a whole, had an undoubted effect in the watering down of the Pact which took place before its signature and which, essentially, rendered it an innocuous engagement.

With respect to his second objective, his prospects of success appeared, until 1935, to be quite favorable. His cordial relations with Alexander of Yugoslavia and Foreign Minister Barthou of France seemed to promise that the Little Entente would not only be maintained but would be the center around which a new security system for eastern Europe was established. This hope was further supported by Russia's rapprochement with

---

[29] On the Conference on Disarmament, see below Chapter 10, §IV and Chapter 13, §II.

[30] For a summary account of Benes' diplomacy between 1932 and 1938, but not including the Munich crisis, see his *Pameti*, pp. 1-73.

the West and her entrance into the League in 1934, which Benes, as chairman of the League Council, helped to effect, and by the subsequent conclusion of a mutual assistance treaty between Czechoslovakia and the Soviet Union, an engagement coordinated with Czechoslovakia's existing ties with France.

These hopes were quickly disappointed. Between 1934 and 1938, the Little Entente disintegrated rapidly. The assassination of Alexander and Barthou in 1934 and the dismissal of Titulescu of Rumania in the following year removed three of its most ardent supporters, and Italy succeeded in detaching Yugoslavia from the partnership through Ciano's treaty with Stojadinovic in the first months of 1937.[31]

Benes' attempts to buttress his security system were weakened further by the fact that Barthou's successors failed fully to exploit their new relationship with the Soviet Union and, simultaneously, developed doubts about the advisability of maintaining the integrity of Czechoslovakia against the threat of external aggression. Benes was, therefore, in a highly exposed position when, in the spring of 1938, Hitler inaugurated the openly aggressive phase of his policy.

In the absence of direct testimony from Benes, who was the suffering protagonist in the dramatic events of the summer and early fall of 1938, it would be difficult, if indeed not unfair to him, to attempt a critical evaluation of his behavior. The testimony of available documents is clear on one point. Neither France nor Britain treated Czechoslovakia as if moral right were on her side. The two Western Powers appeared to be anxious to "steamroll" Czechoslovakia, first, into concessions to the Sudeten German Nazis of such far-reaching nature as to impair the sovereignty of the country and, subsequently, into capitulation to Hitler's demands. The representatives of Great Britain and France showed an *a priori* hostile disposition toward Benes and toward his slow deliberations concerning the course his government should follow.[32] Their impatience with Benes and the peremptory manner in which

---

[31] See below Chapter 16, §11.

[32] This hostility sometimes took curious, but revealing, forms. See, for instance, the private letter written immediately after Munich by the deputy-editor of *The Times*, R. M. Barrington-Ward, a convinced and influential member of the appeasement school. Referring to Benes, Barrington-Ward wrote: "I am sorry for him but . . . I regard him—along with Clemenceau, Poincaré, Austen, Barthou and others—as one of the most active architects of disorder in Europe. No one battled to maintain the disastrous artificialities of the French 'system' with greater diligence and ability than Benes. No one was more adept in using the language of the League to consecrate the *status quo*." *The History of "The Times"*, IV, Part II, 944-945.

they treated him was in glaring contrast to the esteem he had been accorded on earlier occasions.

Confronted with this crisis, Benes did not seem to be in full possession of his diplomatic skill. It was difficult for him to deviate from a principle to which he had adhered most tenaciously, namely that the question of the ethnic minorities in Czechoslovakia was an internal matter not subject to international consideration. It was also difficult for him to realize that the Western Powers—especially France—would actually abandon Czechoslovakia in a showdown. For a long time, Benes indeed seemed to hesitate as to the right course of action. His hesitation, which was interpreted by his Western critics as willful obstinacy, was rather due to his honest inability to face reality and choose to "go it alone" as an alternative to capitulation. In the precarious circumstances in which he found himself, the only tangible offer he seemed to have made consisted in suggesting that any litigation between Czechoslovakia and Germany take place within the framework of the arbitration treaty the two countries had concluded in 1925. In a broadcast to the Czechoslovak people at the height of the crisis he bade them to be calm, for he had "a plan." What his plan was has not been authoritatively revealed. Some people claim that he hoped somehow to weather the first onslaught of German demands and to come to terms with Poland and Hungary in order to free his country's exposed flanks from the danger of attack. It is questionable whether Benes could have carried out his plan successfully under any circumstances. Events, however, moved too rapidly and the efficacy of the plan was not tested.

At Munich, where the fate of the Czechoslovak Republic was sealed, neither Benes nor his emissaries were permitted to participate in the deliberations. In sharp contrast with the beginning of his career, when he managed to secure representation in high international councils without having a state behind him, Benes now had to suffer the humiliating experience of having his country's destiny decided without benefit of consultation with him. It was an ignominious end to a diplomatic career that had begun so brilliantly.

5

....

Diplomats and Diplomacy in the Early Weimar Republic

BY HAJO HOLBORN

THE GERMAN DIPLOMATIC SERVICE could not pride itself on as old a tradition as the French or English services. In the strict sense a corps of German diplomatists came into existence for the first time after the founding of the North Germanic Confederation of 1867. Broadly speaking, only two generations had served in the new Foreign Office when the Bismarckian empire collapsed in military defeat and internal revolution. But even if we consider the German Foreign Office a mere continuation of the Prussian Foreign Office, the German foreign service would not gain a very long or great history. The old Habsburg empire had always trusted the diplomatist's art as much as military valor, and it had picked its diplomatic representatives from among the high nobility of the Holy Roman Empire, Hungary, Italy, and the Austrian Netherlands. Prussia's rise to a Great Power position in Europe was the work of her soldiers and, in a less conspicuous way, of her internal administrators. For these careers Prussia's eighteenth century kings had trained the uncouth scions of the Prussian gentry. The Diplomatic Service was subordinate to the major departments of state activity. A good many Huguenots and Italians were used by Frederick II as diplomatic agents because they had linguistic ability and social versatility.

Diplomacy became a more important business in Prussia during the age of Napoleon, but it was historically significant that before Bismarck's day no Prussian diplomat ever rose to the highest office in the monarchy, as for example Metternich did in Austria. His Prussian colleague at the Congress of Vienna, Hardenberg, was undoubtedly an accomplished diplomat, but he had made his career in domestic administration. Even after 1815 the Prussian Diplomatic Service did not attract outstanding talents, nor was the timid Prussian foreign policy, conducted by reaction-ary officers and bureaucrats, a school for diplomats.

The chief example of new forces in Prussian diplomacy was Otto von Bismarck, who proved to the Prussians and Germans what great diplo-macy could achieve. He defined the place of the diplomats in the pseudo-constitutional system of the new German empire and became the real father of the German Diplomatic Service.

In addition to all the intricacies of the constitutional life of the second German empire, two major problems existed in the formulation of German foreign policy. The army remained the greatest power in the state and, as in the past, was not under civilian supervision. It exercised a strong influence on the conduct of foreign policy.[1] In both the wars of 1866 and of 1870 Bismarck fought bitter fights with the military leader-ship over war policies. As long as Moltke was chief of the Prussian general staff these conflicts did not extend in a serious manner into the peacetime relations of the civilian and military authorities, though cases of friction occurred, which arose chiefly from the insubordination of the military attachés in the German diplomatic missions.[2] They increased once Moltke's influence was superseded by younger men like Count Waldersee and worsened even more with the appearance of Admiral von Tirpitz' ambitious naval attachés. During the first world war the army under Ludendorff's ill-starred leadership emerged not only as dominating the course of German foreign policy but also as the master of German internal affairs.

But the impact of the constitutionally independent position of the armed forces on German foreign policy cannot be discussed without con-sidering at the same time the power that Bismarck had laid in the hands of the emperor-king. The Chancellor was appointed by the monarch and executed officially the policy of the emperor. It was Bismarck's belief that the emperor would normally support the policy framed by his ex-perienced minister with the assistance of an expert staff, the foreign service. William I lived up to these expectations though at times violent

[1] Cf. on the relations between military and civilian leadership most recently Gerhard Ritter "Das Verhältnis von Politik und Kriegführung im bismarckischen Reich" in *Deutschland und Europa, Festschrift für Hans Rothfels*, ed. by Werner Conze (Düssel-dorf, 1951), pp. 69-97. For the older literature see Hajo Holborn "Moltke and Schlieffen" in *Makers of Modern Strategy*, ed. by E. M. Earle (Princeton, 1943), pp. 172-205.

[2] A number of cases are illustrated by Albrecht Mendelssohn Bartholdy, in *Diplomatie* (Berlin-Grunewald, 1927), pp. 51-77. For a historical analysis see Gordon A. Craig, "Military Diplomats in the Prussian and German Service: the Attachés, 1816-1914" *Political Science Quarterly*, LXIV (1949), 65-94.

clashes occurred between Chancellor and emperor over issues of foreign policy, as in 1866 with regard to the peace and, in 1879, to the alliance with Austria. But while William I was malleable, his grandson proved eccentric and untractable, and there was no obstacle in the Bismarckian constitution against direct monarchical government. Differences on foreign policy were not of major importance in the dismissal of Bismarck in 1890, but the personal regime of William II immediately went on the rampage in foreign affairs.

The damage inflicted by the preposterous speeches and ill-considered actions of the emperor on Germany's position in the world was enormous, but William II was too deficient in imagination and consistency to become the exclusive director of German foreign policy. Apart from the management of the routine operations, the Foreign Office retained a considerable measure of policy-making authority. What endangered this authority, however, more than purely personal gestures and interventions was William's propensity to accept the advice of his military and naval chieftains. The determined and reckless machinations of Admiral von Tirpitz overpowered William II, and since Tirpitz was in addition to his diplomacy a master of popular propaganda, the Foreign Office lost the decisive role in the molding of Anglo-German relations. Between 1890 and 1914 the political influence of the German Foreign Office declined rapidly from the height that it had attained under Bismarck.

The first world war completed the breakdown of the policy-making authority of the German Foreign Office. The invasion of Belgium, that made the entry of Britain into the war inevitable, had already been conceded to the military before 1914. But every demand raised by Hindenburg and Ludendorff in the course of the war was granted by the Chancellor and the Foreign Office. The proclamation of a Polish Kingdom in 1916, which killed all possibility of separate peace negotiations with Russia, and the opening of unlimited submarine warfare in 1917, which made the United States declare war on Germany, present only two illustrations of the eclipse of the German Foreign Office. But Ludendorff, protected by Hindenburg's popularity and assisted by Tirpitz' wily gift of mass manipulation, threw the full power of the army behind a program of annexations that only a military victory over all the enemies of Germany could have realized. Moreover, once Hindenburg and Ludendorff had been given supreme command of the German army, they dictated the policies of the civilian government as well. In July 1917 the military leaders forced William II to dismiss Chancellor von Bethmann-Hollweg; in July 1918 they brought about the resignation of the Secretary of

Foreign Affairs, Richard Kühlmann. In these months the personal regime of William II was buried, but so were the last vestiges of Foreign Office authority. The virtual dictatorship of Ludendorff came to an end only when he had to admit defeat in late September 1918 and suddenly demanded a parliamentary German government to conclude an armistice and peace. Then, the German Foreign Office could recover somewhat from the lowly place to which it had fallen.

Whether the German Foreign Office would have provided Germany with a more intelligent foreign policy if it had retained under the reign of William II some of the power that it wielded in Bismarck's days, nobody can say. Undoubtedly, there existed in the German Foreign Office at all times persons who on account of their familiarity with conditions in other countries were conscious of the need for moderation. But though a few of them were ready to take the risk of resignation, none of them showed the willingness to fight for a radical revision of the Bismarckian constitutional system.

This was not surprising. Diplomats are the last people to man barricades, though revolutionaries have often become good diplomats. But the German diplomatic corps that Bismarck created after 1871 was composed of people who supported his constitutional system. Bismarck took great care to make the new German foreign service representative of the new empire. The selection of the German ambassadors to the Great Powers illustrates his policy most clearly. The post in St. Petersburg was in the hands of the Prussian general Hans Lothar von Schweinitz from 1876 to 1893, while Prince Chlodwig Hohenlohe, Bavarian prime minister in the founding days of the German empire, became in 1874 ambassador in Paris. Count Georg Münster, the son of the British-Hanoverian minister who in 1814-15 had restored the kingdom of Hanover, was sent in 1873 as German ambassador to London. A younger son of one of the small reigning princely families of Germany, Prince Henry VII Reuss represented Germany at the Austrian court from 1878 to 1894. When in the 1880's Prince Hohenlohe was made regent of Alsace-Lorraine, Count Münster went to Paris and was followed in London by Prince Paul Hatzfeldt. In Constantinople Joseph M. von Radowitz, the first German specialist on Oriental affairs, attended to German interests.

Each of these six men set a standard of diplomatic performance that compared favorably with that of any ranking member of the older foreign services of other countries. It was obvious that Bismarck tried successfully to expand the Prussian into a German foreign service.[3] Indeed, Swabians and Bavarians were quite numerous in German diplomacy after 1871. There was a European air about Bismarck's ambassadors. By ancestry or marriage many of them were related to the nobility of other countries, and their German national patriotism was tempered by their sense of European responsibility. Up to a point Bismarck also cherished people of independent judgment. He always admonished his diplomatic emissaries to feel themselves not only attorneys of German national interests but also pleaders of the case of the foreign governments to which they were accredited. Bismarck was conscious of profiting from their personal reactions and disregarded, therefore, a certain amount of deviationist opinion. Count Münster, a grandseigneur of stubborn individual convictions, caused him particular worries by his staunch opposition to German colonial acquisitions. On the other hand, none of Bismarck's ambassadors was fully initiated into the arcana of the chancellor's over-all policy. After Bismarck's resignation in the debate over the renewal or nonrenewal of the German-Russian reinsurance treaty, all of them sadly missed the decisive points of Bismarckian foreign policy since they were familiar only with the special problems of their particular posts.

In the Diplomatic Service of the Second Empire a sharp distinction existed between the "political" diplomats and the rest of the Diplomatic Service. Nobody was accepted in the political Diplomatic Service who did not enjoy a private income that was comparable to a high official's salary. Without it he might perhaps be accepted in the consular service or become a legal councillor of the German Foreign Office, but could not normally hope to receive a diplomatic post or enter the political section of the German Foreign Office. In theory at least a separation was maintained among the three sections of the German Foreign Office—the political, the economic, and the legal sections and their dependent diplomatic and consular careers. In practice the distinction often proved surmountable. Quite a few people who started as dragomans in the oriental field went through the consular into the Diplomatic Service. The first Under-Secretary of the German Foreign Office, Dr. Clemens Busch, and the last imperial Foreign Secretary, Dr. Solf, were examples of such advancement. There were also in Bismarck's Foreign Office, as distinct from foreign posts, some special experts who enjoyed the confidence of the Chancellor. The most important personality in this connection was

---

[3] A good description of the German Foreign Office and foreign service in the Bismarckian period is contained in Joseph Maria von Radowitz, *Aufzeichnungen und Erinnerungen*, ed. by Hajo Holborn (Stuttgart, 1925).

Lothar Bucher, the friend of Karl Marx, who was brought back from his English exile and served Bismarck in the political division of the Foreign Office chiefly as councillor in charge of Western European affairs. As a rule, however, members of the political foreign service in rotation served in the political division of the German foreign service, though also in cases like that of Baron Friedrich von Holstein members never returned from the central office to posts abroad.

A strange dichotomy can be noticed in Bismarck's activities as an organizer and educator. He was very conscious of his responsibility as the founder of the German Diplomatic Service and took endless pains to help its members perfect their performance. He never tired of warning them that Germany's role was not that of Europe's policeman or schoolmaster. But he went as well into more special problems of diplomatic conduct. Thus he once remonstrated when at a conference one of his ambassadors had apparently let pass a public pronouncement that spoke contemptuously, with reference to Bulgaria, of the machinations of a small nation undermining European peace. "Our judgment and our vote," Bismarck wrote, "have more weight before Europe the more calmly and dispassionately they are presented. Such an expression weakens the impression that German policy is not exclusively the product of cool reasoning but rather of some sort of touchy sentiment . . . the more I agree politically with your Excellency's interpretation and treatment of the situation the more I would wish that also the form of its expression should be colored by the gentleness and benevolence that we do not inwardly cherish but whose outward appearance will act as the oil in the machine and will not increase the anger of others beyond an unavoidable measure."[4] Admonitions of this type went out to the German diplomats continuously.

Yet at the same time Bismarck wanted to leave the direction of German politics to a young generation imbued with pride in Germany's international position and faith in the worth of Germany's semi-absolutist order. He contributed greatly and deliberately to inflating the autocratic sentiments of Prince William, whom he wished to immunize against the liberal tendencies of his father, Emperor Frederick III, and his mother, the daughter of Queen Victoria. The same policy was noticeable in the 1880's in his selection and preferment of the younger members. His own son, Prince Herbert Bismarck, who was his father's chief assistant in diplomatic affairs during the last years of his reign, already represented a new type of German diplomat, less individualistic and more adaptable to the wind that blew from highest quarters, on the other

---

[4] J. M. von Radowitz, *Aufzeichnungen und Erinnerungen*, II, 256-257.

hand more assertive in international dealings. Herbert Bismarck was profoundly loyal to his father and the Foreign Office tradition that the latter had initiated, but other young members of the service had their eyes on the coming ruler.

Even under William II a good many men of original character and high competence could be found in the German foreign service. Count Paul Wolff-Metternich, German ambassador in Britain, proved his statesmanlike qualities in his long political duel with Admiral von Tirpitz. During the first world war Count Johann Heinrich Bernstorff in Washington and Richard von Kühlmann fought with similar fortitude for the recognition of their own ideas. But none of them prevailed in correcting the course of German foreign policy, and altogether there were too few independent men left in the high places of the German Foreign Service to maintain the distinctive level of the first period. The Foreign Office was internally divided by the factions which were the result of the personal schemes of Baron Friedrich von Holstein, who made himself the actual governor of the office between 1890 and 1906 and drove many of the Bismarckian old guard into the wilderness of peripheral posts or retirement. William II on his part liked people of personal wealth who could glamorize the social functions of diplomacy. He encouraged drastic language and sharp demands if incidents occurred that could be construed as reflections on German national honor. But the emperor paid little attention to the advice of highly experienced diplomats. Dashing smartness and languid servility were rewarded instead, and an atmosphere of mediocre cleverness settled over the *Wilhelmstrasse*. Though the average German diplomat in the age of imperialism was not lacking in self-consciousness, his sense of importance occasionally paled when he had to admit that in the competition with the military and naval coteries for the nod of the imperial majesty, the German Foreign Office more often than not failed to succeed, till during the world war it found itself on the side-lines. "Politics must keep its mouth shut during the war until strategy allows it to talk again," William II proclaimed.[5]

II

When Dr. Wilhelm Solf became Foreign Secretary in the Cabinet of Prince Max of Baden on October 4, 1918, the German Foreign Office was charged with the melancholy mission of concluding an armistice and opening peace negotiations after the war had been lost. At least it was no longer seriously hampered in its task by the army. When Luden-

[5] Otto Hammann, *Bilder aus der letzten Kaiserzeit* (Berlin, 1922), p. 128f.

dorff reversed his political attitude late in October and proposed to break off the armistice negotiations in view of the Allied demands, the new government could depose him without incurring opposition. But the Foreign Office had to cope with the influences emanating from the political parties. Matthias Erzberger, who had led the catholic Center party into the coalition with the Progressive and Social Democratic parties, became the chief German armistice delegate and affected German foreign policy during the whole period very profoundly.[6]

Solf was a liberal and convinced that only democracy could offer Germany a better future. He was a man of considerable learning, wide interests, and foreign experience. Temperamentally he was well-equipped to fit the German Foreign Office into a democratic state. But the November revolution not only swept away the monarchical institutions but also placed the chances of a democratic development into grave jeopardy. After November 10 the executive and legislative power fell into the hands of a council of people's delegates formed by three members of each of the Majority and Independent Socialist parties. The Majority Socialists under Ebert and Scheidemann saw in the council only a temporary authority to be abolished as soon as democratic elections for a national assembly could be held. Meanwhile they were anxious to see the old bureaucratic agencies of the federal government, among them the Foreign Office, carry on under their general supervision. The bulk of the Independent Socialists was not fundamentally but only partly in disagreement with these aims. They, too, wanted a national assembly, but at a later date in order first to gain through revolutionary action more positions of economic and political power. In this connection they took also a far more critical, and even at times hostile, view of the professional civil servants, a feeling naturally reciprocated by the latter.

But under the wings of the Independent Socialist party there also existed extremist groups, which pressed revolutionary action forward and which were willing to do so even in alliance with the so-called Spartacus group, the incipient communist movement of Germany, then under the leadership of Karl Liebknecht and Rosa Luxemburg. In the local workers' and soldiers' councils and on the streets the radical and bolshevist groups displayed formidable strength. In the absence of a properly functioning central authority they could embarrass and possibly even overthrow the moderate elements in the council of people's delegates. The struggle, that went on in Germany in the three months after No-

[6] For the general history, see Arthur Rosenberg, *The Birth of the German Republic* (New York, 1931) and Harry R. Rudin, *Armistice* (New Haven, 1942).

vember 9, 1918, was fought in the first place for domestic ends, but it had from the outset the strongest possible foreign implications.[7] Adherence to democratic forms would mean the creation of a national government that would have the strongest moral right to speak for the whole German people and could take fullest advantage of the democratic principles that Wilson had promised would guide the peacemakers. A democratic Germany, as an equal among the Western democratic nations, could save not only her national unity but also most of her disputed possessions, such as parts of her Polish and Alsatian provinces and perhaps even some of her African colonies. If such a convenient peace could be achieved the internal German conflict would be eased. The democratic principle would protect the continued existence of a strong German national state. It would simultaneously shield the moderate forces from the accusations of the parties on the Right that the Left had been the gravedigger of the Reich. It would equally help to quiet criticism from the socialists that no bourgeois group had ever done anything under the empire to stop official German foreign policy from building up growing anger against Germany among the nations of the world. The first American diplomatic observer, Ellis Lorring Dresel, who visited Germany after the armistice at the end of December 1918, wrote quite correctly: "... there is a strong wish to take up relations again with the United States at the same point where they were before the war, and the hope is cherished that the events of the war will be overlooked and condoned and that by the help of America, Germany will be enabled to rehabilitate herself."[8]

It was with such beliefs and hopes that liberals like Solf placed themselves behind Ebert and the Majority Socialists and appealed for the support of the German bourgeoisie through the founding of the new German Democratic party, which on January 19, 1919, polled about a third of the nonsocialist vote.[9] But before these elections took place the whole democratic program appeared endangered by the growing might of the radical forces in Berlin as well as by Ebert's seeming unwillingness to free himself from the embrace of the sinister Independent Socialists and to put down the terror of the street by force. On December

---

[7] Cf. Hajo Holborn, *La Formation de la Constitution de Weimar, problème de politique extérieure* (Paris, 1931) (Dotation Carnegie, Bulletin 6).

[8] The interesting reports of the first Dresel mission are printed in *Foreign Relations: Paris Peace Conference*, II, 130-172.

[9] In the national elections of January 19, 1919, the Majority Socialists received 37.9, the Independent Socialists 7.6, while the Center party received 19.7, the Democratic party 18.6, the German People's party 4.4, and the German Nationalist People's party 10.3 per cent of the national vote.

9, 1918, Solf appeared at a meeting of the council of people's delegates and caused a scene by accusing Hugo Haase of collusion with the Russians. Both the moment and the target for such an attack were ill-chosen. Haase had no sympathy with Lenin and had readily assented to the continued exclusion of a Soviet diplomatic representation from Germany. But even if Haase had not taken an anti-Soviet stand, Ebert at this stage could not have afforded an open break with the Independent Socialists. He hoped to outvote them easily at the elections and was preparing to meet any attempts at disturbing the elections or refusing to accept their verdict by the use of military force. Solf's sally came too early and he consequently had to be dropped as Foreign Secretary. As his successor the people's delegates selected Count Ulrich von Brockdorff-Rantzau, who was obviously anxious to direct German foreign policy and whom the delegates considered the finest horse in the stable of professional German diplomats.

Brockdorff-Rantzau was undoubtedly one of the best bred among the old-time German diplomats. Descended from an old noble family of Holstein, which in former centuries had seen many of its sons serve in high places in Denmark, and at German courts—in the seventeenth century a Rantzau even had become *maréchal de France*—the count was an unyielding individualist. The artist George Grosz in one of his satirical cartoons of the early 1920's depicted him with his short moustache, cold eyes, and disdainful look as the model of the aristocrat contemptuous of the democratic mob. (See illustrations.) During the first world war Brockdorff-Rantzau as minister to Denmark had seen to it that Germany respected the neutral rights of its small northern neighbor. Since the German legation in Copenhagen by the end of the war had become one of the most important among the few remaining German missions abroad, the minister had been able to acquaint himself with the broad aspects of German foreign policy.

Naturally, Count Brockdorff-Rantzau had been brought up as a monarchist, but he became a critic of German policies under William II. The emperor's flight to Holland in early November 1918 had in his opinion wrecked the moral reputation of the Prussian-German monarchy forever and he used to speak thereafter of William II as "the deserter of Doorn." On the other hand, his twin brother and most intimate confidant, Count Ernst Rantzau, acted in the days of the Weimar republic as the administrator of the large estates and possessions of William II in Germany. Brockdorff-Rantzau was free from a blind chauvinism, prone not to overrate military power in international relations, and a resolute hater of generals meddling in foreign affairs. Apart from a burning German patriotism Brockdorff-Rantzau was motivated by cool reason rather than by sentiment. The Russian and German revolutions impressed him with the strength of the masses and, though he was no genuine democrat, he considered the introduction of democracy as inevitable and as the only bulwark against bolshevism. As conditions of his assumption of office he demanded from the people's delegates the suppression of the power of the revolutionary councils and the earliest possible election of a democratic national assembly. He also wanted to be heard in internal questions and to be assured that in certain circumstances he would have the support of the government if he refused to sign the future peace treaty.[10] From the beginning it was his belief that a united public opinion had to be built behind the official policy at the peace conference in order to impress the Allies and to keep them from imposing humiliating and unbearable conditions. Still Brockdorff-Rantzau did not gain a marked influence on the evolution of Germany's domestic situation even after he had become German Minister of Foreign Affairs in the first republican Cabinet approved by the German national assembly in February 1919. When the critical phase of the peace negotiations arrived in May and June 1919, Brockdorff-Rantzau's policy failed to command sufficient support at home.

Brockdorff-Rantzau realized that he could not become a German Talleyrand. The vanquished Germany could not hope like the defeated France of 1814-15 to safeguard her position as one of the Great Powers by diplomatic finesse. The thought of diplomatic maneuver, in particular between the United States and the European nations but also between Britain and France, was, of course, by no means entirely absent from the minds of German diplomats, but the German peace strategy was fundamentally built upon the loud appeal to world public opinion, which it was confidently hoped would compel the governments of the West to adopt a most liberal interpretation of the Wilsonian peace program. "Open diplomacy," as first practiced in a telling way by Trotsky at Brest-Litovsk and then officially promulgated by Wilson,[11] was to become the chief medium of German diplomacy. The Germans expected that now after the Fourteen Points had been declared as the guiding principles

---

[10] See his letter and memorandum to Scheidemann of December 9, 1918, in Graf Brockdorff-Rantzau, *Dokumente und Gedanken um Versailles* (3rd ed., Berlin, 1925), pp. 29-35. Obviously, Scheidemann must have been in contact with Brockdorff-Rantzau before the actual Solf crisis.

[11] On the historical background of the idea of "open diplomacy" see Hajo Holborn, *The Political Collapse of Europe* (New York, 1951), pp. 80 and 104-105.

of peacemaking they would have an equal voice in debating and settling the application of these principles to the concrete issues.

German diplomacy chose to place an interpretation on the Fourteen Points that favored German claims everywhere. This attitude was understandable if taken at the opening of the great debate, but rather dangerous if maintained to the bitter end. The actual meaning of the Fourteen Points was not easily defined. By and large national self-determination was most strongly emphasized, but certain ideas about free trade and access to the sea were also considered valid. Considerations of national security, too, were not entirely excluded from the Wilsonian peace proposals, and in what form a balance between the various elements of thinking could be struck remained uncertain.

But even with regard to specific problems the quest for the exact sense of the Fourteen Points required more than an abstract philosophical acumen. Point 13 said: "An independent Polish state should be erected which should include the territories inhabited by indisputably Polish populations, which should be assured a free and secure access to the sea and whose political and economic independence and territorial integrity should be guaranteed by international covenant." Broadly speaking, the German-Polish settlement of Versailles, though unnecessarily harsh in details, could be depended on as a fair execution of Point 13. The passionate German assertions that Point 13 excluded the cession of the major part of the province of West Prussia that became the Polish corridor and the creation of the free city of Danzig were untenable. One can indeed go so far as to sympathize with the position that the Poles took even after 1919 when they complained that the Versailles treaty did not give them "secure" access to the sea. Already in the summer of 1920, when Russian armies approaching Warsaw threatened the very existence of the new Polish state, Danzig refused to let arms shipments from the West go through its port. All this is not to say that the German-Polish settlement was not open to criticism on other grounds. It was very questionable whether it was practical policy to impose provisions of this sort upon Germany so long as the Western Powers were not determined to maintain as close a watch over the Vistula as over the Rhine. But such an argument has no direct connection with the search for a correct interpretation of Wilsonian political ideals.

German foreign policy and propaganda under Count Brockdorff-Rantzau represented the Germans as the true champions of pure and politically unadulterated Wilsonianism. The Germans failed to appreciate that their erstwhile enemies would rub their eyes when they saw the

Germans appear in the white garb of liberalism and would become greatly suspicious if the Germans were in any way to twist Wilsonian principles. Their failings in this respect weakened their case with Wilson especially. The German Foreign Office had entertained great hopes that the United States, not having special interests in Europe, would moderate the war aims of her European allies. But the Germans lacked any understanding of the peculiar political circumstances in which Wilson had to pursue his policy.

Wilson's peace program, which embodied the aspirations of the liberal sections of the American people, clashed sharply with the war aims of the European allies, as expressed in the secret treaties. An uneasy compromise between the United States on one side and Britain, France, and Italy on the other had been achieved at the time when Germany urged the conclusion of an armistice. As a matter of fact the German intelligence service, which in contrast to Germany's foreign press analysis was very efficient in this period, had somehow managed to get hold of the key document of these negotiations, the so-called "official" American commentary to the Fourteen Points of October 1918.[12] The document was presented by Colonel House to Clemenceau and Lloyd George to illustrate what the American government considered the practical meaning of Wilson's program as it was to be applied at the conference. It was clear that in all cases the United States would take as benevolent a view of the interests of her wartime allies as was compatible with the letter of Wilson's declarations on peace aims. Nobody, for example, with any political judgment could assume that Wilson's ideas on the reform of the colonial system would be deemed applicable to the colonies of America's European allies. Lloyd George and Clemenceau had agreed to accept the American principles as regulating the future peace settlement with the defeated Central Powers, but not the internal problems of the British and French empires.

Yet the execution of the agreement, reached only under great difficulties, depended to a large extent on the development of the internal political scene. The loss of control over Congress in the November elections of 1918, the fight about American partnership in a League of Nations, and the relative indifference of the American public to all the details of the German settlement narrowed Wilson's freedom of action.

---

[12] The document was printed in Charles Seymour, ed., *The Intimate Papers of Colonel House* (Boston, 1928) IV, 192-200. I first mentioned in my *Kriegsschuld und Reparationen auf der Pariser Friedenskonferenz von 1919* (Leipzig-Berlin, 1932, p. 18n.), that the document had fallen into German hands, a fact later on broadcast by Hjalmar Schacht, "Germany's claim for Colonies," *Foreign Affairs*, XV (1937), 223-34.

Equally grave was the collapse of British liberalism in the British December elections both in its effects on Lloyd George's own policies and on the cooperation between the Prime Minister and the President. Brockdorff-Rantzau did not display a clear insight into the political situation on the Allied side and Count Bernstorff, the former German ambassador in Washington who headed the bureau in the German Foreign Office charged with the preparations for the Paris conference, apparently did not correct Brockdorff-Rantzau's notions.[13] The German diplomats had made a certain attempt to define priorities among the German national interests that they proposed to defend at the conference. They did not wish to put up a fight for Alsace-Lorraine or for Poznania and were prepared to make concessions to Denmark in North Schleswig, but they intended to insist on the retention of the Rhineland, including the Saar, and of all the eastern territories except Poznania. On Austria and what was at a later date called Sudetenland, the Germans were to reserve their claims, but they were not ready to push them too far, since they feared that the merger of Austria with Germany was likely to give the French a chance to demand the whole left bank of the Rhine. Brockdorff-Rantzau also realized that most and possibly all of the German colonies would be lost.

Officially the decision to accept the Allied decision to limit the future German army to 100,000 men was made by the German Cabinet and not by Brockdorff-Rantzau. General Hans von Seeckt, who was the chief military member of the German delegation at Versailles, attacked Brockdorff-Rantzau for making the German army an object of diplomatic barter.[14] And though it is true that the German Cabinet, chiefly under the influence of Matthias Erzberger, adopted this policy, there is no indication that Brockdorff-Rantzau disapproved of the move that was intended to avoid the appearance of German militarism and instead place the restoration of Germany's economic position first. At the last stage of the peace negotiations the German government even went so far as to offer to forego the building of all the battleships that the draft treaty had left to Germany in order to achieve the revision of other sections of the treaty. In addition to the territorial integrity of the German Reich within the limits already mentioned a reasonable settlement of the reparation issue was made the major aim of the diplomatic strategy of the German

---

[13] On the organization of the German preparations for the peace conference see Alma Luckau, *The German Delegation at the Paris Peace Conference* (New York, 1941), pp. 27-53.

[14] The event was the origin of the enmity between Seeckt and Brockdorff-Rantzau; see Friedrich von Rabenau, *Seeckt, Aus seinem Leben 1918-1936* (Leipzig, 1940), pp. 159-186.

Foreign Office. Also, the immediate participation of Germany not only in the League of Nations but also in the drafting of its constitution was considered a highly desirable end.

In itself this program would not have been unrealistic if it had not been followed through in a doctrinaire spirit. German policy was overrating its chances to defend Germany's eastern frontiers. Its desire to partake in the drafting of the League's covenant was hopeless, the more so since the German proposals aimed at turning the League from a federation of governments into an assembly of peoples, ideas that would have made it even more difficult for Wilson to get acceptance of the League of Nations in the United States. But under Brockdorff-Rantzau the original program was adhered to with the utmost determination and, when it began to meet resistance, German diplomatic tactics became stiff and tough-voiced. It should not be forgotten for a moment that the Allies never tried to take cognizance of natural German pride and feeling. The denial of oral negotiations and the humiliating conditions in which the Germans were placed at Versailles were insulting. Still, it is most doubtful whether Brockdorff-Rantzau did a good service to the German cause when he set the style of all subsequent German diplomatic presentations by the tone of his first speech at Versailles on May 7, 1919. It was probably not so important that he remained seated on that occasion as that he purposely used an aggressive language.[15] It was strange to say: "At this conference, where we alone, without allies, face the large number of our opponents, we are not without protection. They themselves have brought us an ally, the law that is guaranteed to us by the agreement on peace principles." While this undiplomatic way of addressing the future partners of negotiations, who had granted Germany the benefit of the Fourteen Points, could perhaps be psychologically explained as an outbreak of honest emotion, other remarks show a rather demogogic attitude. "The hundred thousands of non-combatants, who perished since November 11 on account of the blockade, were killed with cold determination after our opponents had achieved and secured victory. Of this you ought

---

[15] The incident of the German representative remaining seated in his reply to Clemenceau has been interpreted in many different ways. See for example D. Lloyd George, *Memoirs of the Peace Conference* (New Haven, 1939), pp. 453-454. This author believes that Brockdorff-Rantzau's neglecting to get up was the result of his extreme nervousness at that moment. But the count always supported the myth that he had acted this way deliberately and thereby gave belated justification to the understandable annoyance of the conference. That the German representatives were themselves divided concerning the character of this first German speech before an international audience is shown by the discussion that took place on the evening before among the members of the German peace delegation. See Luckau, *The German Delegation*, pp. 63-65, 213-220.

to think when you talk about guilt and atonement."[16] Now, it was true that the armistice of November 11, 1918—and it was an *armistice* and not a peace—had continued the blockade, but by February 1919 the Allies had agreed to lift the blockade and the further delay was as much due to German unwillingness to employ her idle ships and pay for food imports with her own gold as to Allied hesitation to grant credits.[17] These events were fully known to the German minister, and it was not surprising that his speech caused resentment at Paris.

Obviously, Brockdorff-Rantzau felt even at the beginning of the peace negotiations that he would have to use the threat of the German refusal to sign the peace treaty, and no doubt this was the only weapon left to the Germans at the time. But the minister entertained highly exaggerated notions about the possible effects of such a policy. It required a strong and unified popular support in Germany, and it presupposed on the Allied side lack of confidence in the righteousness of their position. Various means were employed to produce both, but most important and, as we may add, most fallacious in its immediate political results was use made of the war guilt question. It was certainly a futile German hope that Allied opinion on Germany's war guilt, the centerpiece of all war propaganda, could be shaken or modified by German arguments, particularly at the very moment when victory had blessed the cause of justice.

On the German side the war guilt question logically became a moral and political issue at the time of the collapse of imperial Germany. The Germans in their vast majority had also been convinced during the war that the others had been responsible for starting the war. The bellicose nature of the pan-Slavism of Tsarist Russia and of British imperialism was singled out for special condemnation. Even most of the German Social Democrats, who before the war had always denounced war as the evil fruit of capitalism and castigated the armaments policy of the German empire, joined in the general German attitude. They justified their own support of the German war effort by the thesis that war had been forced upon Germany by the other Powers and that a socialist party was bound to play its part in the defense of its own national community. Once committed to this new line, however, they had not only made a full contribution to the German defense effort but had also tolerated the

---

[16] See Brockdorff-Rantzau's speech in Brockdorff-Rantzau, *Dokumente und Gedanken*, pp. 70-73. Also in Luckau, *The German Delegation*, pp. 220-223.

[17] W. Arnold-Forster, *The Blockade, 1914-1919* (New York, 1939). Also D. Lloyd George, *Memoirs of the Peace Conference*, pp. 192-199; John M. Keynes, *The Economic Consequences of the Peace* (New York, 1920) and his article on Dr. Melchior in *Two Memoirs* (London, 1949).

disregard displayed by the government for limited war aims. Not even the peace treaties of Brest-Litovsk and Bucarest of 1918 had aroused the Social Democratic party to forceful protestations. The tolerant and conniving policy of the majority of the party with regard to the nationalistic wartime policy of the imperial government had led in 1917 to the secession of a group of Social Democratic members who formed the Independent Socialist party. They asserted that no socialist party ought to forget in its support of national wartime defense its international and social responsibilities. War was a result of capitalistic competition and likely to feed imperialism. It was the sacred duty of the leaders of the socialist workers' movement to oppose with all the force at their disposal imperialistic war aims. Thus the Independents became the only party that voted in the *Reichstag* against the Brest-Litovsk treaties and maintained a sharply critical opinion of German foreign policy before and during the war.

Armistice, revolution, and the ensuing struggle between the Majority and Independent Socialists inevitably brought these problems to the fore and the Independent Socialists endeavored to demonstrate not only the imperialistic character of German wartime policies but to find evidence for the culpability of the German imperial government for the outbreak of war in 1914. The most eminent Marxist scholar of the time, Karl Kautsky, was to devote himself to the perusal of the documents of the German Foreign Office pertaining to the diplomatic crisis of July 1914. In Bavaria, where the revolution had unleashed strong regionalist tendencies, the criticism of the foreign policy of the German empire was presented with an anti-Prussian bias. It was Berlin that since Bismarck's days had falsified the course of German history through the Prussian centralization of German resources and their reckless use for militaristic purposes. Backed by such popular sentiment Kurt Eisner, an independent socialist of doctrinaire complexion whom the foaming Munich revolution had made the temporary master of Bavaria, could open his campaign for a frank German confession of war guilt as the first step toward the purification of German life from the sins of militarism as well as toward the restoration of international confidence in Germany. A repentant democratic Germany could hope to receive from Wilson a just and democratic peace. Eisner did not confine his agitation to public oratory but also began to publish secret diplomatic documents bearing on German policy in July 1914, and he demanded that the Foreign Office be purged of personnel.

The Bismarckian constitution of 1871 had retained Bavaria's right to maintain diplomatic missions abroad, which enabled Eisner to send Professor Friedrich Wilhelm Foerster, one of the few German intellectuals who was a sincere absolute pacifist and a radical critic of the German *Machtstaat*, as Bavarian minister to Berne in Switzerland. Foerster succeeded in making contact with George D. Herron, an American professor who served as an emissary of President Wilson. Nothing seems to have come of all these transactions. Herron apparently was not received by Wilson in Paris, and it is doubtful whether in any event Wilson would have been interested in this approach.[18]

While the war guilt was hotly debated in Germany and used to defame the monarchical system and to criticize the moderate political parties for their lukewarm opposition to the vagaries and excesses of German foreign policy in the past, popular sentiment in the victorious countries was running high with expression of indignation about the responsibility of the imperial German government for the war of 1914 and for many violations of international law in the course of the war. It was said that retribution for the wrongdoers ought to form the chief objective of the forthcoming peace conference. This whole trend was highlighted by the furor of the British election campaign, which also showed that this emotionalism could shift governmental policies away from the original agreement on peace principles. The promises suddenly made by Lloyd George and his ministerial colleagues about reparations were certainly not in harmony with the pre-armistice agreement. Internal and external developments thus conspired to fill the German policy makers with dark forebodings about the political significance of the war guilt question. Within Germany it was an instrument to press the revolution further and to drive a wedge between the radical parties on one side and the moderate as well as the old conservative parties on the other. It also threatened, as Eisner's Independent Socialist and separate Bavarian foreign policy proved, the unity of German foreign policy. Yet even worse was the danger that the war guilt accusation would be employed by the Allied governments to supplant the Fourteen Points in the drafting of the peace treaty. On November 29, 1918, Solf sent a note to the Allied governments proposing to turn over the examination of the causes of the world war to a neutral commission whose members should be given free access to the archives of all the Powers.[19] The proposal met with the rejection of all the Allied governments, who found that it was unnecessary to explore what was self-evident.

[18] Mitchell Pirie Briggs, *George D. Herron and the European Settlement* (Stanford, 1932).
[19] *Foreign Relations: Paris Peace Conference*, II, 71-75.

This result did not allay German fears. In particular democratic groups felt that the political use of the war guilt accusation would have a pernicious effect on the moral resistance of the German people and the foundation of a just international peace. The great German sociologist Max Weber, whose influence on the establishment of the Weimar republic was strong, was also most active in condemning the assertions of a German war guilt raised at home and abroad. A group of democratic political and academic figures, the Heidelberg Association for a Policy of Law,[20] began to address the general public in early February 1919 with manifestos on the question of war guilt. After that the Germans became more and more preoccupied with the expectation that the Allies would base their demands on the allegation of a German war guilt.[21] Such a belief seemed to be confirmed beyond all doubts when the German government came into the possession of a report of a committee of the Paris peace conference dealing with the "authorship of the war." Count Brockdorff-Rantzau consequently did not hesitate at the meeting of the peace conference on May 7, with the big treaty still lying unopened before him, to talk out: "The demand is made that we shall acknowledge that we alone are guilty of having caused the war. Such a confession in my mouth would be a lie."[22]

The Germans when they examined the treaty were apparently not puzzled about the fact that it contained no statement on the German war guilt where one might have expected it most, in a preamble to the treaty, or to the League of Nations, or in Section v, covering the German disarmament, or in Section vii, dealing with war crimes. A reference to German war guilt could be discovered only in Article 231, which opened Section viii, the reparation section of the treaty. This article was now quickly considered to be the result of the already mentioned committee report and thought to demand from Germany the recognition of her war guilt.

Actually the German delegation was mistaken both with regard to the historical origins and the intended legal meaning of Article 231. The committee "for the responsibilities of the authors of the war and sanctions" had considered but, chiefly under American and English influence,

---

[20] On the Heidelberg Vereinigung see Luckau, *The German Delegation*, pp. 46-53. Also Max Weber, *Politische Schriften* (Munich, 1921), pp. 381ff., 394ff., 485ff.

[21] See the report by the representative of the Foreign Office to the committee for peace negotiations of the Weimar national assembly on April 15, 1919, in Luckau, *The German Delegation*, p. 187f.

[22] *ibid.*, p. 220.

rejected a recommendation for the inclusion of an article on war guilt.[23] They were content to write a summary report on the origins of the war of 1914, the very report that came into German hands. But this was only an opinion and no further official action followed from it. The reference to war guilt slipped into the draft treaty of Versailles unintentionally during the discussions of German reparations by the Reparation Commission and the Council of Four. The drafting of the provision for German reparations started from the conditions of the Lansing note of November 5, 1918, which specifically stated that Germany would make compensation "for all damage done to the civilian population of the Allies and their property by the aggression of Germany by land, by sea and from the air." But French and British opposition against this formula was strong, since public opinion in Britain and France expected, and had been made to believe by their governments, that Germany could be forced to make much larger payments than this definition permitted. Lloyd George was also anxious to find a settlement that would give Britain a higher percentage share of the future German reparations than the Lansing note would have made possible. Consideration of Germany's capacity to pay, however, indicated that the actual sum would remain far below popular French and British hopes and be in practice closer to figures that could be derived from the Lansing note.

In order to protect Lloyd George and Clemenceau against the wrath of their parliaments it was decided after long and intricate discussions[24] not to set a final sum that would only cause disappointment. It was also resolved to open the reparations section with a statement that Germany was theoretically responsible for all the loss and damage that the Allies had suffered. But after thus appeasing popular sentiment in Article 231, recognition was taken in Article 232 of Germany's capacity to pay and finally the Lansing formula was reestablished as the ruling principle for eventual German payments and deliveries. However, the appendix to this article, which spelled out the categories of these reparations, expanded the German obligations in an extravagant way by adding war pensions and other items.

Article 231, the first article of the reparations section of the Versailles treaty, was not intended to be a war guilt clause.[25] It was not designed

---

[23] The minutes of this committee were published by Albert de Lapradelle, *La paix de Versailles*, III: *Responsabilités des auteurs de la Guerre et Sanctions* (Paris, 1930).

[24] They are excellently narrated and documented in Philip M. Burnett, *Reparation at the Paris Peace Conference* (New York, 1940).

[25] This opinion was first expressed by R. C. Binkley and A. C. Mahr, "A New Interpretation of the 'Responsibility' Clause in the Versailles Treaty," *Current History*, XXIV

to pass moral judgment on the foreign policy of Germany before 1914, but was meant to affirm a liability of Germany for damages which she was not requested to repair. These exceeded, however, those contained in the Lansing note; and the wording of Article 231 by people who were all convinced of Germany's war guilt could not avoid moral undertones.

The whole difficulty rested with a single word. Article 231 read: "The Allied and Associated Governments affirm and Germany accepts the responsibility of Germany and her allies for *causing* all the loss and damage to which the Allied and Associated Governments and their nationals have been subjected as a consequence of the war imposed upon them by the aggression of Germany and her allies."[26] The insertion of the word "causing" changed what would otherwise have been only a financial liability into a causal responsibility. Thereby "aggression," a word that in the Lansing note (and in Article 232) described only military actions after the outbreak of the war, could change its meaning so as to include events and plans prior to the war.

The German peace delegation read it in this sense, and in their nervous obsession with the war guilt question their German translation of the fateful sentences placed the accent entirely on the moral issue. Their passionate pleas with the Allies against the acceptance of this article produced stern rebuttals. The Allies would probably never have attached to the article the sense of a moral war guilt had it not been for the German remonstrance. In a very strict sense not even the Allied notes dealing with German war guilt linked it with Article 231, but they avoided a denial of such connection and since they expressed the Allied conviction of Germany's guilt with heated acrimony, they were taken by the world as proof that the German interpretation was largely correct. It was impossible for the Allied statesmen to retreat, once they were challenged by the Germans. The article had been written to cap a delicate political compromise among themselves which would have been endangered if they had disavowed its text. Moreover in public they would have

---

(1926), 398-400; then again, with better material, in Binkley's "The 'Guilt' Clause in the Versailles Treaty," *ibid.*, XXX, 294-300. Shortly before the Lausanne Conference of 1932 that buried the reparations problem, two eminent French historians gained wide publicity by their study of the problem. Camille Bloch and Pierre Renouvin, "L'Article 231 du Traité de Versailles. Sa Genèse et sa signification," *Revue d'Histoire de la Guerre Mondiale*, X (1932), 1-24. Cf. also my treatment in *Kriegsschuld und Reparationen auf der Pariser Friedenskonferenz*. A well-balanced and thorough modern historical statement is found in the introduction of Burnett, *Reparation at the Peace Conference*.

[26] Italics mine.

appeared as betraying a main tenet of common faith. For everybody in the Allied camp was convinced of Germany's war guilt.[27]

The German Foreign Office could not, of course, have known what had been going on behind the scenes of the conference of the Allies in Paris. But even if the German reading of Article 231 was bound to be different from what the Allied reparation experts had primarily intended to put into it, the German delegation approached the problem in a frame of mind that was conditioned by the singular circumstances of a Germany in revolution and defeat. It was no doubt desirable to set into motion an objective study of the causes of the world war. But the mills of historical research grind slowly and do not easily produce a standardized result. Moreover it takes a long time to acquaint the general public with the findings of historians who in most cases tend to agree rather on the complexity of the issues raised by the past than on their absolute meaning. From the German point of view, however, it was enough to have made it clear that historical problems could not be settled by simple moral verdicts of a victor and that historical truth, at least in a world that recognized the freedom of the human spirit, was not the monopoly of any single Power.

It was, however, a different matter to make the war guilt issue the hub of a radical fight against the acceptance of the peace treaty. Any cool examination of the treaty was bound to show that the practical provisions, including those for reparations, would have been identical with or without Article 231. Obviously, the treaty of Versailles had been drafted by people who believed in Germany's responsibility for the outbreak of the war of 1914, but they were not likely to change their opinions from one day to the other because of German protests. If Count Brockdorff-Rantzau decided upon making Article 231 the official test case of the sincerity of the Allied nations to conclude a democratic peace, he felt confident that by declaring the article a despicable attack upon German national honor the government could rally the great majority of the German people to resist the acceptance of what soon became known in Germany as "the peace of infamy." Even at Versailles, Brockdorff-Rantzau spoke incorrectly of Article 231 as imposing on Germany the *sole* guilt, and Chancellor Bauer repeated this statement from the rostrum of the national assembly in Weimar.[28]

The fight against the war guilt did, indeed, bring the mass of the Ger-

---

[27] See for example Charles Seymour, *Intimate Papers of Colonel House*, IV, 392, 409.
[28] Brockdorff-Rantzau, *Dokumente und Gedanken*, p. 70; *Stenographische Berichte der verfassunggebenden Nationalversammlung*, CCXXXVII, 1115.

man people together, but it united them on a very dangerous platform. All the German parties with the exception of the reactionary parties and the Spartacus group had been quite irresponsible in their expectations of what a peace on the basis of the Fourteen Points would be like. The government failed to enlighten them before the beginnings of the Versailles discussions about the true feelings of the Allied countries towards Germany. The American diplomatic observer in Germany, Dresel, wrote on May 10, 1919: "The entirely insincere belief that the armistice was only concluded on condition that President Wilson's peace program, as interpreted for the benefit of Germany, would be enforced, had become general. The people had been led to believe that Germany had been unluckily beaten after a fine and clean fight, owing to the ruinous effect of the blockade on the home morale and perhaps some too far-reaching plans of her leaders, but that happily President Wilson could be appealed to, and would arrange a compromise peace satisfactory to Germany."[29] The announcement of the peace conditions was, therefore, a terrific blow to practically everyone in Germany. It could be said now that the introduction of democracy had not saved Germany from a grim fate and that the imposition of the war guilt made it necessary for the Germans to defend their national past. Such at least was the impact of these events on the many bourgeois people who immediately after the revolution had given their vote to the new Democratic party, since they hoped that democracy would protect them against bolshevism at home and foreign nationalism. The Democratic party left the government before the signing of the Versailles treaty, but its power was spent. In the national elections of 1920 the party lost almost half of its members and declined steadily thereafter. The German bourgeoisie went back to the old parties of the Right, the more easily since the spectre of Bolshevism had lost in the course of 1919 much of its terror after the new German armed forces, the so-called "free corps," had established order.

Count Brockdorff-Rantzau hoped through the appeal to German national honor to gain the approval of the nation. This policy was unrealistic. The threat that Germany would not sign the treaty was a practical political device. Lloyd George foresaw the high cost that further or even total occupation of Germany would entail. It might kill the chance of ever getting reparations from Germany and it was certain to reopen all the political issues just laboriously settled with France. The British Prime Minister became the champion of considerable treaty modifications. The most important concessions that the Germans wrested

[29] *Foreign Relations: Paris Peace Conference*, XII, 119.

from the Allies were a plebiscite in Upper Silesia and a number of adjustments with regard to the German-Polish frontier which actually foreshadowed subsequent British support to German claims in this field during the postwar period. Other valuable promises of a more anticipatory nature, like the early accession of Germany to the League of Nations, were added to the final reply of the Allies to Germany.

Still it was entirely unwarranted to assume that Germany could have improved the treaty conditions if it had rejected the Allied ultimatum. It was wishful thinking on the part of the German peace delegation to urge in their final report the refusal of signing the treaty, because, as Brockdorff-Rantzau expressed it, "if our enemies execute their threat and apply force against us, though we are willing to fulfill all their just demands, we are convinced that the progressive peaceful development of the world will give us soon the objective tribunal before which we shall demand our right."[30] It was an optimism born of despair, but with no basis in fact. We know today what would have happened. The Allied armies would have marched into Germany and have occupied northern Germany as far east as the Weser River, cut off southern Germany, and established contact with Czechoslovakia.[31] Most of the German army had dispersed after the armistice and the revolution. After January 1919, however, new troops had been organized on a voluntary basis and the military balance of power vis-à-vis Poland, though not the West, favored Germany. Allied forces had been depleted between November 1918 and June 1919 from 198 to 39 divisions. General Foch was, however, confident that this force was adequate for the occupation of Germany up to the Weser, an estimate in which the German generals fully agreed.[32] For a push beyond the Weser to Berlin Foch demanded additional troops and the authority to conclude armistices with individual southern and western German states.

There is no question that a final German refusal to sign the Versailles treaty would have meant the end of the unity of the German empire. Military resistance, Hindenburg and Groener admitted, was of no avail. In such circumstances a policy of refusing to sign the treaty would have been suicidal. Direct cooperation with the Soviet Union might have changed the German position to some extent. In this case Germany ought

[30] Brockdorff-Rantzau, *Dokumente und Gedanken*, pp. 116-117.
[31] See the discussions of the Council of Four in *Foreign Relations: Paris Peace Conference*, VI, 501-550. On German military estimates, cf. Rabenau, *Seeckt, Aus seinem Leben*, pp. 181-187. Also a book for which its author received much information from General Groener, E. O. Volkmann, *Revolution über Deutschland* (Oldenburg, 1930).
[32] Volkmann, *Revolution über Deutschland*, pp. 278-279.

to have publicly renounced the treaty of Brest-Litovsk and withdrawn her troops from the territories of the prewar Russian empire. This could have opened the way for some sort of diplomatic cooperation between Germany and the Soviet Union that might have impressed the Western Powers. Instead German troops remained in the Baltic states fighting Bolshevism and created a deep gulf between Germany and Russia. Still it was highly doubtful how much assistance Germany could have derived from the economically disorganized and exhausted Russia. The new Russian rulers in 1919 thought in terms of world revolution, and Germany was in their opinion the country that had to be won over first. Lenin would probably have supported with all his might and with all the resources at his disposal a Germany fighting the capitalistic countries with revolutionary means. This, however, would have required a radical workers' government in Germany which would soon have drifted into complete dependency on Moscow. Brockdorff-Rantzau was certainly not planning to promote such a political combination, but for that matter nobody in Germany except the communists and a few adventurers of the extreme Right was willing to take this path. Not even most Independent Socialists were prepared to turn to the East. They denounced the Brockdorff-Rantzau policy of resistance as a revival of German nationalism at the expense of the suffering masses who needed peace and bread.

But would there be peace and bread if the treaty was signed? Did not the treaty contain many provisions which could be used by the victors to commit further hostile acts against Germany, and was not the limitless demand for reparations an absolute block to any economic recovery? And finally would it be possible under such conditions to build a democracy in Germany? These were, indeed, questions that could make any German falter, but there were certain points which could inspire a modicum of confidence. First of all, the unity of the empire was preserved; second, after a respite one could hope to restore the greatest treasure of the nation, the capacity for hard work. Beyond this one might trust that other countries would learn to appreciate the fact that Europe could not recover if Germany did not regain a reasonable prosperity and that if one wished to talk of a comity of democratic nations, Germany could claim the protection of liberal principles.

This belief won out in the councils of the German Social Democratic and Center parties. After the revolution the Center party had come under the leadership of its democratic wing. Matthias Erzberger dominated, and this former Swabian village teacher, who had a quick, if glib mind, became the chief opponent of Brockdorff-Rantzau on the German political scene. As the chairman of the German armistice delegation he had been in contact with Allied representatives since November 11, 1918.[33] Erzberger converted the Center party to the acceptance of the treaty. In the Social Democratic party the sober advice of Hermann Mueller finally prevailed. Mueller had gone to Paris in the last days of July 1914 to establish a common policy of the French and German socialists towards the war crisis. Now, five years later, as the German Foreign Minister he affixed his signature to the Versailles treaty, which showed no influence of the Second International but instead the heavy imprints of nationalism. Even on the German side nationalism had been galvanized into life again by the Allied demands, and German foreign policy had not been conducted with much consideration of the vital internal needs of an infant republic.

III

The actual course of German foreign policy had been finally decided by the parties and not by the old-line diplomats. Hermann Mueller was the first German parliamentarian to assume the wheel in 76 Wilhelmstrasse, and ever thereafter in pre-Hitler days the appointment of a professional diplomat to the post signified a nationalistic policy. According to the Weimar constitution, the German Foreign Office was made the sole agency for the administration of German foreign interests. The Bavarian foreign missions were abolished. Another anomaly disappeared. In the old empire the Federal Foreign Office served at the same time as the foreign ministry of Prussia that maintained legations with all the German courts. Through them the Foreign Office exercised a direct influence in German domestic affairs.

One important development was still instigated through the Prussian minister in Munich, Count von Zech, after the revolution. Relations with the Vatican under the Bismarckian constitution were reserved to the states. Since the end of the eighteenth century Prussia had sent a minister to Rome, but the Vatican had never established a legation in Berlin. The highest diplomatic representative of the Pope was the legate accredited to the Bavarian government, who, in 1919, was Eugenio Pacelli. The communist revolution in Munich in May 1919 forced him to take refuge in the Prussian legation; and, in the conversations between the young Count and the future Pope, the first steps were taken that led to an early visit of the legate to Berlin and to the establishment of a

---

[33] See, on his conversations with American representatives, *Foreign Relations: Paris Peace Conference*, XII, 124-135.

nunciatura in the capital of the German republic in 1920, an event that strengthened the republic internally and externally.

After the dissolution of the Prussian legations the Foreign Office had to gain its popular support through the parliament. The Weimar constitution did not envisage a participation of the state governments in the formulation of German foreign policy; but, since the foreign problems were closely related to those of the internal administration of the states, particularly in the occupied Rhineland, the prime ministers of the states were often consulted. The Weimar constitution had taken a leaf from the book of James Bryce[34] and instituted a special foreign affairs committee of the *Reichstag* that remained in being even between sessions and periods of legislature of the German parliament. Under German conditions the committee was not an ideal instrument for developing a foreign policy beyond individual party opinions. The German parties were profoundly divided in their views on foreign affairs. The presence of communist members, moreover, made the committee unsuitable for confidential discussions. In practice, therefore, meetings between the Minister of Foreign Affairs and leaders or foreign affairs experts of the parties forming the government assumed the functions for which the parliamentary committee had been created.[35]

The Weimar constitution had given the President of the Reich powers greater than those of the French President. In foreign affairs, they included a decisive voice in treaty-making and in the appointment of the diplomatic officers. Both Presidents, Ebert and Hindenburg, guarded these rights jealously but were anxious to avoid friction with the Foreign Office. When Brockdorff-Rantzau was made German ambassador in Moscow in 1922, he made the curious demand that he should be allowed to report to the President instead of to the Foreign Minister. This wish, though a departure from the constitution, was granted, but all reports were sent from the presidential palace to the Foreign Office. The Weimar constitution had also made an attempt to raise the position of the Chancellor above that of the other members of the Cabinet. The Chancellor was supposed to lay down the guiding principles of the policy of his Cabinet. But all the Cabinets of the 1920's were coalition governments over which the Chancellors presided as chairmen rather than as directors. Still, in certain matters, a Chancellor was able to disregard the Foreign Minister. The most important case of this sort was Chancellor Joseph

[34] See James Bryce, *Modern Democracies* (London, 1921), II, 402-420.
[35] Cf. on the Weimar constitution and foreign affairs Heinrich Pohl, *Völkerrecht und Aussenpolitik in der Reichsverfassung* (Berlin, 1929).

Wirth's approval of the independent policy of General von Seeckt in Russia. Since Wirth was simultaneously Minister of Finance, he could provide the funds for the Russian activities of the *Reichswehr*.

Even under the Weimar constitution, there remained additional agencies that were officially charged with foreign policy, or could unofficially concern themselves with it. Among the other federal ministries it was in particular the Ministry of Finance and, to a lesser degree, the Ministry of Economics which were influential in foreign affairs. The old Foreign Office had experience in the negotiation of trade agreements, but in the postwar world economic matters became so intricate and, at the same time, politically so important that members of the Ministry of Economics were brought into the international negotiations. An even more conspicuous role was assumed in all the endless conferences on reparations and loans by the Ministry of Finance. The new "financial" diplomacy was over the heads of old-time diplomats. In Germany it found its first accomplished representative in Carl Bergmann.[36]

A strong hand was needed at the helm of the Foreign Office to hold the course through various currents and to weather the storm of popular resentment and dissension. In the history of the Weimar republic Gustav Stresemann was the only statesman who, through his great ability as a parliamentary tactician and orator, as well as through his diplomatic talents, could make the office fully his own. Under him the German Foreign Office settled down to the execution of foreign policy in greater calm than in the first five years after Versailles. Immediately after the revolution, people had been unanimous in asserting that the German Foreign Office was in bitter need of a drastic reform. Count Brockdorff-Rantzau inaugurated a new internal organization which was realized under his successors.[37] The political and economic divisions of the Foreign Office were merged and then were reorganized along regional lines into three new divisions. Apart from them, four other divisions remained, dealing with legal, cultural, personnel, and press affairs. The merger of the old political and economic divisions was accompanied by the consolidation of the diplomatic and consular services into a single foreign service. Thereby, the selection for higher positions was placed on a broader basis. The change also tended to compel every member of the foreign service to acquaint himself in some measure with economic and social problems.

[36] See Sir Josiah Stamp in the foreword to the English edition of Carl Bergmann, *The History of Reparations* (Boston, 1927).

[37] The details of this organization, which was named in Germany the "Schüler reform" after the official in charge, cannot be treated here.

The German foreign service was small at the end of the war, owing to the closing of many German missions abroad and to the retirement of a good many of the old monarchists. But a substantial number of the middle-aged and younger diplomats of the imperial office remained in the service. Some, like the former ambassador in Washington Count Bernstorff, who was to represent Germany through many years at the disarmament discussions in Geneva, became members of the Democratic party; others such as Baron von Neurath, Germany's ambassador in Rome from 1921 to 1930, and in London till 1932, for the time being suppressed their displeasure with the republic. The old guard saw to it that among the young candidates a goodly number of their relatives, or members of their own elegant student fraternities were selected.

Some of the best representatives of a liberal Germany came from this group, such as Leopold von Hoesch, the greatest of the German professional diplomats of the interwar period. After the mutual recall of the ambassadors in Paris and Berlin during the Ruhr invasion, Hoesch as chargé d'affaires had impressed Poincaré so much that he asked for his appointment as German ambassador. In his eight years in Paris, and again from 1932 to 1936 in London, the sensitive and devoted man proved himself a master of his craft. Dr. Wilhelm Solf went as ambassador to Tokyo, where from 1920 to 1928 he represented a Germany without colonial ambitions and succeeded in establishing close friendly relations in the cultural and economic field.[38] On all levels of diplomatic rank, this list could be extended, and it must at least be added that in general members of this social group, whether liberal or conservative, were less easily swayed in later years by National Socialism. Some of the German nationalists, such as Admiral von Tirpitz' son-in-law, Ulrich von Hassell, even joined the conspiracy against Hitler. But, in the 1920's, these people radiated considerable ill-will toward a republican foreign policy. It is interesting to see how Baron von Neurath spread the idea that the Fascist government of Mussolini would help Germany in a revision of the Versailles treaty, or to find other German diplomats denouncing German parliamentary Ministers of Foreign Affairs as unfit to head their office. Wipert von Blücher, a member of the eastern division of the Foreign Office in the early 1920's and German minister in Finland later on, could complain even in 1951, despite all that had happened in Germany under William II and Hitler, that decisions as such to accept or reject the Versailles treaty could not be made by the discussions of a

---

[38] On German policy in the Far East cf. Kurt Bloch, *German Interests and Policies in the Far East* (New York, 1940).

group of people, such as the Cabinet, since "a multitude of people cannot make foreign policy, for which but a singular will is needed."[39] Ernst von Weizsäcker, a naval officer who strayed into the diplomatic service at the end of the war and within little time acquired the feeling of being a knowing professional diplomat, judged: "The old officials were accustomed from former times to work under the direction of a specialist minister. But . . . the men in charge of the Foreign Office after 1918 were changed frequently and were regarded by us as amateurs. Stresemann was indeed of a higher stature than the general run of Foreign Ministers. But in the Foreign Office he was held to be too trusting in international affairs, a field in which he was not fully at home."[40]

But in the early years of the Weimar republic, chiefly on President Ebert's insistence, an effort was made to have Germany represented in eminent diplomatic posts by men who had made their career outside of the German bureaucracy. None proved a failure; on the contrary, most of them were unusually effective diplomats. Friedrich Sthamer, a former mayor of Hamburg, was sent as ambassador to London and his absolute honesty and tactfulness helped to allay British resentment and, at least after Locarno, to give Anglo-German relations a rather cordial note. Even more successful were the three socialist ministers, a somewhat surprising fact, since the German socialists prior to 1918 had hardly a chance to acquaint themselves with diplomatic affairs and manners. All three were essentially newspapermen. The Bavarian Adolf Müller acted from 1920 to 1933 as German minister in Berne, and the relations between Switzerland and Germany prospered. His influence reached beyond that. Ebert and most republican German statesmen liked to listen to his wise counsel on foreign policy, and much was done from the German legation in Berne to prepare Germany's way to Geneva. From 1922 to 1930, the Swabian Ulrich Rauscher held the most thankless post of the German Foreign Service, the embassy in Warsaw, with extraordinary courage and circumspection. The third socialist diplomat came from Schleswig-Holstein. Adolf Köster came to the Foreign Office as successor to Hermann Mueller when the latter became Chancellor in March 1920. As German representative at the North Schleswig plebiscite, as minister in Riga from 1923 to 1928 and, until his death in 1930, in Belgrade, he proved his mettle.

[39] Wipert von Blücher, *Deutschlands Weg nach Rapallo* (Wiesbaden, 1951), pp. 47ff.
[40] Ernst von Weizsäcker, *Erinnerungen* (Munich, 1950), p. 80; English translation by John Andrews (Chicago, 1951), p. 68. Herbert von Dirksen, *Moskau, Tokio, London* (Stuttgart, 1951), pp. 44, 56-58 is more considerate and restrained in his judgment on this point. So is Erich Kordt, *Nicht aus den Akten* (Stuttgart, 1950), pp. 24-52.

A member of the Bavarian People's party, Wilhelm Mayer-Kaufbeuren, was the first German postwar ambassador in Paris; a Center parliamentarian, Maximilian Pfeiffer, became minister in Vienna; while a board member of the Krupp works, Otto Wiedfeldt, was sent to Washington.[41] It may be mentioned that, after the conclusion of the preliminary trade agreement with the Soviet Union in May 1921, for once in German history an academician was appointed the head of a German diplomatic mission. The selection of Wiedenfeld, professor of economics at Leipzig University, was, however, designed to minimize the political significance of this diplomatic exchange in the eyes of the Western Powers.[42]

In spite of the good results achieved by the appointment of public figures to diplomatic positions, this policy was abandoned after 1923. Soon after his arrival in Berlin, the British ambassador, Lord D'Abernon, who had no special prejudice against German conservatives, confided in his diary that he preferred the Germans whom democracy had brought to the fore. He disliked in the old officials what he termed "Teutonic obstinacy or dourness." At the end of his ambassadorship he wrote: "German negotiators may be, and perhaps are, difficult to deal with, slow to be persuaded, pernickety, and disposed to quibble on small points, overcareful, making an infinity of reserves and precise pre-conditions on conjunctures and developments which, in all human probability, will not arise."[43] These remarks should perhaps not be taken too literally, for there were good reasons for moving cautiously in the years after Versailles, but they point up some of the shortcomings of the old-time professional German diplomats who were soon again to set the style of the foreign service. A good many people with greater and lesser gifts had gained accession to the Foreign Office in Berlin in the early years of the republic. How long they survived the trend toward the restoration of professionalism depended largely on their party support. The Center party was especially anxious to have a number of trusted party members in the office, and, since the Center commanded a pivotal position in German politics from 1920 to 1932, it retained a certain influence on the personnel policy of the Foreign Office. The Social Democratic party never gained representation in the inner councils of the central office after 1920. The examination for admission to the foreign service was stiffened, but

---

[41] Mayer-Kaufbeuren was recalled at the time of the French Ruhr invasion and died in 1923; Pfeiffer died in 1926; Wiedfeldt resigned his post in 1925. About the events leading to his retirement, see Gustav Stresemann, *Vermächtnis* (Berlin, 1932), I, 290-293.

[42] Wipert von Blücher, *Deutschlands Weg nach Rapallo*, p. 150.

[43] Lord D'Abernon, *An Ambassador of Peace* (Boston, 1929), I, 39; III, 28.

this reform did not amount to the introduction of a merit system, since the examination could be taken on invitation only. Moreover, the candidates could not feel certain that, even after passing the entrance examination, their future career would be commensurate with their ability.

Stresemann cared about these problems, but he was not a great administrator nor quite able to see through the cunning of bureaucrats. The tremendous burden of internal and foreign problems that he carried in a continuous struggle with his failing health, forced him to leave the internal administration of the office to the Secretary of State. Carl von Schubert, a slightly gruff, methodical, and immovable *Junker*, held this position from 1924 to 1930.[44] Under him the restoration of the German professional diplomat was fully achieved. The German foreign service had acquired a somewhat broader social and political basis, but its character was determined by the conservative professional diplomat. To secure his dominance Bismarck's IA division, a division to deal with high policy question, was reintroduced in an oblique fashion. So far as the existing six divisions were not directed by old-line diplomats, a deputy director of that ilk was appointed, who received instructions from, and could directly report to, a newly created office of the minister, the *Büro Reichsminister*, which centralized all matters considered of first-class significance.[45] Thus, even in the organizational sense, the old guard, and those who wished to perpetuate the old tradition, had come back. Probably only one group had a greater influence than it used to exert in the days of the imperial office. In a time when so much of the German foreign policy was a fight over the interpretation of the Versailles treaty, the legal division under its ambitious director, Friedrich Gaus, exerted an influence on the formulation and often even the execution of German foreign policy that went far beyond the functions of legal advice.

IV

The internal development of the German Foreign Office in the five years after the revolution reflected closely the general political history of the Weimar republic. During the period from the middle of 1919 to the middle of 1920, the forces which had supplied the strength for the building of a German democracy lost what earlier had seemed an irresistible momentum. The dramatic weakening of the Democratic party in the elections has already been mentioned, but even more important

---

[44] On the Foreign Office at the time of Stresemann's death in 1929, see Julius Curtius, *Sechs Jahre Minister der Deutschen Republik* (Heidelberg, 1948), pp. 146-150.
[45] Dirksen, *Moskau, Tokio, London*, p. 54.

was the crisis of the Social Democratic party. In the elections of June 1920, it lost about a third of its 1919 vote, which went to the Independent Socialists instead. With the great losses which the two democratic parties had suffered, and with the doubling of the Rightist vote in favor of the German People's party and the German Nationalists, the political position of the democratic wing of the catholic Center party grew precarious. Fehrenbach, a conservative member of the Center party, became Chancellor and formed a government consisting of the Center, the Democrats, and the German People's party, with the latter exercising preponderant influence.

The attempt to have a German republic under the leadership of the German workers' movement was shattered and had no actual chance of being renewed for another twenty years or more. It has become a definite tenet of German Social Democratic "self-criticism" that their willingness to accept the Versailles treaty and to support a pacific foreign policy in the period of the Weimar republic was a major cause in the collapse of their influence on German affairs. This is not true. The German Majority Socialists lost their dominant position in German politics because they utterly failed to give their followers the feeling that they were in dead earnest about abolishing the authoritarian state in Germany, and about preparing the way to a socialist economy in accordance with what they had preached for almost a half-century. The members of the working class would have forgiven their leaders for the original delay of any decisive action in the social field, since they agreed with them that the conclusion of peace must take precedence over all other political aims. But once the peace had been signed, the socialist workers expected active leadership directed towards the goals of democratic socialism which the party had inculcated upon its following for many decades. When the Social Democratic chiefs did not take action even after the first open counterrevolutionary move, the Kapp *Putsch* of April 1920, the workers wandered to the Independent Socialist party.

Foreign policy, therefore, was not the major reason in the decline of the Majority Socialist party, and the German worker wanted nothing so much as peace then and later. But he was not easily ready to bear the suffering that the German defeat forced upon him in order to vindicate the honor of a past Germany which had denied him full citizen's rights. During the first world war and again during the resistance to the French occupation of the Ruhr, the vast majority of the German workers proved their willingness to make sacrifices for a foreign policy in which they believed. But the leadership of the Majority Socialist party was unable to formulate a program of a German foreign policy that would have defined the vital interests of a democratic nation and, at the same time, boldly sketched out the practical ideals and obligations of a worldwide society of nations. The foreign policy of the Social Democratic party appeared to many of its followers as just another version of the policy of the Right parties, while the latter could decry its pacifism as sheer supineness. The lack of a clear foreign policy on the part of the Majority Socialists, therefore, was a contributing element to the rise of the Independent Socialists and subsequently of the Communists. In this connection, it should not be forgotten that democratic socialism had been confounded everywhere by the world war and by the advent of the Third International. And both France and England emerged from the war as bourgeois states.

The direction of German foreign policy fell into the hands of the German bourgeois parties after 1920, and among them the German People's party assumed a crucial position, not only because it had startlingly increased its popular vote in the elections, but because it represented the bulk of the German industrialists, including most of the coal and iron magnates of the Ruhr district. Hugo Stinnes, who had just expanded his family holdings into one of the greatest industrial and commercial empires, was the chief political spokesman of this group. There was a streak of the gambler in his nature that appeared even in his business enterprises, which collapsed shortly after his death in 1924. In politics, he was reckless and erratic. The new constellation of German party relations made it impossible to stabilize the German currency.[46] It was asserted from now on that in any event inflation maintained high employment in Germany while on the other hand demonstrating Germany's incapacity for making large reparations. Stinnes even argued that it would be desirable to refuse outright the payment of reparations, even at the risk of an Allied occupation of the Ruhr district. He disregarded the impact that the resulting coal shortage would have on the economic life of the rest of Germany and contended that a military occupation of the Ruhr would prove, once and for all, that nobody could collect reparations from Germany with bayonets.

The policy of negotiating reparations with a stiff upper lip was temporarily defeated when, in May 1921, the Allies, through the London ultimatum, presented an exorbitant bill for reparations and a demand for immediate cash payments, which Germany up to then had not made in any considerable size. The Fehrenbach cabinet resigned and, for another

[46] Cf. C. Bresciani-Turroni, *The Economics of Inflation* (London, 1937).

year and a half, the so-called "Weimar coalition" of the Center, Democratic, and Majority Socialist parties returned to office. But they ruled
largely by sufferance of the Right, which did not at yet feel ready to
launch its policy of firmness and which retained sufficient power even outside of the government, since it could rely on its influence on industry,
the bureaucracy, and the army. The assassination of Walter Rathenau,
the Foreign Minister of the Wirth cabinet, in June 1922 was a dreadful
symptom of the demoralization of the fanatic nationalists. Chancellor
Wirth and Rathenau had proclaimed Germany's willingness to fulfill
the terms of the London ultimatum and had hoped to be able to show
through this "policy of fulfillment" the impracticability of the Allied
demands. This hope proved fruitless, and, in November 1922, a government of the Right under Wilhelm Cuno took the reins again. By this
time, Poincaré was set on the enforcement of French claims for reparations and he expected through the occupation of the Ruhr district to
solve France's security problem, which the nonratification of the mutual
assistance pact of 1919 with the United States and Great Britain had
left unsettled.

The Cuno government called for passive resistance, but within a
period of eight months the French administration slowly succeeded in
establishing control over the occupied area, while the fantastic super-
inflation brought Germany to the brink of complete chaos. The danger
of the loss of the Rhineland, as well as the Bolshevization of the rest of
Germany, was very real. The ultra-radicals of the Right, like Hitler,
would have transformed the passive into an active resistance, but the
military situation was hopeless in the judgment of the chief of the German army, General von Seeckt. Thus, the *Reichswehr* marched to stamp
out the supposed centers of Left socialist and communist agitation in
Thuringia and Saxony. At the same time, it snuffed out the revolutionary
flame that Hitler tried to kindle in Munich. The stage was thereby set
for a new approach to the major political problems of Germany. Now
the liberal leader of the German People's party, Gustav Stresemann,
could persuade the German industrialists to assist in the stabilization of
the mark and attempt to reach an understanding with the foreign Powers.
This led to the Dawes plan on reparations of 1924, the Locarno treaty
of 1925, and Germany's entrance into the League of Nations in 1926.

This survey of German foreign policy with regard to its most urgent
questions in the years after Versailles clearly indicates how little of it
was or could have been made by diplomatic action. The great decisions,
as far as they were at all in German hands, were inherent in the out-

come of the internal social struggle. However, to regard the reparations problem exclusively, as we have done, from a German perspective, is much too narrow a view. On the evolution of French and British thinking about reparations the Germans could exert but a moderate influence. It depended on the economic and political developments of the Western countries, and was also to be determined by the mutual political relations of the wartime allies in the postwar years. Last but not least, the future policy of the chief creditor nation of the world, the United States, was always to be considered. The size of future American capital export or, for that matter, of American imports from Europe, as well as American preparedness to draw conclusions from the practical interrelations between German reparations and inter-Allied war debts, were all contingent elements. It would be a serious error to overrate the role of German foreign policy in bringing about the Dawes plan.

In the immediate postwar years, German officials had always urged the establishment of the total German obligation, instead of accepting an interim plan of reparation payments for a number of years. It was argued that, so long as the final sum was left undetermined, Germany was not likely to receive those credits that were needed to restore the German economy and enable it to produce reparations. Obviously, the argument was self-defeating if the total sum were placed at a very high level, as happened with the 132 billion gold marks of the London ultimatum. The Dawes plan stuck officially to the London figure, but defined a payment schedule only for a limited period. This was done, however, at a time when as a result of the settlement under discussion the influx of foreign capital could be anticipated. The example illustrates the baffling complexity of the reparation question and the novel problems that it presented to modern diplomacy. It is difficult to see how the German government could have managed the reparations question without the active mediation of the British ambassador, Lord D'Abernon, sometimes referred to in those years as the lord-protector of Germany. The Dawes plan was no solution of the reparations question, as later events were to reveal. But thereafter it was impossible for France to use the reparations issue as a means to achieve political and military aims which the peace settlement of Paris had denied her. The active participation of American financiers in the discussions of reparations strengthened the belief that Europe's economic ills could be cured in spite of reparations, a faith to which Americans themselves subscribed in the form of loans and credits of which Germany became the chief beneficiary.

The solution of the reparations question was the foremost task of

German policy all through the 1920's and, even more than the military occupation, it brought German foreign policy under the predominant influence of the Western Powers. But ever since May 7, 1919, the general aim of German foreign policy was the revision of the treaty of Versailles. It was popular with every party from the extreme Right to the extreme Left and, one may say, with every individual German. Revision, however, meant all things to all men. There was, in the first place, the division of opinion on whether the revision should be sought by peaceful means alone or ultimately by military action. In the latter case, it had to be discovered how a situation of war between the major Powers might develop in which Germany could join as an ally of one party and thereby regain a role in world affairs. On the other hand, those who saw the threat of a new war to Europe and Germany took the view that bilateral understandings should only serve for diplomatic, as against military, cooperation.

All these attitudes were reflected in the actual German foreign policy, or rather policies, in the years after the first world war. The prevailing sentiment in Germany discovered the divergence of French and British foreign policies soon after the war. Lloyd George had already fought for amendments of the draft treaty of Versailles. After the signing of the treaty, British diplomacy had continued to assist in its amelioration, in the drafting of a statute for the free city of Danzig, and in foregoing the extradition of German war criminals to Allied courts.[47] British occupation policy in the Rhineland was not overbearing and, in addition, tried to resist unwarranted French schemes of oppression. Again, after the plebiscite in Upper Silesia, Lloyd George favored Germany's political wishes. To be sure, Britain insisted upon the strict execution of the disarmament provisions of the treaty and displayed no willingness to waive her own claim for German reparations, but she showed an interest in the economic recovery of Germany, and her ambassador was using suave words about German disarmament at an early moment.[48] It was clear that Britain did not wish to see France as the absolute ruler of the continent and would, therefore, back Germany as a counterbalancing force.

It became a fundamental principle of German political thought, out-

[47] On the history of the revisions of the Versailles Treaty, see W. E. Stephens, *Revisions of the Treaty of Versailles* (New York, 1939), and the annotated edition of the Treaty prepared at the suggestion of President Roosevelt in the State Department at the end of the second world war and published as Volume XIII of *Foreign Relations: Paris Peace Conference.*

[48] D'Abernon, *Ambassador of Peace,* I, 87, 225.

side the Communist party and a very few other small groups, that the main endeavor of German diplomacy was to be directed towards ingratiating Germany with England in order to induce her to champion the German cause vis-à-vis France. Moreover, Britain seemed to own the best key for opening some doors to American help in European affairs. Practically nobody in Germany questioned the priority of the cultivation of Anglo-German relations on the agenda of German foreign policy. Ebert and most of the ministers were convinced that Britain's support for Germany had to be won by all means. But Ebert's opinion was shared by most of the German Rightists as well. Grand-Admiral von Tirpitz led the procession of the former England-haters who confessed that, after the lost war, a new German attitude towards Britain would be in order.[49] After the acceptance of the Versailles treaty by the national assembly, Count Brockdorff-Rantzau had not joined the ranks of those who persecuted his successors with reproaches and calumnies. In July 1919, he was already warning that Germany, once she had signed the treaty, must abstain from any secret schemes to blow it up. "Where the treaty is incapable of execution, it must be proved to our opponents."[50] And Brockdorff-Rantzau, too, had his eyes on Britain.

As early as 1918 there were, as we shall see in more detail further on, some military men who thought that they could build a close Anglo-German alliance by offering German military strength to Britain for the overthrow of Bolshevism in Russia. Ludendorff and General Max Hoffmann carried this propaganda into the postwar years, accompanied by the journalistic pleas of Arnold Rechberg, a wealthy industrialist and amateur politician. Adolf Hitler's foreign program was reared in the same camp, though he placed greater emphasis upon the necessity of an internal transformation, which in his opinion would make Germany strong enough to pull Britain in the right direction.[51] But the belligerent anti-Bolshevism lost out in the practice of German foreign policy after 1920. General von Seeckt's refusal to cooperate with the group was especially important in this connection.

On one point, however, all the German schools were in agreement. The attempt at an Anglo-German rapprochement was the most promising method of working towards the diplomatic, and perhaps eventually even

---

[49] Foreword to Alfred von Tirpitz, *Politische Dokumente*, 1: *Der Aufbau der deutschen Weltmacht* (Stuttgart, 1924).

[50] Brockdorff-Rantzau, *Dokumente und Gedanken*, pp. 125f.

[51] See on the "antibolshevist" school Max Hoffmann, *Aufzeichnungen*, ed. by Karl F. Nowak (Berlin, 1929), and chapters 13-15 of the second volume of Hitler's *Mein Kampf*, written after Locarno in 1926.

the military, isolation of France. The opposite idea that the most logical way to achieve an alleviation of the treaty burdens on Germany was a firm understanding with France had only a handful of advocates in Germany in the Social Democratic and Democratic parties, and it was not the official policy of either party.[52] But the political and psychological difficulties on both sides were so great that it would have been impossible to base German foreign policy upon an early Franco-German reconciliation. The economic approach, as tried by Rathenau in his negotiations with Loucheur in 1922, might have created some of the preconditions for easing the tension between the two nations, but in both countries the majority of the politically powerful industrialists opposed cooperation. In these circumstances, London acquired an even greater control over German foreign policy than could have occurred if even a remote chance for a direct Franco-German understanding had existed.

It is most doubtful whether German diplomacy could have brought such a chance into being during the years between 1919 and 1925, but there is certainly no indication that German diplomats ever thought seriously about the implications of the situation thus created. They were preoccupied with the hope that the friction between Britain and France would grow into such an antagonism as to force Britain to bury the Entente and to side with Germany. In 1922-1923 these hopes reached their highest pitch. Not only the altercations over Germany but also the clash of French and British policies in Turkey and Greece as well as in Morocco and Tangier appeared from the German perspective as definite proof of the irreconcilable nature of British and French interests. It was a bitter disappointment to these Germans when the Mediterranean and Near Eastern conflicts were composed at the time of the Lausanne conference, which wrote the new Turkish peace treaty replacing the treaty of Sèvres.[53] When British resistance to the French policy in the Ruhr remained lukewarm, it was said that the British government had acquired the oil of Mosul by giving away the Ruhr coal. But then these unhappy events showed even more clearly that Germany must not lose contact with Britain. Stresemann's decision to form a government that could end the Ruhr struggle and work out a compromise with France, under British mediation and guarantees, was greatly affected by the disappointment over British policy.

The Germans, who believed in the incompatibility of future French and British policies, made very serious errors in their appreciation of

---

[52] The main organ of this school was a socialist monthly, *Sozialistische Monatshefte.*
[53] See below, Chapter 6, § IV.

Anglo-French relations. They disregarded the imponderables entirely. Although popular anti-German feeling in Britain lost its shrill emotionalism rather quickly after June 1919, the popular British attitude towards Germany remained reserved for a good many years. It is difficult to decide how much genuine popular sympathy existed between Frenchmen and Britishers, but both knew that they had immensely benefited by the Entente cordiale; and from this practical experience stemmed the readiness to tolerate some friction and to stop it before it poisoned their relations. But even the ponderable political factors should have indicated that the British had no need to fear France. The Germans, with the French upon them, were inclined in those years to overrate the strength of France. Britain was conscious of the security that her vast naval superiority afforded her, and she was also aware of her incomparable economic preponderance over France.

There was never any panic in Britain over the political and military position that France had gained as a consequence of the Paris peace settlement. The British government was not willing to commit too much British strength on the European continent particularly after the withdrawal of the United States. If France ruled the continent within the regulations of the Paris settlement and with reasonable regard to British sensitivities in Western Europe, Britain would be content to devote herself to her own far-flung and knotty imperial problems. Poincaré, however, was unmindful of the British conception of the Anglo-French Entente. French policy became an embarrassing nuisance but not yet a dangerous threat, the less so since some soul-searching brought out past British mistakes in the treatment of the French. Outstanding among them was the gingerly way in which the British had dealt with the French demand for a British guarantee of the Rhine frontier after the draft treaty of June 28, 1919 had come to naught as the result of America's refusal to ratify. British policy would have to be more generous than in the past in order to keep France from adopting a unilateral policy in Europe that would be ruinous to the rehabilitation of the continent, to the collection of any reparations and to the restoration of European markets, which was needed for the economic recovery of Britain. In one respect, the German resistance in the Ruhr was of great consequence. The expense to which the French were put led to a long-overdue crisis of their public finances and of the stability of the franc. Internally it weakened the confidence of the high bourgeoisie in the government and gave the parties of the Left fresh influence, while demonstrating how dangerous it was for France to play a singlehanded game in world affairs.[54] The moment had arrived when British diplomacy could intervene and redefine the European power relationships.

One can say that the British Foreign Office under Austen Chamberlain never intended to steer an anti-French course. On the contrary, the whole British policy was often described as a return to the Entente cordiale. Chamberlain refused to accept the Geneva Protocol that would have meant a British obligation to act in any conflict arising out of the peace settlement,[55] but in the Locarno Treaty France received a British guarantee of the Rhine frontier. On the other hand, if Germany received the same guarantee against an act of French aggression, this signified in the first place the French renunciation of a unilateral policy going beyond the Treaty of Versailles. No doubt the double-sided British guarantee of the Rhine border had, from the German point of view, a certain prestige value as seemingly joining Germany to the Great Powers on a basis of equality. In general, the British were now convinced that a stronger Germany was needed to insure not only the recovery of Europe but stricter French adherence to the general ideas of British policy. "Desiring the maintenance of the Anglo-French entente, I am compelled to desire the existence of a strong Germany," said Lord D'Abernon.[56] He might have gone a good bit farther than official British policy did or could go. For the Versailles provisions were not changed. Germany had to accept the cession of Alsace-Lorraine and, more important, to subscribe voluntarily to the demilitarization of the Rhineland. She had to do so without the evacuation of the Allied troops from the occupied western regions. It was true that the Rhineland was eventually freed of Allied occupation, five years before the final date set by the Versailles treaty. But it had already been stated by the Allied statesmen at Versailles that, once Germany fulfilled her treaty obligations, an earlier evacuation would be possible. In these circumstances, it seemed frustrating that the occupation should come to an end only five years after Locarno and after lengthy negotiations, during which the British had not exerted the harsh pressure on France for which the Germans had hoped. Nor did the British show themselves easy bargainers in reparations questions. Germany's admission to the League of Nations afforded her new political

---

[54] See above, Chapter 2, § II.

[55] See above, Chapter 1, § III and Chapter 4, § III.

[56] D'Abernon, *Ambassador of Peace*, II, 238-239. Cf., for the general historical analysis, Arnold Wolfers, *Britain and France Between Two Wars* (New York, 1940); W. M. Jordan, *Great Britain, France and the German Problem, 1918-1939* (London, 1943); Hajo Holborn, *The Political Collapse of Europe* (New York, 1951), pp. 124ff.

opportunities to plead her case before the world, but it was a promise on her part not to seek revision by extra-legal methods and to work in peaceful cooperation with the other League members. In this respect League membership tied Germany closely to the international system that the Western Powers represented, and it compromised her in other directions. But those Germans who criticize the courageous policy of Stresemann still have to show how Germany could otherwise have overcome the grave consequences of the lost Ruhr struggle of 1923.[57] Other gains accrued, too. The foreign loans which flowed to Germany in the second half of the 1920's enabled her to build the most modern industrial plant of any European country. Of greater significance yet was the fact that Germany was now being listened to in her new position in world affairs. By 1933 no nation, not even France, was willing to rise to the total defense of the Versailles Treaty, which had lost its moral justification in public opinion.

But the Western Powers made important concessions to Germany at the time of Locarno and of Germany's entrance into the League which in the eyes of many Germans made these events the starting point for a new German foreign policy that no longer depended exclusively on the Western Powers and that was the genuine expression of German national interests. Before we can discuss the concessions of the Western Powers to Germany in Eastern European and Russian affairs, we must briefly review German policy in the East since the armistice of November 1918. In this field, the German Foreign Office could develop a greater initiative than in Western European matters. Whereas the Western division of the Foreign Office was continuously under the pressure of the foreign Powers and domestic controversies, the Eastern division could plan and execute in an atmosphere of greater calm. However, it had a competitor or pacemaker in the German army, which was under less observation in the East than it was in the West, and which was determined to take full advantage of this situation.

At the time of the armistice German troops in the east were spread as far as to the Ukraine and the Caucasus in the south and to Finland and the Baltic provinces in the north. They flooded back to Germany in great disorder and dissolved on their march at home.[58] The hostile attitude of populations such as the Polish was a major element in this dis-

---

[57] Dirksen, *Moskau, Tokio, London*, pp. 75-76 is rather serious in his criticism, while Ernst von Weizsäcker's remarks are insipid, *Erinnerungen*, p. 69.

[58] See Forschungsanstalt für Kriegs- und Heeresgeschichte, *Darstellungen aus den Nachkriegskämpfen deutscher Truppen und Freikorps*, 1: *Die Rückführung des Ostheeres* (Berlin, 1936).

integration, as was the influence of the German revolution upon army discipline. In the Baltic provinces—called the "Baltikum" by the Germans—a somewhat different situation developed. German military and political authorities had worked closely together during the war with the German nobility, which formed a small minority in these countries but owned most of the land dearly coveted by the indigenous peasantry. But the retreat of the German troops from the northern Baltikum laid the country open to easy conquest by the Russian Bolshevists, and not only the Baltic Germans but also the democratic national movements were anxious not to lose German military protection. Some German troops remained in the Baltikum, and, beginning early in 1919, they were reinforced by a division sent by the High Command of the German army and, subsequently, by a stream of volunteers hired with the promise of land settlement in the region. In addition, Russian prisoners of war in Germany were induced to serve in the fight against the Bolshevist desecrators of the Russian empire.[59]

The German High Command under Hindenburg and Groener moved to eastern Germany in February 1919 in order to defend the old frontiers of Germany against Polish infringements and Bolshevist dangers. General von Seeckt was in command of the defense of East Prussia from January to April 1919 and was chiefly responsible for the army's decision to make the province secure by creating a protective zone in the Baltikum. His thoughts ranged beyond this immediate aim. In East Prussia and the Baltikum, it might be possible to rebuild a strong German army which would make its weight felt in the peace negotiations at Paris. But other German leaders entertained even bolder dreams, especially after the military situation in the Baltikum developed favorably and the Paris Conference entered its critical stage. Could the Baltic bastion perhaps become the military base for a decisive military action against Bolshevist Russia through the capture of Leningrad? If such a coup were successful, it could be assumed that Britain would join Germany in the anti-Bolshevist struggle. But even if Britain refused to ally herself with Germany one could expect a counter-revolutionary Russia to side with Germany.

All these dreams came to nothing. As in the past, the Germans dis-

---

[59] On the military events, see *ibid.*, II: *Der Feldzug im Baltikum bis zur zweiten Einnahme von Riga* (Berlin, 1937). Also Graf Rüdiger von der Goltz, *Als politischer General im Osten* (Leipzig, 1936). On the political side of the Baltikum developments in 1919, see *Foreign Relations: Paris Peace Conference*, XII, 136-227; *British Documents*, 1st series, III, 1-307; Dirksen, *Moskau, Tokio, London*, pp. 29-34; Wipert von Blücher, *Deutschlands Weg nach Rapallo*, pp. 69-86.

regarded the national movements of the Lithuanians, Letts, and Esthonians and their White Russian companions treated the Baltic countries as provinces of Russia. The Baltic peasant and middle classes waited only for the moment when they could acquire full national freedom by ridding themselves of the Germans. The hour arrived at which the Western Powers had gathered sufficient military and naval strength. Since February 1919 they had been demanding the withdrawal of the German troops; in the fall they saw to it that their orders were obeyed. The whole German Baltikum adventure had to be liquidated. For a while the German Foreign Office still endeavored to keep the White Russian troops of Colonel Bermondt in being and to relate them somehow to the Allied-supported armies of intervention. German diplomatic officials also cultivated relations with prominent Russian refugees. General von Seeckt, who became chief of the *Reichswehr* in the spring of 1920, was the leader in a revision of German policy.[60]

Already during his command in East Prussia it had dawned upon Seeckt that the German military effort in the Baltikum was doing a job for the Allied rather than the German cause. He had always lived in the Bismarck-Moltke tradition and viewed friendly German-Russian relations as the keystone of German security and France as the implacable enemy of the empire. The general, however, was also a child of the age of William II and Tirpitz and had considered the defeat of England to be the major objective of the first world war. Even after the war, he remained cool to the British, who showed no indication of giving Germany a sizable army. Considering the hostile attitude of the Western Powers, Seeckt judged that Germany could not afford to incur the enmity of Russia. Bolshevism in Germany would have to be fought relentlessly, but it was imperative to restore the natural contact between Russia and Germany. The German empire had no real interest in the new eastern European states; on the contrary, the annihilation of the new Poland and the restoration of the Russo-German frontiers of 1914 should form the main goal of German foreign policy. Thus, he welcomed the opportunity for conversations with Soviet emissaries, which were brought about by the intercession of Enver Pasha, the military leader of the Young Turkish revolution of 1908 and of the pro-German groups in Turkey during the world war. In 1920 Enver Pasha had gone

[60] Cf. Rabenau, *Seeckt, Aus seinem Leben*, pp. 251-253; 305-520; Julius Epstein, "Der Seeckt Plan," *Der Monat*, I, No. 2 (November 1948), 42-50. Cf. also George W. F. Hallgarten "General Hans von Seeckt and Russia, 1920-1922," *Journal of Modern History*, XXI (1949), 58-71.

to Moscow, originally working for a Russo-German-Turkish alliance against the West.

Seeckt remained seemingly unmoved when the Russians approached Warsaw in the summer of 1920. He expected a total Russian victory. It is impossible to say whether Seeckt felt confident that the Russians would not cross the frontiers of 1914 into Germany or whether he hoped that, in the case of a Soviet threat to Central Europe, Germany would receive arms from the Allies. In any event, after "the miracle of the Vistula," Seeckt proceeded to set up in the War Ministry the section "R" that was charged with directing the activities of the German army with regard to the Soviet Union. The innermost concern of General Seeckt was the building up of German military strength. To all those Germans who since 1918 believed that economic recovery came before military power, he had replied that without swords plowshares were of no avail.[61] In his opinion, German diplomacy should have centered its struggle for a better peace in Paris around the retention of a German army of 300,000 men. Instead, Count Brockdorff-Rantzau appeared in sheep's clothing, inveighed against imperialism, and fought in the first place for the economic existence of Germany. The general despised the count for his cowardly policy. After June 1919, Seeckt pressed the German government to request a change of the disarmament provision of the Versailles Treaty from the Allies, an entirely hopeless demand that tended only to worsen the atmosphere in which the discussion of the reparations question had to take place.

When the Allies finally turned down the German demand for a moderation of the Allied conditions for German disarmament, and when the London ultimatum on reparations had led to the formation of the Wirth Cabinet, General von Seeckt persuaded the new Chancellor to allow the *Reichswehr* the use of whatever facilities the Russians would provide for the production of armaments forbidden to Germany under the terms of the Versailles Treaty. With public funds, though through the channels of private industry, armament factories were developed in the Soviet Union for the output of artillery, ammunition, tanks, and planes. The ominous plan of building also a factory for the production of gas weapons seems not to have been realized. But the industrial rearmament was accompanied by mutual exchanges of officers for training in staff work and the tactics of large formations. Although information on the details of the German-Russian defense cooperation is still lacking, we may well judge that it did not assume the form of a military alliance

[61] Cf. Rabenau, *Seeckt, Aus seinem Leben*, pp. 117-119.

or planned cooperation for war, but was aimed only at mutual assistance in strengthening the war potential of each nation.

The Foreign Office followed suit on the path opened by the diplomacy of the army. Among the old professional staff of the office, Baron Ago von Maltzan emerged as the most powerful member after the war. He quickly rose from chief of the Russian section to chief of the eastern division and Secretary of State in the Foreign Office. He came from Mecklenburg *Junker* stock and became related by marriage to industrial circles. With great personal means at his disposal, he made his pleasant home the center of enjoyable and interesting social gatherings in the midst of inflation-ridden Berlin. At the Maltzans' distinguished foreigners ranging from the papal nuncio to the Soviet commissar met and rubbed elbows with important Germans from all political camps. Exactly where Maltzan stood on the hard-fought issues of German domestic politics, nobody has ever found out, and he epitomized well the deflation of ideologies which was an aftermath of years of war and revolution. Maltzan used his wide connections exclusively with a view to improving the international position of Germany, and after a brief period of hesitation he accepted Seeckt's ideas on the practicability of a German-Russian rapprochement. The negotiations were carried on through the only diplomatic line that had survived the rupture of German-Russian diplomatic relations in early November 1918. Both in Moscow and Berlin commissions for the repatriation of prisoners-of-war had been created.

As a consequence of the conversations, the Soviet Union and Germany, on May 6, 1921, concluded a trade treaty which laid the foundation for extensive economic intercourse between the two countries. The treaty followed a trade agreement between Britain and Russia of March 1921 and failed to cause any remarkable international reaction. But the German-Russian treaty was in the technical diplomatic sense far-reaching. The repatriation commissions were entrusted with the execution of commercial activities and received all the rights and privileges of diplomatic missions. A bridge had been constructed over the gulf that had separated the two governments since the days of the treaty of Brest-Litovsk.

This is not the place to speculate over all the motives that induced the Soviet government to move closer to Germany. The two countries were undoubtedly pariahs among the nations at that moment, but Soviet policy was never noticeably affected by sentiment. The German talent in military organization and the engineering skill in peaceful and military industries were welcome in Russia on the eve of the inauguration of the New Economic Policy (NEP). But Germany was weak and, worst of all, poor. The centers of world politics and world finance were in the West. The Soviet Union would have liked to gain recognition by the Western Powers. In the West the impact of the postwar depression had created an appetite for new markets, and projects for the opening of the Russian market were freely discussed. Rathenau was not the first to propose such plans, but in his prolific mind the proposal for an international syndicate, supported and financed by all the Western nations and Germany, took definite shape. The expansion of European production and trade, so Rathenau thought, would make German reparations bearable. Rathenau won Lloyd George over for an international discussion of the plan which was to take place at Genoa in April 1922.[62] The idea, as Maltzan apparently felt beforehand, was much disliked in the Soviet Union. It tasted of capitalistic exploitation, which was made even less palatable by the formation of such a union of capitalistic governments.

To break up the common front of the Western Powers was the main objective of Soviet diplomacy. But, to the German delegation, this front did not seem real. They found themselves left out of the discussion and became afraid that the French might falsify the whole plan by offering the Soviet Union a share in German reparations. Article 116 of the Versailles Treaty had reserved possible Russian claims against Germany. It was a great relief to Maltzan that Chicherin offered to sign a separate treaty with Germany, in which Russia and Germany renounced all their mutual claims arising from war damages and war expenses. Beyond this, the treaty that was signed in Rapallo on the morning of Easter Sunday, April 16, was in the nature of a general treaty of friendship. It envisaged, as the most important practical step, the immediate establishment of embassies in Berlin and Moscow.

The treaty was not drafted in Genoa. So far as content went, it had been the result of negotiations in the months before. Chicherin had offered to sign the treaty in Berlin on his way to Genoa, but Rathenau did not wish to do so before the conference. There, on Russian insistence, the treaty had been consummated and turned into a demonstration against the diplomatic plans of the Western Powers. Rathenau was most reluctant to proceed behind the back of Lloyd George, and it was Maltzan's persuasiveness that dragged the minister along. Rathenau's position in reparations discussions was at least temporarily weakened, and the break-

[62] On the Genoa Conference, see, in addition to the works cited above, Chapter 1, note 56, and the memoirs of D'Abernon, Dirksen and Wipert von Blücher, Eric C. Kollman, "Walter Rathenau and German Foreign Policy," *Journal of Modern History*, XXIV (1952), 127-142.

down of the conference, though it did not inspire Poincaré's decision to use sanctions against Germany, brought the Ruhr invasion a few steps nearer.

The precipitate action of the German conference delegation made President Ebert angry. He saw in it a violation of his constitutional authority and was concerned about the reaction of the German parties. Apart from the Communists, no German party supported a Russian orientation of German foreign policy. The Social Democratic party was opposed to it; the Center party very cool; and even the German Nationalists were against close relations with the Soviet Union. Of course, this was true of the militant anti-Bolshevists, but, in addition, the agrarian interests in the party feared Russian economic competition. Genuine popular support came chiefly from a few groups in the German Nationalist, German People's and Democratic parties. But these few people, supported from the background by General von Seeckt, succeeded in getting the Rapallo Treaty easy passage through the German parliament. Public opinion was friendly, because, after so much submissive toleration of Western demands, Rapallo seemed a defiant gesture of German dissatisfaction.

Count Brockdorff-Rantzau was sent to Moscow as German ambassador. He was not in agreement with Seeckt about the aims of German policy in Russia. During the summer of 1922, the two imperious men fought a furious battle of memoranda.[63] There were many misunderstandings between them. Seeckt's critique of Brockdorff-Rantzau's opinion was an expression of unmitigated contempt for the man of 1919, who "cannot understand that ultimately every political activity rests on power." But the Count was a passionate hater, too; he was so aroused that he would have liked to challenge the general to a pistol duel. Brockdorff-Rantzau and Seeckt were in agreement that German foreign policy should aim at the isolation of France and that a British alliance was desirable. Both misjudged the state and trend of Anglo-French relations. The ambassador argued that it was dangerous to have military arrangements with the Soviet Union, since the mere suspicion of such cooperation would bring the British and French closer together. He also warned against Soviet blackmail and wanted to see German-Russian relations confined to the economic field. Seeckt, on his part, denied that the German military activities in Russia would affect the course of British policy. He believed that the clash between France and Britain would

[170]

come as the result of overseas conflicts and that a Germany strengthened by her rearmament would be more *bündnisfähig*.

Count Brockdorff-Rantzau went to Moscow in 1922 as a "Westerner." While he let his great gift for personal diplomacy work on Chicherin in many conversations in the hours after midnight, Seeckt continued to operate his own wires to Moscow. But practically, though not formally, the two German foreign policies turned into parallel directions. Brockdorff-Rantzau came to find greater value in a general cooperation between Russia and Germany.[64] When Germany was about to accept the Locarno Treaty, the German ambassador almost joined forces with Russian diplomacy in its storm against Berlin. It seems improbable that he shared the Russian fears that Germany would become in the League the tool of an anti-Russian coalition and especially a vassal of Britain. It is more likely that Brockdorff-Rantzau, in memory of Versailles, was dumbfounded by the prospect of close Franco-German cooperation. He was, therefore, little impressed by the concessions made by the Western Powers which finally made it possible to conclude the German-Russian Treaty of Berlin of April 24, 1926.[65]

Germany was exempted from participation in possible sanctions against the Soviet Union taken by the League of Nations under Article 16. Her special diplomatic situation vis-à-vis the Soviet Union was thereby officially recognized. The significance of this event was greatly heightened by the absence of a British guarantee for the postwar frontiers in Eastern Europe. Whereas Germany accepted the Rhine settlement of Versailles, she was free to press for revision in the East, though only by peaceful means. The political moderation and circumspection, as well as the strong fortitude of heart, that Gustav Stresemann had shown were the greatest single factor in achieving for Germany this new position in the world. She could feel a new sense of relative independence and at the same time of self-chosen participation in European affairs. For a short period German foreign policy was almost as largely consolidated in the hands of the Foreign Office as in the days of Bismarck. However, this influence of the Foreign Office rested as much on the balance of the domestic social and political forces as upon the gains made in the foreign field. The age in which the professional diplomat could preside over the formulation of foreign policy had passed long ago.

[64] Some interesting material on the later years of Brockdorff-Rantzau was brought together after his death in *Europäische Gespräche*, VII (1929), 1-47.
[65] Cf. Stresemann, *Vermächtnis*, II, 502-542.

6

. . . .

Turkish Diplomacy from Mudros
to Lausanne

BY RODERIC H. DAVISON

TURKEY alone of the nations defeated in 1918 was able to reverse the decision within a few years and to negotiate as an equal with the Allied Powers for a new peace treaty. She was not, like Czechoslovakia, a beneficiary of the Allied victory, nor was she, like Germany or Russia, inherently a Great Power which could be expected to grow in strength. The Turkish struggle to establish a favorable international position was unique also among Muslim peoples in successfully shaking off foreign controls.

It was not the Ottoman government of Sultan Mehmet VI at Istanbul which achieved this success, but a new nationalist government which began in Anatolia as a movement of resistance to partition and foreign occupation. The Turkish nationalists, competing for position both with the Sultan's government and with foreign Powers, were organized first as the Representative Committee of the Union for the Defense of the Rights of Anatolia and Rumelia, and then as the Government of the Grand National Assembly, before the formation of the Turkish Republic in 1923. Each change in name represented a stage in the development of the nationalist movement into an effective government, and a step forward in its international position. By the time the republic was proclaimed, the new nation-state had already created the diplomatic basis for an independent and peaceful foreign policy.

From the beginning Mustafa Kemal [Atatürk][1] was the soul and

---

[1] Personal names in modern Turkey offer a constant source of confusion. They will here be given in the modern Turkish spelling, with explanatory notes where necessary. A Turkish law of 1934 obliged all citizens to take family names, which few Turks heretofore possessed. The new names will be indicated in brackets wherever possible, but since these names were unknown during the period under discussion they will not be used in the text. Mustafa Kemal was given the surname Atatürk by the Assembly.

leader of the nationalist movement. He had served with distinction as an officer in the Ottoman army on several fronts, notably in the defense of Gallipoli in 1915. His wartime experience had taught him to resent the German influence over Turkey, and to oppose the domination of any foreign Power. At the time of the 1918 armistice Kemal, as commanding general on the Syrian front, tried to oppose surrender to foreign occupation of territory he regarded as geographically and ethnographically Turkish.[2] He had by this time developed a Western-style national consciousness of a sort not uncommon among educated Turks, many of them of the officer class. Not yet forty years old, he had already exhibited undoubted military and organizational ability. Since Kemal had also avoided close association with the defeated Ottoman government, and had quarreled with its military leader, Enver Pasha, he was almost ideally suited for the leadership of the new nationalist movement.

To succeed in reversing the defeat and avoiding partition, Kemal had in the first place to organize military resistance and wage war against foreign occupation. But along with the fighting went a diplomatic campaign, no less successful, which is often overlooked. The fruits of military victory in the years 1919 to 1922 could never have been gathered without an astute foreign policy which paralleled the military campaigns, aided them, and won international recognition of the results. The bases of foreign policy were simple—to create an independent and sovereign Turkey for the Turks. To Kemal and his followers this meant not only territorial unity, but complete abolition of all such extraterritorial rights in matters of justice, taxation, and economic exploitation as foreigners had enjoyed, and remarkably abused, under the Ottoman empire. The emphasis on territorial integrity, and absolute Turkish sovereignty within the state, was so constant as to appear monotonous, but Kemal's diplomacy is understandable only as the pursuit of these objectives.

His diplomacy utilized every possible advantage presented by the postwar situation. As best he could, Kemal exploited the divergence of policy between Britain, France, and Italy, and the greater chasm that separated the Western Powers from Soviet Russia. Sometimes Turkish action helped to increase the differences. Kemal would negotiate alternately with Russia or the West, or simultaneously with both; whatever advantages he won on one side increased his bargaining power on the other. At times it looked as if Kemal were the most apt pupil of the nineteenth century Ottoman diplomats who tried to find salvation by

---

[2] See Jean Deny, "Souvenirs du Gazi Mustafa Kemâl Pacha," *Revue des études islamiques* (1927), Cahiers 1 to 3, *passim*, on the war and early armistice periods.

playing one Power against another. There was, however, a significant difference. Ottoman diplomacy had to the end attempted to use Europe's quarrels to preserve a sprawling and heterogeneous empire. The nationalists from the start limited their aim to the preservation of control and complete sovereignty only over those areas which were predominantly Turkish in character. Nationalist diplomacy used all means possible to attain these limited but almost rigid objectives. Its workings can be understood only by following the sequence of events from the establishment of nationalist foreign policy in 1919 to the triumph of its diplomacy at Lausanne in 1923.[3]

I

When Husein Rauf [Orbay], Ottoman minister of marine, signed the Mudros armistice on October 30, 1918, most of the Arab portions of the empire were already under British and Arab control. The armistice terms[4] opened the Straits to the Allies, and permitted them further to occupy any strategic points should Allied security be threatened. The Ottoman army was to be demobilized, except for units necessary to frontier surveillance and internal order. Soon thereafter Allied warships anchored off Istanbul and Allied High Commissioners took up residence there, while British forces not only occupied Dardanelles forts, but pressed forward in the Mosul province against the vain protests of Turkish army commanders.[5] French troops later replaced the British in

[3] In view of the lack of documentary material from the Turkish archives, and of the lack of important memoirs by leading diplomats, it is not yet possible to write the full story of Turkish diplomacy, particularly in the difficult and often disorganized early years. Very little information is available on the exact processes of policy formulation, or on the correspondence between the capital and the diplomats charged with executing the policy. Various books attempt to survey the development of Turkish foreign policy in general, but none is completely satisfactory. All are lacking in diplomatic detail and documentary evidence. Among the more useful are three theses: Frédéric Abelous, *L'évolution de la Turquie dans ses rapports avec les étrangers* (Toulouse, 1928), mostly on the capitulations and rather anti-Ankara; S. Reşat Sagay, *La nouvelle Turquie et la communauté internationale* (Strasbourg, 1936), a fairly good summary of foreign policy; Edward R. Vere-Hodge, *Turkish Foreign Policy 1918-1948* (Ambilly-Annemasse, 1950), concentrating on post-1923. Kurt Ziemke, *Die neue Türkei, 1914-1929* (Stuttgart, 1930) is perhaps the best general treatment. Arnold J. Toynbee, *The Western Question in Greece and Turkey*, 2nd ed. (London, 1923) offers a good background, though diplomacy is not its central theme. Among the most useful but most disappointing studies is Yusuf Hikmet [Bayur], *Yeni Türkiye Devletinin Harici Siyaseti* [The Foreign Policy of the New Turkish State] (Istanbul, 1934), which lists among its sources the archives of the Sublime Porte for the armistice period, and the files of the Representative Committee and of the Foreign Ministry, but cites few documents from any of these sources and gives few details on policy formulation or its execution.

[4] Text in Eliot G. Mears, *Modern Turkey* (New York, 1924), pp. 624-626.

[5] Here Turkish officers, like Kemal, tried to hold the armistice line, giving rise to a

Syria and Cilicia, while Allied armistice control officers and military units occupied various Anatolian cities. British forces were also in the Transcaucasus, where the Russian collapse had allowed Georgia, Azerbaijan, and Armenia to spring up as independent states. Ottoman armies had to retire from this region, where they had at one point in 1918 advanced as far as Baku, and where the districts of Kars, Ardahan, and Batum had voted for union with Turkey.[6]

Nominal authority over the Ottoman Empire was still exercised by the cabinet of Damad Ferid Pasha at Istanbul. To nationalist Turks, however, he appeared too Anglophile, and almost completely subservient to the High Commissioners. There was as yet no organized nationalist movement, but rather a great war-weariness in the empire which had fought the Italians, the Balkan League, and the Allies since 1911. At first the Allied control officers had little trouble with Turkish demobilization. Some of the educated Turks hoped to save their country under an American mandate. A cohesive nationalist movement did not arise until the Allies themselves provided the impetus. Toward the end of April 1919, Italian troops landed at Antalya [Adalia] in an effort to secure territory in southwest Turkey promised them by the secret treaty of St. Jean de Maurienne. This provoked far less of a nationalist reaction than the landing of Greek troops at Izmir on May 15 following.

The fateful acquiescence by Lloyd George and the Supreme Council in Paris in the desires of the Greek premier Venizelos to recapture Byzantine hegemony in those fertile areas of western Anatolia which still had a large Greek Orthodox population had explosive consequences. Ostensibly an Allied occupation, in accordance with the terms of Mudros, the landing was in fact purely Greek. To the Anatolian Turk this was the supreme indignity—that a subject and minority element, fundamentally considered second-class subjects of the Sultan, should rule him or part of his land. Knots of local nationalist resistance sprang up where there were no organized elements of the Ottoman army such as still existed in eastern Anatolia. With the arrival of Mustafa Kemal in Anatolia, four days after the Greek landing, began the painful process of incorporating such groups into a nationalist movement which produced an army, a *de facto* government, and a foreign policy. Kemal had been in Istanbul in the spring of 1919, trying to reinvigorate the Ottoman

---

seven-year controversy with Britain. Turkish documents in *La question de Mossoul de la signature du traité d'armistice de Moudros . . . au 1re* [sic] *Mars 1925* (Constantinople, 1925), pp. 8-73.

[6] Chicherin had already protested the Baku advance and the plebiscite: Degras, I, 83, 102, 109-110, 120-121.

government, when he was appointed inspector of the Third Army, stationed at Erzerum and Sivas. As rapidly as possible he left the Allied-controlled capital, never to return until long after the republic was established. His landing at Samsun on May 19, 1919 marks in Turkish hagiography the beginning of the nationalist movement.

Kemal's immediate aim was to organize military resistance to the partition of Turkey. This necessitated the creation of some unified nationalist authority in Anatolia. Kemal later said that his aim already extended to the creation of a new and independent Turkish state, since continued allegiance to the Sultan's government was unacceptable to him.[7] He could not yet announce such views publicly, but his actions soon led to a complete break with Istanbul. Disregarding an order of recall, Kemal resigned his commission. During the summer of 1919 his leadership produced the Representative Committee, the basis of a foreign policy, and the beginnings of direct though irregular contact with foreign Powers. Two nationalist congresses, one held at Erzerum in late July and the second at Sivas in early September, were the instrumentalities through which this was achieved. Though only the eastern provinces were represented at Erzerum, the Sivas congress brought together elected delegates from all Anatolia. The Union for the Defense of the Rights of Anatolia and Rumelia was formed in consequence. Each congress chose a Representative Committee with Kemal as president. The Representative Committee after Sivas began to function as the executive authority of the national will, and in its name Kemal signed telegrams and conferred with foreign representatives.

On September 9 the Sivas congress issued a declaration elaborating resolutions already passed at Erzerum which, with slight modifications, stated the foreign policy thereafter followed by the nationalists.[8] All Turkish territory inside the armistice frontiers was regarded as an indivisible whole within which no foreign intervention should be allowed, nor any independent Greek or Armenian state. The Muslim majority, "a veritable fraternity," would grant no special status to non-Muslim

---

[7] Mustafa Kemal [Atatürk], *A Speech Delivered by Ghazi Mustapha Kemal . . . October, 1927* (Leipzig, 1929), p. 17. This speech to the Peoples' Party Congress reviews the nationalist movement from 1919 to 1924, and is Kemal's self-justification, partly against the attacks of domestic opponents. It contains important information on foreign policy and its execution, though domestic matters occupy more of its 700-odd pages. Many documents are included *in extenso.*

[8] Text of Erzerum resolutions in Gotthard Jäschke, "Zur Geschichte des türkischen Nationalpakts," *Mitteilungen des Seminars für orientalischen Sprachen,* XXXVI (1933), II, 107-116; summary in Société pour l'étude de l'histoire turque, *Histoire de la république turque* (Istanbul, 1935), p. 38. Sivas declaration in Mears, *Modern Turkey,* pp. 627-628.

minorities such as the Ottoman system had permitted. No mandate or protectorate over Turkey would be considered. Foreign scientific or economic assistance would be accepted only if it were untainted with imperialism. The national will must control the Sultan's government, which should convoke a National Assembly. Though the Sivas declaration still considered the Sultan's government to be the lawful one, it rejected Istanbul's policy of acquiescence to Allied demands.

Most of these ideas were basically Kemal's, though he was no ardent supporter of the Califate and Sultanate. Defense of these institutions was mentioned in the Sivas declaration to satisfy the generally more conservative Turkish opinion, which Kemal could not afford to antagonize until his victories ended the crisis of foreign invasion. Kemal's major insistence was always on national and popular sovereignty. As early as June 3, 1919, he declared in a circular telegram to Anatolian officials that Turkey must have complete independence, and "the majority in the purely national districts of the country shall not be sacrificed in favor of the minority."[9] In August he stated that "we prefer that our negotiations and relations with foreign countries shall be conducted in the name of the nation, founded on the proceedings of the Congress."[10] Soon after, still not attacking the Sultan, he asserted that until a government with the confidence of the people should be formed, the Representative Committee would "remain in office and continue to conduct the affairs of the nation."[11]

It is a question as to how far Kemal in the early days was willing to go in accepting foreign aid of some sort. He proposed at the Erzerum congress that help be accepted from a Great Power with no imperialist interests, presumably meaning the United States, but refused to name that country when the resentment of Anatolian Turks against American support for an independent Armenia was expressed.[12] The Sivas congress debated at length a possible American mandate over all Turkey, evidently after reports by Istanbul delegates of conversations with Wilson's King-Crane commission. Kemal apparently opposed an American mandate, but was interested in possible American support for Turkish independence.[13] When the Harbord Commission in September passed through Sivas on its whirlwind trip to investigate a possible Armenian

[9] Kemal, *Speech*, p. 29.   [10] *ibid.*, pp. 91-92.   [11] *ibid.*, pp. 125-126.
[12] Halidé Edib [Adivar], *The Turkish Ordeal* (New York, 1928), p. 16.
[13] Kemal, *Speech*, pp. 77-100. The King-Crane commission reported that the Sivas congress was expected to declare for an American mandate: "First Publication of the King-Crane Report on the Near East," *Editor and Publisher*, LV:27, 2nd section (December 2, 1922), p. 17.

mandate, Kemal talked with General Harbord. Kemal says only that Harbord was convinced of the justice of the nationalist program.[14] But Harbord reported that Kemal said his aim was "the preservation of the Empire under a mandatory of a single disinterested power, preferably America," and wanted "the aid of an impartial foreign country."[15] Later in 1919 Kemal conferred with M. Georges Picot at Sivas, reportedly proposing to him a French economic "mandate" over Turkey if France handed back Cilicia.[16] All such ideas were undoubtedly tentative, explored as possible means to combat the Greeks and their British backers, and were abandoned as the nationalists gained momentum.

Such reports make it clear that Kemal, from the very beginning, tried to establish contact, however informal and irregular, with the Allied Powers and to win their recognition for the nationalist program. He and other nationalists saw various Allied control officers and special diplomatic agents. On many occasions in 1919 he assured his countrymen that British, French, Italian and American representatives had approved the nationalist aims, or had said that they would not interfere with the nationalist movement; that their representatives at Sivas had reported favorably to their governments; that close relations were already established.[17] Kemal exaggerated to impress the Turks and to win followers but such declarations prove his consciousness of the necessity for a nationalist diplomatic offensive. Kemal directly informed the Great

[14] Kemal, *Speech*, p. 150; Gasi Mustafa Kemal Pascha, *Die neue Türkei, 1919-1927*, III, *Die Dokumente zur Rede* (Leipzig, 1927?), no. 106.

[15] Maj.-Gen. James G. Harbord, "American Military Mission to Armenia," *International Conciliation*, CLI (June 1920), 294-295. It is perhaps significant that Kemal in October 1919, replied to all the written questions of a Turkish journalist of Istanbul except "What was your interview with General Harbord about?" Kemal, *Dokumente*, no. 144.

[16] Comte Roger de Gontaut-Biron et L. Le Révérend, *D'Angora à Lausanne* (Paris, 1924), pp. 12, 204.

[17] Kemal, *Speech*, pp. 136-137, 147-148, 151, 154, 156; Kemal, *Dokumente*, nos. 43-45, 106. A reliable account from the other side is in A. Rawlinson, *Adventures in the Near East, 1918-1922* (London, 1923), pp. 188-190, 231-232. Col. Rawlinson saw Kemal often at Erzerum in 1919, appreciated his character and aims, and reported personally to Lord Curzon on the Erzerum resolutions. Curzon naturally would accord the nationalists no recognition, but sent Rawlinson back to discover unofficially from Kemal what peace terms they might accept. Rawlinson returned ostensibly as an Allied control officer. *Ibid.*, pp. 251-252. General Harbord concluded even this early that Kemal was "no cheap political adventurer," and that his movement had to be taken seriously: Maj.-Gen. James G. Harbord, "Mustafa Kemal Pasha and His Party," *World's Work* XL (June 1920), 188. Harbord's official report included a long letter by Kemal explaining his aims, the Sivas declaration, and a letter from Kemal and Husein Rauf to the U.S. Senate asking that an American committee visit Turkey before the peace treaty was signed: U.S. American Military Mission to Armenia, *Conditions in the Near East. Report . . . by Maj.-Gen. James G. Harbord* (Washington, 1920, 66th Congress, 2nd Session, Senate Document no. 266), pp. 29-40.

Powers on September 11 that Damad Ferid's government was an illegal tyranny, and that the delegation which it had sent to Paris did not represent the nation.[18] British and French agents in Turkey in 1919 recognized that there were already, in fact, two governments in that country.[19]

Kemal refused to concede that there were two governments. Maintaining that the national will was supreme, and the Representative Committee was its spokesman, he tried to capture control of the Istanbul government for the nationalists, and thus to create and guide a unified Turkish foreign policy. This was particularly important because the Allied peace treaty with Turkey was still under discussion. Damad Ferid had led a delegation from Istanbul to Paris in June, where his carefully reasoned statement to the Supreme Council was rebuffed with biting words on the iniquities of the Turks. From Sivas Kemal reproached Damad Ferid with subservience, and set about to cause his downfall. On September 11 he cut off telegraphic communication with the Porte. "This is the last warning we shall give you," said Kemal before the Sivas congress. "The attitude that the nation will take up in the future will be explained to the representatives of the Entente through the foreign officers who are among us."[20] This pressure forced Damad Ferid out at the start of October. Ali Riza, more sympathetic to the nationalists, replaced him as grand vizier.

Thereupon Kemal tried to force his foreign policy upon the new Istanbul Cabinet. To Ali Riza he explained his foreign relations thus far as having "no official diplomatic character. They only consist of certain contacts with different political agents sent by the Allied Powers who, not finding themselves in the capital in the presence of a legitimate government resting on the confidence and strength of the nation, wanted to check the veracity or bad faith of the pronouncements made by the preceding Cabinet against the national forces. In maintaining these relations, the aim we follow is exclusively to make known the national aspirations, the extent and power of the national organizations, so as to gain the respect and confidence of foreign countries."[21] Now he demanded that Ali Riza recognize the nationalist movement, make no binding decisions until a genuine national assembly had met, and choose new delegates to the peace conference from among the nationalists.[22] Salih Pasha,

[18] Kemal, *Dokumente*, no. 97, annex 1.
[19] Kemal, *Speech*, p. 262; Hikmet, *Haricî Siyaseti*, p. 38.
[20] Kemal, *Speech*, p. 121.
[21] Kemal, *Dokumente*, no. 132; see also no. 143.
[22] *ibid.*, no. 128; Kemal, *Speech*, p. 168.

minister of marine in the new Cabinet, was authorized to confer with Kemal. Their three-day conference produced essential agreement. Salih accepted the main points of the Sivas declaration, and the demand that delegates to Paris be approved by the Representative Committee. Salih could not, however, persuade his Cabinet to agree, perhaps because of Allied pressure.[23] The chance for immediate coordination on foreign policy between Kemal and the Sultan's government was thus lost.

Elections for a new parliament were, however, authorized by Mehmet VI. A large nationalist majority was returned. Kemal thereupon gathered most of the deputies together at Ankara, to which he moved his head-quarters from Sivas in late December 1919, to be able to use the railroad to Istanbul. The deputies subscribed to a National Pact, based on the Sivas declaration, which Kemal presented to them; it became for the future the fixed basis of nationalist foreign policy. Most of the deputies led by Rauf, a member of the Representative Committee since the beginning, left for Istanbul in early January, though Kemal did not go because of the danger to him. There the parliament met formally, voting on January 28, 1920, to confirm the National Pact. The Allies were thus notified of the Turkish demands which, in Kemal's view, had to serve as the basis for peace negotiations.[24]

The National Pact emphasized complete independence—territorial, political, judicial and economic; nothing like the capitulations would be accepted. There was no mention now of foreign assistance, as there had had been at Sivas. The territorial claims were extended to include Kurdish areas beyond the armistice lines, while plebiscites were demanded for Kars, Ardahan, Batum and Western Thrace. Only regions with an Arab majority were specifically excluded. Minorities in Turkey would have no special privileges beyond the rights commonly recognized in the minority treaties of the peace settlement. If Istanbul, seat of the Sultanate and Califate, were secure, regulations on traffic through the Bosporus could be made jointly by Turkey and other interested Powers. These principles, said the preamble, represented "the maximum of sacrifice which can be undertaken in order to achieve a just and lasting peace." It was Turkey for the Turks (and Kurds).

Though the pact lived on, the parliament which voted it was soon killed by Allied action. The Western Powers were alarmed not only by

---

[23] *Histoire*, pp. 42-43.

[24] Kemal, *Speech*, p. 306. Texts of the National Pact which differ slightly in translation in *Histoire*, pp. 46-47; Mears, *Modern Turkey*, pp. 629-631; H. W. V. Temperley, *A History of the Peace Conference of Paris*, vi (London, 1924), 605-606.

the Pact's demands, but by the success of nationalist troops in driving the French from Maraş [Marash], news of which burst upon an Allied conference at London in February 1920.[25] The British conceived and executed an Allied military occupation of Istanbul on March 16. Two score prominent nationalist deputies, including Rauf, were deported to Malta, the parliament was dissolved, and Ali Riza dismissed in favor of the more pliable Damad Ferid. Those deputies who could escaped to rejoin Kemal in Ankara. The nationalists jailed a few British armistice control officers as hostages. Kemal meanwhile despatched vigorous protests against the British occupation to many foreign Powers. It is significant that he did this through the Italian representative at Antalya. He was already receiving private assurances from French and Italian officials that British policy was not theirs—that Millerand and Nitti did not agree with Lloyd George.[26]

If the Greek landing of 1919 had created the nationalist movement in Turkey, the British occupation of Istanbul converted the movement into an effective separate government. The establishment of the Ankara government occurred, ironically, at the exact time when Allied statesmen at San Remo were partitioning the Ottoman empire despite the protests of Damad Ferid, whose government declared the nationalists to be rebels. Meeting on April 23, the deputies in Ankara resolved to create the Government of the Grand National Assembly and to secure independence by an honorable peace. They did not declare the Sultan deposed, but called him an Allied prisoner whose acts were therefore invalid. Mustafa Kemal was the next day elected president of the Assembly, and presided also over a council of ministers elected by the Assembly from among its members.[27] This organization was confirmed and elaborated in a law of January 20, 1921, which specifically placed in the Assembly's hands the powers of war and peace, of concluding treaties and receiving foreign diplomats.[28] Though the relations of the Ankara government to Istanbul were ill-defined—inasmuch as the Sultan

---

[25] David Lloyd George, *The Truth About the Peace Treaties* (London, 1938), II, 1285-1294. Lloyd George did not know who Kemal was.

[26] Kemal, *Speech*, pp. 353, 360-362; Kemal, *Dokumente*, no. 229. Count Sforza, Italian High Commissioner in Istanbul early in 1919, had then offered Kemal shelter in the Italian embassy from British arrest: Carlo Sforza, *Makers of Modern Europe* (Indianapolis, 1930), p. 365.

[27] In this period the nationalists used the word *vekil* for minister, which was usually translated as "commissar," "commissary," or "commissioner," probably owing to the Russian example. After Lausanne the translation "minister" became usual. The Foreign Office was often called the "commissariat."

[28] Resolutions of April 23, 1920, and of law of January 20, 1921, in *Histoire*, pp. 52-53 and 83-84 respectively.

was not deposed, Ankara not declared the capital, and the previous constitution not abrogated—the Grand National Assembly was hereafter the real government for most of Turkey. Foreign Powers were notified that it alone represented the people, and that it would "preside over the present and future destiny of Turkey" so long as the unjustified occupation of Istanbul continued.[29]

II

The Government of the Grand National Assembly set out to gain recognition abroad, to negotiate for foreign assistance or the cessation of hostilities, and to carry out by diplomacy wherever possible the stipulations of the National Pact. The task was finished only when the Lausanne treaty was signed in July 1923, but by early 1922 Ankara had won important victories in negotiation both with Russia and the West, and had passed through the first phase of its struggle for international position. Mustafa Kemal was inevitably the leader in this as in military operations, but he now had for the first time an embryonic Foreign Office and a Foreign Minister.

Ankara provided little for the ministries except a central location and a nationalist atmosphere. Space and facilities were scarce. The Foreign Office began life in a room in the agricultural school where Kemal made his headquarters. Here the credentials of the Grand National Assembly's first diplomatic mission were typed on a decrepit machine by Halide Edib [Adivar], the first Turkish woman college graduate. Soon the ministry moved to a larger building once occupied by the Ottoman Public Debt administration. More officials were added: an undersecretary for political affairs, who helped organize the office in the summer of 1920, a legal counselor and others. By November it was found advisable to have a diplomatic agent, Hamid Bey, to represent Ankara in Istanbul, and to deal there with the High Commissioners and other Western representatives.[30]

The foreign service also grew from scratch. Most of the diplomatic

[29] Gotthard Jäschke und Erich Pritsch, *Die Türkei seit dem Weltkriege: Geschichtskalender, 1918-1928* (Berlin, 1929), p. 32; Gaston Gaillard, *The Turks and Europe* (London, 1921), pp. 186-187. See also Donald E. Webster, *The Turkey of Atatürk* (Philadelphia, 1939), p. 86.

[30] Edib, *Turkish Ordeal*, pp. 146-147, 173-174, gives a brief account of the beginnings; she was the typist. See also Berthe Georges-Gaulis, *Angora, Constantinople, Londres* (Paris, 1922), pp. 134-135. Hamid Bey was apparently first known in Istanbul as vice-president of the Red Crescent: Hikmet, *Harici Siyaseti*, p. 83; Jäschke, *Die Türkei*, p. 41. This anomalous Foreign Office post in Istanbul continued to exist even after Ankara became capital of the new republic.

agents sent out from Ankara in the next few years were cultured men with education along Western lines, though not trained diplomats from Ottoman days; they were usually lawyers, army officers, or other professional men. One experienced diplomat who joined Kemal in 1919, Ahmed Rustem Bey, had been ambassador in Washington before 1914, but does not appear to have been employed by Ankara for important missions.[31] In these years much important negotiation both abroad and at home was handled by the Foreign Minister himself. Ankara's first official mission, to Moscow, was headed by Bekir Sami, elected Foreign Minister by the Assembly early in May 1920. Bekir Sami was a huge Circassian who had experience in a wide range of civil service posts from the time of Abdülhamid II on, including important provincial governorships. He had been, with Kemal, a member of the original Representative Committee. In May 1920, he set out to Moscow to establish treaty relationships and seek aid in the face of the British occupation of Istanbul.

Kemal later said that the first decision of the Ankara government was to send this mission.[32] He himself wrote to Chicherin, the Soviet commissar for foreign affairs, on April 26, 1920, apparently suggesting some sort of an alliance.[33] The delegation, which included Yusuf Kemal [Tengirşenk], minister of economy, spent two months in the Transcaucasus region, arriving in Moscow toward the end of July.[34] Despite the long history of Russo-Turkish antagonism, it was advantageous at the moment for each to seek support in the other. Each faced the same opponents, and the opponents controlled the Straits. Contact was easier to establish after Denikin's forces in the Caucasus collapsed in December 1919, and after the British took their troops out of the Transcaucasus region except for Batum.[35]

[31] Possibly because he was a Christian Pole turned Muslim. Mufty-Zade Zia, "How the Turks Feel," *Asia*, XXII:11 (November, 1922), p. 861, makes the obvious point that the nationalists no longer used Greeks and Armenians in their foreign service as the Sultans had done.

[32] Kemal, *Speech*, p. 396.

[33] Louis Fischer, *The Soviets in World Affairs* (London, 1930), I, 390. Gotthard Jäschke, "Urkunden I. Der Weg zur russisch-türkischen Freundschaft im Lichte Moskaus," *Die Welt des Islams*, XX (1938), 132, cites notes appended to the Russian translation of Kemal's *Speech* [E. F. Ludšuvejt, ed., *Put Novoi Turtsii 1919-1927*, III (Moscow, 1934)] to indicate that Kemal's letter proposed military cooperation with Russia against "imperialism," and exhibited willingness to see Turkish-speaking Azerbaijan become a Soviet republic.

[34] Hikmet, *Haricî Siyaseti*, p. 63.

[35] The first contacts between the Turkish nationalists and Soviet Russia are not yet clear from the published records. See discussion of the evidence of relations between the two while the Representative Committee guided nationalist affairs in 1919 and early

Though the immediate opponents were the same, the ultimate aims of Moscow and Ankara were quite different. Bolshevik policy conceived of the Turks as the westernmost of a string of Muslim peoples who would be natural allies against the British, and against capitalist imperialism. In December 1917, the Council of Peoples Commissars had issued an appeal for cooperation to the Muslims of Russia, India, Persia, Turkey, and Arabia, simultaneously denouncing all secret treaties partitioning Persia and the Ottoman empire.[36] When the Sivas Congress was meeting Chicherin renewed the appeal directly to the "workers and peasants of Turkey," naming the British as the enemy and denouncing "pasha landlords."[37] Kemal was interested in a national war, not a class war. Chicherin's reply to him of June 2, 1920, was therefore chiefly in terms of cooperation against "foreign imperialism."[38] Chicherin did not mention alliance or military assistance, but proposed immediate establishment of diplomatic relations. He accepted the principles of the National Pact, but tried to reinterpret two of them to Russian advantage: he noted the Assembly's decision "to allow Turkish Armenia, Kurdistan, Lusistan [Lazistan?], the Batum province . . . to decide their own destiny," and introduced the now-familiar claim that the Straits question was "to be submitted to a conference of states bordering on the Black Sea." These demands Kemal eventually succeeded in avoiding. He never accepted a class war, though in reply to Chicherin he was willing to use Bolshevik terminology like "proletarian masses."[39]

By August 24, 1920, Bekir Sami had reached sufficient agreement in Moscow to initial a draft treaty, but the formal signing was delayed for seven months by considerable friction over the Transcaucasus region. This area had for a century been the scene of Russo-Turkish conflict. Now that it was temporarily in the hands of independent Armenia (Republic of Erivan), Georgia, and Azerbaijan, both Turks and Russians sought to

---

1920 in Jäschke, "Der Weg zur russisch-türkischen Freundschaft," *Die Welt des Islams*, XVI (1934), 27 and note 20; *idem.*, "Urkunden I," p. 122, note 3. Several authorities assert that by April, 1920, Ankara and Moscow had already concluded a military convention, providing supplies for the Turks. None cites documents. See, for example, Harold Armstrong, *Turkey in Travail* (London, 1925), p. 116; Toynbee, *Western Question*, p. 367; John Kingsley Birge, *A Guide to Turkish Area Studies* (Washington, 1949), p. 234. Toynbee in *Survey of International Affairs, 1920-1923* (London, 1925), p. 365, mentions even earlier agreements of December 1919, and March 1920, without citing sources or indicating content. Jäschke, "Der Weg," p. 35 and note 76 discusses some of the evidence and seems to discount the likelihood of a military convention.

[36] Text in Degras, I, 15-17. [37] Text, *ibid.*, pp. 164-167.

[38] Text, *ibid.*, pp. 187-188.

[39] Kemal to Chicherin, November 29, 1920, in V. A. Kliuchnikov and A. Sabanin, *Mezhdunarodnaya Politika noveishovo vremeni v dogovorakh, notakh i deklaratsiakh* III (Moscow, 1928), 27-28.

increase their control there, while the Transcaucasus states tried to secure their independence and their borders. Kemal complained to Chicherin in a letter of June 20, 1920, of Armenian attacks on Turkish areas, and asked assistance and mediation.[40] But while Bekir Sami was in Moscow, Russia signed a treaty with Armenia which recognized Armenian control over territory which the Turks considered theirs, involving also Armenian domination of the land route from Turkey to Russia. Chicherin then demanded that the Turks cede territory to Armenia.[41] This demand brought a suspension of Bekir Sami's negotiations. Undoubtedly Kemal was suspicious of Communist aims, and Chicherin wary of aligning Russia with a Turkish regime that still might collapse. Unofficial Bolshevik agents and propagandists had in fact appeared in Ankara and other Anatolian cities by May 1920, though their arguments and literature won few converts.[42] Despite this friction, Chicherin sent a more formal mission to Ankara in October, and the next month the Grand National Assembly authorized diplomatic and consular representation in Russia.[43] Kemal himself characteristically selected Ankara's first ambassador. Removing Ali Fuat from command of troops on the western front for alleged incompetence, he sent him to Moscow. The Assembly confirmed the appointment.[44]

Kemal was always ready to negotiate with the Western Powers as well as with Russia. The defeat of various French units in southern Anatolia had led in May to a twenty-day armistice concluded with French representatives sent to Ankara. Kemal tried to portray this as tacit French recognition of his government.[45] He became convinced that France would desert Britain and evacuate Adana. To put pressure on France, the Turks gave some encouragement to Arab opponents of French control in Syria.[46] But it was difficult to negotiate with the Western Powers in the spring and summer of 1920, when they were elaborating the Treaty of Sèvres

[40] *Hakimiyeti Milliye* (a nationalist paper in Ankara), no. 44, July 8, 1920, quoted in Jäschke, "Der Weg," p. 29.

[41] Hikmet, *Haricî Siyaseti*, p. 64; Kemal, *Speech*, p. 396. Yusuf Kemal brought this demand back to Ankara, which Kemal categorically refused to grant, even in return for Soviet aid: Hikmet, p. 65; Jäschke, "Der Weg," p. 31.

[42] Edib, *Turkish Ordeal*, pp. 170-182; Rawlinson, *Adventures*, p. 295. Actually a Turkish Communist organization had already been formed in Moscow, and in June of 1920 one was started in Ankara. Kemal curbed it in about a year, and undermined it by having an "official" Communist party founded, which however proclaimed the virtues of Islam and nationalism: Gotthard Jäschke, "Kommunismus und Islam im türkischen Befreiungskriege," *Die Welt des Islams*, XX (1938), 110-117.

[43] Jäschke, *Die Türkei*, pp. 39, 41.

[44] Kemal, *Speech*, pp. 429-430, 436; Edib, *Turkish Ordeal*, pp. 224-225.

[45] Kemal, *Speech*, pp. 390-391.

[46] King Abdullah, *Memoirs*, ed. by P. P. Graves (London, 1950), pp. 190-192.

that would partition the Ottoman Empire for their own benefit and leave only a section of Anatolia to complete Turkish control. On May 11, 1920, a draft of the proposed treaty was handed to the Istanbul government. A month thereafter the Allied ministers agreed, at the Hythe conference, to a Greek offensive to prevent the Turkish nationalist forces from reaching the Straits and blocking the partition of Turkey. News of the treaty, and the Greek war, naturally spurred the nationalists to renewed opposition. Though their ill-equipped troops had to retire before the Greek drives, their deputies in the Grand National Assembly took an oath to support the National Pact in the face of the treaty, and further informed the Powers that no agreements concluded by the Istanbul government since the British occupation could be valid.[47] Damad Ferid also protested the treaty, in the name of the Sultan's government, at the Spa conference in July, but he was powerless to do more, since in Istanbul his government could not escape Allied control. The Allied ministers dismissed his protests, and obliged his representatives to sign at Sèvres on August 10, 1920. On the same day Britain, France, and Italy concluded the Tripartite Treaty, giving the latter two Powers extensive zones of influence in Anatolia.[48]

Since negotiations with Moscow were deadlocked because of Armenia, and since Sèvres created an independent Armenia and an autonomous Kurdistan in eastern Anatolia, the nationalists set out to secure their eastern frontier by force. During the fall and winter of 1920 Moscow and Ankara cooperated to exclude all Western Powers from the settlement of the area, but competed in extending their own control.[49] Azerbaijan was by then already Soviet-dominated, and the last British troops evacuated Batum in July. Ankara then sent an ultimatum to Armenia. General Kâzim Karabekir, at thirty-eight as outstanding in the nationalist military leadership as he was famous for his paternal care of hundreds of Turkish orphans, delivered an attack from Erzerum in late September that swept in six weeks through Kars to Alexandropol.[50] Moscow then engineered a coup to capture the Armenian government, which forth-

[47] *Histoire*, p. 63; Webster, *Turkey of Atatürk*, p. 86. The *Hakimiyeti Milliye* of Ankara published the terms of Sèvres under the headline "How They Tear Us Apart," and observed further that the treaty could not be constitutionally ratified because Istanbul had no parliament: Jäschke, *Die Türkei*, pp. 36, 38.

[48] Text of Sèvres in Great Britain, Treaty Series, 1920, no. 11 (Cmd. 964), and of the Tripartite Agreement, no. 12 (Cmd. 963).

[49] On events in this region see Toynbee, *Survey . . . 1920-1923*, pp. 361-376.

[50] Presumably there were Turkish-Soviet conferences during the campaign about aims in the Transcaucasus: *ibid.*, p. 368. On Kâzim Karabekir in this period: Edib, *Turkish Ordeal*, pp. 203, 400-403; Rawlinson, *Adventures*, pp. 180-181, 282-284; Berthe Georges-Gaulis, *La nouvelle Turquie* (Paris, 1924), p. 97.

with made peace to forestall any further Turkish advance. Kâzim Karabekir signed Ankara's first international treaty at Alexandropol [Gümrü]
on December 2, 1920.[51] It returned the district of Kars to Turkish control, and again made possible direct land connection to Russia. Bekir Sami
and Yusuf Kemal soon thereafter started for Moscow to pick up the
threads of the suspended negotiations.[52]

The developing Russian-Turkish friendship meanwhile survived two
potential threats. The first was the appearance of Enver Pasha in Moscow. There the former Ottoman war minister tried to pose as the real
representative of Turkey, to discredit Kemal, and to win Soviet backing
for his own schemes. The Bolsheviks, unwilling to lose Kemal's possible
help against Britain, and suspicious of the effect on their own Turkish-
speaking millions of Enver's pan-Turanian ideas, gave the latter little
encouragement.[53] The second was the drive of the Comintern to dominate
the Muslims of Asia, dramatically expressed in the Congress of Eastern
Peoples held at Baku just as Kâzim Karabekir was about to start his
offensive against Armenia, not far off. Of the nearly 2,000 delegates
about a third were non-Communist, representing peoples whose anti-
imperialist nationalism the Comintern hoped to exploit. Most of the 235
Turks present were of this group, many of them middle-class. Zinoviev,
president of the Congress, denounced them as Calif-supporters, and
criticized the "pseudo-Soviets such as are now sometimes being offered
to you in Turkey." But he recognized that the Turks, like the Communists, opposed Britain. "We give patient aid," said Zinoviev, "to groups
of persons who do not believe in our ideas, who are even opposed to us
on some points. In the same way the Soviet government in Turkey sup-
ports Kemal. Never for one moment do we forget that the movement
headed by Kemal is not a Communist movement. We know it."[54]

[51] A. Poidebard, ed., *La Transcaucase et la République d'Arménie dans les textes
diplomatiques . . . 1919-1921* (Paris, 1924), pp. 56-58, giving the treaty text from an
Armenian source. Gotthard Jäschke, "Die türkische-armenische Grenze und der Friedens-
vertrag von Gümrü (Alexandropol)," *Mitteilungen des Seminars für orientalischen
Sprachen*, XXXV (1932), II, 167-171, 173-176, gives a partial text from a Turkish source.
See also *Histoire*, p. 71; Kemal, *Speech*, p. 418.

[52] Hikmet, *Harici Siyaseti*, p. 66.

[53] Fischer, *Soviets in World Affairs*, I, 384-390, on Enver in Russia. Enver was the
subject of fantastic speculation and rumor, portrayed both as a Soviet tool against Kemal
and a Turkish tool against Moscow. See reports in *Oriente Moderno*, I, II (1921-1923),
passim.

[54] G. Zinoviev, "Bolshevist Aims in Asia," *Current History*, XIII, part 2, no. 3 (March
1921), 465; Michael T. Florinsky, *World Revolution and the* USSR (New York, 1933),
pp. 57-62. Enver sent a message to the Congress using Communist terminology: "W,"
"Les relations russo-turques depuis l'avènement du Bolchévisme," *Revue du monde
musulman*, LII (1922), 197, giving part of the text. Jäschke, "Der Weg," pp. 29-30,

While renewed Russo-Turkish negotiations were in prospect, opportunity came to Kemal also at the start of 1921 for conversations with the West. Turkish success against Armenia, coupled with the first victory over the Greeks at Inönü in January 1921, worried the Allied ministers, who invited the governments of Athens and Istanbul to a conference at London in February. The Ottoman delegation, they said, should include plenipotentiaries from Ankara. This was a back-handed recognition of his government which Kemal refused to accept. He asserted in a lengthy telegraphic correspondence with Tevfik, the new grand vizier in Istanbul, that only the Grand National Assembly represented Turkey, and that it demanded a direct invitation. To Tevfik's arguments that the two governments had identical aims, and that the Sultan had to maintain his government in Istanbul lest the Allies completely control the city, Kemal replied that the aims might be similar, but free Turkey could never subordinate itself to occupied Turkey.[55] In Ankara there was debate as to whether the London invitation were not merely a ruse to enable the Greeks to recover from their Inönü defeat.[56] Kemal swung the Assembly to his views, which were not those of the extremists: a delegation should set out but should not go to London unless a direct invitation was received. Italy provided a torpedo boat at Antalya to take the delegation to Brindisi. In Rome the nationalists waited until Lloyd George sent a direct invitation through Count Sforza, whose sympathy for the nationalists had frequently been expressed.[57]

Bekir Sami had just returned from Moscow when he set out as head of the new mission to London. His stay in Russia had disillusioned him. He now looked upon the Soviet government as rule by an autocratic minority, insincere in its professions of international goodwill and regard for minority rights.[58] At London his consequent desire to reach agreement with the West was quite apparent, though the demands he presented to the conference were still those of the National Pact. By agreement, Bekir Sami spoke for the Istanbul delegation as well as his own—an exhibition of harmony that astounded the Allied ministers, but reflected the relative power of the two factions. The Allies offered two schemes involving modifications of Sèvres, thereby admitting that Kemal's success so far

---

says that Bekir Sami and Yusuf Kemal attended the Congress on their return trip from Moscow; also *Oriente Moderno*, I:2 (July 1921), 87-88.

[55] Kemal, *Speech*, pp. 469-490.   [56] Edib, *Turkish Ordeal*, p. 243.

[57] Jäschke, *Die Türkei*, pp. 45-46; Kemal, *Speech*, p. 490; Count Carlo Sforza, *Diplomatic Europe Since the Treaty of Versailles* (New Haven, 1928), pp. 51-66, summarizing his Turcophil views. Ankara already had diplomatic agents in Rome and Paris.

[58] Edib, *Turkish Ordeal*, pp. 242-243.

rendered the whole treaty unenforceable. Bekir Sami accepted one scheme with reservations, on instructions from Kemal, and the other *ad referendum*. The Greeks, however, refused to consider modifications of their rights under Sèvres, and launched a new offensive against Ankara at the end of March. Ankara was thereby spared the necessity of refusing proposals which did not meet all the National Pact's demands.[59]

Bekir Sami's success at London was in widening the breach among the Allies by private negotiation with Lloyd George, Briand, and Sforza. His efforts to persuade Lloyd George to call off the Greeks were fruitless; so also his reported proposal that Britain support an anti-Bolshevik union of Turkey and the Caucasus peoples. He did arrange with Lloyd George a mutual exchange of prisoners.[60] With Briand and Sforza he was able to sign formal treaties providing for withdrawal of French and Italian troops from large sections of Anatolia in return for Turkish economic concessions. Briand also agreed to a Syrian-Turkish frontier south of that of Sèvres, while Sforza promised support at the peace settlement for Turkish possession of Izmir and Thrace.[61] France and Italy had deserted the British-backed Greeks for the Turks.

But Bekir Sami's success was also his failure. Things looked different to him than to Kemal and many other nationalists. On his return home Bekir Sami was attacked by Kemal and the Assembly for having made economic concessions which in effect paralleled the zones of the Tripartite Treaty. France and Italy were attacked in the nationalist press as still colonial-minded. Bekir Sami's attitude toward Russia was also questioned; it was important not to alienate this source of help. Kemal insisted that Bekir Sami resign as Foreign Minister, saying he had exceeded his instructions. The Assembly rejected the French treaty and did not even consider the one with Italy. A strong group in the Assembly professed themselves "Easterners," placing more hope in a Russian orientation than in negotiation with the West.[62] Despite his forced resignation, however,

[59] On the London conference see *Oriente Moderno*, I:7 (December 15, 1921), 390-393, including Bekir Sami's demands; Kemal, *Speech*, pp. 490-491; Toynbee, *Western Question*, pp. 93-97; Edouard Driault et Michel Lhéritier, *Histoire diplomatique de la Grèce de 1821 à nos jours*, V (Paris, 1926), 389-395.

[60] Kemal, *Speech*, pp. 497-498; Edib, *Turkish Ordeal*, pp. 254-255. A report of these conversations leaked to Krassin and Chicherin, perhaps in a British effort to block any Turkish-Russian agreement. Britain and Russia were at this time fighting for influence over Muslims from Turkey to China, and indulging in recriminations about attempts to influence the Turkish nationalists. See Degras, I, 230-233.

[61] Texts in *Oriente Moderno*, I:2 (July 15, 1921), 79-81, and II:1 (June 15, 1922), 18 respectively.

[62] Kemal, *Speech*, pp. 409-410, 498-499; *Oriente Moderno*, I:1 (June 15, 1921), 21-23; "W," in *Revue du monde musulman*, LII, 201-202; Michel Paillarès, *Le*

Bekir Sami's work was not lost. The prisoner-exchange agreement was renegotiated with Britain in the fall, the Italians began in June to evacuate forces from Antalya, and the French exhibited eagerness for new conversations. After the London conference it was obvious that Ankara spoke for the Turks, while the Istanbul government represented only the Sultan. Though the Western Powers recognized Istanbul, they had to deal with Ankara to get results.

Mustafa Kemal had in the previous fall gained the legal right to nominate ministers to the Assembly for election, thereby assuring his personal control over top-level personnel. He thus hand-picked Yusuf Kemal, minister of economy, to be Bekir Sami's successor as Foreign Minister.[63] Yusuf Kemal had been obliged in his youth to turn from medicine to law because of severe injury to his right hand. This accident gave the nationalists a successful negotiator with a lawyer's skill in settling cases out of court. Trained at the universities of Istanbul and Paris, Yusuf Kemal was at home in both French and English. He did not have the practiced finesse of the older Bekir Sami, but his direct approach, typical of the nationalist leaders, who were, like him, all about forty years old, enabled him to drive hard bargains. He was a "shirt-sleeve" diplomat, as one of his compatriots called him.[64]

When the Assembly confirmed his appointment as Foreign Minister in May 1921, Yusuf Kemal had not yet returned from Moscow, where he had successfully conducted the final negotiations for a treaty at the same time as Bekir Sami was in London. The Russo-Turkish treaty had threatened to founder on arguments over Batum, which in early 1921 was controlled by Menshevik Georgia. As Bolshevik troops advanced against this last non-Soviet Transcaucasus state, Ankara demanded territory from Georgia by ultimatum. The Georgian ambassador in Ankara, Mdivani, agreed to Turkish occupation of Batum, presumably to keep it out of Bolshevik hands. Kâzim Karabekir thereupon led Turkish troops into the city on March 11, preceding by a week the arrival of Red troops, with whom serious clashes were narrowly avoided.[65] This potential

Kémalisme devant les Alliés (Constantinople, 1922), pp. 355-356. Sforza, Diplomatic Europe, p. 63, confirms Kemal's analysis of the significance of the economic concessions.

[63] Kemal, Speech, pp. 427-428; Jäschke, Die Türkei, p. 49.

[64] Mufty-Zade Zia, "How the Turks Feel," p. 860; Ibrahim A. Gövsa, Türk Meşhurlari Ansiklopedisi [Encyclopedia of Turkish Notables] (n.p., n.d.), p. 378; Mehmet Zeki, Encyclopédie Biographique de la Turquie (Istanbul, 1932), pp. 37-38; Toynbee, Western Question, p. 178; Clair Price, "Mustafa Kemal and the Angora Government," Current History, XVI (1922), 794-795.

[65] Kemal, Speech, pp. 418-419; Fischer, Soviets in World Affairs, I, 392; Edib, Turkish Ordeal, pp. 240-241; Jäschke, Die Türkei, pp. 45, 47; Toynbee, Survey . . . 1920-1923, pp. 369-370; Hikmet, Haricî Siyaseti, p. 66.

Fashoda was settled by compromise, which Chicherin and Yusuf Kemal agreed to make part of the treaty signed on March 16, 1921.[66]

For Chicherin this treaty may have been only one of several to secure anti-British friends; the preamble noted Turkish-Russian "solidarity in the struggle against imperialism." For Ankara, the Moscow treaty was a major victory, securing a favorable and stable eastern frontier and strengthening its hand for bargaining with the West. Yusuf Kemal had to leave Batum to Soviet Georgia, but with stipulations of broad local autonomy and free transit for Turkish goods. Kars and Ardahan were included within Turkey. Chicherin agreed that "Turkey" meant the territories specified in the National Pact, and promised that Russia would recognize no international agreements concerning Turkey not recognized by the Grand National Assembly. Each agreed to recognize no treaties imposed on the other. Russia renounced all capitulatory rights. Yusuf Kemal's greatest concession was to agree that, Istanbul being secure, the Straits regime should be determined by the littoral states of the Black Sea. So long as British warships controlled the Straits and Greek troops attacked, the concession was not surprising, though at Lausanne the Turks successfully avoided implementation of this clause.

The mutual suspicion still existing was revealed by Article 8, wherein each signatory promised to permit on its soil no group aiming at the overthrow of the other government. For Moscow, this was protection against pan-Turanian agitation among Russia's millions of Turkish subjects; for Ankara, protection against Bolshevik conspiracy based in the Caucasus or elsewhere. There was no specific provision against propaganda activity. Communist propaganda was in fact attempted in Turkey, but with little success. Kemal discouraged it by prison and other means, for which he was denounced at the third Comintern Congress in 1921 and, the next year at the second Congress of Communist Labor Unions.[67] This ideological friction did not seriously disturb governmental relations, and Moscow continued to provide military supplies to the Turks in amounts which, to this day, have not been disclosed.[68]

[66] Text in Degras, I, 237-242, from the Russian, and in *Oriente Moderno*, I:6 (November 15, 1921), 340-343, from the Turkish.

[67] *Oriente Moderno*, I:3 (August 15, 1921), 154-155 and II:8 (January 15, 1923), 472; Kemal, *Speech*, pp. 427-428; Fischer, *Soviets in World Affairs*, I, 393; "W" in *Revue du monde musulman*, LII, 193, 202; *Current History*, XV:1 (October, 1921), 144; Gotthard Jäschke, "Protest der Türkischen Volkskommunistischen Partei gegen die Regierung der Türkischen Grossen Nationalversammlung," *Die Welt des Islams*, XX (1938), 135-136.

[68] Fischer, *Soviets in World Affairs*, I, 391; Jäschke, *Die Türkei*, p. 141; *Oriente Moderno*, I:5 (October 15, 1921), 283. Kemal makes no mention of military aid, saying only that "Turkish-Russian relations developed very favorably" in 1921. *Speech*, p. 541.

Kemal was never lured by the early friendship with Russia into accept-ing the position of the "Easterners" in foreign policy. Nor was he a "Westerner," but sought constantly to gain advantages from both sides in carrying out the aims of the National Pact. Reviewing the international position of Turkey for the Assembly on March 1, 1921, he stressed his desire for peace and for good relations with both Orient and Occident. He was ready to negotiate with Britain, but reproached British statesmen for pretending not to understand his pacific aims.[69] A second Turkish victory over the Greeks at Inönü, shortly after the Moscow treaty was signed, led the High Commissioners in Istanbul to declare neutrality in the Greek-Turkish struggle and to deny either belligerent entrance into a neutral zone around the Straits. But the only immediate move toward peace was an Allied offer of mediation in June, which the Greeks rejected, knowing that since Constantine's return to the Greek throne France and Italy were becoming increasingly Turcophile. In July the Greeks aimed a new offensive at Ankara.[70]

Until the Greeks could be defeated, or until Kemal could negotiate agreements conforming to the National Pact, his policy was simply to maintain contact with the Western Powers. Bekir Sami was sent on a roving commission to sound out the Western capitals.[71] Meanwhile Kemal and General Harington, the British High Commissioner, were apparently willing to use their correspondence on prisoner exchange to develop a wider canvass of the situation, but as neither would see the other in the role of petitioner the projected meeting fell through.[72] The Italians began to evacuate Antalya also in June, 1921, and pressed again for an agreement like that of Bekir Sami with Sforza, but Kemal was no more willing now than before to accord the economic concessions asked by the Italian agent in Ankara, Tuozzi.[73]

It was with the French, beset by troubles enough in their Syrian man-date and at odds with Britain over many questions, that Ankara first managed to conclude a treaty on its own terms. M. Franklin-Bouillon,

[69] Text in *Asie française*, XXI:193 (June 1921), 251-252.

[70] *Oriente Moderno*, I:7 (December 15, 1921), 395-396.

[71] Jäschke, *Die Türkei*, pp. 50-52. Kemal, *Speech*, pp. 500-501 again accuses Bekir Sami of a peace-at-any-price policy.

[72] Kemal, *Speech*, pp. 541-543; Rawlinson, *Adventures*, pp. 247-248. Litvinov to Curzon, September 27, 1921, says that the Commissariat for Foreign Affairs had arranged British-Turkish conversations in Moscow: Degras, I, 260-261. Relations be-tween the two countries in 1921 were enlivened by the public trial in Ankara of an Oxford-trained Indian Muslim accused of espionage for Britain: Edib, *Turkish Ordeal*, pp. 229-230; Georges-Gaulis, *Angora*, pp. 242-247.

[73] Hikmet, *Harici Siyaseti*, p. 100; *Oriente Moderno*, I:3 (August 15, 1921), 183, and I:8 (January 15, 1922), 469.

president of the Senate foreign relations committee, came to Ankara in June on an "unofficial" mission, and had long talks with Kemal. Franklin-Bouillon wanted to end the hostilities in Cilicia, but only in return for economic concessions and some remnant of capitulatory privileges to protect the great interests of France in Turkish finance, economic development, and French schools and missions. To achieve this, he tried to negotiate on the basis of the abortive Bekir Sami-Briand treaty. This Kemal would not allow. The National Pact, he said, which emphasized "political, economic, legal, military and cultural" independence, must be the starting point. The French envoy was impressed by Kemal's obstinacy. His government was impressed by Kemal's victory over the Greeks in the Sakarya battle at the end of August, which repulsed the most serious military threat to Ankara. The Treaty of Ankara was therefore signed on October 20, 1921, marking as great a triumph for Turkish diplomacy as the Treaty of Moscow.[74]

The treaty provided that hostilities cease immediately, and that a new frontier between Turkey and Syria revise the line drawn at Sèvres to leave Cilicia and most of the Bagdad Railway track in Turkish hands. As he had been obliged to yield Batum to Georgia, so Yusuf Kemal's greatest concession here was to leave Alexandretta to Syria, but with guarantees of a special regime in which Turkish should be an official language, and with a promise by Franklin-Bouillon to try to arrange for a local flag incorporating the Turkish flag.[75] Yusuf Kemal avoided giving France any guarantees on economic concessions or minority rights which would limit Turkish sovereignty. By the Treaty of Ankara the Turks gained recognition of the Government of the Grand National Assembly by France and a bilateral revision of Sèvres which was essentially a separate peace with France behind Britain's back.[76] Many thousands of Turkish troops were now free to move against the Greeks, while the French turned over to Ankara quantities of military supplies.[77] Turkish-French relations were henceforth close, and Franklin-Bouillon continued to shuttle back and forth until the final armistice.

[74] Kemal, *Speech*, pp. 523-527; *Oriente Moderno*, 1:3 (August 15, 1921), 152. During this period the French were suspected of encouraging the Turks to reject any Allied mediation offers: Toynbee, *Western Question*, pp. 100-101. The Turks rebuffed British attempts to frustrate the conclusion of the treaty by hinting through the Japanese High Commissioner that they were ready to recognize the National Pact: Hikmet, *Harici Siyaseti*, p. 100.

[75] The Turks never ceased to insist that Alexandretta [the Hatay] was a special case, thus laying the basis for its eventual reincorporation into Turkey in 1939.

[76] Curzon protested such recognition and separate peace, which Paris denied was true: Turkey No. 1 (1922), Cmd. 1570.

[77] Gontaut-Biron, *D'Angora à Lausanne*, p. 98.

Not only the British, but also the Russians were worried by Kemal's success in making peace with France. Chicherin demanded explanations, and apparently threatened to use Enver from a Transcaucasus base to weaken or upset the Ankara regime.[78] But Kemal stood firm. So long as he did not also make peace with Britain, his success in negotiation with France served to increase his prestige in Russian eyes. After the Sakarya victory, and just one week before the conclusion of the Franklin-Bouillon agreement, Kâzim Karabekir signed for Turkey the Treaty of Kars with Russia, Georgia, Azerbaijan, and Armenia. Modeled on the Treaty of Moscow, this was a formal confirmation by the Transcaucasus republics under Russian pressure of the new eastern boundary of Turkey, and a declaration of friendship among the signatories.[79] In December 1921, a new Soviet mission arrived in Ankara from the Ukraine, headed by General Frunze, which led to the signing on January 2, 1922, of a Turkish-Ukrainian treaty much like that of Kars.[80] Frunze also arranged for further shipments to Ankara of military supplies, for which Kemal had asked after his Sakarya victory, and he offered military advice for campaigns against the Greeks. Soon after Frunze's three-week mission was over, a new ambassador from Moscow, Comrade Aralov, arrived to receive great acclaim both in Ankara and on a tour of the front with Kemal.[81]

In his diplomatic dealings since the Ankara government was established, Kemal had oscillated successfully between Russia and the West. He had managed also to keep on cordial terms with the Muslim world, which could give at least moral and sometimes diversionary support against the other two worlds with which he dealt. Bekir Sami had not yet left on his first mission to Moscow when the Grand National Assembly issued an appeal for the support of all Muslims.[82] But Kemal was convinced that nationalist Turkey must become essentially a secular state, and keep clear of any pan-Islamic movement. To the Assembly he said that Islamic ties had done nothing for the Ottoman sultans but extend their commitments and cause them trouble.[83] During the war of libera-

---

[78] Ziemke, *Die neue Türkei*, pp. 366-367; "W" in *Revue du monde musulman*, LII, 201-205; Harry N. Howard, *The Partition of Turkey: A Diplomatic History, 1913-1923* (Norman, Okla., 1931), p. 268.

[79] Text in Degras, I, 263-269.

[80] Text in Kliuchnikov and Sabanin, *Mezhdunarodnaya Politika*, III, Pt. i, 164-165.

[81] Fischer, *Soviets in World Affairs*, I, 393-394. In 1922, the Soviet embassy was the best-appointed in Ankara, with a staff of 70. See Grace Ellison, *An Englishwoman in Angora* (London, 1923), p. 151.

[82] In the *Hakimiyeti Milliye*, May 9, 1920. See Jäschke, *Die Türkei*, p. 33.

[83] *Oriente Moderno*, I:8 (January 15, 1922), 467-468; Kemal, *Speech*, pp. 377-378.

tion, however, Kemal accepted gracefully from influential Muslims and Muslim nations the admiration and support which they naturally accorded the Turks, who seemed to be successful in upholding the Califate against the Christian world. The new Turkey would eventually sever its ties with the house of Osman and with Islam, but the time for this step had not come.

The most important international Muslim relationship was established with Afghanistan by a treaty of March 1, 1921, negotiated in Moscow while Yusuf Kemal and the Afghan ambassador were both concluding treaties with Russia.[84] It began with the customary Muslim invocation, "In the name of God, the Merciful, the Compassionate." In its third article Afghanistan recognized the leadership of Turkey for services to Islam, and for bearing "the standard of the Califate." The two countries agreed to a formal alliance against attacks by an imperialistic Power, meaning Britain, and Turkey agreed to supply military instructors to Afghanistan. Sultan Ahmed Khan, the first Afghan ambassador, was a popular figure in Ankara after his arrival there in April 1921. "All of us other Muslims consider the Turkish cause as our own," he said to a Western visitor.[85] In the same year Kemal sent an ambassador to Bokhara, which enjoyed a tenuous independence, and received from the Bokharan ambassador in Ankara the gifts of a Koran and a sword. Kemal's speech of welcome referred to the common ties of religion, though his emphasis on this was less than that of his visitors.[86]

The leading Muslim dignitary with whom Kemal dealt was Sheikh Ahmed esh-Sherif es-Senusi, ex-leader of the influential Senusi brotherhood of Cyrenaica. Sayyid Ahmed, after fighting with the Turks against Italian, French, and British forces, had escaped to Turkey in 1918. In 1920 Kemal received him at a banquet of honor, and apparently allowed him to organize a pan-Islamic congress in Sivas and to aid the Turkish nationalists in the early days by preaching the Holy War and rallying Arabs to oppose the British and French along with the Turks. Though accepting such support tacitly for a time, Kemal never committed himself to any pan-Islamic cause. Sayyid Ahmed later found it wise to leave for Syria when Kemal opposed his ardent support of the Califate. Kemal further refused to be dragged into any attempt to reimpose Turkish

[84] Text in *British Foreign and State Papers*, cxviii (1923), 10-11. This treaty was partly modeled on the Russo-Afghan treaty of the day before. See Degras, I, 233-235.
[85] Jean Schicklin, *Angora: l'aube de la Turquie nouvelle, 1919-1922* (Paris, 1922), p. 317.
[86] *Oriente Moderno*, I:9 (February 15, 1922), 545-547, and I:10 (March 15, 1922), 604-605.

control over the Arab territories which had given the sultans so many headaches.[87]

III

By the start of 1922 the Government of the Grand National Assembly was well-established. Its major task was now to drive the Greeks from western Anatolia and Thrace, and secure a peace incorporating those areas in Turkey. "We could not flatter ourselves," Kemal said later, "that there was any hope of success in a diplomatic way until we had driven the enemy out of our territory by force of arms."[88] But he was willing still to seize any chance of negotiation for a bloodless victory. For this purpose, Yusuf Kemal spent March in London and Paris, trying vainly to persuade Curzon and Poincaré that peace should be made on the basis of the National Pact.[89] The three Allied Foreign Ministers, however, met in Paris in March and proposed a further pro-Turkish modification of Sèvres, an immediate armistice, and a Greek evacuation of Anatolia after the peace.[90] The Greeks, desperate since February, accepted. Kemal was determined not to break off possible peace preliminaries but equally determined not to give the Greeks respite by an armistice to mount a new attack. The reply of April 5 which Yusuf Kemal therefore sent to the Allies, after Kemal and his ministers had conferred, accepted in principle a four-month armistice provided the Greeks began evacuation at once and completed it during the armistice period.[91] This the Greeks and Allies refused. Again on April 23 a Turkish note insisted on immediate evacuation, and tried to seize the initiative by proposing a preliminary conference on peace terms at Izmit, near Istanbul. This the Allies also rejected.[92]

[87] E. E. Evans-Pritchard, *The Sanusi of Cyrenaica* (Oxford, 1949), pp. 130-133; Jäschke, *Die Türkei*, pp. 42, 45; Georges-Gaulis, *Angora*, pp. 239-240; Sforza, *European Dictatorships*, pp. 202-203; *Oriente Moderno*, I:1 (June 15, 1921), 24, 32 and I:11 (April 15, 1922), 653. As late as January 1923, Rauf Bey, then prime minister, attended a banquet given by the Afghan ambassador in Ankara in honor of Sayyid Ahmed, and expressed the thanks of Turkey for help in an hour of danger. *Ibid.*, II:10 (March 15, 1923), 583. Kemal and the Assembly approved the idea of a pan-Islamic congress in March 1921, at exactly the same time as Bekir Sami was in London and Yusuf Kemal in Moscow, and the *Hakimiyeti Milliye* publicly endorsed the idea. France, Ministère des affaires étrangères, *Bulletin périodique de la presse turque*, XIII (April 22, 1921), 3.

[88] Kemal, *Speech*, p. 543.

[89] *ibid.*, pp. 544-545; *Oriente Moderno*, I:11 (April 15, 1922), 650.

[90] Text in *Oriente Moderno*, I:11 (April 15, 1922), 641-645, and II:5 (October 15, 1922), 266-271.

[91] Text in *Oriente Moderno*, I:11 (April 15, 1922), 650-651, where it is also reported that the Russian ambassador in Ankara tried to influence Kemal to reject the offer.

[92] Kemal, *Speech*, pp. 545-559; *Histoire*, pp. 104-108; *Oriente Moderno*, II:5 (October 15, 1922), 271-272.

While Kemal thus refused to accept the responsibility of breaking off potential peace negotiations, he attempted also to win an invitation to the Genoa economic conference in April 1922. Chicherin alone supported his demand. The Turkish ambassadors in Paris and Rome protested the exclusion; the latter went to Genoa to observe and object in person. Ankara announced that it preserved consequently complete liberty of action in economic matters.[93] In July Fethi [Okyar], minister of the interior, was given leave of absence to sound Paris and London again on the chances of a negotiated peace. Poincaré twice received him, but Lloyd George and Curzon would not.[94] Meanwhile the Greek-Turkish war was coming to its climax. To improve their situation the Greeks in July proposed to occupy Istanbul themselves. The Allies refused bluntly. Then the Greek commissioner in Izmir proclaimed there the autonomous state of Ionia, occasioning bitter Turkish protests through Hamid in Istanbul to the High Commissioners. The final Turkish answer was a drive in August which broke the Greeks, captured their commander, and resulted in a victorious entry into Izmir on September 9, as the Greeks evacuated Anatolia precipitately.[95]

Military victory at once placed the Turks in an advantageous bargaining position. They were now less dependent on Russian assistance. Kemal gave an interview to *Izvestya* saying that Turkey wanted normal relations with Britain, France, and Italy, which called forth bitter Russian comments on Turkish opportunism. The Turkish ambassador in Moscow tried to assuage feelings there with a speech of thanks which referred to the solidarity of Muslim peoples and the Russian proletariat.[96] Britain alone, now suddenly deserted by the French and Italians, faced the Turks along the Straits. Demanding that the Greeks evacuate Eastern Thrace at once, Turkish forces advanced into the Straits zone at Çanak [Chanak]. Though they came with rifles butt-forward, the appalling prospect of an Anglo-Turkish war now confronted the two governments. Peace was maintained because General Harington ignored Cabinet in-

[93] Degras, I, 289; *Oriente Moderno*, I:9 (February 15, 1922), 525-526, I:12 (May 15, 1922), 706, 719-721, and II:1 (June 15, 1922), 12.
[94] Edib, *Turkish Ordeal*, p. 247; Jäschke, *Die Türkei*, pp. 61-65. Presumably Fethi telegraphed Kemal from London that no peace would be forthcoming until a final attack on the Greeks.
[95] Jäschke, *Die Türkei*, pp. 63-64; *Oriente Moderno*, II:4 (September 15, 1922), 211-212; Driault et Lhéritier, *Histoire diplomatique*, V, 408-14.
[96] Ziemke, *Die neue Türkei*, pp. 367-368; *Oriente Moderno*, II:4 (September 15, 1922), 214-215. The Russians, seeing the end of the war coming, had tried in a series of notes from July to September to seize the initiative for themselves by proposing a peace conference and insisting that, by the Russo-Turkish treaty of 1921, only the Black Sea powers could deal with the Straits regime: Degras, I, 330-333, 334-336.

structions on an ultimatum to Kemal unless he withdrew, and because Kemal, so close to complete victory, chose not to provoke the British. Yusuf Kemal accepted an Allied offer of September 23 for an armistice and a peace conference on the basis of the return to Turkey of Istanbul and Eastern Thrace, including Edirne [Adrianople]. Though insisting that Thrace be evacuated at once, not after the peace, Yusuf Kemal agreed that armistice talks could begin at Mudanya. The Turks were perhaps influenced to accept the offer by Franklin-Bouillon, who saw Kemal at Izmir. That Kemal now strongly desired peace was evident from the less intransigent tone of his Foreign Minister's note of October 4 to the Allies, accepting a peace conference, though asking that it be held at Izmir, on Turkish soil.[97]

Armistice negotiations began at Mudanya, a small Marmara port, on October 3. Kemal sent Ismet [İnönü],[98] commander of the Western front against the Greeks, as his representative. Ismet provoked a crisis at Mudanya by again insisting on immediate Greek evacuation of Eastern Thrace. Curzon made another hurried trip to Paris, and the three Allied Foreign Ministers yielded. But as late as October 9 the British representative, General Harington, believed the Mudanya negotiations would break down over numerous other, though smaller, points. After repeated telephone calls from Ismet to Kemal the issues were narrowed to six, and finally to one, while Harington left hidden in his pocket two telegrams from London authorizing him to open hostilities against the Turks. The final point in dispute was settled by a maneuver which Ismet later duplicated at Lausanne. After Harington had stated the British position, he and Ismet paced on opposite sides of the room, each intractable. Ismet said he would not agree and then, suddenly, "J'accepte." He had held out as long as he could, but apparently had already been authorized to yield if necessary. "I was never so surprised in my life," said Harington later. Agreement was thus reached on October 10 seventy-five minutes before the British officers at Çanak were to start firing. Next day the formal armistice was signed by Ismet, Harington, and French and Italian generals, though the Greeks ad-

---

[97] On Chanak and the pre-armistice exchange of notes see Col. D. I. Shuttleworth, "Turkey, From the Armistice to the Peace," *Journal of the Central Asian Society*, XI:1 (1924), 61-62; Harold Nicolson, *Curzon: The Last Phase* (Boston, 1934), p. 271; *Oriente Moderno*, II:5 (October 15, 1922), 278-281, and II:6 (November 15, 1922), 338-339; Kemal, *Speech*, pp. 568-570. Kemal is said to have caused a minor crisis by declaring intemperately to the British consul-general at Izmir that the two countries were at war: Edib, *Turkish Ordeal*, pp. 385-386.

[98] Ismet later took his last name from the scene of one of his victories.

hered only three days later.[99] Refet Pasha arrived in Istanbul on October 19 to be Ankara's first governor of Eastern Thrace, thereby completing nationalist control over most of the territory claimed in the National Pact. Lloyd George, his Grecophile policy bankrupt, resigned the same day.

A formal invitation to a peace conference at Lausanne issued by the Allies on October 27 to both Turkish governments—Ankara and Istanbul—spurred the nationalists to clarify the relationship between themselves and the Sultan. This was done simply by a resolution of the Assembly on November 1 declaring the Sultanate abolished, although a Calif of the House of Osman would be chosen by the Assembly. The Istanbul cabinet resigned and Mehmet VI, declared a traitor by Ankara, fled aboard a British warship. Thereupon Abdülmecid [Medjid] was elected Calif by the Assembly. For Turkish foreign policy this meant a final break with the imperial Ottoman traditions, though for purposes of mollifying conservative sentiment at home and of retaining among Muslims abroad the prestige of the Califate, that shadowy institution was allowed two more years of existence. Istanbul no longer contained a government which could be influenced by Allied occupation; it was a provincial city only. Kemal, though not alone in his views, had forced the measure through the Assembly, using Bismarckian terms to a committee deliberating the bill. "Gentlemen," he said, "neither the sovereignty nor the right to govern can be transferred by one person to anybody else by an academic debate. Sovereignty is acquired by force, by power, and by violence.[100] Sovereignty lay with Kemal's victorious nationalists, who alone were represented at Lausanne.

IV

Ismet Pasha led the Turkish delegation to Lausanne. Kemal himself, pleased with Ismet's hard headedness at Mudanya and confident of his personal loyalty, chose him for the most important diplomatic task Ankara had yet faced. Ismet was simultaneously elected Foreign Minister by the Assembly, after Kemal had requested Yusuf Kemal's resignation.[101] The man thus chosen, now only thirty-eight, had had a purely

---

[99] On the Mudanya negotiations: *Oriente Moderno*, II:6 (November 15, 1922), 337-345; Sir Charles Harington, *Tim Harington Looks Back* (London, 1941), pp. 117-128.
[100] Kemal, *Speech*, p. 578.
[101] *ibid.*, pp. 570-572. Rauf, president of the council of ministers, was perhaps a logical choice to head the delegation, as well as Yusuf Kemal. Rauf and Kemal were divided by various arguments over domestic politics. The former, however, served as acting Foreign Minister while Ismet was at Lausanne.

military career, rising to be Under-Secretary of War before he left Istanbul in 1920 to join Kemal in Ankara. Thereafter he had served as member of the Assembly, as chief of the general staff and as commander of the Western front. Aside from his week at Mudanya he had had only slight contact with diplomacy as military adviser to the commission that negotiated peace with Bulgaria in 1913.[102] His new responsibilities weighed heavily on Ismet, and at dinner on the day he became Foreign Minister he was unwontedly somber.[103] Kemal brushed aside Ismet's plea that he was no diplomat. At Lausanne Ismet continued to have misgivings about his new role. "They have sent me, a soldier," he said to an English journalist, "to fight a Bismarck, one of your greatest statesmen."[104] Lord Curzon, who presided over most of the conference sessions, was indeed a formidable opponent, but Ismet acquitted himself well. The meetings in the Hotel du Château, where Curzon hoped to produce a treaty in a few weeks, stretched out for eight months largely because of Ismet's obstinate negotiation. The successful issue of the conference was in part due also to Ismet's sense of timing on compromise.

Ismet found himself in a difficult position at Lausanne. He represented a victorious nation which the Allied delegates tried to treat like a defeated nation. Curzon in particular employed "star chamber proceedings" and "steamroller methods."[105] But the Assembly in Turkey demanded complete equality and a diplomatic triumph. Curzon's tactics tended to make Ankara more obstinate than ever, thus increasing Ismet's difficulties in arriving at viable compromise.[106] It was generally thought by other diplomats at Lausanne that some of the Turkish delegation were there partly to see for the Assembly that Ismet did not make too many concessions in order to secure a treaty. Dr. Riza Nur, the second Turkish plenipotentiary, seemed to be a particularly intransigent watchdog.[107] During the conference Hasan [Saka], Ankara's third delegate, went back to Turkey and returned with, presumably, instructions for greater

[102] Gövsa, *Türk Meşhurlari*, pp. 188-190.

[103] Georges-Gaulis, *La nouvelle Turquie*, p. 95.

[104] Ellison, *Englishwoman in Angora*, pp. 305, 308.

[105] The judgments of the American observers: Richard Washburn Child, *A Diplomat Looks at Europe* (New York, 1925), p. 86, and Joseph Clark Grew, *Turbulent Era: A Diplomatic Record of Forty Years* (New York, 1952), Chapter 18, November 21, 1922, entry. Mr. Grew kindly permitted use of his book in proof.

[106] *Foreign Relations, 1923*, II, 901-902; Grew, *Turbulent Era*, Chapter 18, November 22, 1922, entry; Child, *Diplomat*, p. 98: "I know directly from Ismet Pasha," says Child, "that he is harassed from Angora enough as it is."

[107] Nicolson, *Curzon*, p. 346; *Foreign Relations, 1923*, II, 910; Grew, *Turbulent Era*, Chapter 19, February 4, 1923, entry.

obstinacy.[108] On territorial and political questions, where Ismet had special competence, he was able to accept solutions more often on his own authority, whereas in matters of economics and finance he was forced to rely on the expert advice of others in his delegation.[109]

At the opening session on November 20 Ismet began at once to demand for Turkey complete equality of treatment as an independent and sovereign state. Sometimes this insistence led Ismet to unnecessary extremes, but it was on most occasions his major weapon in combatting any measure of foreign control over Turkish finances, economy, justice, minorities, territory, or anything else. Ismet stood on the National Pact. Curzon grew immensely tired of Ismet's repetitious arguments, professing not to understand why Ismet insisted on undiluted sovereignty. Ismet was too sensitive on the subject, said Curzon; he should deal with realities, not phrases. The question was one of guarantees to minorities in Turkey. Thinking of Ottoman history since Kuchuk Kainarji, Ismet begged Curzon to excuse his insistence on sovereignty. "Turkey was acutely sensitive on this matter, and her fears were unfortunately well-founded, for up to the present day Turkish sovereignty had always been infringed on the plea of humanitarian considerations. The integrity of Turkey had frequently been guaranteed by means of promises from the highest authorities and also by solemn treaties, and yet Turkish sovereignty had repeatedly been violated. . . . How could Turkey help having misgivings?"[110] Ismet likewise opposed an international commission to supervise demilitarization of the Straits. "Turkey has had experience of such systems. For a state to be exposed in any way whatever to intervention in a part of the territories subject to its sovereignty is a calamity worse than death."[111] Curzon was exasperated by the same argument on the question of capitulations. "I am tired of replying to that argument," said Curzon. "Cannot the Turks realize that theirs is not the only sovereignty in the world?"[112] Curzon often assumed the role of a weary schoolmaster admonishing a stupid pupil. Ismet refused to learn. In private negotiation between Curzon and Ismet the same antithesis often developed. When the American observer brought the two men together to discuss the judicial capitulations in Turkey, Curzon shouted and beat the wall with his cane. Ismet held out for complete

---

[108] *ibid.*, January 14, 1923, entry.

[109] France, Ministère des Affaires Étrangères, *Documents Diplomatiques. Conférence de Lausanne* (Paris, 1923), II, 127-129.

[110] Great Britain, Turkey No. 1 (1923). *Lausanne Conference on Near Eastern Affairs, 1922-1923.* Cmd. 1814, p. 219. (Hereafter cited as Cmd. 1814.)

[111] *ibid.*, p. 283.   [112] *ibid.*, p. 496.

sovereignty and said that the adjustment of such matters took time. "Curzon and Ismet had about as much in common as a lion tamer and a grower of azaleas," reported Ambassador Child.[113]

Whenever he stated the Turkish position, Ismet was slow and methodical, which also annoyed Curzon. Because he was deaf, Ismet had frequently to rely on the secretary at his side for the gist of other delegates' remarks. But Ismet used his deafness to gain time to think, and he was often suspected of hearing only what he wanted to. When he did reply, he spoke indistinct French, reading from prepared statements or using notes dictated in Turkish to his secretary, and in a voice so low as to be barely audible. Ismet did not have the necessary details at his fingertips, as Curzon did. He required time to confer with his experts. He was forever reserving his right to reply, or requesting a delay to prepare an answer.[114] Curzon tried unsuccessfully to stampede Ismet into quick and injudicious statements. On the Straits question, Ismet refused to answer directly Curzon's brilliant and rather sarcastic question as to whether Chicherin's views represented the Turkish position.[115] "It must be a terrible experience," said Child, "for Curzon to turn his splendid flow of beautiful English upon this man and then find Ismet, with his little quizzical face, wholly untouched."[116] Ismet was well aware that he could not match Curzon in extemporaneous debate and analysis. He patiently conducted a siege, instead of attempting brilliant assaults. Ismet was also, of course, in constant telegraphic communication with Kemal, who followed the negotiations closely and sent instructions. A courier left each day for Ankara.[117] Even when authorized to compromise, Ismet sometimes bargained until the last possible moment. Having told Curzon point-blank one morning at 10:30 that the Greek Orthodox Patriarchate could under no circumstances remain in Istanbul, he said at 11 out of a clear sky as the two were walking together to a session, "All right, I will yield."[118]

Ismet used as best he could the differences among the Powers for Turkish advantage. Sometimes he was unsuccessful. Repeatedly he sought to strengthen his hand by suggesting to the American observers that they conclude a treaty with Turkey. They refused to do so before the Allies had completed negotiations.[119] At other times he succeeded.

---

[113] Grew, *Turbulent Era*, Chapter 19, January 15, 1923, entry.

[114] Grew, *Turbulent Era*, Chapters 18 and 19, *passim*; Child, *Diplomat*, p. 95; Nicolson, *Curzon*, pp. 298, 319, 333-334.

[115] Cmd. 1814, pp. 127-135.   [116] Child, *Diplomat*, p. 96.

[117] Hikmet, *Harici Siyaseti*, p. 113; Georges-Gaulis, *Nouvelle Turquie*, p. 189.

[118] Grew, *Turbulent Era*, Chapter 19, January 9, 1923, entry.

[119] *Foreign Relations*, 1923, II, 901, 970, 987, 997, 1042-1043.

Ismet had in the early stages of the conference considerable sympathy and support from the Italian and French delegations. He nevertheless made his major concessions to the British, whose warships at Istanbul and troops in Mosul offered the greatest threat. Thereafter he could oppose various French and Italian demands without fear that Britain would back them to the point of breaking up the conference and so jeopardizing her gains.

Ismet succeeded also in walking a narrow path between Russia and the Western Powers. He saw Chicherin nearly every day in the first period of the conference, and presumably received helpful advice from him.[120] After he had made concessions to Britain, he could menace the West with a return to a Russian orientation: "Turkey could look to the East and the North as well as the West."[121] But though Ismet and the Turks remained friendly to Russia, they avoided becoming dependent on her. No Rapallo resulted from Lausanne as from Genoa. The test of this was the Straits question. Chicherin was more Turkish than the Turks in arguing for their complete control over the Straits in order to close the Black Sea to vessels of other Powers. Ismet passed over Chicherin's arguments in silence. Instead he negotiated privately—"clandestinely," as Chicherin complained—with the Allies, ultimately accepting the British view that the Straits be open to all. Along the way Ismet had to made concessions to the Allies on demilitarization around the Straits, and to accept a guarantee of their security less adequate than he desired. But the final result was of inestimable advantage for Turkey. Ismet had on this point carried out the basic demand of the National Pact, but avoided applying that article of the Russo-Turkish treaty which would give a Soviet-dominated coalition of Black Sea states—Russia, Georgia, and the Ukraine—control over Turkish shores in a closed sea. He placed the new Turkey in an advantageous position between the West and Russia. Though the decision on the Straits is sometimes represented as Curzon's triumph in splitting Turkey from Russia, it was as much Ismet's triumph in avoiding dependence on Russia.[122]

By the end of January 1923, essential agreement had been reached between Ismet and the Allies on the Thracian boundary, ownership of various Aegean islands, the Straits regime, the elimination of an Armenia carved out of Turkish territory, and a compulsory exchange of Greek

---

[120] Fischer, *Soviets in World Affairs*, I, 409; *Oriente Moderno*, II:8 (January 15, 1923), 471-472.

[121] *Foreign Relations*, 1923, II, 935.

[122] Cmd. 1814, pp. 127-135, 156-173, 230-287, 447-457. See Nicolson, *Curzon*, chapters 10 and 11 for a good interpretation of Lausanne as Curzon's triumph.

and Turkish minorities.[123] The outstanding questions still in dispute concerned the Turkish-Iraq boundary in the Mosul region, the partition of the Ottoman debt, the Turkish demand for reparations from Greece, the status of foreign economic concessions in Turkey, and the possibility of some substitute regime for the capitulations which would give legal protection to Allied interests and nationals in Turkey. Ismet's strategy had been to drive a hard bargain on territorial questions, but to compromise on all of them except Mosul, whose Kurdish-Turkish majority was included in the claims of the National Pact. On all proposals tending to limit Turkish sovereignty within the boundaries thus laid down he was adamant. He successfully refused international commissions of various sorts to supervise matters as minor as the sanitary regime of the Straits. He would give no blanket validation to foreign economic concessions, nor admit any sort of foreign supervision over Turkish courts. On "Turkey for the Turks" Ismet would not compromise.[124]

The Allies presented the Turkish delegation on January 31 a draft treaty including all points on which agreement had been reached, and their draft of points still in dispute. Curzon, in skillful and forceful language, urged the Turks to accept a good offer. "We are not here to go on bargaining until we all sink into the grave, but to settle and conclude." Bompard and Garroni, for France and Italy, urged on the Turks the clauses on capitulations and finance. Ismet, in the face of this pressure, recounted the concessions he had made, accused the Allies of bringing up new points, and requested eight days to prepare his "observations" on the Allied draft. Curzon, in more of a hurry than Ismet, set a final limit of February 4 for his departure from Lausanne.[125]

There ensued four dramatic days of informal bargaining between the Turks and the Allies, during which more concessions were made by the latter.[126] Among these was an acknowledgment of Ismet's major premise, which eventually appeared in the preamble of the final treaty—that "relations must be based on respect for the independence and sovereignty

---

[123] A convention concerning the last question was actually signed by Venizelos and Ismet on January 30, 1923. See Stephen P. Ladas, *The Exchange of Minorities: Bulgaria, Greece and Turkey* (New York, 1932), pp. 335-352, 787-794.

[124] On some matters Ismet was led into extreme statements which could not stand close examination. "The present state of Turkish law is such as to meet all the requirements and necessities of modern life," he said. (Cmd. 1814, p. 489.) A few years later the Turks themselves introduced a wholesale modernization of the law Ismet had thus praised.

[125] Cmd. 1814, pp. 428-447.

[126] *ibid.*, pp. 832-837. Nicolson says that in this period Dr. Riza Nur, second Turkish plenipotentiary, proposed to him a separate Anglo-Turkish peace. (*Curzon*, pp. 345-346.) Whether Riza Nur had any such authorization is obscure.

of the States concerned." Ismet's reply to the new concessions was received by the Allied delegates at 1:45 p.m. on February 4. Ismet made a few counterconcessions, and accepted many parts of the draft treaty, but held out for the substance of sovereignty on capitulations and finance. He proposed that a treaty incorporating all agreed points be signed then, leaving the others for later negotiation.[127] Such a treaty, involving only questions on which the Turks had agreed but giving them peace, would have strengthened the Turkish position enormously. The Allied delegates met in Curzon's hotel suite and decided to offer a few more concessions. Ismet was summoned to meet them there at 5:40. He came, obviously unhappy and embarrassed; he was essentially a pleasant and agreeable man. Dire warnings and cajolery were alternately applied to Ismet as Curzon laid down post-final concessions: he would not appeal the Mosul question to the League, as he had threatened, unless after one year it remained unsolved by direct negotiation; some economic questions could be left open for six months. Ismet raised objections, saying no in unprovocative but firm tones. He would not accept the economic and judicial clauses, since they imposed "servitudes" on Turkey. Curzon's train left just after 9 that evening. Though he hoped Ismet would agree to signing before then, he had to depart disappointed.[128]

Ismet left a few days later to report to the Grand National Assembly. During a heated two weeks' debate he was both attacked for his concessions and criticized for having failed to make peace. There was general agreement that the Allied draft was unacceptable, but continued argument as to whether to resume negotiations. Mustafa Kemal defended Ismet before the Assembly, opposing the demands of some extreme nationalists that there be no resumption. Kemal's view was finally adopted on March 6, despite the opposition of the Soviet ambassador.[129] A note signed by Ismet and approved by the ministers was sent to the High Commissioners through Dr. Adnan [Adivar], now the foreign ministry's representative in Istanbul. It restated the Turkish views, with some alternative proposals, and asked that the conference be resumed at Istanbul. Along with it the Turks submitted a counterdraft of a treaty which exhibited the usual sensitivity on matters of sovereignty—as, for example, in the severe limitations with which they proposed to surround British ownership of the Anzac cemetery on Gallipoli.[130] A potential

[127] Cmd. 1814, pp. 837-841.

[128] *ibid.*, pp. 842-853; Nicolson, *Curzon*, pp. 346-348.

[129] Kemal, *Speech*, pp. 599-602; Jäschke, *Die Türkei*, pp. 71-72; Rawlinson, *Adventures*, p. 248; Oriente Moderno, II:10 (March 15, 1923), 589-590, 594.

[130] Texts in *Oriente Moderno*, II:11 (April 15, 1923), 643-659.

Treaty of Istanbul was no more acceptable to the Allies than a Treaty of Izmir would have been the previous September, but they were willing to meet again in Lausanne. The Turks agreed to reconvene there on April 23.[131]

During the break in the conference, Kemal lost no opportunity to bolster Ismet's negotiating position. The Turkish army was strengthened. The Turks followed increasingly a practice already begun—to treat the capitulatory rights of foreigners as if they no longer existed.[132] An elaborate economic congress at Izmir produced an Economic Pact which emphasized independence, sovereignty, and the necessity that foreign business houses observe Turkish law. Kemal, addressing the congress, said that Turkey welcomed foreign capital, but refused exploitation. "We cannot permit that this country should become as a city of slaves."[133] Kemal's effort to consolidate his political leadership within Turkey by organizing his own Peoples' party produced also a restatement of foreign policy in the party platform: the peace must assure Turkish financial, administrative, economic, and political independence.[134] A further play for American support was made when on April 9 the Grand National Assembly ratified the Chester concession, granted to the Ottoman-American Development Company. Though American economic aid might be welcome in developing nationalist Turkey, ratification was undoubtedly a maneuver to win American support at Lausanne against European economic claims. The concession involved railroad construction and the exploitation of oil and other mineral resources both in British-controlled Mosul and in regions of eastern Anatolia where the French had prior concessions. France objected to Ankara that this was an unfriendly act. Though the ratification was a diplomatic sensation at the moment, the final outcome at Lausanne was little affected thereby, despite Ismet's efforts to secure American backing on this basis.[135]

The second session of the conference required three months rather than the two weeks Ismet had hoped for. He had strenuous arguments on the Ottoman debt, Greek reparations and foreign economic concessions. In a meeting on the concessions, Ismet was reported to be "re-

[131] Note exchange in *Oriente Moderno*, II:11 (April 15, 1923), 659-662.
[132] *Foreign Relations*, 1923, II, 971, 1047-1049.
[133] *Oriente Moderno*, II:11 (April 15, 1923), 671-672; Mears, *Modern Turkey*, pp. 382-383.
[134] *Oriente Moderno*, II:12 (May 15, 1923), 707-709.
[135] *Foreign Relations*, 1922, II, 966-983 and 1923, II, 1198-1252; Grew, *Turbulent Era*, Chapter 20. I am indebted to Professor John De Novo of Pennsylvania State College for information on this question. The Chester concession was canceled by Ankara late in 1923 when the company remained inactive.

ceiving treatment which would make the third degree in a Harlem police station seem like a club dinner. He had deep circles under his eyes, his hair was standing on end, and he looked completely worn out, but was still holding his ground manfully in spite of all assaults."[136] Finally, Ismet obtained solutions satisfactory to him. He successfully refused any substitute regime for the capitulations. Only the Mosul question, on which Britain was as adamant as Turkey, was reserved for further bilateral negotiation or appeal to the League of Nations.

Ismet sometimes despaired of successful compromise and told Ankara he would resign. Rauf, still Prime Minister and acting Foreign Minister, differed with Ismet on matters of procedure and possible concessions. This was particularly true of Ismet's desire to renounce reparations from Greece if that country restored Kara Agaç, a vital suburb of Edirne, to Turkey. Ismet complained that Rauf did not allow him enough latitude and tried to go beyond giving him fundamental instructions to the point of prescribing negotiations in detail. This, said Ismet, would produce disaster, like the military collapse of 1877 when the Palace tried to direct the campaign against Russia. Kemal gave Ismet full support, forcing Rauf to withdraw his objections.[137] Ismet was then able to compromise the matter of Greek reparations, which had appeared to threaten a complete break and a renewed Greco-Turkish war in Thrace. At a dramatic meeting late in May, the two-hour tension suddenly changed to the hilarity of immense relief when the French chairman wrung from Ismet the admission that his instructions from Ankara, which he had thus far held in secret reserve, allowed him to accept the compromise.[138]

When the Treaty of Lausanne was signed on July 24, 1923, together with seventeen annexes and numerous letters, Ismet could pride himself on having achieved most of the nationalist aims.[139] The contrast to Sèvres was obvious. Now there were no reparations to pay. Turkey's boundaries were substantially those of the National Pact, except for the undefined Mosul frontier. No Armenia existed in eastern Anatolia, and no Greek state in the west. "Turkey for the Turks" was further assured by the population exchange with Greece, which excepted only the Greeks of Istanbul. The capitulations were abolished; foreign residents, businesses, economic concessions and schools were subject to Turkish law. The Turks

---

[136] Grew, *Turbulent Era*, Chapter 20, Speech of September 2, 1923.

[137] Exchange of telegrams between Ismet and Kemal and Rauf in Kemal, *Speech*, pp. 620-641.

[138] Grew, *Turbulent Era*, Chapter 20, speech of September 2, 1923.

[139] Texts in League of Nations, *Treaty Series*, XXVIII (1924), 11ff. and *Oriente Moderno*, III (1923), 461-550 (collated with the Turkish text).

were not completely masters of the Straits, and had accepted a demilitarized zone; their tariff rates were limited for some years; but the restrictions on complete sovereignty were so few as to leave no doubt that the Government of the Grand National Assembly represented a people victorious in diplomacy as well as in arms. Referring to the acknowledgment of sovereignty in the preamble, Ismet told the Assembly that "these are no vague words . . . (but) the result of the battles of a whole epoch."[140] Turkey's independence was more than technical, for with peace and the Straits open to all, Turkey was now balanced between the West and Russia.[141]

Some members of the Grand National Assembly, particularly those from the frontier regions, were not satisfied with the treaty, and criticized severely the cession of parts of Thrace to Greece and of Alexandretta (called by one deputy a "Turkish Alsace-Lorraine") to Syria. But 213 of 227 deputies voted for ratification on August 23, the Allied High Commissioners were at once notified, and the evacuation of British troops from Istanbul was shortly completed.[142] Kemal was proud of the Lausanne treaty, and always regarded it as the logical and necessary outcome of his leadership in the nationalist cause from 1919 on. "I was certain," he said later to his party, "that we would achieve a positive result. . . . What we demanded from the Conference was nothing more than the confirmation in a proper manner of what we had already gained. We only claimed our well-known and natural rights. In addition, we had the power to preserve and protect these rights."[143]

The conclusion of peace gave the nationalist regime the prestige and stability necessary to proclaim Ankara the capital of Turkey on October 13, and to declare formally on October 29 the existence of the Turkish Republic with Mustafa Kemal as its first President and Ismet its first Prime Minister. The peace by no means solved all Turkey's diplomatic problems, though it laid the basis for the conclusion of a host of friendship and commercial treaties in the next few years. The Califate, until its abolition in 1924, complicated Turkey's relations with Muslims outside its borders. The Mosul question brought acute tension between Turkey and Britain before its settlement in favor of Iraq in 1926 and

---

[140] Afet [Inan], "L'indépendance turque et le traité de Lausanne," *Belleten*, 11:7-8 (1938), 300.

[141] Although Russia signed the Straits convention, Chicherin protested that it was a "violation of the rights and interests of the Turkish people." Degras, I, 406-408. He was still more Turkish than Ismet.

[142] *Oriente Moderno*, III:4 (September 15, 1923), 208-209; Jäschke, *Die Türkei*, pp. 75, 148.

[143] Kemal, *Speech*, pp. 586-587.

caused the Turks to sign a nonaggression treaty with Russia in 1925. The Syrian frontier produced incidents only partly solved by a Franco-Turkish treaty of 1926; a similar situation existed on the Persian border. There was friction with Greece over the population exchange and over the status of the Greek Orthodox patriarchate in Istanbul. But the diplomatic victory of 1923 allowed Ankara to negotiate with others as an equal on such matters. It is noteworthy that since 1923 Turkey has enjoyed a period of peace unparalleled in her previous history.

Turkish diplomacy rested, of course, on the military successes which allowed bargaining from a position of comparative strength. It made good use of the collapse of Allied solidarity after 1918, and of the antagonism between Russia and the West. But it could not have been successful without the severe limitation of territorial objectives, laid down in the National Pact and not increased thereafter. The heterogeneous Ottoman Empire could never have served as a basis for Kemal's diplomacy. This he emphasized again and again. "It is necessary that the State should pursue an exclusive national policy and that this policy should be in perfect agreement with our internal organization and based on it," he said of the situation in 1920.[144] These limited objectives were relentlessly pursued in the years 1919 to 1923 by comparatively able and stubborn men like Bekir Sami, Yusuf Kemal, and Ismet. Behind them stood Mustafa Kemal, who throughout the entire period kept in his own hands the control over major diplomatic appointments, the ultimate and sometimes immediate direction of all diplomatic negotiation, and the authority to make the results acceptable to the nationalists and the Grand National Assembly.

[144] *ibid.*, pp. 377-378. For an incisive discussion of the internal nationalist basis for this diplomacy see Lewis V. Thomas, "The National and International Relations of Turkey," in T. Cuyler Young, ed., *Near Eastern Culture and Society* (Princeton, 1951), pp. 167-187; also Thomas and Richard N. Frye, *The United States and Turkey and Iran* (Cambridge, Mass., 1951), pp. 38-71.

....

The Early Diplomacy of Italian
Fascism: 1922-1932

BY H. STUART HUGHES

In February 1932, in a sweeping survey of Italy's international position
addressed to Dino Grandi, Italian Minister of Foreign Affairs, the ranking permanent official in the ministry, Baron Raffaele Guariglia, characterized his country's traditional policy in terms of sober realism: it
was "historically constrained, for intrinsic and obvious reasons, to take
its stand first on one side and then on another; to pursue the execution
of its aims by cutting from the garments of its different adversaries the
material necessary for its own cloak; and to take refuge on rainy days
(so long as this cloak was not ready) under the ample and capacious
mantle of England."[1] This was a substantially accurate statement of the
modest and realistic policy to which the facts of geographic location and
natural resources had condemned the Italian kingdom. For the first half
century of united Italy's existence it had been pursued with fairly satisfactory consistency and success. It was the policy in which career diplomats like Guariglia had been trained and the one in which they still
believed. But since 1922 they had been serving a new master whose
speeches erupted defiance and praise of the heroic virtues. Between the

---

[1] Raffaele Guariglia, *Ricordi: 1922-1946* (Naples, 1950), p. 146. These memoirs are
the most important single source for the inner history of Italian foreign policy during
the decade in question. Guariglia's open admission of his ties with Fascism—and particularly his frankness about his early advocacy of a penetration of Ethiopia—suggest
that his account is to be trusted. Of general histories of Italian foreign policy in this
period the most thorough, penetrating, and original, despite its polemically anti-Fascist
tone, is Gaetano Salvemini's *Mussolini Diplomatico*, revised edition (Rome, 1945);
the most judicious and balanced is Maxwell H. H. Macartney and Paul Cremona's *Italy's
Foreign and Colonial Policy: 1914-1937* (London, New York, Toronto, 1938); while
Muriel Currey's *Italian Foreign Policy: 1918-1932* (London, 1932), is a pedestrian,
pro-Fascist, thoroughly outdated account, valuable only for its translations *in extenso*
of Mussolini's speeches on foreign policy.

old doctrine of slow and patient negotiation toward modest goals and the new program of vast ambitions and quick results, the conflict was obvious.

This conflict is the central problem in the study of Italian foreign policy during the first decade of Fascist rule. Its investigation leads us to two further aspects of the same problem: first, the extent to which the differences between Fascism and tradition were on the one hand real and deep, or, on the other hand, largely a matter of vocabulary and emphasis (i.e., big words in public and practical negotiation in private); second—and here the answer depends heavily on the one already given to the first question—the extent to which the inevitable compromises between the two policies represented something more than a merely temporary postponement of an eventual open break.

I

Italy's intervention in the first world war had been carried out in the classic manner. After carefully weighing the bids from both sides, Prime Minister Salandra and Foreign Minister Sonnino had made the proper decision—that the Entente had offered more than the Central Powers. The proposed reward, however, since it was to be carved out of the Austrian and Turkish empires, rested on certain presuppositions as to the future of those states. The former was to remain in being, the latter to collapse utterly. Actually the reverse happened. The Austrian empire vanished from the map: its southern territories joined themselves to a South Slav state totally unwilling to see a large number of its conationals pass under Italian rule. The Turkish empire—reduced to its ethnically homogeneous core—rose in resistance against the proposed partition of Anatolia. In both cases, the changed circumstances made obsolete the original Italian claims. And to these considerations of *force majeure*, the later stages of the war had added the Wilsonian doctrine of self-determination—which the American President seemed inclined to enforce with more rigor against Italy than against any other of the victorious nations.

The story of Italy's role at the Paris Peace Conference need not be retold here.[2] In retrospect, we may question whether Sonnino's literal-minded and inflexible insistence on the promises contained in the secret treaties with France and Britain was the best possible course for Italy to pursue. With a more accommodating attitude, the Italian statesman

---

[2] It has been told in scholarly detail by René Albrecht-Carrié in his *Italy at the Paris Peace Conference* (New York, 1938).

might actually have come away from Paris with larger territorial gains. Specifically, he might have obtained definite compensation in Africa for Italy's failure to obtain a mandate over any of Germany's former colonies. The basic significance of the Peace Conference, however, so far as Italy's future was concerned, was that it left with the whole nationalist and conservative sector of Italian public opinion the conviction that their country had been swindled of the rewards of victory. This unhappy memory was to overshadow the next two decades of Italian foreign policy.

The three years from the resignation of Sonnino in June 1919 to the advent of Mussolini in October 1922 were dominated, then, by the conflict between the indignant proponents of "sacred egoism" and those of more democratic turn of mind who wished to "renounce" the claims that had proved impossible of fulfillment. This conflict, in turn, reflected and was rendered more bitter by the internal struggle between Socialists and Fascists that was to culminate in the March on Rome. Under the circumstances, it proved impossible for a nation so deeply divided to pursue any coherent foreign policy.

Of the five Foreign Ministers who followed one another in quick succession between 1919 and 1922—Tittoni, Scialoja, Sforza, Torretta, and Schanzer—Sforza alone left a record of accomplishment. Senator Tommaso Tittoni, a politician and diplomat of the old school, had had time to do little more than preside over the final act of Italy's disappointment at Paris. His successor, Senator Vittorio Scialoja, was a man of far larger dimensions. A wit, a renowned student of Roman law, and a member of one of Italy's most distinguished Jewish families, Scialoja had consented to serve as Nitti's second Foreign Minister—as he later consented to serve under Mussolini—in a spirit of profound skepticism: to his intimates he would confess that he was "here to see that, in foreign politics at least, they do not make too many mistakes."[3] In his seven months of office, however, he was able to arrive at one permanent settlement: the agreement with Lord Milner provisionally establishing the frontier between Libya and Egypt.

Count Carlo Sforza—a curious, highly personal amalgam of aristo-

---

[3] In Italian the term is much stronger: *fesserie*. The anecdote is from Daniele Varè's *Laughing Diplomat* (London, 1938), p. 159. These memoirs of a half-British Italian diplomat and writer, while fairly frivolous, are not without value in tracing the backstairs aspects of Italian diplomacy. All references are to the original edition, published only in English. The Italian edition, dating from 1941, while it continues the story from 1932, where the original edition left off, to 1940, omits a good deal of the original material on the 1920's, including several references to Mussolini.

cratic attitudes and democratic sympathies—frankly and fearlessly advocated a policy of "renunciation." He argued that there existed an indissoluble "bond between the destiny of a forward-looking Italy and that of the states created by the war." And so he became the passionate advocate of an Italian understanding with Yugoslavia and Turkey—"whose resurrection Sforza was the first and for a while the only one to call inevitable."[4] His vision of a new era of international reconciliation found its embodiment in the Treaty of Rapallo with Yugoslavia, of November 12, 1920. Under its terms Italy received Istria and the Dalmatian city of Zara, while Fiume was to become a free city. The fact that this treaty could never be carried out does not diminish its historical importance. It remained through the 1920's as an inconvenient reminder of an alternative course that had never received a fair trial—the course of understanding rather than provocation toward Italy's most difficult neighbor.

Sforza had bucked the popular current. His successor, the former ambassador to London, Marchese della Torretta, passed through the Foreign Ministry leaving scarcely a trace—aside from his original declaration to the Senate that he "intended to continue the policy of his predecessor in working for peace in the eastern Mediterranean and for friendly relations with Turkey."[5] And by the beginning of 1922, when the last pre-Fascist Foreign Minister, Senator Carlo Schanzer, took office, Italy's internal situation had deteriorated to such an extent that a firm policy was no longer possible. Nor was Schanzer the man to give a clear lead. "Able, hardworking, conscientious, but timid," he was "a good Secretary of State for the Treasury, but not suited to the Consulta."[6] Before his appointment as Foreign Minister, he had played an effaced role as Italy's chief delegate to the Washington Conference (November 1921 to February 1922)—although he later took credit for having won by his own efforts the principle of naval parity with France.[7] Scarcely back from Washington and just named to the Foreign Ministry, he hurried off to Paris, where he exhibited a profound ignorance of the questions raised by the resurgence of Turkey.[8] Then—after a spring

---

[4] From the author's preface and Alberto Cappa's introduction to *Pensiero e azione di una politica estera italiana: discorsi e scritti di Carlo Sforza* (Bari, 1924), pp. 10-11, 18. On Sforza's sympathy for Turkey, see above, Chapter 6, § 11.

[5] Currey, *Italian Foreign Policy*, p. 65.

[6] Varè, *Laughing Diplomat*, p. 207.

[7] *British Documents*, 2nd series, I, 368 (Sir R. Graham to Mr. A. Henderson, May 28, 1930). The volumes of this series published to date bear on the present study only for the years 1929 to 1932, and almost exclusively in the field of naval relations.

[8] Guariglia, *Ricordi*, pp. 8-9.

interlude of futile international conferring at Genoa—he went in June to London, where, as Mussolini complained, he allowed Lloyd George to treat him in a way "of which the representative of San Marino would have been ashamed."[9] The autumn crisis over a settlement with Turkey brought further humiliation—until the advent of Mussolini, just before the opening of the Lausanne Conference, mercifully put an end to Schanzer's sufferings.

When the Fascists came to power, most of the questions of vital concern to Italy left over from the Peace Conference of 1919 were still pending: the settlements already reached with Yugoslavia and Turkey had become obsolete, and the question of colonial compensation in Africa had made little progress. But this situation was not nearly as grave as the Fascists made it out to be. It had resulted from a combination of normal delays, a lack of governmental prestige, and a too rapid succession of Foreign Ministers. All Fascist propaganda to the contrary, the governments from 1919 to 1922 had made no irrevocable mistakes, and Italy's relative standing among the Powers was just about what it had always been—last among the great or first among the little depending on how one looked at it. Italy's international difficulties were largely psychological. The comparatively shabby treatment she had received at Paris had been only natural—in view of her disappointing contribution to the Allied war effort and the changed circumstances previously alluded to. What had suffered was national pride—little else. And at the same time Italy's permanent and really pressing grievances—the handicaps under which she was laboring in her search for emigration outlets and access to raw materials—were receiving only slight attention from her statesmen. Italy might feel herself to be sick—but she was essentially a *malade imaginaire*.[10]

II

To a career diplomat anxiously pondering Mussolini's utterances for a sign as to what the new regime would do, the last weeks of 1922 brought little but uncertainty. The Duce himself had assumed the foreign portfolio—along with several others—and evidently intended to be more than a figurehead Foreign Minister. The public statements he had made before attaining power suggested that at the very least he would try to startle the diplomatic world with a series of melodramatic gestures. Yet his inexperience of foreign affairs and certain essentially conservative

[9] Varè, *Laughing Diplomat*, p. 207.
[10] Salvemini, *Mussolini Diplomatico*, p. 35.

attitudes of the Fascist movement gave hope that the permanent officials of the Consulta might be able to steer him into more moderate courses.

On the one hand, Mussolini was clearly no "renouncer." He had attacked the previous governments for their timidity toward the French and British, and he was subsequently to define Fascism as a doctrine of "education to combat and acceptance of the risks that combat implies."[11] In allying himself with the Italian Nationalists, he had taken over their whole armory of hyperbolic claims and carefully-nurtured grievances. If an opportunity arose to make a big display, his first instinct was to rush in without regard to the consequences. When, for example, Italy had at length obtained definitive title to the Dodecanese, it was all that his professional advisers could do to dissuade him from sending a naval squadron to take formal possession. Only most reluctantly and with obvious ill-humor did he silently consent to their arguments that the gesture would be both provocative and ridiculous—since, after all, the Italians had already held the islands for more than ten years.[12] With Mussolini, the threat of ridicule was to prove the most potent deterrent from rash actions.

Balanced against these dangers, the Fascist government offered distinct advantages. Primarily, it promised permanence in office and firmness in international dealings: this was doubtless what was uppermost in the minds of certain high officials of the Foreign Ministry when they had made contact with the Fascists shortly before the March on Rome.[13] Similarly the liking and respect for established hierarchies that were to become an increasingly important feature of Mussolini's program were calculated to reassure any permanent corps of functionaries. And the Fascists' own boast of the flexible and adaptable nature of their aims worked in the same direction. Mussolini had scarcely been in office two weeks when he began to exhibit a highly reassuring tendency to take up each outstanding issue in turn and to arrive at a specific, practical settlement as soon as possible. The old guard of the Consulta might well have decided that the balance had tipped in favor of their new master when, early in 1923, he disclaimed any intention of being "original" in the field of foreign policy.[14]

---

[11] From Mussolini's (actually Giovanni Gentile's) article on "The Political and Social Doctrine of Fascism," dating from 1932 and published in the *Enciclopedia Italiana*, which is the most authoritative statement on the subject. The authorized English translation can be found in *International Conciliation*, No. 306, January 1935, pp. 5-17.

[12] Guariglia, *Ricordi*, pp. 27-28. [13] *ibid.*, p. 10.

[14] Speech to the Chamber of Deputies of February 16. For the Italian text, see *Scritti e discorsi di Benito Mussolini*, edizione definitiva (Milan, 1934), III, 59-73. Currey, *Italian Foreign Policy*, pp. 85-87, gives a slightly abridged English version.

III

Shortly after Mussolini came to power, the Italian Foreign Ministry changed quarters. From the elegant, quiet palace of the Consulta, just across the Piazza of the Quirinal from the King's own palace—a building the Foreign Ministry had occupied ever since Rome had become the capital of united Italy—it moved to the architecturally undistinguished Palazzo Chigi, located at the busiest street-corner in the city. The old officials regretted the change and feared that it presaged a new demagoguery in foreign relations.[15] Actually, within the Ministry itself, little was altered except the *décor*.

The ambassadors stayed at their posts. Sforza's abrupt withdrawal from the Paris embassy, immediately upon receiving news of Mussolini's accession to power, remained an isolated gesture.[16] Throughout the first decade of Fascist rule, most of the ambassadors continued to be men of the old type, career diplomats and frequently aristocrats. In Paris, for example, Count Sforza was succeeded by Baron Romano Avezzana, and at the turn of the decade Count Manzoni held the post.

Nor was it only the diplomats who offered the new regime a highly-appreciated contribution of permanence and respectability. Three of Mussolini's predecessors as Foreign Minister—Schanzer, Tittoni, and Scialoja—regularly supported him from their seats in the Senate. Tittoni—president of that body from 1922 to 1929—published a pro-Fascist book on foreign policy to which Mussolini was happy to contribute the preface.[17] And Scialoja served from 1921 to 1932 as Italy's representative on the Council of the League of Nations. In the latter case, however, the support was of a distinctly eccentric variety. "The position of this emaciated, refined septuagenarian, toward Mussolini and Fascism, strangely recalls that of the great aristocrats who 'rallied' to the First Consul and the Empire, a Talleyrand, for example. . . . Neither the King nor the Duce nor the institutions of the regime could escape the sarcasms . . . of this great master of the *bon mot*."[18]

Within the Ministry itself the presence of Salvatore Contarini, the experienced Secretary General (corresponding to permanent Under-Secretary) assured a continuity of administration. All witnesses agree on Contarini's ability and devotion to the state service. The Swiss Minister

---

[15] Guariglia, *Ricordi*, pp. 25-26; Varè, *Laughing Diplomat*, p. 225.
[16] For the exchange of messages between Sforza and Mussolini, see Sforza, *Pensiero e azione*, pp. 282-283.
[17] Tommaso Tittoni, *Questioni del giorno* (Milan, 1928).
[18] Arturo Carlo Jemolo, *Chiesa e Stato in Italia negli ultimi cento anni* (Turin, 1949), p. 653.

regarded him as "a man of a rare competence,"[19] and his subordinates at the Palazzo Chigi had an enormous respect for his judgment. His peculiar office hours (at meal-times only, which made him practically inaccessible), his "theory of the taps" (turn on the argument suited to each type of visitor), and his calculated rages (but never with foreign diplomats), all contributed to the growth of a kind of Contarini legend.[20] "With his exquisite political sensibility, his tact, and his way of doing business, which at first seemed confused but which was always guided by a serene and simple logic, Contarini succeeded in solving the problem" posed by the advent of Mussolini. In this endeavor he was ably supported by another career official, Giacomo Paulucci Barone, who as the Duce's *chef de cabinet*, constantly urged the counsels of prudence and moderation. It took several months of the "patient work of Contarini" to convince Mussolini that the traditional course of alignment with Britain was the correct one. But once the job was done, the Duce, "realizing his complete ignorance" in matters of foreign policy, "let himself be guided with a good deal of docility." Such at least was the conviction of the permanent officials at the Palazzo Chigi.[21]

This happy state of affairs lasted until April 1925. In that month Contarini—whose position had been growing increasingly difficult as Mussolini began to work behind his back in dealing with Yugoslavia—resigned his post as Secretary General. His successor, A. Chiaramonte-Bordonaro, remained in office less than two years. In February 1927 he left the Palazzo Chigi for the London embassy. And a month later Barone went off to Geneva. The old group of career officials was beginning to break up. Moreover, after Bordonaro's resignation from the secretary-generalship, no successor was appointed: the position was simply allowed to lapse.[22]

This change in the internal structure of the Ministry was due to the growing influence of a new figure on the scene—whom the permanent officials had at first distrusted as a Fascist and an outsider but whom they soon came to regard as an ally. In early 1925 somebody—it is unclear who—decided that the Foreign Ministry needed an Under-Secretary. This was a position that in Italy had traditionally been of little importance and had been filled only from time to time. With his customary adroitness, Contarini offered to find the proper man. His choice fell on Dino Grandi—to all appearances a strange selection. For Grandi was

---

[19] Georges Wagnière, *Dix-huit ans à Rome* (Geneva, 1944), p. 106.
[20] Varè, *Laughing Diplomat*, pp. 227-228.
[21] Guariglia, *Ricordi*, pp. 12-15, 24.   [22] *ibid.*, pp. 14, 50.

known as one of the tough young men of the Fascist movement: he had been party leader of Bologna and participated in the March on Rome. But Contarini had learned that Grandi was actually both "malleable" and "understanding," and his expectations proved correct. Once in office the new Under-Secretary indicated not only that he intended to elevate his post from its traditional insignificance but that he realized the way to do it was through working with the career men against their common master, the Duce and Foreign Minister.[23]

"A few weeks . . . sufficed for Grandi to penetrate the mysteries of the Palazzo Chigi." Here, he soon realized, there offered itself a field of action and ambition far broader than the domestic sphere in which his party comrades were rapidly bogging down under Mussolini's all-controlling authority. As sole intermediary between the career officials and the Duce—as interpreter of their concept of the "inherent exigencies" of Italian foreign policy—he could eventually attain to a position of practical independence in the international field. The permanent officials soon found Grandi to be an apt scholar: he worked on his diplomatic behavior as eagerly as he took up the study of English and French. No wonder that in his first important speech in the Senate, his appearance— "measured in movement, placid and almost monotonous in voice, cordial but distant in smiling"—should have satisfied even the "old fogeys of diplomacy."[24]

Nor was it surprising that after two years in office he should have decided, by leaving vacant the position of Secretary General, to concentrate authority in his own hands. This change did not represent the threat to the career officialdom that one might imagine, for a new team was ready to take over. Baron Raffaele Guariglia—later to play an important role in the palace revolution against Mussolini of July 1943—was able to make himself a kind of substitute Secretary General, since his position of political director for Europe, the Levant, and Africa actually embraced the major areas of Italian policy. He and Augusto Rosso— who handled League of Nations affairs—became Grandi's "closest collaborators." Together they continued to uphold the thesis that relations with England were the "keystone" of Italian policy. They were satisfied that Grandi had learned his lesson well—and they believed the British to be satisfied also. "On many important occasions," they found, Grandi was able to "make Mussolini change his ideas and directives—though naturally acting with prudence and clever dissimulation so as not to offend" the Duce's "vanity." Guariglia reported only to Grandi, never

[23] *ibid.*, p. 47.   [24] *ibid.*, pp. 48-50.

to Mussolini. Hence for the career men it meant no real change when in September 1929 the Duce decided to give up the foreign portfolio and to hand over sole direction of foreign policy to his former Under-Secretary.[25]

IV

The best way to judge the extent to which Grandi—and to a lesser extent Mussolini—had actually been "tamed" is to review briefly their actions in the foreign field during the first ten years of the latter's tenure of power. Two main strands of activity immediately appear—a process of liquidating the problems left over from 1919, and an incipient, if controlled, expansionism. They correspond roughly to Mussolini's two contrasting propaganda goals—to reassure foreign Powers, and particularly Britain, as to his pacific intentions, and to show his own people that he had a unique talent for chalking up points for Italy on the international scorecard.

Mussolini's two introductory moves in the international sphere were distinctly propaganda ventures. In their unblushing amateurishness, they belong in a category by themselves. The first of these was the Duce's brief appearance at the Lausanne Conference, which was to make a final settlement with resurgent Turkey. Not yet three weeks in office, Mussolini set out for Lausanne with the resolve to do something dramatic. It occurred to him that if he had his train stopped a bit short of his destination and invited Curzon and Poincaré to come and talk with him it would give a proper impression of Italy's enhanced prestige. The representatives of Britain and France consented—Curzon with amused curiosity, Poincaré more grudgingly. After a brief huddle, the three emerged with a formula: Italy was to be treated "as an equal." Armed with this "success"—actually either meaningless or insulting to Italy, since it implied that she might *not* have been treated as a Great Power— Mussolini consented to go on to Lausanne. Here he spent only one day at the conference—a day in which he seemed ill at ease in his strange surroundings and formal attire, and in which he reportedly said nothing more important than "Je suis d'accord." The next day he returned to Italy in triumph. Actually his country, either before or after Mussolini's departure, exerted little influence at Lausanne—obtaining only the formal cession of Rhodes and the Dodecanese, which she held in any case. And the one effort that the chief Italian delegate made to black-

---

[25] *ibid.*, pp. 53, 60, 63-64.

mail the conference by a threatened withdrawal simply collapsed before one of Curzon's majestic attacks of rage.[26]

The Duce's second eruption on the international scene was more serious. In August 1923, in retaliation for the murder—by undisclosed assailants—of the Italian president of the commission engaged in delimiting the Greco-Albanian frontier, Mussolini ordered the bombardment and occupation of the Greek island of Corfù and presented the Greek government with a demand for an indemnity and the performance of a number of ceremonial gestures of a humiliating character. The Greeks immediately took the question to the League. Here it might have gone badly with Mussolini if the French and British had not decided to shift the case to the more friendly arena of the Conference of Ambassadors. Why they decided to do this is not entirely clear: an attack of weariness on Lord Curzon's part seems to have been largely responsible. In any case, Mussolini got his indemnity—but little else. In the general jubilation over their leader's second "success," Italians forgot that the indemnity was the only one of the Duce's original demands that the Greeks had fully met. And if Mussolini—as appears likely—had actually intended to keep Corfù, he had been obliged to give up that ambition.[27]

The lessons Mussolini drew from these two incidents were conflicting. On the one hand, he remained convinced that in the Corfù case he had scored a victory. Contarini, Guariglia, and the rest, who had tried first to restrain him and then to patch up a bad situation, found that the Corfù precedent encouraged the Duce to start on other expansionist ventures.[28] Yet his experience at Lausanne had been more sobering. It had evidently persuaded him that international conferences were not the sort of place in which his talents shone to best advantage. Between 1925 and 1937 Mussolini for the most part stayed away from them. And in the former year it was only the arguments of his professional advisers that induced him to go in person to sign the Locarno pact. He must have regretted it; for he was hurt by the massive fashion in which the foreign correspondents boycotted the reception he gave. Otherwise he found that it worked better to stay in Italy—and in this more flattering setting to dazzle his visitors. Beginning with the trip to Rome of the new British Foreign Secretary, Austen Chamberlain, in December 1924—an encounter that was to be repeated at frequent in-

[26] Harold Nicolson, *Curzon: The Last Phase, 1919-1925* (London, 1934), pp. 288-290, 303-304; Guariglia, *Ricordi*, pp. 17-21.
[27] Salvemini, *Mussolini Diplomatico*, pp. 61-67; Nicolson, *Curzon*, pp. 368-371.
[28] Guariglia, *Ricordi*, pp. 14, 28-31.

tervals during the next five years—a steady stream of admiring foreigners found their way to the Duce's presence. These meetings the Fascist press regularly reported as virtual "journeys to Canossa."[29]

Aside from these two introductory forays, the early years of Mussolini's rule were dominated by the first aspect—the liquidation phase—of diplomatic activity. In addition to the settlement at Lausanne with Turkey, the Duce tried to come to terms with Yugoslavia on the question of Fiume, and with Britain and France in the matter of colonial compensation. Originally, Mussolini had accepted Sforza's treaty with Yugoslavia—the Free City arrangement for Fiume evolved at Rapallo. But this was only a temporary concession. By July 1923, the Duce was suggesting to the Yugoslavs the incorporation of Fiume in Italy, and two months later, wearied by the way the negotiations were dragging, he simply took over the city. The following January, by the Pact of Rome, the Yugoslavs accepted the *de facto* situation. Although they had acted under duress—the French, fully involved in the Ruhr, had not provided the expected support—the Yugoslavs evidently decided that it was best to treat the Italian annexation of Fiume as simply the liquidation of an untenable situation. In the Pact of Rome and the subsequent Nettuno Conventions, they agreed to the friendly settlement of all pending Italian-Yugoslav questions.[30] These two documents soon became virtually a dead letter—but that story belongs to a later phase of Mussolini's diplomatic activity.

With Britain, the settlement on colonial compensation, while long delayed, was never seriously in doubt. It involved little more than the formal ratification of the pledges already made by the British in the Treaty of London of 1915 and the Milner-Scialoja accord of 1920. In July 1924, Britain ceded to Italy the region of Trans-Jubaland, adjoining Italian Somaliland, and a year and a half later, a treaty between Italy and the now independent state of Egypt finally delimited the Libyan-Egyptian frontier. But with France no such definitive solution proved possible. All through the 1920's and well into the 1930's, the question of a general accord with France held a prominent place on the Italian diplomatic agenda. But nothing substantial ever resulted. Even the boundary between Libya and French Equatorial Africa was not finally settled until 1935. Why did the question of a general understanding with France prove so peculiarly difficult?

With this question we come to the central area of Mussolini's diplo-

---

[29] *ibid.*, pp. 38-39, 99; Salvemini, *Mussolini Diplomatico*, pp. 91, 98-100.
[30] Macartney and Cremona, *Italy's Foreign Policy*, pp. 93-94, 107.

matic exertions. In the first place, in the matter of colonial compensation, Italy's claims on France were both larger and vaguer than her highly specific demands on Britain. Mussolini would speak of an extension of Libya nearly to Lake Chad, and a discussion of colonies invariably branched off into a related problem that was essentially insoluble—the status of the large Italian minority in Tunisia. Then there was the question of the two countries' relations with Germany: in the period up to about 1930 it was Mussolini who feared a Franco-German accord—later it was the French who worried over the Duce's tentative approaches to the Brüning government.[31] Nor could Mussolini resist the temptation to make a success with the crowd by violent anti-French speeches—a tendency that reached its climax in the bellicose tirades he delivered at Leghorn and Florence in May of 1930.[32] And for their part the French possessed propaganda weapons—admittedly unofficial—to which the Duce was peculiarly sensitive. The hospitality extended by the French to the *fuorusciti*, the anti-Fascist refugees, who made their headquarters in Paris, and particularly the light sentences imposed on their "subversive" activities by the French courts, regularly reduced Mussolini to impotent fury. And the attacks of the Leftist sector of the French press had the same effect: as ruler of a country where the whole educated class could read French, he rightly feared the contagion of ideas from across the Alps.[33]

Beyond all these things, however, the greatest reason for the continuation of Franco-Italian tension was the fact that beginning in 1926, Mussolini had embarked on the second phase of his diplomatic activity—the phase of expansion. The Duce's choice of an area for penetration—the new and chaotic state of Albania—implied a threat both to Yugoslavia and, more remotely, to France as Yugoslavia's protector.

In 1920 the Italians, who had occupied the Albanian port of Valona and its hinterland at the start of the first world war, withdrew to the island of Saseno, leaving the Albanians to work out their own destiny. But the following year they obtained a kind of contingent mandate over the country: the four Great Powers on the League of Nations Council declared that in the event of a threat to Albania's independence, they would recommend that Italy carry out the duty of intervention. For the next few years the Italians were too occupied with their own internal

---

[31] Guariglia, *Ricordi*, p. 123; Salvemini, *Mussolini Diplomatico*, p. 154.

[32] For the text of these speeches (slightly abridged in the case of the one delivered at Leghorn), see *Scritti e discorsi*, VII, 199-201, 203-206. In this case, Currey, *Italian Foreign Policy*, pp. 286-287, translates only extracts.

[33] Guariglia, *Ricordi*, pp. 110-111; Salvemini, *Mussolini Diplomatico*, pp. 127-128.

difficulties to take up this virtual invitation to meddle. It was rather the Yugoslavs who more successfully kept Albania in a turmoil. But by 1925, when Ahmed Bey Zogu—originally a Yugoslav protégé—had finally united and pacified the country, Mussolini decided that it was time to resume an active Albanian policy. And Zogu, in desperate need of financial aid, and realizing that the Yugoslavs were unable to supply it, was obliged to turn to Italy for help. The result was the Pact of Tirana, of November 1926, pledging Albania and Italy to mutual support and cooperation that amounted to an Italian right of intervention.

The background of this pact forms a curious chapter in the history of Mussolini's diplomatic dealings. In July 1926, Baron Aloisi, the Italian Minister to Albania, presented Zogu with a series of demands which if accepted would have made Albania virtually an Italian protectorate. Zogu, stiffened by the British Minister, Mr. Reilly, rejected them. But then Austen Chamberlain "went for a yachting cruise in the Mediterranean, met Mussolini for a long conversation off Leghorn, and not long afterwards recalled Mr. Reilly." There followed an Italian-inspired revolt in northern Albania. When Aloisi presented Zogu with a revised—and somewhat mitigated—set of demands, the new British Minister advised the Albanian President to accept. These new demands formed the basis of the Pact of Tirana.[34] They were supplemented the next year by a military alliance called—confusingly enough—the Treaty of Tirana.

The Yugoslav reaction was prompt. In November 1927, a few days before the signature of the Treaty of Tirana, the Yugoslavs concluded an alliance with the French. From this year on, Italian-Yugoslav relations were frankly bad. And they became worse as the conviction gradually spread that Mussolini was sending arms and money to dissident Croats and to Bulgarian terrorists in Macedonia. These activities cannot yet be documented; but indirect evidence strongly suggests that the Yugoslav fears were well-grounded.[35]

A second aspect of Italian expansionism—and one similarly calculated to alarm the French—was Mussolini's sporadic advocacy of revision of the Paris settlement. The idea was logical enough: it might have developed into a systematic exploitation of Italy's psychological position midway between the victorious and the defeated nations. But Mussolini never seems to have thought through exactly what he was trying to do. In his first speech as Prime Minister, on November 16, 1922, he stated

---

[34] Vandeleur Robinson, *Albania's Road to Freedom* (London, 1941), pp. 76-78.

[35] See, for example, Guariglia, *Ricordi*, pp. 54, 91-92, and Salvemini, *Mussolini Diplomatico*, p. 275.

his conviction that "treaties are not eternal, are not irremediable."[36] And in the following years he gave encouragement to the conservative governments of Austria and Hungary—in the latter case with shipments of arms, the discovery of one of which caused something of an international scandal. He probably also gave financial aid to Hitler's struggling National Socialist movement.[37] But at the same time he saw the danger inherent in a reviving Reich: in 1923 he tacitly endorsed Poincaré's occupation of the Ruhr. It was not until June 5, 1928—in the course of an extensive survey of Italy's relations with nearly every portion of the globe—that he clearly declared himself for revision.[38]

Certain historians have seen in this speech the beginning of revision as a "recognized instrument of Italian national policy" and the "real opening of the abyss between Italy and the Little Entente."[39] It is tempting, in the light of what occurred after 1936, to read back the events of the 1930's into an earlier period. Actually, during the whole decade we are considering, Mussolini seems to have been feeling his way. He was well aware of the possibilities inherent in revisionism—but he was not yet ready to exploit it as a fully consistent policy.

The same may be said of the whole expansionist aspect of his activity. Both anti-Fascists and Fascists, for contrasting reasons, have given him too much credit for prescience and careful planning. The former have written that the Mediterranean was "never far from . . . Mussolini's mind."[40] The latter have made much of a supposed "single program" for gradual political and cultural penetration eastward.[41] It is true that the Duce himself declared in February 1924 that the "lines of . . . Italian expansion" lay "towards the east."[42] And it is also true that every Italian government has necessarily devoted a major share of its attention to the Levant and the Balkans. But when we come to look more closely at Mussolini's eastern policy, we find that it is only bits and pieces—penetration of Albania, friendship with Bulgaria, a pact with the Yemen, the encouragement of Italian commercial and linguistic interests in the Levant. There is no clear sign of plan or considered policy. It is rather similar to the Duce's mania for signing pacts of amity with foreign coun-

---

[36] *Scritti e discorsi*, III, 9; Currey, *Italian Foreign Policy*, p. 78.
[37] Salvemini, *Mussolini Diplomatico*, pp. 81-82, 245-248, 250-252.
[38] *Scritti e discorsi*, VI, 203-205; Currey, *Italian Foreign Policy*, pp. 251-253.
[39] Macartney and Cremona, *Italy's Foreign Policy*, p. 197.
[40] *ibid.*, p. 9.
[41] Carlo Capasso, *Italia e Oriente* (Florence, 1932), p. 219; "Latinus," *L'Italia e i problemi internazionali* (Milan, 1935), pp. 395-399.
[42] Capasso, *Italia e Oriente*, p. 192. The speech is lacking in *Scritti e discorsi*. A mistranslation can be found in Currey, *Italian Foreign Policy*, p. 128.

tries of all descriptions: one can count at least eight of them between 1926 and 1930. "No country ever signed so many pacts and treaties as Mussolini's Italy; he never refused his signature to any convention that was proposed to him, even the most contrary to his ideas and purposes."[43]

Rather than a considered plan, the whole thing looks more like a random and uncoordinated striking-out in all directions in the hope of scoring points on the cheap. In the words of his admirers, Mussolini's great aim was "to prevent the crystallization of the European situation." More critically stated, this meant "to keep Europe in a constant state of uncertainty that would permit him now and then to obtain in some fashion or other some sort of advantage. His was a policy of improvisations without a definite aim."[44]

And what had been the results after ten years of this sort of activity? A hostile critic has summed them up as follows: "1) two colossal errors: granting a free hand to Poincaré in the Ruhr and the occupation of Corfù; 2) one sagacious decision: the compromise with Yugoslavia on Fiume; 3) the fulfillment of the British promises . . . [in Africa]; 4) the protectorate over Albania. . . ."[45] Whatever Mussolini had accomplished had actually been based on the work of his predecessors—Sonnino, Scialoja, and Sforza. It had been no more than what any firmly organized Italian government might have done in the same period—and doubtless with less friction. For against Mussolini's actual accomplishments one must balance off the fear and hostility that he had aroused. By antagonizing France, he had alienated the one country that offered even a partial solution to Italy's most pressing need—an outlet for emigration—a problem, incidentally, which Mussolini regularly neglected in favor of more showy issues.[46] And he had opposed every concrete effort for regrouping and coordination among the small states of Central and Eastern Europe. He had alarmed the Little Entente not only by his favors to Hungary but also by his overtures to the authoritarian government of Rumania headed by General Averescu. Likewise he had stood firm against a Yugoslav-Bulgarian rapprochement or any sort of general Balkan understanding.[47] Mussolini might have few real accomplishments to his credit—but he had at least partially succeeded in his goal of keeping Europe in a constant state of flux.

[43] Guariglia, *Ricordi*, p. 40. [44] Salvemini, *Mussolini Diplomatico*, p. 354.
[45] *ibid.*, p. 383.
[46] In his speech of June 5, 1928, he stated: "For the last two years the Fascist Government has followed a policy of voluntary restriction and control of emigration." *Scritti e discorsi*, VI, 183; Currey, *Italian Foreign Policy*, p. 239.
[47] See the frank admissions of Capasso, *Italia e Oriente*, pp. 237, 241.

V

Faced with this puzzling record, can we conclude that the permanent officials of the Palazzo Chigi were right in thinking that they had thoroughly domesticated Under-Secretary Grandi and had had some success in performing the same operation on his chief? The answer is half and half. We may approach it under four headings: first, the relations between the career men and the Fascist movement; second, the goals the former were pursuing; third, the elements of incoherence between the activities of Mussolini and the aims of the permanent officials; and finally, the actual satisfactions that these officials were able to derive from the Duce's rule.

It would be incorrect to picture the cleavage between Mussolini and the Palazzo Chigi as anything resembling a conflict between Fascism and democracy. Aside from a few convinced admirers of Mussolini, the Italian career diplomats—like foreign service men in all countries—were apolitical, that is, simply conservative and nationalist. Most of them had neither a strong liking for nor a strong objection to Fascism; in 1927 they accepted without protest their mass enrollment in the Fascist party. Moreover, from their standpoint, a Fascist government had definite advantages. In its internal solidity and its unpredictability, it gave them leverage for negotiation abroad; they could use it to further the permanent aims of Italian policy. Mussolini's idea was just the reverse; he tried to exploit his diplomatic successes—real or trumped-up—to consolidate his power at home.[48] This difference already represented an initial element of incoherence in the Italian diplomacy of the 1920's.

It was no fundamental opposition of political philosophy that separated Mussolini from the career men. They, like him, wanted to see Italy great and respected, substantially enlarged in territory and influence. But the methods they advocated to achieve this common goal were more patient, modest, and realistic. They well knew that the inadequacy of Italy's financial and military resources made it impossible for her to compete with the more prosperous powers in the game of building up client states, and that for this reason such small nations as Austria, Hungary, and Bulgaria could never be really reliable allies. In default of dependable satellites, then, the Palazzo Chigi continued to insist on the traditional alignment with Britain. Most of the pending questions between France and Italy, they believed, could best be approached from the British direction. Or—to regard the matter from another angle—if

[48] Guariglia, *Ricordi*, pp. 14, 39-40, 53.

only Mussolini would proceed more cautiously in Albania and would conscientiously try to reassure the Yugoslavs, relations with France would automatically improve. The Italian professional diplomats were not particularly impressed by the League of Nations—but they would not neglect whatever advantages it offered: the main reason they had been so enthusiastic about the Locarno Pact was that it enabled Italy to place herself in a position of dignity "above the mêlée" and alongside Britain. Finally, they advocated a penetration of Ethiopia as a safety valve for Italian nationalist yearnings and a field for the exportation of Italian labor and talent. But they believed that this penetration should be preceded by a diplomatic preparation as slow and as thorough as the one that had virtually won the Tripolitan War of 1911-1912 before it was ever fought.[49] Toward this goal they had made a good start with an agreement with Britain, of December 1925, that provisionally recognized an Italian sphere of influence in eastern Ethiopia.[50]

Obviously Mussolini would never have agreed, either publicly or in private, to any such cautious definition of Italy's goals. And many of the things he did in the first decade of his rule—his Albanian-Yugoslav policy, his toying with revisionism, his provocations directed at the French, and his indiscriminate welcome to small nations seeking to sign pacts of friendship—ran directly counter to the advice of his professional counselors. With Grandi it is more difficult to tell exactly where he threw his weight. For the period of the 1920's at least, it is nearly impossible in most cases to distinguish his opinions from those of the Duce above him and those of the Palazzo Chigi career men, his technical subordinates. Usually, however, in his delicate position of middleman, Grandi seems to have sided with the professional diplomats.

Yet the curious thing about Mussolini's direction of the Foreign Ministry is that he appeared quite content to let these rather obvious situations of incoherence drag along without any clear decision. Only in the crucial case of relations with Albania and Yugoslavia did he recognize in organizational form the cleavage between his own policy and that of the permanent officialdom. We have seen how Mussolini's independent dealings with Yugoslavia had driven Contarini in early 1925 to resign his position as Secretary General. And under Guariglia's direction of the political department, the handling of Albanian and Croat affairs escaped his control entirely. The former area Mussolini assigned to a special

---

[49] *ibid.*, pp. 38-39, 64-66, 92, 114-115, 119, 142, 153-154, 169-170, 176.
[50] For details of this agreement, see Macartney and Cremona, *Italy's Foreign Policy*, pp. 290-294; Salvemini, *Mussolini Diplomatico*, pp. 171-173.

unit headed by Ambassador Loiacono; somewhat later, "when the contacts with certain Croat spokesmen began," these questions also were removed from Guariglia's jurisdiction. Even "Grandi did not succeed in this most important matter in *coordinating* . . . the activity aimed at an Italo-Yugoslav accord (which he also *heartily* endorsed . . .), with that into which [Mussolini's] Albanian policy had forced us, and with the policy of favoring the Croats in order to put political pressure" on the Yugoslav government.[51]

Otherwise, however, Mussolini seems scarcely to have realized the extent of the existing divergence of view on Italian foreign policy. Or he saw it simply as the inevitable and not particularly troubling gap between what he was obliged for propaganda purposes to say in public and what any well-run Foreign Ministry would naturally do on the official level. In May 1930, when Grandi—now Foreign Minister—came to the Duce in great distress to protest against the way in which his inflammatory speeches at Leghorn and Florence had contradicted his own policy of general pacification, the latter seemed sincerely surprised: "What does it matter what I say to my crowds?" he queried. "Why do you think I made you Foreign Minister except to be able to talk here exactly as I please!"[52] This gap between public and private utterance frequently proved extremely useful to Mussolini, and he was probably honest in giving it as his reason for having resigned the Foreign Ministry. Under this system, for example, it was always possible to disavow what some Fascist propagandist had written in the newspapers—and even to get foreign statesmen to believe that the journalist in question had spoken without official authorization.[53]

Moreover, Mussolini similarly failed to realize (or simply chose not to see) the contradictions inherent in his *own* policies—the incompatibility between two lines of activity that he might be following at the same time. We have seen how his revisionism was never strictly consistent. It was certainly inconsistent to talk about a general revision of the Paris settlement and at the same time to oppose any move toward *Anschluss* between Germany and Austria—as he did in the case of the proposed customs union of 1931.[54] It was difficult to court the favor of Austria and at the

---

[51] Guariglia, *Ricordi*, pp. 54, 74.

[52] *British Documents*, 2nd series, I, 368.

[53] Even Sir Austen Chamberlain was apparently taken in. See Tittoni, *Questioni*, pp. 210-211.

[54] For a statement of opposition to the *Anschluss*, see Mussolini's speech to the Senate of May 20, 1925: *Scritti e discorsi*, V, 78; Currey, *Italian Foreign Policy*, p. 150. In the case of the customs union, Mussolini was at first in favor of it, but was subsequently persuaded by Grandi to change his mind. Guariglia, *Ricordi*, pp. 80-81.

same time to pursue a rigorous policy of Italianization against the German-speaking inhabitants of the South Tyrol. Nor was Mussolini's support of Hungary's grievances consistent with his policy of friendship toward Italy's "Latin brothers" the Rumanians—threatened as they were with the loss of more than a third of their national territory.[55]

When everything else has been said, however, it is not too paradoxical to conclude that Mussolini, in lightheartedly dismissing all this incoherence as inevitable and unimportant, came closer to the heart of the matter than the permanent officials of the Palazzo Chigi who sighed and grumbled over his extravagances. Aside from the one great cleavage over relations with Albania and Yugoslavia, none of the questions at issue between the Duce and his professional advisers was important enough really to change in one direction or the other the main course of Italian policy. During the 1920's—under the surface of his inflammatory rhetoric—Mussolini, like the career men of the Palazzo Chigi, was essentially a believer in slow expansion based on the maintenance of the traditional alignment with Britain. And, in his curious way, he actually kept up the Anglo-Italian understanding rather well. He was certainly most successful in cultivating the good will of Austen Chamberlain and other prominent Tories, and even the change to a Labor government in June 1929 did not seriously alter his standing with the British. Moreover, Mussolini's attitude toward the League of Nations was quite similar to that of the career officials. While he had no belief in what he called the "almost mythological virtues" attributed to the League, he never seriously proposed leaving it.[56] He was "always on the verge of withdrawing without ever doing so."[57]

Thus the permanent officials of the Palazzo Chigi could take comfort in that fact that Mussolini, "despite his outbreaks of ill humor, his oratorical manifestations, and his directives to the press . . . , showed himself convinced of the necessity of not departing from . . . the fundamental lines" of traditional Italian foreign policy.[58] And the Duce offered them other satisfactions. Among the amateur diplomats of the 1920's, Mussolini was far better than average in the clarity of his aims and the precision of his utterance. His reports on foreign policy to the Senate and Chamber of Deputies were distinguished for their brevity of expression, their lucidity, and their grasp of detail. To his diplomats he usually

[55] Salvemini, *Mussolini Diplomatico*, p. 245; Guariglia, *Ricordi*, p. 75.
[56] Speech of June 5, 1928, in *Scritti e discorsi*, VI, 215; Currey, *Italian Foreign Policy*, pp. 253-254.
[57] Macartney and Cremona, *Italy's Foreign Policy*, p. 244.
[58] Guariglia, *Ricordi*, p. 106.

behaved with understanding and generosity. One of his first acts on becoming Foreign Minister was "to put an end to the lingering paralysis" that had descended on their careers since the end of the first world war.[59] With Mussolini in power, promotions began again, and the diplomats could rest assured that their chief was taking a personal interest in the internal reorganization of the Italian foreign service.[60] Abroad, they enjoyed a fair degree of independence—provided, of course, they followed major instructions and did not openly criticize the Fascist regime. A German representative at Geneva noted that the Italians there—Scialoja, Rosso, and the rest—"were not much bothered by what the Party had prescribed in Rome. They did what Italian foreign policy seemed to demand, and in this they were supported by the authorities at home."[61] Provided he had a certain dose of skepticism about his country's international role and his own activities—and such an attitude was not totally foreign to Mussolini himself—the Italian diplomat of the 1920's could ride comfortably along with scarcely a thought for the noisy vagaries of the Fascist party.

And so for a certain time in Italian foreign relations the traditions of the old diplomacy and the impatience of the new came to a kind of happy compromise. But this was a special and peculiar case. It was possible only because Italy was a lesser Power and most of the international issues in which she was involved were relatively unimportant. During the 1920's, after all, it was France and Britain that were really making the great decisions. Italy remained on the fringes of major diplomacy. So long as she stayed there, the divergences of view between Mussolini and his professional advisers could be compromised or glossed over. But once there should come a radical change in European alignments and Italy could succeed in forcing her way into the main stream of international negotiation, the fragile compromise between Fascism and tradition could scarcely fail to collapse.

VI

The year 1929 marked the high point of Mussolini's diplomatic prestige—and of the accompanying sense of qualified satisfaction in the Palazzo Chigi. In that year, Italy's relations with nearly all the nations of Europe were in a state of happy tranquility. The British were demonstrating their customary reserved friendliness, the French were giving

[59] Varè, *Laughing Diplomat*, p. 215.
[60] See the statements in his speech of June 5, 1928: *Scritti e discorsi*, VI, 217-227.
[61] Ernst von Weizsäcker, *Erinnerungen* (Munich 1950), p. 89; Eng. Trans. by John Andrews, *Memoirs of Ernst von Weizsäcker* (Chicago, 1951), pp. 74-75.

few signs of alarm, and the Austrians were settling into a relationship of amity with their protector south of the Alps that the Italian professional diplomats could characterize as answering "the purposes of sound policy." Even the Yugoslavs were enjoying a sense of precarious *détente*: in the autumn of 1928 they had at length ratified the long-pending Conventions of Nettuno. And the following winter, in February 1929, Mussolini scored the most substantial success of his whole career—the signature of the accords with the Vatican. This amicable settlement of the vexed Roman question, although based, like nearly all the Duce's diplomatic triumphs, on the less showy work of his predecessors, had enormous repercussions throughout Europe and the Catholic world: the thesis that Mussolini was essentially a moderate and constructive statesman now seemed to have found irrefutable confirmation. The Duce had conducted the whole negotiation himself. The Palazzo Chigi—apparently even Grandi—were kept in ignorance of what was going on. But when they heard the news, the professional diplomats were delighted.[62] Seven months later, Mussolini turned over the Foreign Ministry to Grandi. And the latter, convinced that international conciliation had now become the accepted goal of Italian policy, began to devote his major attention to preparations for the London Naval Conference that was to meet in January 1930, and more particularly to the crucial question of a naval agreement with the French.

The Naval Conference, however, failed to arrive at a general Franco-Italian understanding. After its adjournment in April, Grandi continued the negotiations on a two-Power basis, with the British and Americans as interested mediators. These supplementary negotiations were to drag along for a year and three-quarters, finally to end in total failure in January 1932. As they pursued their tortuous course, Grandi began to succumb to a sense of bewilderment and frustration. The "admirals and naval party," he knew, were systematically hampering his work with their insistence on a building program that would give Italy parity with the French in all major classes of warships.[63] What he did not know was that Mussolini himself had turned against his new Foreign Minister and was beginning to undermine the whole policy of conciliation.

In May 1930, the Duce emerged from an exclusive concentration on internal questions that had made him "almost inaccessible to foreign

[62] Guariglia, *Ricordi*, pp. 107-108.

[63] For details of these negotiations, see *British Documents*, 2nd series, I, 354-472, and particularly Doc. No. 198 (Sir R. Graham to Mr. A. Henderson, May 3, 1930). Other details, *ibid.*, II, 383-434.

representatives,"[64] and went on an extended speaking tour of northern Italy. His stops along the way—Leghorn, Florence, Milan—witnessed those provocative oratorical displays whose disturbing effect on the French we have already noted. Five months later, on October 27, in an address to the provincial directors of the Fascist party, he made a number of statements that were widely interpreted as an abandonment of the idea that Fascism was not a product for export. "Yesterday," he declared, "it was Italy, today it is the world, because everywhere there are people fighting for or against Fascism." And he added a more categorical endorsement of treaty revision than he had ever given in earlier years.[65]

From now on—this time in earnest—revisionism was to be a dominant element in Mussolini's foreign policy. The insistent and increasingly successful demand for international equality on the part of the German government headed by Chancellor Brüning had at length opened that crack in the post-Versailles alignment of European diplomacy for which the Duce had been waiting. Now he was ready to offer his friendship to a resurgent Reich. In 1931, the semi-official Fascist propagandists began to warn the French against the dangers and pitfalls of a Franco-German understanding.[66] And in August of that year, Brüning and his Foreign Minister, Julius Curtius, paid a visit to Rome: their reception was warm, and the exchange of toasts strongly suggested that in the forthcoming general Disarmament Conference Italy would take a pro-German line. This assumption proved correct. When the Conference opened, in February 1932, the initial Italian proposal—to consider as aggressive arms all weapons forbidden to the conquered countries by the peace treaties—was close to the German demand for complete equality.[67]

Meantime, the Palazzo Chigi had taken alarm. Guariglia, who had begun to worry about Mussolini's revisionism as early as 1928 and had been insisting for some time on the urgency of coming to an understanding with France, was pleased when he was asked to accompany Grandi on the latter's journey to Berlin to return Brüning's visit: at least it would give him a chance to caution his chief and to assess on the spot the strength of the German nationalist resurgence.[68] But Grandi was becoming a feeble support to lean on. He also was beginning to feel the ground slipping from beneath his feet. Back in March 1930, at the time of the

---

[64] *ibid.*, I, 379 (Sir R. Graham to Mr. A. Henderson, June 27, 1930).
[65] *Scritti e discorsi*, VII, 225-228; Currey, *Italian Foreign Policy*, pp. 295-297.
[66] See, for example, Arrigo Solmi, *Italia e Francia nei problemi attuali della politica europea* (Milan, 1931), pp. 120, 132.
[67] Macartney and Cremona, *Italy's Foreign Policy*, pp. 161, 269.
[68] Guariglia, *Ricordi*, pp. 129-131.

London Naval Conference, he had confessed to Prime Minister Mac-Donald that he detected in a recent declaration of the Grand Council of Fascism "a veiled admonition against himself for having gone as far as he had" toward a compromise with the French.[69] The following June he had complained to the French Ambassador of the activities of the "strong party . . . which wished to throw Italy into the arms of Germany" and had characterized his own position as "one of extreme difficulty."[70] Part of this lament, of course, had been for effect—to induce the French to come closer to the Italian viewpoint. But the distress had been real. Grandi had proved his sincerity nine months later, in March 1931, when, faced with a new and totally discouraging turn in the two-party naval negotiations, he had "placed his resignation in Signor Mussolini's hands in case the latter thought somebody more suitable could be found."[71]

This time the Duce had refused to accept his Foreign Minister's resignation. But a year later he was ready to do so. On June 16, 1932—just as the Conference on Disarmament at Geneva was beginning to adjourn its inconclusive labors—Mussolini gave an interview to the *Daily Express*, in which he voiced his pessimism about the League of Nations and about the Conference itself.[72] To the initiated it was a clear indication that Grandi's time had come. Five weeks later, on July 21, Mussolini, in effect, simply fired his Foreign Minister—with none of the usual "internal or external preparation" and "without any reason given."[73]

As a consolation prize Grandi received the London embassy. And he was allowed to find suitable positions for his two close collaborators, Guariglia and Rosso: the former went as ambassador to Madrid, the latter to Washington. The professionals in the Palazzo Chigi had now lost their adopted leader. They were left to the tender mercies of the Duce himself and, subsequently, to those of his son-in-law, Count Ciano.

---

[69] *British Documents*, 2nd series, I, 275 (record of an interview between Mr. MacDonald and Signor Grandi, March 24, 1930).

[70] *ibid.*, I, 377 (Sir R. Graham to Mr. A. Henderson, June 25, 1930).

[71] *ibid.*, II, 392-393 (Graham to Henderson, March 28, 1931).

[72] Salvemini, *Mussolini Diplomatico*, p. 376.

[73] Guariglia, *Ricordi*, pp. 176-178.

8

· ·

Soviet Diplomacy: G. V. Chicherin, Peoples Commissar for Foreign Affairs, 1918-1930

BY THEODORE H. VON LAUE

IN 1923, five years after the humiliating treaty of Brest-Litovsk, the government of Soviet Russia, according to its new federal constitution, considered itself the nucleus of a global association of Soviet socialist republics. To an observer unencumbered by ideology and judging international relations by prewar standards, the millennial goal of the new regime might have seemed preposterous. With the resources of imperial Russia, which had been so recently found wanting and which were further reduced by loss of territory and civil war, the Bolsheviks tried to sustain a political ambition far exceeding the boldest aspirations of the Tsars. The discrepancy between a weakness so recently demonstrated and an ambition so boldly proclaimed would have forever discredited the Soviet leaders, had they not developed, at ferocious cost, two novel sources of power: a totalitarian dictatorship to expand Russia's military and industrial potential; and a totalitarian type of foreign relations. With their new plenitude of controls the Bolshevik leaders were able to manipulate every phase of the relations between Soviet Russia and the outside world; they could fit every point of contact between Soviet citizens and foreign nationals into their central scheme of foreign relations. The new regime thus evolved an armory of foreign policy instruments exceptionally complete for that time. It had at its disposal the Comintern, Profintern, the secret police and military intelligence, as well as the traditional channels of diplomacy, the foreign trade agencies, the Society for Cultural Relations with Foreign Countries (VOKS), Intourist, and a host of other organs. This multitude and variety of agencies with contacts abroad helped Soviet foreign policy to offset the weakness of Soviet Russia and gave the Soviet impact on other countries an unusual intensity.

Through these channels the Bolsheviks made bold to transmit their techniques of class warfare and social disintegration into the struggle between states. And by the example of their intentions, properly interpreted by Bolshevik ideology, they also claimed the leadership of all "progressive" causes. In short, they arrogated to their rule as universal a significance as was implicit in the cultural preeminence of the Great Powers of the West; and, in doing so, they issued a profound challenge to the world order inherited from the nineteenth century.

It was understandable that the role of diplomacy, the traditional tool of international relations, should be changed under an avowedly revolutionary regime, for it found itself in an alien milieu. In the competition for power, in which the Bolsheviks, after their revolution, joined with such seemingly unlimited aims, diplomacy had to accommodate itself to an inferior role. It was the tragedy of Chicherin, who assumed the post of Peoples Commissar for Foreign Affairs after Trotsky's resignation in March 1918 and who carried the burden of office longer than any contemporary Foreign Minister, that he was placed in the center of the turbulent confluence of diplomacy and social revolution. In order to be intelligible, Soviet diplomacy, and Chicherin's role in it, must therefore be viewed not in isolation but as a fragment, and a rather unrepresentative one, of Bolshevik policy in world affairs. This chapter will deal, above all, with the relationship between the two seemingly discordant instruments of Bolshevik foreign relations, between diplomacy and revolution, leaving out the other less important agencies of policy and treating the main lines of Soviet foreign policy proper in a necessarily summary fashion.

I

Strictly speaking, Soviet diplomacy did not begin with Chicherin, but with Trotsky; and Trotsky began by abolishing diplomacy. Named Peoples Commissar for Foreign Affairs after the seizure of power, he took an optimistic view of his tasks at the Foreign Office, now renamed Peoples Commissariat for Foreign Affairs (Narkomindel): "I will issue some revolutionary proclamations to the peoples and then close up the joint."[1] Admittedly he exaggerated, but not without reason. Diplomacy—if one may extend Trotsky's unspoken thought—was part of the capitalist superstructure, like the national state. The revolutionaries of all countries would know how to deal more simply and honestly among themselves; and the advanced national states, now locked in ferocious imperialist

---

[1] L. Trotsky, *Mein Leben* (Berlin, 1930), p. 327. See also Lenin's startled comment: "What, are we going to have foreign relations?" *Ibid.*

war, would disappear in the world revolution which had begun in Petrograd. What was needed most at this historic moment in the foreign relations of the new regime were stimulants to set the sluggish masses of Europe and the European dependencies throughout the world into revolutionary motion, primarily to assist in the revolution at home, and perhaps, in a series of chain reactions, to spread and even complete the world revolution.

From the first, Bolshevik foreign policy aimed at world revolution. Asked early in the world war what he would do if he should come to power, Lenin gave the daring answer: "We would propose peace to all the belligerents, the liberation of all colonies and all dependencies, all the oppressed, and those peoples who do not have equal rights. Neither Germany nor England and France would accept these conditions with their present governments. Then we would have to prepare and conduct a revolutionary war: i.e. not only would we carry through our whole minimum program with decisive means, but we would at once systematically start to incite rebellion among all the peoples now oppressed by the Great Russians, all the colonies and dependent countries of Asia (India, China, Persia, and others). And we would also raise in rebellion the socialist proletariat of Europe against their governments.... There is no doubt that the victory of the proletariat in Russia would create very favorable conditions for the development of the revolution in Asia and Europe."[2]

Having seized power in Petrograd, Lenin proceeded at once to put that master strategy into effect. The opening act of the new regime was its Proclamation on Peace, the starting-point of Soviet foreign relations, which outlined a revolution in international relations no less drastic than that accomplished in civil society. First of all, by its peace proposal the Bolshevik regime eliminated itself from the traditional European system. As a socialist government, it considered itself outside the pale of "capitalist" nations. Bent upon liquidating the most Westernized elements in its population (and later, by the same token, in the Bolshevik party), and following an ideology which, in strict theory at least, permitted no dealings with "capitalism," Soviet Russia lapsed into profound isolation. A citadel of suspicion and hostility, she lived henceforth as though in a different world, which remained obscure to the outside and, in turn, permitted only a distorted picture of the alien realities of Western democracy. Secondly, in calling for world revolution, Lenin's Proclamation on Peace envisaged a global, rather than a European, system of

[2] Quoted from D. Shub, *Lenin* (New York, 1948), p. 144.

international politics. Although, in its special appeal to the workers of England, France, and Germany, it obliquely recognized the traditional preponderance of Europe, it counted more on the nationalist and anti-Western stirrings of the non-European, and particularly the Asiatic, world; for the new regime was dedicated to the overthrow of the global balance of power inherited from the nineteenth century. Finally, in preferring revolutionary agitation to traditional diplomacy, Lenin's Proclamation introduced a new dimension into the field of power politics, the dimension of social revolution. What was the use of armament factories, of imposing armies and navies, and of strategic strongpoints, if the social structure was crumbling underneath them? Thus, cohesion again took its place as a factor of political power, and subversion became a potent weapon of power politics. As for the Bolsheviks, who in the months after November 1917 commanded practically none of the traditional weapons, revolutionary agitation was almost the sole effective instrument at their disposal. Besides, from their own upbringing, it was one especially dear to them; they were superior to all statesmen of the liberal tradition in handling it. Circumstances in due time apprenticed them in the use of the traditional tools as well, even of diplomacy; but to this day revolutionary agitations remain closest to the revolutionary core of the party.

The attempts which Lenin made before the foundation of the Communist International to exploit war-born and war-nurtured unrest in Europe and Asia may be studied in Merle Fainsod's *International Socialism during the War*. With the formation of the Comintern in March 1919, the preliminary, experimental phase of these efforts was ended. Henceforth, revolutionary agitation became institutionalized as a permanent feature of Soviet foreign relations. To be sure, the Comintern, with its related agencies, was not a flawless tool of Soviet policy; it could not be as freely wielded as was sometimes assumed. But, at a time when they possessed few other resources, it brought great advantages to the Soviet leaders. Through it, they could extend the techniques of revolutionary agitation into the realm of international relations. The conditions for admission into the Comintern were such as to mold its members in the Bolshevik pattern. They were ordered to establish an underground organization beside their legal party apparatus and to infiltrate not only into every proletarian organization but also into the armed forces of their country. And above all, they were commanded to observe Bolshevik discipline, which made them subject to the decisions of the Comintern Executive, dominated in turn by the Russian Communists. Lenin himself was the chief Russian delegate; Trotsky, Bukharin, and Zinoviev were his associates on the Executive Committee.[3] This revolutionary organization, which soon had its own information service and intelligence center in Moscow, followed closely Lenin's original aim: the immediate preparation for the dictatorship of the proletariat.

In the center of that struggle, as the guiding policy of the Comintern stated,[4] stood the Soviet Republic. It was surrounded and protected by the proletarian vanguard of all countries and the liberation movements of the colonial and suppressed peoples—the revolutionary *glacis*. Beyond lay the hostile capitalist world, doomed by the very laws of its existence to be reborn into Soviet socialist society. It was the task of the Comintern to hasten the dialectical development, with the active assistance of the Soviet Republic. How far that active assistance might go was made clear by events. In March 1919 Lenin dispatched troops to help Bela Kun, although he had to recall them almost immediately because of the advance of Denikin's White Armies; and in the following year, during the offensive against Poland, he undertook to "break the crust of the Polish bourgeoisie with the bayonet." Soviet Russia's weakness again interfered, and for the next two decades its revolutionary agitation abroad was carried forward with minimum effort and without the active assistance of the Red army. But, according to the main strand of Bolshevik theory, revolutionary war remained part of the revolutionary outward thrust, as it was part of the domestic attack. As Stalin expressed it in 1924: "The victorious proletariat of one country should stand up against the remaining capitalist world, attracting to itself the oppressed classes of other countries, raising revolts in those countries against the capitalists, in the event of necessity coming out even with armed force against the exploiting class and their governments."[5]

The policies of the Soviet regime or its novel techniques of agitation and organization within the framework of the Comintern may be studied elsewhere. The record is clear: between 1919 and 1930 Soviet domination increased until it amounted to tightest possible control. Through the far-flung activities of international communism, the Politburo manipulated to a considerable extent the revolutionary forces of Europe and Asia in order to suit its own ends according to its interpretation of world affairs.

---

[3] The close ties between the Comintern and the Politburo were inadvertently revealed by Zinoviev at the Twelfth Party Congress, when he spoke of immediate consultation with the Politburo on a matter of Comintern policy. See P. Miliukov, *La Politique Extérieure des Soviets* (2nd ed. Paris, 1935), p. 135.

[4] Lenin, Theses on the Nationality and Colonial Question, submitted at the Second Comintern Congress, July 1920.

[5] In "The October Revolution and the Tactics of the Russian Communists," quoted by Historicus, "Stalin on Revolution," *Foreign Affairs*, Jan. 1949.

Through the Communist parties it reached into the center of domestic politics in other countries where, at least in the recent history of the sovereign state, no foreign Power had ventured in such strength.

But while the Bolsheviks perfected their revolutionary instruments of foreign relations, they were confronted with new situations in which these instruments were patently inadequate, or even harmful to their interests. Even at the time of the foundation of the Comintern, revolutionary agitation, in which Trotsky had put such hope, had ceased to be the sole tool of Soviet foreign relations. What, in the eyes of the faithful, had been intended to do away permanently with power politics had become merely another dimension of the same old evil. For, contrary to Trotsky's prediction, the Narkomindel had not yet closed shop. Almost from the beginning, its diplomatic activities were expanding, with aims that were eventually to differ radically from those of the Comintern. Diplomacy, indeed, had been implicit in Lenin's Peace Proclamation (which, in regard to the relation between revolution and diplomacy, maintained a revealing ambiguity). And when the Central Powers, who alone among the belligerents had accepted the Soviet proposal for peace negotiations, pressed home their ruthless terms, and when the German revolution did not come to the rescue, the Bolshevik leaders were forced to resort to the traditional forms of international relations. "The given relation of forces in the world arena," read a party resolution of March 1918, left no choice except negotiating with the Central Powers and signing the Treaty of Brest-Litovsk. In its precarious position, both at home and abroad, the Soviet government was thus compelled to recognize the existence of capitalist governments and to adapt itself, for the time being, to the conditions of capitalist encirclement. While the international revolutionary movement gained momentum, with active Soviet assistance but still far too slowly, "we must . . . stick to our tactics of waiting," Lenin reported to the party on May 14, 1918, "taking advantage of the conflict and antagonisms among the imperialists and of slowly accumulating strength. . . ." He promised "everything diplomacy can do," in the execution of that policy. On July 4, 1918, before the Fifth All-Russian Congress of Soviets, Chicherin reported on the new situation in yet greater detail. After the revolutionary offensive which had followed immediately upon the seizure of power, he explained, a radical change had come over Soviet policy. It was now on the defensive, trying to gain time while the international revolution matured and Soviet institutions took hold at home. There were certain assets upon which Soviet foreign policy could draw: the split among the capitalist Powers just then fighting the fiercest battles of the war, and disagreements within each capitalist Power between military and industrial groups, and between those who favored intervention in order to restore the Russian front and those who wanted thereby to overthrow the Bolshevik regime. Bolshevik diplomacy, he claimed, had already been maneuvering among these forces.

The record of Soviet diplomacy in the two years after the seizure of power (which need not be told here) substantiated Chicherin's analysis.[6] But, of course, while there was still a chance for a White victory in the civil war, Soviet diplomacy could make little headway among the "capitalist" Powers. The only direction in which it could move with greater assurance was Asia. But even on that continent, its actions were rather in the nature of gestures; and, despite their enthusiastic reception, particularly in China, they brought no immediate relief to the hard-pressed Soviet regime. The full opportunity for Soviet diplomacy inevitably lay in the West.

When at last in 1920 the struggle between the White armies assisted by foreign intervention and the Bolshevik outward thrust for revolutionary penetration had been fought to a stalemate, Soviet diplomacy came into its own. Peaceful coexistence between capitalism and socialism, proclaimed by the Narkomindel long before capitalist stabilization was conceded by the Comintern, demanded machinery for formal relations. The New Economic Policy, a reluctant retreat on the home front, called even for capitalist assistance in the construction of socialism in Soviet Russia. At the Genoa Economic Conference in April 1922 (a time of famine in Russia), the Soviet delegation, headed by Chicherin, officially made its debut in European diplomatic circles. The old-time diplomats noticed with pleasure that the Soviet representatives, in frock coats and striped trousers, behaved exactly as diplomats were expected to behave. Chicherin even went to a royal reception and exchanged toasts with an archbishop. Henceforth, Soviet diplomats became known as sticklers for diplomatic etiquette.

Soviet diplomacy, indeed, had come a long way in the five years since Trotsky's casual repudiation of diplomacy. It now occupied a legitimate place in the Soviet scheme of government, helping the revolutionary

---

[6] The length to which Soviet diplomacy would go in this period in order to attract attention and aid might be seen in Litvinov's and Vorovskii's letter to the Norwegian lawyer Ludwig Meyer, in which they offered the reinstatement of the political emigrés, reconsideration of the repudiation of the Tsarist debt, and cessation of all propaganda. These promises, needless to say, would never have been honored by Lenin. See Degras, I, 133.

regime to adjust itself to its capitalist environment and even to derive a limited benefit from it. On this unrevolutionary plane of its policy, the Soviet republic was merely one state among others. It had to be informed of the plans of other governments so as to know how to cope with their presumably hostile designs, to exploit their separate needs, and to support within each of them the groups most favorable to itself. For that reason it had to maintain normal relations, and to cultivate at least a minimum of goodwill. Thus, by the logic of survival in a capitalist world, diplomacy was foisted upon a revolutionary regime. But it was tainted from the start with defense, retreat, concessions, insincerity, and the weakness of revolutionary Russia in general.[7]

II

Needless to say, in the process of evolution these two almost antithetical planes of Soviet policy—the revolutionary one close to the Bolshevik core and the more peripheral one of diplomacy—became only gradually differentiated. At the very beginning, of course, diplomacy and revolutionary agitation were almost indistinguishable. Even after Trotsky's resignation, the Narkomindel, barred from formal relations with other governments, continued in his spirit. It was the first Foreign Office to put the "new diplomacy" into effect. All diplomatic correspondence was conducted in the open with an eye to its publicity value both in revolutionary and nonrevolutionary circles. In July 1918 Chicherin frankly admitted that assistance to non-Russian revolutionary movements was a recognized function of revolutionary diplomacy,[8] and in the following January the invitation to the first Congress of the Comintern went out through his Commissariat; moreover, he attended it in person. In his more strictly diplomatic utterances he tried to mobilize Western labor unions over the heads of their governments on behalf of Soviet interests. In the inner councils of the Narkomindel he, Karakhan (its eastern expert), and Radek functioned as a triumvirate, joined for a time by Kamenev. Radek was in charge of the central European department, whose main function consisted of agitation among German prisoners of war; he founded the Karl Liebknecht brigade from their ranks. But, as a brilliant journalist,

---

[7] One can detect a defensive note even in Chicherin's formal and informal analyses of Soviet diplomacy. Particularly in the early years he constantly stressed the complexity of international relations, as if to justify his work as a necessary and autonomous field of government activity.

[8] Quoted by Bruce Hopper, "Narkomindel and Comintern," *Foreign Affairs*, July 1941. Chicherin had told Bruce Lockhart already in the spring of 1918 of the coming Third International.

Radek was also the commissariat's chief publicist. Only later, when diplomacy and revolution had become divorced, did he drift into work with the Comintern in order to stay nearer the center of revolutionary power. (He remained, however, always closer to diplomacy than Zinoviev.) Among the Soviet plenipotentiaries abroad the identity of revolutionary action and diplomacy was still more prominent. Joffe, who was sent to Germany after the Treaty of Brest-Litovsk, at once formed close relations with the Independent Socialists and worked to the utmost to strengthen the revolutionary movement. A few days before the revolution in Germany he was expelled for his machinations—his baggage had burst open (not entirely by accident) in a Berlin railway station and was found stuffed with revolutionary propaganda. Lenin at the time fully conceded that the Soviet embassy in Berlin was "a carrier of the revolutionary contagion";[9] and Chicherin, in his annual report to the Seventh All-Russian Congress of Soviets in December 1919 commented upon the incident in a telling formulation, saying that "the rising revolutionary wave in Germany [had] gradually forced the technical diplomatic work into the background."[10]

Even the very paraphernalia of diplomacy were affected by the original association with revolution. The first Soviet delegation to the Brest-Litovsk negotiations was distinguished by the presence of a worker, a peasant, and a soldier; the proletarian touch was even preserved, although in a far more dignified manner and for more concrete reasons as well, in the Genoa delegations which contained top representatives of Soviet trade unions. A further revolutionary note was carried into diplomacy in June 1918, when it became clear that diplomacy was here to stay: all diplomatic ranks as established by the Congress of Vienna were declared abolished, and equality was decreed between diplomatic and consular agents. Henceforth the heads of Soviet missions abroad were to be known simply as "plenipotentiary representatives." In this connection the old distinction between small and Great Powers, another hangover from the capitalist system, was also considered dropped. Unfortunately, when formal relations were later established with capitalist countries, it proved rather difficult to determine the exact position of a "plenipotentiary

---

[9] Speech on the anniversary of the October Revolution, November 6, 1918; also the following day before the Extraordinary All-Russian Congress of Soviets.

[10] Quoted by T. A. Taracouzio, *War and Peace in Soviet Diplomacy* (New York, 1940), p. 76, note 40. Later when the Soviet government began to insist upon the fiction of the complete separation of the two spheres, the incident was fiercely denied and the blame cast upon White agents, who were accused of having smuggled the compromising material into Joffe's suitcase.

representative" in the diplomatic corps of a foreign capital; and the Soviet government had to recognize the old titles, albeit in an indirect way. In the same year (1924) the government also prescribed for all Soviet diplomats abroad "the simplicity of form and the economy of expenditures fitting the ideals of the Soviet regime."[11]

After the formation of the Comintern and the end of the civil war, the separation of the two spheres of Soviet foreign relations proceeded apace. If the Soviet government wanted to deal with capitalist governments it had to conform to their standards of diplomacy. The issue of revolutionary propaganda cropped up at once as an almost insurmountable obstacle to diplomatic recognition and even to the resumption of trade relations. The result was a strict outward separation of the two spheres.[12] The Soviet government denied any complicity whatever with the activities of the Comintern; it always protested any contrary view as an unfriendly act.

Underneath the fictional separation, however, the relationship between the two spheres was always a troublesome problem. In most areas of the East, where from the Leninist point of view national and revolutionary movements tended to coincide, there were far fewer sources of conflict.[13] But where, as in the West or in Japan, there was a sharp distinction between the established government and the revolutionary movement, the two branches of Soviet policy were bound to collide. One strained its utmost to overthrow the governments with which the other tried to

---

[11] T. A. Taracouzio, *The Soviet Union and International Law* (New York, 1935), app. viii. This regulation, incidentally, did not prevent Rakovsky from wearing silk breeches in his audience with the King of England. How far Soviet diplomats would go in submitting to capitalist or feudal ceremonial practices depended to a large extent upon the current political situation. If the Politburo desired good relations, its diplomats could conveniently drop their Bolshevik simplicity. There seemed to be almost no end to Soviet adaptability: in 1926, at the death of the Mikado, the Soviet representative deposited the official wreath with the Soviet insignia, but without the inscription: "Proletarians of all countries unite," which was part of it. See Bessedovsky, *Den Klauen der Tscheka Entronnen* (Leipzig, 1930), p. 99.

[12] The clearest formulation of this separation was given by Chicherin in 1922: "The Communist party stands at the head of a great government. As a government it enters into relations with all other governments and establishes close friendly relations, guarding the political and economic interests of its republic. . . . Speaking in the name of the government organs we leave [party policy] on the side. The fate of the communist movement, the successes and experiences of communist parties belong in the realm of other organs. Our attention is given to the fate of the Soviet government." "Za piat liet," *Mezhdunarodnaia Zhizn*, 1922, No. 15. There is, of course, much discussion of this point in Soviet literature on international law, which obscures rather than clarifies the relationship.

[13] After the Congress of the Peoples of the East in September 1920 no more revolutionary congresses were held. In relations with the Near and Middle East, the Comintern did not seem to have played an active part. Thus, communications with the Indian communists were maintained, according to M. N. Roy, through diplomatic channels.

maintain friendly relations. Which branch would prevail in the conflict depended upon circumstances. According to Chicherin's felicitous phrase, a rising revolutionary wave would always force "the technical diplomatic work" into the background; in that respect diplomacy was forever inferior to revolution. But in the uncertain setting of the 1920's a twilight zone developed, with revolution and diplomacy holding each other in balance. In the end, the relative success of each branch determined to a large extent its standing in regard to the other. Insofar as the revolutionary ventures of the Comintern and its chief, Zinoviev, collapsed, diplomacy gained;[14] and, insofar as diplomacy failed, revolutionary agitation again advanced. The two branches were in constant adjustment to each other through most of the 1920's for reasons of foreign as well as domestic policy. The period ended, however, with a net gain for diplomacy.

While the prevailing impression is thus one of considerable friction, there is no doubt that the two branches also supplemented each other. The members of the Comintern were always bound, unless otherwise instructed, to support the diplomacy of the Soviet government in their own countries, often much to their chagrin.[15] And without the diplomatic immunity which Comintern agents enjoyed as members of a Soviet foreign mission, they could not have done their work either. Despite their friction, then, a degree of cooperation was indispensable to both.

At the top level of the Politburo, foreign relations, of course, appeared again as one. All disputes between the two main instruments of foreign policy were submitted to it, and it chose the tool, or more commonly the combination of tools, that seemed best to fit the particular occasion. Sometimes diplomacy won an outright victory, as in the case of the Soviet Union's friendly relations with Mussolini in the mid-1920's. Sometimes the Politburo seemed to pursue two seemingly contradictory policies, as in regard to the Kellogg-Briand Pact, which it supported on the diplomatic level while the Comintern denounced it. Sometimes again, as in relations with Germany in the fall of 1923, the revolutionary impulse gained the upper hand without, however, depriving diplomacy of its

---

[14] This may be the point to comment on *Pravda's* famous cartoon, showing Zinoviev haranguing a revolutionary crowd while Chicherin, in the background, held his head in despair. This cartoon appeared before the Fifth Congress of the Comintern in June 1924, when a new equilibrium between diplomacy and revolution was in the making. But the pictorial design of the cartoon still leaves no doubt of Zinoviev's superiority. (See illustrations).

[15] At the Fourth Congress of the Comintern in 1923, Bukharin found it necessary to justify the ways of Soviet diplomacy to the members of the Comintern. See B. Moore, *Soviet Politics: The Dilemma of Power* (Cambridge, Mass., 1950), p. 208.

usefulness. One might say then that each of the two main branches of Soviet policy had an area of maximum effectiveness, with a relatively small area of friction separating them. In the case of the divided attitude towards the Kellogg-Briand Pact, the Soviet leadership tried to make the most of each dimension of its foreign relations, the contradiction not really being as prominent as one might expect (except in the eyes of a few intellectuals) because both dimensions were usually kept apart also in the life of most contemporaries.

The Politburo's analysis of the basic factors of Soviet strength in world affairs likewise counted on the two dimensions. As Stalin put it in the Political Report to the Fifteenth Party Congress, the position of the Soviet Union depended upon three interrelated elements: the inner strength of the Soviet Union; the strength and weakness of the capitalist states; and the strength and weakness of the suppressed classes all over the world and of their revolutionary movements. The first element, the only one entirely under Soviet control, remained, of course, uncomfortably insufficient from the Politburo's point of view, despite all strenuous effort to build up Russia's internal security, her army, and—above all—her industrial potential. All the more significant were the other two, in which the Soviets operated as much as their preoccupation with their internal reconstruction permitted. Their joint significance was also revealed in the chief party documents. In the Political Reports of the Central Committee, particularly in Stalin's methodical rendition from 1925 on, one is apt to find a passage dealing with the world situation in general, analyzed in Marxist terminology, followed by a section on the tasks of the party in the international revolutionary movement and another one on the tasks of diplomacy.[16]

In assessing the scope of Soviet foreign relations, one cannot overstress the fact that from the beginning the Soviet leaders insisted in their dealings with capitalist countries upon the combination of revolutionary activity, with all its illegal components, and traditional diplomacy. The Soviet regime had reverted permanently and wholeheartedly to a more brutal interpretation of the nature of international relations than had become customary in the West. As with diplomats in the age of royal absolutism, Soviet foreign missions were designed to spy, to lie, and to intrigue abroad for the welfare of their masters. But while the Machiavellian diplomat combined the legitimate with the illegitimate business

---

[16] The fact that the spokesman of the Central Committee gave a Leninist analysis of the world situation, from which Soviet diplomacy in its official reports was barred, showed again the relative inferiority of that branch of government.

in his own person, the Soviet regime, recognizing that the standards of diplomacy had been raised in a liberal age, relieved its diplomats[17] of the more unsavory functions. It created a number of separate agencies for spying and subversion, for which, in the eyes of the gullible, it need not assume responsibility. The advance over the days of cabinet policy lay in the vastly improved technique of socio-political agitation, the chief contribution of Leninism. To be sure, in the period under consideration, much of its revolutionary agitation in Europe and Asia remained an idle boast and an act of self-deception. The revolutionary tide had receded and the bulk of Soviet effort came to be concentrated at home. But, for the conduct of Soviet foreign relations, the combination of diplomacy with revolution remained standard practice. In an age of almost universal social and political crisis the Soviets had opened up, for better or worse, the cohesion of society as a new field of power politics, which demanded new instruments, new organizations, and new concepts of theoretical analysis. The Soviets thus started their career with a more comprehensive grasp and control of the factors of power in the twentieth century than their liberal-democratic opponents were to possess for another generation.

And to ask the Soviet regime in its weakness to refrain from making use of its revolutionary tools was as futile as to ask the British Empire to scrap its fleet.

III

One can imagine the difficulties of Chicherin as Soviet Russia's chief diplomat in such a setting. The Soviet Foreign Office had lost the monopoly over the conduct of foreign relations. In the Comintern, it always had a jealous rival and one which was closer to the ears of its superiors.[18] Traditionally, the Foreign Minister had always enjoyed a leading position in the government, and the Foreign Office was an honored branch of the government. There had been notable exceptions to the undisputed monopoly of foreign relations in the hands of Foreign Offices, but never had diplomacy fallen to such a humble and suspect position as it now did. In an avowedly revolutionary society, diplomacy was an anomaly, a standing contradiction to the essential spirit of the regime. Its imitation of the formalities practised by other states was—even while patently insincere—disconcerting and unpleasant to the hard-bitten professional revolutionaries who dominated the government. No

---

[17] Except Joffe, who on all his foreign assignments (in Berlin and Vienna, and on his trip to the Far East) combined the two elements.

[18] For a long time Radek (and never Chicherin) was the Politburo's rapporteur on foreign affairs. See Bessedovsky, *Revelations of a Soviet Diplomat* (London, 1931), p. 62.

one, for instance, could have been unhappier than Kalinin, when he was forced, in his capacity as Chairman of the Presidium of the all-Union Congress of Soviets, to receive King Amanullah of Afghanistan.[19] It is not surprising that the Narkomindel was often by-passed. When something really important seemed in the offing, as for instance the revolutionary upsurge in Germany after July 1923, the Politburo took over, acting through the Comintern; and, for the promotion of the Chinese revolution, it appointed a special Chinese Affairs Commission, in which the Narkomindel was represented by a Far Eastern expert only.[20] In short, at the slightest pretext the Politburo was always inclined to deal directly with all matters within the jurisdiction of the Narkomindel, thus reducing its significance. In many ways, an early uncomplimentary characterization of the Narkomindel as "just a diplomatic chancellery attached to the Central Committee"[21] stated the simple truth. And as a true clerk it was not necessarily admitted into the secret purposes of its masters.

Chicherin's low position in the Communist party, the center of Soviet power, also reflected the inferior status of his office. A former Menshevik, admitted into the party in January 1918, Chicherin could not expect to be heard in the inner councils. Even foreigners knew how much he depended upon Lenin in all major decisions.[22] An early tiff with Stalin over the nationality question, in which he lost out, may have also shown him his powerlessness.[23] His timidity towards the chief leaders increased with the years; rarely did he dare to assert himself. Party distrust was also expressed in the appointment of Litvinov, an old Bolshevik, who in April 1919 joined the *collegium* of the Narkomindel as an informal party guardian over his chief. Joffe, Krestinsky, Rakovsky, Krassin, and others who in the 1920's represented the Soviet government abroad, stood

[19] A. Barmine, *Memoirs of a Soviet Diplomat* (London, 1938), p. 221.

[20] Bessedovsky, *Revelations*, p. 122. This commission was headed by Unschlicht, the head of foreign military intelligence.

[21] Ascribed by Bessedovsky to the acting head of the Ukrainian Narkomindel, Yakovlev, in 1920. *Revelations*, p. 20. Important notes were drafted by members of the Politburo themselves; so Trotsky drew up the reply to the Curzon Ultimatum in May 1923. It is significant also that the official *History of the Communist Party* barely mentions Soviet diplomacy in the period under discussion.

[22] Lenin's private opinion of Chicherin may be gathered from his letter to Trotsky after Chicherin had suggested that substantial concessions be made at the Genoa Conference: "Send Chicherin at once to a sanitarium." Trotsky, *Mein Leben*, p. 455.

[23] At the Tenth Congress (March 1921) Stalin attacked Chicherin over a series of articles in *Pravda* written by the latter, entitled: "Against Stalin's Theses." Although nominated to the Committee on the National Question at that Congress, Chicherin was not elected to it. See the stenographic protocols of the Tenth Congress (ed. N. N. Popov, 1933).

higher in the party than their official chief. Until the Fourteenth Party Congress in 1925, the Narkomindel had not even a voice in the Central Committee, while its rival, the Comintern, had from the beginning several spokesmen in the Politburo, not to mention Radek on the Central Committee. At the Party Congress of 1925, because of the changing balance of power in the party and the successes of Soviet diplomacy in the previous year, Chicherin was promoted to the Central Committee, but by that time this body had lost its original significance; and in 1930, at the Sixteenth Congress, he was deprived of this preferment without his successor Litvinov at once being elected in his place.[24] Obviously, the Narkomindel was left very much on the outer fringes of the party.

Under these circumstances it was not easy to organize and operate an efficient foreign service. Soviet diplomacy, to discuss briefly its internal organization, was handicapped from the outset because, unlike most other branches of the Soviet government and unlike its foreign equivalents, it had to start entirely from scratch. The Narkomindel's historian has described the tense scene when Trotsky took over the Foreign Office.[25] Upon his arrival he ordered the entire staff inherited from the previous regime to assemble and announced to them curtly: "Those for us go to the left, those against us go to the right." The *chinovniks*, after deliberating among themselves, went right to a man. Only the menials remained to shake hands with the new Commissar. Shortly thereafter all Foreign Office personnel abroad was recalled or repudiated. Within two months, however, the personnel of the Narkomindel already numbered about two hundred, including the revolutionary guards from the Siemens-Schuckert works and a nearby pipe-rolling mill. But even after the arrival of Chicherin, the organization and routine of the new Peoples Commissariat reflected for some time the shiftlessness of that hectic phase of Soviet rule. By 1921 it had at last achieved some stability. Its internal organization was sanctioned by a decree of the Council of Commissars; and the treaties with Soviet Russia's neighbors, the trade negotiations with England, and expanding relations with the outside world in general provided its officials with a steadily growing volume of business. But for a long time it had a reputation for amazing inefficiency.[26]

The top personnel, constituting the *collegium*, which ran the Narkomindel in the mid-1920's, was a remarkable body in the annals of

[24] Litvinov was elected in 1934, at the Seventeenth Congress.
[25] See the Narkomindel's publication *Desiat Liet Sovietskoi Diplomatiia* [*Ten Years of Soviet Diplomacy*] (Moscow, 1927), p. 4.
[26] See O. Blum, *Russische Köpfe* (Berlin, 1923), p. 406.

diplomacy. Georgii Chicherin himself, his country's chief diplomat, was considered rather an oddity.[27] A shy, timid little man with an intelligent and gentle glance, utterly negligent of dress, an aesthete and hypochondriac, he had little of the outward polish of the diplomat, despite his aristocratic birth. Those who knew him closely called him a visionary who had shut out all reality and who lived with his job twenty-four hours a day—although occasionally he would lock himself up in a room adjoining his study and for hours play Mozart on the piano. They praised him as a man above pettiness and party intrigue, almost too fragile for the rude hurly-burly of Bolshevik politics. The foreign correspondents discussed his unorthodox methods of work, his custom of receiving foreign diplomats and other callers in the small hours of the morning, his dislike of modern office equipment. The gossipers traded stories of how, because he was unable to delegate work, he drafted, wrote, typed, sealed, and posted diplomatic notes himself; or how, in his absent-mindedness, he mislaid important documents, for which then the whole department had to search. In such an event, they related, he even routed his colleagues from bed or the ballet. But everyone who knew Chicherin respected his abilities as diplomat: his brilliant mind, his sharp repartee, and that amazing memory which made foreign diplomats wince.

Only revolution could have placed such an unusual man in charge of Russian diplomacy; but even among the revolutionaries he remained a stranger. Among the matter-of-fact life stories of Old Bolsheviks, Chicherin's authorized biography (which only he himself could have written) reads like a chapter from Dostoievsky.[28] There were no revolutionary deeds in the underground to record; there was only the tortuous metamorphosis of a Russian aristocrat into a Menshevik, who during the world war found himself in agreement with Lenin's revolutionary internationalism rather than the "social chauvinism" of the bulk of European socialists.[29] In his case the making of a Menshevik consisted of a series of inner crises: the adjustment problems of an only child reared in an emotionally surcharged and highly religious atmosphere; the sufferings and inhibitions of a poor relation in the fast and superficial northern capital; the tensions which led to his final break

[27] Characterizations of Chicherin's personality can be found in Louis Fischer, *Men and Politics*; Bruce Lockhart, *Memoirs*; Lincoln Steffens, *Autobiography*; Louise Bryant, *Mirrors of Moscow*; G. Bessedovsky, *Revelations*; O. Blum, *Russische Köpfe*; E. Cerruti, *Visti da Vicino*; etc.

[28] Printed in *Entsiklopedicheskii Slovar Russkago Bibliograficheskago Instituta Granat* (hereinafter cited as *Granat*), XLI, part III, 215ff.

[29] See Trotsky, *Mein Leben*, p. 334, for Chicherin's initial leanings towards patriotism.

with his aristocratic past. His intense spiritual struggles, which he later described with introspective detail, carried him from bourgeois respectability, Nietzschean yearning for the superman, and tortured compulsions towards self-destruction to the optimistic collectivism of Marxism. They left his physique undermined from an early age; he was not fit for active revolutionary duty. But there was also a more stable side to his development: his interest in foreign policy.

Diplomacy had been in the family. His father, before he took up pietism and retired to his estate in the province, had been secretary to the Piedmont legation in 1859 and, shortly thereafter, counselor at the Paris embassy. His maternal grandfather, Count Stakelberg, had been the Russian ambassador at Vienna, at the time of the Congress of Vienna; hence the self-avowed Metternich touch in Chicherin's diplomacy.[30] This tradition compelled the young Chicherin to join the Tsarist Foreign Office. He entered, however, not as an active diplomat, but as an archivist and scholar, who was set to work on Russian foreign policy between the Crimean war and the Congress of Berlin, a fact which may account for his special interest in the Near and Middle East and for his anti-British bias in later years.

After 1904 the two strands of his life interests, diplomacy and social justice, separated to be united again only after the revolution. Quietly giving up his position at the Foreign Office, he left Russia and studied the social-democratic movement in Germany, where he became a close friend of Karl Liebknecht. It was indicative of his ability that, within three years, he assumed an important post in the revolutionary movement by becoming secretary of the foreign bureau of the Russian Social-Democratic party, which tried to coordinate the work of the various Marxist emigré centers. At the same time he took a deep interest in the socialist youth movement. After the outbreak of the war, he shifted from Paris to Brussels and London, where he worked for the relief of Russian political refugees and took a hand in the antiwar agitation of the Independent Labor party. After the March Revolution, he headed a committee for the repatriation of political exiles, was arrested after the Bolshevik coup for his propaganda activities, and was finally exchanged in January 1918 for Sir George Buchanan, the British ambassador to Russia. Upon his return he joined the Bolshevik party. As he was the only comrade with Foreign Office experience, an excellent linguist, and otherwise well-qualified except perhaps in party staunchness, Lenin assigned him at once to the Peoples Commissariat for Foreign Affairs, and, even before

[30] See his biography, cited in note 28 above.

[250]

Trotsky's resignation as Commissar in March 1918, he assumed control. Thus, at the age of 45, "a new page of his life," as he wrote, began for him. It was not to be an altogether happy one, for, as he confessed in his autobiography, the revolutionary and the aesthete did not always blend in him, either before or after the revolution.

Next in importance in the Narkomindel, and eventually to replace his chief, came M. M. Litvinov, Vice-Commissar, whose work will be evaluated in a subsequent chapter of this book. Beside Litvinov stood L. M. Karakhan, also Vice-Commissar and specialist for Far Eastern affairs.[31] His background was rather undistinguished both from a revolutionary or intellectual point of view. Born in the Transcaucasus (his name indicates Armenian origin) and trained in the law, he joined the Russian Social-Democratic Workers party in 1904, and worked for a while in its Far Eastern organization. Later he went to the capital where he became a permanent member of the international committee. He was said to have proved himself a competent agitator, propagandist, and organizer, who remained outside the factional strife. A "defeatist" during the war, he was banished to Tomsk, where he continued his revolutionary work and extended it into eastern Siberia. He joined the Bolsheviks after the March revolution and appeared for the first time in the limelight as a member of the Brest-Litovsk delegation, owing his selection to Lenin. His background in Asiatic Russia seemed to fit him particularly for Soviet relations with the East; in 1925 he was Soviet ambassador in Peking. He was generally described as an able, but by no means outstanding person, who impressed some of the younger Bolsheviks like Barmine as the department's diplomatic dandy.[32]

A fourth member of the *collegium*, who joined it in 1923, was V. L. Kopp, who, like Karakhan and Litvinov, stemmed from petty bourgeois background. He had studied engineering but had soon followed the revolutionary call and became a member of the "transport administration" which received and distributed revolutionary materials within Russia. After organization work among St. Petersburg metal workers in 1905, he had gone into foreign exile and newspaper work with Trotsky and the German Social Democratic party. After the outbreak of the

---

[31] The following biographies are based on *Granat*, XLI. It should be noted, however, that these official biographical sketches are by no means reliable. All revolutionaries had to censor their *curricula vitae* both before and after the revolution. See also Bessedovsky's characterization of Karakhan as "the ass with the classical profile."

[32] Barmine, *Memoirs*, p. 155. Maybe Trotsky's quip was directed at him (or was it Litvinov?): "I absolutely cannot understand those revolutionaries who like to become ambassadors and swim in their new role like a fish in water." Trotsky, *Mein Leben*, p. 348.

war, he served in the Russian army—an unusual turn for a future Bolshevik commissar—but was captured by the Germans in 1915. Joffe obtained his release in the fall of 1918 and made him counselor at the Berlin embassy. He then served as Soviet representative in Berlin until his promotion to the *collegium*. In 1925 he was Soviet ambassador in Japan, where he proved quite susceptible to the geopolitical teachings of Haushofer.

The *collegium* of the Narkomindel, in which the Commissar was *primus inter pares* rather than undisputed chief, was far from a unanimous body. Litvinov, the Old Bolshevik, had been set to watch over Chicherin. In the ensuing jockeying for power, which divided the Commissariat ever more deeply towards the end of the 1920's, Karakhan sided with Chicherin, Kopp with Litvinov. It was said that a fifth member, T. A. Rothstein, was appointed to break the deadlock. Rothstein, however, who had been an editor of the London *Daily News* and had his sons educated at Oxford, proved unequal to the task. More of a scholar than a diplomat, he was put in charge of publicity and press affairs. At times other men also joined the *collegium*—Rakovsky as Ukrainian delegate and Vice-Commissar, and after him the party economist Schlichter. As a body, the *collegium* may be said to have been made up of the least revolutionary type of Bolsheviks, most of whom had fairly extensive knowledge and experience of western European life. They were "halfway men," making their career in the twilight zone between the outside world and the Bolshevik core. But, apart from Chicherin, its chief members would have hardly qualified for Sir Ernest Satow's characterization of a diplomat as an "educated gentleman." The *collegium* was apparently not a congenial environment for profitable common work. Bessedovsky, a minor diplomat, found it shot through with intrigue and scandalmongering.

Under the *collegium* there operated, besides the numerous secretariat, the various geographical and functional departments.[38] The latter dealt with administrative and personnel affairs, the press, economic and legal matters. As to the geography of its foreign relations, the Narkomindel knew only East and West, the Eastern Department being divided into Near East (including Africa), Middle East, and Far East, and the Western, according to the decree of November 12, 1923, into Central Europe, the Baltic limitrophes and Poland, Scandinavia, Anglo-Roman

[38] *Desiat Liet,* p. 19. They were organized under the *Sovnarkom* decree of November 12, 1923. This decree is reprinted in French in the Yearbook of the Narkomindel for 1929.

(Britain, France, Italy, Spain, United States, and Latin America), and the Balkans. In 1927, as an economy measure, the Balkan division was dissolved and its countries assigned either to the Anglo-Roman or Central European divisions.[34] Altogether, between 450 and 550 men and women seem to have been employed at the central offices during the mid-1920's,[35] a number roughly comparable to the personnel of the central offices of the Comintern.[36] Paul Scheffer, the German correspondent, found the department overworked and somewhat neglected.[37] Indeed, a position in the Narkomindel was not considered an easy berth, particularly in the early 1920's, not only because of Chicherin's unusual hours but because of the low pay scale. Other government departments paid their officials three to four times as much[38]—a further indication of the relative unimportance of the Narkomindel in the Soviet scheme. By comparison the experts of the Comintern, mostly pampered foreign comrades, lived like kings.

The Narkomindel as part of the formal government structure was subordinate to the Council of Peoples Commissars and through it responsible to the all-Russian Congress of Soviets and its Central Executive Committee (VTSIK).[39] Occasionally Chicherin or Litvinov reported before these bodies on the state of international relations, and their Commissariat submitted its annual report to them. One may assume that the few public discussions on foreign affairs in these bodies,[40] prepared beforehand, were no problem to the Narkomindel; at least Soviet diplomacy was spared the worry over parliamentary pressure groups or public opinion. The relations of the Narkomindel with other executive agencies, however, were more complicated. Within its extensive bureaucracy the Soviet government found it difficult to coordinate all its formal foreign relations. In 1927, for instance, the Naphtha Trust was discovered negotiating on its own with the Spanish government[41] (which had not yet recognized the Soviet Union), despite the recent decree of *Sovnarkom* that all business between the branches of the Soviet government and

---

[34] *Desiat Liet,* p. 23.

[35] *ibid.,* p. 17. For 1924 the number of "responsible workers" (corresponding roughly to the Tsarist *chinovniki*) was given as 484, 376 of them being party members.

[36] P. Scheffer, *Sieben Jahre Soviet Union* (Leipzig, 1930), p. 286.

[37] *ibid.,* p. 416.

[38] *Desiat Liet,* p. 12.

[39] For the place of the Narkomindel in the constitutional structure of the USSR, see J. Towster, *Political Power in the USSR, 1917-1947* (New York, 1948).

[40] See, for instance, the debates of the Third All-Union Congress of Soviets in May 1925, and the analysis of them in Towster, *Political Power,* pp. 217ff.

[41] Bessedovsky, *Revelations,* p. 205.

foreign governments be conducted through the Narkomindel.[42] Under that decree only strictly nonpolitical matters could be handled directly; otherwise the Narkomindel was to be informed immediately. Military and naval authorities were to arrange with the Commissariat their modes of communication with their attachés (who were outside the jurisdiction of the Narkomindel). That decree incidentally suggests that, even within the relatively narrow legitimate sphere of foreign relations, the Narkomindel had found it difficult to enforce its monopoly. The very size of government in the twentieth century—the Soviet government took the lead in "big government"—created new problems for the conduct of diplomacy.[43]

The Narkomindel's relations with other government departments, however, were far less of a problem to it than its relations with the Comintern, the OGPU, and the party, i.e. with those interlacing agencies which by their nature were closer to the Bolshevik core. The full extent of the domestic pressures bearing down upon the Narkomindel will probably never be known with certainty; but the few available glimpses into that fluid and carefully hidden realm of internal Soviet politics, although to be interpreted with caution, tell their own story. There is no evidence of any routine liaison between the Narkomindel and the central office of the Comintern (the OMS—International Liaison Section) headed by O. A. Piatnitsky. But there were two indirect ties, one through the Politburo acting as arbiter between the two agencies; the other through the foreign missions. If Bessedovsky's case was at all typical, a Soviet diplomat about to assume a new post abroad was briefed not only by the Narkomindel but also by the Comintern and the Politburo—not to mention the OGPU and military intelligence.[44] In his embassy then he would have to shift back to the position of mere diplomat. There his job was to come to some working relationship with the Comintern agents and other nondiplomatic personnel who were part of his suite and enjoyed full diplomatic privileges no matter how subversive their real concerns.[45]

[42] Joint decree of *Vtsik* and *Sovnarkom*, August 27, 1926, reaffirming an earlier one of 1921. See Taracouzio, *Soviet Union*, Appendix x.

[43] There is no room here to discuss the federal aspects in the organization of the Narkomindel. There is no reason to assume, however, that they were of any special concern either to Chicherin or Soviet diplomats in general.

[44] Bessedovsky, *Revelations*, pp. 127ff.

[45] As the presence of Comintern agents in Soviet diplomatic missions was public knowledge, it was the desire of all governments to limit the size and number of Soviet missions in their territory; hence the protracted negotiations over the status of Soviet trade delegations in England and other countries.

Inevitably, the relation between revolution and diplomacy within the walls of a Soviet foreign mission were often stormy. Nowhere else was their rivalry so keen and so intimate. Naturally the Narkomindel wished to rid its embassies of their most compromising members, or at least curtail their powers.[46] And many times it carried the dispute over the disciplinary rights of its diplomats to the Politburo.[47] Over the years the position and influence of the subversive agents in Soviet embassies and trade delegations was reduced. After the failure of the German revolution in 1923 the Comintern agents were given more subordinate functions as translators or press agents, and their work was organized separately to reduce friction with the diplomatic staff. But individual Comintern agents with strong backing in Moscow occasionally defied these regulations. And while the Narkomindel succeeded in limiting the power of the Comintern in its foreign missions, it never could eliminate it altogether; diplomatic immunity was too essential for its work. Sometimes it would even occur that a diplomat was asked to aid directly in some Comintern transaction, which he was apt to refuse if he was worth his salt.[48] But while individual diplomats might resist such compromising orders at some risk to their careers, diplomatic mail pouches would unfeelingly carry dynamite, weapons, propaganda, or money for revolutionary purposes. And the couriers of the Narkomindel were all said to be OGPU men.[49]

The Narkomindel's relations with the secret police resembled somewhat its relations with the Comintern. As part of the subversive machinery abroad and closely related to the Comintern at the center,[50] the police agents constituted an equally compromising part of foreign missions. In the home office in Moscow, the presence of a Cheka man was reported in the early 1920's.[51] In 1927 Chicherin confessed to Bessedovsky that his office (like most others in the government) was wired with hidden microphones by the OGPU.[52] That agency also interfered in matters of policy. Paul Scheffer, the German correspondent, reported that after 1927 the OGPU, staffed ever since Dzerzhinsky's days with Poles, manufactured anti-German incidents to the embarrassment of

---

[46] The second secretary of the mission was usually the Comintern agent, the third secretary the OGPU man (or woman). Miliukov, *Politique extérieure*, p. 136.

[47] Bessedovsky, *Revelations*, pp. 69ff.

[48] *ibid.*, p. 166.

[49] Krivitsky, *In Stalin's Secret Service* (New York, 1939), p. 38.

[50] Piatnitsky, the head of the OMS, was a close friend of Trillisser, in charge of the foreign section of the OGPU. G. Agabekov, *OGPU* (New York, 1931), p. 269.

[51] Louise Bryant, *Mirrors of Moscow* (New York, 1923), p. 191.

[52] Bessedovsky, *Revelations*, p. 196.

Chicherin.[53] It meddled furthermore in the censorship exercised by Rothstein of the Narkomindel's press department over foreign correspondents, often stopping dispatches previously passed by him.[54] Litvinov, who could afford to be bolder than his chief, took a vigorous stand against OGPU penetration, with scant success.[55] Here, still more than in the case of its struggle with the Comintern, Soviet diplomacy had its hands tied. This does not mean that harmony prevailed between the agencies closer to the core of the party—there was some friction also between the OGPU and the Comintern; but the two were apt to present a common front against diplomacy. And yet, no doubt, Soviet diplomacy also benefited from the code cracking and espionage services of the OGPU.

The link between the Narkomindel and the party was kept fairly well out of sight, for obvious reasons. Of course, all its chief officials were party members and thus under party discipline. Lenin commented proudly on the close penetration of the Narkomindel by the party. Chicherin's speeches, and still more Litvinov's, although adapted to diplomatic non-Marxist parlance, reflected the official line. At party congresses, Chicherin after 1921, and later Litvinov and Karakhan, appeared only as nonvoting delegates for their department; they took no part in the discussion. The report on foreign policy, as part of the Political Report, was entirely in the hands of the leading member of the Politburo, Lenin, Zinoviev, or Stalin.[56] But while Soviet diplomacy was silent at party congresses, the head of the Comintern submitted a lengthy and fully publicized report. As to the attitude of the Politburo towards the Narkomindel, it was what would be expected: tolerance because of a limited usefulness but not respect. In public, Lenin had treated Chicherin and his work with a certain friendly solicitude; even Zinoviev in delivering the Central Committee's report in 1923 found a few good words for him, but Stalin was cool. Only after 1928 was he said to have taken a greater interest in the department, when Chicherin was already

---

[53] P. Scheffer, *Sieben Jahre*, p. 441.   [54] *ibid.*, p. 421.

[55] Agabekov, *OGPU*, p. 269.

[56] Litvinov once spoke, at the Fifteenth Party Congress in December 1927, reporting on the Preparatory Committee on Disarmament of the League of Nations, in whose work he had recently participated. But his speech was an exception prompted by a very special reason. At that congress Stalin played a difficult and ambiguous game. On one hand he had been forced to set a sharp Left course, which implied bitter hostility to the League. On the other hand, he had already determined upon a policy of cautious rapprochement with the Western Powers. It was left to Litvinov, just back from Geneva, to reconcile the two incompatible policies by giving a strongly Left interpretation to Soviet policy at Geneva. Judging by the hilarious reception of his speech, he acquitted himself successfully of his difficult task.

See also Towster, *Political Power*, on the discussion of foreign policy at party congresses.

on his way out. Bessedovsky reports many instances when Stalin ignored the views of the department; he also tells of Stalin's private correspondence with diplomats over the heads of their chief and of errands on which he sent them contrary to official diplomatic policy.[57] Needless to say, the fact that the Politburo was occasionally divided in itself on foreign policy was another source of complications to Chicherin.[58] Of cordiality between the Narkomindel and the chief figures in the party there was no trace; Chicherin disliked Stalin, and both he and Litvinov disliked Molotov.

While Soviet diplomacy at the center was hampered by internal friction and hostile crosscurrents, Soviet diplomatic missions abroad operated on the whole—if one may trust Bessedovsky or Barmine—no more efficiently or harmoniously. And yet they did not lack able diplomats. During its first ten years the Soviet government drew on the services of Krassin, who in the past had followed an unusual, but successful, career as an electrical engineer, big businessman, and revolutionary, and who was also its Commissar for Foreign Trade;[59] of Joffe, who as a young man of means had given his time to studies and revolutionary underground work until he was exiled to the Siberian *taiga* to rise after his return to the inner circles of the party;[60] of Krestinsky, who had been a lawyer, a Bolshevik candidate for the Fourth Duma, and later chairman of the Ural committee of the Communist party before he was made secretary of the Central Committee; and finally of Rakovsky, the Ukrainian communist who for years had practiced medicine in France before he became chairman of the Ukrainian Council of Peoples Commissars and its Commissar for Foreign Affairs.[61] To be sure, Krestinsky and Rakovsky were sent to their foreign posts as a form of political exile; they had become *personae non gratae* in Moscow. In the years of Stalin's rise, assignment to the diplomatic service became a favorite method of isolating potential opponents, a practice which reflects again the relatively inferior position of diplomacy. During the

[57] Bessedovsky, *Revelations*, p. 210. The issue here was Bessarabia.

[58] As in the Ghilan affair. See L. Fischer, *The Soviets in World Affairs* (new ed., Princeton, 1951), I, xv. (Not to mention the party division over the Chinese revolution.)

[59] His biography in Lubov Krassin, *Leonid Krassin, His Life and Work*; and more revealingly in Simon Liberman, *Working for Lenin's Russia*, which contains interesting glimpses of Soviet diplomacy in the early years.

[60] *Granat*, XLI. Also for the following.

[61] One might also mention Vorovsky, who was of Polish noble background and had received a scientific education. He was the Bolshevik representative among the Polish Social Democrats and lived in Stockholm, as a contact man, during the war. After the February revolution he became a member of the foreign bureau of the Bolshevik Central Committee, to be sent back to Scandinavia after the seizure of power.

struggle against the "left deviation," Kamenev thus became ambassador in Rome, and Mme. Kollontai, the Soviets' first woman diplomat (and much advertised as such), minister to Norway and later ambassador to Mexico. Unfortunately, no study of the background of Soviet diplomats in the 1920's is available. It appears, however, that not only Bolsheviks secured diplomatic assignment. Bessedovsky, a career diplomat, had been a Ukrainian Social Revolutionary and forestry expert; Leonid Obolensky, Soviet plenipotentiary in Warsaw until 1925, an aristocrat and Tsarist tax collector in Siberia.[62] In the subordinate positions, at least in the first years after the revolution, all sorts of revolutionary riffraff could be found. In general, the conditions were such that the Narkomindel was forced from an early time to undertake the training of suitable Bolshevik cadres to make the most of the opportunities for distinction which Soviet diplomacy afforded.

The position of Soviet diplomats in foreign capitals, indeed, was a very challenging one, although not without obvious physical dangers.[63] Their job was twofold: to overcome the often extreme hostility against the Soviet regime—a feeling so intense on occasion that Litvinov, upon his first arrival in Copenhagen for negotiations with the British over the return of prisoners of war, was unable to secure lodging in any respectable hotel—and to make a position for themselves which would enable them to wield at least some political influence. Their situation was not unlike that of the diplomats of an earlier period, when, in the absence of instantaneous communication with their home office, they had to rely upon their own resources. The Soviet diplomat, of course, could always resort to the telegraph. But as his success depended upon adaptation to a very alien scene, the home office could not always assist him. This suggests, incidentally, that it was not only modern communications but also the increased uniformity of conditions and diplomatic practices among the Western governments that deprived diplomats in general of their former independence. Where there was little common ground between governments, as between the Soviet Union and the outside world, the diplomat—at least potentially—had a chance to regain his former stature. That was true, not only of Soviet diplomats with spirit and boldness, such as Rakovsky in Paris, but also of foreign diplomats in Moscow, when political circumstances favored their assignment, as was

[62] Bessedovsky, *Revelations*, p. 40. He was appointed, it seems, because he had done a favor to a Bolshevik exile in Siberia.

[63] Two Soviet diplomats, Vorovsky and Voisky, and a courier, Nette. were assassinated in the 1920's. Throughout, Soviet embassies lived in fear of attack.

the case with Brockdorff-Rantzau. The independence enjoyed by these men, however, could not last. Rakovsky's attempts to manipulate French domestic politics (entirely without recourse to revolutionary forces) finally led to a demand for his recall;[64] and the tightening control of the Stalinist regime soon limited whatever opportunity existed for Soviet diplomats abroad or Western diplomats in Moscow. What Stalin expected of his diplomats may be gathered from his admonition to Bessedovsky as he set out for Tokyo: "Talk to the Japanese as little as possible and telegraph us as often as possible. And don't think yourself the cleverest of us all."[65]

Here, in short, was the constant dilemma of Soviet diplomats. They had to attempt to bridge the profound gap between the core of the revolutionary regime, with its Leninist-Stalinist sense of reality, and the "capitalist" governments to which they were accredited. If they played too much the professional revolutionary or kept too much to themselves, they could not hope to make their way abroad and to be of maximum usefulness to their government. If, on the other hand, they made their way too well, they laid themselves open to the charge of submitting to capitalist influences. Few members of the Soviet foreign service knew how to strike a balance acceptable to their masters and true to their craft. Some, like Krassin, found their influence increasingly limited; others, like Bessedovsky, Solomon, and Dimitrievsky, fled from Soviet service when the disparity between the Soviet Union and the outside world, between the Stalinist regime and their political ideas, became too uncomfortable. These dramatic defections were followed by the adoption of greater security measures. But, as the later examples of Barmine and Kravchenko show, the loyalty problem was never completely solved, despite very strict supervision within Soviet missions abroad.

Apart from the supervision of the diplomats by the agents of the secret police and the Comintern within their mission, there was the scrutiny by the party cell, the secretary of which reported directly to party headquarters. In appointments to foreign posts, loyalty checks played a great part by 1930, with the chief of the foreign section of the OGPU and the members of the Central Committee in charge of party cells abroad conferring with the Narkomindel or the Commissariat for Foreign Trade on every candidate.[66] The activities of the party cells in

[64] The official reason was that he had signed a manifesto of the Left opposition which encouraged foreign soldiers to desert to the Red Army in case of war with the Soviet Union.

[65] Bessedovsky, *Revelations*, p. 131.

[66] Agabekov, *OGPU*, p. 269. The penalties for desertion were further increased in the 1930's.

foreign missions often descended to a rather unpleasant personal level. Relatively idle and almost completely isolated from "capitalist" society, Soviet missions abroad, particularly the lesser ones, often stagnated in their own sordid little messes. A touch of scandal or insurmountable personal animosity often led to the transfer of personnel from one post to another. These circumstances may have contributed in part to the low esteem in which diplomats were held in inner party circles.[67]

Nor could they, on the whole, make a good impression abroad on grounds of their professional integrity or competency. How could a Soviet diplomat fulfill the conditions which Lord Balfour set for the good diplomat?[68] As a party member and representative of the Soviet government, he could not expect to gain the confidence of the government to which he was accredited. Nor could he honestly and clearly convey the policies of the Politburo to that foreign government, for he voiced only the surface segment of Soviet foreign relations. And again, if he reported to his Soviet superiors accurately and understandingly on the intentions and policies of foreign governments, and particularly on general conditions abroad, he always ran the danger of being accused of lacking in revolutionary rectitude. The safest procedure for a Soviet diplomat under the circumstances was to forget professional standards and, as a diplomatic technician, adapt himself to the outlook demanded of him, at whatever cost to Soviet interests or world peace.[69]

The individual diplomat's dilemma, however, only reflected the larger quandary of Soviet diplomacy. In all countries the Diplomatic Service must mediate between foreign reality and domestic pressures; for that reason, it is bound to encounter hostility at home. Particularly in countries where social cohesion is insufficient for the purposes of government, those who urge the need for adjustment to the nature and the needs of foreign peoples are under suspicion, for they introduce an alien element into a society which fears any challenge to its orthodoxy. In Soviet Russia, the Bolshevik norm was increasingly narrowly defined; hence the professional handicaps of diplomacy increased during the 1920's. In order to win successes abroad, Soviet diplomacy was forced to indulge

---

[67] That is the picture conveyed by Bessedovsky, and to a lesser extent by Barmine. There was, however, also the example of Iureniev, Soviet representative in Rome, who conducted his embassy according to the best Bolshevik ideals. See Barmine, *Memoirs*, p. 206.

[68] Lockhart, *Memoirs*, p. 271.

[69] The effects upon diplomatic negotiations resulting from such close supervision of diplomats may be seen in Philip E. Mosely, "Some Soviet Techniques of Negotiation," in *Negotiating with the Russians*, ed. Raymond Dennett and Joseph E. Johnson (New York, 1952).

in a degree of adaptation to "capitalist" environment; by its very nature, then, it had a bias towards the "right deviation"—just as, in the case of capitalist countries dealing with socialist governments, the conscientious diplomat is apt to be accused of Leftist sympathy. No wonder, then, that Soviet diplomats were put under very strict observation.

What, then, was the outward appearance of Soviet diplomacy as a halfway station between the revolutionary core and the capitalist world? As the legitimate segment of Soviet policy it had to serve as a shield of the revolutionary core; its task in carrying out its assignments was to explain away, to conceal, to deny, or to ignore the revolution. For all its actions, it had to find nonrevolutionary motives. And here Soviet diplomacy, which was to be "open diplomacy," presumably averse to all secrecy or camouflage, found itself often in another insoluble dilemma, from which it escaped only by employing the most preposterous lies, half-truths, or arguments which, in strict theory, were incompatible with Soviet ideology.

Among the outright falsehoods frequently employed was the contention that the Soviet government had nothing to do with the Comintern. In his speech to the Central Executive Committee of the all-Russian Congress of Soviets on March 4, 1925, to quote but one example, Chicherin rejected a German protest that a member of the presidium of that body had signed a revolutionary appeal to the German Communist party: "We have already been forced once before to advise the German government formally that our government is not responsible for the activities of the Comintern and has nothing in common with it." The German government, bound to Soviet Russia by political necessity, did not pursue the point further. In 1921 and 1922, the British government under Curzon had disputed the same Soviet assertion and had been met with a series of evasions[70] and claims that British information about the connection between the Comintern and the Soviet government was false (it was in form, although not in substance); that it was fabricated by White agents (who, indeed, were active forgers in that period); and that the British, too, were employing subversive agents against Soviet influence (which presumably was also true but beside the point); and that members of the British Cabinet were also members of international organizations (which again was irrelevant). If Soviet diplomacy admitted the existence of the Comintern at all, it argued—and this was another

[70] See the documents in Degras, I, 209, and Krassin, *Leonid Krassin*, pp. 135ff.

half-truth—that capitalist and colonial conditions inevitably made for revolution, regardless of Soviet propaganda.[71]

When Soviet diplomacy was not rubbed so hard against uncomfortable verities, it resorted to more congenial subterfuges. It took a line which might be called homeopathic revolution; it would be progressive, anti-capitalist, even proletarian, but without the Bolshevik sting. Chicherin's speech at the opening session of the Genoa Conference, carefully prepared with Lenin's help, may serve as an illustration of this mode. He said that the Russian delegation came in the interest of peace and the economic reconstruction of Europe and recognized, without surrendering their Communist principles, the parallel existence of the old and the new order in the present historical period. He even put the economic opportunities for foreign business under the NEP in a rather favorable light. But then he introduced issues not on the agenda: various measures of disarmament; a better League of Nations, in which the distinction between small and Great Powers, between the victorious and the vanquished, was abolished; and even a plea for planned global distribution of industrial resources. In short, he presented a picture of the Soviet government as the leader in progressive reforms of international relations, advocating drastic but not necessarily revolutionary measures for an admittedly bleak postwar world. On other occasions, Soviet diplomacy harped on the foibles of capitalist international relations in general, the brutal character of the Versailles settlement, the shortcomings of the League, the friction between the Great Powers, and the high cost of power politics in general; it delighted in pointing out the injustices of the existing balance of power and the hypocrisy of all capitalist diplomacy (as it was quick, in retaliation, to show up the dirt in the politics of any other government). In the 1920's, the climax of this propaganda policy without the revolutionary corollary was of course Litvinov's famous first performance before the Preparatory Commission on Disarmament in November 1927. While Chicherin did not approve of Litvinov's policy, he himself had many times sung a similar gloating tune on other issues; it was the *basso continuo* of Soviet diplomacy. The closest Soviet diplomacy came to admitting an interest in revolution—and it did this only in the early 1920's—was to claim that it represented the foreign policy of the international proletariat.

Another motif of Soviet revolutionary not-so-revolutionary diplomacy,

[71] In Chicherin's circular to Soviet representatives abroad (September 10, 1920) concerning a note from the American Secretary of State Bainbridge Colby to the Italian ambassador in Washington. Degras, I, 210. Also Stalin, Political Report to Sixteenth Congress.

in which Chicherin, the Metternich pupil, felt particularly at home, was its frank *Realpolitik*. It sought to exploit the "contradictions" among the capitalist powers. These "contradictions" were always listed in any Soviet survey of the foreign situation and often much exaggerated, particularly in the case of Anglo-American relations. Soviet diplomacy tried to aggravate these cleavages and thus sided with the revisionist powers and with the weaker against the stronger, like any practitioner of the traditional balance of power policy. At the same time—and here it reverted somewhat to Marxist analysis—it made much of the divisions among capitalist groups within a given country, attempting particularly to bait certain commercial and industrial interests with concessions in Russia. On this level of its diplomacy, social revolution played no part whatever; any traditional practitioner of power politics might have acted likewise.[72]

Considering Chicherin's background (and also the fact that the Bolshevik revolution represented a strong upwelling of Russian national feeling), the strong trace of nationalism in the rationalizations of Soviet diplomacy should not cause surprise; it again helped to obscure the revolutionary segment of Soviet foreign relations. In many cases, the same policy could be equally interpreted from a revolutionary or from a nationalist point of view, as was true, for instance, of the monopoly of foreign trade. Justified on grounds of socialist theory, this was equally acceptable to non-Bolshevik Russian mercantilists.[73] Similarily, the revolutionary fear of contamination through contact with the West reappeared in diplomatic talk as the nationalist fear of Western economic and political penetration, which had been quite widespread in Russia before and during the war. In the same category, also, belongs Chicherin's championship of the protection of Russian boundaries, shores, and access to its shores, his claim to Bessarabia, his clash with Curzon over the Straits, and his demand for Soviet participation in all diplomatic arrangements involving traditional Russian interests like the Aaland Islands and Spitzbergen. In September 1926, he even pressed for Soviet participation in the current Tangiers negotiations, because Tsarist Russia, he argued, had been a signatory to the Algeciras Treaty,[74] (although the foreign debts of the regime had been repudiated, it will be remembered, precisely because they had been contracted by that government). And

---

[72] How much Chicherin was at home in the intellectual milieu of *Realpolitik* may be gathered from his articles, signed *postscriptum*, in *Mezhdunarodnaia Zhizn*, the Narkomindel's organ.
[73] Krassin, *Leonid Krassin*, p. 167.
[74] Reported in *Osteuropa*, I (1926), 697.

who could not hear the voice of traditional Russia in Chicherin's impassioned fulmination against Curzon at the Lausanne Conference in 1923: "The Russian revolution has transformed the Russian people into a nation whose entire energy is concentrated in its government to a degree hitherto unknown in history; and if war is forced upon that nation it will not capitulate. You are uneasy because our horsemen have reappeared on the heights of the Pamirs and because you no longer have to deal with the half-witted Tsar who ceded you the ridge of the Hindukush in 1895. But it is not war that we offer but peace. . . ."[75]

England, with whom Russia had clashed so often in the past, was also the main enemy of Soviet Russia in Chicherin's eyes. Hoetzsch, the German observer, was right in saying that the second Commissar for Foreign Affairs had always at his heart the *Staatsgedanke* of Russia; it was enshrined by him at the Narkomindel.

No further illustration is needed to show Chicherin's efforts to motivate and conduct Soviet diplomacy as if it were the sole instrument of Soviet foreign policy, and a nonrevolutionary one at that. Those familiar with the discussions of Soviet foreign relations on the Politburo level will be amazed how much Chicherin's conception of foreign policy differed from his masters'. But it must be remembered that, quite apart from the Soviet leadership's ability to accommodate itself to halfway stations, Bolshevik theory permitted any conceivable expedient in the relations with the capitalist world.[76] And no matter how unrepresentative the stated motivations of Soviet diplomacy—to take a view above the quarrels and disabilities from which it suffered at home, and to see it from the perspective of the Politburo—its successes aided the revolution, too, at least indirectly. In the security of its boundaries, its prestige in the world (even a "capitalist" world), in the matter of foreign economic assistance and loans, national and revolutionary interests overlapped or coincided. The only conflict on this higher level arose perhaps from a difference of emphasis. A diplomatic course which represented the *Staatsgedanke* of Russia was apt to consume prematurely the national

---

[75] Degras, I, 348. Chicherin, indeed, often interpreted the Bolshevik revolution as a source of renewed unity and energy in Russian foreign policy.

[76] The variability of Soviet attitude towards the western world goes probably far deeper than mere expediency. Soviet foreign relations in the first decade show the same "variability in depth" that can be found in the personal attitudes of the revolutionary leaders. They could range from the surface level of polite and seemingly sincere compliance with western standards, the give-and-take with foreign visitors through a whole gamut of intermediary moods to the raw revolutionary inner core of relentless hate. Under Stalin, however, this variability, born of the prerevolutionary contact between Russia and the West, has been greatly reduced.

resources which Bolshevik leadership wanted to husband for the further domestic development of the revolution. There prevailed in this period, from the Treaty of Brest-Litovsk to Stalin's willingness to surrender the Russian claim to Bessarabia and the sale of the Chinese Eastern Railway, a considerable inclination at the revolutionary center (not shared by the Narkomindel) to make territorial concessions for the sake of strengthening the revolution at home. But there was no reason why the territorial and strategic viewpoint should not again come to the fore and be justified in Leninist-Stalinist terms, once "the given relation of forces in the world arena" had changed in favor of the Soviet government.

IV

In conclusion, the analysis set forth in the previous pages will be illustrated by a brief and necessarily casual survey of Soviet foreign relations in the crucial period between 1921 and 1928. The following sketch will change the observer's vantage point from the Narkomindel to the Politburo and cast into bold relief what appears so flat from a survey of Soviet foreign policy premised on the fiction of the Narkomindel's effective monopoly of foreign affairs. As seen from the Kremlin, foreign relations stretched over a broad and deep front, with the revolutionary detachments of the Comintern and Profintern deployed on the left flank, along with the OGPU and military intelligence, with its various organizations for foreign cultural contact and foreign trade arrayed in the center, and with diplomacy engaged on the right flank. Unfortunately no picture of the fascinating complexity of interaction along this extended phalanx, of its coordinated maneuvers, sallies, feints, and ambushes, can here be given. Only the barest outline of the chief ventures on both flanks, the diplomatic and revolutionary, in their interplay and common relation to domestic conditions, is possible.[77]

[77] No history of Soviet foreign relations in the Chicherin period has yet been written from the Politburo point of view, covering the entire foreign policy phalanx and coordinating its actions with domestic development. Most existing texts suffer from an overemphasis upon Soviet diplomacy. Louis Fischer's indispensable volumes were conceived largely from the Narkomindel's point of view (in unusually close collaboration with Chicherin himself). P. Miliukov, *La Politique Extérieure des Soviets*, does far greater justice to the complexity of the subject. I. Deutscher's account of "Foreign Policy and Comintern I" in his biography of Stalin gives the best general background to the study of Soviet foreign policy in the Chicherin period, without devoting, however, much space to Chicherin's work. The essays by Boris Nikolaievskii, "Vneshnaia Politika Moskvy"; "Sovietskoie IAponskoie Soglashenie 1925 g"; "Revoliutsia v Kitaie, IAponia i Stalin" (in *Novyi Zhurnal*, 1942-1944); and "Russia, Japan, and the Pan-Asiatic Movement to 1925" in *The Far Eastern Quarterly*, VIII (May 1949), no. 3, show by far the greatest insight into the problems encountered in a detailed study of Soviet policy in this period. Least helpful, of course, from the point of view here taken is the official

As the Soviet government considered itself the spatial nucleus around which other Soviet Socialist republics might eventually gather, its relations with its immediate neighbors assumed special significance. In the West, the postwar settlement, based on Soviet weakness, had surrounded Russia with a *cordon sanitaire* of buffer states. A barrier had thus been established separating the Soviet regime from other countries with a revolutionary potential, such as Germany. While communist parties were forbidden by law in all of these border countries, the Bolsheviks maintained the usual underground organizations with the help of whatever local communist forces they could rally. The establishment of White Russia as a Union Republic and the creation of an autonomous Moldavian Republic were, at the same time, designed to create pro-Soviet sympathy among the Russian minorities in Poland and Rumania respectively.

In Soviet relations with all the border states, diplomacy necessarily stood in the foreground. In a series of treaties in 1920 and 1921, the Soviet government recognized the existence of these states with stipulations safeguarding Russia from attack through their territories; only relations with Rumania, which had seized Bessarabia in 1918, remained unsettled. Chicherin succeeded also, by playing Lithuania off against Poland, in preventing the creation of a Baltic bloc under Polish leadership. It seems in the last analysis, however, that it was the obvious threat of Russian power which discouraged dangerous adventures on the part of the border states. As things stood, they continued to be unfriendly to the Soviet Union, and they effectively blocked her revolutionary outward thrust; but, at the same time, by their very existence, they afforded the Soviet government a measure of protection against foreign intervention.

In the Near and Middle East, Soviet Russia faced an entirely different situation. Lenin had stressed the revolutionary importance of anti-western nationalism in colonial and semicolonial countries. In accordance with this, Soviet policy towards Turkey and Persia at once repudiated the Tsarist heritage and supported the national aims of the new governments. Thus, Soviet Russia supported Kemalist Turkey in her struggle with the Western Powers, helped the rise of Riza Khan in Persia and granted assistance to King Amanullah in Afghanistan. In their relations

---

version of Soviet diplomacy in V. V. Potemkin's volumes: *Istoriia Diplomatii.* On the other hand, the introductory paragraphs of the article on "Soviet Foreign Policy" in the official *Diplomatic Dictionary* (II, 650ff.) confirm, although in general terms, the tenor of Soviet foreign relations as viewed in this chapter.

with Turkey, the men of the Politburo appear to have played a straight-forward game, although the sincere friendship which Chicherin displayed toward Kemal's government was probably no more than mere expediency to Stalin.[78] In the vast territory stretching from Azerbaijan to Manchuria, however, Soviet policy and Tsarist expansion tended to coincide, despite Soviet professions to the contrary. In repudiating imperialism, the Bolshevik leaders were careful to hold on to the many concrete advantages they had inherited, such as the fishery rights in the Southern Caspian, the domination of Outer Mongolia, the operation of the Chinese Eastern Railway, and the disposition of the Russian share in the Boxer indemnity.

In the long run, the Politburo counted on the natural dissemination of its ideals and accomplishments in the Asiatic hinterland. Its agents were not only its diplomats, consuls, trade officials, OGPU and Red army men, but also its telegraphs, railways, tractors, and the example of Uzbek and Turkmen autonomy. It was as though Soviet Russia had attached a series of suction cups[79] to adjacent territories. How successfully and quickly these cups would work depended on local circumstances and the world balance of power.

In the last analysis, however, the important question was not that of Soviet Russia's relations with the border states, but rather of her relations with the three great capitalist Powers of the West, Great Britain, France and the United States. Germany and Japan, which—in Stalin's mind—occupied somewhat analogous positions, were more ambiguous factors; they were capitalist Powers which nonetheless contained strong anti-Western elements. Finally, there was a lesser Power, Italy, and the host of the small ones, which, apart from certain propaganda and nuisance aspects, counted for little. It was towards the centers of world power that the Politburo directed its diversified foreign policy instruments.

In 1920, Lenin had confidently set them all to work in order to break the blockade that had been imposed upon Soviet Russia. He had built up the Comintern to intensify the revolutionary pressure; he appealed to labor organizations and humanitarian groups for political and economic assistance; he held out the promise of concessions to foreign businessmen, trying to draw rival business groups into competition for Soviet favor; through his diplomats, he shouted peace to the victorious Allies

[78] Bessedovsky, *Revelations*, p. 187. On Soviet policy with regard to Turkey, see above, Chapter 6, §11.
[79] Scheffer, *Sieben Jahre*, p. 355.

and whispered consolation to the wounded nationalism of the defeated; and he tried to stir up the colonial peoples of the East. The question was: on what part of his broad foreign policy front the first breakthrough would occur and which foreign policy instruments would be the most effective in the long run. The first opening—there never was a breakthrough—occurred on the diplomatic flank, in relations with Great Britain. Lloyd George, in an attempt to secure the Russian market for British business, met the Soviet offer for a trade agreement, and thus *de facto* established relations. The Soviet government, through Krassin, proved most accommodating and even curtailed its anti-imperialist propaganda in the East. Yet trade relations nevertheless developed rather slowly. At the same time, Lenin directed his special attention towards Germany. As early as 1919, Radek, from his prison cell in Berlin—(he had been caught while organizing the revolutionary underground in Germany)—had negotiated with German industrialists and militarists; and in the next two years, against a backdrop of retreating revolutionary waves in Germany and Soviet threats of a rapprochement with France, the groundwork for future nonrevolutionary German-Soviet collaboration was laid.[80]

A still more satisfying gain was made, again on the economic-diplomatic wing (but with the support of the revolutionary wing),[81] in 1922 at the Genoa Conference, the first European diplomatic gathering to which the Soviet government was invited. The invitation was made possible by a widespread anxiety among European business groups to overcome the postwar depression by restoring the prewar economic ties between Russia and Europe. The danger for Soviet Russia in this juncture lay in the creation of a European consortium strong enough to force a breach in the Soviet monopoly of foreign trade. The Politburo, however, succeeded in dealing separately with interested parties, selecting one, the Urquhart interests, as proof that it was possible to do business with Russia (but repudiating the contract the moment the demonstration had outlasted its usefulness). Despite these maneuvers, the Politburo (acting through Chicherin and Krassin) could not create such competition among Western economic interests for the Russian trade as to weaken their demands for a prior settlement of the Tsarist debt and for concessions limiting its monopoly of foreign trade. The Genoa Conference thus failed, as did the subsequent Hague Conference. But at the same

---

[80] See Wipert von Blücher, *Deutschlands Weg nach Rapallo* (Wiesbaden, 1951), p. 155.

[81] The Comintern had been instructed to agitate everywhere for economic relations and political recognition.

time a more important matter than economic relations was decided: a course of German-Soviet collaboration.

The Rapallo Treaty, skillfully brought forward at Genoa by Chicherin at a time when the Germans were feeling their isolation most keenly, signified that with Soviet help Germany would try to pursue an independent national policy; it sanctioned a major split among the capitalist Powers. Through Radek, the Politburo had made a strong bid to enlist on its side the anti-Western elements of German nationalism and had succeeded. This tie not only weakened the force of capitalist encirclement but, through the influx of a variety of German experts, directly assisted the socialist reconstruction of Russia. This guarantee of a Soviet-induced and partly Soviet-controlled division of the capitalist world remained one of the major features of Soviet diplomacy, as well as of Politburo policy, throughout the Chicherin period.

It cannot be claimed, however, that at the time even the combined power of Germany and Soviet Russia altered the political situation appreciably. In the following year the French occupied the Ruhr, and Russian diplomacy, unable to prevent an adverse settlement of the Straits question, had also to back down before the Curzon Ultimatum, by which the British Government, in terms so peremptory as to suggest an imminent rupture of relations, demanded compensation for outrages against British subjects and a cessation of anti-British activities in the Middle East. Obviously, it was more difficult than Lenin had anticipated to raise Soviet Russia's position in the world. And he had to face the fact that the concrete gains (such as they were) had been won by diplomacy rather than revolutionary measures.

In 1923 revolution, however, seemed to be in the ascendancy. In that year the entire front of Soviet foreign policy was on the move, with revolution and diplomacy in close interaction. The Ruhr occupation—to concentrate upon the events in Germany—had set the stage for intensified revolutionary agitation and incited the hopes of Soviet leaders. For half a year after the French had moved, Soviet policy still stuck to the spirit of the Rapallo agreement. Chicherin vigorously protested against the Ruhr occupation, branding it a crime; protest demonstrations were held in Soviet cities; and the Red Army forwarded munitions to the *Reichswehr*. Through the Comintern, Radek preached the Schlageter line: communist cooperation with German nationalism. In thus supporting the German government's policy of passive resistance, the Soviet leaders hoped, at best, for a national war of the defeated against the victors. In mid-August, however, the Politburo abruptly changed its tune from diplomatic alliance to social revolution. What had happened to cause this sudden shift of initiative from the right flank of the Soviet foreign policy front to the left?

For one thing, seven months of French occupation had increased the likelihood of a genuine revolution in Germany. On August 12, a series of bitter strikes broke out throughout the country. Secondly, faced with such turmoil, the German government, now headed by Stresemann, decided to abandon passive resistance. With British mediation it now pursued a more moderate course of fulfilment and worked for pacification at home. At this point of Stresemann's retreat—which seemed also a retreat from Rapallo—the Politburo began to play for revolution through the Comintern.[82] Its agents had been ready since the beginning of the year; now they set up the necessary organizations. Thousands of Russian party members with a knowledge of German were alerted and the government of the new Soviet Socialist Germany was actually designated.[83]

But in preparing the German revolution, the Politburo faced two major decisions: how much direct aid could it give to the Germans, and what was it to do if a revolutionary victory should be followed by foreign intervention in Germany? Considering the unprepared state of her army and the conditions of the country in general, Soviet Russia was in no position to face war. Territorially separated from Germany, its leaders—at the time of Lenin's illness divided among themselves—could not send armed force without provoking a major international conflict. They dispatched, therefore, a variety of experts, but kept their material contributions at a minimum. The German communists thus had to fend for themselves, the Politburo staking all on their native strength and determination, although it gave serious thought to what would follow a communist victory.

Unable to prevent French meddling, as the French were already in occupation of the Ruhr, the Bolsheviks at least set out to neutralize hostile intervention from the east. They did this on the diplomatic front by sending Kopp to Poland and the Baltic limitrophes to arrange with them an agreement keeping them neutral and permitting the Soviet government to transship grain and other supplies to Germany. Kopp went so far as to threaten the Poles with an attack from the rear if their army should move against Germany. On the revolutionary side, the

[82] See Ruth Fischer, *Stalin and the German Revolution* (Cambridge, Mass., 1951), pp. 300ff.
[83] Bessedovsky, *Revelations*, pp. 46ff.

Politburo's program called for diversionary sabotage in Poland, not to mention aid to the German workers enjoined upon all communists through the Comintern. The risk taken by the Politburo thus included war only in case of Polish intervention in Germany, and it was assumed that the Russian threat would in itself prevent the emergency creating that risk. During these months diplomatic, economic and military relations with the German government of course continued as before, as though nothing had been changed. And after the failure of the German revolution in November 1923, the Politburo conveniently fell back upon its formal ties and the Rapallo policy, having lost very little ground in its unsuccessful revolutionary offensive.

The setback in Germany (and a simultaneous failure in Bulgaria), however, prepared the regrouping of units in the Soviet foreign policy phalanx resulting in greater freedom of action for the diplomats, particularly as the failure on the revolutionary flank was followed by further gains on their sector of the front. Early in 1924 both Great Britain and Italy granted *de jure* recognition to the Soviet government; later in the year France followed suit. The "objective circumstances" seemed to favor the diplomats. The change of government in England and France and the more relaxed atmosphere of international relations raised the position of the Soviet Union as a state among others in the comity of nations. It was in this new situation, calmer than any Soviet Russia had yet experienced, that Lenin's death occurred and the problem of the succession became acute. For the next four years—highly complex years in Soviet foreign relations—Soviet foreign policy was conditioned not only by the changes in world politics but more than ever by the changing internal scene.

At the time of Lenin's death, Soviet policy was determined by the "troika" of Zinoviev, Kamenev, and Stalin, who still followed the basic directives evolved by Lenin. Zinoviev, as head of the Comintern, naturally wielded a dominant influence over foreign relations, which meant continued strong emphasis upon revolutionary agitation. The failures of 1923 weakened his standing in the party, but during 1924 the Left course represented by him still prevailed. For that reason the Politburo remained cool, even hostile, towards the friendly overtures of the Mac-Donald government. Nor could it share the optimism welling up in Western Europe. The new calm in the international sphere began to reduce communist voting strength abroad; and this made the revolutionary weapons of Soviet foreign relations less effective. Furthermore, under the Dawes Plan, Germany was drawn into economic cooperation with

Western countries, which portended a weakening of the Rapallo policy. Finally, there were signs of outright hostility, such as the raid upon the Berlin trade delegation in April, and the reaction of the British public to the Zinoviev letter in the elections of October. In the face of such facts, Soviet leaders were divided. The old policy seemed no longer adequate; the direct incitement of revolution became increasingly ineffectual and even ridiculous. Zinoviev's miserable Reval putsch in December 1924 was the last expression of that policy. What new line should be taken?

Considering the unsettled situation in the party, it is not surprising that the answer came from domestic politics. While Zinoviev's policy still prevailed, a new trend based on internal considerations gained ground in the party. A group called "the economists," eager to rebuild Russian prosperity, even with foreign assistance, advocated less revolution and more foreign trade, which could be obtained only with the help of diplomacy. Zinoviev himself, in delivering the Central Committee's report at the Thirteenth Party Congress in May 1924, alluded to this trend, saying that now more than ever foreign policy stood in close relation to domestic policy. More than that, he even played up Chicherin's significance. There existed, indeed, an intimate connection between Soviet diplomacy and the Russian peasants. The more plentiful the supply of foreign capital for industrial development and the better Soviet Russia's standing with the capitalist Powers, the less sacrifices were demanded of the peasantry. For that reason, as Zinoviev put it, the Narkomindel should be one of the most popular Peoples Commissariats in the villages. In this manner a right turn in Soviet domestic policy meant also a promotion for Soviet diplomacy.

Such a turn took place in the spring of 1925. The uprising in Georgia, a minor Kronstadt, had demonstrated the necessity for greater concessions to the peasants; and the trend abroad was patently against revolution and for diplomacy. At the Fourteenth Party Conference, the new line in domestic as well as foreign policy was proclaimed; as to the latter, its aims were now to be based on the assumption of capitalist stabilization. The Fourteenth Party Congress confirmed the new orientation and also accepted the implicit corollary that, at a time of capitalist consolidation in the world, Soviet socialism would have to advance first of all within Russia. The new status of diplomacy, however, did not mean surrender of the revolutionary flank of the Soviet foreign policy front. But the previous direct incitement of violent revolution wherever possible was now replaced, under Bukharin's guidance,[84] by a more peaceful policy of gradual transition. Communists everywhere were instructed to cooperate with socialists; a link between Soviet trade unions and the British Trade Union Council was established in the form of the Anglo-Russian Trade Union Committee. Bukharin himself admitted, at the time of the English general strike, that revolution in England might not conform to the Bolshevik prototype. In China, too, Borodin was committed to a policy of cooperation with the Kuomintang rather than to outright sovietization. In the mid-1920's, in short, Soviet foreign policy, somewhat in line with the spirit of the times, had moved towards greater moderation. The original predominance of revolutionary agitation was ended; diplomacy had risen to equal rank. But the extreme hopes of some Soviet diplomats for a return by their government to prerevolutionary power politics and a settlement of spheres of influence with the leading colonial powers, were not fulfilled; although with clipped claws, revolutionary agitation continued. And furthermore, the preferment of diplomacy did not imply greater tractability on the part of the Soviet masters. It only meant a partial shift back to European standards in the choice of foreign policy instruments. The total effect of the change upon foreign capitals was thus bound to be negligible, as was fully revealed in 1927.

While diplomacy now enjoyed greater prestige with the Politburo, it did not become more conciliatory and cooperative in its relations with Western governments. Its elevation coincided with the conclusion of the Locarno agreements and the preparation for Germany's entry into the League of Nations. In order to offset such capitalist solidarity under League auspices Chicherin undertook in 1925 and 1926 a vigorous diplomatic offensive. He strengthened Soviet ties with Turkey, secured the continued adherence of Germany to the Rapallo policy (with a commercial treaty and a 300 million mark credit added) and then set out to construct an anti-League of Soviet Russia's neighbors through non-aggression pacts, not all of which, however, could be concluded even after protracted negotiation. Only Lithuania, Turkey, Afghanistan, and Persia responded favorably. After a while the diplomatic offensive bogged down amidst signs of mounting British hostility. Chicherin's diplomatic weapons could not provide an effective antidote to determined British counteraction against the revolutionary wing of Soviet foreign

[84] See B. Nikolaievskii, *Novyi Zhurnal*, no. IV, 1943, pp. 302ff., for an analysis of Bukharin's views. Zinoviev, incidentally, was dropped from the Presidium of the Comintern Executive Committee in 1926.

policy; and, in May 1927, disaster overtook him in the rupture of diplomatic relations by that country.

The chief activities on the revolutionary wing of Soviet foreign policy under the new course, which had so provoked the British conservatives and caused Chicherin's failure, had been the offer of extensive Soviet financial support to the British strikers (who rejected it) and particularly Borodin's energetic promotion of the Chinese revolution. From the summer of 1926 on, the events in China claimed the intense attention of the men in the Politburo, who again set to work all the foreign policy instruments to attain their end. Only a few features of an extremely complex situation can here be mentioned.

Formal Soviet relations with the Far East were established in the spring of 1923, after the Japanese evacuation of Siberia and the absorption of the Far Eastern Republic by the Soviets. In a short time the Politburo negotiated with the chief authorities in China: to wit, the official government in Peking, Chang Tso Lin, the *tuchun* of Manchuria, and Sun Yat Sen in the south, dealing with each in their own terms. Most promising from the Soviet point of view was the incipient nationalist movement of Sun Yat Sen. The Politburo at once dispatched Borodin, an acquaintance of Sun's, together with military advisors, arms and money, to help organize the Kuomintang as a militant mass party with a progressive social and strongly anti-imperialist program. It was clear to the Politburo that the success of such a movement in China with its 400 million population would create a valuable ally and have immense repercussions through eastern and southeastern Asia and affect even the balance of power in the Pacific. In support of the Kuomintang, the Politburo also enlisted the help of Soviet diplomacy: for a time Karakhan was stationed in Peking; in Manchuria the Soviet officials of the Chinese-Eastern railroad defended Soviet interests against Chang Tso Lin, an enemy of the Kuomintang. In 1925 a settlement with Tokyo was negotiated, stabilizing Soviet-Japanese relations and creating a new *point d'appui* in the Tokyo embassy. In addition, Comintern agents were busy in all major cities of China, among the Korean nationalists, and in the Japanese Communist party. Finally, there was the Red Army, a far more active and influential agent in the Far East than in Europe, stationed along the Manchurian border.

After June 1926, with the Kuomintang striking north to the Yangtse, a decisive period was reached. Would the left or the right wing of the Kuomintang prevail? If the right wing under Chiang Kai-shek won out, the Kuomintang would be lost to Soviet Russia, as the seaboard cities with their Western orientation would determine its foreign policy. The Politburo, therefore, supported the left wing, without, however, advocating an all-out Bolshevik social policy. There were bitter disputes in and around the Politburo as to how far to the left the course ought to be set, with Stalin taking a relatively moderate view. The diplomats at the Narkomindel, on the other hand, worried about English reaction and, uninitiated into the projects of the Politburo, stood vigorously opposed to any revolutionary venture, even to the extent of Stalin's commitment.[85] They argued that China was not ready for more than a Kemalist revolution and they warned of Japanese hostility to a Soviet China. The clash between diplomacy and revolution assumed here a novel form, that of a conflict between an Eastern and Western orientation. The Politburo, having been repeatedly disappointed in its revolutionary expectations in Europe, had now turned to the East; for the present it braved British hostility and staked all upon success in China. The diplomats, considering the European scene with its global repercussions of greater importance, sought to minimize first of all friction with the British conservatives whom they greatly feared. In this dispute, the position of Japan also had to be considered, not only because of the extensive Japanese interests in northern and eastern China, but because Chinese nationalism was also anti-Japanese. In order not to antagonize Japan it seems that Stalin, through Comintern agents, tried to stifle the anti-Japanese agitation in the Kuomintang, while through his diplomats he cultivated friendly relations with the Japanese government. He valued the anti-Western potentialities of Japanese nationalism as highly as he did those of German nationalism.[86] During the height of the Chinese crisis in the spring of 1927 and the sharply rising British reaction, he even put his diplomatic representative in Tokyo under unusual pressure to wrest, in a sort of Far Eastern Rapallo, from the Japanese government a Soviet-Japanese nonaggression pact, in order to forestall active British intervention in China (which he thought possible only with Japanese help).[87] Yet even Japanese neutrality could not save the revolutionary venture in China.

The final crisis in the relations between the right and left wings of the Kuomintang merged with a general crisis in Soviet foreign relations and domestic politics. While at home the left opposition prepared its final demonstration, the foreign situation went from bad to worse. In

[85] Bessedovsky, *Revelations*, pp. 120ff.
[86] Nikolaievskii, *Novyi Zhurnal*, no. III, pp. 205ff.
[87] Bessedovky, *Revelations*, pp. 156ff.

April the Soviet embassy in Peking was raided; elsewhere in China consulates were searched. At the end of May the British government, after the Arcos raid, broke off diplomatic relations. British hostility radiated into other quarters. In June the Soviet ambassador in Warsaw was assassinated. In the same month Borodin was ordered home and the Chinese revolution, for all practical purposes, written off. In October the French government demanded Rakovsky's recall, after which Franco-Soviet relations reached a low point. Even in Germany the former enthusiasm for the Rapallo policy had waned. The trend of adversity even extended to Russia's hitherto reliable mid-eastern auxiliaries. In Persia and Afghanistan Great Britain won back lost ground; Turkey grew cooler as her relations with the Western Powers improved. Obviously the anti-imperialist shibboleths of the immediate postwar years no longer carried their old weight. At the end of the year the Soviets had lost all ground in China, and in Japan Count Tanaka, the protagonist of an active Manchurian policy, had been made Prime Minister. The crisis extended throughout the entire length of the Soviet foreign policy front. It was a defeat of diplomacy as much as of revolution; it affected Chicherin as adversely as Bukharin and the Comintern, not to speak of Stalin, who in the eyes of the left opposition was also responsible for the alarming turn of events. And yet, in the end, it helped to thrust the party's General Secretary, whose hand had been noticeable here and there even during the period of Bukharin's greatest influence, to the fore in a field in which he had hitherto held back. With his rise, the confusion and uncertainty in Soviet foreign relations dating from Lenin's last days began to disappear. Soviet foreign relations were reconstituted around a new set of convictions, Stalin's convictions.

The serious setback in the tenth year of the revolution on both the diplomatic and revolutionary flanks of the Soviet foreign policy front brought into sharper focus again the old bleak assumptions about the incompatibility of socialism and capitalism and the isolation of revolutionary Russia. A different leader might have chosen the other alternative and abandoned all revolutionary agitation and reverted to the traditional scope of power politics; and this would have also been the inclination of Chicherin. With Stalin there was no chance of such a course. His ascendancy deepened the distrust of the outside world. The former optimism about the imminence of world revolution or of universal formal recognition by "capitalist" governments—both had been conspicuous earlier, despite their contradictory nature—had gone. The "objective circumstances" of the world situation that had seemed to favor the Soviet regime in earlier years had changed. The instruments of international revolution designed to draw strength from these favorable constellations for the Soviet regime therewith also lost much of their reliability. The failures of 1927 thus put the naked fact of Soviet weakness back into bold relief: Soviet Russia could not play the part of a Great Power without the internal resources of a Great Power. In 1927, therefore, Stalin put the course of domestic politics again to the left: he answered the failure in foreign relations with terror at home and increased antiforeign agitation; he fabricated a war-scare that would justify the drastic measures to come, particularly the policy of rapid industrialization at all costs, out of Russian resources and at the expense of the Russian peasant. Only through the fastest possible development of Russian industries could he provide Soviet Russia with the means for victorious participation in the intensified struggle for world power which he saw ahead. At the Fifteenth Party Congress in December 1927 and the Sixth Congress of the Comintern in 1928, which ended Bukharin's uncertain influence over Soviet foreign policy, the ideological foundation for the new line (for which, of course, there was much cause from purely domestic considerations) was laid down. The brief era of capitalist stabilization was declared ended. Instead Stalin envisaged a new period of capitalist disintegration with attendant wars and crises, which would require that Russia be ready, not only to repel any capitalist attack, but to throw in her weight for the ultimate decision which would decide the fate of the world. In terms of practical politics, Stalin's policy, which he presented as a continuation of the old Left course, meant a drastic break with it. Now, the order of the day was concentration upon the domestic tasks of the First Five Year Plan. Foreign policy, despite the revolutionary flourishes of the Fifteenth Congress, was relegated, for a long time to come, to second place. Its sole task was to work relentlessly for peace and Soviet security in the period of socialist industrialization. No realignment of its forces was needed; the foreign policy phalanx remained roughly in the order in which it had been cast in 1925. But the freedom of the diplomats was sharply curtailed and the units on the revolutionary wing were reorganized. The Comintern was thoroughly "Bolshevized," i.e. transformed into a pliant tool for extensive foreign espionage and underground work. All along the policy front, the aggressive tactics of the earlier years gave way to a new defensive quiescence. The millennial hopes of the early period, although not forgotten, were replaced by ruthlessly realistic aims for the immediate future.

In Soviet diplomacy the change became obvious even before the break with England. Even in the latter part of 1926, foreign observers had noticed increased anxiety and uncertainty in Soviet foreign policy, fore-shadowing a change of course.[88] In the following spring the new policy emerged as the crisis of Soviet foreign policy deepened. A renewed but fruitless effort was made to win American recognition. As to Europe, the Narkomindel in a sharp reversal gave up its former unconditional hos-tility towards the League and dispatched a delegation under Sokolnikov to the World Economic Conference in Geneva, where it stoutly main-tained the possibility of peaceful coexistence and cooperation between the two systems.[89] Even more significant was Litvinov's participation, after November 1927, in the work of the preparatory Commission on Disarma-ment, not to speak of Soviet support of the Kellogg-Briand pact in the following year. Soviet weakness drove the regime to seek closer diplo-matic ties with the League of Nations, thus dimly foreshadowing a reac-tion which, in the 1930's, led to membership in it.

The new turn of Soviet foreign relations also affected Chicherin's posi-tion[90] and aggravated the physical ills that had always plagued him. Quite apart from the incompatibility between his temperament and that of Stalin, their political differences made further cooperation difficult. Chicherin, who had much in common with the Right opposition, refused to concede the necessity for the change in Soviet diplomacy dictated by Stalin. He had always opposed the League and did not agree now with the Stalin-Litvinov policy of cautious rapprochement; nor did he accept the necessity for the anti-German agitation that was part of the domestic course. He could not share the dictator's apprehension about the immi-nence of capitalist attack. And finally he who had always stood for the defense of Soviet state power in critical border areas, as well as in the world in general, could not willingly consent to such a far-reaching sub-ordination of foreign relations to domestic reconstruction. For that reason, he spent much time away from his desk, ill and grumbling, leav-ing most of his business to Litvinov, who was better adjusted to the totalitarian spirit of the Stalinist regime and found the new policy more congenial to his talents. After an absence of a year and a half, the ailing Commissar was finally released from his position by the Sixteenth Party Congress in July 1930, to die six years later in utter obscurity. As

---

[88] See P. Scheffer, *Sieben Jahre*, p. 304. Also O. Hoetzsch in *Osteuropa*, II, 397.

[89] In order to make Soviet attendance possible, the Narkomindel, after having rejected the original invitation, suddenly asked for another invitation. See Nikolaievskii, *Novyi Zhurnal*, no. VIII, p. 376.

[90] On Chicherin's position in the late 1920's, see L. Fischer, *Men and Politics*; and Bessedovsky, P. Scheffer, and O. Hoetzsch in the books previously quoted.

Chicherin disappeared from the scene, Stalin abandoned for the time being any intention to engage in competition for new power abroad and rallied all his energies to the single task of strengthening his home base. He drew the line which he was prepared to hold with his foreign policy phalanx in his report to the Sixteenth Party Congress, insisting that: "We do not seek a single foot of foreign territory, but we will not surrender a single inch of our territory either." By this statement, it is safe to say, he also implied: We will not seek any foreign revolution even during the tempting opportunities of a world depression.

In summary, then, what were the aims of Soviet policy in world affairs as they evolved during the first dozen years of capitalist encirclement? The principal one, which overshadowed all others, was to guarantee the absolute independence and security of the revolutionary development within its world base, Soviet Russia. This, incidentally, implied a far stricter interpretation of sovereignty (manifested in an extreme reluctance to enter binding political, economic, or even technical arrangements with non-Soviet governments) than prevailed in Western countries. From the first aim followed the second: to make the Soviet government as strong as possible through the planned organization of its human and material resources. Throughout the Chicherin period (and for at least a decade afterwards) Soviet Russia was, despite her often pathetic attempts to exaggerate her significance in world politics, if a Great Power at all, certainly a very weak one. Consequently, her main energies as well as her chief domestic controversies were concerned with the best and quickest ways of overcoming that weakness. The aims and means of her relations with other countries in turn were all conditioned by that weakness. From its narrow base of yet undeveloped strength, the Politburo conducted what might be called "negative" power politics; it counted less on the determining force of its material power than upon the opportunities provided by unrest and disunity among its opponents. The greatest desideratum of Soviet foreign relations was foreign revolution fomented by propaganda and local organization, not alliance or territorial gain. In the absence of such revolution (which, to be sure, in a country like Germany might have made all the difference), the position of Soviet Russia in the world depended to an amazing extent upon the minor ups and downs of parliamentary politics in the West, the turn of the business cycle, local, social and economic conditions, and still other factors not normally controlled by foreign governments. No wonder then that, given its soaring political ambition, the Soviet regime perfected its revolutionary techniques so as to gain at least some measure of control over these hitherto so elusive and hence neglected factors of power politics; no wonder that it strove to intensify its impact abroad by manipulating all phases of its foreign contact and by putting to maximum use every shred of sympathy and loyalty which it could find. Such dependence upon foreign conditions also made the Soviet regime unusually sensitive to regional and national differences; it was forced at the risk of being contradictory to identify itself very closely with local circumstances and the political forces there at play. In other words, it had, in its weakness, to seek for sources of power where the powerful countries had hitherto not yet penetrated, because their traditional resources of strength seemed still adequate.

In the new dimensions of international relations thus opened up by the Bolsheviks, Chicherin and the Narkomindel could play only a limited part. Social agitation was a highly specialized field which called for an experience and a mental outlook far different from those required in the conduct of strait-laced diplomacy. As a result, Soviet diplomacy was excluded from a large share of Soviet foreign relations. And Chicherin faced in acute form many of the difficulties which sooner or later beset diplomats everywhere when their governments are driven to cope with the instability of state and society in vital areas of the world. Within his restricted sphere of activity, he proved a very able craftsman, who justly earned the respect of his critics. His tactical skill in the negotiations at Genoa and Rapallo and his sallies against Curzon at Lausanne raised his prestige even in party circles. But his major successes, like Rapallo, and his failures, like the breach with Britain in 1927, were not of his own making. They were caused by the policies and actions of the Politburo, over which Chicherin had very little control. He was, after all, Foreign Minister in name only. His importance was exaggerated by foreign journalists who were guided in their interpretations by the example of Western governments, where Foreign Ministers enjoyed a large measure of influence in foreign relations, and who failed to realize that this was not true in Russia. Chicherin succeeded, however, in giving credence to their fiction, largely, one suspects, because it was his ambition to make it a reality. Whether unintentionally or by design, he thus effectively camouflaged the real politics of his masters.

Chicherin's main contribution, however, should be sought, not so much in the history of international relations in the 1920's, as in the changing formulations of Soviet foreign policy among the inner circles of the party. He stood for a continued validity of *Realpolitik* in the tradition of Metternich and Bismarck at a time when the professional revolutionaries were all but throwing diplomacy overboard. In his efforts to preserve the *Staatsgedanke* of Russia, he carried over into the new regime the heritage of Tsarist diplomacy. He was responsible for the element of continuity which links Tsarist and Soviet foreign policy and which, despite the great contributions of Leninism, seems to grow stronger as the years go by.

9

The Department of State and
American Public Opinion

BY DEXTER PERKINS

THE emphasis in the essays in this volume is placed upon the role of distinctive personalities in the evolution of foreign policy, and this emphasis is an eminently proper one. The study of social history, highly desirable and fruitful, has led in some instances to a distorted concentration on trends and movements, and to an undue minimization of the part played by highly individual decisions. In American foreign policy, as elsewhere, the importance of resolutions taken *in camera* by a few persons is not to be disregarded. Yet in a fundamental sense, the diplomatic history of the United States does not resemble the diplomatic history of Europe. Essentially, the professional diplomat has always played a subordinate role. There are few Légers, few Vansittarts, few Holsteins in the record of American action. Occasionally, we have a House, or a Hopkins, or a Harriman—a non-professional—who plays a significant role; and, in the 1930's, a career diplomat, Sumner Welles, had great influence. But, for the most part (and the longer the perspective the truer is the generalization), men of this type are rare. The elements in the formation of policy are at once more subtle and more complex than they are in many other states. We may, therefore, before describing the diplomacy of the 1920's, properly examine the various factors that enter into it.

In a sense that is true in no such degree in other nations, American diplomatic action has been determined by the people. There were ardent debates on foreign policy in the first days of our national history. There have been such debates ever since. Uninstructed though the average citizen may be in the facts of international life, he still has an opinion with regard to them. If he does not know, he thinks he knows. And this conviction on his part is one that cannot be disregarded. Nor do those who conduct our affairs in the main desire to disregard it. The democratic tradition is deeply rooted in our history. The men who stand at the levers of control are almost always men with substantial political experience. Their habits, their prepossessions, their convictions all lead them to pay heed to the voice of the great body of citizens, to shape their decisions with that voice in mind.

This does not mean that the minutiae of diplomatic action can be determined by the masses. Nor does it mean, if we are careful in our use of terms, that "public opinion," in the sense of a carefully thought-out view of a specific problem, is the fundamental factor. It means, rather, that the general sentiment of the people lies at the root of every great issue. There have been times when the mood of the American people was essentially militant. The government has responded to this militancy. There have been times when the mood was essentially one of withdrawal, of *reculement* as the French would put it. The government has responded to this mood likewise. Presidents have been powerless to withstand these deep-seated feelings. President McKinley was a man of peace, yet he was swept into war. President Franklin D. Roosevelt was certainly by conviction no isolationist, yet his first administration was essentially isolationist in spirit. This overmastering popular emotion rationalized, perhaps, into convenient slogans, often influences policy. To say this is not to praise or condemn. It is simply to state a fact. One may believe, if one is a convinced democrat, that in the main the popular instincts are sound. Or one may be cynical enough to distrust them. The important thing is to recognize that they exist.

But once this essential generalization has been made, there are others that need to be added to it. So far as individuals make policy, the balance of influence in the United States is always tipping, now this way or that, now to the executive, now to the legislature, and rarely to the professional diplomat. For example, there have been many Presidents of the United States who have exercised a remarkable personal influence on diplomatic action. This was true of Polk, of Theodore Roosevelt, of Woodrow Wilson, of Franklin D. Roosevelt, to mention only a few. But there have also been Presidents who delegated a large part of their power to their Secretaries of State. Except perhaps at the beginning of his administration, Lincoln did so. Grant did so. Harding and Coolidge did so. The role of the Chief Executive in foreign policy is a shifting thing, now great, now small, depending upon the type of individual happening to hold the office.

It is the same way with Secretaries of State. Some have been strong personalities, the true makers of policy. Others have recorded the views of Presidents, or depended upon their professional staffs. The one thing that is certain is that no definite and fixed role can be assigned to the Secretary under our constitutional system.

But we cannot end here. The conduct of American diplomacy is substantially affected by our constitutional forms. It is not, of course, merely that the legislative body, through the treaty-making power, participates in the formation of policy. In other states some control of foreign affairs can be exerted by the law-making power. What is more important is that, under our type of government, there is no certainty of harmony between the executive and the legislature. Under the parliamentary system with cabinet responsibility there naturally exists between the government of the day and its majority in parliament an intimate and cooperative relationship. But in the United States the Congress does not feel bound to pay any very extraordinary deference to the views of the executive, and its attitude is all the more likely to be critical if the Congressional majority is, as it may be under our system, of a different political complexion from that of the executive. Furthermore, the chairmen of the great committees, especially the chairman of the Senate Committee on Foreign Relations, may be veterans in political life, and men of strong convictions who feel no obligation to take their views from the other end of Pennsylvania Avenue. They may insist not only on being consulted but on being heeded.

Let us look for a moment at the manner in which these generalizations apply to the period under examination in this essay. It is the period of the Harding, Coolidge, and Hoover administrations, from 1921 to 1933. First, as to the mood of the American people. When the Harding administration entered power, the country had just emerged from a great war. There had been much disillusionment and a severe letdown from the mood of exaltation induced by the leadership of Woodrow Wilson. The question of the role of the United States in world affairs had been under constant and vigorous debate. On the whole, I think it fair to say, the country had reacted against a policy of extensive commitments in the world at large. In the struggle over the League, there was so much pettiness and partisanship that it is difficult to discover its essential meaning. Yet it seems reasonable to say that between the President and his opponents there was a real issue involved and that this issue centered upon that part of the Covenant which projected the United States most deeply into the international scene. Article 10, with its pledge of territorial sovereignty and political independence, may or may not have been, as Wilson claimed, the heart of the whole matter. But, if one reads the

Senate reservation to that article,[1] one becomes convinced that there was a real and fundamental question at stake, the question whether the United States should participate in the fullest sense in the development of a system of collective security for the maintenance of peace. And the answer that the American people gave, with the election of Harding to the Presidency, was that they did not care much about the matter. This renunciation must not be understood as implying that the withdrawal of the United States from world affairs was to be anything like total, or that there was not much devotion to the peace ideal as an abstraction. It merely means that the American mood was not one in which a sense of world responsibility played a dominant part.

Moreover, the mood of 1920 was the mood of virtually all of the period we shall consider. The immense prosperity of the United States, and the profound reaction from that prosperity, both concentrated American attention upon domestic rather than foreign matters. Those who conducted the foreign affairs of the nation, while often far ahead of public opinion in the breadth of their vision and in their sense of the large role which the country ought to play, had to take account of that essential fact.

As to the role of the Executive, neither President Harding nor President Coolidge was fitted to assume the function of leadership in the field of foreign affairs. Harding was an easygoing man of very mediocre intellectual gifts, if the word gifts may be used at all, and when he thought at all he thought in stereotypes. Coolidge was congenitally cautious, incapable of powerful or effective leadership, essentially the exponent of the laissez-faire philosophy. Neither exercised any really powerful influence on the diplomacy of the period. The same thing cannot be said of Herbert Hoover. Few Presidents were more conscious of their responsibilities than he, and, as we shall see, in some essential matters the opinion of the Chief-Executive was of great significance during his administration.

The Secretaries of the period we are examining present an interesting

---

[1] The Senate reservation reads as follows: "The United States assumes no obligation to preserve the territorial integrity or political independence of any other country by the employment of its military or naval forces, its resources, or any form of economic discrimination, or to interfere in any way in controversies between nations, including all controversies relating to territorial integrity or political idependence, whether members of the League or not, under the provisions of Article 10, or to employ the military or naval forces of the United States, under any article of the treaty for any purpose, unless in any particular case the Congress, which, under the Constitution, has the sole power to declare war or authorize the employment of the military or naval forces of the United States, shall, in the exercise of full liberty of action, by act or joint resolution so provide." D. F. Fleming, *The United States and the League of Nations* (New York, 1932), p. 433.

picture, and interesting contrasts. Charles Evans Hughes, Secretary from 1921 to 1925, was undoubtedly one of the ablest men who ever held that office. His personal role in the formation of policy was a most important one. Secretary Kellogg, on the other hand, was much less disposed to initiate action of any kind, much more conscious of the limits imposed upon him by public opinion and by the Congress. Henry L. Stimson, Hoover's Secretary of State, was a man of powerful and strongly-held convictions, but was compelled in some matters, as we shall see, to defer to his chief.

All three Secretaries had to consider the legislative branch. The great concentration of powers inevitable to the waging of the first world war had inevitably led to a reaction, and the Congresses of the 1920's were in many respects jealous of their own position, and none too disposed to defer to the Executive. Despite the obstacles thrown in his way, Hughes often succeeded in by-passing the legislators, and in shaping policy by his own personal force. Kellogg was exceedingly deferential to Senators, and he had to deal with a man of great force, and of capacity superior to his own, in William E. Borah, chairman of the Senate Committee on Foreign Relations. Stimson was, on the whole, on good terms with the Senate, and was more confined by the views of his chief than by the opposition of the legislature. Yet on some questions, as we shall see, he could make little headway over Congressional resistance. The pattern, in other words, changed with each Secretary of State.

As for the permanent personnel of the Department, it is not easy to estimate its role. But it seems fair to say that Hughes dominated his department, Kellogg was often much influenced by his professional advisers, and Stimson, like Hughes, had strong views of his own. From all of which it can be understood how difficult it would be to write the diplomatic history of this period in terms of any single personality.[2]

Since the personal interpretation of American foreign policy is denied to us by the facts of the American scene, it seems wise to center our examination of the 1920's about certain key ideas. The emphasis, as in all these essays, is on Europe, and much, therefore, will be omitted that is not relevant to the European picture. Such emphasis is wholly justified. For whatever may have been the case before 1914, the relations of the United States with the great communities of the West are, in the period with which we are dealing, of great significance to the world as a whole.

---

[2] It is relevant to remark that in the brief period between 1921 and 1933 there were no less than six Under-Secretaries of State. No single fact indicates more strikingly the contrast between the American and the European diplomatic scene.

II

Let us choose, as the first theme for our examination, the attitude of the United States towards the idea of collective security, as it was reflected in the three administrations from 1921 to 1933. First of all, it is necessary to reiterate that the opposition to the famous Article 10 of the Covenant was nothing more or less than opposition to the collective security idea. That article was designed by its framers to prevent physical aggression on the part of one state against another. The members of the League agree, it read, "to respect and preserve as against external aggression the territorial integrity and existing political independence of all members of the League." This was not, as has sometimes been said, a freezing of the *status quo*. It was a prohibition on the alteration of the *status quo* by force. But it involved, and involved very deeply, the notion of common action against an aggressor, and it became the focus of the most fundamental attacks upon the Covenant itself. While the materials for a judgment are not so satisfactory as we might desire, it seems clear that a majority of the Senate were not ready to accept such an obligation, and when President Wilson attempted to make an issue of the matter in the election of 1920, he utterly failed. The great vote for Harding in that year showed, so it seems to me, that the mass of the people, to put it mildly, attached no very great positive importance to this central idea—if, indeed, they apprehended it at all clearly.

It seems clear, too, that Mr. Hughes, soon to become Secretary of State, was not enamored of the collective security idea, either. He was not a foe of the League idea in general but, as his correspondence shows, he thought of it in quite a different way from Wilson. "There is plain need for a league of nations," he wrote, "in order to provide for the development of international law, for creating and maintaining organs of international justice and machinery of conciliation and conference, and for giving effect to measures of international cooperation which may from time to time be agreed upon."[3] There is not a word in this interesting statement with regard to the machinery of coercion. It is, moreover, abundantly clear that he was opposed to Article 10. Indeed, he expressed such opposition as early as March of 1919, and this position he consistently maintained. Whether or not the treaty was to be ratified by the new administration, there seems no reason to believe that Hughes was ready to fight for the principle of common action against aggression. In point of fact, however, the question was never discussed in the early

[3] C. E. Hughes to Senator Hale, July 24, 1919, quoted in M. J. Pusey, *Charles Evans Hughes* (2 vols., New York, 1951), I, 397.

days of the Harding regime. For so bitter was the opposition of the irreconcilable Republicans to the whole Wilsonian edifice that Hughes, despite his own desire to see the Versailles pact ratified with reservations, was obliged to abandon this idea, and to abandon it even in the face of the assurances that he had offered to the American people in the campaign of 1920 that a vote for Harding was a vote for entry into the League under reasonable conditions.[4]

Despite the rebuff administered by the new administration to the idea of collective security, the idea itself showed a remarkable vitality. This is not to say that it was ever close to general acceptance in the 1920's; such a proposition, I think, cannot be maintained. But there were important discussions of the problem, and we should understand these discussions before we can examine the American attitude with regard to them.

First of the attempts to strengthen the machinery of the Covenant was the Draft Treaty of Mutual Assistance of 1923. This treaty gave to the Council considerably greater power than that conceded in the League constitution itself. It permitted that body, for example, in case of the outbreak of hostilities to designate the aggressor nation, and bound the contracting parties to furnish each other mutual assistance against the nation so designated, on a basis determined by the Council itself. It assumed that both military and financial aid would be accorded the aggressed state, and implied that an international force would be created to give effect to the obligations of the treaty. It sought at the same time to limit the operation of sanctions by declaring that in principle no state in a continent other than that in which the operations would take place would be required to cooperate in military, naval, or air operations.[5] The draft treaty was transmitted to the various governments by the Fourth Assembly, and comment invited.

There is little reason to believe that there was ever much chance of the adoption of this ambitious scheme, even by the members of the League. Indeed, the opposition to more extensive commitments than those of the Covenant had been expressed by not a few states in the deliberations which preceded the drafting of this instrument, and in the Fourth Assembly itself. In the debates at Geneva, indeed, it is possible to discern a distinct reaction against the idea of collective security, a reaction by no means wholly due—perhaps not even chiefly due—to the

---

[4] For a discussion of this point see Pusey, *Charles Evans Hughes*, II, 431-434.

[5] For a scholarly discussion of the mutual assistance treaty, see B. S. Williams, *State Security and the League of Nations* (Baltimore, 1927), pp. 151-182. See also Chapters 1, § III and 4, § III above and Chapter 10, § I below.

attitude of the United States. Nevertheless, it is interesting to observe the extremely cold tone in which Mr. Hughes replied to the note of January 9, 1924, in which the Draft Treaty was presented to the American government. Delaying his answer until June 16, and expressing a "keen and sympathetic interest" in "every endeavor" for the reduction of armaments, an end towards which the treaty was directed, he pointed out that wide powers were given to the Council of the League of Nations. "In view of the constitutional organization of this government," he declared, "and in view of the fact that the United States is not a member of the League of Nations, this Government would find it impossible to give its adherence."[6]

The reference in this note to the constitutional obligations of the United States deserves a word of comment. What Hughes is talking about is perfectly clear. Obviously effective action under any agreement looking to the application of collective measures for the maintenance of peace can, under our form of government, only be taken by the Congress of the United States. But this is not to say that the Executive cannot enter into an engagement which would bind Congress to act. Many another treaty, and not merely a treaty of the type we have been discussing, can be made effective only by affirmative action of the legislative branch. The question is not constitutional but moral. When an obligation is incurred, it is morally imperative that the Congress should carry it out. It should not be incurred, of course, unless there is good reason to believe that it would be honored. But it is quite unnecessary to speak, as did Mr. Hughes, as if our governmental forms prevented the signature by the United States of agreements for the maintenance of peace.

Practically speaking, we repeat, the Hughes note was not of very great importance. The Draft Treaty was probably doomed from its inception. The point to be made is that in this instance the Secretary showed no enthusiasm for—indeed no interest in—the idea of collective security.

The Secretary was to take a still more drastic stand with regard to the Geneva Protocol.[7] In 1924 the European diplomats tried their hand once again at the problem which the Treaty of Mutual Assistance had failed to solve. The result was the Geneva Protocol for the Pacific Settlement of International Disputes. This Protocol erected an elaborate system for the solution of international difficulties, first by extending the compul-

---

[6] *Foreign Relations*, 1924, I, 79.

[7] For a discussion of the Protocol, see Williams, *State Security and the League*, pp. 182-205, also D. H. Miller, *The Geneva Protocol* (New York, 1925), and P. J. Noel Baker, *The Geneva Protocol for the Pacific Settlement of International Disputes* (London, 1925); and Chapters 1, §III and 4, §III above and Chapter 10, §I below.

sory jurisdiction of the Court of International Justice, and, second, by
providing for the settlement, either by the Council of the League or
by compulsory arbitration, of all disputes which did not fall within the
jurisdiction of the Court. At the same time it made it possible to define
an aggressor with more precision than was possible in the Covenant, and
bound the signatories to participate loyally and effectively in the application of sanctions, but with the proviso that aid should be given by each
state "in the degree which its geographical position and particular situation as regards armament allows." It is important to note that the
Geneva Protocol was unanimously approved by the Fifth Assembly of
the League on October 2, 1924.

The Geneva Protocol has a far greater significance than the Draft Treaty. The leaders of the greatest states of Europe were at the meetings of that
famous Assembly of 1924, Ramsay MacDonald for Great Britain, Eduard Herriot for France. The Protocol was launched at a favorable
moment and under favorable auspices, with the end of a period of tension
in the relations of France and Germany, and in an atmosphere favorable
to constructive achievement. It is true that the position was somewhat
altered by the fall of the Labor government in November of 1924. Still,
without overstressing the matter, it is possible to say that, on the mere
basis of the significance of the instrument, the attitude of the United
States towards the Protocol was bound to be of considerable importance.

The Foreign Relations of the United States for 1925 contain a very
remarkable account of conversations on the subject between the Secretary
and the British ambassador in Washington. The first occurred on January 5, 1925. It is important to quote this document, recorded in a memorandum by Mr. Hughes himself. It was Sir Esmé Howard who opened
the conversation. Declaring that "it was a cardinal point in British policy
to maintain friendly relations with the United States, and to cooperate
with this Government wherever possible," he added that "there might
be interference with this policy if contingencies should arise in which
through the operation of the Protocol the British Government was
brought into opposition to the interests of the United States." "On the
other hand," he continued, "it seemed to the British Government that
it would not be well to throw out the Protocol entirely. . . ." "The only
alternative to such a competition in armament with all its possible consequences would seem to be the adoption in some form of such an arrangement as the Geneva Protocol proposed."[8]

In reply to these observations the Secretary took what can only be

[8] *Foreign Relations*, 1925, I, 16-17.

described as a rather high tone. "There were," he remarked, "two aspects, at least, of the Geneva Protocol which might give concern to this Government." "If the Protocol were taken as having practical value and actually of portending what it set forth," said Hughes, "there would appear to be a proposal of a concert against the United States, when the Powers joining in the Protocol considered that the United States had committed some act of aggression, although the United States might believe itself to be entirely justified in its action, and in fact be acting in accordance with its traditional policies. The Secretary said that he did not believe that such a concert would actually become effective but he supposed that the Protocol must be taken as it is written and in this view the United States would be compelled to view it with disfavor. The Secretary said there was another class of cases where the action of the United States itself might not be involved but that of some other country with which the United States had trade relations, and the action of the Powers who had joined in the Protocol might turn out to be inimical to the interests of the United States in such relations with the country in question." Alluding still further to the possibility of collective action against some other nation, Mr. Hughes went on to remark that "there was one thing he believed could be depended upon, and that was that this Government from its very beginning had been insistent upon the rights of neutrals and would continue to maintain them." He "did not believe that any Administration, short of a treaty concluded and ratified, could commit the country against assertion of its neutral rights in case there should be occasion to demand their recognition."[9]

All this could hardly be described as encouraging. But Mr. Hughes went further. He declined at one and the same time to approve or to disapprove the Protocol. He intimated that the British sounding was a mere maneuver and excuse for inaction, and expressed the hope that if other governments did not approve of the Protocol, they should deal with the matter from the point of view of their own interests and not put the responsibility on the United States. To the suggestion that the matter might be handled by a reservation on the part of the British, he declared that he would not wish anything to be said that might imply that this way of dealing with the problem might be satisfactory to the United States.

It is difficult to describe this commentary of Mr. Hughes as other than a dash of cold water thrown in the face of Sir Esmé. Indeed, it is hard to see how the tone could have been much more intransigent and un-

---

[9] *Foreign Relations*, 1925, I, 17.

conciliatory. Nor was the effect of this interview diminished three days later when the British ambassador returned to the State Department and was told that the Secretary had consulted with the President and that the Chief Executive approved the point of view previously expressed.[10] And it is worth noting that the position then assumed was in no sense due to any particular political pressure. The date, it will be noted, was January 1925. The presidential elections were over, and the Republican party had been brilliantly victorious. It may be that Mr. Hughes believed that he was expressing the mood and temper of the American people. It is certain that he was not acting on the basis of any particular exigency of the moment.

On the other hand, it is by no means clear that the action taken by the Secretary was a determining factor in the final collapse of the effort to strengthen the League through the Protocol. The British elections of November 1924 brought the Conservatives into power with an overwhelming majority, and the new Secretary of State for Foreign Affairs was not an enthusiast for the arrangements that had been worked out at Geneva. The Dominions, when consulted, also were disposed to avoid the rather sweeping commitments contained in the League proposals.[11] True, the position of the United States afforded an excellent argument against these new commitments, and the British government made a good deal of this argument in its memorandum of March 1925.[12] But the most that can probably be said is that the position assumed by Mr. Hughes reinforced a point of view that the London government might have assumed in any event. It is useless to speculate, of course, on what would have been the course of events in the 1920's if the United States had wholeheartedly accepted the engagements of the Convenant itself.

The dislike of the League idea, it must be stressed, did not, in the secretariat of Mr. Hughes, prevent the taking of steps which expressed American interest in the idea of peace. There was, for example, in 1923, a proposal put forward by the administration for American adhesion to the protocol creating the Court of International Justice.[13] Such a proposal was consonant with American traditional thinking, which connected peace, not with power, but with orderly process. But this proposal got nowhere. When the United States Senate in 1926 voted to adhere to the protocol,

---

[10] *Foreign Relations*, 1925, I, 19.

[11] See some of their comments in Williams, *State Security and the League*, pp. 310-320. See also Chapter 1, note 91, above.

[12] Williams, *State Security and the League*, p. 306.

[13] On the World Court question, see D. F. Fleming, *The United States and the World Court* (Garden City, 1945).

it did so with reservations that created new problems and that carried the whole controversy with regard to the Court over into the Roosevelt administration.[14]

But let us return to the movement for collective security. The failure of the Protocol was followed by the very significant negotiations, lasting through a great part of 1925, that finally resulted in the treaties of Locarno. By these treaties specific agreements strengthening the principles of collective security were approved in place of generalized understanding. Thus the French, British, Italian, Belgian, and German governments entered into engagements by which the territorial *status quo* with regard to the frontiers between France and Germany and Belgium and Germany were guaranteed, and by which the countries concerned mutually undertook in no case to attack each other or resort to war against each other. They also agreed to settle all disputes arising between them by resort to arbitration, and to extend mutual assistance to one another against any one of their number which resorted to war in violation of the pact. The Eastern frontier settlements of Versailles, that is, the frontier between Germany and Poland and Germany and Czechoslovakia, were not similarly guaranteed. But treaties of arbitration were drawn up between Germany and Poland and Germany and Czechoslovakia, and these treaties were buttressed by antecedent agreements between France and Poland and France and Czechoslovakia to give each other immediate aid and assistance in case of an unprovoked recourse to arms. The Locarno agreements, signed at the end of 1925, represent the high-water mark of the movement for collective guarantees in the period between the wars.[15]

By the time the Locarno treaties were under discussion, Secretary Hughes had laid down his charge at the State Department and had been succeeded by Secretary Kellogg. The new director of American foreign policy was a man of far less force than his predecessor, far less likely to adopt any initiative in the field of foreign policy. Yet the very fact that the Locarno agreements were regional in their character was calculated to relieve the United States of any embarrassment with regard to them. To such partial understandings the American government could have no such objections as pertained to the strengthening of the Covenant. Mr. Kellogg, of course, when informed of what was going on, firmly declined to have anything to do with any guarantee.[16] But Presi-

---

[14] *ibid.*

[15] For a convenient summary see Williams, *State Security and the League*, pp. 206-226. See also G. Glasgow, *From Dawes to Locarno* (New York, 1926).

[16] *Foreign Relations*, 1925, I, 21.

dent Coolidge speaking in July of 1925 gave the negotiations his bless-ing,[17] and in his message of December 1925, the cautious Chief Executive declared that the recent agreements "represent the success of the policy on which this country has been insisting . . . of having European coun-tries settle their own political problems without involving this country," and went on to suggest that the way was now clear for the reduction of land armaments, while underlining the fact that this was primarily a European problem.[18]

III

The question of American participation in the movement for the reduction of land armaments was, in due course, to take another turn. In no little time the American government began to participate in dis-cussions at Geneva looking to such reduction. But, since the climactic moves in this discussion came in the early 1930's, it will be convenient to postpone discussion of this subject for a moment, and to examine first that remarkable movement which culminated in the famous Kellogg Pact, or the Pact of Paris, for the maintenance of peace.[19] This pact, finally signed on August 28, 1928, was a simple pledge on the part of the contracting parties "not to have recourse to war as an instrument of national policy, and to settle all disputes arising between them by peace-ful means." At first blush this compact looks like a denial of the very principle of collective security, a substitution of peace by promises for peace by common action. But whoever studies the background of the Kellogg Pact in detail will, I think, come to a somewhat different con-clusion. For the friends of the Pact were by no means always clear on the matter of sanctions. Mr. S. O. Levinson of Chicago, who very early espoused the idea of the outlawry of war and who was one of those who pressed it most tenaciously throughout the 1920's, though certainly not depending on force as the essential element in his own view of the prob-lem, at one time seems to have believed that in flagrant violations of a no-war pledge force might be used.[20] Senator Borah, who had a great deal to do with the promotion of the Kellogg Pact, on one occasion de-

---

[17] See the *New York Times*, July 4, 1925.

[18] The *New York Times*, December 9, 1925.

[19] On the Kellogg Pact, see the full discussion in *Foreign Relations*, 1928, I, 1-234. See also J. T. Shotwell, *War as an Instrument of National Policy and its Renunciation in the Pact of Paris* (New York, 1928), D. H. Miller, *The Peace Pact of Paris. A Study of the Briand-Kellogg Treaty* (New York, 1928), and D. P. Myers, *Origins and Con-clusion of the Paris Pact; the renunciation of war as an instrument of national policy* (Boston, 1929).

[20] See J. E. Sloner, *S. O. Levinson and the Pact of Paris: A study in the techniques of influence* (Chicago, 1943), esp. pp. 27 and 185.

clared that it was "quite inconceivable that this country would stand idly by in case of a grave breach of a multilateral treaty to which it was a party."[21] Statements such as these ought not, it is true, to be given an exaggerated importance. They certainly do not represent the prevailing mood or conviction of the two men just mentioned, both of whom seem to have had a naive faith in the power of public opinion. But neither can they be entirely disregarded. To this fact must be added another. Some of the friends of the pact were quite clear as to what they hoped would flow from it. Believing in the principle of collective action against aggression, they took the view that once the treaty was ratified there would arise, almost inevitably, a demand that it be "implemented." And this demand, they hoped, would in due course lead the United States into closer relations with the League of Nations. If once the principle that war was inherently illegal, as well as immoral, were accepted, a way would be found by which the American people would take action in support of the principle they had affirmed. This point of view appears most clearly in Professor Shotwell's interesting book on *War as an Instrument of National Policy*.[22] But one can find it in many other pronouncements of the period as well.[23]

Perhaps the most interesting thing about the Pact of Paris, however, is the illustration it affords of the way in which American foreign policy on occasion comes up from the grass roots rather than down from the State Department or its Secretary. It is a well-known fact that the initial step in the negotiations that led to the pact came from a proposal of the French Foreign Minister Aristide Briand, made on April 6, 1927, to enter into a bilateral treaty for the renunciation of war. This proposal, incited by Professor Shotwell on a visit to Paris, passed almost unnoticed at the time, and was indeed completely ignored by Secretary Kellogg. The situation was in some degree changed when Nicholas Murray Butler, then president of Columbia University, in a letter to the *New York Times*, called attention to the significance of the Briand offer, and when Professor Shotwell and Professor Chamberlain put the idea in the form of a draft treaty. In June of 1927, the French government presented a formal proposal to the United States.[24] Still the administration hesitated, indeed the State Department declared that no such compact was necessary, and that it would not even be desirable.[25] But the outlawry of war

[21] See Shotwell, *War as an Instrument of National Policy*, p. 224.
[22] *ibid.*, pp. 254ff.
[23] See, for example, Miller, *The Peace Pact of Paris*, and J. B. Whitton, *What Follows the Pact of Paris* (New York, 1932).
[24] Shotwell, *War as an Instrument of National Policy*, p. 72.   [25] *ibid.*

proposal aroused an increasing interest, and the crucial factor in securing official consideration for it was doubtless the attitude of Senator Borah, the powerful chairman of the Senate Committee on Foreign Relations. On December 27, 1927, Borah introduced a resolution calling for the outlawry of war, the establishment of an international code, and of an international court by the decisions of which the nations of the world should be bound to abide.[26] On the very next day, Secretary Kellogg, in a note to the French government, proposed that "the two governments, instead of contenting themselves with a bilateral declaration of the nature suggested by M. Briand, might make a more signal contribution to world peace by joining in an effort to obtain the adherence of all of the principal powers of the world to a declaration renouncing war as an instrument of national policy."[27] Thus were initiated the negotiations that finally led to the Pact of Paris.

I do not think it desirable to trace these negotiations in detail. There were substantial obstacles to be overcome. The French were by no means enthusiastic about the alteration of their original proposal, and they feared that the proposed agreement might weaken the structure of the League of Nations, and the machinery of sanctions embodied in the Covenant. Other difficulties soon arose. The British, in particular, seemed to fear that their freedom of action in certain parts of the world might be limited by the proposed engagement. Matters ended happily, however. By making it clear, as he did in a speech of April 28, 1928, that the Pact did not affect the right of self-defense, Mr. Kellogg calmed the apprehensions of the critics, and at the same time (having regard to the flexibility of the term self-defense itself) whittled away some of the significance of the Pact itself.[28] By the spring of 1928, with a Presidential election coming on, there was only one course of action to be followed, and that was to press matters to a conclusion. And so the Pact was signed.

What effect did the Pact have on American diplomacy in the years that followed? The first attempt to invoke it concerned a dispute between China and Russia in 1929 and need not concern us here save to remark that the appeal made by the American government exposed the United States to a severe rebuff from the Soviet Union.[29]

The fiasco which resulted in this particular case led Mr. Stimson to

[26] The resolution is found most easily in Shotwell, *War as an Instrument of National Policy*, pp. 108-109.
[27] *Foreign Relations*, 1927, II, 626-627.
[28] The speech is in the *New York Times*, April 29, 1928.
[29] The voluminous correspondence is in *Foreign Relations*, 1929, II, 186-435.

meditate on possible means by which the Kellogg Pact might be made more effective. Thus arose the idea of consultation, or of a consultative pact.[80] This idea was discussed with the French ambassador in the fall of 1929.[81] It also came up at the London naval conference of 1930. At that conference the French again brought it forward and threw out the hint that the reduction of their own naval armament might be facilitated by some understanding on the matter. The Secretary was at first cold to the suggestion since it smacked of a diplomatic bargain, and President Hoover was still more opposed. But, as the conference proceeded, it appeared possible that the French and the British might agree on some strengthening of their association under the Covenant of the League, and Stimson played with the idea of encouraging such a strengthening by some agreement for consultation. On March 25 he issued a somewhat cryptic statement to the press on the matter, intimating that some positive step might be taken. He seems at this moment to have had the support of the American delegation of which he was the head. There was, however, less enthusiasm in Washington; the President was distinctly nervous with regard to the matter and feared the reaction in the Senate. He was, indeed, strongly opposed to any generalized engagement to consult. Though he gave his approval to a watered-down version of a consultative clause in the naval treaty, the project was, in the last analysis, abandoned.[82]

But Stimson was tenacious of the general objective. When the Manchurian crisis broke in the fall of 1931, he maintained close contact with the League, even to the extent of permitting the American representative at Geneva to sit in on meetings of the Council, and of sending General Dawes to Paris to participate at arm's length in the League deliberations. There was an American member on the commission which the League appointed to investigate the situation and make recommendations, and the League and the United States cooperated in the winter of 1932 in proclaiming the so-called Stimson doctrine by which it was declared that there could be no recognition of an illegal situation arising out of the violation of the Kellogg Pact. In the course of the year 1932, moreover, both party nominating conventions declared in favor of the principle of consultation,[83] and Stimson underlined the desirability of

[80] For this whole matter of consultation, see R. M. Cooper, *American Consultation in World Affairs for the Preservation of Peace* (New York, 1934).

[81] See *Foreign Relations*, 1929, I, 59-64.

[82] See *Foreign Relations*, 1930, II, *passim*, esp. pp. 36-92.

[83] Cooper, *American Consultation in World Affairs*, p. 58.

accepting this principle in a speech of August 8.[34] Nonetheless, no formal engagements were entered into during any part of the period which we are reviewing.

Taken all in all, however, it cannot be said that the American government, between 1921 and the advent of the Roosevelt administration, had gone very far towards the acceptance of the idea of collective security. There was very distinctly a difference between the attitude of Hughes and the attitude of Stimson,[35] but the difference was by no means so wide as practically to affect the policies of the European nations. On the whole, the dogma of freedom of action dominated American policy during the period, and none was more deeply attached to it, it should be said, than was President Hoover.[36] It seems likely that in this respect he expressed the dominant opinion of the nation.

Interesting as it is to speculate on "what might have been," in summarizing the attitude of the United States in the years under review, all that can really be said is that the general line of policy was unfavorable towards common action against an aggressor, but that the Kellogg-Briand Pact, by branding war as immoral, reflected something of the sentiment of the American people, and may have provided a basis for the more active diplomacy of the United States at a later period.

IV

The dislike of the administrations of this period for the League idea is well illustrated in the manner in which they dealt with the problem of reduction of armaments. There was, at the end of the war, an immense sentiment for such reduction, and Mr. Hughes, in the very first year of his administration of the State Department, boldly capitalized on such sentiment. The Washington Arms Conference of 1921-1922 was, in many ways, a great diplomatic achievement. Though the British would have liked the credit for calling it, Mr. Hughes insisted on garnering that credit for himself. He electrified all observers when, at the very outset, he laid down a plan for the scrapping of a substantial part of existing building programs and for the establishment of fixed ratios in capital ships and aircraft carriers. He secured that parity with the British which American opinion (for no very clear reason, it must be conceded) demanded, and he persuaded the Japanese to accept a subordinate position. He brought about these striking results without what the enemies

---

[34] *ibid.*, p. 59.

[35] Stimson was disposed to acquiesce in sanctions against Japan in 1931.

[36] See President Hoover's recent article in *Colliers, The National Weekly,* for April 19, 1952, p. 57.

of the League would have described as "entanglement." The nearest approach to such an entanglement, indeed, was a Four Power pact, consultative in nature, with regard to "the regions of the Pacific." (Somehow or other, such a pact could, even in 1922, be regarded as innocent if it applied to the Orient.) In the course of the negotiations, moreover, assisted by the pressure exercised by the Dominions, and especially by Canada, he broke up the Anglo-Japanese alliance which had existed since 1902. But this story is not for us to tell here in detail.[37] The point is that the American theory with regard to arms reduction was essentially different from the thesis upheld by many influential Europeans, and especially by the French. To the latter, the building of a system of external security was a condition precedent to the reduction of armaments, and it was only under very heavy pressure that the Quai d'Orsay yielded even on the partial limitation of naval armaments at Washington. But American statesmanship stoutly insisted that there was no necessary connection between the curtailment of armed forces and a network of treaties to punish aggression. It succeeded, in this particular instance, in making its point of view prevail by giving up, in the face of Japanese pressure, the right to fortify Guam and the Philippines. In other words, it abdicated so far as the use of force in the Far East was concerned. No doubt, as was frequently maintained at the time, because of the state of American public opinion, it would have been impossible to secure funds for such fortifications in any case. But however this may be, the significant thing is that the American outlook on the whole question of armaments was so very different from that involved in acceptance of the League.

The success of the Washington Conference in the field of naval armament was to be repeated and extended in the administration of President Hoover. For a time after 1922 it seemed as if the rivalry of the United States and Great Britain, partially exorcised so far as capital ships were concerned, was to break out in new construction of vessels of inferior tonnage. An attempt to come to an agreement in 1927 in a conference at Geneva aborted, largely because the preparations for the conference were inadequate and because the admirals were allowed a very important, if not a central, role in the negotiations. But at London in 1930, the three Great Powers, the United States, Great Britain, and Japan, came to an agreement which limited ships of every kind and which was, indeed, a remarkable achievement.[38] It ought, perhaps, to be

---

[37] The best brief account of the Conference is in A. W. Griswold, *The Far Eastern Policy of the United States* (New York, 1937), pp. 269-332.

[38] The London negotiations are given in much detail in *Foreign Relations*, 1930, I, 1-186.

said parenthetically, that one of the reasons for the success of both the Washington and London conferences was the appointment of influential Senators as members of the American delegations. This specific is not infallible, but it has frequently proved efficacious in smoothing the way to successful negotiation.

The naval agreements of the period seemed at the time to be remarkable achievements. In the short run they were rightly so regarded. But they did not survive the tensions of the 1930's, and their long-time effects were certainly not entirely happy. The United States was for a time lulled into a false security and neglected its naval establishment, failing to build up to the agreed quotas. The British were compelled at London, or in the negotiations preceding London, to reduce their cruiser strength in order to propitiate the American government, and this was to be a serious handicap in the 1940's. Naval disarmament was an expression of the temper of the 1920's and of a distinctively American point of view. But it was very far from affording a long-time guarantee of peace, and it contributed little to the stabilization of Europe. It is for this reason that I have dealt with it so summarily.

Let us turn to examine the American role in the effort carried on from 1925 to 1933 to reduce land armaments. As early as 1925, eschewing the very cautious view of the matter expressed by Secretary Hughes, and responding, no doubt, to the pressure of powerful elements in American opinion, Secretary Kellogg permitted the United States to take part in the deliberations of the Preparatory Commission on Disarmament that assembled at Geneva. For years a long discussion went on in this Commission which finally culminated in the Geneva Conference of 1932. In this conference bold proposals were put forward for the curtailment of land armaments as well as sea armaments, and in June of 1932 President Hoover presented a sweeping program which laid the emphasis on the abolition of "offensive weapons."[39]

But firmly, at all times, the United States adhered to its idea of no entanglement, of making no engagements that might tie its hands. And, equally firmly, the French insisted that such engagements were essential to any understanding. Thus the arms conference was to end in a fiasco; the way was blocked to any concrete accomplishment, and though the attitude was slightly changed when the Roosevelt administration came into power, the advent of Hitler in Germany dimmed the prospects of any accord. The world, instead, was to march down the long road to war.

[39] See *Foreign Relations*, 1932, I, 180-182.

Let us summarize at this point the policies of the United States with regard to peace and security as they relate to Europe. We shall have to begin by saying once again that these policies were narrowly circumscribed by public opinion. There are those who believe that if the American government had been able to take part wholeheartedly in a program of military guarantees the catastrophes of the 1930's might have been avoided. Certainly, in this year of grace 1953, the assumptions of American diplomacy are based on the idea of such guarantees. But different times, different manners. Neither Secretary Hughes nor Secretary Kellogg ever believed in the principle of collective action, and Stimson, believing in it more, had to contend with a President who was deeply set against any such conception. It is easy, if one will, to bewail the situation. But it is perhaps more judicious merely to recognize the fact that in democratic countries it is not possible to proceed in defiance of, or in opposition to, a powerful body of opinion.

V

Let us turn from the questions of politics to the principal economic problems that vexed the administrations of the 1920's. And here the two principal matters to be considered are the war debts[40] and reparations. On the former a position had been taken at Paris by President Wilson from which it was impossible at any time in the next fifteen years to depart. This position was that the cancelation of the debts could not be considered. It is obvious that, in assuming this position, Wilson was interpreting American opinion. It would have been impossible to take any other course. In the wave of postwar nationalism most Americans saw only that they had come to the rescue of the Western democracies in a great war, that they had played a decisive part in the winning of that war, and that the United States had little to show, in the way of material gain, for the immense sums of money that had been expended and for the loss of American lives. The suggestion that they should now forgive borrowings which had been understood to be such at the time they were made was hardly to be tolerated.

Accordingly, the Harding and Coolidge administrations were bound to base their own policy on the position assumed by the previous administration, and to turn a deaf ear to European appeals for a scaling down of both the war loans and reparations. The American attitude was first defined in an explicit manner, that is, by legislation, in the winter of

---

[40] On the war debts, see especially H. G. Moulton and L. Pasvolsky, *War Debts and World Prosperity* (Washington, D.C., 1932).

1922. The act of February 9 of that year created a special War Debt Commission to preside over the liquidation of these debts into long-term obligations. The Secretary of State, the Secretary of the Treasury, and members of both Houses of Congress were to constitute this commission. The original act narrowly confined the Commission as to the terms on which refunding could take place. No new bonds were to be issued the date of maturity of which was later than June 15, 1947, and the rate of interest was not to be fixed at less than 4¼ per cent.

The legislation of 1922 produced no great enthusiasm in the breasts of our European debtors for refunding, and it was indeed fundamentally vulnerable. For as the rate of interest fell in the United States so that the American government could borrow at a rate substantially lower that that of the war years, it seemed unreasonable to exact a high rate from other governments. It was also apparent, as time went on, that if interest payments were to be added to principal, there was little chance of arriving at agreements which stipulated for the complete discharge of the debt by 1947. The Congress was therefore obliged to enact a much more flexible statute in the winter of 1923, which gave far more latitude to the Commission. It was undoubtedly influenced to that end by the negotiations with Great Britain which took place in January of the same year. Secretary Mellon was chairman of the Debt Commission, and it does not appear that the American Secretary of State took the leading part in the discussions. The first of these discussions, carried on for the British by Stanley Baldwin, who came to America for that purpose, ended in a deadlock. The problem was complicated, moreover, by the wholly unauthorized assurances of George Harvey, our ambassador in London, as to the rate of interest that the United States would demand, and as to the possibility of floating a tax-free loan in the United States.[41] Hughes had good reason to lament the good old American custom which confided the charge of the most important embassies to political supporters of the administration. But, in due course, an arrangement was arrived at, the rate of interest reduced, and the period of payments extended to 62 years, and this agreement was approved by the Congress. The method adopted, that is, legislative approval instead of the negotiation of a treaty, undoubtedly made easier the arrival at an accord, and is an interesting example of a method, which was to be more and more employed in the future, of circumventing the Senate.

Other debt agreements followed. It was the French who were the most obdurate in negotiation, and who were particularly insistent that

---

[41] Pusey, *Charles Evans Hughes*, II, 585.

the war debt problem be linked up to the question of reparations. Against any such proposition the War Debt Commission and the State Department alike took a very strong and unyielding stand. No connection between the two subjects was admitted, though it was obvious, of course, that if Germany defaulted on reparations, the burden of repayment of the debts would fall squarely upon the taxpayers of the debtor nations, and would, to some extent, at least, create a new situation. The first flurry with the French took place in 1925. When the French went home without an agreement, and in a good deal of a huff, the Italian government, nicely calculating the moment for a deal, took up the thread of its own negotiations, and, for reasons that are somewhat obscure, emerged with a settlement that reduced the average rate of interest on the Italian obligations to something like .4 of one per cent. A new effort at dealing with the French was undertaken in 1927, and in a much more favorable climate of opinion. Though the French continued to press for a recognition of the relationship between debts and reparations, an agreement was signed and payments began to be made.

In these negotiations for debt refunding, the principal burden was borne by the Treasury. But it was not so with reparations. Here the State Department played an important role, and this was particularly true under Secretary Hughes.

At Paris in 1919, it was impossible to arrive at any settlement with regard to Germany's payments to the victors. The problem was, at best, a very complicated one, and it was rendered more complex by the strong public feeling in both France and Great Britain. The exaggerated hopes of the mass of people had been encouraged by the politicians, and economic realism flew out the window. Accordingly, what was done was virtually to adjourn the settlement of the matter, to entrust the determination of Germany's indebtedness to a Reparations Commission set up by the treaty, which should by May 1, 1921, following certain principles laid down in treaty, determine the facts of the situation. In the meantime Germany was compelled to make certain types of payment, which we do not need to examine in detail.

Originally, it was expected that the United States would be one of the five nations represented on the Commission, and that the American member would be chairman. But the treaty of Versailles failed in the Senate, and when a separate treaty was negotiated with Germany, the Senate tacked on a reservation by which the representation on any of the numerous bodies functioning under the pact was forbidden, unless the explicit consent of Congress had been given. Mr. Hughes thus found himself in a most embarrassing situation. He could, of course, and did, appoint "unofficial" representatives to the Commission. But these individuals could wield very little authority; they could not vote on any issue. As a consequence, the control of the Commission gravitated into the hands of the French, and the attitude assumed became more and more rigorous. On a problem where the relatively objective attitude of the United States might have been of very great value, it became of almost no value at all.

The hamstringing of the State Department did not prevent Mr. Hughes from taking an active interest in the reparations question. At the outset of his term of office he was approached by the German government and asked to mediate the reparations question, and to fix the sum to be paid by Germany to the Allies.[42] This hot potato the Secretary naturally laid down hastily enough, but he urged that the German government itself formulate proposals that would form a proper basis for discussion. This suggestion was promptly accepted, and an offer made to pay a sum of 50,000,000,000 gold marks, present value, which would have amounted to something like four times this sum in annuities. The very afternoon it was received, the German proposition was submitted to the British and French ambassadors, and in the conversation that ensued Mr. Hughes raised the question whether a point had not been reached where it was better to take the proposal as a basis for further negotiations.[43] But the various European governments concerned remained obdurate. And on May 2 the word went forth to Berlin that the United States "finds itself unable to reach the conclusion that the proposals afford a basis for discussion acceptable to the Allied Governments."[44] The first American effort at a solution of the reparations question had met with failure.

As is well known, the reparations question became more and more aggravated in 1922, and the French government in particular manifested a more and more rigid point of view. The situation was shaping up towards sanctions and military pressure on Germany in the fall of the year. Very obviously, this development the Secretary profoundly deplored. Indeed, in December of 1922, he held a long conversation with Jusserand in which, in none too gentle a tone, he pointed out the difficulties to which further coercive measures by France would surely lead.[45] Moreover, there was germinating in his mind as early as September a proposal that the reparations question be taken out of the field of

[42] *Foreign Relations*, 1921, II, 41.   [43] *Foreign Relations*, 1921, II, 48.
[44] *Foreign Relations*, 1921, II, 54.   [45] *Foreign Relations*, 1922, II, 187ff.

emotional debate, and submitted to the examination of financial experts, and this idea, too, he presented to Jusserand. On the other hand, he rejected as impracticable a proposal that came from Ambassador Houghton in Berlin, and which looked towards easing the general international tension by canceling the war debts in exchange for measures of disarmament, and a pledge on the part of the great nations of Europe not to go to war without a public referendum.[46] At the end of December, in a step only less remarkable than the dramatic proposal for arms reduction at the Washington Conference in November 1921, he laid bare to the public his views on the reparations question, in a speech before the American Historical Association at New Haven. The speech, it is true, indicated no concessions on the part of the United States. But it contained a key idea, which the Secretary stated as follows, "Why should they (the Allies) not invite men of the highest authority in finance in their respective countries—men of such prestige, honor and experience that their agreement upon the amount to be paid (by Germany), and upon a financial plan for working out the payments, would be accepted throughout the world as the most authoritative expression obtainable. I have no doubt that distinguished Americans would be willing to serve on such a commission."[47]

At the time that it was pronounced, the New Haven speech produced no effect whatever. On January 2, Britain dissenting, the Reparations Commission declared Germany to be in default, and authorized sanctions against her. Not many days later the French moved into the Ruhr, and there began one of the most disastrous political moves of the postwar decade.

During the summer and early fall of 1923 the situation in the Reich deteriorated in sensational fashion. There was, in Hughes' opinion, nothing that the United States could do that would not make the situation worse; any suggestion in favor of Germany would, he felt, irritate the French and weaken the force of the suggestion that he had made at New Haven. Only experience could alter the situation and provide a means of settlement. And experience did precisely that. Slowly the French, in the face of British and American criticism and German passive resistance, yielded ground. They haggled over terms of reference to be laid down for the committees of experts and sought to limit the conclusions of the inquiry in time. But Hughes stood his ground, and at last he had his way. On November 23, 1923, the Reparations Commission approved of an inquiry of the type the Secretary had suggested,

[46] *Foreign Relations*, 1922, II, 181.   [47] *Foreign Relations*, 1922, II, 199-202.

and two committees of experts were appointed to consider means of balancing the budget and stabilizing the currency and to investigate the amount of German capital that had been exported abroad. Since the Commission itself appointed the members of the committees, the limitation that the Senate had appended to the treaty of peace with Germany with regard to official representation on international bodies was of no effect, and that body was neatly outflanked.

The deliberations of these committees, appointed in November 1923, resulted, of course, in the Dawes plan. It is not possible to analyze that plan here. But it is important to note the part which Hughes played in seeing that its recommendations were carried into effect. Ostensibly going to Europe as President of the American Bar Association (a camouflage that seems a bit ineffective), he visited the various capitals of Europe and lent his influence to persuading the governments concerned to accept the program that General Dawes and his associates had laid down. He appears to have had his greatest difficulties in France, where Premier Herriot, himself not unfavorable to the plan, was mortally afraid of the hostile influence of Raymond Poincaré. But he saw both Herriot and Poincaré and made it clear that rejection of the scheme would have a very unfortunate effect.[48] Whether his role was decisive it is not possible to say. But, at any rate, the Dawes plan was put into effect.

Of course the new arrangements did not last long. They had to be revised in 1929 when the same technique of committees of experts was again employed. And then came the depression of 1929, forcing still further readjustments.

These readjustments we must for a moment examine if only for the light they throw on the character of American foreign policy in general. As the depression deepened, it became increasingly clear that the whole structure of international indebtedness erected in the postwar years rested on a flimsy foundation. The crisis came in 1931, with the collapse of the Austrian bank, the Credit-Anstalt, and a serious deterioration in the economic situation of Germany. Though Congress was not in session, and though his only recourse was to telegraph Congressional leaders in both Houses, the President came forward with a proposal for a year's moratorium on reparations and war debts alike. In his recent memoirs Mr. Hoover declares that this proposal was his own.[49] Certainly there have been few examples of more forthright action on the part of the

---

[48] Pusey, *Charles Evans Hughes*, II, 591-592.
[49] *Collier's*, May 10, 1952, p. 72.

Chief Executive, and no one will deny that the decision took political courage. Even so, it was necessary to attenuate its effects by declaring that no question of cancelation was involved, and by stating (somewhat illogically, it must be confessed) that the question of German reparations was a "strictly European problem."

The President's bold initiative did not alter the fundamentals of the situation. It was accepted by the French only after some diplomatic haggling, and it did not prevent an increasing agitation for the reduction of German reparations. The European conference which met at Lausanne in the summer of 1932 reduced the obligations of the Reich to a minimum, while at the same time drawing up a "gentleman's agreement" which stipulated that these reductions would not go into effect if the United States persisted in maintaining its attitude with regard to the war debts. What followed is no part of our story, except to say that both reparations and war debt payments had broken down entirely by 1934. The essence of the matter is that here was a problem that the diplomats simply could not settle, one in which the prejudices and resistances of the masses were more powerful than any appeal to intelligence could be. And outside the gesture of the Hoover moratorium, it is to be stated that American statesmanship in the last years of the debt question was never ready to face up to explaining to the American people the cold realities of the situation.

There is a peripheral aspect of this question of war debts and reparations that deserves a word of attention. The tariff attitude of the United States in the 1920's and early 1930's was in glaring contrast with its position on the refunding of the war obligations. It is an extraordinary commentary on the architects of American policy that they seem to have been so oblivious of the fact that if Europe were to pay up, it would be necessary to tear down, or at least to lower, customs barriers. Yet Secretary Hughes appears to have been little interested in the tariff act of 1922, and Secretary Stimson, though apparently more clearly aware of the problem, offered no effective resistance to the still higher tariff bill of 1930. The coordination of economic and political factors in the evolution of American diplomacy would, in any case, have been difficult; but in this one phase, at any rate, it does not seem even to have been attempted.

It is further to be noted that the edifice erected in the 1920's, the edifice of the naval treaties, of the Kellogg Pact, of the Dawes plan and the Young plan, was virtually completely to collapse in the 1930's, and here again the principal reasons were economic. When economic collapse came, and economic collapse for which the uncontrolled inflation in the United States must be regarded as a heavy contributing cause, the diplomats found their work in large degree undone. In the face of popular pressures based on economic discontent, they were powerless to prevent the deterioration of the general international situation in the 1930's.

The central question raised by this essay is, then, the question as to where, in the last analysis so far as America is concerned, foreign policy is made. And the conclusion is one suggested by the first pages of this text. It is made by the people, to no inconsiderable degree. It functions only within a frame of reference which they prescribe. Today, we seem to have embarked upon courses of action entirely antithetic to those of the 1920's. Then the thought was all of keeping American freedom of action, of avoiding Leagues and treaties which implied commitments. Today we think in terms of massing collective strength against a new menace, of alliances, of common action, and warning to aggressors that aggression will meet with punishment. Such policies are today dictated by the public mood, or are at least consistent with it. But the statesmen of the 1920's labored in a different climate of opinion, and were circumscribed by the prejudices which were typical of that climate. In the long run, they failed to erect a structure of peace. Will the formulas of the 1950's make success possible where it was not possible three decades ago? That is a question, not for the historian but for the prophets.

1. Poincaré and Lloyd George

2. Curzon

3. Austen Chamberlain

4. The British Delegation at Locarno. Sir Cecil Hurst, Miles Lampson, Austen Chamberlain

5. The Signing of the Locarno Treaties in London, December 1925. Prime Minister Baldwin and the three British delegates are at the head of the table with the Italian and German delegations, headed by Scialoja and Stresemann, to their right and with Briand, Berthelot, Benes, Count Skrzynski, and Vandervelde to their left.

6. Chicherin and Litvinov at the Narkomindel

Дружеские шаржи.

7. The Famous *Pravda* Cartoon. Zinoviev and Chicherin

8. Benes at Geneva in the early 1930's

9. Brockdorff-Rantzau. (From George Grosz, *Das Gesicht der herrschenden Klasse*, Malik-Verlag, Berlin)

10. Ismet Pasha at Lausanne

11. Secretary of State Kellogg

12. Ramsay MacDonald with Secretary of State Stimson

13. On the Paris-Calais train: Berthelot, Brüning, Curtius, Briand, Laval, François-Poncet

14. In the Hotel Excelsior in Rome: Mussolini, Brüning, Grandi, Curtius

15. Litvinov addressing the League Assembly

16. Arthur Henderson holding a press conference at Geneva

17. Papen and Neurath at the Lausanne Conference 1932

18. Opening of the Conference on Disarmament, 1932. In the aisle seats are Brüning, Belgian Foreign Minister Hymans, and Sir John Simon. German Secretary of State Bülow is beside Brüning.

19. André François-Poncet, French ambassador to Germany, 1932-1938

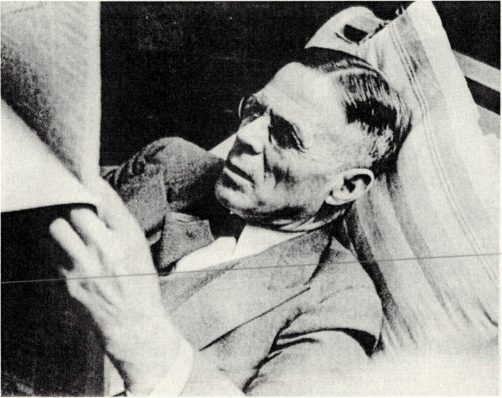

20. William E. Dodd, U.S. ambassador to Germany, 1933-1937

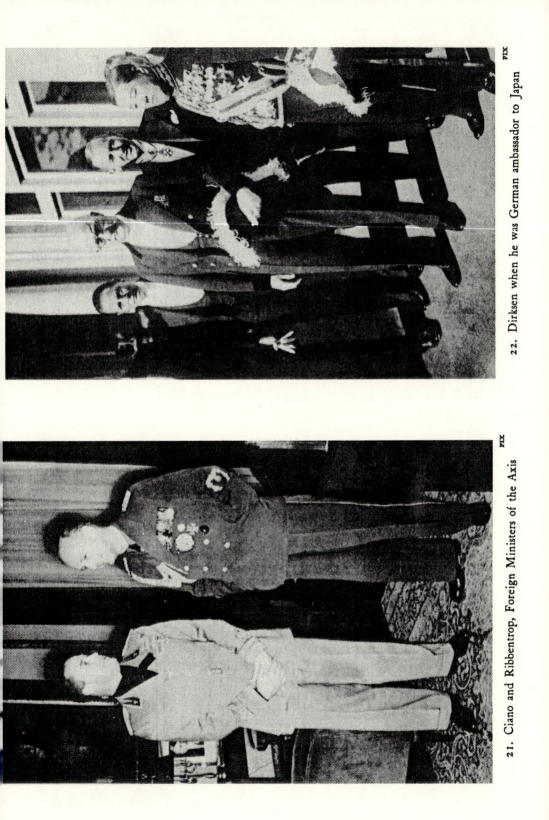

22. Dirksen when he was German ambassador to Japan

21. Ciano and Ribbentrop, Foreign Ministers of the Axis

23. Alexis Léger, Secretary General at the Quai d'Orsay, 1932-1940

24. Jozef Beck, Foreign Minister of Poland, 1932-1939

25. The Earl of Perth signing the Anglo-Italian Declaration of November 1938 in the Hall of Victory of the Palazzo Chigi

26. Nevile Henderson at the Victoria Station, March 1939

27. Pierre Laval signing the Franco-Soviet Pact in the Quai d'Orsay on May 2, 1935, while M. Potemkin (seated right), the Soviet minister to France, looks on

28. Ribbentrop taking leave of Georges Bonnet, French Foreign Minister, after signing the Franco-German Declaration of December 1938

29. The Conclusion of the Tripartite Military Pact of October 1940. Italian ambassador Indelli, Dr. Heinrich Stahmer (Ribbentrop's special envoy), Japanese War Minister Hideki Tojo, Japanese Foreign Minister Yosuke Matsuoka, and German ambassador Ott

30. At a meeting in Paris, William C. Bullitt in conversation with Polish ambassador
Lukasiewicz, on whose left is Sir Eric Phipps

31. Joseph P. Kennedy, U.S. ambassador to Great Britain, arriving at La Guardia field

Book Two: The Thirties

10

Arthur Henderson

BY HENRY R. WINKLER

WHEN ARTHUR HENDERSON came to the British Foreign Office in the summer of 1929, prospects for a European pacification appeared better than at any time since the end of the war. Locarno had been followed by Germany's entrance into the League of Nations, Russia was participating in the Preparatory Commission for the Disarmament Conference, and the Pact of Paris, if it did no more, seemed to symbolize a genuine will to achieve a lasting settlement of international tensions on a new basis.[1] In such a setting, Henderson prepared with characteristic directness to carry out the foreign policy advocated by the Labor party in the decade since Versailles. Two years later, when he was swept aside in the Labor debacle of 1931, the auguries for permanent peace were grim. In the wake of world economic crisis, the explosion of German nationalism was a striking repudiation of the policy of conciliation he had patiently undertaken. And in the aftermath, his experience as President of the Disarmament Conference was a tragic epilogue to the program he had attempted. Yet when he stepped down, the prestige of Great Britain was perhaps at its height and his tenure of office appeared to have been fruitful of real results. His approach to foreign affairs, despite the fate for which it was destined, had captured the imagination of large sections of the British public. It had, indeed, made a profound, if not always a convincing, impression on his European colleagues. Since that time, however, critics have divided sharply on the merits of his policy. His reputation among Labor writers as the greatest Foreign Secretary of the twentieth century is challenged by the picture of a well-meaning, bumbling amateur, blindly following the will-of-the-wisp of disarmament and conciliation in a world that was ready for neither.[2]

---

[1] This view was held in both the major British parties. See Anthony Eden's speech in the Debate on the Address, Parliamentary Debates: Commons, 5th series, CCXXIX, 425-426; and Margaret Cole, *Growing Up into Revolution* (London, 1949), p. 133.

[2] Harold J. Laski, "Ramsay MacDonald," *Harpers*, CLXIV (May 1932), 749; C. M.

While neither portrait is entirely accurate, the aims and nature of Henderson's policy form one of the more revealing chapters in the history of interwar diplomacy. He was in a sense a watershed figure and a survey of his role throws considerable light on the position of Britain as the hopes of the 1920's changed slowly into the fears and disillusionment of the 1930's.

I

Henderson's conduct of foreign affairs must be assessed in the light of his attitudes during the preceding decade. The British Labor party, within whose ranks he worked them out, moved slowly in developing its approach to foreign policy. Its reaction to the peace settlement was bitter. The unilateral disarmament of Germany was damned as unjust. The implication was drawn that other countries had both a legal and a moral obligation to scale down their armaments to the German level. France was accused of harboring aggressive intentions and German grievances were considered a major possible source of a new war. The redress of these grievances and the revision of the peace treaties became therefore a prime element in Labor policy.[3] Labor had been in the forefront of the campaign for a League of Nations, but the actual organization that came into being profoundly disappointed its hopes.[4] In the first shock of disillusionment, substantial groups within the party rejected the League as a coalition of the Allies whose main purpose was the maintenance of their own predominance. While the rank-and-file did not accept the left-wing thesis that peaceful international cooperation could not in any circumstances be organized by an alliance of capitalist governments, there was considerable feeling that the League as it existed fell far short of the genuine internationalism which Labor had demanded. Nevertheless, as time went on, the conviction grew that a reformed and strengthened League could be made to work in the interests of European conciliation and international peace.[5]

That Labor, despite its suspicions, came gradually to support a "League of Nations policy" as its first principle for the conduct of

---

Lloyd, "Uncle Arthur," *New Statesman and Nation*, x (October 26, 1935), 591. Cf., D. C. Somervell, *British Politics since 1900* (New York, 1950), pp. 186-187, 210; Quintin Hogg, *The Left Was Never Right* (London, 1945), pp. 121-123.

[3] W. R. Tucker, *The Attitude of the British Labour Party Towards European and Collective Security Problems, 1920-1939* (Geneva, 1950), pp. 244-246.

[4] See Henry R. Winkler, "The Development of the League of Nations Idea in Great Britain, 1914-1919," *Journal of Modern History*, xx (June 1948), 107-109, 112.

[5] Maxine Whitney, *The Attitude of British Labor Toward the League of Nations, 1919-1924* (unpublished M. A. thesis, Stanford University, 1930), pp. 130, 144-145.

foreign affairs was in part at least the work of Arthur Henderson. The simplicity and directness which were his distinguishing marks in the eyes of his contemporaries concealed a very complex personality.[6] Until the war Henderson's career had glided steadily along in the grooves of trade union activities and Labor party organization. He had displayed little interest in and perhaps less knowledge of British relations with the rest of the world. The coming of the war marked the turning point of his career. Unlike Ramsay MacDonald and a sizable group within the party, Henderson supported the war once Great Britain was involved. At the same time, he soon became one of the leaders in the search for means to prevent its recurrence. While his aspiration was genuine, he made it clear that he realized, as perhaps few within the Labor movement did, that the organization of peace must be attempted within the limits of the possible. As a Methodist lay preacher, he was emotionally attached to the pacific ideal, but his years of experience as a trade union official and party worker offered unmistakable evidence of the practical day-to-day need for negotiation and compromise. His speeches and his tactics even in this early period demonstrate that he was convinced that the will to peace was not enough, that real results must be sought within the framework of generally accepted machinery and techniques of international organization.

During the war Henderson had worked closely with Sidney Webb and Ramsay MacDonald on the important "Memorandum on War Aims" which defined Labor's demands for the postwar settlement. As the outstanding official Labor spokesman in the campaign for a League of Nations and a moderate peace, he shared the disappointment of the party with the results of Versailles. Nevertheless, from the very start he urged the Labor movement to accept the machinery which existed and to work for its improvement in order that it might be used effectively in the construction of a viable international order.

The Labor policy in the early postwar years was essentially one of conciliation. Its details, as outlined by Henderson, were relatively simple. He insisted that the burden of reparations be reduced and that Germany and Russia be admitted as equals into the League. The authority of the Assembly should be increased, with the Council becoming primarily an executive body. The rule of unanimity, which in his view reduced the League to impotence, should give way in most cases to a system based

---

[6] For an assessment of Henderson by a close collaborator, see Mary Agnes Hamilton, *Arthur Henderson* (London, 1938). See also her *Remembering My Good Friends* (London, 1944), especially pp. 251-252; C. M. Lloyd in *New Statesman*, X, 591-592; and Margaret Cole, *Makers of the Labour Movement* (London, 1940), pp. 256, 260.

on majority decision. Some of these demands were eventually brought to fruition. Others were quietly dropped as adjustments were made to the environment of the postwar world.

Changes in the composition and structure of the League, however, were not really the major theme of his policy. To achieve a true pacification it was necessary to deal with the basic causes of war. Militarism must be attacked at its roots by a progressive limitation of armaments in all the states. But Henderson recognized, as he indicated in a speech before the World Peace Congress in December 1922, that disarmament was hardly an adequate guarantee for the maintenance of peace. Each nation, in his view, must find such a guarantee in the League of Nations itself. To that end, he proposed to amend the Covenant so as to make compulsory the submission of every dispute, whatever its nature, for inquiry and decision to the Council, the Assembly, or the Permanent Court of International Justice. Not only should arbitration be required in certain types of disputes, but decisions in such cases must be binding. Once such a system was in full use, the League could more effectively take the lead in promoting the economic, no less than the political, cooperation of the nations of the world.

The development of this approach as early as 1922 revealed the road that the Labor party and Henderson were to follow with considerable consistency for the next decade. It has been customary to emphasize this aspect of the policy and to point out that in contrast Labor opinion gave very little thought, and Labor spokesmen very little emphasis, to the means by which such a system was to be enforced. It is true that a large part of the Labor party shrank from sanctions with an unrealistic aversion to the use of force under any circumstances. It is equally evident that Ramsay MacDonald, the party's leader, displayed a rather vague reliance on the development of the international spirit far more often than he revealed any genuine willingness to face the unpalatable realities that characterized postwar Europe.[7] But it is also clear—and this has often been neglected—that Henderson, who was increasingly to become a major architect of Labor policy, recognized quite early that disarmament, arbitration, the use of the League to promote peaceful settlement, in the final reckoning depended on the willingness of the Powers to commit themselves to the task of enforcement. From the beginning he warned his party that an essential preliminary to disarmament was the assurance that all members of the League would come to the assistance of any

[7] See, for example, J. R. MacDonald, *The Foreign Policy of the Labour Party* (London, 1923), pp. 20-24; Hamilton, *Remembering My Good Friends*, p. 104.

victim of aggression.[8] In so arguing, he was, of course, leading the party closer to the conception of security which had from the first been urged by France. Quite clearly, he did not share the French view that preponderant power must be retained by the beneficiaries of the postwar settlement. At the same time, he saw that the ideal of a European community based on friendly understanding might be long in coming. Meanwhile he accepted the need of making at least some concessions to the requirements of security. He was, in a word, preparing the way for the Geneva Protocol in whose formulation he played a significant part.

The first Labor government, despite MacDonald's success in conciliating France and in ending the Ruhr impasse, had little time to promote its positive program for European pacification. Actually, a major plank in Labor's foreign policy, the revision of the Versailles Treaty, was dropped with the assumption of the responsibilities of office.[9] The question continued to be raised by the left-wing minority, but the leaders of the party came to accept Article 19 of the League Covenant as a sufficient vehicle for possible change. This turn from treaty revision was one aspect of a policy which saw the Labor government draw closer to France. Although it rejected the Draft Treaty of Mutual Assistance, in part because the all-too-concrete guarantees of military support were not combined with any clear-cut definition of aggression, its delegation proceeded at the Fifth Assembly of the League to cooperate with the French in the development of the Geneva Protocol. As a member of the Third Committee of the Assembly, Henderson took a leading part in hammering out its details.[10] Stripped to its simplest terms, this complex proposal made provision for the use of "arbitration," that is, some kind of peaceful settlement, as a key to the equation of disarmament with security.

The Geneva Protocol was a logical application of the policy Henderson had been advocating for several years. It provided for the growth of the machinery of international conciliation along the lines that he had proposed in 1922. In order to achieve this development of the League system, he was willing to make concessions to the French demand for hard-and-fast military commitments, particularly since the Protocol was not to

[8] Arthur Henderson, *Labour and Foreign Affairs* (London, 1922), pp. 6-11 and "War against War. Political Action for Peace," *Labour Magazine*, 1 (January, 1923), 392-393; Tucker, *Attitude of Labour Party*, pp. 94-95, 99.

[9] W. M. Jordan, *Great Britain, France and the German Problem* (London, 1943), p. 207; Tucker, *Attitude of Labour Party*, pp. 99, 103.

[10] Lord Parmoor, *A Retrospect, Looking Back over a Life of More than Eighty Years* (London, 1936), p. 241; Cole, *Makers of the Labour Movement*, p. 261; W. N. Medlicott, *British Foreign Policy since Versailles* (London, 1940), pp. 93-94.

come into force until its signatories had agreed upon a scheme to limit national armaments. Within the Labor party, however, there was considerable doubt as to its wisdom. Some groups were disturbed over its implied support of the post-Versailles *status quo*. Others, probably a substantial majority within the party, suspected a system of security based upon armaments and looked askance at its emphasis on sanctions. MacDonald himself minimized the possibility of the use of force. He referred to the sanctions provisions as a "harmless drug to soothe nerves" and underlined their purely deterrent aspect.[11] The terms of the Protocol were never formally accepted by the Cabinet, and there are observers who believe that the Labor government, had it remained in office, would not have adopted them without serious revision.[12]

Even Henderson argued that if the nations could be persuaded to use arbitration there would eventually be little need for military force. He stressed the role of the Protocol in developing methods of peaceful settlement and in making possible a move in the direction of disarmament. But with a realism relatively rare in Great Britain at the time, he refused to neglect its security features. In October 1924, for example, he commented on the provisions for sanctions in a speech at Burnley. He insisted quite categorically that "we are solemnly pledged that our force shall be used to make the decisions come to effective, if sanity, reason, right and justice fail and these sanctions have to be employed. Let that be clear."[13] This was as close to the concept of collective security as any important group in Britain ever came in the years before the emergence of the Nazi power. It was closer, as has been noted, than the bulk of the Labor movement was prepared to go. For the thought of the Labor party, no less than that of its rivals, was attuned to a popular opinion that had not yet learned to accept the thesis that "if peace is to be obtained, it must be paid for by certain sacrifices, the assumption of certain obligations."[14] The fact that Henderson went as far as he did in accepting the coercive features of the Protocol, rather than his obvious emphasis on its value in fostering arbitration and disarmament, is the most striking element in his position.

[11] Arnold Wolfers, *Britain and France between Two Wars* (New York, 1940), pp. 347-353; Jordan, *Great Britain, France and the German Question*, pp. 208-209; Tucker, *Attitude of Labour Party*, pp. 102-106, 246-248.

[12] See, for example, C. E. Sipple, *British Foreign Policy since the World War*. University of Iowa Studies in the Social Sciences, x, No. 1 (Iowa City, 1932), 85-86.

[13] Arthur Henderson, *The New Peace Plan* (London, 1924), pp. 14-15. See also *idem, Labour and the Geneva Protocol* (London, 1925), pp. 5-16. This is a reprint of his speech in the House of Commons on March 24, 1925.

[14] Quoted in Jordan, *Great Britain, France and the German Question*, p. 207.

Whatever may have been Labor's interpretation of the Protocol, its fate was sealed when the Baldwin government assumed office. The substitution of the Locarno treaties for the Protocol posed a serious dilemma. The Labor party was suspicious of a policy which appeared to turn from the League toward individual agreements between individual nations. It was perturbed because Locarno made no specific provision for disarmament and did not commit Great Britain to the fullest use of arbitration procedures. In addition, Labor spokesmen argued that the new treaties contained military obligations in some ways more binding than those which the Conservatives had rejected in the Geneva Protocol. Moreover, they reasoned, the chances of war, since Austen Chamberlain had deliberately renounced British participation in the stabilization of eastern Europe, were perhaps greater than ever. On the other hand, there was real satisfaction over the arbitration treaties which had been signed and, above all, over German entry into the League of Nations. In the event, therefore, the Labor movement accepted Locarno as a first step toward the conciliation of Europe. In the years that followed, however, that acceptance was tempered by the belief that the Conservative government was throwing away the opportunity to build a genuine peace. When Hugh Dalton later referred to the policy of "the fumbling fingers and the faltering feet," he was reflecting Labor's conviction that Chamberlain could have taken advantage of the "spirit of Locarno" to strengthen the League and obtain substantial disarmament.[15]

During the Locarno era, the Labor party continued to advocate its own prescription for the organization of peace. The apparent return of some measure of economic stability and the presumed reconciliation of Germany and France made the time seem ripe for a further development of the international system. In principle, the Geneva Protocol was proclaimed to be at the core of Labor policy, but emphasis tended to shift more and more to the aspect of the Protocol which had provided for the development of the machinery of arbitration.[16] At its annual conference in 1926, the party demanded that the government sign the Optional Clause of the Permanent Court, which pledged its signatories to submit justiciable disputes for settlement at The Hague. A pamphlet explaining the resolution pointed out that Labor believed all dangerous quarrels

[15] Hugh Dalton, "British Foreign Policy, 1929-1931," *Political Quarterly*, II (1931), 505; C. R. Attlee, *The Labour Party in Perspective—And Twelve Years Later* (London, 1949), p. 150; J. R. MacDonald, foreword to George Glasgow, *From Dawes to Locarno* (New York and London, 1926), pp. ix-xi; Tucker, *Attitude of Labour Party*, pp. 110-115, 145.

[16] Arthur Henderson, "The Principles of the Protocol," *Labour Magazine*, VI (November, 1927), 298-300.

should be submitted either to arbitral decision or conciliation. If conciliation broke down then in the last resort the nations should be bound to accept "compulsory arbitration." This was the program of the Geneva Protocol, but Labor recognized that such a general treaty might take some time to bring into operation. Meanwhile, in its place but as an immediate practicable step toward the same end, it supported the signature of the Optional Clause.[17]

Within the next two years, other elements were added to the Labor scheme for the conduct of international affairs. The adoption of the Kellogg-Briand Pact was hailed as a positive step toward the outlawry of war. When MacDonald warned the party that the "public sanctions" of the League were not acts of war and must be maintained, he was hinting at the future Labor program of bringing the Pact of Paris and the League Covenant into closer conformity with each other. The renunciation of war, in the Labor view, must be accompanied by the progressive development of substitutes for war. This was a postulate upon which pacifists and those who accepted the role of compulsion could unite. Hence the emphasis which was placed on the promotion of the policies embodied in the Optional Clause and the General Act of Arbitration, Conciliation and Judicial Settlement proposed in 1928 by the League Assembly.[18]

By 1928 the party had prepared a full-dress statement on international affairs. The Birmingham Conference of that year was one of the most important in its history. After an acrimonious debate, a document called "Labour and the Nation" was adopted. While historians of the Labor party have been concerned with the domestic aspects of this policy statement, it was actually more important in the field of foreign affairs. Its social and economic clauses were never considered seriously by the Labor government after 1929. In contrast, its international section came to be the program upon which Arthur Henderson later based his foreign policy. As a consequence, it merits some attention.

It is stretching a point too far to insist, as has recently been done,[19] that the international section of "Labour and the Nation" contained conflicting statements on the organization of peace. Superficially, there was perhaps a contradiction. The manifesto laid stress, on the one hand, upon the collective renunciation of war as an instrument of national policy and upon disarmament and arbitration, while on the other it supported the

[17] Labour Party, *Arbitrate! Arbitrate! Arbitrate!* (London, 1927), pp. 1-11.
[18] *Report of the Annual Conference of the Labour Party* (1928), pp. 183-184.
[19] Tucker, *Attitude of Labour Party*, p. 145.

concept of "pooled security" against aggression. But in the minds of Labor leaders like Henderson, it is clear, the problem was resolved by the belief that such security must be looked for within the framework of the League of Nations. They saw a significant difference between war as an instrument of national policy and sanctions as a bulwark of League guarantees. It may be that this was a naive reading of the realities of the international scene and it is certain that many in the party did not share this view, but it was at least a conscious effort to relate the vague promises of the Pact of Paris to the presumably more substantial machinery of the League Covenant. At any rate, "Labour and the Nation" pledged the party to try to implement the renunciation of war by the signature of the Optional Clause, by the international reduction of armaments, by the promotion of international economic cooperation, and by the systematic use of the League to achieve those ends. When, a short time later, the party urged acceptance of the General Act, it had laid down the program which Henderson was subsequently to follow, for his one remaining aim, the conciliation of Germany and Russia, had long been an element of Labor policy.[20]

II

When the Labor government was formed in June 1929, Henderson insisted upon the Foreign Office. He was given the post despite the reluctance of Ramsay MacDonald, who seems to have had the curious notion that in some way J. H. Thomas was qualified for the position. But Henderson, who had taken the leading role in hammering out the international program of "Labour and the Nation," was unquestionably looked upon as the man to carry it out. As we have seen, he had been one of the major architects of Labor's foreign policy. If, therefore, the press expressed some surprise at his appointment, this was an indication not so much of his ignorance of foreign affairs as it was of the press's unawareness of developments within the Labor party since the war. MacDonald made no secret of his resentment, but the new Foreign Secretary held to the objective of carrying through the decisions of the party.[21]

The policy of drift which seemed to characterize the domestic side of

[20] *Report of the Annual Conference of the Labour Party* (1928), pp. 196-200, 264-266; Labour Party, *Labour and the Nation* (London, 1928), pp. 41-49; *Labour's Appeal to the Nation* (London, 1929), p. 3; *Arbitration: Tory Record and Labour Policy* (London, 1929), p. 5. The latter two were campaign leaflets in 1929.

[21] For views of Henderson's appointment and his relations with MacDonald, see Philip Snowden, *An Autobiography* (2 vols., London, 1934), II, 760-764, 767; Laski in *Harpers*, CLXIV, 749, 752; Viscount Cecil, *A Great Experiment* (New York, 1941), p. 207; Parmoor, *Retrospect*, p. 296; Hamilton, *Remembering My Good Friends*, p. 250.

the Labor government's program was certainly not apparent at the Foreign Office. Henderson made it clear from the beginning that he had firm conceptions of his general aims and that he intended to take full responsibility for implementing them. He apparently found it possible to work within the framework of the Foreign Office. For, despite Labor criticism of its organization in past years, he seems to have made no substantial change in either its routine or its structure during these years. His absolute honesty, which a recent writer has summed up as that of a man who was "an almost solid block of integrity,"[22] strikes one as a major element in his conduct of his office. The opinion of those closest to him at this time is that he quickly gained the affection of his subordinates. Often enough, however, civil servants may feel well-disposed to a minister who is sufficiently weak and malleable to be influenced towards positions which they, rather than he, determine. But there is no evidence to indicate such a relationship. Henderson seems to have won the respect as well as the affection of his permanent staff. As one of his associates has put it, they understood that, when he had heard the evidence on any given matter, it was his views and not theirs that were going to prevail.

At the same time, Henderson had a real consciousness of his personal limitations. He showed no feeling of inferiority about surrounding himself with first-rate advisers of whose training and abilities he made the fullest use. The Foreign Office staff under Henderson was surely one of the most competent of its period. In the position of Permanent Under-Secretary, Sir Robert Vansittart succeeded Sir Ronald Lindsay (who went to Washington) early in 1930. The Parliamentary Under-Secretary, Hugh Dalton, and the Parliamentary Private Secretary, Philip Noel Baker, had the background and the brilliance which Henderson lacked. He depended heavily on them, and especially on Dalton, for advice. But in the final analysis, he made the basic decisions, and it reveals much that these products of the best in English (and American) education should have respected the judgment of an almost uneducated ironfounder with a conviction that apparently still persists. Equally striking is the attitude of Viscount Cecil, whom he brought into the Foreign Office to help pursue his League of Nations policy.

His methods of work were singular. He spent little time reading long memoranda or other papers. He preferred to listen to oral explanation of a subject, to ask questions, and to reach his conclusions on the basis of such conversation. Such methods quite obviously have their dangers, but those who worked with him have described his grasp of the problems

[22] Raymond Postgate, *Life of George Lansbury* (London, 1951), p. 171.

which he faced and his ability to cut to the heart of an issue without burying himself in the minutiae of detail. Whatever its defects, the system seems to have worked quite well for him.[23]

While Henderson settled easily into the routine of the Foreign Office, his relations with Ramsay MacDonald were a constant irritant and often a positive deterrent to the efficient conduct of foreign relations. From the start he encountered, as one journalist has described it, "a steady stream of criticism, disparagement and, what was far more galling to the new Foreign Secretary, of contemptuous indifference from No. 10 Downing Street."[24] MacDonald's personal antipathy has been documented again and again, but its effect on the pursuit of a consistent foreign policy requires some comment. In a sense, Great Britain had two foreign policies from 1929 to 1931. MacDonald jealously kept virtually every aspect of American relations in his own hands. From his well-staged trip to America in 1929 through the negotiations which followed the announcement of the Hoover moratorium in 1931, he was almost exclusively in control of this important aspect of British policy. Henderson was deliberately kept in the background and was, apparently, left to keep the rest of his policy consistent with MacDonald's American program as best he could.

In other spheres, MacDonald was difficult to work with. His extraordinary sensitivity to public criticism and his tendency to make ill-considered public statements without consulting his colleagues often caused embarrassment where they did not do worse. Two examples will perhaps reveal how difficult was the position of a Foreign Minister under so perplexing a personality. Scarcely more than a week after he had taken office, MacDonald permitted the publication of an article in the *Sunday Times*, in which he castigated the treatment of minorities in various European countries. With almost breathtaking lack of tact—if one considers that cooperation with France was to be one of the central pivots of his Foreign Minister's policy—he included Alsace and the Saar in his catalogue of minority problems. The explanation that the article had been written before he had assumed office hardly was sufficient to assuage irritation on the Continent or to make the position of Henderson any less difficult.[25]

---

[23] I am indebted to the Rt. Hon. Philip Noel Baker (letter of February 22, 1952) and the Rt. Hon. Hugh Dalton (letter of March 22, 1952) for informative and sympathetic accounts of Henderson at the Foreign Office. See also Hamilton, *Henderson*, pp. 285-286; Major General A. C. Temperley, *The Whispering Gallery of Europe* (London, 1939), p. 163; Cecil, *A Great Experiment*, p. 200.

[24] George Slocombe, *A Mirror to Geneva. Its Growth, Grandeur and Decay* (New York, 1938), p. 239.

[25] Tucker, *Attitude of Labour Party*, p. 118.

Several months later, Henderson was at Geneva supporting British adherence to the Convention for Financial Assistance. The Foreign Office had examined it carefully and had decided that it involved no dangerous new commitments. But MacDonald became frightened by the opposition of a section of the press, and just before Henderson was ready to deposit the signature of Great Britain he wrote the Foreign Secretary a "not very temperate letter," in which the implications pointed quite clearly to a repudiation of Henderson's policy.[26] Henderson struck back with some heat. After tracing the way in which the British decision to sign had been reached and pointing out that MacDonald himself had agreed, he expressed himself in blunt terms to the Prime Minister. "Surely, we shall stultify our whole attitude, if, on being confronted by the first issue that gives us an opportunity of giving some effect to our policy, we turn back because a few hostile and ill-informed critics elect to make a fuss. If we give way to the stunt Press on this, they will seek to make the Government position on Russia, Egypt, etc. impossible.

"I wrote strongly, because . . . there is not that confidence when working in the international sphere one is entitled to expect."[27]

These examples illustrate a situation which continued as long as the Labor government remained in office. On the other hand, despite the problems caused by MacDonald's unreliability, Henderson was from the beginning determined to carry through his program. That program has already been described. At the suggestion of Hugh Dalton, he circulated "Labour and the Nation" among the principal officials. This was perhaps a unique method of explaining his policy, but his Under-Secretary was later to testify to the loyalty and helpfulness with which officials and diplomatic representatives pursued that general policy.[28] Parenthetically, it should be noted that Henderson was well served by his diplomats abroad, particularly by Sir Horace Rumbold and Basil Newton at Berlin and by Lord Tyrrell at Paris. The Berlin embassy was alert to the rising current of German nationalism and the dangerous development of Nazi strength.[29] It recognized the complex difficulties—and also the tortured maneuvering for position—of the Brüning regime and reported what it saw to London. At Paris, Tyrrell outlined with sympathy, but with considerable insight, the French reaction to the changing spirit in Germany which soon cast its shadow over Henderson's entire program.[30]

[26] Hamilton, *Henderson*, p. 326.
[27] Henderson to MacDonald, September 12, 1929. *Ibid.*, pp. 327-328.
[28] Dalton to author, March 22, 1952; Dalton in *Political Quarterly*, II, 489.
[29] See below, Chapter 14, § I.
[30] See, in particular, *British Documents*, 2nd series, I, chapter VI, and II, chapter IV.

When Henderson felt that his representatives could not give him loyal service, he acted with firmness. Soon after coming to the Foreign Office he became convinced that Lord Lloyd, the High Commissioner of Egypt, was unalterably opposed to the policy he intended to pursue. He demanded and received Lord Lloyd's resignation. A parliamentary attempt, led by Winston Churchill, to make it appear that he had brutally dismissed the High Commissioner for political reasons, reacted in his favor. He was able to document the difficulties which Sir Austen Chamberlain had had with Lord Lloyd and to maintain the obvious position that representatives abroad must be willing, whatever their own views, to carry out the policy determined by the government.[31]

With the Egyptian policy itself, he had less success. Although he recognized that Chamberlain had made a start in erasing the bitterness which had followed the murder of Sir Lee Stack, he hoped by extending the policy of cooperation to create an entirely new atmosphere. Working closely with the Cabinet, he took the opportunity of an Egyptian initiative to reopen negotiations for a treaty. He explained the spirit in which he approached the question in a statement to the Commons on December 23, 1929. Irritating restrictions, he remarked, "have been removed, because of the conviction that such restrictions, sought to be imposed from without, can only defeat the main purpose which both countries had in view. That purpose, as far as His Majesty's Government are concerned, is the establishment of a firm and lasting friendship with the Egyptian people, by the removal of those sources of suspicion which in the past have been the cause of so much damage to the interests of both peoples."[32] In contrast was the reaction of Sir Austen Chamberlain to the proposal that both Egypt and Great Britain should undertake not to adopt in foreign countries an attitude which was inconsistent with the alliance or would create difficulties for the other party to it. Chamberlain poured ridicule on the idea that the foreign policy of Great Britain should be governed by the interests and circumstances of Egypt. "The elephant undertakes to protect the mouse, and thereafter the elephant's march is to be conditioned by the mouse's trot."[33] The difference in approach was considerable.

In any event, Henderson's proposals went substantially beyond those made by Chamberlain in 1927 and 1928. He was willing to withdraw troops to the region of the Suez Canal, but refused to accept the Egyptian

[31] Parliamentary Debates: Commons, 5th series, CCXXX, 1301, 1635-1646.
[32] *ibid.*, CCXXXIII, 1977.
[33] *ibid.*, 1959-1960.

demand for control of immigration into the Sudan.[34] Although Henderson was eager to achieve a *détente* in Anglo-Egyptian relations, he declined to sacrifice important British interests in order to accomplish his purpose. Nevertheless, the contrast between the spirit of his policy and that of Chamberlain affords an interesting insight into his approach to other questions of perhaps greater significance.

III

Prominent among those other questions were relations with Germany and Russia. Reconciliation with Germany and closer relations with Russia were of course standing tenets of the Labor creed. The party had long argued that such a policy was an indispensable prelude to the constructive development of international cooperation. Henderson and his advisers believed, in these last days before the onset of the world depression, that there was at last an opportunity to establish an enduring peace in Europe. Hugh Dalton reflected this optimism when he explained the government's policy during the debate on the Address from the Throne. "I myself hope and believe that we are now entering upon a new and more hopeful phase of history," he said. "I think we now have an opportunity to go forward which, if we miss it, may not come again in our own day. Therefore, I hope and believe that we shall be able, in the months and years that lie ahead, to make a forward movement in the direction of arbitration, disarmament, the better economic organization of the life of the world, and the general establishment of reconciliation between old enemies and firmer friendship between old friends."[35] This was more than rhetoric. In 1929, Henderson, like Dalton, saw the Labor government's main problem of foreign policy as the removal of the political antagonisms that stood in the way of a peaceful international order. He was convinced that it could not be solved until Germany and Russia participated as equals in the development of disarmament, machinery for pacific settlement, and the rational economic organization of the world. In retrospect it seems clear that, whatever the possibilities when Henderson took office, the conditions for such a policy were swept away after 1930 by the great depression, which precipitated the trend toward political conflict and eventual war.[36] In the atmosphere of 1929, however, the policy appeared sound. If it was stubbornly maintained even when the German challenge made it unrealistic, it should be remembered that few policy-

---

[34] The Egyptian negotiations are summarized in Arnold J. Toynbee, *Survey of International Affairs*, 1930 (London, 1931), pp. 188-222.

[35] Parliamentary Debates: Commons, 5th series, CCXXIX, 457-458.

[36] Medlicott, *British Foreign Policy*, pp. 107-108.

makers indeed were perceptive enough before 1931 to understand the changes that had come upon the world of the 1920's. Henderson, as we have said, stood at the watershed and the fate of his policy reflected the end of the old era as it symbolized the tragic emergence of the new.

The first step in the reconciliation of Germany was taken almost immediately after the Labor government took office. Henderson was determined to heal the German "wound in the west" by promoting the early evacuation of the Rhineland. He announced his policy to the House of Commons on July 5, 1929, when he declared that the Germans had carried out, so far as he was able to see, the conditions imposed upon them by the Versailles Treaty. The evacuation, therefore, should be carried out as quickly as possible.[37] But his attitude toward the German question was a good deal more complex than has sometimes been represented.[38] He realized that it was not primarily a matter of Anglo-German relations. It meant above all a reconciliation between Germany and France. And while suspicion of France still maintained a strong hold on the Labor party, he was as convinced of the necessity of working closely with France as he was that Germany must have her legitimate demands satisfied. While he was prepared as a last resort to withdraw British troops independently, he realized that such a move might mean a more galling occupation under Belgian and French forces and the increase of tension between Britain and France. On this matter, at least, he received the wholehearted concurrence of Sir Austen Chamberlain, who shared his belief in the desirability of a collective withdrawal.[39]

Henderson's discussion of his plans was in anticipation of the conference which had been scheduled to deal with the experts' report on reparations and the future of the Rhineland. At The Hague in August, he undertook, as chairman of the Political Commission, to promote withdrawal by fostering a Franco-German agreement. Stresemann was insistent that Germany would accept the Young Plan only on condition of a Rhineland evacuation. Briand for his part put the financial settlement first and demanded guarantees of German performance. During the course of the negotiations, Henderson announced explicitly that British troops would be withdrawn beginning in September regardless of the decision on the Young Plan. This pressure on the French, although he worked closely with Briand, apparently had much to do with the successful outcome of

[37] Parliamentary Debates: Commons, 5th series, CCXXIX, 417.
[38] See the comments on this in Floris Delattre, "La Psychologie de la diplomatie britannique depuis la guerre," *L'Année politique française et étrangère*, VI (October 1931), p. 279.
[39] Parliamentary Debates: Commons, 5th series, CCXXIX, 406, 416.

the political negotiations. Actually, the political problem was not the most difficult at the conference. Philip Snowden threw the discussions into an impasse by demanding a greater share of the reparation annuities than had been recommended in the experts' report. Although his stand was hailed with delight in Great Britain, it seems clear that he helped create needless tension in Anglo-French relations, to say nothing of jeopardizing the outcome of negotiations. In the light of the later history of reparations, of course, Snowden's insistence on a share of payments that were never to be made seems like one of the more trivial aspects of the problem. For the moment, the Rhineland settlement appeared about to be shattered in the ruin of the financial negotiations, but in the long run a compromise, rather favorable to Snowden's demands, was reached. Snowden later paid tribute to Henderson's support, but the documents are not yet available by which to judge his role in the financial struggle.[40] In any case, the final agreement called for evacuation to begin in September and to be completed by the French within eight months. In the event, although there were a few qualms about French intentions,[41] the withdrawal went off on schedule. Henderson's policy had been a success at The Hague. He believed it to be a final step for bringing the world war to an end.[42] Its effect in Germany will have to be looked at later.[43]

The Labor movement had insisted for years on the importance of proper relations with Russia. Although the majority of organized labor had little illusion about the nature of the Soviet regime, it is possible to discern, as one French scholar puts it, a kind of "socialist mystique" in the promotion of this demand.[44] But the Foreign Office felt that there were imperative reasons for the resumption of diplomatic intercourse. Henderson accepted a doctrine of recognition that has become unfashionable in recent years. He contended that unsatisfactory relations, far from being an argument for the abolition of normal diplomatic machinery, were a further reason for more regular contact. Acting on the information of his legal advisers that diplomatic relations had never been severed but merely suspended, he proceeded to negotiate for their reestablishment. The Russian refusal to accept responsibility for the activities of the

---

[40] Compare Snowden, *Autobiography*, II, 819, with the account in Hamilton, *Henderson*, p. 316.

[41] See *British Documents*, 2nd series, I, 475-478.

[42] *Verbatim Record of the Eleventh Ordinary Session of the Assembly of the League of Nations*, first plenary meeting, September 10, 1930, p. 5.

[43] For an account of the first Hague Conference, based on press reports and Commons debates, see *Survey of International Affairs, 1929*, pp. 180-188. Also Tucker, *Attitude of Labour Party*, pp. 119-121.

[44] Delattre in *L'Année politique*, II, 278.

Third International proved a particular source of difficulty, but finally on October 3, 1929, an accord was signed which simply confirmed the article in the treaty of 1924 which had prohibited propaganda.

During the course of the next year, the policy of the government was under constant attack in the House of Commons, particularly on the issue of the continuation of Soviet propaganda. In defending his position, Henderson argued that normal relations at least provided a mechanism through which the problem could be discussed. He did not deny that propaganda was going on, but he failed to see how cutting off relations could improve the situation. He was especially anxious for better relations in order to promote British trade in Russian markets.[45] But perhaps an even more important reason of the government was revealed by Philip Noel Baker, who took a major part in defending its policy in the House. Noel Baker laid stress on its value in the maintenance of peace. The prevention of another war, he declared, depended on two things: the realization of the government's policy of disarmament and the spread throughout the world of the spirit of peace. The world knew that unless Russia was brought in, a policy of general disarmament was impossible. Negotiations at Geneva made it clear that in every circumstance the attitude of Russia had to be considered. In Central Europe, where disarmament was vital, nothing was possible without Russian help. It was imperative to resume relations in order to exorcise the suspicion of Britain which existed in Russia and thus work together more effectively for world disarmament.[46] Whatever its purpose, the Russian rapprochement was a disappointment. The problem of propaganda was never solved, as the Conservative press and politicians continued to point out. The best that Henderson's colleague, Hugh Dalton, was later able to say for the policy was that it had succeeded in making Anglo-Russian relations less unsatisfactory than they would otherwise have been.[47] In a sense, however, it did serve as a symbol of the desire for fuller Russian collaboration in the work of European pacification and so formed an integral part of the program which Henderson was attempting to achieve.

IV

The major element in that program, beyond any question, was the changed British attitude toward the League of Nations. In essence, the Rhineland withdrawal and the resumption of relations with Russia aimed

---

[45] Parliamentary Debates: Commons, 5th series, CCXXIX, 418, 466; CCXXXI, 900-902; CCXXXIII, 1447-1498; CCXXXIX, 2581-2633.

[46] *ibid.*, CCXXXI, 920-921.

[47] Dalton in *Political Quarterly*, II, 499-500.

at European appeasement as a preliminary to disarmament and the development of a real collective system through the League.[48] No more than the Conservatives, however, were the Labor leaders ready to consider collective security in terms of the French thesis of automatic sanctions and mutual assistance. Firm in the belief that the war had been liquidated and that it was now imperative to foster a spirit of cooperation, the Labor party, even after conditions had changed radically in 1930 and 1931, clung to the illusion that the collective organization of substitutes for war was more immediately pressing than a collective stand against the unilateral transformation of the European system. This policy, with its emphasis upon disarmament, the use of arbitration in international disputes, and the promotion of measures of economic cooperation, was so tragically divorced from the realities of 1931 that it is somewhat too easy to forget that in 1929 it represented a bold, and on the whole a relatively well-founded, approach to international affairs. Its strength was in its recognition that the problem of maintaining a healthy Europe was more than a problem of military alliance to prevent the disruption of the *status quo*. Labor recognized more clearly than its opponents the imperative need for erecting the framework in which the tensions leading to war might be kept at a minimum. On the other hand, it is essential to point out that so long as the tensions existed, as they did in this period, it was disastrous to act as though they were unimportant or as though some vague spirit of good will would dissolve them. While it was desirable to work for the fullest development of a system of real international law, it was even more essential to recognize that law must be enforced. This was the corollary which many within the Labor party were unwilling to face. Even Henderson, who accepted the need for a system of sanctions, never really faced up to the problem of power relationships in Europe. So long as Germany, for example, had the military and industrial potentialities which she possessed, it was folly to expect France and her allies to agree to substantial disarmament which would leave them at a comparative disadvantage. The French policy, understandable as it was, remained curiously negative. It offered little hope for a progressive development of genuine cooperation. But the British Labor position, correct in its assessment of the long-term goal to be sought, vitiated its usefulness by the optimistic belief that the Europe of the depression and the explosion of German nationalism was a suitable starting place for the inauguration of the millennium.

[48] A. L. Rowse, *The End of an Epoch. Reflections on Contemporary History* (London, 1948), pp. 50-51.

In 1929, however, when Henderson went to Geneva as the working head of the British delegation to the Tenth Assembly of the League, the prospects for the success of his policy appeared promising. The delegation, which included William Graham of the Board of Trade, Cecil, Dalton, and Baker, was an able one. Henderson himself felt at home in Geneva. He got on well with Briand and the dying Stresemann and quite clearly hoped that his close contact with them would promote the fuller development of the League, which was central to his program of action. As a result, he kept himself free for the kind of consultation and conversation that had virtually become the hallmarks of postwar diplomacy.[49] He would probably have agreed with Briand, who explained to the Assembly: "I have often been told that I am rather too fond of conversations. After drafting dispatches and reading dispatches from other people, I soon felt that this method was out of harmony with the modern love of speed. It seemed to me that many difficulties might be solved by a personal conversation—You understand one another, or at least try to understand one another. You make an effort to find a solution, and in the end do find a solution for a situation which appeared to admit of none."[50] Such diplomacy had its dangers, as was strikingly illustrated by the experiences of Lloyd George or MacDonald or even Briand himself. In the case of Henderson there is some doubt. Certainly he was a practitioner of the method. The agreement to resume relations with Russia had been reached at an informal meeting in a little inn at Lewes. At Geneva he pursued his policy in much the same fashion. But he was not particularly flexible nor did he have the capacity for brilliant improvisation which rested on little more substantial than the inspiration of the moment. He came to his "friendly talks" with Briand well prepared, and while the records are not fully available, the documents for the later stages of his Foreign Office tenure show that at such occasions he hewed closely to the fundamentals of his program. There is no indication that at any time the Foreign Office was confused as to the nature or the direction of his personal negotiations.

Actually, there was little need for subtle negotiation with France or Germany about the major item of the British program at the Tenth Assembly. Both states welcomed the new British view of the value of the Optional Clause. The real difficulty came from the British Dominions. They were particularly concerned, as their attitude toward the Geneva

[49] For descriptions of Henderson at Geneva, see Hamilton, *Henderson*, pp. 319-323, 330; Temperley, *Whispering Gallery*, pp. 116-117; Slocombe, *Mirror to Geneva*, pp. 228-229.

[50] *Record of the Tenth Assembly*, sixth plenary meeting, September 5, 1929, p. 5.

Protocol had demonstrated earlier, that their signature should not involve them unnecessarily in continental quarrels and that intra-Imperial questions should be kept from the jurisdiction of the court. Henderson and his advisers worked hard in London and later at Geneva to achieve a compromise which might satisfy the Dominions. The solution was reached in the decision to reserve certain types of questions, even of a justiciable nature, from the province of compulsory arbitration.[51] Here again was another illustration of the complexity of the British position as the center of the empire on the one hand and as a part of the European system on the other.

In his speech to the Assembly on September 3, Ramsay MacDonald announced the intention of the British and the Dominion governments to sign the Optional Clause.[52] Henderson, a few days later, explained to the Assembly what he hoped to accomplish by this move. The British government, he pointed out, believed arbitration to be more likely to bring about a wise and just settlement of a dispute than any other method. It was the true alternative to war for the solution of international quarrels. Above all, it was important because of the new spirit it would bring to the relations between the governments of the world. "A nation which relies on arbitration and is ready to accept the verdict of an impartial judge," he declared, "does not rely on the use of armed force. Its national mind is turned in a new direction, and it is precisely in this new spirit which the practice of arbitration may induce that lies perhaps the most powerful single factor in bringing to the nations security from war." He emphasized that the signature of the Optional Clause was only a first step in the direction of real peace. On the basis of an expanded system of arbitration it would be possible to move ahead to the next step, the formulation of a general treaty of disarmament.[53]

Although he based his hopes on the development of substitutes for war and the consequent disarmament it might make possible, Henderson had some conception of the difficulties of the program. At the annual conference of the Labor party in October he rebuked the delegates who proposed immediate and complete British disarmament—disarmament by example—as the proper road to world peace. "We will not attempt that which is practically impossible," he warned. "The world will have

[51] *Survey of International Affairs, 1929*, p. 75; Dalton in *Political Quarterly*, II, 496. The reservations concerned intra-Imperial questions, disputes in which the parties had recourse to other means of settlement, disputes arising out of questions posed before British ratification (i.e. questions arising out of the peace treaties), and those in which one of the parties preferred to refer the case to the League Council first.
[52] *Record of the Tenth Assembly*, third plenary session, September 3, 1929, pp. 2-5.
[53] *ibid.*, seventh plenary session, September 6, 1929, pp. 5-6.

to be very much more advanced and human nature very much more perfect before you will be able to do without policing forces."[54] Such "policing forces," whatever they might have been, were clearly rather far removed from the sort of security arrangements the French insisted upon. Henderson, like other British Foreign Secretaries before him, was not convinced that the French reading of security was accurate. Unlike them, at least, he had a positive program for achieving it. His policy marked a significant change in attitude on the part of the British government. It might have succeeded if Europe had been favored with years of relative prosperity and quiet. It had little if any chance in the Europe of the 1930's.

At the Tenth Assembly, however, it would have been a prescient observer who could have predicted the cataclysm of the 1930's. The British position on the Optional Clause was almost symbolic of the changed atmosphere. The British plans for future development—Henderson's proposals for a reform of the Secretariat, Willie Graham's appeal for economic cooperation and for a tariff truce, plans to harmonize the League Covenant with the Pact of Paris—testified to the optimism at Geneva about the future. When its work was finished the Tenth Assembly appeared to have made a real start—certainly the most impressive since the Fifth Assembly of 1924—toward the imperative task of rebuilding the political stability of Europe.[55]

At the Tenth Assembly, Aristide Briand broached his tentative scheme for the formation of a European Federal Union. Couched in vague terms, it laid particular stress on the economic association of the European nations.[56] By the time Briand circulated his proposals to the European governments in May 1930, the emphasis had been changed to subordinate economic to political problems.[57] Although Henderson had assured Briand that he would give it his greatest interest, the British reaction to the scheme was not enthusiastic. A Foreign Office memorandum, circulated on May 30, analyzed the basis for criticism. It pointed out that the proposed federation might be regarded as hostile to the American or other continents and might weaken the political cooperation of Britain with other members of the Commonwealth. Above all, the European Union might become a rival of the League of Nations and thus adversely

---

[54] *Report of the Annual Conference of the Labour Party* (1929), pp. 215-216.

[55] F. P. Walters, *A History of the League of Nations* (2 vols., London, 1952), I, 430.

[56] *Record of the Tenth Assembly*, sixth plenary meeting, September 5, 1929, p. 6.

[57] "Mémorandum sur l'organisation d'un régime d'union fédérale européenne," in *British Documents*, 2nd series, I, 320.

affect its prestige and utility. While the memorandum recognized that Briand's plan could be construed as an attempt to stereotype the territorial *status quo*, it suggested that since Briand was a "good European" the sincerity of his desire for fuller European cooperation should be assumed. It proposed, therefore, that the plan be received with general sympathy and with a promise to give the French proposals the fullest consideration in consultation with the Dominions. At the same time, however, it suggested that Briand be made cognizant of the British criticism of the methods which he had proposed.[58] In somewhat amended form the memorandum was presented to the Cabinet in explanation of a proposed draft reply which was then approved.[59] The British note to France emphasized in particular that the European Union would set up new and independent international institutions as possible rivals of the League of Nations. It recommended that Briand submit his memorandum to the next Assembly for its consideration.[60] After a meeting of delegates from some twenty-seven European states, the plan was discussed at the Eleventh Assembly, approved in general terms, and referred to a Commission of Enquiry for European Union to draw up definite proposals. The action of the Assembly effectively pigeonholed the project. It has often been alleged that the action of the British government was the kiss of death for the Briand plan.[61] Actually, Henderson knew that Italy was opposed to the proposal and that Germany was cool.[62] It is possible that if it had been elaborated earlier there might have been some chance of a limited accomplishment. But by the fall of 1930, the project for a European federation, which offered no special concessions to Germany, was almost inevitably greeted with suspicion in revisionist circles. Whatever the attitude of the British government, the Briand plan had little prospect of success. From the point of view of Henderson's policy, the consistency of his approach to the problems of Europe is the significant thing. His coolness to the idea, despite his real confidence in Briand, was motivated, not only by the unique relations of Britain to the Dominions and the United States, but above all by his conception of the League as the central instrument for the promotion of real international cooperation.

[58] *British Documents*, 2nd series, I, 313, 330-331.
[59] *ibid.*, pp. 336-345.   [60] *ibid.*, pp. 345-347.
[61] Jacques Bardoux, *L'Ile et l'Europe, la politique anglaise, 1930-1932* (Paris, 1933), pp. 294-299; Jean-Felix Charvet, *L'Influence britannique dans la S. D. N. (Des origines de la S. D. N. jusqu'à nos jours)* (Paris, 1938), pp. 134-135.
[62] *British Documents*, 2nd series, I, 334 (Graham to Henderson, May 31, 1930) and 335 (Newton to Henderson, July 26, 1930). Newton's dispatch was received after the British note to France had been sent. But see, also, *ibid.*, pp. 324-326 (Rumbold to Henderson, May 28) for a conversation on the Briand plan with Brüning.

Henderson's conception of constructive British leadership was to co-operate in strengthening the League Covenant. This—and of course disarmament[63]—was at the heart of his approach. "We have always believed," he told the Eleventh Assembly, "that true security can only be obtained by a cooperative action through the machinery of the League. We are equally certain that this purpose can far more effectively be sought through measures designed to prevent the outbreak of war, rather than through measures designed to suppress war once it has begun.[64] He proposed accordingly to push on from the Optional Clause, in particular by harmonizing the League Covenant with the Pact of Paris and by signing the General Act of Arbitration, Conciliation, and Judicial Settlement.

The first of these measures was held to be necessary because of the "gap" in the Covenant which permitted members of the League to go to war after having fulfilled the requirements for delay. Since most states had accepted the Pact of Paris and thus presumably had repudiated the right of "private war," Henderson proposed to amend the Covenant so as to ban a right which was now obsolete.[65] This was not a move to do away with sanctions, as a discussion of the amendments in the Labor party's magazine was careful to point out. Acceptance of the new pledges, an article in the *Labour Magazine* declared, would imply acceptance of the obligation to enforce them. Most of the opposition to the draft amendments came from people who were really opposed to the principle of sanctions. "But it must be applied as loyally as any other principle of the Covenant, for it is an integral part of the whole edifice."[66] Despite Henderson's efforts the draft amendments were never accepted. What they would have accomplished, in any case, is difficult to see, for, as Lord Cecil later pointed out, war, when it did erupt, came each time in defiance of the League and not by creeping through the celebrated "gap" in the Covenant.[67]

With the General Act Henderson had more success. The Labor party was pledged to accede to it, but he moved slowly. Once again, it was the problem of the Dominions which posed the difficulties. In September

---

[63] See below §v.

[64] *Record of the Eleventh Assembly*, fourth plenary meeting, September 11, 1930, p. 3.

[65] *League of Nations Official Journal*, XI (February, 1930), 78-79. An attempt to work out an agreement between France and Britain to ensure the incorporation of the amendments into the Covenant foundered in the general failure to reconcile Franco-Italian differences at the London Naval Conference. Actually, the discussion of this issue revealed once again the difference between the British and the French concept of security. *British Documents*, 2nd series, I, 293-301.

[66] *Labour Magazine*, VIII (April, 1930), 540.

[67] Cecil, *A Great Experiment*, pp. 204-205.

1930, he announced to the Assembly the British intention to sign, but indicated that the government wished to proceed in close accord with the members of the Commonwealth.[68] The subsequent Imperial Conference finally reached agreement—except for South Africa—but, as in the case of the Optional Clause, insisted on the usual reservations. Henderson was anxious for accession. The Optional Clause and the General Act were in his view the prelude to effective disarmament. By early 1931 the date for the Disarmament Conference had been set and he himself had been chosen its president. He was convinced, he told the House of Commons, that at the Conference "nations will be prepared to reduce and limit their national forces in proportion to the measure of their confidence in the constructive machinery of peace. If they are convinced that Governments have renounced war, not in name only, but in real intention, as shown by their willingness to support the League proposals for peace, they will be more ready to dispense with the machinery of war."[69] Accession to the General Act came at the Sixty-third Council on May 21, 1931. With the British signature virtually the whole of Henderson's program that had any chance of success had been carried out. Now, as he saw it, he had laid the foundations for a substantial measure of disarmament.

V

Disarmament had of course been in the forefront of his program from the beginning. At the Tenth Assembly, the question had been shelved pending the results of the naval conversations among the major Powers. The London Naval Conference was largely Ramsay MacDonald's show. Henderson participated, but his role was not decisive. He looked upon a naval agreement, in much the same way that he considered his steps at Geneva, as one of the necessary preludes to a

[68] *Record of the Eleventh Assembly*, fourth plenary meeting, p. 3.

[69] Parliamentary Debates: Commons, 5th series, CCXLIX, 825-831. Henderson was clearly most concerned with convincing France of British intention to fulfill the obligations implied in his program. A draft declaration, drawn up at the London Naval Conference, had pledged Britain (and France) to make fullest use of the Covenant (including Article 16), the Optional Clause, the General Act, and to work to close the "gap" in the Covenant. It had included a declaration that "Our Governments are convinced that this declaration will dissipate all uncertainty regarding their common intention fully to carry out, should need arise, the duty which the Covenant of the League of Nations lays upon them; and that by so doing it will effectively help to prevent any situation arising in which, as the result of the failure of preventive action, the question for the community of nations would be no longer the maintenance but the reestablishment of peace." The declaration was never issued, but Henderson's subsequent policy was in part at least directed to assure the French of British intention to carry out the provisions of the Covenant in order to promote French acceptance of disarmament. *British Documents*, 2nd series, I, 300-301.

successful world disarmament conference. The French position at London disturbed him. The European situation, he insisted, had improved in recent years. Germany was a member of the League. She was to be subjected to even firmer control since he and Briand had decided to work toward incorporating the Kellogg Pact into the machinery of the League. Moreover, the Optional Clause had now been ratified. All in all, he professed not to understand the caution of the French delegates.[70] But European agreement was not possible. Although the United States, Japan, and Great Britain signed an accord which provided little in the way of naval disarmament, France and Italy could not see eye to eye on the Italian demand for theoretical parity with France. After the Conference adjourned, Henderson worked to bring the two together. As at London, he continued to deprecate the French attitude. Tyrrell warned him not to undercut Briand's position in France, for "you will achieve more by cooperation with Briand than you will by any appeal to Caesar, or in other words, public opinion."[71] Henderson acted on the same assumption, though he was later to comment that the underlying difficulty in reaching an agreement was that France was evidently determined to effect a rapid and substantial increase in naval armament at a time when all other Powers were attempting to make reductions.[72] By that time, it should be noted, the German touchstone of French policy was as real as the Italian rivalry.[73] For a brief moment in March 1931, it appeared that real progress had been made. The story of the "Bases of an Agreement" and their subsequent fate is well enough known and the recently published documents do no more than fill in some of the details of Henderson's single-mindedness on the issue. Throughout the complicated negotiations his main purpose was to facilitate the holding of the Disarmament Conference. He insisted to Grandi and especially to Briand that a compromise was essential before the Preparatory Commission could complete its task with any hope of success.[74] Despite his efforts, however, when the Disarmament Conference met in 1932 the French and Italian governments were as far apart on the issue as they had ever been.

His diplomatic pressure on France and Italy was paralleled by his more public exhortations. On the issue of disarmament he came as close

---

[70] *British Documents*, 2nd series, I, 213-214.

[71] *ibid.*, pp. 390 (Tyrrell to Henderson, July 11, 1930) and 456 (Tyrrell to Henderson, February 20, 1931).

[72] *ibid.*, II, 417 (Henderson to Lindsay, May 3, 1931).

[73] See, for example, Vansittart to Rumbold, December 20, 1930, *ibid.*, I, 544.

[74] *ibid.*, pp. 359-360 (Henderson to Graham, May 7, 1930) and 401-402 (Henderson to Tyrrell, October 1, 1930).

to eloquence as was ever possible for him. Beginning with the meeting of the League Assembly in September 1930, he joined the German campaign for a rapid termination of preparatory work and for calling the long-delayed Disarmament Conference. Even if his reports from Germany had not documented the dangerous flaring of nationalist impatience, the position of the German representatives at Geneva testified to the German temper. But Henderson, instead of reassessing the bases of his policy, continued to hope that Germany might be appeased by adequate concessions. He lectured the Eleventh Assembly on the long delay in fulfilling the intentions of the Covenant. Its authors, he declared, never believed that international cooperation could succeed if national armaments remained unrestricted and if armament competition revived. Article 8 contained quite definite pledges for a general reduction and limitation of national forces. Britain had undertaken significant new obligations, but was determined to go no further until disarmament became a reality. "The pace is slow," he warned, "and the peoples of the world are growing impatient and doubtful, in many cases, of our good faith."[75] At the Council meeting the following January he took issue with the growing certainty of the French leaders that the changing temper in Germany posed a real threat that must be met. "It may be true," he declared, "that anxiety and fears do exist. But what I want to ask is this: In how great a measure is this anxiety, this fear, the result of the armaments that now exist? How far is it the result of the uncertainties as to whether war can be prevented by the League of Nations?" Given disarmament, the League could enforce the peace. No government, however powerful, could then flout it and violate the obligations it had undertaken.[76] Finally, in November the draft convention of the Preparatory Commission, vague as it was, was adopted. The date for the Disarmament Conference was set for February 1932. For the next year, Henderson continued to pin his hopes on what it would accomplish, despite the rapid deterioration of the European situation.

Henderson's disarmament policy depended to a large extent on his assessment of the German situation as the shadow of the depression lengthened in Europe. From the beginning, the German response to his program of appeasement was not encouraging. The evacuation of the Rhineland, far from being welcomed with enthusiasm, was a signal for raising other demands. Dr. Curtius, who had suc-

[75] *Record of the Eleventh Assembly*, fourth plenary meeting, September 11, 1930, pp. 3-4.
[76] *League of Nations Official Journal*, XII (February 1931), pp. 159-160.

ceeded Stresemann at the Ministry of Foreign Affairs, almost immediately brought up the issue of the Saar.[77] In August, Herr Treviranus, a Cabinet minister, created something of a panic by the incendiary speech in which he brought to the fore the question of the eastern frontier. This German intransigence was not unanticipated in London. In May, Sir Robert Vansittart pointed out in a memorandum that all the German objectives had not been achieved by the Hague settlement. These he defined as the reestablishment of Germany as a world Power, the *Anschluss* with Austria, rearmament so as to obtain at least parity with Poland, and a drastic modification of the German-Polish frontier. These objectives must be assumed to be "inevitable," whatever the urgency with which they were pressed.[78] Even earlier, a memorandum from the Chief of the Imperial General Staff had described in some detail the German contravention of the military terms of the Versailles Treaty. But the report concluded that the German army was not a menace to the peace of Europe. Germany was rather trying secretly to lay the foundations for a large expansion at some future date, when the political situation might permit it.[79]

In the light of such information, Henderson apparently acted on the assumption that he was racing for time against the extreme elements in Germany. On occasion he could be firm. When Curtius sounded out Rumbold, toward the end of the year, on a possible moratorium or revision of the Young Plan, Henderson quashed the idea. Pointing out that the depression had probably hit England harder than Germany, he warned Curtius that to raise the question would frighten foreign investors from Germany and, by inflaming nationalist hopes in Germany and fears elsewhere, might cause serious tension in Europe.[80] Perhaps he occasionally shared the feeling of Rumbold, who had wryly commented: "It is an unattractive feature of the German character to display little gratitude for favours received, but when the receipt of favours is followed up by fresh demands, there are grounds for feeling impatient."[81] But even after the ominous revelation of Nazi strength in the election of September 1930, Henderson hewed to his main course. He remained convinced that by granting concessions to Germany—as in his disarmament program—he might strengthen the moderate elements and preserve their collaboration in working toward European pacification. "The fall of the Brüning Government," he explained to Rumbold in February 1931, "might easily have far-reaching detrimental effects on interna-

[77] *British Documents*, 2nd series, I, 489.   [78] *ibid.*, p. 501, note 5.
[79] *ibid.*, pp. 598-603.   [80] *ibid.*, pp. 536-538.   [81] *ibid.*, p. 486.

tional relationships. If, therefore, there is a real danger of its not being able to weather the storm to which it is likely to be exposed in the near future, it ought, I consider, to be the policy of His Majesty's Government to give it such support and encouragement as they properly can, in order to fortify its position."[82]

The German government, pressed as it was by its domestic critics, did not make Henderson's position any easier. Its growing impatience on the disarmament issue had been apparent for some time. In February, he instructed Rumbold to tell Curtius quite plainly that he expected full cooperation in preparing for the Disarmament Conference. He denounced the view that Germany, being virtually disarmed, had no role to fill beyond that of complainant. Curtius was to be warned that it was essential to restrain the responsible leaders of German opinion from provocative utterance and action and to try to create "that atmosphere of international loyalty and confidence in which alone the conference can hope to succeed."[83]

How well Curtius heeded his advice was revealed in March, when the project of an Austro-German customs union burst upon the European scene. To France and the Little Entente the customs union seemed a clear portent of the *Anschluss* that had been prohibited at Paris and again in the Austrian Reconstruction Protocol of 1922. Their reaction was agitated and immediate. While Henderson refused to go along with a joint *démarche* at Berlin and Vienna, he was seriously disturbed. It is a striking misreading of the implications of his position to write that he "gave no signs of disapproval of the customs union."[84] He received the project with "reserve," but he made his attitude clear in his instructions to his representatives at Vienna and Berlin. His first reaction was that if nothing were done to calm existing fears the task of those who were anxious for the Disarmament Conference to meet under the most favorable circumstances would be seriously compromised. He instructed Rumbold and Phipps to emphasize that the position of Briand in France had become extremely difficult, and that his influence "in controlling more extreme tendencies among his own countrymen" would be unquestionably affected. He appealed to the two governments to give the League Council the opportunity to judge whether the treaty was compatible with the Protocol of 1922 before proceeding further.[85] At Paris,

---

[82] *ibid.*, p. 559.   [83] *ibid.*, pp. 554-555.
[84] Tucker, *Attitude of Labour Party*, p. 125.
[85] *British Documents*, 2nd series, II, 12-13. In the House of Commons on March 30, Henderson repeated almost verbatim the instructions, omitting only the reference to Briand's position. Parliamentary Debates: Commons, 5th series, CCL, 717-720.

where he had gone for a meeting of the Organization Committee of the Commission of Enquiry for European Union, he quickly found that Briand appreciated his intent. On the evening of March 25 a statement was issued from the British embassy indicating that the two Foreign Ministers were in consultation and announcing that Henderson would ask the Council to take up the question at its May meeting.[86] Meanwhile, although both the German and Austrian Foreign Ministers had replied that in their view there was no incompatibility with the 1922 commitment, Phipps was reporting from Vienna that the Austrians were showing signs of wanting to back down.[87] In the event, both accepted the appeal to the Council, despite the fact that Germany kept insisting that the proposal was really an implementation of the Briand plan for European Union. Henderson, for his part, sat tight. Eventually, the Council took up the question and in turn requested an advisory opinion from the Permanent Court of International Justice. By the time a split opinion unfavorable to the customs union was handed down on September 5, Henderson was out of office and the Austrian government, under severe financial pressure from France, had declared its intention not to proceed.[88] The entire incident had embittered the European atmosphere, already tense with the strain of the economic crisis, and was an ominous prelude to the Disarmament Conference. That Conference, it is clear, was Henderson's main concern in the matter. He resented the method chosen by Germany to foster economic union and felt strongly that he must protect Briand's position in France. If his public position was cautious and legalistic, it was because he judged such tactics to be best suited to keep the way open for cooperation in disarmament. He did not want the German government, desperate for a success in foreign affairs to silence its domestic critics, to lose face. He believed that his proposal gave it a way out while at the same time it would satisfy opinion in France. That he was not entirely successful was almost entirely a function of the deteriorating economic situation in Central Europe and above all in Germany.

The summer months of 1931 were taken up, in large part, with the problem of the financial difficulties of Germany. The complicated negotiations, highlighted by President Hoover's proposal of a moratorium on intergovernmental debts and culminating in the unsuccessful London Conference of July 20 to 23, need only be mentioned, since in the final

---

[86] *Survey of International Affairs, 1931*, pp. 305-307; *British Documents*, 2nd series, II, 17-18.
[87] *ibid.*, p. 31. [88] *Survey of International Affairs*, 1931, pp. 318-321.

reckoning their results were negative. MacDonald played a much more prominent role than Henderson in the discussions and in any case Great Britain was hardly in a position to be of much real assistance. Henderson, however, continued to be optimistic. As late as July 30, after he and MacDonald had made a quick visit to Berlin, he wrote to Briand that the Brüning government was receiving an increasing amount of support at home for its handling of the very serious financial situation.[89] Actually, he seemed as much concerned, during this period, to persuade the Germans to give up plans to construct a second pocket battleship.[90] More and more, disarmament had become the touchstone of his policy.

By the time the Disarmament Conference met in February 1932, the foundations for its work had long since been eaten away. In the face of the deterioration of the German situation, it would have been difficult to persuade France to reduce her military superiority except in return for rigid guarantees of collective support to compensate for the sacrifice. Henderson's policy in part had aimed to provide such guarantees, but even his position was not entirely satisfactory to France. When the National government took over, the greater reluctance of Great Britain to make such commitments became quickly apparent. In any case, it is not easy to see how the triangular struggle between Britain, France, and Germany could have ended otherwise than in failure. The German Nazis and their Nationalist allies were not really concerned with disarmament. By 1932 they were well on their way to power. A compromise on disarmament might have permitted Brüning to hang on a little longer. But he too was committed to a demand for equality which the French could not accept. The disintegration of the German political system in the solvent of the economic depression was the final precipitant of the collapse of the disarmament dream.

To recapitulate the history of the Disarmament Conference would have no purpose. But a word on Henderson's role is necessary. The meeting of some sixty-odd nations at Geneva should have been the fulfillment of his career. Instead, it came as a personal tragedy. He had been elected President in May and was grimly determined to take the chair even though the collapse of the Labor government had driven him from the Foreign Office. From the beginning, his position was impossible. The bitterness of the political cleavage at home was reflected in the hostility of the British delegation. He himself was seriously ill. But he kept doggedly to his task, never missing a meeting of the General Commis-

[89] *British Documents*, 2nd series, II, 245.
[90] See, for example, *ibid.*, pp. 115, 119, 161.

sion, working stubbornly with the Bureau, endeavoring by sheer force of will to extract an agreement that had become patently impossible. By exhortation and persuasion he attempted to make up for the fact that he no longer had the authority and bargaining power of a Foreign Secretary. He had no other weapon at his disposal.

The sheer horror of any future war made it inconceivable to him that a treaty would not be achieved. In his speech at the opening of the Conference he elaborated the familiar arguments for disarmament—the expense of huge military establishments, the insecurity caused by arms competition, and the rest. Almost passionately he pleaded: "The world wants disarmament. The world needs disarmament. We have it in our power to help fashion the pattern of future history. Behind all the technical complexities regarding man-power, gun-power, tonnage, categories, and the like, is the well-being of mankind, the future of our developing civilisation."[91] But behind the technical complexities also was the growing reality of the Franco-German antagonism. The French demand for security, the German claim to equality added up to a dilemma for which the Conference had no solution.

The almost interminable haggling of the first six months of the Conference set the tone for its labors. By July, all that had been accomplished was the drafting of a general resolution as a proposed basis for further negotiation. When the resolution was presented, the German delegate, Herr Nadolny, made it clear that he could not accept a formula which made no provision for equality of armaments.[92] Henderson did not conceal his disappointment with the resolution. He tried, however, to salvage something from the wreckage. Whatever its defects, he argued, it would put the Conference on the right road to disarmament. Eventually, success would come and he pledged himself to lose no time in getting on with the task. Nevertheless, Germany, along with the USSR, voted against the resolution.[93] Although it was carried, the fate of the Conference was clear. Thereafter, from the first German withdrawal through her final departure on October 14, 1933, its work went on in a vacuum of unreality. The triumph of the National Socialists should have been proof enough of the failure of its efforts. But Henderson, at least, continued to hope against hope. He literally grasped at every straw. In May 1933, he seized upon President Roosevelt's proposals to the Conference to suggest a compromise which might be ac-

---

[91] *League of Nations, Records of the Conference for the Reduction and Limitation of Armaments*, series A, Plenary Meetings, I, 40-47.
[92] *ibid.*, series B, Minutes of the General Commission, II, 186-188.
[93] *ibid.*, pp. 204-205.

ceptable to Germany.[94] The next month he was in London, trying to convince the heads of governments assembled for the World Monetary and Economic Conference to break the deadlock at Geneva. Again, he had little success. A sketch of his activities at London is surely one of the tragic portraits of this period. John W. Wheeler Bennett wrote: ". . . there have been few more pathetic figures than that of Mr. Henderson sitting alone in one of the lounges in the delegates' *foyer* and gazing enviously at the milling groups of representatives who surged up and down the floor and cast not a glance at the lonely, rubicund, kindly figure in the corner. On the outskirts of these scrimmages hung, like a half-back, Mr. Henderson's faithful Achates, M. Aghnides, Director of the Disarmament Secretariat, who spared no effort to 'collar' delegates as they broke away from their groups and to transform the picture of Mr. Henderson from 'Solitaire' into 'Conversation Piece.' But even when M. Aghnides' efforts were crowned with success, his prey would vanish from his clutches into another group before they had crossed the brief distance to Mr. Henderson's sofa."[95]

Nevertheless, a little later, he was making a swing around the circle of the major European countries to seek a way out of the impasse. He brought back to the Conference only a greater awareness of the real difficulties to be faced, though he still hoped they might be overcome.[96] Even after the final German break he continued his efforts. He met with the Bureau and various committees in 1934 and 1935, but the Conference was finished, although its formal existence dragged on almost without end. The award of the Nobel Peace Prize in 1935 must have been scant recompense for his labor. When he died on October 20, 1935, the world which had come into being furnished a bitter testimony to the failure of his hopes.

VI

The temptation is great to let the final tragedy of Henderson's efforts obscure the full picture of what he tried to achieve. His last-ditch stand for disarmament by exhortation has captured the imagination of admirers who have seen him as the archetype of the aspiration of all men for peace—and of critics who have summed him up as a sentimentalist, if not a well-intentioned fool. But seen as a whole, as we have tried to see it here, his program comes into a different focus. More than most states-

[94] *ibid.*, II, 462-464.
[95] John W. Wheeler Bennett, *The Disarmament Deadlock*, p. 164, quoted in William E. Rappard, *The Quest for Peace since the World War* (Cambridge, 1940), pp. 459-460.
[96] *League of Nations, Records of the Conference for the Reduction and Limitation of Armaments*, series C, Minutes of the Bureau, II, 178-179.

men in British public life, he had a surprising conception of the issues posed by the catchwords of disarmament and security. He accepted the thesis that it was necessary to strike at the tensions caused by the post-war settlement in order to prepare the way for a viable international order. But at a time when the British people felt themselves secure and most British leaders were unwilling to make any sizable commitments in Europe, he had some sense of the real difficulties faced by the beneficiaries of the Versailles system on the continent. While he was perhaps never willing to go as far in the direction of explicit military guarantees as the French might have wished, he collaborated fully in trying to erect a genuine structure of international guarantees through the League of Nations in order to make disarmament possible. He realized that armed forces would be necessary, but he hoped that they might be reduced as security came more and more to rest upon the collective action of the League. His policy of appeasement, the development of the League, and then disarmament came closer to being one of effective collective security before 1930 than any within the realm of serious possibility. Seen in the light of the 1920's, it was a thoughtful, perceptive, and practicable line of approach. It is tempting, also, to commit the cardinal sin and to speculate, unhistorically, on what might have been if the world had not plunged into economic disaster. Temptation aside, the cataclysm of 1930 and 1931 turned a practical program of action into a shambles. By 1932, all the basic assumptions of the campaign which was supposedly to culminate in the progressive reduction of armaments had disappeared. It was now time for rigid resistance to the demands of an importunate German nationalism—and time also for equally firm support of France and the European order. The threat to the stability of Europe itself was too great to be ignored. In such a pattern, there was little place for the chimera of disarmament by international agreement. To change a way of thinking overnight, however, was difficult, and there were few who saw the issues clearly. If Henderson did not have the insight of a Winston Churchill after 1932, he had at least, in the brief hopeful era before the decade of nemesis, opened up to Europe some of the avenues for a constructive approach to the problem of an enduring peace. That was the significance of his role in international affairs, and this, rather than his tragic part at the Disarmament Conference, should be the balance in which to weigh his diplomatic career.

11

....

Maxim Litvinov

BY HENRY L. ROBERTS

MAXIM LITVINOV, Peoples Commissar for Foreign Affairs from 1930 to 1939, was undoubtedly the Soviet diplomat most widely and familiarly known in the West during the interwar period. At international conferences and at sessions of the League of Nations his chubby and unproletarian figure radiated an aura of robust and businesslike common sense that was in striking contrast to the enigmatic brutality of the Politburo or the conspiratorial noisiness of the Comintern. Although he was an old revolutionary—he was born Meyer Wallach in 1876 and like Lenin, six years his senior, and Stalin, three years his junior, he assumed a *nom de guerre* while dodging the Tsarist police—to him perhaps more than to any other single person may be traced the impression that revolutionary Russia was returning to the family of nations and could be counted upon as a force for stability and peace. Indeed, the most perplexing problem in Litvinov's career is that of the relation of his role to the totality of aims and intentions of the Soviet regime.

This problem was most sharply posed in the blatant contrast between Litvinov's appeals after 1933 for collective security against Nazi Germany and the provisions of the German-Soviet agreement of August 23, 1939. Was Litvinov really striving for the determined cooperation of the peacefully inclined Powers or was Lord Lothian right in his belief that the ulterior aim of Litvinov's policy was "to maintain discord in Europe?"[1] Is it correct to assume that there was a distinctive "Litvinov policy"[2] or was his role throughout an essentially subordinate one in the Soviet hierarchy?[3] Were there important differences between Lit-

[1] See his speech of April 2, 1936, in *Germany and the Rhineland* (London, Royal Institute of International Affairs, 1936), p. 55.

[2] "Soviet foreign policy between 1929 and May 1939 followed the pattern of Litvinov's mind more than of his chief's." Louis Fischer, *Men and Politics* (New York, 1941), p. 127.

[3] Max Beloff, reflecting on his study of Soviet foreign policy, commented, in 1950:

vinov's outlook and that of the Politburo? If so, how did he survive the great purges which decimated the Foreign Commissariat; if not, why was he so abruptly retired in May 1939? Finally, did his retirement represent a real turning point in Soviet policy or was it only a tactical shift, the importance of which should not be overrated?

In attempting to come to closer grips with these questions—their definitive resolution seems impossible in the absence of evidence from the Soviet archives—this paper will consider in turn three topics: (1) the content of Litvinov's diplomatic policy, so far as it can be ascertained from his public pronouncements and recorded conversations; (2) the connection of this policy with the aims of the Politburo; (3) the relations between Litvinov, the Foreign Commissariat, and the Bolshevist high command.

I

Although it may be a matter of temperament one can detect a definite and largely consistent flavor in Litvinov's diplomatic attitude and behavior. Never the firebrand or the theoretician, he was always valued for his efficiency and practical abilities. Before the 1905 Revolution, the nickname Papasha (little father) was given to him by party comrades. In 1918, when hopes of general revolution were running high, when Chicherin was suggesting that the League of Nations be based on the expropriation of the capitalists of all countries and was intimating to President Wilson that the latter's government was to be replaced by a Council of Peoples Commissars,[4] Litvinov, writing to Wilson two months later, struck a quite different note. He attempted to explain the Red Terror as a defensive measure, protested against the intervention as leading only to the final devastation of Russia, and concluded: "The dictatorship of toilers and producers is not an aim in itself, but the means of building up a new social system under which useful work and equal rights would be provided for all citizens, irrespective of the class to which they had formerly belonged. One may believe in this ideal or not, but it surely gives no justification for sending foreign troops to fight against it, or for arming and supporting classes interested in the restoration of the old system of exploitation of man by man."[5]

One cannot be sure, of course, whether Litvinov's moderation was

---

"It is probable, too, that I did not lay enough stress upon the essentially subordinate nature of Litvinov's role." "Soviet Foreign Policy, 1929-1941: Some Notes," *Soviet Studies* (Oxford), 11 (October 1950), 127.

[4] See his note to Wilson of October 24, 1918 in Degras, I, 112-120.

[5] Telegram from Litvinov to Wilson, December 24, 1918, *ibid.*, pp. 129-133.

merely adroit diplomatic address—it was clearly to the advantage of the struggling regime to persuade the Western Powers to give up their intervention—or whether it actually reflects the absence of revolutionary expectation and belligerence. Louis Fischer reported Litvinov as saying to him some years later, "The prospect of world revolution disappeared on November 11, 1918."[6] In any event, this tone of unrevolutionary reasonableness remained a permanent trade mark of Litvinov's dealings with the outside world.

During the years when Litvinov served as Chicherin's second in the Narkomindel, the principal goals of Soviet diplomacy were, after the flurry of revolution and civil war, to achieve recognition and to increase the security of the Soviet Union by means of treaties of neutrality and nonaggression. The reason for these goals is evident and requires no discussion. Less evident is the Soviet purpose in entering the League discussions concerning disarmament, discussions which first brought Litvinov's name to general prominence.

The initial Soviet attitude on the subject of war and peace is stated in the Narkomindel's Appeal to the Toiling, Oppressed and Exhausted Peoples of Europe, of December 19, 1917: "We do not attempt to conceal the fact that we do not consider the existing capitalist Governments capable of making a democratic peace. The revolutionary struggle of the toiling masses against the existing Governments can alone bring Europe nearer to such a peace. Its full realization can only be guaranteed by the victorious proletarian revolution in all capitalist countries."[7] As a logical consequence the League of Nations was viewed as a "mere mask, designed to deceive the broad masses, for the aggressive aims of the imperialist policy of certain Great Powers or their vassals."[8] Despite this hostile attitude, Litvinov appeared at the Preparatory Commission of the Disarmament Conference to propose "the complete abolition of all land, marine, and air forces."

Litvinov never denied these Soviet views concerning peace under capitalism. In 1922 he granted that the present social-economic structures of the majority of countries made the removal of the possibility of armed international conflict "unthinkable."[9] In 1927 he reiterated the Soviet Union's lack of confidence in the readiness and capability of capitalist countries to destroy the system of war between nations.[10] Nevertheless,

---

[6] Fischer, *Men and Politics*, p. 127. Litvinov's American biographer, Arthur Upham Pope, states that as early as 1920 Litvinov had declared that the project of world revolution was impossible. (*Maxim Litvinoff*, New York, 1943, p. 334).
[7] Degras, I, 19.   [8] *ibid.*, I, 381.
[9] *The Soviet Union and Peace* (New York, n.d.), p. 117.   [10] *ibid.*, p. 134.

this fundamental skepticism did not, in Litvinov's view, preclude the possibility of negotiating for disarmament. On November 6, 1930, he made this point quite clearly: "To us, the representatives of the Soviet Union, and exponents of definite socio-economic theories, the impossibility of removing the politico-economic antagonisms of capitalist society, and hence the ultimate inevitability of war, is perfectly clear. We believe, however, or we should not be here, that the danger of war might be considerably diminished, or made comparatively remote, by some measure of real disarmament."[11] It would appear that something which is ultimately inevitable may, however, be reduced as an imminent likelihood by appropriate action.

But was the Soviet proposal for complete disarmament such an appropriate action? Did it represent an effort, as Litvinov put it, "to find a common language" with the other Powers? It is easy to understand the embarrassed and irritable reaction of the other nations, which were trying—without notable success—to fit disarmament into a more general program encompassing security and arbitration. But to the charge that the Soviet scheme could not guarantee security or destroy international distrust, Litvinov simply answered that he was not offering a universal remedy ("We cannot recommend you any such panacea, for we know you would not entertain it for a moment.").[12]

The other Powers also had suspicions, though they were reluctant to express them, that the real intent of the Soviets was to weaken other states militarily and increase the effectiveness of the Communist weapons of insurrection and subversion. To this charge Litvinov replied with a mixture of frankness and disingenuousness. He stated that the Soviet government had no intention of participating with any other government in working out questions "regarding the class war or the struggle against revolution," and asked caustically if the purpose of armaments was to put down possible revolution. He also gave the customary Soviet denial of any responsibility for the actions of the Comintern.

A more serious doubt about the sincerity of the Soviet disarmament proposal arises from the basic premises of Leninism. The argument has been advanced that the Soviets by their own theory could not be advocates of disarmament: True peace is achievable only in a classless and stateless world. Such a world cannot come about by a process of peaceful evolution, but involves the establishment of the dictatorship of the proletariat. This dictatorship explicitly rests on force, of which the Red

[11] *The Soviet's Fight for Disarmament* (New York, n.d.), p. 34.
[12] *The Soviet Union and Peace*, pp. 188-189.

Army is, equally explicitly, a vital element. Hence, complete disarmament would be, for the Soviets, a "suicidal act."[13] This argument, however, is not wholly conclusive since the Communist response would be that their analysis and consequent tactics were based on the real nature of modern imperialist states. If these states were to prove capable of overcoming their own nature by the act of disarmament, then the Soviet Union could likewise disarm the Red army. Such indeed was the implication in Litvinov's report to the Fifteenth Congress of the Russian Communist party: "If the capitalist governments doubt our sincerity, they have a simple means of proving it. This means is their adherence to our programme. Let them decide on this. If they do not do this, if they cannot do this, if they do not wish to do this, then, before the whole world, against their will, they testify to the fact that a proposal for full disarmament and abolition of war can emanate only from the Soviet Government; that it can be accepted and executed only when the Soviet system has been adopted by all the countries of the world, when their policies and principles will, of course, be at one with those by which the ussr is guided."[14]

In retrospect the real criticism to be made of Litvinov's stand on disarmament in the 1920's is not that it was insincere propaganda but that by viewing the world in the black and white of Communism versus Capitalist Imperialism it misrepresented the significance of the relations between the non-Communist Powers, and reduced them to the sinful bickerings of reprobates.[15] By making the sweeping generalization that "economic competition is the true cause of war" it falsely placed the issue of security, which could not be separated from disarmament, on an all-or-nothing basis.

With such an outlook collective security was, of course, impossible. In 1924 Chicherin had said: "The Soviet Government therefore rejects any plan for an international organization which implies the possibility of measures of constraint being exercised by any international authority whatsoever against a particular State. . . . In the present international situation, it is impossible in most cases to say which party is the aggressor. Neither the entry into foreign territory nor the scale of war preparations can be regarded as satisfactory criteria. . . . The Soviet Government con-

---

[13] See T. A. Taracouzio, *War and Peace in Soviet Diplomacy* (New York, 1940), pp. 266-276, for an able expression of this argument.

[14] *The Soviet Union and Peace*, p. 162.

[15] In his report to the Fifteenth Congress Litvinov said: "It may be said that on all questions considered by the Commission, a clear sharp line was drawn between us and the other delegates. It was a case of *we* and *they*. And this is as it should be."

siders, therefore, that it is absolutely impossible to adopt the system of deciding which State is the aggressor in the case of each conflict and making definite consequences depend upon such decision."[16] In 1928 Litvinov expressed somewhat the same view: "Owing to the lack of exact criteria as to what constitutes an offensive and what a defensive war, the system of regional guarantee pacts based upon mutual assistance . . . may end in something perilously akin to the prewar system of alliances and other military and political combinations."[17]

Even the innocuous Kellogg Pact was regarded with deep suspicion. Chicherin, in August 1928, flatly termed it "an organic part of the preparation for war against the USSR." Litvinov, too, intimated that the proposal to prohibit war as an instrument of national policy implied the possibility of war as an instrument for the defence of "civilization" against "barbarism"—i.e. against the Soviet Union.[18] Nevertheless, after having criticized its origins, its omissions, and its reservations, Litvinov not only announced that the USSR would subscribe to the pact but then turned it to advantage by achieving a regional reaffirmation of its terms through the Litvinov Protocol, signed by the Soviet Union and most of its Western neighbors, in February 1929. The Protocol, however, represented "negative security"; it was not a step toward positive cooperative action. When, in 1929, the United States government attempted to invoke the Kellogg Pact in the Russian-Chinese dispute in Manchuria, Litvinov brusquely rejected all efforts at diplomatic intervention and declared that the Pact did not provide any one of its signatories with the function of being its guardian. Clearly, he was not thinking of collective security at this point.

In July 1930, Chicherin, who had been in ill health for some years, was retired, and Litvinov became chief of the Narkomindel. It is generally agreed that the relations between the two men were far from friendly. Their temperaments clashed, each was suspicious of the other's intentions, and Litvinov, who, despite his amiable appearance, was not an easy person to get on with, appears to have been not overly scrupulous in his ambitions to become Foreign Commissar.[19]

[16] Degras, I, 432-433.

[17] *The Soviet Union and Peace*, p. 167.

[18] Louis Fischer (*Men and Politics*, pp. 88-89) states that neither Litvinov nor Chicherin really believed that the Soviet Union was threatened with attack in 1927-1928. Litvinov is quoted as saying, "That was merely idle gossip here of some people and the press. . . . It is wrong to suppose, as many of us do, that Russia is the center of all international affairs. . . ."

[19] See A. Barmine, *Memoirs of a Soviet Diplomat* (London, 1938), pp. 217-218.

With regard to a new course in foreign policy, Litvinov, on July 25, 1930, informed correspondents that his appointment did not imply any change, not only because he had been for ten years a close associate of Chicherin's but because, under the dictatorship of the proletariat, foreign policy was determined by the will of the working masses and hence not subject to fluctuations.[20] Nevertheless, the German ambassador in Moscow, Dirksen, felt, or so he related twenty years later, that his task had become more difficult because Litvinov was not a really convinced adherent of the Rapallo policy but gave it only lip service.[21] Dirksen went on to say, however, that Litvinov did not really deviate from the German orientation until the Nazi seizure of power gave him the perhaps not unhoped for opportunity to be one of the first to abandon the Rapallo connection.

In fact, it was not his new post as Foreign Commissar but rather developments abroad between 1931 and 1933 which led Litvinov to a new course. The process was gradual, but several stages may be observed.

The Soviet Union continued its policy of signing neutrality and nonaggression pacts with its neighbors. Treaties were made with Turkey, Lithuania, Iran, and Afghanistan between 1925 and 1927. A new treaty with Afghanistan was signed on June 24, 1931. Then, in September 1931 Japan launched its attack on Manchuria. On January 21, 1932, the Soviet Union and Finland signed a treaty which resembled its predecessors, but included a significant new clause: "Should either High Contracting Party resort to aggression against a third Power, the other High Contracting Party may denounce the present treaty without notice." This clause appeared in all subsequent Soviet nonaggression treaties up to but definitely not including the pact with Germany of August 1939.[22]

If this double negative—denouncing a nonaggression pact—be considered a positive step, it may be concluded that this initial move toward collective security, at least by indirection, was stimulated by the first overt aggression of the 1930's.

Litvinov, however, still challenged the possibility of improving international relations except by the path of disarmament. On February 11, 1932, at the Disarmament Conference he declared: "Security against

[20] M. Litvinov, *Vneshniaia politika* SSSR (Moscow, 1937), p. 59.

[21] Herbert von Dirksen, *Moskau, Tokio, London: Erinnerungen und Betrachtungen zu 20 Jahre deutscher Aussenpolitik, 1919-1939* (Stuttgart, 1950), pp. 94-95. Dirksen also commented: "Although he [Litvinov] almost passionately denied any deviation from the pure Rapallo doctrine, his sympathies were with Great Britain, where he had passed the years of his exile and met his wife. So he had to be earnestly admonished from time to time when he was disposed to deviate from the correct faith to the Western heresy."

[22] Such pacts were signed with Estonia, Latvia, Poland, and France in 1932, and with Italy in 1933.

war must be created. This security can never be achieved by roundabout ways, but only by the direct way of total general disarmament. This is no communist slogan. The Soviet delegation knows that the triumph of socialistic principles, removing the causes giving rise to armed conflicts, is the only absolute guarantee of peace. So long, however, as these principles prevail only in one-sixth of the world, there is only one means of organizing security against war, and that is total and general disarmament."[23]

A year later, on February 6, 1933—that is, after Hitler had come to power—Litvinov took a different line. He expressed, somewhat reluctantly, his willingness to consider the French security proposals, and in conjunction with a French plan submitted a draft definition of aggression. He was now attempting to supply the criteria which in 1928 he had said were lacking. Litvinov's original draft, which defined as aggressions declarations of war, invasions without a declaration, bombardments and naval attacks, landings and unpermitted occupations, and blockades, did not include a notable phrase, subsequently added by a subcommittee of the Disarmament Conference: "Provision of support to armed bands formed on its territory which have invaded the territory of another state, or refusal, notwithstanding the request of the invaded State, to take on its own territory all the measures in its power to deprive these bands of all assistance or protection."[24] Moreover, Litvinov's original draft in its second clause was far more vigorous than the subsequent convention in spelling out the political, military, economic or other considerations which could *not* serve as an excuse or justification for aggression as defined: in substance, revolutionary regimes were not to be subject to retaliation for their revolutionary acts of expropriation and civil violence, "backward areas" were not to be exploited by force or penalized by gunboat assault for their actions against capitalist exploitation. It is interesting to note, in view of the publicity later given to the definition of aggression, that Litvinov said frankly, "I admit, however, that the Soviet delegation itself attributes infinitely greater importance to the second clause in its declaration."[25] Thus, the Soviet Union was at this time definitely less interested in establishing a criterion for aggression—which

[23] *The Soviet Fight for Disarmament*, p. 23.
[24] It is worth noting that when the USSR in November 1950 presented a definition of aggression to the Political Committee of the U.N. General Assembly, it reverted to the original Litvinov formulation—i.e., without mention of indirect aggression by armed bands—and not to the revised formula accepted by the Soviet Union in 1933 and used in its treaties with neighboring powers.
[25] League of Nations, *Records of the Conference for the Reduction and Limitation of Armaments*, Series B, Minutes of General Commission, II, 238.

could provide the basis for collective measures—than in protecting its position as a revolutionary state in a presumably hostile world.

A modification of the convention was proposed by a subcommittee on May 24, 1933, and was accepted by the Soviets. While it fared no further at the Disarmament Conference, at the London Economic Conference Litvinov proposed that Russia and its neighbors sign this convention. The proposal was accepted, and in July 1933 a series of treaties bound the Soviet Union, Afghanistan, Estonia, Latvia, Persia, Poland, Rumania, Czechoslovakia, Turkey, Yugoslavia, Finland, and Lithuania to accept this definition of aggression.

On December 29, 1933, shortly after his return from the United States, where he had successfully negotiated for American recognition,[26] Litvinov delivered an important speech to the Central Executive Committee of the USSR. In this speech a distinct change in outlook was apparent. The era of "bourgeois pacifism" had come to an end; new and dangerous ideologies were arising. But whereas Litvinov had previously tended to lump all capitalist states together, he now differentiated between actively belligerent powers, those that were temporarily passive but that would not mind a bit of fighting in the world, especially if it were directed against the USSR, and those powers actively interested in the preservation of peace. With regard to the latter, "I am not entering into an estimation of the motives for such a policy, but am merely stating a fact which is highly valuable to us." Moreover, while stressing that the Soviet Union was perfectly capable of defending itself, "and even the approaches to it," he went on to say that "the maintenance of peace cannot depend upon our efforts alone. It depends upon the cooperation and assistance of other countries as well. By striving, therefore, toward the establishment and maintenance of friendly relations with all countries we devote particular attention to the strengthening of relations and maximum rapprochement with those countries which, like ourselves, furnish proof of their sincere desire to preserve peace and show that they are prepared to oppose any violators of peace."[27]

[26] For the negotiations leading to the establishment of American-Soviet diplomatic relations and for an account of the mutually disappointing aftermath, see *Foreign Relations: Diplomatic Papers: The Soviet Union, 1933-1939* (Washington, 1952). American-Soviet relations are not discussed here primarily because they were not of great importance to Litvinov's major diplomatic efforts. As George F. Kennan wrote from Moscow in November 1937: "When he can be found in Moscow, Litvinov has frequently shown a reluctance to discuss topics other than those he considers to be major political matters. These seem at present to be the success or failure of efforts to induce other states to take strong measures against Germany, Italy and Japan. The result is that few of the current problems of Soviet-American relations attract his interest." *Ibid.*, p. 447.

[27] *Vneshniaia politika* SSSR (Moscow, 1937), pp. 74-96.

The chief trouble makers, of course, were Germany and Japan, to whom Litvinov devoted a considerable amount of attention. He pointed out that for ten years Germany and Russia had enjoyed particularly close political and economic relations, which were advantageous to both Powers. Nevertheless, relations had deteriorated beyond recognition in the course of the last year. The new German regime was showing itself openly hostile to the Soviet Union; its leaders in the past had frequently advocated an anti-Soviet policy, which they had not disavowed since they had come to power. He denied that the Nazi attack on the German Communists was the source of friction: "We have, of course, our own opinion of the German regime. We are, of course, sensitive to the sufferings of our German comrades, but we Marxists are the last who can be reproached for permitting our feelings to dictate our policy." He emphasized that the Soviet Union desired good relations with Germany, but that the responsibility lay with the new regime to desist from its current attitude. In concluding, Litvinov fell back upon the older view that the USSR was, after all, surrounded by capitalist Powers and had ultimately to rely upon the Red army, navy, and air force.

In passing, it is interesting to compare this speech with the one delivered by Stalin to the Seventeenth Congress of the Communist party a few weeks later, on January 26, 1934.[28] While the main lines of foreign policy were quite similar, there was a certain difference in emphasis. Stalin's speech, naturally, was more pontifical and grimmer in tone. He expounded at greater length on the reasons for the changes in the world scene, stressing, as always, the economic crisis of capitalism (Litvinov had given less weight to this, and suggested such other factors as the rise of a new generation which had not experienced war). His talk was more "revolutionary": "The masses of the people have not yet reached the stage when they are ready to storm capitalism; but the idea of storming it is maturing in the minds of the masses." While criticizing the attitude of the new German regime, he was by no means friendly to the "peaceloving" capitalist Powers. He denied any new orientation: "Our orientation in the past and our orientation at the present time is towards the USSR, and towards the USSR alone."

The year 1933 seems definitely to have marked a major turning point in Litvinov's diplomatic orientation. To be sure, in subsequent years Communist spokesmen would say that the Soviet Union had anticipated the mounting crisis of the 1930's and point to a multitude of statements about the precarious state of the capitalist world and the emergence of

[28] J. Stalin, *Problems of Leninism*, 11th edition (Moscow, 1940), pp. 470-486.

fascism. But in these earlier statements the jeremiads against the capitalist world were general volleys against all the Western Powers, just as the term fascism was a general epithet for quite indiscriminate use in domestic politics. The specific menace of a National Socialist Germany was something else again, and it took the unpleasant experiences of 1933 to bring Litvinov, and the Soviet Union, to the position he adopted in his speech at the end of the year.

For the next two and a half years, however, Litvinov proceeded in high gear down the road of collective security and cooperation with the peace-loving Powers. These were the years when the USSR joined the League, when mutual assistance pacts were signed with France and Czechoslovakia, and when Litvinov made some of his most constructive pronouncements on the means to preserve peace, which he now declared to be "indivisible."

In the spring of 1934, on May 29, Litvinov was prepared to admit that "international life and particularly political events in some countries during recent years had prevented the [Disarmament] Conference from carrying out its direct task of drawing up a disarmament convention." After all, however, disarmament, was only a means to an end: "Could not the Conference feel its way towards other guarantees for peace?"— a possibility he had categorically denied some years earlier. He then went on to say that, "Even if there should be dissident States, that should by no means prevent the remainder from coming still more closely together to take steps which would strengthen their own security."[29]

In line with this approach was a new and amiable view toward the League of Nations. As late as December 1933 Litvinov had denied that Russia was likely to join the League in any foreseeable future, but by the following spring his attitude was quite different, and in September the USSR obtained a permanent seat in the Council. Of course, one specific reason for joining the League was that a mutual assistance pact with France, the negotiations for which began in 1934, could be reconciled with the Locarno Treaty only if France's partner were a member of the League.[30]

Although Litvinov was unsuccessful in persuading Germany to join in guaranteeing the Eastern European frontiers or in creating an Eastern Locarno pact, France and Russia did achieve a mutual assistance pact, which was signed on May 2, 1935. On May 16 was also signed a Soviet-

---

[29] League of Nations, *Records of the Conference for the Reduction and Limitation of Armaments*, Series B, III, 657-661.

[30] Max Beloff, *The Foreign Policy of Soviet Russia* (2 vols., London, 1947, 1949), I, 135.

Czech mutual assistance pact, with provisions similar to those of the French pact, but stipulating that they should come into force only if France gave assistance to the country attacked.

Although the Soviet Union was thus drawing closer to some of the capitalist Powers, at the same time, in 1935 and 1936, the Fascist states struck three decisive blows at the structure of European peace: Germany's repudiation of disarmament, the Italian attack on Abyssinia, and the march into the Rhineland. While each of these events did not directly concern the USSR and while the Soviet government did not actually take any important measures, a good deal of Litvinov's positive reputation rests on the speeches he delivered in response to these actions.

In his speech of April 17, 1935, he stated that while the Soviet Union neither favored the Versailles Treaty nor was bound by it, the German action did violate the Covenant of the League, and "one of the foundations of peace is the observance of international relations directly affecting the security of nations."[31] He agreed in principle to the right of equality of armament, but not "if a country which demands or assumes the right to arm is exclusively led by people who have publicly announced as the programme of their foreign policy a policy which consists, not only in revenge, but in the unrestricted conquest of foreign territory and the destruction of the independence of whole States."

On September 5, 1935, when Italy was threatening Abyssinia, he pointed out that while the USSR had no interests involved, the Italian action could set a dangerous precedent: "The repetition of the precedent would certainly have a cumulative effect and, in its turn, would stimulate new conflicts more directly affecting the whole of Europe."[32]

On September 14, in speaking of the Fascist Powers' technique of advocating bilateral pacts, he stated: "We know of another political conception that is fighting the idea of collective security and advocating bilateral pacts, and this not even between all States but only between States arbitrarily chosen for this purpose. This conception can have nothing in common with peaceful intentions. Not every pact of nonaggression is concluded with a view to strengthening general peace. While nonaggression pacts concluded by the Soviet Union with its neighbors, include a special clause for suspending the pact in cases of aggression committed by one of the parties against any third State, we know of other pacts of nonaggression which have no such clause. This means that a State which has secured by such a pact of nonaggression its rear or its flank, obtains the

[31] Maxim Litvinov, *Against Aggression* (New York, 1939), pp. 18-19.
[32] League of Nations, *Official Journal*, 16th Year, No. 11, November 1935, p. 1142.

facility of attacking with impunity third States."[33] Perhaps this statement indicates why Litvinov was not quite the man to negotiate the
German-Soviet pact of August 1939.

When Germany marched into the Rhineland in March 1936, Litvinov
again urged collective action: "One cannot fight for the collective organization of security without taking collective measures against the
violation of international obligations. We, however, do not count among
such measures collective capitulation to the aggressor."[34]

His funeral speech, on July 1, 1936, for the demise of Abyssinia was
one of his best. "We are gathered here," he began, "to close a page in
the history of the League of Nations, the history of international life,
which it will be impossible to read without a feeling of bitterness." The
League had been unable to maintain the territorial integrity and political
independence of one of its members, and it was possible that the League
itself would be declared bankrupt. Litvinov undertook to combat this
defeatist mood and to strengthen the collective security provisions of
the Covenant: "I say we do not want a League that is safe for aggressors.
We do not want that kind of League, even if it is universal, because it
would become the very opposite of an instrument of peace. . . .

"We must educate and raise people up to its lofty ideas, not degrade
the League. We must seek to make the League universal, but we must
not by any means make it safe for the aggressor to this end. On the contrary, all new members and all ex-members wishing to return must read
on its portals: 'Abandon all hope of aggression and its impunity all ye
who enter here.' . . .

"As for myself, I would rather have a League of Nations that tries
to render at least some assistance, even if it proves ineffective, to a
victim of aggression, than a League of Nations that closes its eyes to
aggression and lets it pass unperturbed. . . .

"In an ideal League of Nations military sanctions, too, should be obligatory for all. But if we are yet unable to rise to such heights of international solidarity, we should make it our concern to have all continents,
and for a start, at least all Europe, covered with a system of regional
pacts, on the strength of which groups of States would undertake to protect particular sectors from aggression."[35]

Finally, on September 28, 1936, he warned against the sense of apathy
that was spreading under the impact of the Axis: "The legend of the
invincible aggressor is being created even outside his country; it is

[33] League of Nations, *Official Journal, Special Supplement to No. 138*, p. 73.
[34] *Against Aggression*, p. 23.   [35] *ibid.*, pp. 35-45.

engendering fatalistic and capitulatory sentiments in some countries, which gradually—sometimes even without their noticing it—are beginning to lose their independence and are becoming vassals of the aggressor. Thus begins the process of the formation of a hegemony which is to culminate in the crushing of all refractory countries by force of arms."[36]

Toward the end of 1936, however, there were signs that the Soviet Union's new policy was not proving particularly fruitful. The growing menace of Germany, Italy, and Japan was not being checked. The efforts at collective security did not develop into anything substantial, and indeed the outbreak of the Spanish Civil War introduced new strains in the relations between the Soviets and France and Great Britain. The Popular Front adopted by the Comintern did not diminish the suspicions of the non-Communist states which continued to find that the activities of domestic Communists were a major impediment to collaboration with the Soviet Union. The great purges within Russia were under way and served to weaken Western confidence in the character and stability of the Soviet regime.

In Litvinov's speech before the Extraordinary Eighth Congress of Soviets, on November 28, 1936, a new note, or rather an old one, made its appearance. After commenting on the danger of fascism, not as a form of government but as a source of external aggression, after stressing the specifically anti-Soviet content of the anti-Comintern pact (he clearly had very accurate information on its secret terms), Litvinov waxed bitter over the policy of nonintervention in Spain, and uttered a definite word of warning to the non-Fascist Powers:

"The Soviet Union, however, does not beg to be invited to any unions, any *blocs*, any combinations. She will calmly let other States weigh and evaluate the advantages which can be derived for peace from close cooperation with the Soviet Union, and understand that the Soviet Union can give more than receive. . . .

"Other States, other territories are menaced most. Our security does not depend upon paper documents or upon foreign policy combinations. The Soviet Union is sufficiently strong in herself."[37]

From this time on, in Litvinov's speeches and reported statements two distinct themes are detectable: on the one hand, a continued appeal for collective security; on the other, increasing animus against Great Britain and France and the threat of a Soviet return to isolation. The first theme needs no further development as it is largely the exposition of the prin-

[36] *ibid.*, p. 49.   [37] *ibid.*, pp. 78-79.

ciples set forth in the preceding two or three years. The second and ominous theme tends to become more and more dominant.

On February 4, 1937, Litvinov complained to the United States ambassador, Joseph E. Davies, that "he could not understand why Great Britain could not see that once Hitler dominated Europe he would swallow the British Isles also. He seemed to be very much stirred about this and apprehensive lest there should be some composition of differences between France, England and Germany."[38] On February 15 he said that "Germany was concerned solely with conquest and it was a mistake to magnify Hitler's importance by engaging in discussions of the character which France and England were projecting."[39]

In a speech to the electors of Leningrad, on November 27, 1937, Litvinov reiterated the old theme that imperialism was inherent in all bourgeois states, and was heavily sarcastic about the efforts of France and Britain to pretend that the Fascist Powers were not aggressive: "I see it is a puzzle to you how experienced bourgeois diplomats could fail to understand the meaning of the aggressor's tactics. You think they are only pretending to disbelieve the aggressor's statements and, under cover of negotiations for confirmations and explanations, they are groping for a deal with the aggressor. You can think so if you like, but my position does not allow me to express such doubts, and I must leave them to your responsibility."[40]

In December Litvinov had an interview with a foreign correspondent in which he was reported, some years later, to have made the following significant remarks:

"Anti-Comintern Pact? What nonsense! Can you never look at things without your cheap bourgeois prejudice? The Anti-Comintern Pact is no threat to the Soviet Union. It is dust in the eyes of the Western democracies. . . . Ideologies mean little to the Fascist brigands. The Germans have militarized the Reich and are bent on a brutal policy of gangsterism. Those contemptible peoples, the Japanese and Italians, are following at the German heels, hoping to share in the spoils of German conquest. It is the rich capitalist countries which will fall an easy prey. The British and French peoples are soft under leaders who are blind. The Soviet Union is the last foe to be attacked by the Anti-Comintern powers. They will loot your countries, but we have the Red Army and a vast extent of territory. . . .

"Hitler and the generals who control Germany read history. They

---

[38] Joseph E. Davies, *Mission to Moscow* (New York, 1941), p. 60.
[39] *ibid.*, p. 79.　　　　[40] *Against Aggression*, pp. 106-107.

know that Bismarck warned against war on two fronts. They know that he urged the reinsurance policy with Russia. They believe the Kaiser lost the first world war because he forgot Bismarck's admonitions. When the Germans are prepared at last to embark upon their new adventures, these bandits will come to Moscow to ask us for a pact."[41] According to this report, he predicted the *Anschluss* and the attack on Czechoslovakia, and pointed out that the Soviet Union need not come to Czechoslovakia's aid unless France did: "Well, France won't fight. France is through."

By the spring of 1938 Litvinov had adopted a comparatively passive role, though still affirming that the Soviet Union was ready to join in collective action to arrest further aggression, and was willing to discuss measures within the League or outside it. In March 1938 he told Davies that Czechoslovakia would probably fall because it lacked confidence in France; for that matter "France has no confidence in the Soviet Union, and the Soviet Union has no confidence in France. . . . The only thing that would prevent a complete Fascist domination of Europe was a change of government or policy in Great Britain." He appeared to envisage within the near future a Europe dominated by fascism and opposed only by Great Britain on the West and the USSR on the East.[42]

The prolonged Czechoslovakian crisis of 1938 is far too complex for even summary discussion here. In general, it may be said that Litvinov, publicly and apparently privately, stood by the position that the Soviet Union would honor its obligations to Czechoslovakia if France came to the latter's aid. On the other hand, he repeatedly indicated that the responsibility for taking the initiative lay with France, and this included the thorny question of obtaining Polish and/or Rumanian permission for Russian troops to come to Czechoslovakia's assistance.

There does not seem to be much evidence, however, that he was expecting Russia to be required to take forceful action. It is striking that neither the British nor the German diplomatic representatives in Moscow felt that the Soviet government showed any sign of preparing itself or the Russian people for the defense of Czechoslovakia. The German ambassador, Schulenburg, commented that Litvinov's speech of June 23, 1938, showed distinct aloofness and a desire to retain freedom of action. Moreover, "the tone of the speech has remarkably little aggressiveness and strives to leave open all possibilities. The attempt to arrive at an objective attitude toward the policy of the Third Reich is striking."[43]

[41] J. T. Whitaker, *We Cannot Escape History* (New York, 1943), pp. 207-208.
[42] Davies, *Mission to Moscow*, p. 291.   [43] *German Documents*, series D, I, 924.

On August 22, 1938, Litvinov, in a conversation with Schulenburg was quite frank in charging Germany with aggression and a desire to destroy Czechoslovakia. He went on to say, however, "If the old democratic Germany still existed, the Czech question would have a quite different aspect for the Soviet Union." While the Soviet Union approved of national self-determination and had had no part in the creation of Czechoslovakia, the threat to its independence affected the balance of power: an increase in Nazi strength would be bad for the Soviet Union.[44] According to a British report the Germans felt that in this conversation Litvinov was opening the door for a possible German-Russian rapprochement.[45] Schulenburg, however, did not thus interpret his conversation, and its content as reported need not lead to such an interpretation.

Was Litvinov considering the possibility of independent Soviet action even if France failed to act? This question remains somewhat obscure. In May 1938 he asked the French ambassador Coulondre what France, the ally of Poland, would do in case the latter, having attacked Czechoslovakia, was itself attacked in turn by the USSR? Coulondre replied that the answer was obvious since France was also allied with Czechoslovakia, and both treaties were defensive. Coulondre also pointed out that France recognized that Russia was not bound to move unless France intervened. Litvinov replied, "That is right, but there is another hypothesis: the case in which the USSR for one reason or another should intervene without France having moved."[46] The question naturally presents itself, as it did to Coulondre at the time, whether the Soviet Union was envisaging military action against Poland and whether such action was possible without a preliminary understanding with Germany.

As far as the Czechs themselves are concerned, it is still not altogether clear whether, and if so how, they were led to believe that Russia would aid them even if France did not. Apparently Litvinov, through the Soviet minister in Prague, Alexandrovsky, did inform the Czech government that if the case were submitted to the League of Nations and Germany were found an aggressor, the Soviet Union would give assistance regardless of France.[47] This was clearly not a very rash promise under the circumstances. It has also been stated, though the evidence seems less satisfactory, that Alexandrovsky later informed the Czech government that the Soviet government would come to the support of Czechoslovakia as soon as Moscow was informed that the League had been

---

[44] *ibid.*, II, 604, 630. [45] *British Documents*, 3rd series, II, 141, note 3.
[46] Robert Coulondre, *De Staline à Hitler* (Paris, 1950), p. 153.
[47] Cf. Beloff, *Foreign Policy*, II, 151.

seized of the case and would not wait for a decision to be reached at Geneva.[48] Some years later Benes referred to "the fact that, in spite of the insistence of Moscow, I did not provoke war with Germany in 1938."[49] Some light on this remark may be cast by a statement in a recent Soviet work: "More than that, J. V. Stalin, in conversation with K. Gottwald, said that the Soviet Union was ready to give military aid to Czechoslovakia, even if France did not do this, but on the condition that Czechoslovakia defend itself and ask for Soviet assistance. Gottwald told Benes to that effect."[50] Although this statement requires a good deal of elucidation, it would indicate that such approaches, if made, may not have been through diplomatic channels but through the Communist party. In any event there appears to be no direct evidence connecting Litvinov with any measures more extensive than those to which the USSR was publicly committed: the Czech Treaty and the League of Nations. Furthermore, although Litvinov told the Germans that he thought France and England would assist Czechoslovakia, he seems to have been thoroughly skeptical. On September 16, in discussing with a foreign journalist ways and means of Soviet assistance, he remarked, "This is also unrealistic. . . . They have already sold Czechoslovakia down the river."[51]

In his last major speech in the League, on September 21, 1938, Litvinov bitterly criticized the record of the last few years: "A fire brigade was set up in the innocent hope that, by some lucky chance, there would be no fires. Things turned out differently, however. Fires have broken out in defiance of our hopes, but luckily not in our immediate vicinity: so let us dissolve the fire brigade—of course not forever, but merely temporarily. Directly the danger of any fire disappears, we shall reassemble the fire brigade without a moment's delay." He also carefully relieved the Soviet Union of any responsibility in the debacle: "At a moment when the mines are being laid to blow up the organization on which were fixed the great hopes of our generation, and which stamped a definite character on the international relations of our epoch; at a moment when, by no accidental coincidence, decisions are being taken outside the League which recall to us the international transactions of prewar days, and which are bound to overturn all present conceptions of international morality and treaty obligations; at a moment when there is

---

[48] John W. Wheeler-Bennett, *Munich—Prologue to Tragedy* (New York, 1948), p. 127.
[49] Letter from Eduard Benes to L. B. Namier, in Namier, *Europe in Decay*, p, 284.
[50] *Diplomaticheskii Slovar'* (1950), II, 198.
[51] Fischer, *Men and Politics*, p. 561.

being drawn up a further list of sacrifices to the god of aggression, and a line is being drawn under the annals of all postwar international history, with the sole conclusion that nothing succeeds like aggression—at such a moment, every State must define its role and its responsibility before its contemporaries and before history. That is why I must plainly declare here that the Soviet Government bears no responsibility whatsoever for the events now taking place, and for the fatal consequences which may inexorably ensue."[52] He concluded: "The Soviet Government takes pride in the fact that it has no part in such a policy, and has invariably pursued the principle of the two pacts I have mentioned, which were approved by nearly every nation in the world [the League Covenant and the Briand-Kellogg Pact]. Nor has it any intention of abandoning them for the future, being convinced that in present conditions it is impossible otherwise to safeguard a genuine peace and genuine international justice. It calls upon other Governments likewise to return to this path."

Despite these concluding remarks it was generally felt among European diplomats that the Munich agreement did mark the bankruptcy of the Litvinov policy and that the USSR would inevitably examine other possibilities. The German reaction is particularly interesting. Counselor of embassy in Moscow, von Tippelskirch, on October 3 and 10, 1938, wrote: "That the policy of Litvinov has suffered a complete fiasco, that the war, from which chaos and weakening of Germany were expected, has not broken out, that the policy of pacts and alliances has failed, that the collective idea has collapsed, and that the League of Nations has disappointed the hopes reposed in it, can in my opinion not remain without consequences for Soviet policy. . . .

"In the light of our experiences it seems to me probable that Stalin will draw conclusions about personalities from the failure of Soviet policy. In that connection I naturally think in the first place of Litvinov, who has made fruitless efforts in Geneva throughout the crisis. . . .[53]

"Litvinov will certainly try to convince the Soviet Government that the policy hitherto pursued by him was the only right one and that it must be continued in the future as well. . . . If I judge Litvinov correctly, he will continue to defend his policy of collective action in the conviction that Germany's growth of power . . . will lead to a change in the European balance of power in which sooner or later a definite role must quite automatically fall to the Soviet Union. . . . In other words he will con-

[52] *Against Aggression*, p. 127.
[53] *German Documents*, series D, IV, 602-605.

tinue to recommend measures against the aggressors in the hope of having more success next time."[54]

This German observer was, perhaps, unduly persuaded that Litvinov still had the opportunity to pursue his policy, or that he really felt capable of pressing it vigorously any longer. Shortly after Munich, Potemkin, Litvinov's assistant, after coldly receiving Coulondre, burst out: "My poor friend, what have you done? As for us I do not see any other outcome than a fourth partition of Poland."[55] And on October 16, Litvinov himself said: "Henceforth the USSR has only to watch, from the shelter of its frontiers, the establishment of German hegemony over the center and southeast of Europe. And if by chance the Western Powers finally decide to wish to stop it, they must address themselves to us, for— he added throwing me a sharp look—we shall have our word to say."[56] He then went on to remark that he had made the following declaration to Lord Halifax: "Once its hegemony is solidly established in Europe, and France neutralized, Hitler will be able to attack either Great Britain or the USSR. He will choose the first solution because it will offer him much greater advantages with the possibility of substituting the German Empire for the British Empire, and, to succeed in this undertaking, he will prefer to reach an understanding with the USSR."

In his discussions with the British after Munich Litvinov was distinctly cool; he saw no evidence that the Western Powers would cease their policy of capitulation, and said that the Soviet Union would probably remain "aloof" henceforth, since its interests were not directly threatened.[57] In late March 1939, in a conversation with R. S. Hudson, Litvinov was reported as saying: "He foresaw in the not far-distant future a Europe entirely German from the Bay of Biscay to the Soviet frontier and bounded, as it were, simply by Great Britain and the Soviet Union. Even that would not satisfy German ambitions, but the attack, he said smiling happily, would not be directed to the East."[58]

It is true that Litvinov was willing to embark on the final round of fruitless negotiations after the German march into Prague, but it was

---

[54] *ibid.*, p. 605.

[55] Coulondre, *De Staline à Hitler*, p. 165. On September 29, 1938, Potemkin said to Schulenburg: "The Powers now taking part in the destruction of Czechoslovakia would bitterly regret their submission to militant nationalism. In the first place, Poland, for there were a 'great many' Germans in Poland; in particular it must not be forgotten that several million Ukrainians were living in Poland, who were already beginning to 'move'." *German Documents*, series D, II, 998.

[56] Coulondre, *De Staline à Hitler*, p. 171.

[57] E.g., his conversation with Sir William Seeds, February 19, 1939. *British Documents*, 3rd series, IV, 124.

[58] *ibid.*, p. 585.

clear that he displayed no confidence in the Western Powers. On May 3, 1939, he was relieved of his post.

From this review of Litvinov's diplomatic career several general observations may be made. In the first place, his advocacy of collective security was limited in time: before the rise of the Fascist Powers, he denied the possibility of such methods of providing international security. Moreover, from 1936 on there is an increasing note of isolationism: if the other Powers would not cooperate the Soviet Union could follow its own interests independently. In the second place, the idea of collective security was restricted conceptually. Basically the world was still divided into two camps and the Fascist Powers belonged to the capitalist camp. "Peaceful coexistence" was not in the permanent order of things, nor were the motives inducing certain capitalist Powers to be peaceloving necessarily fundamental or enduring. Litvinov's collective security is not to be identified with the idealism of some of his Western admirers.

On the other hand, it is difficult to find evidence that Litvinov had any revolutionary expectations in these years or that by his diplomacy he was bent on fomenting strife. To be sure, the Soviet Union's total impact abroad, its unofficial as well as its official activities, remained troublesome and disturbing. It is also true that Litvinov's speeches to Soviet audiences displayed a truculent and scornful attitude toward the capitalist world which was moderated though not entirely eliminated in his diplomatic addresses to the League. Even so, his speeches on collective security in the League and elsewhere do have a most convincing ring of sincerity and urgency. By 1938 most foreign diplomatic observers in Moscow—Germans as well as French and English—seem to have felt that Litvinov was an ardent supporter of the course he had advocated since 1933.

If, with the above-mentioned qualifications, Litvinov's campaign for collective security was something real and not merely misleading oratory on his part, then the question arises whether his views and those of the Politburo coincided.

II

From all that is known of the structure of the Soviet state and the Communist party it would be absurd to assume that Litvinov could have pursued a diplomatic course at odds with that desired by Stalin and the inner circle of the Politburo. Clearly the general lines of his foreign policy had the official blessing. Nevertheless, an examination of the available record does reveal a number of instances during his career in which Litvinov was reportedly not in agreement with his superiors. Some of the more illuminating examples may be given, in chronological sequence:

In 1919 a British naval officer, who had an interview with Litvinov in Reval, reported that "M. Litvinoff stated that from the first he had opposed his Government's repudiation of their external debt, as he felt certain that such a course would tend to unify the resistance of other nations against them."[59]

In 1924, according to Christian Rakovsky, Litvinov wished to recognize Rumanian sovereignty over Bessarabia in order to settle the matter. Opposed to his view were Rakovsky, Chicherin, and Stalin, who felt it desirable to maintain Bessarabia as a "Soviet irredenta."[60]

Litvinov seems not to have been convinced of the value of Soviet and Comintern maneuvers in the colonial and Asiatic world at the expense of relations with the Western Powers. He is reported as having said, in March 1929, "I think an agreement with England about Afghanistan and the East generally is possible, but the government takes a different view."[61]

In 1938 it was the opinion of the German ambassador that the new evidence of Soviet antiforeign feeling shown in the closing of numerous consulates was not Litvinov's doing: "Litvinov has to accommodate himself to this predominance of domestic policy."[62]

In January 1938 both Zhdanov and Molotov publicly criticized the Foreign Commissariat, though not Litvinov in person, for its presumed lenience with France, which was accused of harboring anti-Soviet elements, terrorists, and diversionists.[63]

In the summer of 1938 Coulondre told Schulenburg that Litvinov was willing to agree to Soviet participation in defraying expenses occasioned by the withdrawal of volunteer troops from Spain, but had encountered opposition in the Politburo. Litvinov seemed willing to cut losses in the Spanish affair, but the Politburo had prestige considerations.[64]

On March 1, 1939, Schulenburg, referring to Soviet economic negotiations with Germany and Japan, remarked that "M. Litvinov does not regard M. Mikoyan's negotiations with a friendly eye at all. If by obstinacy toward Japan he can sabotage the zealous activities of the Commissar for Foreign Trade, he will intensify rather than moderate this line of action.[65]

---

[59] *British Documents*, 1st series, III, 659.   [60] Fischer, *Men and Politics*, p. 135.
[61] *ibid.*, p. 128. See also David Dallin, *The Rise of Russia in Asia* (New York, 1949), p. 240.
[62] *German Documents*, series D, I, 905.   [63] Beloff, *Foreign Policy*, II, 113-114
[64] *German Documents*, series D, III, 714.   [65] *ibid.*, IV, 628.

Louis Fischer has remarked that Litvinov "has never by word or hint approved of Stalin's pact policy with Hitler."[66] It is obvious, of course, that the German-Soviet rapprochement of 1939 was hardly in the spirit of collective security, that the nonaggression pact of August 23 did not contain the escape clause in the event one of the signatories attacked a third Power. On the other hand, as should be apparent from the above, it is not difficult to find a number of hints of a possible German-Soviet agreement in Litvinov's private remarks from 1937 on. Still, it is worth noting that after the German attack on the USSR in June 1941, and after Stalin in his speech of July 3 had defended the wisdom of the nonaggression pact, Litvinov, in a broadcast in English on July 8, indicated that agreements of any sort with Hitler were worthless because the Nazi gang considered themselves above all conceptions of international obligations. While commenting on the failure to organize collective resistance, he stressed Hitler's technique of dividing his prospective victims: "His strategy is to knock down his victims and strike them one by one in an order prompted by circumstances. He intended first to deal with the Western countries so that he would be free to fall on the Soviet Union." Not only was this no defense of the German-Soviet pact—which would hardly have been a tactful approach to the British and American audience at whom the broadcast was directed—but the whole line of argument was that Hitler's treachery was inevitable and predictable.[67]

Finally, evidence of Litvinov's disapproval of Soviet policy following World War II has been provided by two American reporters writing shortly after his death. C. L. Sulzberger stated that on April 5, 1945, Litvinov, then an isolated figure in Moscow, expressed his pessimism about East-West relations: "The situation is developing badly. First, the Western Powers make a mistake and rub us the wrong way. Then we make a mistake and rub you the wrong way."[68] Richard C. Hottelet wrote that in June 1946 Litvinov indicated to him that the Soviets would continue pressing demands on the West. "As far as I am concerned the root cause is the ideological conception prevailing here that conflict between the Communist and capitalist worlds is inevitable." He declared that the Soviet rulers would not call on him for advice and had reverted to the outmoded concept of security in terms of territory.[69]

While it is difficult to weigh the importance of these scattered examples, they do seem to have a certain consistency: in each case Litvinov

[66] Louis Fischer, *The Great Challenge* (New York, 1946), p. 46.
[67] *New York Times*, July 9, 1941.   [68] *New York Times*, January 3, 1952.
[69] *New York World-Telegram*, January 28-February 1, 1952.

appears to have favored practical accommodation with the Western Powers as against moves to create or abet revolution, disturbance, or international disorder. To be sure, such an attitude would be part of his diplomatic function: his job as Foreign Commissar was not made easier by the Communist temptation to kick things around.

Less tangible than these evidences of disagreements on policy but perhaps as important are the subtler indications of a difference in emphasis and interpretation. In a political system where all action and policy is dependent upon a "party line" enunciated by the supreme authority, emphasis and interpretation are all-important, especially since the "line" is often not wholly unambiguous. For example, the theme which underlies Soviet diplomacy throughout most of the interwar period—"the temporary coexistence of the two systems"—can in practice be given two entirely different meanings depending upon the emphasis accorded "temporary" or "coexistence." Although it is perilous to draw conclusions from purely external evidence, there appear to be a number of respects in which Litvinov's interpretation differed from that of the Politburo—Stalin and the rather murky figures of his inner circle.

While Litvinov always acknowledged that the possibilities of cooperation with the capitalist Powers were temporary, that ultimately the capitalist system was doomed to destruction, in the period after Hitler came to power he recognized the Nazi menace as something requiring the cooperative resistance of the peace-loving Powers, not as the turbulent prologue to the victory of Communism. This mood is quite apparent in his speech of December 29, 1933. Yet at the same time, on December 31, 1933, the official journal *Bolshevik* could still give the following interpretation of the German situation: "In Germany the proletarian revolution is nearer to realization than in any other country; and victory of the proletariat in Germany means victory of proletarian revolution throughout Europe, since capitalist Europe cannot exist if it loses its heart. . . . He who does not understand the German question does not understand the path of the development of proletarian revolution in Europe."[70] Stalin's speech of January 26, 1934, while less far out on the limb, is much more revolution-conscious than Litvinov's.[71] One receives the impression that the Politburo was reluctant and regretful in accepting the new course.

Indeed, Litvinov as a diplomat seems always to have found the irrepressible revolutionary yearnings of the Bolsheviks an uncomfortable

---

[70] Quoted in David Dallin, *Russia and Post-War Europe* (New Haven, 1943), p. 62.
[71] See above, §1.

problem. In a letter to an English negotiator in December 1919, he said: "From the point of view of the vital interests of both countries there should be no obstacle to the establishment of real peace, excepting the bogey of revolutionary propaganda. If formal guarantees from the Soviet Government on this point be considered insufficient, could not means of preventing this propaganda be devised without barring the way to mutual representation?"[72]

The change in the Comintern line at the Seventh Congress in 1935 did not really eradicate this difference. Although Litvinov's diplomatic policy of "collective security" and the Popular Front are often identified, it is doubtful whether this identification should be pressed too far, even though both had Stalin's approval in some fashion. A reasonably attentive reading of Dimitrov's speeches at the Seventh Congress can dispel the popular notion that the Comintern had now really concealed its hard revolutionary core. Certainly, the energetic behavior of the comrades under the new line caused Litvinov perpetual embarrassment. In 1936, for example, Coulondre pointed out to him that the interference of the Comintern in French internal affairs was imperiling the Franco-Soviet pact. In response, Litvinov, after assuring him that the Soviet Union had no intention of interfering and that the Soviet ambassador in Paris had received instructions to that effect—which he would make even more precise—was obliged to fall back on the old claim that the Comintern had nothing to do with the foreign policy of the Soviet government. Coulondre felt, however, that Litvinov was fully aware that this customary disclaimer of responsibility for the Comintern carried no conviction. "But the question went beyond him. It concerned the other side of the double ladder on the top of which sat Stalin alone."[73]

Although Litvinov frequently expressed disapproval and suspicion of the capitalist nations and, in the years after 1936, was extremely critical of the policies of France and Great Britain, he does not seem to have been so deeply imbued with that xenophobia which has increasingly blighted the perception of Soviet leaders. It should not be forgotten that he lived a decade in England, from 1908 to 1918, during which time he settled rather thoroughly into a middle-class existence and married an English wife.

With regard to Germany, while Litvinov certainly subscribed to the general line that the Soviet Union did not desire bad relations with Germany and would welcome a resumption of cordial relations should

---

[72] *British Documents*, 1st series, III, 740.
[73] Coulondre, *De Staline à Hitler*, pp. 32-33.

the German government drop its menacing attitude, he does not seem to have shared the enthusiasm which a number of Russians and Germans had for the Russo-German connection. Dirksen, as mentioned earlier, felt that Litvinov was not a true believer in the Rapallo policy and was pro-English at heart. In March 1936, following the march into the Rhineland, the Soviet statements concerning Germany seemed to display some confusion. On the one hand, Litvinov in the League castigated Germany's recent actions in very sharp terms; on the other, Molotov said to a French editor: "The main trend among our people, the trend which determines the policy of the Soviet Government, considers an improvement in relations between Germany and the Soviet Union possible. . . . The participation of Germany in the League of Nations would be in the interest of peace and would be favorably regarded by us." "Even of Hitler Germany?", asked the French journalist. "Yes, even of Hitler Germany."[74] While there may be no logical contradiction between the two Soviet statements, they have a quite different flavor.

The German-Soviet pact of 1939 inevitably created the suspicion that some Soviet leaders, including Stalin, were always eager for a rapprochement with Germany and had made secret contacts with Hitler even during the period of so-called collective security. Coulondre, who said that he was convinced that Litvinov was, like himself, "a sincere worker for the Franco-Soviet entente within the framework of the League of Nations,"[75] also commented, "I am not even sure that during all that period of my mission in the USSR, certain clandestine contacts had ever ceased between Moscow and Berlin."[76] He was of the opinion that something was definitely in preparation in the spring of 1937, only to be dropped in April.[77] The former Soviet intelligence officer, Krivitsky, professed to know that in the spring of 1937 an agreement had been drafted by Stalin and Hitler, with one David Kandelaki as the intermediary, but had broken down.[78] This source also stated, however, that the Commissariat for Foreign Affairs had no part whatever in this undertaking.

[74] See Beloff, *Foreign Policy*, II, 51-54.   [75] Coulondre, *De Staline à Hitler*, p. 32.
[76] *ibid.*, p. 45.   [77] *ibid.*, p. 125.
[78] W. G. Krivitsky, *In Stalin's Secret Service* (New York, 1939), pp. 225-226. The thesis that Stalin was, all along, seeking for a deal with Hitler encounters difficulties in having to explain all the anti-German steps taken by the Soviet Union between 1933 and 1938. Krivitsky contended that the entry into the League, collective security, the pact with France, the intervention in Spain were all undertaken with a view to making Hitler find it "advantageous to meet his [Stalin's] advances." This seems a singularly round-about way to achieve a rapprochement. Still, this tactic of trying to win an ally by making things uncomfortable for him is not unknown in the history of diplomacy. William II and Holstein tried to woo Britain by the threat of a continental bloc against it.

In general, even after one has made deductions for the fact that Litvinov, as a diplomat dealing with the outside, capitalist world, was likely to adopt a less revolutionary stance than Communists dealing with Communists or, perhaps, dictators with dictators, there still seems to remain a not unimportant difference between the diplomatic policy advocated or desired by him and the temper of the Politburo, a difference occasionally showing up in specific disagreements but more persistently if less tangibly in shadings of interpretation and emphasis. These, however, form a sufficiently coherent pattern to warrant the conclusion that there was a tension of ideas within the monolithic framework of the Soviet government. If so, is it possible to form any notion of the political or bureaucratic relations behind this tension?

III

A preceding chapter has shown that diplomacy as such did not stand very high in the hierarchy of instruments developed or revamped by the new Soviet order. Foreign considerations tended to rank below domestic considerations during most of the interwar period, and even in the field of foreign relations the diplomatic arm lacked the prestige of the revolutionary and the military arms. At the same time, because of the peculiar sensitiveness attaching to foreign policy decisions there came to be "a particularly close, direct, and continual relationship . . . between the Politburo and the Narkomindel in the conduct and control of foreign affairs."[79] Consequently the post as Peoples Commissar for Foreign Affairs did not, in itself, carry a great deal of weight in the Soviet system.

Nor did Litvinov, despite the fact that he was an "old Bolshevik,"[80] rank high in the Party. He was never in the all-important Politburo, though he was a member of the Party's Central Committee for a number of years. Two reasons may help to explain why he was never admitted to the inner circle despite his obvious ability and long record as a party member. He had not returned to Russia from England to participate in the Bolshevik revolution. From the very first he was concerned not with the establishment of the revolutionary state but with its relations abroad. Moreover, even before the revolution he seems to have been valued pri-

[79] Julian Towster, *Political Power in the* USSR., *1917-1947* (New York, 1948), p. 162. Towster points out that in the late 1920's while nearly all the governmental organs were scheduled to report before the Politburo, the Narkomindel apparently was not, presumably because decisions concerning foreign issues were continuously on the agenda of the Politburo itself.

[80] He joined the Russian Social Democratic Labor party in 1898 and was on Lenin's side when the latter formed the Bolshevik faction against the Mensheviks in 1903.

marily as a competent technician. In Lenin's references to him during the war as "our legal representative in the International Socialist Bureau," the term "legal" is charged with the characteristic double meaning of being official and public but not really part of the illegal or extralegal revolutionary core. While part of his function as Chicherin's second in the 1920's may have been as Bolshevik guardian over a former Menshevik,[81] it is doubtful whether in the long run his party status was any higher than that of his predecessor; in the opinion of the German ambassador who worked with both men, it was lower.[82]

Consequently, neither as Peoples Commissar nor as a party member was Litvinov in a position to follow his own policy or even to initiate policy. Indeed, late in his career he is reported as remarking rather sourly: "You know what I am. I merely hand on diplomatic documents."[83]

It is, therefore, difficult to see just how Litvinov was in any position to differ significantly with the Politburo. Moreover, Litvinov's term in office overlapped the years of the Great Purges, in which, so it seems, even half-formed or possibly-to-be-formed disagreements were sufficient to destroy a man. Yet Litvinov retained not only his health but his post.

His success in surviving the purges was something of a surprise and miracle to contemporary observers. He was an old Bolshevik; old Bolsheviks were dropping like flies. He headed the Foreign Commissariat; the Foreign Commissariat and the embassies abroad were swept clean. The former Soviet diplomat, Alexander Barmine, comments on Litvinov's "inexplicably surviving all his friends and collaborators": "Two of Litvinov's four assistants were executed, the third was put in prison and the fourth disappeared. His old friends and personal protégés, Ambassadors Yurenev and Rosenberg, disappeared also. Almost all the heads of departments of his ministry and the leading diplomatic personnel abroad, gathered and trained by him over fifteen years, were shot. But Litvinov continued to smile enigmatically. 'They were traitors; all is well!' Was he so confident because he deemed himself indispensable, or did he have to keep a good face because his family were held as hostages?"[84] Litvinov does seem to have been jolted by the arrest of his assistant Krestinsky,[85] but in general his recorded remarks indicate approval of the purges as a necessity to rid the Soviet Union of treasonous elements.

[81] See, for example, Simon Liberman, *Building Lenin's Russia* (Chicago, 1945), p. 111.
[82] Dirksen, *Moskau, Tokio, London*, p. 94.
[83] Fischer, *Men and Politics*, p. 497.
[84] Alexander Barmine, *One Who Survived* (New York, 1945), p. 121.
[85] Davies, *Mission to Moscow*, p. 262.

Inasmuch as the underlying intent of the purges remains one of the major riddles of Soviet history,[86] it is impossible here to unravel their meaning in the Foreign Commissariat. While some observers have been inclined to regard the diplomatic housecleaning as a preparation for the agreement with Hitler, the part played by foreign policy considerations is by no means clear beyond the fairly obvious fact that people with foreign contacts and foreign experiences were frequent victims, but this may have been for reasons other than the direction of foreign policy itself. The effect of the purge was to reduce even further any independence of action or decision on the part of foreign service officials, an increasing number of whom apparently were attached to the NKVD, and to leave Litvinov a general without an army.

As to Litvinov's own survival, a few comments may be made. In the first place, he may have been fortunate in the fact that while an old Bolshevik he had *not* been one of the inner circle which made the revolution, and consequently had not become enmeshed in the struggle for power within the party, a struggle which produced a very high death rate among the contestants. Moreover, so long as the policy of "collective security" was officially upheld by the Soviet Union, Litvinov's removal or disappearance would have had unfavorable foreign repercussions. By the time he was dropped the purges had subsided. Finally, it is clear that Litvinov must have possessed in some sense or another Stalin's confidence. It is difficult to believe that for all his international political value he could have survived those years of unimaginable suspicion had Stalin not had confidence in his personal as well as his political loyalty. The thesis, however, that Litvinov really believed that Stalin was purging the Foreign Commissariat to rid it of a Fascist fifth column seems quite unlikely, especially since the course of the purges generally started with a suspected chief and spread out through the ranks of his associates and subordinates. Nor does the contrary thesis that Litvinov and Stalin were clandestinely retooling the Narkomindel for a German rapprochement carry conviction; besides making utter nonsense of Litvinov's public policy it increases the difficulty of accounting for his dismissal.

The conclusion that seems able to deal with these confused and contradictory problems most satisfactorily is the one which sees Stalin as always having several strings to his bow. If one assumes that he was capable of considering simultaneously two separate and even conflicting

[86] Two authors, with firsthand experience in the purges, have recently enumerated seventeen theories which have been advanced to explain the purges: F. Beck and W. Godin, *Russian Purge and the Extraction of Confession* (New York, 1951). With unusual reserve they do not pretend to know the answer.

lines of policy, not making up his mind in advance but waiting to see how events developed, then it is possible, perhaps, to reconcile the elements of difference discussed above and the fact that Litvinov was not a victim of the purge.

According to this interpretation, which is the most this paper can attempt to offer, there were at least two contending lines of foreign policy within the Politburo, and perhaps within Stalin's own mind, in the 1930's: one, the "Litvinov policy," of which Litvinov himself was not only the agent but probably also the advocate and possibly even the formulator (even in a monolithic state ideas cannot all originate at the apex of the pyramid); the other, the policy which emerged with the pact of August 23, 1939, and acquired explicit characteristics in the two years following. Stalin, while perhaps inclined toward the second, was willing to give the first a trial, especially since no other alternative appeared profitable after 1933: the revolutionary line had brought few results and did not fit well with domestic developments, the Rapallo connection seemed impossible with Hitler's Germany behaving in an exceedingly unfriendly fashion. On the other hand the "Litvinov policy" depended upon achieving results. When these failed to come about the balance—whether between persons in the Politburo or between ideas in Stalin's own mind—would swing away from it. Thus, Litvinov's warnings after 1936 that "collective security" could be wrecked if the Western Powers did not change their ways may be regarded as a reflection of a decision still in suspension in the Politburo, a forewarning of a course which he himself may not have favored but which was in the cards if collective security failed.[87]

This interpretation also seems able to meet the question of Litvinov's resignation on May 3, 1939. The terse Soviet announcement merely stated that his resignation had been at his request because of ill health. Since the war, however, the official Soviet explanation has been that in the spring of 1939, when the international situation was deteriorating, when the Soviet Union was threatened with a hostile combination of capitalist Powers, "it was necessary to have in such a responsible post as that of Peoples Commissar for Foreign Affairs, a political leader of

[87] When discussing the possible failure of collective security, Litvinov often indicated that the USSR might do well to return to isolation. Now the Molotov-Ribbentrop Pact was scarcely a return to isolation but, as it proved, a decision to collaborate in aggression (the purely defensive interpretation of Russia's advances during the period of the pact seems inadequate in light of the documents published in *Nazi-Soviet Relations*, esp. pp. 258-259). Hence in his occasional predictions that the Germans would seek a pact with the Soviet Union, Litvinov may have been predicting a development which he himself did not approve.

greater experience and greater popularity in the country than M. M. Litvinov."[88]

While this statement is true in the sense that the authority of the Politburo was now concerned with the immediate direction of foreign relations, it does not suggest the possibility of a change in policy. At the time, quite naturally, the Soviet government and its representatives abroad assured the other Powers that the switch in Foreign Commissars meant no alteration in the direction of Soviet policy. These assurances were received with justified skepticism, however, and one of the most interested parties, Hitler, later said, "Litvinov's dismissal was decisive."[89] To be sure, Stalin's speech of March 10 at the Eighteenth Congress of the Communist Party had served to pave the way, as had the remarks on April 17 by the Soviet ambassador in Berlin.[90] Nevertheless, it can be concluded that Litvinov's retirement was a very important step in the German-Soviet rapprochement, if only because he was a Jew and had come to symbolize the effort at collective security against German aggression.

While Litvinov's retirement certainly facilitated the German-Soviet negotiations which led to the pact, was it a mark of "no confidence" in him or his diplomacy? His American biographer, whose account of the event was obtained directly from Litvinov during the latter's ambassadorship in the United States during the war, denies that he was discharged or abruptly dismissed. According to this account, Litvinov, after Munich, decided that a rapprochement with Germany was necessary, that he was an obstacle, and suggested his own retirement. The resignation took place untheatrically after a series of conferences with Stalin, and Litvinov himself proposed his friend Molotov as a successor.[91]

This interpretation has Litvinov's authority for its authenticity. And while it is true that he was, in 1942-1943, an official representative of the Soviet government and therefore not likely to stress conflicts in the conduct of Soviet diplomacy, it is also true that he was often surprisingly frank in such matters and not inclined to allow personal concerns to flavor his thinking. Nevertheless, there are certain difficulties with this interpretation. The postwar Soviet explanation seems to imply, quite ungraciously if the change had been marked by full harmony, that Litvinov was not a

---

[88] *Falsifiers of History*, Supplement to "New Times" (Moscow), No. 8, February 18, 1948, p. 9. See also *Diplomaticheskii Slovar'*, II, 162 and 675.

[89] "Notes on Hitler's Conference with his Commanders-in-Chief, August 22, 1939," *Documents on International Affairs 1939-46*, I, 446.

[90] *Nazi-Soviet Relations*, pp. 1-2.

[91] Pope, *Litvinoff*, pp. 441-442. The author is grateful to Mr. Pope for his letter explaining that Litvinov had personally confirmed this account of his resignation.

big enough man for the job. The picture of Litvinov, not a member of the Politburo, nominating the powerful Molotov to be his successor, appears incongruous. Moreover, there is some evidence that Litvinov was in disgrace with fortune and Stalin's eyes. Early in May 1939 the unusually communicative, and perhaps unreliable, Soviet chargé in Berlin, Astakhov, told Coulondre that for six months Litvinov's fall had been foreseeable, since he and Molotov were no longer in accord, and Stalin, while esteeming him, did not like him.[92] After his retirement he seems to have received a cold shoulder at Soviet public functions.[93] In a speech on August 31, 1939, Molotov criticized those "short-sighted people even in our own country who, carried away by oversimplified anti-Fascist propaganda, forgot about this provocative work of our enemies [the machinating Western European politicians],"[94] a remark that may be interpreted as a slap at Litvinov. On February 20, 1941, Litvinov was dropped from the Central Committee of the Communist party for "inability to discharge obligations."[95]

It is possible, then, that Litvinov was under a cloud; that Stalin had weighed his policy and found it wanting. At the same time he was not officially damned, partly because the policy connected with his name had been Stalin's also, at least nominally; partly, it would seem, because he might still be useful should circumstances change, as they did in June 1941. Still, the remainder of his career is an anticlimax. During his brief ambassadorship in the United States from 1941 to 1943 he was not the leading figure he had been in the 1930's. After the war he sank again into obscurity. At his death on December 31, 1951, he was a minor Soviet hero—with members of the Foreign Ministry as pallbearers, but no one from the Politburo. In the second volume of the Soviet Diplomatic Dictionary, published in 1950, the favorable but brief biography of Litvinov occupies 92 lines, as compared with 54 for Chicherin and 292 for Molotov. Stalin's accomplishments as a diplomat were, of course, too vast for inclusion or comparison.

[92] Quoted in Georges Bonnet, *Fin d'une Europe* (Paris, 1946), p. 184.

[93] It may be worth mentioning that the daughter of a former NKVD official attached to the Foreign Commissariat has recently written that immediately after Litvinov's resignation and replacement by Molotov her father was purged as a part of a general, though unexplained, house cleaning in that ministry. Nora Murray (née Korzhenko), *I Spied for Stalin* (New York, 1951), pp. 116-129.

[94] V. M. Molotov, *The Meaning of the Soviet-German Non-Aggression Pact* (New York, 1939), p. 8.

[95] According to Pope, *Litvinoff*, p. 460, this step was taken because "Stalin was determined to give no offense to the Germans." In that case it is difficult to see why Maisky, Soviet ambassador to Great Britain, should have been elevated to alternate membership on the Central Committee at the same time.

IV

In retrospect Litvinov's "collective security" can be seen to have been largely a phrase, never a reality. Neither the Soviet Union nor the Western Powers were ever really guided by the principle of common action against the rising danger from Germany; both ardently hoped that the hurricane, if it developed, would not come in their direction. The "appeasement" policies of France and Great Britain have been thoroughly criticized by disapproving citizens of those states. There was also, however, a corresponding tendency in Russia which sought a reconciliation with Nazi Germany. This tendency was naturally less apparent so long as the major force of Hitler's propaganda was directed against Soviet Communism.

Even Litvinov's position appears reasonably clear and unambiguous only during the short span from 1933 to 1936—before Germany was equipped to fight a war. After it was clear that the Third Reich was, willy-nilly, going to become a powerful military state, his pleas for collective measures were interspersed with warnings of a Soviet return to isolation. By the time of the Munich crisis his support of collective security was form without content: he was sure that France and England would not move; the French, the British—and the Germans—were equally convinced the Russians would not move.

Nor, in the long run, did Litvinov's efforts to "find a common language" between the Soviet Union and the rest of the world succeed. This failure needs no emphasis today. Indeed Litvinov may have been a cause for deepening the rift. The atmosphere of practical cooperativeness which he created partly concealed but in no way softened the hard core of the Stalinist regime. As a result, collisions with that hard core were not only bruising but carried the additional sting of disillusion.

Still, after this has been said and after one recognizes that future documentary revelations may further darken the picture of Soviet policy between the wars and present Litvinov in a more doubtful light, the late Foreign Commissar does have claim to two things of lasting significance: his ideas and his acumen as a diplomat. Regardless of the aims of Soviet foreign policy or of Litvinov's connection with those aims, the ideas he expressed in his major League speeches are important in themselves. Indeed, whole paragraphs describe, in mood as in content, the tasks facing the world today in its effort to check the new danger of Soviet expansion. His ability to detect the major trends in the 1930's and to anticipate the course of events indicates an extraordinary understanding of that decade.

The most recent historian of the League of Nations has remarked on Litvinov's role in that organization: "No future historian will lightly disagree with any views expressed by Litvinov on international questions. Whatever may be thought of the policy and purposes of his government, the long series of his statements and speeches in the Assembly, the Council, the Conferences, and Committees of which he was a member between 1927 and 1939 can hardly be read today without an astonished admiration. Nothing in the annals of the League can compare with them in frankness, in debating power, in the acute diagnosis of each situation. No contemporary statesman could point to such a record of criticisms justified and prophecies fulfilled."[96]

While one might quarrel with the inclusion of the years 1927-1933, it is difficult to disagree with this conclusion for the six years between Hitler's coming to power and Litvinov's retirement from the diplomatic scene.

[96] F. P. Walters, *A History of the League of Nations* (2 vols., London, 1952), II, 712.

12

Alexis Saint-Léger Léger

BY ELIZABETH R. CAMERON

DIPLOMACY, says Alexis Léger, is imagination, foresight, suggestion, representation, execution. The diplomat is the master of critical analysis and the creator of large designs. He must have courage, he must have patience, he must accept humbly the limits of the possible. In disagreement with his ministers, he must combat the false to the best of his ability, but always as their loyal subordinate. In construction and prevention alike, his role remains hermetic and anonymous. This is Léger's conception of the diplomat: he is an innovator, but also an executor bound by the disciplines of the civil servant.[1]

Léger's career as a diplomat spans the quarter of a century from 1914 to 1940. He entered the service at the beginning of the first world war. He was dismissed from the highest post in the French Foreign Office only a few weeks before the defeat of France by Nazi Germany.

From the start he was no ordinary diplomat. He was a poet, and, as a poet, lived in a world not much frequented by other diplomats. But he was also capable of their world, experienced in many worlds, and not least in the worldly society of the French capital. His courtesy was famous though not always comfortable, and often of a kind to put him out of

[1] The story of Léger's diplomatic career as found in French and foreign sources is extremely fragmentary. The available British and German documents cover only a fraction of the period, and in them the role of the permanent services remains, for the most part, anonymous. The *French Yellow Book*, the only official publication of the Ministry of Foreign Affairs for the period just before the war, has been carefully tailored and contains nothing on the work of Léger. A large part of the archives of the Quai d'Orsay was burned in Paris in May 1940, and of the part saved still more was afterwards lost at sea. There are memoirs, in profusion, by French politicians, soldiers and journalists, and despite their controversial character, they yield some valuable information on Léger's attitudes and accomplishments. There is further evidence, unfortunately not free of political bias, in the report and hearings of the French parliamentary commission charged with investigating the events of the war and prewar years in France. But the reader will see how important Léger's personal testimony is in this study. Wherever references to his record and opinions are not documented, they are taken from conversations between Léger and the writer in Washington in December 1951.

reach.[2] Many, and most of all the worldly and the ambitious, were made uneasy by his aloofness, the subtleties of his language, and the sinuous progressions of his thought.

Léger's life presents a series of contrasts, and it does not yield to simple analysis. As one writer has said, he is a man of East and West, and of both shores of the Atlantic; he is a man also of silence and of the word; a man of worldly possessions and a man stripped of them; a solitary and a lover of the human race; a man of pleasure and an ascetic; a man of culture and a man at home with the elements.[3] These contrasts suggest deep layers in Léger's character and experience. And in their own way, they help to explain his loyalties, the friends and enemies he made through his long and critical course in French foreign policy.

Léger was born in the late 1880's on a small coral island in the Antilles, "the son of a family French as only the colonials are French." From the age of eleven, when he left the scene of an idyllic childhood in the tropics, he was educated in Paris, in literature, medicine, and the law. He completed his training for the Diplomatic Service, and went out to China in 1916 as a junior secretary. Here he lived in Peking in a rented temple, "sat with the philosophers and sages," and broke the life of diplomatic conversations and official cables with journeys overland across the Gobi Desert, and overseas to the far islands of the Pacific. In the East, writes another poet, Léger "learned the art by which a man defends his life from others and even from himself."[4]

The China post was his only foreign service, a fact always held against him by his colleagues in the field. The rest of his professional life was spent within the walls of the Quai d'Orsay. He served first on the Asiatic desk, and later went to the political and commercial division, of which he became chief in 1929. He succeeded to the office of Secretary General with the rank of ambassador of France in 1933, following Philippe Berthelot.

From the mid-1920's, when Léger's rapid rise in the diplomatic hierarchy began, his professional career falls into two periods of equal length: seven years of service under Briand (1925-1932), and seven years as "the permanent master of French foreign policy" (1933-1940). The first was a period of design and realization. The second was "*décadence*," a phase

[2] André Gide in *Les Cahiers de la Pléiade* (St-Jean Perse issue), Summer-Autumn 1950, pp. 23-24.
[3] Gabriel Bounoure, *ibid.*, pp. 107-108.
[4] Archibald MacLeish in *Exil and other Poems*, by St-Jean Perse (New York, 1949), pp. 143-144.

of contraction when all diplomatic operations were conducted on a steadily narrowing base.

The long contact with Briand began in 1921 at the Washington Disarmament Conference, to which Léger was called as a Far Eastern expert. Impressed by the insight of the young diplomat, Briand later invited him to join his personal secretariat, and in 1925 Léger became Briand's *chef de cabinet*. This was a political appointment, and in it Léger had great influence on the shaping of French foreign policy. In effect, he became the intimate collaborator in all Briand's plans for peace and security.

Léger, by 1925, was already a poet of reputation, though under a different name. But when he took service with Briand, he turned himself over completely to diplomacy. He published no verse from 1924 until the years of his exile from France in the 1940's, and the story goes that when Briand asked Léger about the early works of "St-Jean Perse," Léger refused to claim their authorship.[5] He never allowed the private labors or public acclaim of the poet to impinge on the professional dedication of the diplomat.

In Briand Léger found many of the qualities upon which he has always patterned himself: "the boldness of the dream . . . tempered . . . by the dictates of common sense"; the speed of suggestion and retort equaled only by "indifference to the exploitation of success." Briand, he writes, "had no need of duplicity or violence to win. . . . He hated equally stupidity, cowardice, clumsiness and vulgarity. . . . He hunted with the lightest arms, and fished with the finest lines. . . . He brought the refinement of the artist to the handling of men."[6] The skills of the master entered deeply into the consciousness of the pupil, and in Léger they were reflected in a subtlety and complexity often misunderstood by the diplomats and politicians with whom he worked.

From Briand Léger had also learned the rules which guided French diplomacy in the period of construction, and in a published tribute to Briand they are stated in Léger's own words:

First: "To insure for France in particular all possible elements of immediate security."

Second: "Under cover of this immediate security, and in rhythm with its development, to seek the broader bases of European peace."

Third: "To extend beyond Europe the solidarity of nations against war."

Fourth: "In case of pressing risks, to put aside the ambitious plans, and

[5] Louis-Marcel Raymond in *Cahiers de la Pléiade*, p. 125.
[6] Alexis Léger, *Briand* (Aurora, N.Y., 1943), pp. 6-7.

[380]

to concentrate exclusively upon assembling all the forces necessary for the exercise of collective action in prevention."[7]

In Briand's time, says Léger, "these directives were followed so clearly that French foreign policy could never be accused of the least ambiguity."[8] For her own "immediate security," France had her pacts of mutual assistance with Poland and Czechoslovakia. And in the West, Briand had finally succeeded in winning British recognition of the principle of shared responsibility. The Locarno Pact of 1925 was his contribution to the insurance of the critical Rhineland area, and in it Léger had worked with him in all the difficult preparatory stages and in the drafting of the final texts. To its designers, the peculiar virtue of Locarno was that it was both "collective" and "automatic," committing the guarantors to defend the Rhine, committing them further to act in case Germany violated the forbidden demilitarized zone.

With this agreement as the solid base of French security, Briand and Léger moved on to explore "the broader bases of European peace." Together they drafted a plan for an organic statute of Europe, and this plan was first rehearsed in Briand's Commission for European Union. Outside Europe, their device for drawing America in, to make her "first gesture of moral and psychological solidarity," was the Kellogg-Briand Pact.

Taken as a whole, it was an ambitious scheme of diplomacy, ranging from precise guarantees at the chief danger point, to long-range planning for new international ties and institutions. But by 1930, political danger signals in Germany had begun already to expose France to the "pressing risks" which Briand had foreseen. And, as Léger points out, the last painful efforts of Briand's life were expended in the "most urgent of diplomatic campaigns,"[9] the effort to alert the Powers to real and pressing danger.

When Briand died in 1932, Léger was in the small circle which stood beside his deathbed. He inherited many things from Briand which were deep and lasting in their effect on his diplomacy. But the immediate inheritance, the thing that came to Léger most directly, something to which he felt an almost personal commitment, was the burden of the watch on security. In the year of Briand's death, a member of the British embassy had a long conversation with Léger, who was deeply depressed about the prevalence in Germany of what he called the "mentality of prewar imperialist Germany." "What was so alarming, M. Léger continued, was that it seemed impossible to reach finality; each concession,

---

[7] *ibid.*, p. 13.   [8] *ibid.*   [9] *ibid.*, p. 16.

freely granted in the desire to conciliate, was promptly followed by fresh and yet more extravagant demands. If Germany were now to take the law into her own hands in the armament question, and were not brought to book, her next move would assuredly be to proceed to some flagrant act in the demilitarized zone which might even bring into play the Treaty of Locarno. The only way, in M. Léger's opinion, to meet this situation which he considered fraught with great danger, was for the British and French Governments to unite in saying to Germany: 'Thus far and no further.' They must speak their mind clearly and make it plain that there would be no wavering. Otherwise a situation would develop in which war in the relatively near future was absolutely inevitable."[10]

From the moment when he took over the highest post in the French Foreign Office, Léger became a fighter for lost causes. His chief function now was a function of prevention. It fell to him to guard the guarantees of the 1920's. It fell to him also to stand in the way of policies prompted by new threats of violence against France. Léger says of Briand that "he would never have committed the psychological error of practising, at the wrong moment, the policy called appeasement."[11] And this too was Léger's intent.

II

With Briand gone, the task of the Secretary General was complicated by differences which divided him from his Foreign Ministers: in succession, from 1933 to 1940, Paul-Boncour, Barthou, Laval, Flandin, Delbos, Bonnet, Daladier and Reynaud. The list speaks for itself. After Briand, with the single exception of Barthou in 1934, Léger never had a minister who combined, as he says, the vision with the will to carry on "the great rules of French diplomacy." Boncour was a man of integrity but not strong; Delbos was a man of narrow vision and distrustful of himself. Of the rest, all contributed sooner or later to the abandonment of safeguards and the snow-balling of appeasement.

Léger had always regarded Briand's attempt to conciliate republican Germany as the most courageous act of his diplomacy. But after the Nazi revolution the setting itself was changed, and Léger saw no chance of agreement with the new masters of the Reich. The problem now was a problem of containment: of mobilizing, by diplomatic action, the force needed to hold Germany to the terms imposed on her at Versailles; above all, to the contract she had freely agreed to at Locarno. "The

---

[10] *British Documents*, 2nd series, IV, 101-102.   [11] Léger, *Briand*, p. 16.

structure of Locarno," says Léger, "was for a decade our only corner-stone in Europe; the only one which inspired the respect of Hitler by the precision and strictness of its mechanism, the only one which he felt obliged to acknowledge officially and repeatedly until the moment when he discerned the inner weaknesses of the beneficiaries of the system."[12]

But in France, already in the year when Hitler became Chancellor of the Reich, internal weakness began to show itself in alarming outbreaks of political strife. Trouble came to a head in serious riots in Paris in February 1934, and here the evidence suggests an actual conspiracy, a prepared plan to seize the Chamber, disperse the deputies and proclaim an authoritarian government.[13]

Though the attack came close to succeeding, at the last moment the Chamber was defended against the rioters, and the government of the Republic was saved. But in the years ahead, political crosscurrents ran stronger and deeper under the disturbed surface of a shaken republican system and ideal. And having only narrowly escaped a revolution in 1934, France continued to live under stresses and strains which unsettled her diplomacy. The Foreign Ministers whom the Quai d'Orsay now served were personally involved in the sharpening conflict between profascist Right and procommunist Left in their own country. And, at the same time, they were swayed, one way or another, by the political and diplomatic experiments of Italy, Germany, and the Soviet Union abroad.

Léger was not blind to these pressures, but his was not a politically oriented diplomacy. And conscious as he was of the need for a wider circle of allies, for him there was one ruling principle in foreign policy. No new ally was worth the price of estrangement from Britain. Her position must be reckoned with, her confidence maintained against all odds, even if necessary at the high cost of sacrificing the initiative for France.

In his relations with the totalitarian states, Léger was never one to think in terms of hand-to-mouth agreements. On the contrary, through all efforts made to woo them by politicians of differing political persuasions in France, he stubbornly resisted the bait of hasty deals and undercover bargains. And as late as the dark spring of 1940, when Sumner Welles made his tour of exploration in Europe, he was struck by the "magnificent clarity and logic" which Léger "as always" showed, and no less by the "innately liberal nature of his political philosophy."[14] Yet

---

[12] *ibid.*, p. 15.
[13] *Commission d'Enquête parlementaire sur les événements survenus en France de 1933 à 1945, Rapport de M. Charles Serre, député au nom de la Commission d'Enquête parlementaire* (Paris, 1951), I, 13-14.
[14] Sumner Welles, *The Time for Decision* (New York, 1944), p. 125.

none of these qualities were to spare the civil servant the execution of policy decisions which he disapproved.

The first overture of the 1930's which led away from the settled course of French diplomacy came from Italy in a proposal for a Four Power Pact. The French government was reluctant to turn the cold shoulder to Italy, but it was forced also to consider the suspicions of its small allies. In this dilemma, the permanent services of the Foreign Office played a restraining part. The Four Power Pact was concluded in 1933, but by their efforts to emasculate the revisionist clauses suggested by Italy, the French diplomats succeeded in rendering the pact harmless.[15]

This kind of check exercised by the Quai d'Orsay was one basis for the legend, which grew up later, that Léger was the saboteur of all attempts to reach an understanding with Italy. An exaggerated charge, says Paul-Boncour who was Léger's minister in 1933, and one motivated chiefly by political prejudice: "It is a legend, exploited today for reasons of party politics, which attributes to the Quai d'Orsay, and particularly to Alexis Léger . . . an indefinable hostility toward Italy." In Boncour's opinion, "the mind of Léger, supple to excess, was incapable of any kind of phobia," and he adds that he always found him, "like all my collaborators of the Ministry of Foreign Affairs, the intelligent and loyal executor of the directives transmitted to him."[16]

In 1935 Léger appears again in negotiations with Italy, this time with Laval as his minister. The Quai d'Orsay had been working on the draft of an agreement to adjust unsettled Italian claims against France in Africa. But Léger found that Laval cared nothing for the substance of the contract, only for the sensational *voyage de Rome*, which he insisted on carrying through before the diplomats had completed their interminable arrangements, their endless *"chinoiseries."* This time friction between Léger and the Foreign Minister reached the point where Léger threatened to resign. Laval, fearful that Léger's withdrawal would compromise the negotiations with Mussolini, was reluctant to part with him, and here, as at other later critical junctures, the civil servant made the decision to remain.

In many precarious exchanges between French ministers and the heads of foreign states, the known integrity of the French Secretary General served as a cover. His presence was used to disarm suspicion that secret commitments had been made or rights signed away in some se-

---

[15] John Wheeler-Bennett, *The Pipe Dream of Peace* (New York, 1935), pp. 134ff.
[16] Joseph Paul-Boncour, *Entre deux guerres: souvenirs sur la troisième république* (Paris, 1946), II, 339.

cluded corner of Roman parks, Polish railway stations, or Paris museums. Yet in the case of the Rome interviews Léger has asserted that he had no idea of the extent of Laval's private concessions to Mussolini.[17] He was certain however that they existed, and would be used by Italy in preparing her dangerous adventure in East Africa. He was also sure that France would never make an ally of Italy on the basis of such bargains as Laval's.

Since Léger became Secretary General, France had also been approached by the Soviet Union. And, for the record, it should be said again that Léger was no more inclined toward the Left deviation than toward the Right in diplomacy, no more ready for a communist than a fascist orientation in foreign policy. Indeed, Léger regards the Russian proposal of 1933 as "the most cynical of all projects": a top-secret plan for bilateral agreement with France outside the League, devised as a shield for Soviet imperialism in Asia. At first, at the suggestion of the Russians, the secret was carefully guarded in a locked iron box, whose contents were known only to Paul-Boncour, Léger, and the Russian ambassador.[18] Hoping to persuade the Russians to negotiate on a different base, Léger set to work to remove "the inadmissible conditions." Drafts and counterdrafts were worked out between himself and Potemkin over long months, and, as Léger describes it, the Russian negotiator "visited the dentist twice a week." Little by little, progress was made, and the victim responded to repeated extractions, to "moral embarrassment" and "hard usage."

When Barthou succeeded Paul-Boncour in 1934, he first told Léger that he would be dropped from the service. The suspicion was then that Léger was too soft with the Russians. But, after listening to Léger's progress report, Barthou reversed himself, refused to remain in the ministry unless Léger stayed, and gave him a free hand in the negotiations ahead.

Characteristically, Léger first made it his business to set British suspicions at rest. He went to London with Barthou in the summer of 1934, took the British into his confidence on the French tête-à-tête with the Russians, and pressed his case on the merits of drawing Russia into the collective circle.

Léger's design now took shape as an elaborate dual scheme: first, a regional agreement (Germany, Russia, Poland, Czechoslovakia, and the Baltic states); second, a Franco-Soviet Pact of mutual assistance, open also to Germany if she wished to adhere to it. The regional proposal was

[17] Général M. Gamelin, *Servir* (Paris, 1946), II, 172.
[18] Paul-Boncour, *Entre deux guerres*, II, 366-369.

Léger's most ambitious effort of the 1930's, a plan for insuring Eastern Europe as Western Europe had been insured in the 1920's at Locarno. No commitment was asked of the British in the East, and after the London conference with the French, they approved the proposals. Meanwhile, Litvinov had yielded on the principle of a multilateral pact, and, more important, he had agreed to Russia's prior entry into the League.

But how to overcome the obstacles still standing in the way of an Eastern Locarno? Germany and Poland were both hostile for their own reasons, and in view of their obstruction, time and effort expended in the furtherance of the scheme appears essentially unrealistic on the part of its designer. Yet for months Léger persisted in the pursuit of his goal.

The assassination of Barthou in October 1934 deprived Léger of his strongest backer, and with Laval in Barthou's place, there was an immediate demand for a tactical victory. Laval's *voyage de Moscou*, which followed within a few months his journey to Rome was, as Léger says, a *voyage de cabotin*, a stage on the circuit of the strolling player. The permanent services of the Quai d'Orsay opposed Laval's contracting in haste for this engagement. But when Léger objected to the plan for an insufficiently prepared visit to Moscow, Laval only replied: "Vous couchez avec les affaires." He then summoned Potemkin, and Potemkin, seeing the rift which divided the diplomat from the minister, was able to advise his government that the time was ripe for a deal with the French.

In practical terms, what emerged from the Moscow journey was the most realistic part of the complex dual design. Léger's Eastern Locarno, for reasons which seem obvious, had fallen by the way, but a treaty of mutual assistance was concluded between France and Russia in the spring of 1935. The signature of the pact was an important step, but in the last analysis its effectiveness depended on staff talks between the military of the two countries. These were indispensable to common action, and they were never to materialize.

Léger's chief object in the Franco-Soviet Pact was to drive a wedge between Moscow and Berlin, to divorce Russia from her old military liaison with Germany. But for France he was never convinced of the wisdom of a policy which would throw her into too close and exclusive a dependence on Moscow.[19] As late as December 1938, during the conversations held between Bonnet and Ribbentrop in Paris, Léger told the Germans that "the bilateral nature of the Franco-Russian Pact had not

[19] Pertinax, *The Gravediggers of France* (New York, 1944), p. 245.

been designed by the French partner. . . . It was only through the development of circumstances that the pact had become a purely bilateral affair."[20]

For all the agreements made with Rome and with Moscow, 1935 had been a bad year for French diplomacy, and there was reason enough for the pessimism which Léger expressed to Gamelin at the end of the year: "If France commits herself definitely to Russia, [Germany] will reply by occupying the left bank of the Rhine; if Italy emerges weakened from her current difficulties [in Abyssinia] that means *Anschluss*; if there is war between Britain and Italy [in the Mediterranean] and we come in, Germany is prepared to move against us. Only the closest understanding between France and Britain can keep the peace from now on." And he added that even that insurance was in doubt.[21] In effect, the search for allies had accomplished no closing of the ranks. On the contrary, it seemed only to accentuate divergences of interest and purpose, and Léger saw these divergences as dangerous obstacles to common action against the main enemy, the Reich.

III

In the spate of *ex post facto* polemics which in recent years have been centered on the progress of German rearmament, there has been a race on all sides in France to pass the buck. And many have tried to make the Quai d'Orsay the ultimate recipient. For one, the French ambassador to Berlin, M. François-Poncet, maintains that he tried repeatedly to find out what measures the Ministry of Foreign Affairs had prepared to counter treaty violations by Germany. To no avail, he says, since all warnings delivered, all questions asked, all suggestions offered resulted only in the refusal to consider any preventive or punitive measures outside the League.[22] François-Poncet adds that he favored the application of "drastic sanctions" when Germany reintroduced conscription in 1935,[23] but recognizing his government's unwillingness, suggested that efforts be made to seek a compromise with the Reich on the status of the Rhineland. "The Quai d'Orsay, however, replied that it would be rash to admit that the Locarno contract could be modified in any of its details, since there was

---

[20] *German Documents*, series D, IV, 476.

[21] Gamelin, *Servir*, II, 177. Throughout his service as Chief of the General Staff, Gamelin testifies to free and frank exchange of information between himself and Léger. They often conferred, and Gamelin trusted both Léger's integrity and his judgment on foreign affairs.

[22] *Commission d'Enquête parlementaire, Témoignages et Documents recueillis par la Commission d'Enquête parlementaire* (Paris, 1951), III, 762.

[23] *ibid.*, III, 764.

always the danger that England and Italy as guarantors might seize the occasion to draw out."[24]

The French consul general in the Rhineland, M. Dobler, has also some harsh things to say of the negligence, the obstinacy, and the inexperience of the permanent services: "It is the inadequate professional training of the diplomats at home (he cites specifically the fact that Léger had never served abroad except in a junior post in China twenty years earlier); it is the barrier which they opposed to the diffusion in France of information from their foreign agents; it is this deplorable state of affairs which in my opinion was the initial cause of the French government's disastrous failure to act against Germany before March 1936 and at that time."[25]

Dobler cites a number of examples to prove his point. Each is designed to show that reports from Germany to the Quai d'Orsay, all of them containing alarming information on German preparations for remilitarization, had never reached the responsible authorities in Paris. Various excuses had been made and obstacles raised: either the Foreign Minister had been too busy to read the dispatches;[26] or foreign service agents, attempting to bring their reports directly to the Minister, had been turned aside by high officials of the permanent services, and made to understand that their jurisdiction did not extend to political questions.[27]

But other witnesses are more guarded in their judgment of the methods and policies of the Quai d'Orsay. Léger was accused of working too much with the ambassadors of foreign Powers in Paris, doing so in order to exclude his own agents from their proper share in policy decisions. The investigating commission questioned the secretary of the Berlin embassy, M. Tarbe de Saint-Hardouin, on this point but, under pressure of interrogation, he refused to commit himself: "It is certain that there was a tendency to take action on the ground [in Paris] wherever possible. But I think it would be a mistake to generalize or treat this assertion as an indictment."[28]

[24] *ibid.*, III, 766.
[25] *ibid.*, II, 500-502.
[26] *ibid.*
[27] *ibid.*, II, 503-504. Yet Dobler claims that Léger's predecessor, Philippe Berthelot, had intended the Cologne consulate to serve as an outpost of political intelligence in the Rhineland (*ibid.*, II, 470).
[28] *ibid.*, VI, 1526. In an interview with the author in December 1952, Robert Coulondre, former ambassador in Moscow and Berlin, expressed little sympathy for the view that the permanent services had put up a screen between the ministers and the envoys in the field. In Coulondre's view, failure to reach the ministers was always the fault of the ambassador. See, however, Chapter 2, note 34, above. On the methods of the Quai d'Orsay, see also Chapter 2 at note 53.

No doubt, in France as elsewhere, there were sharp jealousies between the foreign and sedentary services, and inadequacies in the diffusion of intelligence.[29] But these in themselves are not sufficient to place the responsibility for the confusions which hampered decision when Germany made her crucial move in the Rhineland. In Paris, it appeared that the professional diplomats, the responsible ministers, and the General Staff were not agreed on the rights to independent action which French diplomacy claimed to have won at Locarno. Gamelin and the Minister of War were both uncertain on this point,[30] whereas others, including Léger and Sarraut, who headed the government, insisted that France had the clear right to move without waiting for the verdict of Geneva.[31]

The possibilities of military reprisals against Germany were also shrouded in doubts and confusion. The fact is that the French army had neither the plan nor the organization to enforce the treaties by military action. And after Germany announced remilitarization on March 7, it became clear that any deep penetration of the Rhineland by the French would involve nothing less than a general mobilization.[32] This fact certainly came as a shock to those who had thought a simple police operation would suffice. Léger had no such illusions. He recognized that heavy sacrifices would be called for to meet the risk of German resistance on the Rhine.

Even severe critics recognize that Léger and the permanent services were determined to preserve demilitarization at whatever cost.[33] Unfortunately, they did not succeed in overcoming the confusions and hesitations which prevailed at the top level. After three days of ministerial conference and consultation in Paris, Léger accompanied his minister to the meetings of the League Council in London in mid-March. And it is worth noting that it was at this moment, so critical for the policy of con-

[29] In 1932, Léger had served on an interministerial commission to study the reorganization of the Ministry of Foreign Affairs. The parliamentary report on the foreign affairs budget for 1933 also concerned itself with the lack of cohesion in the permanent services, the inadequacy of Quai d'Orsay intelligence, and the poverty of diplomatic information sent to French representatives abroad. The report, however, suggested that what foreign policy most needed was to be taken out of the realm of political *sautes d'humeur*, and placed in the hands of professional diplomats, *Journal Officiel de la République Française, Chambre des Députés, Documents parlementaires*, Annexe 1535 (March 9, 1933), pp. 510-525. See also Chapter 2, §1 above.
[30] See note of March 11, 1936, from the Ministry of War, Gamelin, *Servir*, II, 208.
[31] *Témoignages et Documents*, III, 574. Yet Sarraut asserts that rights aside, his government had decided before Germany acted that France could not afford to reply without consulting the Locarno guarantors (*ibid.*).
[32] Gamelin, *Servir*, II, 209.
[33] See Dobler in *Témoignages et Documents*, II, 505.

tainment, that Léger was first locked out of the decisive conversations. Léger believes that Flandin followed the *politique de complaisance* from the start, and if this judgment is correct, it is not hard to see how Léger's presence would stand in Flandin's way. As Léger says, it is true that the British encouraged French inaction by rolling out "a velvet carpet for retreat,"[34] and he could see how relieved they were that the French had not ventured to act before them or without them. Still, he remained convinced that, had France moved, the British would have followed. Britain had given her pledge to the French on the Rhineland, and it was a principle of Léger's diplomacy that one could always count on the British to honor their commitments.

For Léger, the decision to leave Germany in military control of the Rhineland spelled the collapse of the whole structure of security: "It was the London Conference of March 1936, not Munich, which must bear the responsibility for Hitler's flooding over the banks."[35] This decision lost France the buffer which protected her from direct attack; it also seriously compromised her power to check Germany's Eastern adventures by threats of counterattack in the West. After the return of the French mission from London, Léger told his subordinates that war was inevitable. It was only a matter of time and of Germany's choosing. And the significance he attached to this warning is indicated by the fact that he has called it his "political testament."

This was the end of Locarno, and it brought Europe to the watershed in the precarious diplomacy of the 1930's. From the start of Léger's regime at the Quai d'Orsay, French diplomacy had fought a losing campaign of prevention. After 1936, he felt that the battle was lost. Yet despite his pessimism, Léger continued in an attitude which he describes as "irréductible dans l'irréductibilité." In this intransigence he became a thorn in the side of all politicians and journalists who favored solutions by compromise. And it was at this time that the pro-appeasement press began to attack him systematically.

The years 1936 and 1937 were the years of the Front Populaire. Léger was now in the service of governments of the Left, and his enemies, ever since, have tried to link his name with all that they found to excoriate in its policies. He was, he claims, a man of the Left, "an

[34] Winston Churchill, *The Gathering Storm* (Boston, 1948), p. 194. Léger holds that Churchill, who gave Flandin the benefit of the doubt in writing of his attitude in March 1936, was perhaps influenced to some degree by his expectation that he might, at a future date, have to work again with representatives of the French Right.
[35] Léger, *Briand*, p. 15.

opponent of everything antirepublican." But under governments of Right and Left alike, it was his settled purpose to keep his judgment clear of political sympathies—a purpose well illustrated in his attitude toward the war in Spain.

When war broke out in the peninsula in the summer of 1936, once more Léger's first concern was with the state of opinion in Britain. He saw with alarm that the new socialist government in France, the turmoil of French strikes and workers' agitation, had raised a red scare across the Channel. Accordingly, he persuaded Blum to accompany him to the diplomatic conferences scheduled for London.[36] Léger's *cauchemar* was nothing short of a British alignment with White Spain, Germany, and Italy "in a new Holy Alliance in the style of Metternich." And however right or wrong his judgment, he was convinced that British neutrality could not be assured unless the French government agreed to forego the shipment of arms and volunteers to the legal government of Spain. Therefore, against all Blum's sympathies, he got him to propose nonintervention as the best available insurance against the spread of conflict.

For the obvious reasons, nonintervention placed Blum in the direct line of fire from his supporters on the Left in France, and it often fell to Léger to defend it on behalf of his ministers. Thus, in the Spanish question, Léger became the scapegoat of the communist Left, while at the same time, on other counts, he was still under attack by the pro-fascist Right.

In January 1937, the Spanish crisis gave Léger the chance to show his hand once more, at a critical moment in French relations with Germany. Rumors of German troop movements in Spanish Morocco had started a scare, and Léger, acting in the absence of Blum and Delbos, protested to the German ambassador in Paris. At the same time, the French ambassador in London, M. Corbin, an agent with whom Léger always maintained relations of confidence, secured, at Léger's instance, a promise of energetic support from Vansittart of the British Foreign Office. Such steps Léger regards as only the routine procedures of his office. The Germans, however, thought differently, as their reports on the Quai d'Orsay *démarche* clearly show.[37] They had felt a strong hand at the helm of French foreign policy, and they didn't like it. Thus, the incident

[36] Léger was anxious to show the British conservatives what kind of a man the new head of the French government really was. And one incident, reported by Léger, shows the kind of thing which he did to make his point: as the French delegation passed through the corridor which led to the conference room at 10 Downing Street, Léger deliberately held Blum in conversation beside the statue of Disraeli, a Jew, but obviously a gentleman and a statesman.

[37] *German Documents*, series D, III, 223-224.

added another black mark to their dossier on Léger as a public enemy of the Reich.

With the Blum government, Léger, and to a far greater extent than with those who came before or after Blum, was in a position to exert a decisive influence on foreign policy. Yet with this influence in his hands, it cannot be said that he made a positive approach to the complex issues of the war in Spain. The ideological conflicts were already deep, but he still clung to the view that security could be defended as an interest independent of ideological concerns. A more flexible policy in a rapidly changing world would surely have sought the balance between national security, insurance against war, and the political realities. Léger declares that nonintervention was always distasteful to him politically, but he persisted in upholding it through all the later and more dangerous developments of the Spanish crisis. This he did in the conviction that England would still separate herself from France if France reversed her course.[38]

There is good reason to believe that Spain was the last important issue of the 1930's on which the Quai d'Orsay had sufficient weight with its government to make policy, and its influence here is to be attributed to the confidence and respect in which Léger was held by Blum and his Foreign Minister. Blum, for one, has denied the charges leveled at the Quai d'Orsay for a deliberate blackout of political intelligence: "During this entire period, I myself read all the diplomatic correspondence including the mails from Berlin."[39] And his testimony certainly suggests that the "ignorance" of other ministers had causes more complex than the "screening" of field reports by the home services.

But with Chautemps in Blum's place, relations between the Foreign Office and the government were more strained. Late in 1937 Delbos and the Quai were still advocating the fulfillment of treaty obligations in the East, while Chautemps was inclined to be "soft."[40] But Delbos himself was "terribly tired and fearful," and Léger and Massigli were hard put to it to prop him up.[41] To the British, at least, there was no doubt that Léger was "much more powerful" than his ministers.[42]

After *Anschluss* in March 1938, the whole question of the French alliances was brought up for debate at the Quai d'Orsay. The French ambassadors in Central and Eastern Europe were summoned to Paris

---

[38] See *Procès-verbal du Comité de la Défense Nationale* (March 15, 1938) in Gamelin, *Servir*, II, 322-328.

[39] *Témoignages et Documents*, I, 126.

[40] *German Documents*, series D, I, 83. [41] *Documents and Materials*, p. 70.

[42] Keith Feiling, *The Life of Neville Chamberlain* (London, 1946), p. 333.

for consultation for the first and only time in Léger's term as Secretary General, a point on which some of them were sensitive.[43] They were in the mood to blame the Foreign Office for all the trials of their missions, and the debate between the two sides of the service was acrimonious. When, for instance, Noël, the ambassador to Poland, took the position that France could do nothing for her allies while she was so weak in arms and so disturbed internally, he says that one of the principal chiefs of service of the Quai d'Orsay replied by crying "defeatism." Noël has subsequently retaliated by a bitter indictment of the policies of his accuser, and though Léger is not mentioned by name, it seems clear that he is the target of Noël's attack: "Shot through with generous but disastrous illusions; led astray by unbounded confidence . . . in the principle of collective security and the multiplication of international agreements; convinced that it was possible, then and there, to block Hitlerism and defeat it, my colleague revealed the profound lack of realism which afflicted our diplomacy."[44]

Quite apart from the motivation of this attack, Léger admits some grounds for complaint on the crucial question of the alliances. He acknowledges that the disparity between diplomatic commitments and military potentialities was the cardinal weakness of French diplomacy after 1936. However, he argues that it was not the diplomats but the military in France who held most tightly to the Eastern allies. Treaty obligations which the diplomats had come to regard as "charges," both "morally and juridically embarrassing," the military still looked upon as assets. They thought, he says, in terms of Poland and Czechoslovakia holding a large number of German divisions in a part of Europe remote from the Rhine.

These considerations reveal the desperate hand-to-mouth planning of the military at this late stage in French unpreparedness. But they hardly absolve the diplomats of their share of responsibility for a system conceived too much in the abstract, too little in terms of the power to act. This, in effect, is the burden of the accusation which the postwar investigating commission has laid to the charge of the French Foreign Office.[45]

---

[43] This conference occurred in the short Foreign Ministry of Paul-Boncour (March-April 1938). François-Poncet was apparently not present, and he claims that he was summoned only once, by Flandin, when the ambassadors of the threatened Locarno Powers met after German remilitarization of the Rhineland (*Témoignages et Documents*, III, 767).

[44] Léon Noël, *L'agression allemande contre la Pologne* (Paris, 1946), pp. 196-197. In 1940 Noël served on the French commission to negotiate an armistice with Germany; and, for a short period, he was Vichy's first delegate general to the German military administration in occupied France.

[45] *Commission d'Enquête, Rapport*, I, 86: "The diplomats negotiated. They arrived

There is no doubt, however, that there were strong incentives to begging the question of the alliances at this late date. Had France publicly renounced her commitments in Eastern Europe, while German pressure was rising ominously in this area, her renunciation would have amounted to a public declaration of bankruptcy, to open admission that she no longer regarded herself as a first-class Power. This was certainly the position in which M. Bonnet found himself when trouble started in Czechoslovakia in the spring of 1938. Officially, he stated and restated his government's determination to honor its foreign commitments. At the same time, and increasingly without the knowledge and participation of the permanent services, he was on the look-out for ways of avoiding the fatal contingency.

Léger was no willing accomplice of the champions of appeasement. He was their enemy in 1938, and has remained so ever since. Yet hating both the tawdry politics and the foreseen damages of further surrender to Nazi demands, he nevertheless followed a line which hewed closely to that of the appeasers on the need for concessions to Germany in Czechoslovakia. At the time he was convinced that even a French government dedicated to resistance would have had no alternative to diplomacy by conference. For he believed that France stood alone, without allies among the Great Powers, and that alone it would have been nothing short of folly for her to fight. Here, once again, his judgment was swayed by his analysis of the position of Great Britain. Britain had consistently refused to commit herself to support France in a war for Czechoslovakia,[46] and with Léger the conviction that Britain would not move held even through the disputed British Foreign Office communiqué of late September. As to Russia, he maintains that his doubts of Russian aid antedate Munich by a year. And on this point, at least, the latest evidence appears to confirm his judgment.[47]

The part which Léger took in the Munich negotiations has given rise

---

at juridical constructions, which reflected rigid adherence to a system rather than political views grounded on realities." And in a recent summary of the findings published in the Paris press, the *rapporteur général* of the Commission refers again to the "intellectual acrobatics of M. Alexis Léger and his small coterie." (*Libération*, January 18, 1952.)

[46] More than once the British had thrown cold water on the French by warning them not to overinterpret Britain's concern for the fate of Czechoslovakia (*British Documents*, 3rd series, I, 346-347).

[47] See W. L. Langer and S. E. Gleason, *The Challenge to Isolation* (New York, 1952), p. 56. It is still, however, dangerous to be categorical about Russian intentions in 1938. France's ambassador to Moscow, Coulondre, believes that an effective agreement—that is, one which could have prevented Munich—could have been made as late as March 1938, if the Western Powers had been more responsive to Russian proposals then.

to charges against him of aiding and abetting the dismemberment of Czechoslovakia.[48] By his own admission, he felt that his country was in no position to fight, and, in the end, on September 28, after a long night of argument with Bonnet over the issue of his instructions to act as negotiator for the French government, Léger complied with his minister's orders to board the plane for Munich.

But on arrival, there is no doubt that he did all he could to stand out for the best possible terms for the Czechs. Indeed, it is from German and Italian reports that we learn how important a part he played in stiffening the resistance of Daladier. An Italian account describes Daladier refusing to start operations without Léger: "But where is Léger? I won't begin if Léger is not there. . . . He knows all the tricks of the trade and I know nothing."[49] And Paul Schmidt, who was Hitler's interpreter, tells how Léger sat by Daladier's side, prompting him to raise objections.[50]

In these perilous negotiations, Léger claims to have made headway by stubborn insistence on a line which would make the rump state of Czechoslovakia a reasonable risk for international guarantee. He also claims to have embarrassed Hitler, in the midst of one of his irrational seizures, by asking the direct question whether he was for or against the survival of Czechoslovakia. In the upshot, the Munich agreement upheld the geographical as against the ethnic principle, and the British concede that it was the French delegation which obtained "a form of words" which took some account of Czechoslovakia's economic needs and fortified areas.[51] Hitler's resentment against Léger was expressed on the evening of the conference, when he declared that Léger was a *martiniquais*, a black man, and that it was unthinkable that the French should have sent such a person to represent them.[52]

According to the French Secretary General, it was not the decisions taken at the Munich conference which were disastrous in their consequences but what happened afterwards, when the International Commission of Ambassadors yielded to Hitler's most extreme demands for the transfer of debatable zones in Czechoslovakia.

After Munich, two important officials of the Quai d'Orsay, its political director, Massigli, and the head of its press section, Comert, lost their

---

[48] Paul Reynaud, *La France a sauvé l'Europe* (Paris, 1947), II, 129. Charles Serre also points the finger at those who preferred the plane for Munich to the plane for Moscow (*Libération*, January 18, 1952).
[49] Filippo Anfuso, *Roma Berlino Salò* (Milan, 1950), p. 94.
[50] Paul Schmidt, *Statist auf diplomatischer Bühne, 1923-45* (Bonn, 1949), p. 414.
[51] See Horace Wilson's account of the Munich conference, *British Documents*, 3rd series, II, 632.
[52] Anfuso, *Roma Berlino Salò*, p. 98.

jobs.[53] Both were recognized opponents of the Munich policy. Léger remained, some say "because the fish was too big," others because Bonnet needed him as a front of firmness. Plainly, he did not remain because they were in agreement. And at the half-way mark between Munich and Prague, when Ribbentrop made his controversial visit to Paris to negotiate a Franco-German agreement, the Germans saw clearly the differences between Bonnet and his Secretary General. At these meetings, as the Germans themselves report them, Léger laid "great stress" on the promised four Power guarantee of Czechoslovakia. Bonnet, on the other hand, suggested that France had been maneuvered into the offer "by force of circumstances."[54] In other words, he was not prepared to insist.

In the end, no guarantee was given the Czechs, and the Germans entered Prague in March 1939. Léger, at this time, urged the recall of Coulondre from Berlin, as a sign to the Germans of the "seriousness of the situation." He also complained to Daladier, "evidently against what he thought the weak attitude and hesitancy of M. Bonnet, and against his being himself 'surrounded with reticence.' "[55] It was therefore no accident that when Bonnet went to London for conferences four days later Léger did not accompany him.

In his analysis of the possibilities of resistance in the spring of 1939, Léger appears to have misjudged the "probable attitude" of Britain and Poland. As to Poland, he had always regarded the policy of M. Beck as entirely "cynical and false." He guessed that Beck would ask the British for an alliance, but he believed that the British would still refuse to "undertake a definite commitment," and that Poland, in her "hand-to-mouth policy," would choose the alternative of leaning on Germany.[56] He saw that "France and Great Britain were at the turning of the road," but he told Sir Ronald Campbell of the British embassy that he hoped Britain would not "put the cart before the horse," by subordinating her decision to the demands of small Eastern Powers like Rumania: "These governments would decide their attitude in accordance with the intentions of France and Great Britain. In any case, they were only what he called 'corollaries.' "[57]

Contrary to Léger's expectations, Britain did reverse her policy of "no commitments beyond the Rhine," and gave her first guarantee, to Poland, on March 31. Here Léger had guessed wrong, but this was not nearly

[53] Reynaud blames Léger for allowing the removal of his "rival," Massigli, on the count of *bellicisme. La France*, II, 129.
[54] *German Documents*, series D, IV, 474.
[55] *British Documents*, 3rd series, IV, 382.
[56] *ibid.*, IV, 373.   [57] *ibid.*, IV, 382.

so serious as the charge brought against him for misjudging the position of the Soviet Union. He has been accused of contributing directly to the "diplomatic Waterloo of French history, the Stalin-Hitler Pact of August 23, 1939." The Quai d'Orsay, says Reynaud, gave no help in the laborious negotiations for a French and British agreement with Russia, but Léger did worse. It was he who was chiefly to blame for "blocking," "taking lightly" and "denying" reports that Moscow and Berlin were preparing a pact of nonaggression."[58] In this attack on Léger, Reynaud cites in evidence reports from the French consul in Hamburg, and here again the substance of the charge, highhanded treatment of field subordinates who were discouraged from passing on field intelligence to the authorities in Paris, agrees with Dobler's testimony on the Rhineland. The Foreign Office may or may not have been ignorant of secret exchanges between Germany and Russia, but it seems clear that Léger was overoptimistic for the British and the French. He told Bullitt at the end of June that "there were eighty chances in a hundred" that Anglo-French talks with the Russians "would be successfully concluded in the near future."[59]

As to the old charge of making trouble with the Italians, there is nothing in the record to bear it out. Since the breakdown of the Stresa front in 1935, when Italy became involved in Abyssinia, the French Foreign Office had searched every possible ground for cooperation with Italy. And at the end of 1938, the British ambassador in Paris made his report on the stalemate which had been reached: "In taking stock of Franco-Italian relations as they now are, the French government feel that they have made repeated and persistent efforts during the past two years to improve the atmosphere, only to be met with a rebuff on each occasion."[60]

By 1939, Léger was persuaded that further British or French efforts to win the Italians would be worse than useless. He insisted that they must be allowed to carry their experiment to the end: "Every effort to bring them back to us is destined to fail; it will only encourage them in their two-faced policy, leading them to name the highest price for their

[58] Reynaud, *La France*, II, 132-135.
[59] Charles Callan Tansill, *Back Door to War, Roosevelt Foreign Policy, 1933-1941* (Chicago, 1952), pp. 533-534. Tansill cites an unpublished despatch of Bullitt to Hull, June 28, 1939, 740.00/1822, *Confidential File*, MS, Department of State.
[60] *British Documents*, 3rd series, III, 480. To illustrate the French "examen de conscience," the ambassador enclosed a detailed memorandum from Léger demonstrating in parallel columns that every concession Paris had offered had served as a spring-board for hostile words or actions from Rome: *ibid.*, pp. 484-486. But see also *ibid.*, pp. 506-507 for Perth's objections to Léger's memorandum.

assets, and making them value even more highly the benefits the Axis can offer them."[61]

While the Quai d'Orsay stood out against further concessions, pro-Italian politicians like M. de Monzie were still promoting unofficial Roman missions, conducted without the knowledge or blessing of the permanent services. And François-Poncet, who had asked for transfer to the Rome embassy in the vain hope of "detaching" the Italians, urged that fresh efforts be made with Rome after Prague. Again, he says the Quai d'Orsay rebuked him, telling him to stick to his day-to-day business.[62] This, to François-Poncet, was only another instance of Foreign Office obstruction of the proper function of the ambassadors. He never forgave Léger, and two weeks before Italy entered the war in 1940 he told Ciano that a great part of the responsibility for the errors of French foreign policy lay with Léger, calling him a "sinister man."[63] There can be no doubt that, in the spring of 1939, Léger was fundamentally opposed to concessions to Italy; he does not seem to have believed that Italy could be "bought off."[64] Yet the fact that, without Franco-Italian agreement, Italy stayed neutral in 1939 and entered the war only when France had been defeated can be regarded as a justification of Léger's attitude. He had been entirely right in his judgment of Italy's role, as right as François-Poncet was wrong. And this particular attack, far from implicating Léger, succeeds only in drawing attention to the confusions of his attacker.

As the Polish crisis deepened in the summer of 1939, Léger took a position quite different from his position in 1938. Britain's guarantees to Poland and other small states threatened by Germany had brought to an end the isolation which had made earlier action "impossible" for France. France had now a sure partner in arms, and resistance became a collective enterprise containing, in Léger's eyes, the possibility of ultimate success. And he was anxious that British and French loans and planes should be given to Poland "at once in order to convince the Germans that France and England are determined to support Poland if Poland should become involved in war with Germany."[65]

[61] Grégoire Gafencu, *Derniers jours de l'Europe, un voyage diplomatique en 1939* (Paris, 1946), p. 209. Gafencu was the Rumanian Foreign Minister. The English edition is Grigore Gafencu, *The Last Days of Europe* (London, 1947).

[62] *Témoignages et Documents*, III, 778.

[63] Galeazzo Ciano, *Diario* (Milan, 1948), I, 271.

[64] See *British Documents*, 3rd series, IV, 335-337 and 353 where Lord Halifax expresses his fear that "M. Léger may be exercising his influence to prevent any response" to Mussolini.

[65] Bullitt to Hull, June 28, 1939, as quoted by Tansill, *Back Door*, p. 534.

The *French Yellow Book* shows only how tightly Bonnet tried to hold the reins in the eleventh hour negotiations which preceded the outbreak of the war.[66] The fact that Léger hardly appears in the *Yellow Book* is in itself no proof of his exclusion, but from other sources we learn that the Secretary General was deliberately shut out of the final negotiations, and that Bonnet took pains to avoid him both before and after the German attack on Poland on September 1. Yet on the next day Bonnet made an occasion at his press conference to suggest that it was Léger who had made it impossible to stave off the struggle.[67]

In one sense, though not in the sense in which he intended it, Bonnet was right on Léger's attitude at the moment of decision. Léger was convinced now that there was no way out, but he was still afraid that his minister would try to find one, where none existed. When he learned on the last day of August that the Italians had proposed another conference to save the peace, he said at once that the English were right, that the conference could not take place with German troops on Polish soil: "If such negotiations were to be started by a retreat on the part of the allies and under threat of German force, the democracies would soon find themselves faced with wholly unacceptable Axis terms. There would be war anyway, and under especially unfavorable conditions. No, the trap is too obvious."[68]

IV

After the war was on, Bonnet was forced out of the Foreign Ministry, and Daladier replaced him. Much less confident than Bonnet of his ability to handle the complexities of diplomacy, he made a practice of reviewing foreign policy in daily conference with Léger and Coulondre.[69] At every turn, freedom of action was hampered by military weakness, and once more the French government was forced to take refuge in a calculated ambiguity. The policy that Daladier decided on, says Léger, was to delude Hitler into thinking that France would entertain proposals for an early peace; and at the same time to pursue rearmament. Active prosecution of the war was to be postponed until France could give a better account of herself. It was a dangerous game, as Léger saw, but he believes that Daladier chose the only course open to him.

The coming of the war, far from putting the quietus on quarrels be-

[66] Ministère des Affaires Etrangères: *Le Livre Jaune Français. Documents diplomatiques, 1938-1939* (Paris, 1939).

[67] Pertinax, *Gravediggers*, pp. 408-410.

[68] Pierre Lazareff, *Deadline* (New York, 1942), pp. 239-240.

[69] Pertinax, *Gravediggers*, p. 103. During these conferences, Daladier, like Blum, had the diplomatic correspondence "methodically laid before him by the career diplomats."

tween conflicting factions in France, served only to intensify them, and in the spring both Daladier and Léger were caught in the currents of political intrigue. The Daladier government fell on bad days over the failure of allied aid to Finland, and Daladier's enemies found it a convenient handle for pulling him down. His government resigned in March, and Reynaud succeeded Daladier as Prime Minister and Minister of Foreign Affairs.

This change of government produced the most paradoxical situation of Léger's career as Secretary General. Why was he kept on by such partisans of appeasement as Bonnet and Laval, only to be dismissed by the man who had a long and famous record as the voice of resistance?

Reynaud was a man of many abilities, but he was vain, impatient and uncertain in his judgment of situations and men. Moreover, from the start, his government was in an extremely precarious position politically, and Reynaud was unable to divorce himself from the intrigues and pressures which surrounded it. He felt that his only hope was an immediate and demonstrable victory in foreign policy. And it was this which dictated his first dealings with the British. Drafts of an agreement pledging France and Britain to full cooperation in the war, above all pledging them not to entertain proposals for a separate peace, had been worked on by Léger and the British Foreign Office during the winter, and after long delay, the Franco-British alliance was concluded in London on March 28.

But this, for Reynaud, was not enough. He knew even better than Daladier the weakness of the military position, but he felt that he could no longer delay the activation of the war. Consequently, what he insisted on with the British in London was that steps be taken to retrieve the Finnish fiasco by an expedition to Norway. Léger, on the other hand, recognizing that the Chamberlain government was already politically embarrassed by the recent government upset in France, begged Reynaud not to press the British too hard. He saw that they were anxious and reluctant, and he himself was anxious at all costs to avoid any possible disagreement between the Allies. But in the end Reynaud had his way. The British agreed to the Norwegian expedition, but only with the gravest misgivings.

Léger says that he was on good terms with Reynaud until he took office, and that they had seen eye to eye on many important issues. But there were differences of method and temperament, and in the balance they weighed more heavily with Reynaud than agreement on ultimate goals. These differences first came to the surface in friction over the plan

for Norway, with Reynaud in London arguing his case with the ruthlessness of a lawyer in court, impatient of delay and resentful of Léger's
cautions and warnings. One day, when someone in Paris asked Reynaud
if things were not going well with Léger, he is said to have replied:
"Yes, but we haven't the same kind of mind. I don't know how to deal
with his infernal socratic method."[70]

Léger's preoccupation with what he calls the "lightning of syntax,"[71]
his tireless search for an expression precise and pure of the banal, his
refusal to compromise his integrity—all, in the end, acted as intolerable
goads to politicians who found him an uneasy presence both in the
methods and substance of his diplomacy. And Léger had made many
enemies.

How extensive this hostility was is reflected by Elie Bois. As editor
of *Le Petit Parisien*, Bois had fought many of the same battles in the
press which Léger had fought in the government service. Léger, he says,
had against him all the former ministers, deputies, senators, journalists,
financiers, and industrialists "who made up the party which Georges
Bonnet defined to Sumner Welles as the party of peace." They never
pardoned Léger for standing guard over the Franco-British partnership,
indeed many hoped by his removal to deal it a blow; and, indifferent to
the record, they consistently represented him as the wrecker of agreement with Italy. "Wherever difficulties arose he was blamed, even if he
had foreseen them and warned his governments to take action in prevention. But if a desired goal was achieved, he had no part in it, even if he
had prepared the way with infinite pains. . . . He was not even in a
position to defend himself or take pride in his accomplishments. The
nature of his task condemned him to silence and impassivity."[72]

As things went from bad to worse for the French and British in April
and May, Reynaud became more and more erratic, and it became more
and more difficult for the permanent services to hold his policy on an
even keel.[73] With one ear he listened to the counsels of patriots like
Mandel and de Gaulle, but "his house, his Cabinet, his anterooms were
soon transformed into the most active and dangerous cell where defeatists
of all kinds were to attack the nerve centers of the state."[74]

And here there was an actual conspiracy. At the center were Paul
Baudouin, secretary of Reynaud's War Cabinet, and Reynaud's mistress,

[70] Elie J. Bois, *Le Malheur de la France* (London, 1941), p. 192.
[71] *Exil and other Poems*, by St-Jean Perse, p. 27.
[72] Bois, *Le Malheur*, p. 189.
[73] Pertinax, *Gravediggers*, p. 241.
[74] Bois, *Le Malheur*, p. 175.

the Comtesse Hélène de Portes. Both were prime movers in the campaign to unseat Léger.[75] To them and their circle, he was the creature of the Front Populaire, the accomplice of Daladier and Gamelin, the prop of the Russians, the willing vassal of the British.

Léger's dismissal came eight days after the German attack on Holland and Belgium, three days after the break through into France. On May 16, Paris was thrown into panic, expecting the arrival of the Germans from hour to hour. On the afternoon of that day, the archives of the Ministry of Foreign Affairs were set on fire in the garden of the Quai d'Orsay.[76]

In the vain hope of restoring public confidence, Reynaud decided to call on Pétain and Weygand. In a Cabinet reshuffle, he himself would take the key Ministry of National Defense, while Daladier would go to the Quai d'Orsay. Therefore, in order to make sure of Léger's removal, Mme. de Portes and the politicians in Reynaud's personal secretariat, using every device of threat and persuasion, got him to sign the decree of replacement before he left the Foreign Ministry on the night of the 18th. Mme. de Portes boasted that "Léger's scalp" was worth over seventy votes to Reynaud in the Chamber.[77]

In the landslide of bad news, Léger's dismissal was only another item. But it did not pass unnoticed. Berlin was triumphant, as were all Léger's enemies in Paris. On the other hand, he still had the confidence of such important Frenchmen as Blum, Herriot, and Daladier, and strong supporters in the London government. Mandel had warned Reynaud in advance that Léger's dismissal would be interpreted as a first step toward policies which he, Reynaud, had fought consistently ever since the appearance of Hitler. And Lazareff of *Paris Soir* wrote in his diary: "The ouster of Alexis Léger has certainly not been well received. The very circumstances of the dismissal of the Secretary General of Foreign Affairs are particularly alarming because they reveal a new Paul Rey-

---

[75] Pertinax, *Gravediggers*, pp. 244 and 246. According to Pertinax, Baudouin had been talking of reversing the French alliances and urged that "a Secretary General less firmly rooted in the tradition of the British entente should be appointed."

[76] Pertinax maintains that the order for the destruction of the archives was given by Reynaud himself, and that Léger did all he could to prevent the measure from being carried out, yielding only after he had telephoned his minister "and received direct instructions" (*Gravediggers*, p. 238). On the other hand, both Baudouin (*The Private Diaries of Paul Baudouin*, London, 1946, p. 31) and Reynaud (*La France*, II, 131) claim that the destruction took place on Léger's initiative. This charge is repeated in some of Vichy's most vituperative propaganda against the discredited officials of the Third Republic.

[77] Pertinax, *Gravediggers*, p. 246.

naud. One cannot help wondering what this man might be planning to do."[78]

Léger only learned the news on the morning of the 19th, when members of his staff brought the published announcement to his attic room in the Quai d'Orsay. There followed a meeting with Reynaud in which Reynaud was thoroughly ill at ease. According to report, he tried first to persuade Léger that, far from being humiliated, he was slated for the honors of the Washington embassy, where he was to perform the miracle of persuading the United States to immediate action in Europe. But Léger refused to lend himself to this maneuver, insisting that if Reynaud had intended him for Washington, he had surely wrecked the chances of a difficult mission by disgracing his agent in advance. And nothing could be more in character than Léger's final words to Reynaud: "I have the right to the whole injustice."[79]

Reynaud, in his memoirs, has tried to incriminate Léger on a variety of counts. His accusations range from Léger's alleged pacifism in the Briand period, through support of appeasement at Munich, to the turncoat *bellicisme* of post-Munich days, "when the wind had changed." Léger is blamed for the failure to foresee and forestall the Nazi-Soviet Pact, and for ordering the state archives burned to destroy the evidence of gross mistakes in foreign policy. He is further charged with calculated leaks to the press, which insured him a following among such powerful journalists as Lazareff, Pertinax, and Bois. François-Poncet is quoted against him to prove the dictatorial nature of his regime at the Quai d'Orsay. Finally, Reynaud accuses Léger of offering his services to Pétain in the Vichy period.[80]

How much substance there is in this last charge can be seen from the action of the Vichy government. It passed against Léger the sentence of "national indignity," and, as a result, Léger lost his citizenship and all his property in France. He lost too the manuscripts of his unpublished verse which fell into the hands of the Germans in his apartment in Paris, and on the table it is said that there was left only a copy of the Versailles Treaty, inscribed by the Germans with the words, "Much good may it do you now, last defender of the last French victory."[81]

[78] Lazareff, *Deadline*, pp. 289-290.
[79] Pertinax, *Gravediggers*, p. 247. Léger holds that Reynaud's last minute appeals for U. S. aid were only for the record: Reynaud did not expect them to succeed, but believed that refusal would give him an easy out. On this question, and for Bullitt's corroboration of Léger's views, see the *Memoirs of Cordell Hull* (New York, 1948), I, 767-768.
[80] Reynaud, *La France*, II, 129-132.
[81] Louis-Marcel Raymond in *Cahiers de la Pléiade*, p. 125.

During the years which followed his dismissal and the defeat and occupation of France, Léger has lived in retirement in the United States. In his retirement he has been deeply concerned with the fate of his country, more so indeed "than many of the extravagant partisans who noisily occupied the center of the stage."[82] He never touched Vichy or Pétain, but he also refused to join de Gaulle. Yet, in a letter to Léger— a piece of evidence whose authenticity Reynaud has since tried to impugn—de Gaulle has asserted that "the grave injustice" committed against Léger was "one of the worst results of the bad influences" which surrounded Reynaud in 1940.[83]

Many of Reynaud's charges against Léger are patently false, and are all vitiated by the animus of the accuser. Léger has never answered his enemies publicly. It has been said that he spoke frankly to Reynaud on the day of his dismissal, accusing him of going to pieces and debasing himself in the hour of his country's greatest danger.[84] And Léger is convinced that Reynaud, as early as May 19, 1940, had decided to reverse himself, to direct his whole policy toward liquidation of French commitments in the war. The removal of Léger has always been one of the blackest marks on Reynaud's record in the eyes of those who have come to regard him as the fallen angel of French resistance.

V

But how are we to judge Léger's own place in the "decadent" diplomacy of the 1930's? Were his methods, more or less than others of the period, equal to the task of coping with a new situation and meeting the accumulation of new threats? And if not equal to the challenge, what were the shortcomings of these methods, and where precisely did they fall down? At times he was too much the disciple of concepts better adapted to the emotional climate of the 1920's, counting too heavily on the ambitious collective design, or bound by too narrow a vision of national security. Again he was too fearful of striking out for France on the gamble of British support. There was something unyielding in the pattern of this diplomacy, a lack of the resilience, perhaps even of the nerve needed to complement the high qualities of his integrity. Léger's resources as an innovator would appear to have been depleted after the failure of his Eastern Locarno in 1935; and virtually exhausted after 1936, with the collapse of the Western Locarno which had been his

[82] Denis de Rougemont, *ibid.*, p. 136.
[83] *Journal Officiel de la République Française, Débats de l'Assemblée Nationale Constituante*, 1946, III, 2623.
[84] Lazareff, *Deadline*, pp. 293-294.

master plan for the containment of Germany. As violence mounted, a lead in dealing with it was desperately needed, but the lack of it was certainly not confined to the French Foreign Office. Léger was always out of sympathy with the worst causes of the 1930's, but like so many of his colleagues powerless to salvage the good ones. And at the last what distinguished him from many diplomats in the democracies was a kind of dogged intractability in the delaying actions of retreat.

It can be argued that Léger, at odds with the trimming policies of successive Foreign Ministers, should have resigned his post, before Rome in 1935, before London in 1936, or before Munich in 1938. Since he was compelled as a civil servant to execute the decisions of these ministers if he remained, the only possible protest against counsels overborne was resignation. Yet it can also be argued, and perhaps with greater cogency, that by remaining he could still hope to exercise a restraining influence, a small but valid function of prevention even on the road to surrender.

Since 1940 the end of Léger's life as a diplomat has served as a release for Léger as a poet. At first, as he told a literary colleague in America, "there could be no thought, no possibility of poetry again." Yet within a short time, "he faced not only his exile from his country, but the demand upon him" of creative powers long held in reserve.[85] Since then, with the verse published in the last decade, he has found a secure place among living poets.

This poetry of exile brings to light Léger's vision of the universe and the part that man plays in it. It is a world of great designs constantly renewing themselves from the "abyss" of failure and catastrophe. The innovator and the guardian are familiar figures in his *Exil*. Both are exiles, and both touch nearly Léger's experience in the world of politics. Here he had labored for "the new idea," and here it had fallen to him "to stand guard over the purity of great crystal lenses between two wars."[86] But in the *décadence* of diplomacy, the innovator is caught in the storm of "partiality" and "secession," and the guardian finds himself barred from "the threshold of Lloyd's" where his "gold has no standard," and his "word no currency."[87] But man's design and man himself persist. In the East in his youth Léger had learned early the art of self-defense; he had maintained it later through the heavy pressures of his service as a diplomat; and, in the sequel, it is this persistence of man and the idea which lies at the heart of his poetry.

[85] MacLeish in *Cahiers de la Pléiade*, p. 118.
[86] *Exil and other Poems*, p. 22.   [87] *ibid.*, p. 26.

13

....

The German Foreign Office from Neurath to Ribbentrop

BY GORDON A. CRAIG

ADOLF HITLER's appointment, on January 30, 1933, to the position of Chancellor of the German Reich caused what used, in a more elegant age, to be described as a twittering in the diplomatic dovecotes. The Fuehrer's assumption of office quite clearly forecast a revolution in Germany's domestic affairs. If there were any doubts on this score, they were resolved before the winter of 1932-1933 had turned to spring. But did it also presage a revolution in German foreign policy? Could Hitler be expected to act in that spirit of intransigent nationalism which had characterized his speeches when he was merely a struggling politician? Would he, indeed, revert to the grandiose ambitions expressed in the pages of *Mein Kampf,* and seek to overthrow the accepted diplomatic conventions and the public law of Europe in order to fulfill them? Or would power bring a new sense of responsibility, convert the demagogue into a statesman, and induce him to seek his objectives by peaceful negotiation and collaboration with the other Powers?

If these questions were debated in the Foreign Offices of Germany's neighbors, they caused no less speculation in Germany's own legations and embassies abroad and in the Wilhelmstrasse itself. But, naturally enough, there was yet another question which was of even more pressing concern to the staffs of those establishments. How was the coming of Hitler to affect their own careers? Would the new Chancellor dispense with their services in favor of the men who had fought with him in the streets, or could they expect to have an honorable and influential role in the new order? One German diplomat, at least, viewed the future unhappily. In Washington, Ambassador von Prittwitz, in a conversation with Under-Secretary of State Castle on February 2, spoke in terms of unrelieved gloom and expressed the opinion that, if the new government became entrenched in power, "his days as ambassador would be numbered," and all diplomats "with a Stresemann taint" would lose their positions.[1]

This pessimism was not, however, generally shared. In the embassy at Ankara, the staff members were advised by a visiting party official from Germany that it would be wise for them to join the National Socialist movement as quickly as possible; but they were simultaneously reassured by his statement that Hitler was not as wild a man as he sometimes sounded and that much of his talk about radical change was mere election propaganda which need not worry them overmuch, since "the soup is never eaten as hot as it is cooked."[2] In Geneva, the members of the German delegation to the Conference on Disarmament listened to an informal lecture by one of their number on the attitude of professional diplomats in times of revolutionary change. Referring to the attempt of the Russian diplomatic corps to embarrass the Bolshevist regime in 1917 by refusing to serve it,[3] he argued that this gesture had served no useful purpose. The German diplomats and Foreign Office officials of 1918, he said, had followed a wiser course by remaining at their posts, where their services were soon recognized as indispensable by the revolutionaries and where, incidentally, they had been able to prevent dangerous adventures in foreign policy. More recently, the professional diplomats of Italy had enjoyed similar success in convincing Mussolini that it was well to leave foreign affairs in the hands of experts. There was no reason to suppose that Hitler could not be persuaded of the same truth, provided the professionals did their jobs with their customary efficiency and were sufficiently firm with the Chancellor.[4]

This cheerful belief was probably more representative of the reaction of the foreign service to the *Machtübernahme* of January 1933 than were the prognostications of Prittwitz in Washington. It was certainly a belief that was strongly held in the German Foreign Office. The permanent head of that establishment in 1933 was the Secretary of State Bernhard von Bülow. Member of a family which had supplied the German state with many servants, including Emperor Wilhelm II's favorite Chancellor, Bülow was a precise, methodical, and tireless official, a mas-

---

[1] *Foreign Relations*, 1933, II, 187. Prittwitz seems, however, to have regarded Hugenberg, rather than Hitler, as the man who would clean house.

[2] Rudolf Rahn, *Ruheloses Leben* (Düsseldorf, 1950), pp. 95-96.

[3] For a description of the situation in the Narkomindel in 1917, see Chapter 8, § 1 above.

[4] Erich Kordt, *Nicht aus den Akten* (Stuttgart, 1950), pp. 51-52. On the situation in the German Foreign Office in 1918-1919, see also Chapter 5, § III above.

ter especially of the legal aspects of diplomacy, and a man who disliked amateur dabblers in foreign affairs.[5] It was perhaps his family pride which prevented him from taking Hitler and his movement very seriously. Throughout the latter half of 1932, and as late as January 1933, Bülow had refused to believe that the former corporal could ever attain the Chancellorship, and he had sent reassuring circulars to the missions abroad predicting the imminent destruction of Hitler's "splinter party."[6] When these prophecies proved false, the Secretary of State was not particularly discomfited. It was, in his eyes, inconceivable that the new Chancellor would attempt to disregard Foreign Office advice in matters in which he had no experience whatsoever. Bülow was forced, before the end of his career, to correct these initial impressions, but there is no evidence that he foresaw trouble in the opening months of 1933; and the opinions of the diplomatic corps were naturally colored by his attitude of calm.[7]

Bülow's opinion was matched by that of the Foreign Minister, Freiherr Konstantin von Neurath. A professional diplomat since the first world war, Neurath had served successively as minister to Copenhagen from 1919 to 1922, ambassador in Rome from 1922 to 1930 and ambassador in London from 1930 until the formation of the Papen Cabinet in June 1932, when he was recalled to Berlin and made Foreign Minister. He had apparently accepted this post because of an urgent personal appeal by President von Hindenburg;[8] but—as Neurath told the British Foreign Secretary at the time—in the political discussions which had preceded the formation of Papen's government, the Nazis had also urged his appointment, "which, he understood, was not intended to be a stop-gap but was made with the intention of leaving foreign affairs in his hands after the German elections."[9] A man of no very penetrating political insight and possessed of an inflexibly sanguine temperament,[10] Neurath comforted himself during the turbulent events of January 1933 with the thought that the Nazis respected him and that, if they showed signs of ceasing to do so, he would be protected by the President's authority. This conviction doubtless inspired his con-

---

[5] On Bülow, see André François-Poncet, *Souvenirs d'une ambassade à Berlin* (Paris, 1946), pp. 240-241.

[6] See *British Documents*, 2nd series, III, 160; Rahn, *Ruheloses Leben*, p. 95.

[7] Thus, Ambassador Hoesch in London told Sir John Simon on January 31 that "these domestic changes did not betoken any change in the line of German foreign policy." *British Documents*, 2nd series, IV, 401.

[8] *ibid.*, III, 149-150; *Conspiracy and Aggression*, Supplement B, p. 966.

[9] *British Documents*, 2nd series, III, 152-153.

[10] See the analysis of his character in François-Poncet, *Souvenirs*, p. 49.

fident statements to Sir Horace Rumbold on February 4. His first impressions of Hitler, he said, were favorable. The Chancellor was "proving reasonable"; he did not always agree with the other Nazi members of his Cabinet; and he had, on various occasions, "spontaneously" solicited Neurath's advice. As for his own position, Neurath said that "the President had made a point of his being included in the new government, and that he had only accepted on condition that he was given a free hand and that no experiments in foreign policy were to be tried. He knew that he had the President's full support."[11]

In the light of our present knowledge of the history of the Third Reich, Neurath's attitude and that of his colleagues in the Foreign Office and the diplomatic corps appear to have been singularly feckless. Hitler was not to prove as amenable to instruction as the professionals believed. The Foreign Office, indeed, was entering an era in which its formerly proud position was to be systematically destroyed, in which its hitherto uncontested right to advise the government in foreign affairs was to be ignored and its legitimate functions usurped by other agencies, in which the Foreign Minister and the Secretary of State were often kept ignorant of pending political actions, and in which the Wilhelmstrasse was to be degraded to the role of a mere "technical apparatus,"[12] to carry out decisions in the formulation of which its staff had had no share.

The confidence which the professionals expressed was not, however, entirely unreasonable, considering the situation which confronted Hitler in the first months of 1933. For the Fuehrer was in no position to set forth on a foreign policy which was radically different from that of the past. His most urgent consideration was the task of consolidating his power within Germany itself. Until that was accomplished, his steps in foreign policy were necessarily conservative and in line with precedents already established; and for that very reason they not only won the approval of the professional diplomats but strengthened their belief that the Chancellor was a reasonable, and a manageable, man. It was not, indeed, until the beginning of 1934 that the first serious doubts began to creep in.

II

The first subject of international importance to engage the new government's attention was the problem of disarmament. At the end of

---

[11] *British Documents*, 2nd series, IV, 406-407.
[12] The phrase is that of Ernst von Weizsäcker, Secretary of State from 1938 to 1943. *Erinnerungen* (Munich, 1950), p. 129.

January 1933, the delegates to the Conference on Disarmament re-assembled at Geneva, to grapple once more with the questions that had proven so intractable the year before. Remembering Hitler's frequent assertions, in the days before he attained power, that he would end the shame of Versailles and rebuild the German army,[13] the Conference would probably not have been surprised if the Fuehrer had appeared personally on the scene to issue a cease and desist order and to march his delegation back to Berlin. In fact, nothing of the sort happened. The German representatives remained at Geneva and remained, moreover, under the direction of Rudolf Nadolny, the former ambassador to Turkey, who had headed the group during 1932. Nadolny's complete authority over his delegation was, furthermore, strikingly vindicated shortly after the resumption of negotiations when he peremptorily ordered two Nazi dignitaries to return to Berlin because they were attempting to negotiate behind his back and were indulging in undigni-fied political gestures, and when his action was approved personally by the Fuehrer.[14] Meanwhile, in Berlin, Hitler assured visitors that "there would be no change in the policy Neurath had laid down" in 1932;[15] and for the most part he seems to have left the direction of Conference strategy to the Foreign Minister and his Secretary of State, intervening rarely and then only to moderate views expressed by them.

In the course of the first year's negotiations at Geneva, Germany had won important concessions from the other Powers. At the very outset of the Conference, Brüning had made it clear that "the German people look to the present Conference to solve the problem of general disarma-ment on the basis of equal rights and equal security for all peoples";[16]

---

[13] These promises were made so frequently that they had a perceptible influence in weakening the allegiance of the officers—and especially the junior officers—of the *Reichs-wehr* to the Weimar Republic; and there is little doubt that the bulk of the army expected that rearmament would follow Hitler's victory and supported him for that reason. See, *inter alia*, Friedrich Hossbach, *Zwischen Wehrmacht und Hitler, 1934-1938* (Wolfen-büttel and Hannover, 1949), p. 9; Friedrich Meinecke, *Die deutsche Katastrophe: Betrachtungen und Erinnerungen* (Wiesbaden, 1947), especially Chapter VI; Ignaz Pollmüller, "Die Rolle der Reichswehr von 1918 bis 1933," *Frankfurter Hefte*, 1. Jahrg., Heft 9 (December 1946), *passim.*; and Gordon A. Craig, "Reichswehr and National Socialism: The Policy of Wilhelm Groener, 1928-1932," *Political Science Quarterly*, LXIII (1948), 199-200, 205-208, 213, 228-229.

[14] These amateur diplomats were Reinhard Heydrich and a certain Krüger who, among other things, insisted on hoisting a swastika banner over the German delegation's hotel. Kordt, *Nicht aus den Akten*, p. 53.

[15] *Foreign Relations*, 1933, II, 218. Statement to Norman Davis in April.

[16] The protocols of the early meetings of the Conference can be conveniently located in *British Documents*, 2nd series, III, 505ff. For an excellent short account, see John W. Wheeler-Bennett, *The Disarmament Deadlock* (London, 1934). See also F. P. Walters, *A History of the League of Nations* (2 volumes, London, 1952), II, 500-516, 541-555.

and, after Brüning's disappearance from the political scene, this theme had continued to be reiterated by his successors, although, it is true, with increasingly menacing overtones. Attempts to satisfy the Germans by means of qualitative limitations on the armed establishments of all Powers had broken down because of France's reluctance to make concessions to a country in which extreme nationalism was patently on the increase and her suspicion, moreover, that concessions would merely lead to new German demands.[17] The first six months of negotiation had resulted only in an eloquent but innocuous draft resolution which Germany, seconded by the Soviet Union, promptly rejected; and, in July 1932, as the Conference prepared to adjourn for a period of some months, Nadolny had informed the startled delegates that, unless the Powers gave clear recognition of "the equality of all States in the matter of national security" before they reassembled, Germany could not "undertake to continue its collaboration."[18]

This announcement caused general consternation and, in the months that followed, the Western Powers sought to convince themselves that the Germans really didn't mean it. The British and French ambassadors in Berlin believed, at least temporarily, that the hardening of the German line was the result of the increase of *Reichswehr* influence in government counsels;[19] and Rumbold suggested that the Foreign Office did not approve of the new course and would seek, under Neurath's leadership, to check "the ebullitions of General Schleicher," who, as Papen's Defense Minister, had been making minatory speeches about Germany's right to rearm.[20] In reality, both Neurath and Bülow, who was specially charged with the guidance of disarmament policy,[21] soon proved themselves to be convinced and intransigent supporters of the position taken in July; and they steadfastly refused to engage in renewed discussions of any kind until the British government had persuaded the French to give them what they wanted.[22] In December, having apparently been assured beforehand that his case was won,[23] Neurath went to Geneva to meet with the other Powers and to receive, from the British, French, and Italian governments, the assurance that "one of the

---

[17] See Alexis Léger's views on this matter, Chapter 12, § 1 above.

[18] *British Documents*, 2nd series, III, 589.

[19] *ibid.*, IV, 178. The American ambassador, Frederic M. Sackett, also believed in September that Germany was "now being governed virtually by a military directorate." *Foreign Relations*, 1932, II, 314.

[20] *British Documents*, 2nd series, IV, 201.   [21] *ibid.*, pp. 195-196.

[22] Rumbold, who was inclined to think of Neurath as a "reasonable man," found Bülow "suspicious and unhelpful." *Ibid.*, pp. 178, 272.

[23] *ibid.*, pp. 285-286.

principles that should guide the Conference on Disarmament should be the grant to Germany . . . of equality of rights in a system that would provide security for all nations."[24] In return for this first clear recognition of the German claim to equality, Neurath promised that Germany would resume her participation in the Conference.

By January 1933, then, Germany was in a much stronger position at Geneva than she had been when the Conference opened, and Neurath and Bülow were determined now to make the most of their victory. Even if he had wished to do so, there was little reason for Hitler to take personal charge of the negotiations which followed, as the Powers tried to translate the formula of December into regulations governing the armed forces of the signatories. With a dialectical skill which he could not have improved upon, the German diplomats, having achieved recognition of Germany's right to equality, now fought stubbornly to assure her right to achieve that equality in her own way. Between January and March, Nadolny rejected all plans for implementing the December formula, arguing that the French were seeking to repudiate their pledge by giving precedence to security issues and insisting that the only way in which progress could be made was for the other Powers to begin forthwith to reduce their armed forces.[25] When, however, the British government, in order to forestall another deadlock, came forward on March 16 with a plan which actually did envisage a general reduction of armaments but which provided also for effective supervision and investigation of German armaments for a period of five years,[26] Nadolny reacted with suspicion and coldness, and his attitude was reflected by that of his superiors in the Wilhelmstrasse. Although Neurath told Norman Davis in April that he was willing to accept the British plan as a basis for future discussion,[27] he permitted his delegation chief to use tactics which seemed clearly designed to make such acceptance impossible.[28] Moreover, on May 11, the Foreign Minister himself cast serious doubts on Germany's willingness to admit any limitations on her future progress in armaments. In an article in the *Leipziger Illustrierte Zeitung*, Neurath wrote that, whatever the result of the Conference, Germany intended to rearm in military and naval aircraft, heavy artillery, and manpower. "Germany's standpoint is morally and legally beyond criticism," he added. "What is right for others is right for Germany.

---

[24] *ibid.*, pp. 328ff.   [25] Wheeler-Bennett, *Disarmament Deadlock*, pp. 86-98.
[26] *British Documents*, 2nd series, IV, 539ff.; Walters, *History of the League*, II, 542-544.
[27] *Foreign Relations*, 1933, II, 218-219.
[28] Wheeler-Bennett, *Disarmament Deadlock*, p. 113.

Such weapons and armaments as others hold to be necessary for their security can no longer be dispensed with for Germany's security."[29]

The sharp reaction to this in London and Paris, coupled as it was with growing horror and indignation at the excesses which the Nazis were perpetrating inside Germany, induced Hitler now to intervene openly .in the disarmament question for the first time. Sensing that the tactics of his diplomats were placing Germany in the position of being responsible for sabotaging the Conference, the Fuehrer, in a speech to the *Reichstag* on May 17 which has since, by collectors of Hitler's works, been solemnly entitled the *Friedensrede*, obliquely repudiated his Foreign Minister's words of the previous week. With certain conditions which did not at the time seem serious, he announced his acceptance of the British plan as a starting point for the solution of the disarmament problem, his readiness to agree to a transitional period of five years in which Germany would not enjoy full equality, and his willingness to forswear the use of instruments of aggression, and to admit international supervision even over his storm troops and other party formations, during that period.[30] As an essay in appeasement, the speech, it has been said, "could scarcely have been equalled by Stresemann or Bruening"[31] and, if it fell on skeptical ears in Paris, in other capitals it aroused an enthusiasm which confounded the critics of the Nazi regime.[32] As a diplomatic stroke, the speech was masterly, for it effectively passed the responsibility for making the Conference on Disarmament a success, or a failure, back to the French.

In the general euphoria that followed the speech, the Conference adjourned its labors for three months. Part of the interval was employed by Mr. Arthur Henderson, its President, to visit the capitals of the Great Powers and exhort their statesmen to heightened efforts in the approaching session.[33] In Berlin, Henderson had interviews with both Hitler and Neurath. In the first of these—to which the Fuehrer came, rather disconcertingly, armed with a large whip[34]—no matters of great

---

[29] *ibid.*, p. 115.

[30] The complete text is in *Dokumente der deutschen Politik*, I (Berlin, 1935), 92-103. The greater part of the speech, in translation, is in *The Speeches of Adolf Hitler*, edited by Norman H. Baynes (2 volumes, Oxford, 1942), II, 1041-1058.

[31] Wheeler-Bennett, *Disarmament Deadlock*, p. 118.

[32] The speech, says Walters, "comforted the hearts of all who were still hoping, against their own instinctive convictions, that the new Germany might become part of a tranquil Europe." *History of the League*, II, 547.

[33] See above, Chapter 10, § IV.

[34] Kordt, *Nicht aus den Akten*, p. 65. The whip was apparently a relic of Hitler's Munich days. See Alan Bullock, *Hitler: A Study in Tyranny* (New York, 1953), pp. 349-350.

moment seem to have been discussed. In his talk with the Foreign Minister, however, Henderson had to listen to professions of Germany's desire to cooperate tempered by dark hints concerning the wrecking policy of other Powers.[35] When the recess had passed and the Conference was scheduled to resume its work, Neurath was more open in his language. On September 15, he announced bluntly that it was time now for the Conference to produce equality for Germany or to see the utter collapse of the idea of disarmament.[36]

It seems clear that the Foreign Minister confidently expected that the French would raise new objections to the British plan of March and that he was preparing the ground for the most vigorous kind of retaliation. His expectations were soon confirmed, for the French government, alarmed by growing evidence of illegal military activities inside Germany, were no longer prepared to consider weakening their own military establishment. Instead, they proposed the stabilization of existing forces under strict supervision for a period of at least four years, at the end of which time gradual disarmament might begin; and they succeeded in persuading the American, British, and Italian governments to modify the original British proposals in this sense. Thus, when the Conference convened at the end of September the delegates were handed a plan which departed sharply from the proposals so generously accepted by Hitler in May.

It was this turn of events which prompted Germany's second and final withdrawal from the Conference and her simultaneous resignation from the League of Nations on October 14, 1933. The gravity of this step was not lost upon the German diplomats who effected it. Nadolny, for one, seems to have doubted its wisdom and to have gone to the President's Palace to try to persuade Hindenburg that the new Four Power Plan be provisionally accepted for consideration.[37] But the very fact that he took this unusual course indicates that his views were not shared by his superiors in the Foreign Office. Of Bülow's opinions at this time, we know nothing; but he had always had strong nationalist views on the disarmament question and was a bitter critic of the Geneva system, and there is no reason to suppose that he opposed the October decision. As for Neurath, it is perfectly clear that he greeted the severance with enthusiasm. In pre-trial testimony at Nuremberg, after the

---

[35] Wheeler-Bennett, *Disarmament Deadlock*, p. 165.   [36] *ibid.*, p. 175.
[37] Speaking of this in May 1942, Hitler said that when Nadolny, who had just been appointed ambassador to the Soviet Union, finished his remarks, Hindenburg answered curtly: "You're slated for Moscow. Get yourself there!" Henry Picker, *Hitlers Tischgespräche im Führerhauptquartier, 1941-1942* (Bonn, 1951), p. 432.

second world war, Neurath not only defended the departure from the Conference and the League, but admitted freely that he had advised Hitler in September that no further results could be expected in Geneva and that the break should be made.[38]

It is wholly likely, of course, that Hitler would have taken this action regardless of the advice given him by his diplomatic advisers. The important point here, however, is that in this first marked sally of Nazi foreign policy, the Foreign Office and the Fuehrer were at one. The diplomats had, indeed, every reason for satisfaction. They had, for the most part, been left free to follow to its logical end the line they had laid down in 1932; the cooperation between the *Reichskanzlei* and the Wilhelmstrasse had at all times been amicable and effective; Hitler had preferred the services and advice of the professionals to those of party diplomats like the two Nadolny had expelled from Geneva; and the result of the joint effort had been a diplomatic success, or at least a diplomatic sensation.

The enthusiasm of the professionals for this stroke of policy rested in part, of course, on the conviction that it involved no serious risks. Existing differences between the Great Powers of Europe suggested no possibility of a union on their part against Germany. A period of strained relations with London and Paris could be expected; but Germany was on cordial terms with the other Powers and need not fear isolation. Italy had always been sympathetic to the German claim to equality in arms, and Mussolini was himself so critical of the Geneva system that it was improbable that Germany's repudiation of it would trouble him. As for the Soviet Union, the Treaty of Berlin of 1926 was still in force, and, despite certain signs of Soviet uneasiness—like their request in June that the hitherto close liaison between the *Reichswehr* and the Red Army be discontinued[39]—the Soviets were apparently anxious to preserve their ties with Germany and had sent one of their ablest diplomats, the former ambassador to Ankara, Suvich, to work to this end.[40]

---

[38] *Conspiracy and Aggression*, Supplement B, p. 1504. This advice formed the basis for the first charge in the indictment of Neurath at Nuremberg, and he was adjudged guilty of it. Papen, a member of the Cabinet in October 1933, says that he opposed the withdrawal from the League and that he tried to persuade the Foreign Minister that it was a mistake but that "Neurath was very little help." Franz von Papen, *Memoirs* (London, 1952), p. 297.

[39] Herbert von Dirksen, *Moskau, Tokio, London: Erinnerungen und Betrachtungen zu 20 Jahren deutscher Aussenpolitik, 1919-1939* (Stuttgart, 1950), pp. 124-125.

[40] Erich Kordt, *Wahn und Wirklichkeit* (Stuttgart, 1947), p. 62. Hitler's conclusion in July 1933 of a Concordat with the Papacy—the first Reich concordat since the Reformation—also seemed a sign that Germany's external relations were in good condition. Mussolini, for instance, had said: "The signing of this agreement with the Vatican

Yet, almost before the initial exaltation had died away, German diplomats were confronted with two disturbing developments which led some of them at least to revise their opinion of the new Chancellor. In the first place, Hitler had become increasingly interested in the possibility of a National Socialist revolution in Austria which would promote a union of that country with Germany; and the obvious aid and encouragement sent to the Austrian Nazis from party headquarters in Munich produced a progressive deterioration of relations between the Austrian and German governments. In the late fall of 1933, Franz von Papen had become sufficiently alarmed over this to go, with General von Blomberg, to Hitler and to urge the advisability of a gesture of friendship to the Dollfuss government, so that the tension—which was attracting the anxious attention of other Powers—might be relaxed. This advice Hitler rejected, and he proceeded to commit himself definitely to the course which was to precipitate the disorders in Vienna in 1934.[41] Thus, at the very moment when he was antagonizing the Western Powers by withdrawing from Geneva, the Fuehrer was embarking on a policy admirably designed to alienate Mussolini.

The second development was even more serious. Throughout 1933, Hitler had been considering, in fits and starts, the possibility of a rapprochement with his fellow dictator in Warsaw, Pilsudski;[42] and, at the end of September, he had instructed Neurath to talk with the Polish Foreign Minister Beck about "the best means of creating a better atmosphere in the relations between the two states." Two months later—after the break with Geneva had been effected—the Fuehrer authorized the negotiations which eventuated in the famous Declaration of January 26, 1934, whereby Germany and Poland undertook to refrain for a period of ten years from the use of force in the settlement of disputes between them.[43]

---

will establish the credit of your Government abroad for the first time." Papen, *Memoirs*, pp. 280-281.

[41] *ibid.*, pp. 299-300. Papen claims that his efforts were defeated primarily by Neurath, who convinced Hitler that he could not stab the Austrian Nazis in the back. Papen's animus against Neurath is so strong, however (see, for instance, his remarks on Neurath in the apologia which he wrote at Nuremberg, in *Conspiracy and Aggression*, Supplement A, p. 447), that this need not be accepted as wholly reliable. In general, Papen's *Memoirs* must be used with caution. Some doubt, for instance, is cast on the accuracy of the incident mentioned above by Herman Rauschning's recollection of a remark by Blomberg, who told him that he would "never dream of saying anything to [Hitler] about Austria. . . . It is a point on which he is not quite sane." Rauschning, *Germany's Revolution of Nihilism* (New York, 1939), p. 153. Rauschning indicates, however, that Blomberg said this sometime in 1934.

[42] Dirksen says that Hitler spoke to him of the possibility of a treaty with Poland as

However much this agreement could be praised as a shrewd blow against France's eastern alliance system, it was obvious that it could not help but be disturbing to the Soviet Union and that it might even be the decisive factor in persuading the Soviets to turn to the West. This was all the more likely since Hitler's speeches immediately after the conclusion of the Declaration began to contain open references to the Bolshevist menace. And if Russia turned to the West, Germany, in view of developments on other fronts, would be effectively isolated.

This danger was probably realized by many members of the German diplomatic corps; it was strenuously combatted by only one. Rudolf Nadolny, who had gone to Moscow as ambassador after Germany's departure from the Conference on Disarmament, bombarded Berlin with warning despatches, statistics on the size of the Red Army and recommendations that something be done to reassure the Soviet government.[44] During trips to Germany, he delivered lectures to the officers of the East Prussian military district, urging the importance of cooperation with Russia.[45] And finally he carried his case directly to the Chancellor.

According to Nadolny's friend and former colleague, Rudolf Rahn, the interview with Hitler was a stormy one. The ambassador pointed out that German isolation was imminent and might, in time, lead to a disastrous war. If Hitler were not prepared to remain within the Geneva system, as Nadolny had previously urged, then it was absolutely essential that he preserve the tie with Russia, who protected Germany's rear. Hitler answered that no compromise was possible with Bolshevism and that the Western Powers were not prepared to satisfy Germany's just claims. There was, therefore, only one course left: for Germany to break loose from all international obligations and to become so strong, militarily and economically, that she could attain her goals by her own power. "I am not mistaken," Hitler said angrily. "For fourteen years I have predicted developments accurately." "And I," Nadolny answered, "have been making foreign policy for thirty-two years, and there is no man living who can point to a mistake that I have made in that time." "As far as I am concerned," said the Fuehrer, "this con-

---

early as April 1933. *Moskau, Tokio, London,* p. 123. See also DeWitt C. Poole, "Light on Nazi Foreign Policy," *Foreign Affairs,* xxv (1946), 134.

[43] The pertinent documents will be found in *Polish White Book,* pp. 11-24, and *Vorgeschichte,* pp. 54-66. A convenient chronological record of Polish-German relations will be found in *Speeches of Hitler,* II, 1029-1038. For Polish motives in concluding the agreement, see Chapter 19, § VII below.

[44] Kordt, *Wahn und Wirklichkeit,* p. 63.

[45] Hossbach, *Zwischen Wehrmacht und Hitler,* pp. 37-38.

versation is finished." "As far as I am concerned," the ambassador answered, "it is only beginning"; and he proceeded to repeat his arguments.[46] They did not, however, convince the Fuehrer, and led only to Nadolny's resignation, or dismissal, a few weeks later.

Nadolny's position was almost certainly supported by Bülow, for the Secretary of State knew the importance of the Russian connection, and it had been on his personal initiative that the term of the Berlin Treaty had been prolonged, when it came up for renewal in May 1933.[47] But Neurath had vigorously combatted Nadolny's point of view from the beginning, denying flatly that there was any danger of a Russian rapprochement with the West.[48] In his decision to ignore realities—for Russia, after all, did change her policy and had, by the end of 1934, become a member of the League—we can detect some of the basic weaknesses of Neurath as a Foreign Minister. The French ambassador in Berlin has written of him that he was not a strong man but gave in easily to pressure, and that he was a covetous man and one desirous of holding on to his office.[49] It seems clear—we have Hitler's own testimony on the point[50]—that Neurath had by now decided to cast his lot completely with Hitler; and, despite his efforts to prove the contrary at Nuremberg, he does not seem to have opposed the Fuehrer on any major issue from this time on. In the dispute with Nadolny, moreover, there were other motives at work. There was a long record of hostility between the two men;[51] Nadolny had been a competitor for the post of Foreign Minister in 1932;[52] and, if his arguments were accepted, he might become so again. Neurath's advocacy of Hitler's policy was in all likelihood determined more by personal considerations than by an objective appraisal of the international situation.

It cannot be said, however, that his attitude enhanced his reputation, or that of the Foreign Office, in Hitler's eyes. It was, indeed, precisely at this point that the decline of the Foreign Office began. It may have been the brush with Nadolny which awakened all of Hitler's latent distrust of the aristocrats who filled the offices of the Wilhelmstrasse, although it would be unwise to attribute too much importance to that incident. It is safer to say that, by the middle of 1934, Hitler had inaugurated a foreign policy of his own, a policy which defied the cautious canons of professional diplomacy, and that he was inclined to place its implementation in the hands of new men.

---

[46] Rahn, *Ruheloses Leben*, pp. 83-84. [47] Kordt, *Wahn und Wirklichkeit*, p. 63.
[48] *ibid.* [49] François-Poncet, *Souvenirs*, p. 49.
[50] *Hitlers Tischgespräche*, p. 431. [51] Kordt, *Nicht aus den Akten*, p. 49.
[52] Rahn, *Ruheloses Leben*, p. 83.

III

Until the middle of 1934, the Foreign Office had had little reason to complain of party interference or of illegitimate usurpation of functions reserved to it. There had, it is true, been some annoying incidents. The empire-building proclivities of Joseph Goebbels had early become apparent and, in the course of 1933, he had annexed most of the staff and the duties of the press section of the Foreign Office, leaving it only a skeleton force with little responsibility. The new Propaganda Ministry had at the same time arrogated to itself the dissemination of cultural information, which had been within the jurisdiction of the Wilhelmstrasse before 1933.[53] But the loss of these prerogatives, which had always been regarded as of minor importance, was not considered very serious. The core of the Foreign Office's functions and by far the greatest part of its personnel had remained unaffected by the first eighteen months of National Socialist rule; and, in comparison with other Reich agencies, the foreign establishment had reason to be thankful.[54] Whatever satisfaction there might have been, however, was now marred by the sudden irruption of Joachim von Ribbentrop into the field of foreign policy.

It is impossible to write anything but a damaging portrait of Ribbentrop, for there is no evidence upon which to base a charitable account of his activities. Except for some fragmentary, incoherent, and contradictory reports written at Nuremberg, he has left no memoirs;[55] and his former colleagues have been uniformly contemptuous in their appraisals.[56] Geyr von Schweppenburg, who served as military attaché during his mission in London, has admitted grudgingly that Ribbentrop was reputed to have been a brave officer in the first world war; the wife of Italian ambassador Cerruti in Paris has called him "one of the most diverting of the Nazis." These are perhaps the kindest references to Ribbentrop in diplomatic literature, and even their weight is diminished by the fact that Geyr proceeds to excoriate Ribbentrop's conduct of

---

[53] Kordt, *Nicht aus den Akten*, pp. 91-92.

[54] See H. Gerth, "The Nazi Party: Its Leadership and Composition," *American Journal of Sociology*, XLV (1940), 517-541.

[55] When Ribbentrop was sentenced at Nuremberg, he murmured, "Death! Now I won't be able to write my beautiful memoirs." G. M. Gilbert, *Nuremberg Diary* (New York, 1947), p. 432. Considering his mental state in those last months, it may be doubted that the world has lost anything of value. Extracts from his testimony, which may be considered an apologia for his career, can be found in *Conspiracy and Aggression*, Supplement B, pp. 1177-1251.

[56] See the comments of his fellow prisoners at Nuremberg in Gilbert, *Nuremberg Diary*, *passim*. Neurath's views are on pp. 201, 225, 229-230.

embassy business, while Mme. Cerruti says that only in Nazi Germany could a man of his superficiality have attained high office.[57]

The subject of these unkind remarks had, in the period between the wars, been a *marchand de vins*, the head of Ribbentrop and Co., and allied by marriage to Henkell and Co., the foremost German manufacturer of sparkling wines.[58] This pleasant calling allowed him to live in affluence and to visit foreign capitals frequently; he had a more than superficial acquaintance with London and Paris, some influential friends in business circles, and a good command of languages. It seems probable that these evidences of cosmopolitanism impressed Hitler when he was entertained by the Ribbentrops for the first time in the spring of 1932; and the Fuehrer was further flattered by the attentions of Ribbentrop's wife, who catered to his unorthodox dietary habits, talked to him about landscape painting, and listened raptly to his interminable political monologues. By 1932, the Ribbentrops had developed political ambitions and, although they could not be described as old party comrades, they came into Hitler's life at a crucial point and had the wit to recognize him as the coming man in Germany.

Once Hitler had become Chancellor, he did not forget the pleasant household at Dahlem and Ribbentrop did not give him an opportunity to do so. Indeed, he became the most constant attendant in the Chancellor's anteroom, where, by the simple expedient of making a fine art of hanging around, he managed to have frequent talks with Germany's new ruler. In these conversations *à deux*, he stumbled on the technique that was to be the foundation stone of his career. This was the gift of storing away in his memory pet ideas of the Fuehrer and then introducing them on later occasions as ideas of his own—a procedure which could not help but persuade Hitler that Ribbentrop was a man of discernment and judgment. To this he added the further talent of being more Hitlerian than Hitler himself and encouraging the Fuehrer in those moments when he developed doubts about the possible success of his plans. This coarse form of flattery might have proved obnoxious to a man of finer sensibilities than Hitler; the Fuehrer, however, never fully recovered from the conviction that Ribbentrop was a man of parts.[59]

---

[57] Freiherr Geyr von Schweppenburg, *Erinnerungen eines Militärattachés: London, 1933-37* (Stuttgart, 1949), p. 112; Elisabetta Cerruti, *Visti da vicino* (Milan, 1951), p. 241.

[58] See Paul Schwarz, *This Man Ribbentrop: His Life and Times* (New York, 1943), pp. 54-70. Dr. Schwarz, a former member of the Foreign Office, knew Ribbentrop before he entered politics. His book is interesting but is filled with such startling inaccuracies that it must be used with extreme caution.

[59] This paragraph follows closely an eloquent passage in François-Poncet, *Souvenirs*, p. 291.

Ribbentrop chose the field of foreign policy as the one in which he could most easily make himself indispensable to Hitler, for it was a sphere in which none of the other leading men of the Third Reich possessed his own dubious qualifications.[60] The man who had been widely considered as Hitler's expert in foreign affairs before the *Macht-übernahme*—Alfred Rosenberg—was already a spent force, because, on a visit to London in the summer of 1933, he had discredited himself and his master by painfully maladroit attempts to get into the good graces of the "English ruling class"—attempts in which, it should be added, he was encouraged by the London embassy staff in the hope that he would, as he did, cover himself with ridicule. With Rosenberg out of the way, Ribbentrop had a clear field as far as as the National Socialist party was concerned.

He had now, of course, to contend with the official foreign policy agencies of the state, and this at first promised to be difficult. Throughout 1933, as Hitler and the Foreign Office seemed to work in perfect harmony, he made little headway in establishing his claims to competence in foreign affairs. In 1934, however, a more favorable wind arose. As the professional diplomats began to express their first doubts about Hitler's course and to betray a pessimistic belief that he had, by injudicious behavior, isolated Germany, Ribbentrop undertook to prove to Hitler that these doubts and fears were groundless and that the Chancellor—and he himself—had a more realistic view of the international situation than the gentlemen in the Foreign Office.

Perhaps the most astonishing feature of this experiment was the temerity which Ribbentrop displayed in attempting it. In the spring of 1934, for instance, the French government lost patience with the long-distance correspondence between Berlin and the Western capitals concerning the possible resumption of disarmament talks; and on April 17, in the so-called Barthou note, they accused Germany of bad faith and declared that they would henceforth look to their own security. The menacing tone of this communication seems to have made Hitler nervous; he feared the possibility of a French attempt to persuade the other Powers, at the forthcoming meeting of the Bureau of the Disarmament Conference, to concert on retaliatory action against Germany. Ribbentrop offered to persuade the other governments to postpone their meeting at Geneva; and, with Hitler's permission, he set forth on a whirlwind trip

[60] At Nuremberg, Goering, who yielded to no man in his contempt for Ribbentrop, admitted that, in 1933-1934, his qualifications impressed most of the Nazi leaders. See Poole in *Foreign Affairs*, XXV, 133.

to London and Rome. It was from the outset a hopeless undertaking. In their respective capitals, Sir John Simon and Mussolini listened politely to this extraordinary envoy who came armed with nothing but a proposal that they adjourn the meeting of an organization of which Germany was no longer a member, and went ahead with their plans.[61] Ribbentrop's debut as negotiator was therefore a failure, but it was not one which handicapped him in any way. The fact that nothing eventful transpired when the Bureau of the Disarmament Conference held its meeting may have persuaded Hitler that Ribbentrop's wanderings had not been without result. In any event, he encouraged his eager friend to extend his activities.

Ribbentrop did this by establishing an agency of his own—the so-called *Dienststelle* (or *Büro*) *Ribbentrop*—in a building that faced the Foreign Office across the Wilhelmstrasse and staffing it with a horde of exjournalists, disappointed businessmen, graduates from the *Hitler-jugend*, and aspiring party members who had hitched their wagons to his star. This organization was presumably intended to collect and analyze foreign intelligence, but it tried whenever possible to absorb other Foreign Office functions as well. Before his trip to London, Ribbentrop had been appointed Special Commissioner for Disarmament Questions and had been given the right to see all diplomatic correspondence dealing with this subject. This privilege was now widened, on Hitler's express orders, to include all dispatches which were not specially marked "For the Foreign Minister" or "For the Secretary of State." The former wine merchant developed a habit of scanning the incoming correspondence, seizing upon telegrams which required action and securing Hitler's assent to replies which he had himself drafted, before the Foreign Office had had time to consider the cases.[62]

The *Büro Ribbentrop* took the whole world for its province; its chief, on the other hand, was especially interested in Anglo-German relations, which he knew to be a subject close to Hitler's own heart. The possibility of achieving that natural combination with Britain of which Hitler had written so warmly in *Mein Kampf* seemed to have become extremely remote by the fall of 1934, when the continuing reaction to the Blood Purge of June 30 and to the abortive *Putsch* in Vienna in July seemed to confirm the isolation of Germany which had been predicted by Nadolny. But here again Ribbentrop elected to disregard what the professionals considered to be realities and to persuade Hitler that what

[61] For further details, see Kordt, *Nicht aus den Akten*, pp. 69-73.
[62] *ibid.*, pp. 79-80.

the Fuehrer wanted to believe was true: namely, that Germany's isolation was more apparent than real and that the British government was yearning for a comprehensive agreement with Germany. In November he made another journey to London where he talked with such notables as Lord Cecil and Sir Austen Chamberlain, who were decidedly cool, and George Bernard Shaw, who was sardonic; but where he also encountered persons, like Lord Lothian, who expressed their complete sympathy with Germany's right to rearm and their belief in the natural affinity of the two countries. In high good humor, Ribbentrop returned to Berlin and told Hitler that all classes of English society—members of Parliament, journalists, businessmen, and ordinary citizens—desired close collaboration with Germany. Hitler was delighted to have his hopes confirmed so authoritatively. He is reported to have remarked that Ribbentrop was the only man who told him the truth about foreign countries; and he made available to his informant increased funds for the expansion of his Bureau.[63]

The Foreign Office would have been well-advised at this juncture to take some kind of a stand against the interloper. Nothing of the sort, however, could be expected from the Foreign Minister. Neurath had, indeed, helped give Ribbentrop his *entrée* into the sphere of foreign affairs when, in deference to Hitler's wishes, he had overcome President von Hindenburg's resistance to Ribbentrop's appointment as Special Commissioner for Disarmament Questions in the spring of 1934.[64] Aside from this, Neurath had developed a nimbleness in side-stepping awkward questions of competence. He absented himself from Berlin for long periods during hunting season,[65] and—as he explained solemnly at Nuremberg—went to bed early when he was in the capital.[66] The job of dealing with Ribbentrop's incursions into the Foreign Office domain was therefore left to Secretary of State Bülow, and Bülow was betrayed once more by his tendency to underestimate his adversaries. Bülow could not regard as a serious competitor a man who had had no formal training in diplomacy, who could not write a report in correct German, who did not listen carefully enough to the remarks of foreign statesmen to interpret them correctly, and who insisted upon seeing possibilities of alliance where none existed. He took the line, therefore, that no formal

---

[63] *ibid.*, pp. 83-88.
[64] Kordt, *Wahn und Wirklichkeit*, p. 95.
[65] Dirksen, *Moskau, Tokio, London*, p. 184.
[66] Professing ignorance of many of Hitler's plans, Neurath told the prison psychiatrist: "He must have done his conspiring with his little group of henchmen late at night. But I couldn't stay up so late." Gilbert, *Nuremberg Diary*, pp. 75-76.

protest against Ribbentrop's activities was necessary, since their patent foolishness could not long be hidden even from Hitler.

It would be unfair to be too critical of Bülow's tactics in this matter. Who after all could have foreseen that the British government would act in a manner which seemed to confirm Ribbentrop's wildest statements and that this would make his position unassailable? Yet that is precisely what happened in the spring of 1935.

The events of these months are well enough known to make unnecessary any detailed description of them. This was the spring when Europe first experienced Hitler's "Saturday Surprises," as the Fuehrer countered a final Anglo-French attempt to secure agreement on an armament convention by announcing, first, the creation of a German air force and, second, the complete repudiation of the military clauses of the Versailles Treaty and the institution of universal military service in his country. The second announcement, which was made on March 16, created a situation in which momentarily the isolation of Germany seemed to be confirmed, for in April representatives of the British, French, and Italian governments met at Stresa and agreed that further aggression must be resisted. Yet, as subsequent events showed, only the French government took this plain warning to Germany seriously and continued to act in its spirit. Mussolini's attention was already wandering off in the direction of Africa. As for the British, within six weeks of the Stresa meeting, they had so far forgiven Hitler's violation of the military clauses of the Versailles Treaty that they were willing to authorize him to disregard its naval clauses as well. In June 1935, they concluded a naval pact with Germany, permitting her to build up to 35 per cent of British strength in capital ships and to build submarines virtually without restriction.

The conclusion of this agreement, which effectively destroyed the Stresa front, was Hitler's greatest victory to date, and it was one which redounded especially to Ribbentrop's credit. This was due less to the fact that he had negotiated the agreement personally—although that, of course, had its importance—than to the fact that he had done so after the professional diplomats had declared categorically that an agreement was impossible. The London embassy and the Foreign Office were in complete agreement on this point[67] and, far from being indignant over the choice of Ribbentrop as negotiator, they seem to have welcomed it, in the certain assurance that the amateur would now discredit himself totally. In the memoirs of the German diplomats who had an opportunity to observe Ribbentrop's diplomacy in London, some traces of this attitude

[67] *Conspiracy and Aggression*, Supplement B, pp. 144-145.

are still to be found, for their authors have carefully recorded all of his *gaffes* and discourtesies and breaches of diplomatic usage.[68] This latterday jeering has a rather hollow sound. As negotiator, Ribbentrop had few of the qualities which are considered indispensable by Callières and Sir Ernest Satow; but he did, after all, come back from London with his treaty.

That he had confirmed Hitler's high opinion of him, there is no doubt. For some time now, the idea had been growing in Hitler's mind that the career diplomats were blind to realities (*Wirklichkeitsfremd*)[69] and over-cautious. Years later he was to say: "In 1933-34 the reports of the Foreign Office were miserable. They always had the same quintessence: that we ought to do nothing."[70] Now he had found a man who possessed the dynamic spirit which should characterize a revolutionary regime and whose judgment equalled his energy. He tended, therefore, increasingly to give Ribbentrop his head, using him as his Special Ambassador on all sorts of mysterious missions in the months that followed. In a Europe which in the last part of 1935 was distracted by the tensions engendered by the Abyssinian crisis, Ribbentrop darted busily from capital to capital, seeking to register new triumphs and startling foreign statesmen with ingenious schemes, like his offer to the Belgian government of a solemn renunciation of Germany's claims to Eupen and Malmédy in return for a Belgian declaration of neutrality in any future conflict.[71]

The Foreign Office found itself more and more in the position of not knowing what the Special Ambassador was up to—a situation which was embarrassing when foreign governments directed questions to it—and increasingly uncertain concerning the direction of Hitler's policy as a whole. Even before Ribbentrop's London triumph, communication between the Wilhelmstrasse and the *Reichskanzlei* had become intermittent, and the Foreign Office had learned, for instance, of the projected repudiation of the military clauses too late to express any opinion on its political consequences.[72] As 1935 gave way to 1936, this situation grew progressively worse. Hitler's personal liking for Neurath apparently continued, but he had lost confidence in his organization. It is significant that the working up of the legal case which was to justify Hitler's next

---

[68] See especially Paul Schmidt, *Statist auf diplomatischer Bühne, 1923-1945* (Bonn, 1949), pp. 311-316; and Kordt, *Nicht aus den Akten*, pp. 98-113.

[69] The phrase is taken from a conversation in 1942. *Hitlers Tischgespräche*, p. 86.

[70] *ibid.*, p. 97.

[71] See Kordt, *Wahn und Wirklichkeit*, p. 119.

[72] Kordt, *Nicht aus den Akten*, p. 93. But the leaders of the army do not seem to have been consulted until the eve of the declaration either. See Hossbach, *Zwischen Wehrmacht und Hitler*, pp. 94-96.

adventure in foreign policy—the entry into the Rhineland and the repudiation of Locarno in March 1936—seems to have been handled in the *Büro Ribbentrop* rather than in the Foreign Office.[73]

When the Rhineland invasion was launched, it gave rise to an incident which was scarcely designed to increase Hitler's respect for professional diplomats. In the anxious pause which followed the march-in of the troops, the staff of the London embassy became convinced that military action by Britain was highly likely and, with the apparent approval of Ambassador von Hoesch, the military attachés sent reports home underlining this possibility. Hitler was in an extremely nervous state—in contrast to Neurath, who said phlegmatically, "Jetzt sind mer drinne und bleibet drinne"—and his nervousness increased perceptibly when the reports from London were communicated to him by General von Blomberg.[74] He resented this unnecessary, and undignified, strain and did not forget it when the crisis had passed; the attachés were severely reprimanded, and it seems likely that Hoesch would have suffered also had he not died in April, worn out by his exertions during the crisis.

To Hitler the incident was additional proof of a lack of healthy realism on the part of career diplomats, and there is some indication that, at this moment, he considered a thoroughgoing shake-up of the diplomatic establishment. An opportunity was provided for such a step by the sudden death, in June 1936, of Bernhard von Bülow, and Hitler's first intention seems to have been to make Ribbentrop Secretary of State.[75] His desire for a comprehensive settlement with Great Britain was still, however, unfulfilled, despite the notable advance made toward it in the previous year; and it appeared that Ribbentrop's talents would be better used in London. The creator of the naval pact was, therefore, appointed to succeed Hoesch, a preferment which—having come so close to his real goal—he resisted vigorously, but in vain.[76]

With Ribbentrop's posting to London, the Foreign Office secured a

[73] Kordt, *Nicht aus den Akten*, pp. 129-130. How much the Foreign Office knew about Hitler's exact intentions is not clear. At Nuremberg, Neurath admitted that he knew and approved of the step but did not say whether his permanent officials had been consulted in any way. *Conspiracy and Aggression*, Supplement B, p. 1495. In conversations with François-Poncet in January 1936, Bülow stated flatly that Germany had no intention of denouncing the Locarno Treaties. The former ambassador believes that this was merely an evasion, but it may not have been. *Souvenirs*, p. 249.

[74] Geyr von Schweppenburg, *Erinnerungen*, pp. 87-88; Hossbach, *Zwischen Wehrmacht und Hitler*, pp. 97-98.

[75] Neurath claimed that Hitler had suggested this and that he himself had flatly refused to accept Ribbentrop's appointment. Gilbert, *Nuremberg Diary*, pp. 229-230. Neurath was not, however, by this time given to strong stands against Hitler and, if the Fuehrer changed his mind, it was probably for reasons other than Neurath's opposition.

[76] Kordt, *Nicht aus den Akten*, pp. 149-150.

respite, but nothing more. In the eighteen months that followed, its prestige and influence sank to their nadir, new aspirants to its privileges and functions appeared, and the administration of German foreign policy became completely chaotic.

IV

In illustrating the serious diminution of Foreign Office influence in this period, it may be noted at the outset that, in two important areas of Germany's foreign relations, the Wilhelmstrasse now had no effective role. Ribbentrop was not, like other ambassadors, subordinate to the Foreign Office and, while that office was informed of his activities, it had no power to issue instructions to him and found it useless to submit advice. Anglo-German relations thus became a private preserve of the Special Ambassador and the Fuehrer. An exactly similar situation obtained in matters affecting Austria. After the murder of Dollfuss in July 1934, Hitler had appointed Franz von Papen as minister to Vienna. Papen made his acceptance of the post conditional upon his being "free from the jurisdiction of the Foreign Office but . . . responsible to Hitler alone."[77] He was expected to send copies of all his reports to the Foreign Office, and he probably did so; but the personal coolness which existed between him and Neurath probably kept his consultation with the Foreign Minister at a minimum. Moreover, Papen staffed his Vienna legation with men who had been his aides when he was Vice Chancellor,[78] a circumstance which certainly weakened the normal liaison between the legation and the home office. Even in such an important development as the negotiations leading to the Austro-German agreement of July 1936, the Foreign Office played no part, and the drafting of that treaty was Papen's work alone.[79]

At the same time, Foreign Office control over all embassies was affected by another development. This was the growth in influence of the National Socialist party's Foreign Organization (*Auslandsorganisation*).[80] The AO, as it was usually called, had been established in 1931 and was originally concerned only with maintaining contact with party members who resided abroad. After 1933, however, it rapidly developed a kind of foreign service of its own, sending agents abroad to spread National Socialist propaganda, maintain contact with subversive elements and extend party discipline over German nationals. Between these agents

---

[77] Papen, *Memoirs*, pp. 340-341.   [78] *ibid.*, p. 365.
[79] *ibid.*, pp. 362-364; Weizsäcker, *Erinnerungen*, p. 130.
[80] A convenient outline of the origins and activities of the organization will be found in *Hitler's Speeches*, II, 1063-1079. See also *Trials of War Criminals*, XII, 220-221.

and the official diplomatic representatives of the Reich there was continual friction. Foreign Office protests against the embarrassment caused by AO activities had no result, however; and it finally became injudicious for it to raise any objections. For on January 30, 1937 Hitler issued an order which stated that "in order to unify the care of German citizens living abroad there is created the post of Head of the AO in the Foreign Office, to whom at the same time the conduct and administration of all matters affecting German citizens living abroad falling within the competence of the Foreign Office are entrusted."

This sweeping ukase was a grievous blow to the independence of the foreign service as a whole. In a public interpretation, Neurath sought to explain that the AO would henceforth operate within lines set by him. This was contradicted by the fact that, while E. W. Bohle, the appointee to the new post, was nominally subordinated to Neurath, he remained, in his capacity as Head of the AO of the party, responsible to the Fuehrer's Deputy Rudolf Hess and was furthermore, in all matters touching his sphere of competence, a member of the Cabinet of the Reich. Later in the year, a Foreign Office circular to the field advised Germany's diplomats, in rather obscure language, that Bohle was in fact independent of the Foreign Minister's control.

The net result of Hitler's order, then, was, first, that the AO received jurisdiction over all Germans residing abroad and, second, that it was placed in a position to pass judgment on the loyalty and efficiency of Germany's diplomatic representatives. As one newspaper expressed it: "Henceforth, no German diplomat or consul can be employed who has not given proof of his National Socialist attitude in the closest cooperation with the *Auslandsorganisation*."[81] The effect of this on the morale of the foreign service can easily be imagined. While Bohle prowled about the corridors of the Wilhelmstrasse, accosting officials who were not wearing the party insignia in their lapels, his agents abroad exercised surveillance over the mission chiefs and their staffs and often sought to undermine their reputation and authority.

In addition to this, the AO undertook to make policy on its own. In Austria, for instance, AO agents were active as early as 1935 and were indulging in undercover maneuvers which Papen believed, or claims to have believed, jeopardized the fulfilment of the policy upon which he had agreed with Hitler.[82] In Spain, they were laying the basis for German support of General Franco even before the outbreak of the civil

---

[81] The *Allgemeine Zeitung*, cited in *Hitler's Speeches*, II, 1068.
[82] Papen, *Memoirs*, pp. 355-356; *Trials of War Criminals*, XII, 221.

war, as was later proved when Loyalist authorities raided the AO headquarters in Barcelona and seized their files.[83] It is not too much to say
that the policy adopted by Germany in Spain was an AO policy. Immediately after the beginning of hostilities, two of Bohle's agents traveled from Spain to Berlin with a letter from Franco to Hitler. Through
Bohle's influence, they were received by the Fuehrer and, as a result of
this conversation, Hitler summoned Goering, Blomberg, and a member
of his naval staff to a meeting which agreed in principle to the support
of the rebel forces.[84] It is significant that the Foreign Minister was not
present at these deliberations, and the head of the Political Department
of the Foreign Office has written that the decision took the Foreign
Office completely by surprise.[85]

The surprise was accompanied by a feeling of dismay which grew
steadily in the months that followed. The Foreign Office experts were
not opposed to the idea of exploiting the situation in Spain to Germany's
advantage, but they were frightened by the possibility that a thoroughgoing commitment in Spain would sharpen the opposition of the Western
Powers and even involve Germany in a disastrous war.[86] Memoranda
prepared in the Wilhelmstrasse repeatedly stressed this idea and urged
the necessity of leaving open the way for retreat from support of the
Caudillo; as late as July 1937, the director of the Political Division was
writing: ". . . our goal should be rather the prevention of a general
conflict than the unconditional and complete victory of the Franco party
in the Spanish Civil War."[87] In this attitude, the Foreign Office was
strongly supported by the army high command, including War Minister
von Blomberg, General von Fritsch, the Commander in Chief, and the
Chief of General Staff Beck, all of whom regarded the military commitment in Spain as politically unwise and materially wasteful.[88] These
chance partners were always, however, uncertain of Hitler's real intentions and continually fearful of the influence upon the Fuehrer of other
groups and individuals who were seeking to direct Germany's Spanish
policy.

There were many of these: Johannes Bernhardt, German businessman
and director of the Economic Agency of the AO in Tetuán, who by virtue

---

[83] On this, see *The Nazi Conspiracy in Spain. By the Editor of the Brown Book of the
Hitler Terror* (London, 1937).

[84] *German Documents*, series D, III, 1-2.

[85] Weizsäcker, *Erinnerungen*, p. 129.

[86] *German Documents*, series D, III, 225-226.　　　　[87] *ibid.*, p. 391.

[88] *ibid.*, pp. 50, 149, 168. For further details on the army's attitude, see Hossbach,
Zwischen Wehrmacht und Hitler, pp. 41-43, and Walter Görlitz, *Der deutsche General-
stab: Geschichte und Gestalt* (Frankfurt-am-Main, 1950), pp. 441-442.

of his transmission of Franco's letter to Hitler in July 1936 looked upon himself as "the Fuehrer's delegate to Franco" and who was instrumental in organizing the Spanish trading company *Hisma* and its German counterpart *Rowak* to facilitate the exchange of Germany military supplies for Spanish raw materials;[89] Colonel-General Hermann Goering, who also had an interest in *Hisma* and *Rowak* and who furthermore welcomed intervention in Spain as a means of testing the fighting qualities of the *Luftwaffe*; the Ministries of Economics and Propaganda and the *Dienststelle Ribbentrop*, which sought to exploit the Spanish situation for their own ends;[90] the shadowy figure of Admiral Canaris, head of the Counter Intelligence Section of the War Ministry, a personal friend and admirer of Franco and consequently much more cordial to the idea of an all-out commitment than Blomberg and Fritsch;[91] and even the newly accredited ambassador to the Burgos government, an ardent party member and retired general named Faupel who, far from sharing the doubts and hesitations of his nominal superiors in the Wilhelmstrasse, used his right of personal access to the Fuehrer to plead for a policy which would have involved the employment of as many as three German infantry divisions in the peninsula and the gradual assumption of direction over Franco's war effort by a German staff, presumably under his own leadership.[92]

With this welter of irresponsible agents wandering about in Spain, the pursuit of any clear-cut line of policy became well-nigh impossible. The continuation of the work of the Non-Intervention Committee in London, which was the best assurance against the outbreak of war among the Powers and which was participated in by Germany for that very reason, was constantly threatened by injudicious releases by the Propaganda Ministry[93] or experiments in brutality by Goering's air force. The policy of cooperation with Italy in Spain, which had the incidental advantage of diverting Mussolini's attention from the Danubian area by nailing his military forces down in the peninsula, was jeopardized by Faupel's rather obvious attempts to give Germany a stronger position in Franco's counsels than Italy.[94] Even the hope of winning solid economic advantage in return for the military aid sent to the Nationalists was weakened and eventually defeated by Bernhardt's clumsy attempts to blackmail the Burgos government into granting extensive mining concessions to Ger-

---

[89] *German Documents*, series D, III, 88, 111-114, 245-247.
[90] See, for instance, *ibid.*, p. 225.
[91] Karl Abshagen, *Canaris* (Bonn, 1949), pp. 161-164.
[92] *German Documents*, series D, III, 134, 137-139, 155-156, 159-162, 207, 236.
[93] See Weizsäcker's remarks on propaganda, *ibid.*, p. 429.   [94] *ibid.*, p. 219.

many.[95] All in all, Germany's Spanish adventure is a striking illustration of the confusion and lack of coordination which had come to characterize the administration of German foreign policy; and there is no more telling example of the extremes to which the Foreign Office had been reduced than the subterranean methods which it seems to have employed, in informal conspiracy with the army leaders, to discredit and unseat its own ambassador in Spain before his personal ambitions should produce a completely chaotic situation.[96]

It can nevertheless be noted, as one of the few victories won by the Foreign Office in this period, that the line of caution advocated by the Wilhelmstrasse and the Army Command was generally adhered to in the Spanish war, and that both military commitments and political risks were kept within careful limits by Hitler. In another field of policy, however, the Foreign Office and army partnership suffered a decisive defeat in this same period: namely, in the Far East.

Their antagonist here was Ribbentrop, whose appointment to London had neither put a stop to his interest in other aspects of Germany's foreign relations nor interrupted the activities of his Bureau. In the course of 1935, Ribbentrop, doubtless inspired by an expression of interest by the Fuehrer, had conceived the idea of effecting a closer relationship between Germany and Japan. While he himself had entered into conversations with Oshima, the Japanese military attaché in Berlin, his Bureau had made preliminary studies and drafts for a political treaty between the two countries, oriented against Russia although explicitly expressing only a common opposition to communism.[97] These studies and negotiations were kept strictly secret from the Foreign Office, and it was not until April 1936 that the officials there had any inkling of them.[98] Even after that date, they refused—as they had on other occasions—to be concerned; and the negotiations were permitted to continue until they eventuated in the Anti-Comintern Pact, which Ribbentrop returned from London to sign in November 1936.

The Pact was so innocuous in content that the Foreign Office attitude

---

[95] *ibid.*, chapter v, pp. 496-619 for details.

[96] *ibid.*, pp. 168, 423-424, 434. Faupel's recall came after Franco had requested it, but it seems clear from the German documents that the Foreign Office and its army allies helped effect this result.

[97] It was apparently Raumer of the *Büro Ribbentrop* who invented the term Anti-Comintern Pact, taking advantage of the frequently repeated claim of the Soviet government that it was not responsible for Comintern activities. See Poole in *Foreign Affairs*, xxv, 136.

[98] They learned of the negotiations for the first time from the ambassador in Tokyo, Dirksen, who had received hints from friends in the Japanese General Staff. Dirksen, *Moskau, Tokio, London*, p. 184.

seemed to have some justification. The treaty was, however, an earnest of Ribbentrop's intention of effecting close cooperation with Japan in world politics generally, and for this reason was worthy of more attention. Cooperation with Japan would, after all, involve taking her side in her struggle with China, and this was in flat contradiction to the policy of friendship with the Chinese National government which the Foreign Office and the army had championed ever since the 1920's and which had recently been strengthened by arrangements for military and economic aid to that government.[99] The issue was not clearly posed until the outbreak of the China Incident in July 1937; but, after that time, the Japanese government had no hesitation in demanding the cessation of German aid to Chiang Kai-shek, basing their demands upon the spirit of political collaboration which had been expressed in the Anti-Comintern Pact.

The Foreign Office brusquely rejected the Japanese request, arguing that Japan's military action was in itself inconsistent with the spirit of the Anti-Comintern Pact, since it could only serve to drive China into the arms of communism, and insisting further that Germany intended to remain neutral in the Far Eastern conflict.[100] But this was a position which it could not long maintain. Ribbentrop, disappointed in his earlier hopes of obtaining a comprehensive agreement with Great Britain, had now swung to the opposite extreme and had convinced himself that a union of Germany, Italy, and Japan would assure his country of effective control of continental affairs.[101] Throughout the fall of 1937 he was working feverishly—and, characteristically, behind the Foreign Office's back—to secure Italy's adhesion to the Anti-Comintern Pact, an objective which he attained in November.[102] Simultaneously, he had accepted the Japanese position completely and was making every effort to persuade the Fuehrer that, since definitive Japanese victory in the Far East could not be long delayed, it would be the part of political wisdom to yield to Tokyo's desires.[103] The first intimation of his success came in October, when Goering ordered the stoppage of military deliveries to China.[104]

[99] *German Documents*, series D, I, 852-853.   [100] *ibid.*, pp. 733-734.

[101] See, for instance, the confused, illogical, and often hopelessly inaccurate memorandum which he wrote in December 1937 and submitted to Hitler in January. *Ibid.*, pp. 162-168.

[102] In the preliminary negotiations, the Foreign Office informed the Italian government that Germany preferred a separate Italo-Japanese agreement. On the following day, Raumer of the *Büro Ribbentrop* contradicted this, saying that Germany preferred Italian adhesion to the Japanese-German treaty. *Ibid.*, pp. 15-18. See also Galeazzo Ciano, *L'Europa verso la catastrofe* (Verona, 1948), pp. 212-226; Ciano, *1937-1938 Diario* (Bologna, 1948), pp. 37-38; Kordt, *Nicht aus den Akten*, p. 169.

[103] *German Documents*, series D, I, 758-759.   [104] *ibid.*, pp. 767-769, 772.

The Foreign Office and the army command were able to have this order reversed; but this was a temporary victory and, in the spring of 1938—after a German attempt to mediate the eastern conflict was defeated by Japanese intransigence[105]—the last links with China were broken.[106]

By any measure, therefore, the period that stretched from the middle of 1936 to the end of 1937 was one of steady decline for the Foreign Office. Even in Spain, one area in which it could claim that its advice had not been wholly disregarded, a major part of its energies had been expended in seeking to discover and control the activities of other agencies which were trying to usurp its legitimate functions. Elsewhere, its consultative prerogatives had been ignored and its advice overruled, while it was frequently left in ignorance of pending agreements with other Powers or important changes in the direction of national policy. And now the professionals were to experience their crowning humiliation, for, in February 1938, in the major reorganization of the state administration which prefaced the opening of a new and aggressive phase of his foreign policy, Hitler dismissed Neurath and made Joachim von Ribbentrop Foreign Minister of the Reich.[107]

V

This was a shattering blow to a diplomatic corps which had persisted in believing that Ribbentrop would, sooner or later, overreach himself. Some attempts were made, of course, at self-reassurance. Ambassador Dirksen, who was to take over at London, comforted himself with the reflection that at least the ruinous competition between the Foreign Office and the Ribbentrop Bureau would now come to an end.[108] Ernst von Weizsäcker, head of the Political Department, who was now invited

---

[105] The documents bearing on the mediation attempt are in *ibid.*, pp. 787-825.

[106] For the further development of German-Japanese relations, see Chapter 20 below.

[107] The reasons for Hitler's action are by no means clear. At Nuremberg, Neurath claimed that he himself had taken the initiative; that he was so shocked by Hitler's revelation, in the famous conference with his generals on November 5, 1937, of his intention of proceeding against Austria and Czechoslovakia that he had a heart attack and subsequently submitted his resignation to Hitler; and that Hitler had accepted it reluctantly, saying, "But I will never make this Ribbentrop Foreign Minister!" *Conspiracy and Aggression*, Supplement B, pp. 969, 1491. Hossbach, who was present at the meeting of November 5, does not mention either objections or perturbation on the part of Neurath (*Zwischen Wehrmacht und Hitler*, pp. 217-220); and it is significant that Neurath did not resist his new appointment as head of the so-called Secret Cabinet or his subsequent elevation, after March 1939, to the position of Reich Protector of Bohemia and Moravia. On the other hand, Ribbentrop does not seem to have expected any change in his own position, as Erich Kordt tells us. (*Nicht aus den Akten*, p. 178.) It seems likely that Hitler believed that Ribbentrop's energy was more suited to the coming period of action than Neurath's lassitude and hesitations. See François-Poncet, *Souvenirs*, p. 290.

[108] Dirksen, *Moskau, Tokio, London*, p. 199.

to take Bülow's old post of Secretary of State,[109] also concluded that all might yet be for the best. In a mood which was reminiscent of that which pervaded the diplomatic corps at the time of Hitler's accession in 1933, he told himself that Ribbentrop, despite his "fantastic political imagination," could be influenced;[110] and that the Foreign Office might now regain its legitimate influence over the course of state policy.

There were, indeed, some aspects of Ribbentrop's activity which were immensely reassuring to the professionals of the Wilhelmstrasse. "He used to say," the chief of the Legal Division testified at Nuremberg, "that everything that the Foreign Office lost in the way of terrain under Neurath he wanted to win back and, with all his passion, he fought for this aim in a manner which can only be understood by somebody who actually saw it." "My main activity," the legal adviser added, "was nearly 90 per cent concerned with his competency conflicts.[111] The new Foreign Minister did what Neurath had never dared, or at least attempted, to do. He put up a strong defensive against the incursions of the AO, both within the Foreign Office itself and in the field missions, and gathered his strength for a successful offensive against Bohle's pretensions which was finally carried through in 1941. At the same time, he sought to regain the ground ceded earlier to the Propaganda Ministry and, by 1939, had persuaded Hitler to permit him to make known his "wishes and instructions" to Goebbels and to maintain liaison with the Propaganda Ministry. Against party comrades who sought to employ the tactics which he had himself used so successfully, Ribbentrop was a pitiless and effective antagonist; and his "paranoical battle to broaden (or at least defend) the jurisdictional sphere of the Foreign Office assured the latter of its institutional survival in a sea of competitors."[112]

It was essentially, however, a survival without meaning. In Ribbentrop's conception, the Foreign Office was meant to be a technical apparatus and nothing more. His most explicit definition of its functions was not made until the war years, when Steengracht von Moyland succeeded Weizsäcker as Secretary of State, but it may be taken as expressing his belief at the time of his entrance into the Foreign Office. "Your

---

[109] For other changes which took place at this time, see *Trials of War Criminals*, XII, 149. A complete list of officials as of December 1, 1937 will be found in *German Documents*, series D, I, 1187-1198, and a list as of June 1, 1938 in *ibid.*, II, 1031-1040.

[110] *Trials of War Criminals*, XII, 922. See also Weizsäcker, *Erinnerungen*, pp. 152-155.

[111] *Trials of War Criminals*, XII, 1190.

[112] Paul Seabury, "Ribbentrop and the German Foreign Office," *Political Science Quarterly*, LXVI (1951), 554. This article, from which some of the details in the paragraph above are taken, is the most intelligent treatment yet to appear of Ribbentrop's administration of the Foreign Office.

sphere of tasks," Ribbentrop said, "includes these points: you must handle routine contacts with diplomats in Berlin; you must maintain discipline in the Foreign Office; and you must protect the competencies of the Foreign Office towards all agencies with ruthless energy." Steengracht said modestly that he supposed that he would have a voice in policy matters also. Ribbentrop denied this absolutely. Policy, he said, "was exclusively the concern of Hitler and himself. The Foreign Office and myself [Steengracht] were just to carry out the orders we received."[113]

From the time of the *Anschluss,* which was effected before he had formally assumed charge at the Wilhelmstrasse, until the outbreak of the war and after, Ribbentrop directed the Foreign Office in this spirit. The virtue which he prized most highly in his subordinates was loyalty,[114] and he was fond of lining them up and gazing into their eyes, as if seeking to divine the extent of their devotion. But their advice on policy was not desired by a Foreign Minister who believed that his own chief function was to execute the Fuehrer's wishes and to protect Hitler from doubts and from the considerations which might instill them. It was for this reason that reports from Germany's embassies abroad which seemed to challenge the bases of the aggressive policy which Hitler was now following were carefully prevented from reaching the Fuehrer's eyes; the futility to which this reduced the ambassadorial function will be described in a later chapter.[115]

The Foreign Minister insulated himself and his master just as fully from the cautionary advices of his immediate aides. In August 1938, when Weizsäcker sought to convince the Foreign Minister that an attempt to solve the Czech problem by force of arms would almost certainly lead to war, Ribbentrop reminded him that it was not his duty to make comments of this nature. "Herr von Ribbentrop sought to represent the question of responsibility in such a way that I was responsible to him alone, he to the Fuehrer alone, and the Fuehrer solely to the German people, while I maintained that it was necessary to be deeply rooted in the theory of . . . policy in order to carry it out to the best advantage. Herr von Ribbentrop declared that the Fuehrer had never yet made a mistake; his most difficult decisions and acts (occupation of the Rhineland) already lay behind him. It was necessary to believe in his genius, just as he, R., did from long years of experience. If I had not yet reached the stage of blind belief . . . then he desired of me, in a

---

[113] *Trials of War Criminals,* XIII, 25.
[114] Kordt, *Nicht aus den Akten,* pp. 199-200.   [115] See Chapter 15 below.

friendly manner and urgently, too, that I should do so. I should certainly regret it later, if I did not succeed in doing so and the facts then contradicted me."[116]

In May 1939, as Germany began her preparations for the operation against Poland, Ribbentrop was more threatening in the advice which he gave to his permanent officials. Even if the Polish government elected to resist German claims and war came as a result, he is reported to have said, Poland would collapse within twenty-four hours and Britain would not dare to intervene; and, if he should hear a Foreign Office official expressing contrary views on this matter, he would personally shoot him and assume responsibility for this action before the Fuehrer.[117]

In the face of these admonitions, the Foreign Office became little more than a stenographic bureau. Even those officials who were dismayed by what was obviously a headlong rush toward war and the probable destruction of Germany were powerless to influence the course of policy. They were reduced to such methods as sending secret warnings of pending actions to friendly circles in foreign countries—warnings which were rarely understood or believed and never acted upon—and talking of conspiracies and putsches which never materialized until it was too late. Aside from this, they could only go about their customary dignified business of inditing notes and sealing diplomatic pouches, while they waited for the inevitable to happen.

[116] *German Documents*, series D, II, 593.
[117] Kordt, *Nicht aus den Akten*, p. 332.

14

Three Observers in Berlin:
Rumbold, Dodd, and François-Poncet

BY FRANKLIN L. FORD

THE position of the ambassador is one of the points where diplomatic history relates most clearly to the history of institutions, ideas, and social forms in general. For the envoy is the product of one society, transplanted into another which inevitably possesses certain unfamiliar characteristics. With the latter he must deal as best he can, combining the fullest possible comprehension and even sympathy with a steady awareness of the interests of his own nation. It is a balance more easily prescribed than achieved, and to analyze the performance of any given ambassador is to accept a challenge demanding the exploitation of every tool and every insight into human experience at the historian's disposal.

The above applies with particular acuteness to the case of foreign envoys to Germany in the 1930's, since the complexities of the ambassador's position are never greater than when the country to which he is sent is undergoing internal convulsions. In such a setting the foreign diplomat is no longer merely called upon to adjust to traditions and social forms differing in some degree from those of his own country, but not in themselves incomprehensible. Now he must describe, assess, even predict and recommend, in the light of changes that threaten his most comfortable assumptions about the state to which he is accredited.

Such was the situation confronting the three men, British, American, and French, respectively, with whom this chapter is concerned. Each of them served in Berlin during some portion of the decade preceding the second world war. Each brought with him some prior knowledge of and experience in Germany. Each had to decide what kind of a Germany was emerging under Nazi leadership. Would other nations be able to live with this Third Reich, and if so, on what terms? Ultimately the conclusions of each envoy were determined by his personal temperament and aspirations, by his conception of his country's vital interests, by his historically oriented judgment of the prospects, and finally—a point not easy to put succinctly—by his more or less conscient selection of those values in modern civilization which he felt must be defended. Obviously these separate elements differed from one man to the next, not only in specific content but also in their order of importance to the individual concerned. To appreciate the resulting variations of response, one need only refer to the body of diplomatic documents and personal memoirs now available for the period. Such records are by no means as yet complete, but already they offer a substantial basis for investigation.

I

On August 10, 1928, Sir Horace Rumbold, P.C., K.C.B., 9th Bt., presented his credentials to President Hindenburg. When Sir Horace took up his duties in the big embassy on the Wilhelmstrasse, just off Unter den Linden, Germany's Chancellor was a Social Democrat, Müller, and her Foreign Minister was Stresemann. In May 1933, when Sir Eric Phipps succeeded to the ambassadorship, Müller's party had just been suppressed and Stresemann's foreign policy was well on its way to oblivion. During a tenure of slightly under five years, Rumbold had seen Germany adhere to the Kellogg-Briand Pact in 1929, had seen Brüning advance to the Chancellorship in March 1930, and had seen economic disaster break upon central Europe in the spring of 1931. Then he had watched the procession of Chancellors, from Papen in May 1932, through Schleicher the following December, to Adolf Hitler in January 1933. When he left Berlin that spring, he had just witnessed the legalization of Nazi dictatorship in the Enabling Act of March 23.

Sir Horace, like his father and grandfather before him, was a professional, "the ideal diplomatist," Harold Nicolson was to call him.[1] Born in 1869 in St. Petersburg, he had passed his competence examination for the foreign service at the age of twenty-two. Between 1892 and the outbreak of the first world war he had served in Cairo under Lord Cromer, in Teheran, Vienna, Madrid, Tokyo, and finally, as counselor of embassy, in Berlin during the tense summer of 1914. Thereafter, he had been minister to Switzerland and to Poland, High Commissioner in Constantinople from 1920 to 1923, and ambassador to Spain until 1928. With this remarkable odyssey behind him he returned to Berlin after an absence of fourteen years.

He was now almost sixty, a heavy-set man possessed of impeccable manners, a certain wry wit, and very few discernible emotions. The

---

[1] In the dedication of *Diplomacy* (London, 1939).

personality which emerges from his dispatches and from his book on 1914[2] is that of an analyst who resists extreme views. Yet Rumbold was not easygoing. He could be stubborn, and intelligently so, as when he and General Sir Charles Harington refused in 1922 to deliver the British Cabinet's ultimatum to Turkey over Chanak, and subsequently received their government's thanks![3] For all his apparent blandness, he could become extremely upset and extremely angry; and in the long run the Nazis both upset and angered him. Speaking the careful, faintly archaic language of diplomacy, at times confused by false analogies drawn from a rich store of experience, at other times tripping over his own social and professional prejudices, he nonetheless won through to a strikingly prescient view of the dangers which appeared on the European horizon with the advent of Hitler.

Rumbold's judgment of the Nazi movement and its rise to political hegemony is, of course, the most significant aspect of his career in terms of the present chapter. It would be well, however, to pause long enough for a brief look at his methods and certain of his opinions regarding developments prior to Hitler's triumph. This is important, because the ambassador's performance in dealing with pre-1933 diplomats and politicians under relatively normal conditions in Berlin provides a background for his later comments on the pathology of Nazism.

Sir Horace was an assiduous reporter for his Foreign Office. His dispatches to London were frequent and detailed (in the second series of the British documents, there appear 303 messages from Rumbold sent between January 4, 1930 and March 25, 1933—and even these represent a selection). In return, he appears to have enjoyed the full confidence of his superiors in England. Nothing suggests that he was ever rebuked for indiscretions, as Nevile Henderson was to be later,[4] or that he ever felt that negotiations were by-passing him. In pursuance of his duties as an observer he used several sources of information, of which the easiest to identify was a definite circle of German officials chiefly notable for the moderation of both their views and their manners: Foreign Minister Curtius, Secretary of State Bülow of the Wilhelmstrasse, Secretary of State Weismann of the Prussian Ministry of Interior, Chief of the Presidential Chancellery Meissner, Secretary of State Planck of the Reich

---

[2] *The War Crisis in Berlin: July-August, 1914* (London, 1940).

[3] Harold Nicolson, *Curzon: The Last Phase* (Boston, New York, 1934), p. 275. In *Water under the Bridges* (London, 1945), Sir Nevile Henderson comments repeatedly and enthusiastically on Rumbold's firmness and intelligence during his period as High Commissioner in Turkey, at which time Henderson was himself a principal aide at Constantinople.

[4] See Chapter 17, § 1 below.

Chancellery, and others. His Majesty's representative had little personal contact with Germans who would have felt ill at ease in the deep arm-chairs of his own Travellers' Club in London.

In all fairness to Rumbold, however, it must be said that his assess-ment of events generally went well beyond anything suggested to him by highly placed Germans. Several explanations for this fact suggest themselves. For one thing, the embassy staff offered some variety of opinions. Further, although Sir Horace long retained a relative aloofness toward his fellow ambassadors, from time to time he mentions having compared notes with French, American, Dutch, or Italian colleagues, especially during his crowded final year in Berlin. Most important of all, he read the newspapers and periodicals. His spoken German was not fluent (he knew Arabic better and Japanese almost as well), but he con-ducted his own press survey day in and day out. Some of his shrewdest comments relate to items from *Der Tag*, the *Frankfurter Zeitung*, or *Vorwärts*.

As regards general outlook, many Western diplomats who were later to be far more conciliatory than Rumbold toward the Germany of Hitler were far harsher than he toward the Germany of Stresemann and Brüning. His tone was one of caution during the Weimar period and became one of unequivocal alarm with the proclamation of the Third Reich, but it cannot be said that he let degrees of German strength alone determine his attitude in speaking to or about the Germans themselves. There is in Rumbold's record none of that transition from arrogance to fawning which looms so unpleasantly in the case histories of some of his contemporaries.

Not that he could be called, by any stretching of the term, a Germano-phile. He never forgot the Kaiser or Tirpitz or Schlieffen, and he came to Berlin a convinced believer in Germany's war guilt of 1914. His book on the outbreak of the first world war makes no concessions on this point of history. Nor was he a partisan of any balance of power theory based on distrust of France and reliance on Germany. In the spring of 1930, he hoped that France would not delay its scheduled evacuation of the Rhine-land,[5] but added subsequently that Germany "has little to fear of French aggression."[6] Referring to reactions in Berlin after the French did leave the Rhineland, he wrote in July 1930: "It is an unattractive feature of the German character to display little gratitude for favours received, but when the receipt of favours is followed up by fresh demands, there are

[5] *British Documents*, 2nd series, I, 477. Rumbold to Henderson, May 2, 1930.
[6] *ibid.*, 563. Rumbold to Henderson, February 26, 1931.

grounds for feeling impatient."⁷ While he reported in detail German complaints over the Versailles boundaries, he indulged in no expressions of sympathy for irredentist arguments.

Perhaps the fairest way to sum up Rumbold's attitude toward traditional nationalism in Germany is to say that he took it for granted. He seems to have assumed that the Weimar Republic would make certain claims and that men he admired, including Stresemann and later Brüning, would press their country's case, especially given the political pressure they themselves were under from the steadily growing mass chauvinism in the country. An old-fashioned kind of irredentism was something a seasoned diplomat could understand and presumably could parry. It had to be controlled by precautionary arrangements, might even have to be met head-on someday. Nevertheless, it was to be accepted as an inevitable product of returning German vitality.

Rumbold's treatment of three major issues of the pre-Hitler period, though none of them can be gone into in detail here, will at least illustrate his underlying assumptions. The first was the question of the German-Polish frontier. The ambassador was sure that, even under Weimar, this was the greatest point of danger in German foreign policy. In July 1930, he informed London of his concern over a talk he had had with Curtius, in the course of which the Foreign Minister had referred to Germany's eastern boundary as "absurd."⁸ The following month he summarized a belligerent speech by Treviranus concerning the Polish Corridor and betrayed his own misgivings by saying that he *hoped* the flareup represented only an episode, not a developing trend.⁹ Despite the official efforts in Berlin to play down the problem of *Ostpolitik*, Rumbold was still sure in February, 1931, that the Polish frontier dominated all other considerations in German thinking on foreign policy.¹⁰ He never abandoned this conviction.

The second problem on which he spent much time and thought was that of Germany's armaments. Rumbold was sure that the Germans would rearm, especially in view of their hostility to Poland. In repeated dispatches he passed along reports of illegal activity. It should be stressed that he never argued for complacency toward these treaty violations, as did his military attaché on at least one occasion.¹¹ He did, however, in-

---

⁷ *ibid.*, 485. Rumbold to Henderson, July 3, 1930.
⁸ *ibid.*, 490. Rumbold to Henderson, July 3, 1930.
⁹ *ibid.*, 491. Rumbold to Henderson, August 12, 1930.
¹⁰ *ibid.*, 563. Rumbold to Henderson, February 26, 1931.
¹¹ *ibid.*, 11, Appendix IV. Colonel Marshall-Cornwall, in a report dated December 9, 1931, and forwarded by Rumbold to Simon, observed that there was much to be said for

sist that many German officials were going no further than nationalist agitation demanded, and he believed that left-wing opposition would keep rearmament within reasonable limits. The prevailing tone of his reports, on this point as on so many others prior to 1933, was a mixture of wariness and hope—wariness based on his fear of the potential violence of German nationalism, hope stemming from his belief in the essential moderation of the existing German government.

Third and last of these illustrative problems centered on the proposed German-Austrian Customs Union, the plan for which was communicated to the ambassador by Bülow in a talk on March 13, 1931. Rumbold's first move was to send London a factual account of the interview, attempting no analysis of its implications but giving full coverage to the Secretary of State's arguments, especially the plea that "the great point was to set the ball rolling and to revive trade."[12] Within ten days the British and French governments had been officially advised of the project by the accredited Austrian and German representatives, and the Western Powers' hostile reaction to the Union, as both a threatening preliminary to *Anschluss* and a discriminatory trade agreement, had begun to harden.[13] In Berlin, Rumbold carried out his instructions faithfully, representing to various officials his government's opposition to any special Austro-German arrangements. By July, in fact, he was able to report that his discreet urging had led influential members of the German Cabinet to accept the view that the plan should be withdrawn as soon as this could be done without a disastrous loss of face.[14]

This, however, was not the whole story from Rumbold's side. Equally important was the line he adopted toward his own Foreign Office in London. As early as March 26, less than a fortnight after learning of the proposed Union, the ambassador was emphasizing the dangers inherent in any public rebuff in Germany.[15] The next day he expanded this theme by conceding that the proposal had been badly presented but adding that Brüning "has to show the country some results" and that the Chancellor might be broken politically by a bullying reaction on the part of Britain and France.[16] Rumbold was particularly opposed to any move which would make the issue "devolve into a personal and public

---

the *Wehrgeist* as a defense against Bolshevism and added that "most decent Britons, were they Germans today, would be Stahlhelmers."

[12] *ibid.*, I, 587. Rumbold to Henderson, March 13, 1931.
[13] *ibid.*, II, 2-11. Vansittart to Rumbold, March 21 and 23, 1931.
[14] *ibid.*, 210. Rumbold to Henderson, July 17, 1931.
[15] *ibid.*, 16. Rumbold to Tyrrell (for Henderson), March 26, 1931.
[16] *ibid.*, 21. Rumbold to Henderson, March 27, 1931.

struggle between MM. Briand and Brüning."[17] One gets the impression that the ambassador was fully alive to the danger of a slide toward full *Anschluss* if the Union were effected, that he was willing to examine the economic technicalities involved and to press quietly for abandonment of the scheme, but that his attention remained riveted on the political aspects of alternative Franco-British attitudes and their repercussions in German domestic politics. There can be no doubt that he was relieved when other public questions appeared on the scene to divert attention from the Customs Union; but he could only deplore the damage already done by those elements of humiliation for Germany which remained to exacerbate rancorous nationalism and to endanger German leaders on whom he felt the West had no choice but to rely.

Rumbold had admired Stresemann greatly—perhaps more than the record would seem to warrant—and on the whole he maintained a kindly feeling toward the succeeding Foreign Minister, as he revealed when the latter left office in October 1931: "My principal colleagues and I regret Dr. Curtius' departure from the Ministry of Foreign Affairs. Although he had neither the imagination, the wide outlook, nor the political genius of his predecessor, he was a level-headed man, while his quiet and courteous manner made him pleasant to deal with."[18] His feeling toward Wilhelmstrasse officials was assuredly not one of uncritical confidence, as he had shown in his analysis of even Curtius' playing with fire on the Polish boundary issue,[19] and again in his reservations about the suave and amiable Bülow, "whom I suspect of Nationalist tendencies."[20] Nevertheless, the ambassador counted on such men for realism and a conservative resistance to chauvinistic gambles. At any rate, he had no difficulty in imagining much worse. His early admiration for Chancellor Brüning, whose "courageous frankness" in the face of economic depression and political agitation he pointed out to London early in 1931,[21] and his generally good opinion of President Hindenburg must be discussed in connection with the events of 1932 and 1933, since the latter modified in some respects his views concerning both men. The important point, however, is that, until Hitler came to power, Sir Horace never displayed any deep or consistent alarm with regard to

---

[17] *ibid.*, 24. Rumbold to Henderson, March 30, 1931.

[18] *ibid.*, 278. Rumbold to Reading, October 6, 1931.

[19] *ibid.*, I, 524. Rumbold to Henderson, October 27, 1930. "Whilst I am satisfied that he [Curtius] will not embark on a foreign policy of adventure, there are signs that he will, if I may use the expression, 'increase the *tempo*'."

[20] *ibid.*, II, 211. Rumbold to Tyrrell (for Henderson), July 18, 1931.

[21] *ibid.*, I, 573. Rumbold to Henderson, March 4, 1931.

German foreign policy. Hence, to understand how he arrived at the views which he was to expound on the eve of his departure from Berlin, it is necessary to examine his analysis of the overshadowing development in German domestic politics during his time there, to wit, the accession of the Nazis.

National Socialism began to figure prominently in the ambassador's dispatches only in the fall of 1930. Writing to London on September 7 of that year concerning the *Reichstag* election campaign, he noted the Nazis' intense activity as an exception to the general apathy and reported that some predictions gave this "new and vigorous movement" as many as 50 or 60 seats.[22] Actually it won 107 seats, as compared with its previous 12, in the voting a week later; but Herr Weismann hastened to dismiss the Nazis' success as ephemeral,[23] and Rumbold himself initially adopted the reassuring thesis that Hitler's party, unprepared for its sudden gains, would now have to quiet down and accept some parliamentary responsibility.[24] Though not inclined to take Nazism lightly, Sir Horace still felt in March 1931, that "a nation of such stout fibre, containing as it does unplumbed reserves of strength, especially in the business community, is not going to fail eventually to master its difficulties."[25]

An interesting aspect of the subsequent evolution in Rumbold's thinking was the change in his opinion as to where the Nazis should be placed in the political spectrum. On this point he originally accepted the view of his German informants that Nazism, like Communism and Social Democracy, was a proletarian movement. As late as December 1932, he called the NSDAP one of "the three great parties of the Left."[26] But he took due note of the Harzburg conference between Nazi and right-wing leaders in the fall of 1931;[27] and in a dispatch of June 28, 1932, he spoke of "those many better class people who regard the Nazi movement as a timely revival of nationalism which it will not be difficult for the right people to control and exploit."[28] The major change in Rumbold's thinking on this matter, however, came with the crisis in the Nazi high command at the end of 1932; for he felt that the defection of Gregor Strasser removed the last check on Hitler's own inclination to

---

[22] *ibid.*, 504. Rumbold to Henderson, September 7, 1930.
[23] *ibid.*, 510. Rumbold to Henderson, September 18, 1930.
[24] *ibid.*, 512. Rumbold to Henderson, September 25, 1930.
[25] *ibid.*, 573. Rumbold to Henderson, March 4, 1931.
[26] *ibid.*, IV, 92. Rumbold to Simon, December 7, 1932.
[27] *ibid.*, II, 295. Rumbold to Reading, October 14, 1931.
[28] *ibid.*, IV, 3. Rumbold to Simon, June 28, 1932.

join forces with big business.[29] The first dispatch following the selection of Hitler as Chancellor bluntly pairs him with Hugenberg as "reactionary and anti-parliamentary";[30] and a few days later Rumbold wrote that "the ship is definitely going to the starboard again."[31]

Concerning the Nazi leaders Rumbold had to sift widely differing judgments. He was told of Hitler's interest in fortune tellers,[32] heard him described by General Hammerstein as "a very mediocre personality,"[33] by General Groener as something worse than the "visionary but decent individual" he had at first appeared,[34] by Meissner as "quite reasonable and moderate" in private conversation, though apt to rave if excited.[35] Rumbold's first unequivocal assessment on his own authority was that "Hitler may be no statesman, but he is an uncommonly clever and audacious demagogue . . . fully alive to every popular instinct."[36] Of the other party chiefs Sir Horace generally spoke with contempt. The one exception was Strasser, whom he called "the ablest of the National Socialist leaders and a strong man."[37] Goebbels he considered "vulgar, unscrupulous and irresponsible";[38] Goering, a ruthless adventurer inclined to overplay his hand.[39] Before he left Germany, however, Rumbold had to concede that these "gangsters" had succeeded in their aim of "bringing to the surface the worst traits in the German character, i.e., a mean spirit of revenge, a tendency to brutality, and a noisy and irresponsible jingoism."[40]

As long as the issue in Germany was still in doubt, Rumbold placed his hopes in "that union of the bourgeois parties for which the situation seems to call."[41] He never sought to conceal his aversion to Communism; and he showed no particular warmth toward the Social Democrats until 1932, when they began to win his sympathy as victims of reactionary violence. Time and again it was the Center party to which he assigned the crucial role, pressing his hope that the moderate conservatives would rally to the support of Brüning. He neither expected

[29] *ibid.*, 385. Rumbold to Simon, January 11, 1933.
[30] *ibid.*, 398. Rumbold to Simon, January 30, 1933.
[31] *ibid.*, 409. Rumbold to Simon, February 7, 1933.
[32] *ibid.*, III, 99. Rumbold to Simon, February 17, 1932.
[33] *ibid.*, 101. Rumbold to Simon, March 1, 1932.
[34] *ibid.*, 113. Rumbold to Simon, April 13, 1932.
[35] *ibid.*, IV, 56. Rumbold to Simon, September 28, 1932.
[36] *ibid.*, 423. Rumbold to Simon, February 22, 1933.
[37] *ibid.*, 28. Rumbold to Simon, August 13, 1932.
[38] *ibid.*, 3. Rumbold to Simon, June 28, 1932.
[39] *ibid.*, 49. Rumbold to Simon, September 13, 1932.
[40] *ibid.*, 452. Rumbold to Simon, March 14, 1933.
[41] *ibid.*, II, 280. Rumbold to Reading, October 7, 1931.

nor thought desirable a restoration of the Hohenzollern monarchy, observing on one occasion that to ask a German if he were a monarchist would be like asking a drowning man how he felt about music and painting.[42]

It was to President Hindenburg that he looked for stability. Despite his awareness of Papen's hold over the old man and the influence of the President's Junker friends in blocking even timid reforms, Sir Horace long clung to his faith in Hindenburg's beneficent role. The fall of Brüning, whom he saw as an honest and moderate politician, disturbed him deeply. Nevertheless, in a dispatch written four months after that event, he conceded that Brüning's use of emergency decrees had helped to undermine the parliamentary system;[43] and he deplored the ex-Chancellor's efforts to reach an understanding with Hitler. As for Papen, the ambassador considered him a frivolous and cynical opportunist, whereas Schleicher impressed him as an intelligent political general who at least had stuck to his post after 1918.[44]

These few references will, I hope, have sufficed to reveal Rumbold as an observer of the German scene who was critical but until the Nazi coup d'état never blackly pessimistic. It is only against the background here sketched that one can appreciate the dramatic change in tone involved in his dispatches of late winter and spring 1933. Turning even on Hindenburg, he then wrote: "The Left parties are largely responsible for the President's re-election and are now compelled to witness the forces of reaction ruling this country with an irresponsibility and a frivolous disregard for all decent feeling which is without precedent in its history. There can be no other language to apply to the action of the present Government in ousting hundreds of Prussian and Reich officials from their posts for no other crime than the holding of political views to which they are constitutionally entitled."[45] This, be it remembered, was a seasoned professional diplomat and a baronet, speaking in defense of Germans, many of whom he disagreed with to the core of his political beliefs.

What could one expect of the "new Germany" in international affairs? Rumbold's valedictory, a dispatch sent on April 26, 1933, is explicit enough.[46] Reviewing the bellicose pronouncements in Hitler's speeches

---

[42] *ibid.*, IV, 83. Rumbold to Simon, November 24, 1932.

[43] *ibid.*, 54. Rumbold to Simon, September 21, 1932.

[44] *ibid.*, 92, 389. Rumbold to Simon, December 7, 1932, and January 25, 1933.

[45] *ibid.*, 423. Rumbold to Simon, February 22, 1933.

[46] This dispatch, which postdates those so far published in the *British Documents*, appears as an appendix to Rumbold's *War Crisis in Berlin*, 344-358. All quotations used here are from that text.

and in *Mein Kampf*, the ambassador concludes that "the outlook for Europe is far from peaceful. . . . It would be misleading to base any hopes on a return to sanity or a serious modification of the views of the Chancellor and his entourage. . . . I cannot help thinking that many of the measures taken by the new Government of recent weeks aim at the inculcation of that silence, or *Schweigsamkeit*, which Hitler declares in his memoirs to be essential to military preparations."

For Rumbold, the Germany of 1933, like that of 1905, was in transition. "The task of the present German Government is more complicated [than that of Admiral Tirpitz]. They have to rearm on land and . . . to lull their adversaries into such a state of coma that they will allow themselves to be engaged one by one." It was difficult to believe that a European government, after the experiences of the first world war, would embark on so dangerous a policy, "but the actions of the new Government have already shown the world that, like former German Governments, they are capable of almost any degree of self-deception." When Sir Horace went home to an exceedingly active retirement in May 1933, he expected the worst. When he died in May 1941, at his family home, Pythouse, in Wiltshire, his fears had long since passed into a terrible reality.

II

During those same spring weeks of 1933, while Rumbold was sending his final reports from Berlin, the United States government was hunting a replacement for Frederic M. Sackett, who in March retired as ambassador to Germany. The newly inaugurated President Roosevelt considered several possibilities for the post, including James M. Cox, Nicholas Murray Butler, and Newton D. Baker; but ultimately the choice fell on a professor of history at the University of Chicago, William E. Dodd. Roosevelt had never met Dodd; but the Secretary of Commerce, Daniel C. Roper, had known him since the campaign of 1916, when both had worked for Wilson, and the nomination had the support of the aging Colonel House, of Assistant Secretary of State R. Walton Moore, and of Secretaries Ickes and Swanson.[47] Roper recalls that he personally "believed that Dodd would be astute in handling diplomatic duties and, when conferences grew tense, he would turn the tide by quoting Jefferson."[48] Cordell Hull, though he knew and liked

---

[47] *Ambassador Dodd's Diary, 1933-1938*, ed. William E. Dodd, Jr. and Martha Dodd (New York, 1941), pp. 9-10.

[48] Daniel C. Roper, *Fifty Years of Public Life* (Durham, N.C., 1941), pp. 334-335.

Dodd, was less enthusiastic because of the latter's tendency to "run off on tangents every now and then, like our friend William Jennings Bryan."[49] The Secretary of State announced himself agreeable, however, and on June 8, 1933, the President telephoned his offer to Professor Dodd in Chicago. On the 10th the Senate confirmed his nomination.[50]

The ambassador-designate was an experienced teacher, a man of transparent integrity and a distinguished historian of America, especially of the South. Born sixty-three years before in Clayton, North Carolina, he had received his scholarly training at Virginia Polytechnic and at the University of Leipzig, where he took his Ph.D., with a thesis on Jefferson, in 1900. He had been on the faculty at Chicago since 1908. The long list of his published works included biographies of Nathaniel Macon and Jefferson Davis, *The Cotton Kingdom, Statesmen of the Old South, Lincoln or Lee, Woodrow Wilson and His Work*, in addition to the six volumes of Wilson's public papers which he edited with Ray Stannard Baker. Dodd's particular contribution to the historiography of the South had been a rare balance in treating the weaknesses and the virtues of southern society in the pre-Civil War era. For the rest, his writings reveal a devotion to Jeffersonianism at its most idealized, a Wilsonian faith in internationalism, and, in articles composed after Roosevelt's election in 1932, a lively enthusiasm for the New Deal as an antidote to the power of "big interests." Roosevelt's precise reasons for appointing him will probably never be known, but Dodd's belief that he was to go to Berlin as a living sermon on democracy seems to have reflected his early instructions honestly enough.

The President was also getting an envoy who would set forth with high hopes for German-American friendship. Through half a lifetime, Dodd had cherished the memories of his university life in the old empire. In addition, though only an irregular Baptist churchgoer, he looked with reverence upon the Lutheran Reformation and honored "this ancient realm of religious liberty."[51] He considered the Germans to be "by nature more democratic than any other great race in Europe,"[52] deplored the harshness of Versailles and felt considerable hostility to-

---

[49] Cordell Hull, *Memoirs* (New York, 1948), I, 183.

[50] There has long been current a story, actually published by E. J. Flynn in *You're the Boss* (New York, 1947), p. 148, to the effect that the call to Dodd resulted from a confusion in names, since Roosevelt had decided to appoint Walter F. Dodd, a former law professor at Illinois and Yale, but by 1933 in private practice in Chicago. However, Flynn retracted the story almost immediately after the appearance of his book (*New York Times*, November 2, 1947). It is in any case flatly contradicted by Hull's and Roper's memoirs.

[51] *Ambassador Dodd's Diary*, p. 400.   [52] *ibid.*, p. 447.

ward French policy since 1918. As he boarded the *S.S. Washington* in New York on July 5, 1933, he issued the following statement: "The realities of the American past as well as the dilemma of the present reconcile me to the adventure I am about to undertake. Germany can hardly fail to realize the importance of friendly cooperation with the 120,000,000 people of the United States, and the United States can hardly fail to realize the value of economic and social cooperation with the land of Luther, Stein and Bismarck. Though difficulties lie ahead, one can hardly think that an honest, frank mission to Berlin can fail of good result."[53]

The Dodds, husband, wife and two grown children, docked at Hamburg on July 13 and went directly to Berlin, where after some delay they succeeded in renting a comfortable house on the Tiergartenstrasse. Dodd was insistent that the family should live within his salary of $17,500, since he had no extra funds of his own to spend.[54] Nevertheless, his daughter recalls that, at least during the first part of his ambassadorship, "our house was always full of people—young Germans, students, Foreign Office attachés, Government officials, newspapermen, and officers in the S.A., or S.S., or Reichswehr."[55] In addition to the American journalists, with whom he got along well on the whole, Dodd quickly acquired several confidants in the diplomatic corps, chief among whom were the Spanish ambassador, Zulueta (a former philosophy professor), and the aristocratic Dutch minister, Limburg-Stirum. Toward his other fellow diplomats he felt less cordial, though he liked Sir Eric Phipps better than he had expected to and enjoyed what he took to be passages of wit with François-Poncet at social functions or on strolls in the Tiergarten. One of François-Poncet's aides, young Armand Berard, came often to the house; and it was he who represented the real link between the French and American embassies, so far as Dodd was concerned.

A combination of nervous indigestion and boredom at formal affairs led the ambassador to keep his personal routine as simple as possible, given his position. On his occasional pleasure trips he studiously avoided luxury, and it was a point of pride with him that his modest habits made for closer contact with the German people than usual diplomatic be-

[53] *New York Times*, July 6, 1933.
[54] Not long after reaching Berlin, Dodd wrote to thank President Roosevelt for arranging to have the embassy salaries paid in gold, which action "prevented the necessity of resignation on my part." Franklin D. Roosevelt Library [hereafter cited as *R.L.*], P.P.F. (President's Personal File) 1043. Dodd to Roosevelt, October 28, 1933.
[55] Martha Dodd, *Through Embassy Eyes* (New York, 1939), p. 47.

havior would have permitted. He was careful to sidestep any honorary degrees under Nazi auspices, but he loved to visit the university towns. Only shrines of the Reformation attracted him as much. When in Berlin, he insisted on keeping up his scholarship, completing the first volume (and the only one to appear) of his *Old South* while still ambassador. I am told by one of his principal deputies in the embassy that, at least in 1936 and 1937, Dodd could frequently be found in his office thumbing through a card file containing genealogies of Virginia families. During his earlier, more optimistic and energetic period, however, he seems to have simply added his research and writing to the normal round of appointments and social appearances.

Dodd was ambassador to Germany for four and a half years. The period between his arrival and the Blood Purge of June 30-July 1, 1934, was a time of first impressions, of mounting indignation, but still of hope. In August, for example, he wrote to President Roosevelt, recommending that the U.S. government keep an open mind on the Nazis: "This is given not in defense of German armaments and anti-semitic attitudes (both contrary to all liberal philosophy), but to explain the tense situation and the possibility of worse things ahead. Fundamentally, I believe a people has a right to govern itself and that other peoples must exercise patience even when crudities and injustices are done. Give men a chance to try their schemes."[56]

His first interview with Hitler, on October 17, was not as alarming as he had expected it to be. Dodd's "final impression was of his belligerence and self-confidence," but the Chancellor promised to punish any Storm Troopers who subsequently attacked Americans and only ranted in a general way about the Treaty of Versailles.[57] At a second interview, the following March, Hitler was more truculent but still not wholly unconciliatory, declaring that "Germany wants peace and will do everything to keep the peace; but Germany demands and will have equality of rights in the matter of armaments."[58] In the interval between these two talks Dodd had written to Roosevelt that at least Hindenburg represented a moderate policy.[59]

All of this suggests, I think rightly, that well into 1934 the ambassador still believed in a wide range of future possibilities. Nevertheless, al-

---

[56] *R.L.*, O.F. (Official File) 523. Dodd to Roosevelt, August 12, 1933.

[57] *Foreign Relations*, 1933, II, 396-397. Dodd to Hull, October 17, 1933. Also *Ambassador Dodd's Diary*, p. 50.

[58] *Foreign Relations*, 1934, II, 220. Dodd memorandum, March 7, 1934.

[59] *R.L.*, P.S.F. (President's Secretary's File), Box 10, *Dodd* folder. Dodd to Roosevelt, February 8, 1934.

most from the day he arrived, he engaged in a campaign of admonition-by-analogy which left little doubt as to his feelings about the Nazi dictatorship. Speaking at the Columbus Day dinner of the American Chamber of Commerce in Berlin, just six weeks after having presented his credentials, he said in part: "There are not many forms of human association, though many new names have been invented from time to time. Half-educated statesmen of today swing violently away from the ideal purpose of Gracchus and think they find salvation for their troubled fellows in the arbitrary modes of the man who fell an easy victim to the cheap devices of the lewd Cleopatra. They forget that the Gracchus democracy failed upon the narrowest of margins and Caesar's succeeded only for a short moment as measured by the tests of history."[60] On the third day after this address, he wrote in his diary: "It is evident some dislike of me is arising here now in official circles. I believe it is simply Nazi opposition."[61]

Through the first months of 1934 Dodd maintained normal social contacts with leading Nazis—a *Bierabend* with Rosenberg, tea with Goebbels, a visit to Goering's hunting lodge, a chat with Ribbentrop. He had even invited S.A. leader Ernst Roehm to a dinner he was planning for July 6. Then came the Blood Purge—the execution of Roehm, Strasser, and scores of other party functionaries, the attack on Papen, the assassination of General Schleicher and his wife. So far as analysis was concerned, Dodd saw these measures as eliminating extremists, on both the Right and the Left, particularly the latter.[62] His emotional reaction, however, practically overpowered any effort at objectivity. Through the tense hours of the crisis, his daughter recalls, he was pale, excited, silent. On July 1, having learned that Papen was under house arrest, he made a point of stopping by to leave a card for the ex-Chancellor with the message, "I hope we may see you soon."[63] Of Hitler, Dodd wrote on July 13, "I have a sense of horror when I look at the man."[64] He never again had a private interview with the Fuehrer, though they met several times subsequently at large receptions for the entire diplomatic corps.

The next two and a half years, down to the end of 1936, constituted the second period of Dodd's service in Berlin, a period of worry over

[60] *New York Times*, October 13, 1933.
[61] *Ambassador Dodd's Diary*, p. 48.
[62] For Dodd's coverage of these events, see *Foreign Relations*, 1934, II, 229-243.
[63] *Ambassador Dodd's Diary*, p. 117; Martha Dodd, *Through Embassy Eyes*, pp. 148, 154-155.
[64] *Ambassador Dodd's Diary*, p. 126.

international conditions and of growing isolation from official life. He carried out his routine functions in the tedious and futile economic negotiations. He attended such social gatherings as he could not politely avoid. He had welcome trips to the United States in the winter of 1934-1935 and in the spring of 1936 (he had previously been home in the spring of 1934 for a rest). Back in Berlin, however, he remained hostile and despondent.

During those years Dodd never ceased to plead the cause of collective security. In August 1934, he urged Roper to sponsor more use of the League, especially after Russia's entry the following month, in order to restrain Germany and Japan.[65] In March 1935, the U.S. minister to Austria, Messersmith, noted Dodd's concurrence in a warning to Washington that no trust could be placed in Nazi promises and that Germany's aim was "unlimited territorial expansion."[66] The following October Dodd wrote to the President denouncing the Italian campaign in Ethiopia.[67] Germany's remilitarization of the Rhineland in March, 1936, he viewed as sending France into "a definite decline toward the position of Spain."[68]

The last year of Dodd's ambassadorship was, from his point of view, a near nightmare which included his involvement in the Supreme Court fight back in America, the Nuremberg Party Congress incident, and finally, his recall from Berlin. The first of these incidents can be briefly summarized. Dodd had never ceased to state his opinions on American political questions to anyone who would listen. Now, on May 11, 1937, the *Richmond Times-Dispatch* printed a letter written by Dodd to several United States Senators, and subsequently quoted by all leading papers, in which he urged support of Roosevelt's proposal for enlarging the Supreme Court, then went on to say: "There are individuals of great wealth who wish a dictatorship and are ready to help a Huey Long. There are politicians who think they may gain powers like those exercised in Europe. One man, I have been told by friends, who owns nearly a billion dollars, is ready to support such a program and, of course, control it."[69] Senator Borah promptly denounced Dodd as "an irresponsible scandalmonger" and "a disgrace to his country." Senators Van Nuys and King demanded his immediate recall. Senator

[65] *R.L.*, O.F. 523. Dodd to Roper, August 14, 1934.
[66] U.S. Department of State, *Peace and War: United States Foreign Policy, 1931-1941* (Washington, 1943), No. 44. Messersmith memorandum, March 22, 1935.
[67] *R.L.*, P.S.F., Box 10, *Dodd* folder. Dodd to Roosevelt, October 31, 1935.
[68] *ibid.*, Box 19, *Dodd* folder. Dodd to Roosevelt, April 1, 1936.
[69] *New York Times*, May 12, 1937.

Nye tried unsuccessfully to have him subpoenaed by Congress and forced to name his billionaire. The target of all this did not reveal the name, and he was not then recalled from Berlin. Nevertheless, there was no question that he was now *persona non grata* with influential groups in two capitals.

Dodd came home on leave for the fourth time in early August 1937, and did not return to Germany until the end of October. Just before leaving Berlin he had learned from François-Poncet that all or most of the diplomats accredited to the Reich would for the first time attend the Nazi Party Congress in a body that September. Dodd had curtly reiterated his view that ambassadors should not appear at party rallies.[70] This time, however, the State Department overruled him. American newspapers of September 4 not only discussed the appearance at Nuremberg of Prentiss Gilbert, our *chargé* in Germany during the ambassador's absence, but also printed sections of a confidential letter of protest which Dodd had written to Hull ten days before. Dodd was furious over the leak, which of course damaged still further his standing in Berlin, and over the public repudiation of his views. From Williamstown, Massachusetts, where he was attending a conference, he issued a statement calculated to suggest his possible resignation. The State Department for the moment sought only to terminate the incident as quickly and quietly as possible.[71]

Meanwhile, the question of the ambassador's position in Germany was becoming critical. On arriving in Norfolk on August 4, he had made a debarkation statement to the effect that "the basic objective of some powers in Europe is to frighten and even destroy democracies everywhere." The next day German Ambassador Dieckhoff cabled Berlin a report of his formal protest to Hull and Under-Secretary Sumner Welles; but he advised the Wilhelmstrasse to let the matter drop for the time being, so as "not to cool the inclination to recall Dodd from Berlin, which has existed in various quarters here for some time."[72] It is clear that Roosevelt found disquieting the reports concerning his envoy's health, emotional state, and general effectiveness. In early April 1937, the President notified the State Department that he would accept Dodd's resignation, effective September 1.[73] Under this plan the ambassador would not even have returned to Germany after his summer leave

[70] *Ambassador Dodd's Diary*, p. 425.

[71] *New York Times*, September 4-5, 1937; *Ambassador Dodd's Diary*, p. 427.

[72] *German Documents*, series D, I, 627. Dieckhoff to Neurath, August 5, 1937. See also pp. 627-630.

[73] R.L., P.S.F., Box 27, *Dodd* folder. Roosevelt to Moore, April 5, 1937.

of absence. By August, however, possibly because of his reluctance to have it appear that he was yielding to Nazi pressure, Roosevelt had changed his mind. When Dodd lunched with him a week after arriving in the country, the President remarked, "I wish you to return to Berlin for two to three months."[74] Dodd left his signed resignation for use at the discretion of the White House and the State Department when he started back to Germany, but his own suggestion was that he be retained until the following March.

There can be no doubt that he was startled and hurt when on November 23, less than a month after his return to Berlin, he received orders from Hull to present the name of Ambassador Hugh Gibson, then in Belgium, to the Foreign Office as his successor and to wind up his own affairs by December 31. Although the Secretary cabled that these were the President's wishes, Dodd was certain that it was Sumner Welles who had engineered his recall.[75] Gibson declined the appointment, but Hugh Wilson, our minister to Switzerland, was approved in time to maintain the indicated deadline. Dodd left Berlin on December 28, quietly and without prior notice to the German press. He arrived in New York on January 6, 1938, stating to American newsmen that he "doubted if any American envoy who held his ideals of democracy could represent his country successfully among the Germans at the present time."[76]

Almost immediately he began a series of speeches to anti-Nazi meetings, always on the threat of Axis aggression and the need for concerted action by the democracies. He joined the American Friends of Spanish Democracy out of sympathy for the Loyalists, correctly predicted the sequence of German moves against Austria, Czechoslovakia, and Poland, and urged strong resistance to Japan. Publicly Berlin deprecated "the retiring ambassador's habitual lack of comprehension of the new Germany";[77] and at Nuremberg in September, Goebbels reserved for Dodd some of his choicest invective. In secret, Dieckhoff tried vainly to shake Secretary Hull's disclaimer of responsibility for statements by the ex-ambassador, which the latter, as a private citizen once more, could not be prevented from making.[78]

By the end of 1938 Dodd was failing rapidly from a combination of nervous, respiratory, and abdominal ailments. In December he was arrested in Virginia on charges of hit-and-run driving; and his subsequent conviction, accompanied by temporary loss of his state citizenship, un-

---

[74] *Ambassador Dodd's Diary*, p. 426.   [75] *ibid.*, pp. 433-434.
[76] *New York Times*, January 7, 1938.   [77] *New York Times*, January 9, 1938.
[78] U.S. Department of State, *Peace and War*, No. 103. Hull memorandum, January 14, 1938.

questionably shook his fragile health still further. He was hospitalized in Washington in January 1939, and in July underwent an operation, complicated by bulbar palsy and bronchial pneumonia. He rallied briefly, but the following winter pneumonia struck again. On February 9, 1940, he died at Round Hill, Virginia, his family home, having lived just long enough to witness the beginning of the Nazis' war, which he had dreaded for so long.

I have thus far minimized references to Dodd's relations with Washington, in order that this aspect of his period as an ambassador might receive a few words of separate treatment. It is quite clear that so far as the State Department was concerned, he was never a key figure in the formulation of policy. The volume, *Peace and War*, which the Department published as a review of American foreign relations from 1931 to 1941, contains dispatches on the Third Reich sent by the U.S. ministers to Austria and Switzerland, the consul at Berlin and, our military attaché there; but not a single report by the ambassador himself was thought important enough to be included.

Secretary Hull, whose misgivings in 1933 have already been cited, clearly welcomed the retirement of a man whom he considered "sincere though impulsive and inexperienced."[79] During the summer of 1937 Dieckhoff informed his Foreign Office superiors that Hull had referred to the ambassador as "somewhat insane" on topics such as ideal Jeffersonian democracy and world peace.[80] It is impossible to be sure just whose words are being used in Dieckhoff's subsequent report to the effect that the Secretary of State had called Dodd "the sort of fool with whom one could not reason," but the tenor of the remarks was clearly unflattering.[81] Dodd himself never ceased to rely on Hull's good will and on that of his friend, Judge Moore, who in 1937 became Counselor of the Department. In addition, he felt some cordiality toward certain of his colleagues abroad, notably Messersmith in Vienna and Cudahy in Warsaw. However, he never dissembled the hostility he felt toward most career diplomats and businessmen in the Foreign Service. His diary bristles with remarks about "rich men," not only those in the Department or other missions, but certain of his own principal aides as well.

It was Sumner Welles who supplied the most consistent focus for Dodd's animosity. Even in 1934, on his first visit home, the ambassador had a rather tart interview with the then Assistant Secretary, whose

[79] Hull, *Memoirs*, I, 572.
[80] *German Documents*, series D, I, 627. Dieckhoff to Neurath, August 5, 1937.
[81] *ibid.*, 679. Dieckhoff to Neurath, January 14, 1938.

house in Washington irritated Dodd by its very size.[82] His later conviction that he knew precisely whom to blame for his recall finds partial confirmation in the German documents. In September 1937, when Welles met Dieckhoff aboard the *Europa* en route to New York, he reportedly told Hitler's ambassador that Dodd seemed to him quite incomprehensible and that he would "take up the Dodd case immediately upon his return."[83] A few days later, the Under-Secretary called Dieckhoff in to inform him that Dodd's recall had now definitely been decided upon.[84]

It would, however, be unfair to assume that Welles had to wage anything like a one-man campaign to oust the ambassador in Berlin. For some months before the events just described there had been press reports of Dodd's impending resignation. The following, written by Arthur Krock for the *New York Times* amid the uproar over the Supreme Court letter, is a representative sample: "[Mr. Dodd] has long been one of the Department's worries. He has impressed his diplomatic associates as a man who is inclined to forget his responsibilities as an envoy in his zeal as an historian and in his views as a contemporary observer of governing trends. For these impulses the Department is disposed to award Mr. Dodd full credit as a man. But it is no secret in those generally discreet corridors that a change at Berlin has long been desired and would be welcomed at any time."[85]

Not the least of the official grievances against Dodd was the personal correspondence he was known to carry on with the President outside regular departmental channels. Now that this correspondence is available at Hyde Park,[86] it is possible to examine an interesting example of the late President's personal diplomacy, marked by all the verve and charm which he knew so well how to introduce into his relations with devoted subordinates. I have already quoted from certain of these letters for purposes of the general narrative; but they merit comment in their own right.

The prevailing tone, on both sides, is one of confidence and cordiality. "My dear Dodd," the President wrote in December, 1933, "that is an exquisite pen picture of yours [of Hitler, Goebbels, and Goering]. It confirms my impression. Merry Christmas! You are doing a grand

---

[82] *Ambassador Dodd's Diary*, p. 94.

[83] *German Documents*, series D, I, 630. Dieckhoff to Neurath, September 27, 1937.

[84] *ibid.*, 632. Dieckhoff to Neurath, October 1, 1937.

[85] *New York Times*, May 14, 1937.

[86] *R.L.*, O.F. 523; P.P.F. 1043; and P.S.F., Boxes 10, 19, and 27, *Dodd* and *Germany* folders.

job."[87] Even after the ambassador's position became more complicated, Roosevelt repeatedly sent words of encouragement and thanks for letters received. Dodd, on his part, wrote about whatever topic was uppermost in his mind: the Nazi leaders, collective security, personal finances, Japanese aggression, plans for selling the burned-out Blücher Palace (which was to have housed the U.S. embassy), predictions concerning German foreign policy, American history, and contemporary politics.

On only one point did the President introduce a distinctly official note into the correspondence. In March 1936, he asked Dodd to notify him "if in the days to come the absolutely unpredictable events should by chance get to the point where a gesture, an offer or a formal statement by me would, in your judgment, make for peace."[88] The following summer, he became more specific: "I should like to have your slant, in the utmost confidence, as to what would happen if Hitler were personally and secretly asked by me to outline the limit of German foreign objectives during, let us say, a ten-year period, and to state whether or not he would have any sympathy with a general limitation of armaments proposal."[89] Dodd carried out his assignment but had to report in October that his approaches to the Foreign Office had met with no success.[90] A few weeks later, Dieckhoff, then still Secretary of State in the Wilhelmstrasse, expressed to the ambassador his puzzlement as to "why people in America were so particularly worried" and admitted that Germany "would place no great hopes in a big disarmament conference."[91]

For the two years left to Dodd after his retirement, there are relatively few items in the Hyde Park collection. The correspondence really terminates with a birthday greeting which Dodd wrote, in a shaking longhand, in January 1939, from Georgetown University Hospital. After a pessimistic section—"What a world we live in!"—the old admiration comes through, now almost incoherent: "You are the greatest leader in the world and I hope you may be able to block things before too late. A master's job. Unequalled in history. Congratulations!"[92] The remaining messages from Dodd to the President offer pathetic evidence of their writer's desperate pessimism and declining mental, as well as physical, powers. The last is an expression of regret, written

---

[87] *R.L.*, O.F. 523. December 8, 1933.

[88] *ibid.*, P.P.F. 1043. March 16, 1936. Also printed in *F.D.R.: His Personal Letters, 1928-1945*, ed. Elliott Roosevelt (New York, 1950), I, 571.

[89] *R.L.*, P.S.F., Box 19, *Dodd* folder. August 5, 1936. Also printed in *F.D.R.: His Personal Letters*, I, 605-606.

[90] *R.L.*, P.S.F., Box 19, *Dodd* folder. October 19, 1936.

[91] *German Documents*, series D, III, 153. Dieckhoff memorandum, December 5, 1936.

[92] *R.L.*, O.F. 523. January 28, 1939.

three months before his death, that he could not attend the laying of the cornerstone for the very library where the letter, with all its predecessors, now reposes.[93]

It is not easy to dissociate one's sympathy for William E. Dodd as a sincere and humane individual, horrified by the vicious regime with which he was expected to deal, from one's judgment of him as a diplomat. Yet in this context the distinction must be made, even at the risk of dehumanizing diplomacy. Dodd's sense of defeat is apparent throughout his diary. In July 1934, he wrote, "Ought I to resign?"; in July 1935, after talking to Luther, the German ambassador to Washington, "I intimated that both of us ought to resign"; in December 1936, "I wait and watch for my time to retire"; in October 1937, "In Berlin once more. What can I do?"[94] Even his anger when finally recalled bespeaks reluctance to lay aside a piece of work while it still appeared a failure. But in what did this failure consist? To his way of thinking, it unquestionably lay in his inability to affect the course of German internal developments. His daughter has written (and his diary confirms) that he set off in 1933 thinking that "he could have some influence in moderating the policies of the Nazi regime," that there would be "a chance to bring them back to reason, to recall forcefully to them their recent democratic past."[95]

It is my own feeling that Dodd was ineffectual as an ambassador less because he failed to achieve his aim of changing the Third Reich by example and persuasion than because that was the aim he set himself. Once he discovered that he could not convert the Nazis, his despondency practically incapacitated him as a diplomatic representative. His general prophecies, it is true, proved accurate in their broad outlines; but one is struck, in reading the available reports from Dodd to Washington, by the comparative lack of concrete intelligence concerning *immediate* Nazi objectives and power. Finding the party chiefs unbearable, he fell back on contacts with German scholars, with aristocrats, and with men whom he considered "decent" officials: Neurath, Bülow, Dieckhoff, Schacht, even Papen. The result was that he could neither tell Washington as much as Rumbold had told London or Coulondre was to tell Paris about affairs within the Reich, nor present the American position to the German government with any hope of being taken seriously. Even if the latter task was frustrating—and would have been for any man—

[93] *ibid.*, P.P.F. 1043. November 10, 1939.
[94] *Ambassador Dodd's Diary*, pp. 123, 262, 375, 430.
[95] Martha Dodd, *Through Embassy Eyes*, pp. 15-16.

the ambassador's basic responsibility for close, accurate reporting still remained. Had Dodd made the most of his opportunities in that regard, he might conceivably then have demanded a hearing for whatever specific policy recommendations he cared to submit to his own government.

Viewed simply as a reporter, however, he suffered from several serious weaknesses. One was his lack of knowledge concerning modern German history. I make this statement fully aware of the frequency and scorn with which Dodd himself leveled the same charge against his contemporaries, but it is a conclusion which a study of his record makes inescapable. A case in point is the anachronistic standard he sought to apply. Nazi Germany was built on brutal fraud, and it was dangerous for the rest of the world. No honest man could—though many men did—try to make it appear otherwise. For Dodd, however, the alternative, the gauge to be used, was always a Germany that had once been, when it was not a Germany that had never been, save perhaps in "The Student Prince." Admiration for the land of Luther, Stein, and Bismarck offered few guideposts for setting a diplomatic course vis-à-vis the land of Hitler.

Even Dodd's Jeffersonianism, attractive enough in some connections, played him false in others. His individualistic orientation led him to see in Nazism nothing but the demonic work of certain evil leaders. Thus he poured his wrath upon Hitler and other prominent Nazis, while remaining singularly uncritical of groups which, if less blatantly murderous, were no less deeply implicated. "It all stems from Hitler himself," he wrote of anti-Semitism in a momentary surrender to the *Führerprinzip*.[96] This inability to appreciate the full significance of the Jewish question, here treated in terms simply of Hitler's personality, is a striking example of the ambassador's lack of historical perspective. He was horrified by physical cruelty to the Jews; and as a humane man he did what he could to help individual victims, while fulminating publicly against the moral lapse which such brutality represented. Yet he understood, to some extent he even shared, the older, subtler, admittedly nonviolent anti-Semitism of many members of the German professorial class. One may search in vain for any evidence that he appreciated how deep were the roots of German persecution of the Jews or how crucial was such persecution to the Nazis' hold on political power in Germany. History no more permits one to view anti-Semitism as incidental to Nazism than it permits him to view Nazism itself as an outburst which broke upon Germany as a result of some mistakes at Versailles and some

[96] William E. Dodd, "Germany Shocked Me," *The Nation*, August 20, 1938.

[459]

providential bad luck. Dodd talked much of history, but in the sense just noted, he applied it little. He could not fully understand the forces underlying Nazism because he could not think in terms of either the industrialized, urban society or the kind of farming community which had combined to produce the Third Reich. His nostalgia for a loosely organized polity of self-reliant freeholders, like his nostalgia for pre-1914 German university life, was profoundly misleading.

The alternative to a Dodd need not have been a morally neutral technician, smoothly rationalizing away what he saw in Germany. My critique presupposes no such model of diplomatic performance. George S. Messersmith, for example, distrusted the Nazis as much as did the ambassador, yet during the 1930's, both as consul-general in Berlin and then as minister to Austria, he managed to give far greater substance to his warnings. If Dodd could have retained his human values but served them more by cool assessment of the situation and less by self-conscious outpourings, if he could have buttressed his generally sound premonitions with evidence better calculated to impress Washington, he might have had less cause to look back on his record in Berlin as one of failure.

III

André François-Poncet came to Berlin as French ambassador a year and a half before Rumbold left and remained there until almost a year after Dodd's departure. It was on September 22, 1931, that he moved into the old embassy on the Pariserplatz, with Brüning still Chancellor and the Nazis, in the opinion of many observers, only an overrated band of swaggerers. He moved out, to become French ambassador to Italy, in October 1938, in the weeks just after the Munich Conference. Thus he supplies a sort of personal continuum for seven years of watching and maneuvering.

François-Poncet was born in Provins (Seine-et-Marne), the son of a Court of Appeals magistrate. He made a brilliant record at the Ecole Normale Supérieure, completing his thesis on Goethe's *Elective Affinities* in 1909, then accepting a professorship at the Lycée de Montpellier. The first world war, however, interrupted his promising career as a scholar and teacher. It also, by sending him to Switzerland for the French government and later to Washington as an adviser to the International Economic Mission, shifted his professional interests from academics to applied economics. Through his marriage he had acquired substantial holdings in the steel industry, and it was as a public defender of that industry, or more precisely of the powerful Comité des Forges, that he founded the Société d'Etudes et Informations Economiques at Paris in 1922. His connection with German affairs continued, however, at least during the Ruhr occupation, when he was economic adviser to the commanding general. He also entered politics as a member of that protean group, the Alliance Démocratique; and from 1924 until his departure for Berlin in 1931, he represented Paris (VIIᵉ) in the Chamber of Deputies. By the late 1920's he had distinguished himself as a skillful opponent of organized labor[97] and as one of French industry's cleverest parliamentary spokesmen. His rise in the government service began in 1930, when Tardieu made him Under-Secretary for Foreign Affairs; and at the time of his appointment to Berlin he was Laval's Under-Secretary to the Premier's Office.

He was forty-six when he went to Germany, a dapper, mustachioed, voluble man with a reputation for wit, flexibility, and an excellent command of German. For all his love of conversation, however, François-Poncet impressed those who knew him in Germany as rather inscrutable, except in the company of any of his eight children.[98] He and his strikingly handsome wife maintained a veritable court at the embassy, where on formal occasions liveried pages lined the big stairway in a setting reminiscent of Louis XIV with Napoleonic overtones.[99] The ambassador might relax over weekends at his villa on the Kleine Wannsee outside Berlin, but his working day was full enough. By eleven o'clock he had reviewed the daily press summary before it was telephoned to Paris, and then there were telegrams to be drafted and dispatches prepared for the courier pouch. The bound copies of his own reports, he tells us, eventually ran to forty volumes.[100]

Several circumstances complicate the study of François-Poncet's record during his period at the Pariserplatz. One is the intricacy of the narrative itself, seen from any point of view. Another is the extreme paucity of French documents available. The *Yellow Book* supplies a few, of course, for 1938-1939; and occasional French texts have found their way into other collections. For most of the 1930's, however, one must

[97] See his *Une formule nouvelle: le contrôle syndical* (Paris, 1921) and *La France et les huit heures* (Paris, 1922), both published by his Société d'Etudes.

[98] On his personality see Bella Fromm, *Blood and Banquets* (New York, 1942), pp. 28, 30-32, 37-38, 78, 118, 204; *Ambassador Dodd's Diary*, by index; Martha Dodd, *Through Embassy Eyes*, pp. 41-42, 150, 326-330; and scattered references in memoirs such as those of Henderson, Weizsäcker, and Paul Schmidt. See also the personal sketches from *Je Suis Partout* and *Marianne* in *The Living Age* (October 1931), 135-137, and (March 1937), 56-5⁷.

[99] *Ambassador Dodd's Diary*, p. 54.

[100] André François-Poncet, *Souvenirs d'une ambassade à Berlin* (Paris, 1946), p. 6.

depend on German, British, and American official sources, supplemented by memoirs and occasional press reports of more than average value. A third difficulty arises from the nature of the ambassador's own account, in his *Souvenirs*. This volume contains several excellent descriptive passages and some interesting judgments of men and events. Nevertheless, it fails to mention a number of important aspects of its author's performance; and the latter's recollections of his own role, even where clearly set forth, differ sharply at several points from the versions to be found in other sources. All one can do is to cite these discrepancies where relevant.

The new French ambassador of 1931 had been identified with a policy of toughness toward Weimar Germany, because of his criticism of Briand in the Chamber and his known hostility toward the German-Austrian Customs Union of the preceding spring. He made no secret of the misgivings he felt about Brüning, who had just declined a French proposal for a ten-year truce on all boundary disputes. It appeared at first that François-Poncet might continue to espouse "hard" policies. In January 1932, for example, while on one of his frequent trips to Paris, he told the British ambassador there that he was apprehensive over German attempts to escape completely from further reparations;[101] and in the matter of armaments, he warned Sir Horace Rumbold against Germany's efforts to "force the pace in the question of equality of status"—admittedly an ambiguous statement.[102]

On one issue, however, François-Poncet could from the first be called conciliatory. This was the possibility of closer industrial ties between Germany and France. He recalls that his own government, having despaired of immediate progress in the political field, expected him now to explore the economic.[103] Even before his appointment to Berlin, while still an Under-Secretary in Paris, he had proposed a complex international cartel plan.[104] And in his initial press conference upon reaching the German capital he spoke with enthusiasm of an alliance between French and German industries, the former rich but technically inferior, the latter well-equipped but lacking capital.[105]

It is impossible, pending release of his actual dispatches, to reconstruct François-Poncet's coverage of the Nazi triumph inside Germany. The

---

[101] *British Documents*, 2d series, III, 23. Tyrrell to Simon, January 12, 1932.
[102] *ibid.*, IV, 178. Rumbold to Simon, September 19, 1932.
[103] *Souvenirs*, p. 23.
[104] *British Documents*, 2d series, II, 45. Rumbold to Henderson, May 6, 1931. Rumbold had learned of the scheme from Bülow at the German Foreign Office.
[105] Bella Fromm, *Blood and Banquets*, pp. 30-32.

discussion in his *Souvenirs* is an historical essay, not a portrayal of his on-the-spot reactions. At times he seems to have entertained hopes that Papen, or if not he then Schleicher, could hold together a conservative regime resting on the authority of Hindenburg. At other times, unlike Rumbold, the ambassador toyed with the prospect of a monarchist restoration. In the summer of 1932 a Paris weekly quoted him as saying, "Before spring comes a Hohenzollern, if not William II himself, will be seated again on the throne of his fathers. . . . A Hohenzollern would be a guarantee of at least ten years of peace."[106] So far as the Nazis were concerned, he states that during the year before January 1933, he never had any contact with their leaders.[107]

For the first eighteen months after Hitler became Reich Chancellor, the French envoy moved suavely through the social and official life of Berlin in his normal fashion. He continued to negotiate with the Foreign Office over the German demands for equality of armaments. He began to form personal impressions of the energetic new masters of Germany, including especially Hitler, whom he saw on official business about once a month. But he also saw Papen and many other gentlemen of the *Herrenklub*, remained the personal friend of Schleicher and had at least social contacts with Roehm and his circle. Hence, when the Blood Purge struck, he experienced several days of near panic. "It is popularly supposed [Dodd cabled Washington on July 2, 1934] that France was the foreign power with which, according to official version, Roehm was dealing. This allegation would find certain confirmation in known desire of French Ambassador for reform in German Government such as would be conducive to less *intransigeance* in international politics."[108] Although the official version here referred to was restated by Hitler before the Reichstag on July 13, and although François-Poncet had certainly followed closely the feuds within the Nazi party during the preceding months, there is no evidence to contradict his assertion that he never offered the support of his government to any dissident group. The Nazi chiefs, including Hitler, were apparently convinced within a few weeks that the French embassy was not a danger spot after all.[109]

François-Poncet was at this time engaged in revising his own views in a direction which made for easier personal relations with German leaders. By early 1934 he was convinced, he tells us, that the only hope lay in permitting the Reich to rearm under international surveillance, since a

[106] *New York Times*, August 30, 1932.   [107] *Souvenirs*, p. 142.
[108] *Foreign Relations*, 1934, II, 230-231. Dodd to Hull, July 2, 1934.
[109] *Souvenirs*, pp. 9 and 194.

formal convention might retard the German pace and would, at the very least, establish some limits, the infraction of which would alert the democracies to their danger.[110] Here he began to sound a note that was to recur over and over again in his subsequent arguments, a note of pessimism concerning the chances of blocking Hitler by frontal resistance, but also of hope that a policy of accommodation might leave the Allies with some measure of control still in their hands.

There remained one alternative which he was prepared to advocate: a close alliance of the Western democracies with Italy. Only with the aid of Mussolini could he envisage the resumption of a hard policy. For François-Poncet, the Stresa Conference of April 1935, after Hitler had announced full rearmament, represented the high point in European solidarity. Mussolini's Ethiopian venture, however, destroyed the "Stresa Front" before it had even begun to affect international relationships; and in Berlin the French ambassador resumed his advocacy of what was coming to be regularly referred to as "business pacifism." By November 1935, questions were being raised in the French press concerning Laval's efforts at Franco-German rapprochement, with François-Poncet identified as the go-between. Although Laval, in the Chamber of Deputies, flatly denied any secret intentions, the uneasiness in Paris continued, fed, as one American analyst has put it, by "the known enthusiasm of the Ambassador for the National Socialist system and the suspicion of proposals made behind closed doors."[111]

Whatever Laval might tell the Chamber, there were such proposals. As early as November 1935, François-Poncet recommended to the Quai d'Orsay that a conference with Germany be held at once on the question of the Rhineland, in order to anticipate Hitler's remilitarization of the area and to limit him to light forces.[112] When the Spanish civil war broke out in mid-1936, the ambassador began a long series of talks with Neurath and Dieckhoff, in which he made clear his lack of sympathy for the Spanish government but urged the Germans not to precipitate a crisis through too open support of Franco.[113] In his memoirs François-Poncet cites only his desire that the fighting in Spain, regardless of its outcome, should remain localized. While the civil war was in progress, however, he was much more explicit about his sentiments, on one occasion complaining to the German ambassador in Rome that Bonnet had

[110] *ibid.*, pp. 174-179.
[111] Elizabeth R. Cameron, *Prologue to Appeasement* (Washington, 1942), p. 177.
[112] *Souvenirs*, p. 248.
[113] *German Documents*, series D, III, Doc. Nos. 29, 32, 37, 45, 46, 54, 66, 166, 177, 195, 270, 371, 427, 430.

made a blunder in not recognizing Franco in the general confusion after Munich and thus having done with the Spanish government, "this last stronghold of the Popular Front."[114]

Meanwhile the ambassador was seeking to convince the German Foreign Office that friendship between Berlin and Paris was both desirable and attainable. With this end in view, he had to make clear his own dislike for the Franco-Soviet pact of 1935. In September, 1936 he asked Secretary of State Dieckhoff whether Germany was interested in negotiating a Western agreement or would demand first that France renounce its Russian alliance. "If Germany followed the first course," Dieckhoff records, "he [François-Poncet] believed he could say that the Franco-Russian ties would gradually cool, particularly since they had never been popular with a large sector of the French people."[115] More than a year later, after Flandin's visit to Berlin had failed to produce any explicit pledges from the Germans, Papen, home on leave from Vienna in December 1937, found the French ambassador dejected over the slow pace of negotiations. "Flandin, as is well known," Papen added, "is very close to François-Poncet politically."[116]

The year 1938, which was to witness his greatest personal triumphs, began unpleasantly for François-Poncet, with a cold rebuff from Ribbentrop on the subject of what the new Foreign Minister was pleased to call the "family affair" in Austria.[117] When, on March 11, Seyss-Inquart invited German troops to enter Austria, it was the duty of the ambassador, who in his memoirs has almost nothing to say about the *Anschluss*, to deliver the sharp French note of protest.[118] Affronts such as this were damaging to the policy of accommodation, especially given the manner in which they were perpetrated. The French envoy's argument, as he now repeats it, however, was still that since France had been timid while Germany was weak, she could scarcely become intransigent as the Reich grew stronger.

It was the Czech crisis which gave François-Poncet a chance to influence directly the course of Franco-German negotiations. In May 1938, when the first Sudeten scare was brewing, he suggested to the sympathetic Sir Nevile Henderson the possibility of Germany's accepting the good offices of the Western Powers in its dispute with Czechoslovakia.[119] "It

[114] *ibid.*, IV, 460. Mackensen to Ribbentrop, November 22, 1938.
[115] *ibid.*, III, 66. Dieckhoff memorandum, September 1, 1936.
[116] *ibid.*, I, 129. Papen to Weizsäcker, December 16, 1937.
[117] *ibid.*, 529. Ribbentrop memorandum, February 17, 1938.
[118] *ibid.*, 578. François-Poncet to Neurath, March 11, 1938.
[119] *British Documents*, 3rd series, I, 238, 286. Henderson to Halifax, May 3 and 12, 1938.

is time," he told Henderson, "that Europe revised its opinion of M. Benes."[120] Back in Paris, early in June, he made clear to his old colleague, Sir Eric Phipps, now ambassador to France, that he did not trust Benes and that the Allies should offer Hitler a deal on the Sudeten question.[121] By the end of that month he and Henderson were agreed that "allied to Russia, [Czechoslovakia] constitutes a perpetual menace to Germany."[122]

Toward the Germans, he was simultaneously holding out hopes of conciliation, expressing his anxiety to Ribbentrop in mid-May,[123] by late June urging the possibility of a Great Power settlement and "evolutionary changes" in existing alliances,[124] a month later assuring Weizsäcker of British and French sincerity in urging Prague to be reasonable.[125] Throughout this busy summer he asked only that the Reich avoid injuring French dignity and do what it could to minimize the general tension.

Reducing tension, however, scarcely fitted into Hitler's scheme of things, and the Fuehrer's blustering at Nuremberg in early September seemed to spell the doom of any settlement by negotiation. François-Poncet seems to have lapsed into despondent inactivity even before the Party Congress (his nervous state has been described by the diplomatic correspondent, Bella Fromm, who called on him at the Wannsee villa late in August).[126] Or perhaps he had been temporarily restrained from further advances by instructions from Paris. In any event, as late as September 27, when Chamberlain's Berchtesgaden and Godesberg visits seemed to have come to naught, the Polish ambassador to Germany was told by Weizsäcker that "François-Poncet had not set foot in the Foreign Office for nearly a fortnight."[127]

Actually, however, the French envoy was about to take the center of the stage. During the night of September 27-28, he received orders from Bonnet to see Hitler and to reopen with him the discussion of possibilities for a peaceful solution. By eleven o'clock the next morning he was at the Chancellery. Once in the presence of the Fuehrer, Ribbentrop, and the chief translator Paul Schmidt, he spread out a map showing the phases for a Czech evacuation of the disputed borderlands and then launched

[120] *ibid.*, 273. Henderson to Halifax, May 10, 1938.
[121] *ibid.*, 452. Phipps to Halifax, June 8, 1938. See also p. 460.
[122] *ibid.*, 534. Henderson to Halifax, July 1, 1938.
[123] *German Documents*, series D, II, 284. Ribbentrop memorandum, May 17, 1938.
[124] *ibid.*, 428. Ribbentrop memorandum for Hitler, June 23, 1938.
[125] *ibid.*, 515. Weizsäcker memorandum for Ribbentrop, July 26, 1938.
[126] *Blood and Banquets*, p. 280.
[127] *Documents and Materials*, p. 230. Lipski to Beck, September 27, 1938.

into an address on the horrors of the war which threatened.[128] "You are naturally confident of winning the war, just as we believe that we can defeat you," Dr. Schmidt quotes him as saying to Hitler, "but why should you take this risk when your essential demands can be met without war?"[129] It was while this discussion was in progress that Hitler was called out of the room to speak to the Italian ambassador Attolico, bearer of Mussolini's offer to propose an immediate four Power parley.

Hitler's acceptance of the Duce's initiative and what followed from that acceptance are too well known to require recapitulation here. François-Poncet went down to Munich for the conference, was in fact present at the second session; but his real contribution had occurred in Berlin on the 28th. Recalls Paul Schmidt, "The Munich Conference was regarded at the time as the decisive turning point in the Sudeten crisis. Actually this had occurred the day before, in Hitler's talk with Attolico, after the vital preparatory work carried out by François-Poncet."[130] The ambassador's memoirs tend to minimize his own importance in this instance, stressing instead the decisive role of British policy throughout the crisis.[131] He is content to argue that the deal on Czechoslovakia bought the Allies a precious year for further arming before war broke out and that the British air victories of 1940 were in effect won at Munich. He is not impressed by the counterargument that the same year saw an even more rapid increase in Germany military power, the absorption of the Skoda works into the Reich's industry, the liquidation of Czechoslovakia's strategic value (even if only nuisance value) in a two-front war, and the neutralization of Russia.

The remaining month of François-Poncet's ambassadorship in Germany was an active one for him. For one thing, as a member of the International Commission which met in Berlin to supervise the transfer of the Sudeten areas, he made some short-lived attempts to maintain the appearance of a negotiated solution. His own Foreign Office failed to support him, he complains, and it was only a few days before the German interpretation prevailed on every important point.[132] The other

---

[128] *Souvenirs*, p. 328.
[129] Paul Schmidt, *Statist auf diplomatischer Bühne* (Bonn, 1949). The translation here quoted is from the American edition, *Hitler's Interpreter* (New York, 1951), p. 106. François-Poncet's command of German left Schmidt no function save that of recording the discussion.
[130] *ibid.* (American edition), p. 108.
[131] *Souvenirs*, p. 328. Hitler, on the other hand, is reported to have said later on several occasions, "François-Poncet was the only one who made a sensible proposal." Schmidt, *Hitler's Interpreter*, p. 107.
[132] *Souvenirs*, pp. 334-335. See also *German Documents*, series D, IV, 12, Minutes of

development of that October was François-Poncet's culminating effort to achieve better relations between Paris and Berlin. To his own Foreign Office he wrote that no effort should be spared to strengthen French powers of resistance and that the Nazis would bear watching, even during this breathing spell, but that France must not let any show of intransigence on her part cost her the moral advantage in world opinion. The Fuehrer, though dangerously mercurial, was capable of astounding changes of front; and should he, for any reason, try the road to peace, "it is possible that he will end by not being able to turn back again, even if he wished."[133]

To the German Foreign Office, on October 13, he suggested a non-aggression pact, to be signed on the occasion of Ribbentrop's projected visit to Paris. "Such an agreement," noted Weizsäcker, "would fulfill an idea which he, Poncet, had already urged for a long time."[134] Five days later occurred the final visit with Hitler in the Berchtesgaden "eagle's nest," so eloquently described by the ambassador.[135] It was a long discussion, for the last hour of which the two principals were alone. In the course of a review of the entire European situation, the Fuehrer complained of his disappointment over the continuing international tension and burst forth once or twice against Great Britain. In general, however, it was a cordial talk. François-Poncet declared that Munich had proved the value of Great Power collaboration; and before he left, he had Hitler's assurance of interest in a Franco-German friendship pact. Back in Berlin, the ambassador was able to report to Weizsäcker and to Goering that Paris accepted in principle the ideas discussed at Berchtesgaden on the 18th.[136] In his interview with the former, he mentioned that Britain, Italy, even Belgium should be kept informed and later drawn into the arrangement. "It would, however, be a mistake," he went on, "not to strike while the iron was hot in the matter of purely Franco-German relations."[137] The Ribbentrop-Bonnet declaration of friendship, mutual acceptance of common boundaries, and determination to remain in contact on all questions was actually signed in Paris on

the International Commission, October 1, 1938; and II, 53, Weizsäcker memorandum, October 10, 1938.

[133] *The French Yellow Book*, published by authority of the French government (New York, 1940), Doc. No. 18. François-Poncet to Bonnet, October 20, 1938. See also Doc. No. 16 for François-Poncet's dispatch of October 4.

[134] *German Documents*, series D, IV, 436. Weizsäcker memorandum, October 13, 1938.

[135] *French Yellow Book*, Doc. No. 18. François-Poncet to Bonnet, October 20, 1938.

[136] *ibid.*, Doc. Nos. 19-21. Bonnet to François-Poncet, October 21, 1938, and François-Poncet to Bonnet, October 22 and 24, 1938.

[137] *German Documents*, series D, IV, 438. Weizsäcker memorandum, October 22, 1938.

December 6. Six weeks earlier, its most ardent sponsor had left Berlin to take up his duties in Rome, where he remarked to the German ambassador that it had been time for him to leave the Reich: "You should stop while it tastes best."[138]

François-Poncet's activities in Italy during the next year and a half can here be treated only as they relate to his views of the Axis problem in general. He had long admired Mussolini and as recently as Munich had reaffirmed his conviction that the Duce offered the best hope of restraining Hitler.[139] Hence, though he insisted that France would yield not an inch of territory, he was willing to swallow the insults he received in Rome and to keep at the task of securing an Italo-French rapprochement to fortify the Franco-German. In his first talk with Mussolini, according to the version he gave his British colleague, he announced that "he had come to develop the policy of the Munich Agreement" by converting into reality the dream of a four Power system.[140] In a public address on New Year's Day, 1939, he further elaborated his view of the "Munich Spirit" which was to bring France, Italy, Germany, and Britain into closer association. The onrushing events in the north, however, paid little heed to this vision. When war came the following September 1, the ambassador could only support Mussolini's unsuccessful effort to mediate once again, as he had done over Czechoslovakia.[141] All was to no avail. On June 10, 1940, when Ciano called him in to receive the Italian declaration of war, he managed a sarcastic reply, then shook the Foreign Minister's hand and said, "Don't get yourself killed."[142]

Back in France, after the defeat, he served under the Vichy government as a member of the National Council and as Controller-General of the Press, only to be arrested by the Germans in August 1943 (having been incriminated in their eyes, he believes, by captured documents) and held in confinement in the Austrian Tyrol until his liberation in May 1945. In 1948, he was appointed adviser to the Military Governor of French-occupied Germany and a year later became French High Commissioner in the former Reich.

Concerning François-Poncet's feelings toward the Nazis there will probably always remain some disagreement, though the external aspects of his relations with them are clear enough. He was generally conceded

[138] *ibid.*, 460. Mackensen to Ribbentrop, November 22, 1938.

[139] *Souvenirs*, p. 307.

[140] *British Documents*, 3d series, III, 461. Perth to Halifax, November 29, 1938.

[141] *French Yellow Book*, Doc. Nos. 306, 332, 360 and 363. François-Poncet to Bonnet, August 31-September 2, 1939.

[142] Galeazzo Ciano, *Diario* (Milan, 1948), I, 278.

to be the Fuehrer's favorite ambassador, once the suspicions of the Blood Purge period had disappeared. François-Poncet, on his part, adopted a tone of easy familiarity with Hitler. Sometimes he was jocular, as when he arrived for the historic interview on the day before Munich exclaiming cheerfully, "You know, Mr. Chancellor, I have always been your good star."[143] Sometimes he was more acid, as during the 1937 Party Congress when, referring to a recent speech by Goebbels, he remarked, "You see, Herr Reich Chancellor, the 'stupid cow nations' did not hesitate to come to Nuremberg."[144] The recently published collection of the Fuehrer's "table talks" confirms the warmth of Hitler's feelings for an ambassador who was so broad in his European views and so generous with chocolates specially shipped from Paris.[145]

The discrepancy in interpretation arises only over the question of François-Poncet's true sentiments. Ambassador Dodd classified him as "not far from being a fascist,"[146] sections of the French press spoke bluntly of his high regard for Nazism,[147] and the German newspaper-woman, Bella Fromm, described him as "hypnotized by Hitler."[148] Judgments such as these, according to François-Poncet, are just so many tributes to his success in playing a part. "National Socialism I had always found revolting, for I was brought up as a liberal and a humanist. The spectacle of tyranny trampling human values, exalting brutality and glorying in savagery, I found odious. The earliest manifestations of Nazi rule filled me with an enduring aversion. . . . I did not display my feelings, but I did not seek to conceal them. Usually I gave vent to them in the ironic mode, in a form that would not offend. Most of the epigrams circulating in Berlin about the Nazis were attributed to me; but since I also showed my interest in Nazi ideology and in the reforms the Nazis introduced in every field, instead of holding these sallies against me, they found them amusing. My relations with the Nazis were not bad, or, to be more exact, I ended by being on fairly good terms with some of them."[149]

I have seen no evidence that the ambassador was an uncritical admirer of the government to which he was accredited. If he liked Goering and was impressed by Hitler and Goebbels, he certainly was not attracted to

---

[143] Ernst von Weizsäcker, *Erinnerungen* (Munich, 1950), p. 210.

[144] *New York Times*, September 12, 1937.

[145] Henry Picker, *Hitlers Tischgespräche im Führerhauptquartier, 1941-42* (Bonn, 1951), pp. 105-106.

[146] *Ambassador Dodd's Diary*, p. 347.   [147] See above, at note 111.

[148] *Blood and Banquets*, p. 280.

[149] *Souvenirs*, p. 8. The translation quoted here is from the American edition, *The Fateful Years*, tr. Jacques LeClercq (New York, 1949), x-xi.

Rosenberg and, like most other diplomats, loathed Ribbentrop. If he approved the social and political discipline enforced by the regime, he did not approve its tawdry racism or its risky foreign policy. About all that can be said with confidence is that nothing about Nazism so repelled him as to inhibit his efforts to arrange an understanding between the French government and French industry, on the one hand, and Hitler's Reich, on the other.

François-Poncet put little stock in a violent overthrow of the Nazis, at least after 1934. In his memoirs he insists that even had the French army resisted the reoccupation of the Rhineland in 1936, no German group could have ousted Hitler.[150] It is worth noting that in his dispatches of autumn 1938, he remained unimpressed by General Beck's efforts to organize a military coup the previous summer and spoke of future changes only in terms of the Fuehrer's own personality. The strange concept of Hitler's possibly going so far along the road to peace that he could not turn back presumably grew out of François-Poncet's hopes that an eventual increase in the influence of traditional conservatives would modify the ambitions of the Nazi leaders.

One final topic, concerning which it is necessary to compare carefully the ambassador's account and the evidence from other sources, is the part he played in formulating French policy during the decade before 1940. Of his indirect influence, as an assiduous observer and analyst, there can be no doubt. As he himself remarks, the political atmosphere of Berlin lent itself to clever exploitation for purposes of gathering information.[151] Not only was he in touch with a wide variety of leading Germans, he also, at least during the first years of his mission, had informal monthly dinners with his foreign colleagues.[152] His successor at the Pariserplatz was duly impressed by the intelligence operation which François-Poncet had organized.[153]

What did he do with all the information he assembled? Some of it he communicated directly to the French General Staff through his personal liaison officer. The rest, he tells us, simply disappeared into the labyrinth of the Quai d'Orsay: "What I thought personally mattered little. I gave my opinion of my own accord. I was never asked for it."[154] Ambassadors of the Third Republic he describes as nothing but "prefects abroad— préfets de l'extérieure," rigidly subordinated to the centralized control of their government.[155]

[150] *Souvenirs*, p. 256.   [151] *ibid.*, p. 212.   [152] *ibid.*, pp. 161-164.
[153] Robert Coulondre, *De Staline à Hitler* (Paris, 1950), p. 204.
[154] *Souvenirs*, p. 12.   [155] *ibid.*, p. 13.

The British and German documents, however, give a strikingly different picture. We have, for example, Rumbold's and Campbell's references to François-Poncet's initiative in negotiations for a truce on boundary disputes in 1932,[156] as well as German records of his overtures from 1935 to 1937 (at least partly self-motivated, it would appear).[157] It is for 1938 that evidence of his personal influence is most abundant. His sympathy for German grievances and how he expounded his views in Paris and Berlin have already been mentioned.[158] There is a further hint of his pre-Munich role in a note which Bonnet handed to Sir Eric Phipps summarizing the September 28 interview between Hitler and François-Poncet. The latter, according to this document, had advised Paris that "it seemed to him that the business had been badly joined, under imprecise conditions, and that if it were possible to have some more precise proposals and especially to answer the essential objection made by Hitler on the subject of protection for the Sudetenlanders, it would not be impossible to arrive at an agreement."[159] Yet, in speaking of Munich François-Poncet's memoirs portray their author as "only an informant, an intermediary, an assistant, an executor, who was never consulted when the major decisions were made."[160]

Certainly not even he would deny his contribution to the Franco-German rapprochement following the Sudeten crisis. Beginning with remarks to Weizsäcker, reaching a decisive point in the farewell visit to Berchtesgaden, continuing in Berlin and then back in Paris, the ambassador's efforts to secure a treaty of friendship overshadowed all other aspects of relations between the two Powers that autumn. "M. A. François-Poncet had caught the ball on the rebound in inaugurating this negotiation," writes his successor, Robert Coulondre, "and the French Government was logical with itself in pursuing it."[161] From Paris the German envoy informed his government: "Yesterday François-Poncet called on me and gave me, quite spontaneously, details of his conversation with the Fuehrer. According to his account, the initiative in the matter of continuing the Munich conversations with a view to a settlement of and improvement in Franco-German relations had come from him—François-Poncet."[162]

[156] *British Documents*, 2d series, III, 135, 137. Rumbold to Sargent, May 4, 1932; Campbell to Sargent, May 13, 1932.

[157] See above, notes 113, 115.   [158] See above, notes 119-121.

[159] *British Documents*, 3d series, II, 607. Bonnet note, transmitted by Phipps to Halifax, September 29, 1938.

[160] *Souvenirs*, p. 314.   [161] *De Staline à Hitler*, p. 195.

[162] *German Documents*, series D, IV, 444. Welczeck to Weizsäcker, November 1, 1938.

The policy for which François-Poncet was agitating, once identified beneath the disavowals that burden his *Souvenirs*, is not in itself very surprising, certainly not unique. It was, in fact, the common property of a substantial section of the French Right. Fear of the Russia of Stalin, indifference toward the Czechoslovakia of Benes, reliance on the Poland of Beck, admiration for the Italy of Mussolini, all were implicit in the ambassador's attitude, as they were explicit in the speeches of Fabre-Luce or Louis Rollin and the articles of d'Ormesson or Pierre Gaxotte. But the argument inevitably centered on Germany. François-Poncet had been tough toward the Weimar Republic, as had his political intimates in Paris. Concerning the formidable Third Reich, however, he argued, as did they, that given Anglo-French pacifism, all that could be done was to put obstacles in Hitler's way, hamper him with public agreements, and thus either divert him from warlike undertakings or, if he could not be diverted, leave him exposed as a perjurer and an aggressor.[163]

A natural question arises as to François-Poncet's basic attitude toward the Reich, judged by his performance over the whole decade of the 1930's. Was the underlying reason for his seeking to conciliate Hitler a fatalistic sense of Germany's irresistible strength? Or did his early interest in Franco-German cartel arrangements assert itself ever more strongly as an independent factor in his calculations? The answer is necessarily a matter of guesswork, and an "either-or" formulation should probably be avoided. On his record, the ambassador would appear to have favored close industrial cooperation under the dominance of France. Even after the change in Germany's power position destroyed all hope of realizing this dream in its original form, the dream remained—modified to allow, if necessary, for German leadership, but a consolation still. So long as there remained a chance for wealthy Frenchmen to have a share in the prosperity of the New Order, one might reconcile himself to the changed balance of forces in European diplomacy.

The all-important thing, François-Poncet had maintained in a little book published in the mid-1920's, just after his election to the Chamber, was to look facts in the face. Speaking for his parliamentary group, he wrote: "We belong to the school of contingencies. Politics appears to us as essentially the art of the real and the possible. . . . For 'realists' truth is never finished or closed. By definition it cannot be, for truth is a perpetual becoming. . . . They [the realists] are steeped in reality, opposed to abstractions and utopias, liberal and conciliatory but not, for

---

[163] *Souvenirs*, p. 12. On this general subject, see C. A. Micaud, *The French Right and Nazi Germany, 1933-1939* (Durham, N.C., 1943).

all that, skeptical; because they install themselves in that which is; they accept it, they wish to live with it; their dominant concern is to organize it, ameliorate it, get the best out of it."[164] Now, in the 1930's, realism demanded that a Frenchman identify correctly the posture of affairs and the locus of his own and his country's interests therein. Having Germany strong was not in itself a welcome circumstance. The fact that Germany had become strong, however, had to be accepted. If Hitler was amenable to reason, a deal could be arranged. If he was not, one might then still claim credit for having sought to save the peace.

IV

Between Sir Horace Rumbold's introduction to Hindenburg in 1928 and André François-Poncet's farewell to Hitler in 1938 lay a decade surpassed in violence but not in complexity of action by that which followed. An essay of the present length, even using the vicarious vantage point of Berlin, can recreate those ten years only in the broadest outlines or in selected vignettes of greater detail but tiny scope. It would be possible, with the wisdom of hindsight, to erect a sort of scoreboard for tallying the accuracy of any man's detailed predictions and the soundness of his advice during the period in question; but it would be neither very fair nor particularly useful. The main question here is simpler and at the same time larger: when all was said and done, how did these three observers see Nazi Germany?

Rumbold, cool, tolerant, rather skeptical of the reality of supposedly new departures, not easily hurried or readily flustered, ended by lashing Nazi behavior with measured strokes and by warning London to stand by for trouble. Drawing to the close of a long career, he could speak with detachment of his nation's stake in the struggle ahead. Not unnaturally, he saw that struggle in relation to his own experience with the Germany of 1914. It was to recollections of the Kaiser and Tirpitz and Schlieffen that he turned for illustrations and insights. Britain must assume that this Third Reich, to whatever extent it surpassed the Second in power and insatiability, would to that extent be more dangerous.

Beyond the realm of purely national interests, however, Rumbold perceived some other issues. He sensed, in his undramatic fashion, that Western man could no longer relax comfortably with a hodgepodge of half-formulated, frequently conflicting values. It might soon be necessary to distinguish between those features of our civilization without which the word itself would become meaningless and those which could, if

[164] A. François-Poncet, *Réfléxions d'un républicain moderne* (Paris, 1925), pp. 16, 27-28.

necessary, be modified. When Rumbold came to the defense of the German Social Democrats' constitutional right to their views, he was in effect saying that if he *had* to choose, at least for Germany, he would uphold civil liberty, even at some risk to private property. Since he personally felt not the slightest aversion to the latter, this was, I submit, a value choice of some moment.

For Dodd also, the threat of Hitler's Germany and the need to resist were starkly apparent. Like Rumbold, he spoke at the end of a long career; like Rumbold, he employed an historical frame dominated by comparisons with the old Empire. But here the similarities end. Nervous, self-conscious, loving the startling analogy, the sharply drawn distinction, the categorical prophecy, Dodd combined the didactic techniques of the professor with those of the preacher. When he referred to pre-1914 Germany, it was to evoke the picture of a genial, sturdy, intellectual nation and to despair of this new race which seemed to have forgotten all that he recalled.

America must be prepared, he felt, to defend its democracy against foreign as well as domestic enemies, and he had not the slightest doubt that the developing threats at home and abroad were related. His chosen value *sine qua non* was individual freedom. Without that golden talent, western civilization could not survive as he knew it. Forced to its conclusion, his plea set resistance to Hitler, even at the cost of war, above the value of peace, if the latter could be bought only at the price of acquiescence in tyranny.

François-Poncet, still in mid-career, ambitious, supple, highly resistant to any lasting despair, simply kept adjusting his definition of realistic optimism to fit changing conditions. In one respect, he was less bound by history than were the preceding two men. That is, he was inclined to view Nazism as an unprecedented phenomenon and hence to sustain the hope that it might evolve in an acceptable manner. Hitler's regime was obviously capable of breathtaking abruptness in its formulation of demands. Might it not also, unlike the deep-keeled state of the turn of the century, be capable of an equally rapid change of course toward peaceful development of its resources? In another respect, however, he too was the captive of history. The problem was for him definable, and hence soluble, in terms of traditional European power relationships. The possibility that the great non-European nations, America and Russia, might hold some high cards, might in fact play the final cards, entered into his calculations almost not at all.

The accommodation for which François-Poncet was working would promise little to victims of Hitler's internal policies and scarcely more to the small states in Germany's sphere of influence. It would, however, keep Europe's industrial output high and its economic organization stable. This made some sense if one assumed that the basis of our civilization is its material productivity and its existing social structure. The French ambassador might add that his distaste for Nazi crudities implied a lingering respect for certain aesthetic values in Western culture.

After all, François-Poncet seems to have asked himself, what does the new Reich represent? An industrial giant, to be sure, one with which French business could either compete, at grave risk, or cooperate, to its own profit. A potential threat to international peace, unquestionably, but surely not a Power capable of defying a judiciously constructed Anglo-French-Italian entente. A state directed by some dangerously changeable adventurers, but also by some sensible conservatives whose influence might increase with time. For the rest, a mighty bulwark against Communism and a not unwelcome model of social discipline in an otherwise disturbingly clamorous age.

The three ambassadors here discussed influenced the policies of their respective governments in different ways and to varying degrees. Rumbold's dispatches must have been buried in the files so far as Chamberlain was concerned, but their impact was not spent so long as a Vansittart or an Eden had any influence in London. Dodd was important primarily for whatever part his views may have played in strengthening the personal forebodings of Roosevelt. Of the three, François-Poncet had the most easily discernible influence, in that he fortified the Laval-Flandin-Bonnet line in French thinking on foreign policy questions. Even he, however, could not overcome the distrust of Mussolini and Franco felt by many at the Quai d'Orsay, nor prevent recurrences of interest in reliance on Russia.

It would be a mistake to think of any of the three envoys as personifying his own nation's reactions to Hitler. In the late 1930's, it was a Frenchman, Coulondre, who represented a continuation of Rumbold's attitude more clearly than did leading British policymakers. By the same token, it was Sir Nevile Henderson who clung most tenaciously to the hope of a deal with Hitler after François-Poncet left Berlin. Needless to say, there were American diplomats of all persuasions, ready to echo the voices of one or another of the men here discussed. Thus the records of these three serve not to illumine national differences of outlook but to exemplify emotional and intellectual crosscurrents simultaneously operative in London, Paris, and Washington during those tormented years when the West sought a way out, between war and capitulation.

15

....

Two German Ambassadors: Dirksen and Schulenburg

BY CARL E. SCHORSKE

IN THE RAPIDLY SHIFTING INTERNATIONAL SCENE of 1938 and 1939, no positions in the German foreign service had greater importance than the ambassadorships to London and Moscow. The men who held these crucial posts were both diplomats of the old school, men who sought to exploit the possibilities afforded by their positions to promote Germany's revisionist aims without jeopardizing its national existence. Each saw the key to this objective in the development of close ties between Germany and the country to which he was accredited. Each developed his own variation on one of the two traditional themes which have always been heard at the Wilhelmstrasse: those of eastern and western orientation of Germany's foreign policy. During the period from the Munich Conference to the signing of the Nazi-Soviet Pact, the themes played by Dirksen in London and Schulenburg in Moscow formed a kind of diplomatic counterpoint, which could be heard in full clarity by neither of the two players but only by the music-masters in Berlin. In this contrapuntal relationship between Dirksen and Schulenburg one can study in microcosm the formation of Nazi foreign policy in the final prewar years and the ironic, almost bizarre fate of those career diplomats whose loyalty to that great abstraction, *der Staat*, led them into the attempt to serve the Nazi Foreign Office as they had served its predecessor.

Before Munich, the work of the two ambassadors was not on the same level of importance. A totally negative policy toward the USSR was not only ideologically congenial to Hitler but essential to his policy of softening up the ruling classes of Western Europe. While Dirksen led an active, often hectic diplomatic life in the heyday of appeasement in London, Schulenburg sat quietly in Moscow as a mere observer, too well aware of the realities in the Kremlin and the *Reichskanzlei* to indulge in idle talk of a Russo-German *détente*. After Munich, which unraveled the tenuous cords that bound the Soviet Union to the Western Powers, new diplomatic possibilities opened up in Moscow. The November pogroms depressed Anglo-German relations to a point where Dirksen was obliged to operate on the same level as his Moscow colleague. Thenceforth until August 1939, the two ambassadors were engaged in a kind of unwitting competition, each trying in his way to save his country from the catastrophe of a two-front war if not from war itself. As Germany's leaders took the decisions which led to war, the field of diplomatic possibilities progressively narrowed and the lines pursued by Dirksen and Schulenburg became increasingly conflicting and incompatible. In order to realize its aims against Poland, Germany could, in late July and early August, choose either London or Moscow, not both. In a nightmarish kind of way, the diplomatic counterpoint of the two ambassadors became transformed into a game of musical chairs, in which Hitler and Ribbentrop would decide when to stop the music and who—Dirksen or Schulenburg—would sit on the last remaining chair.

I

Of the two ambassadors, Herbert von Dirksen was the more complex in temperament and character—and the closer to the Nazis. He came from a line of hard-working bourgeois civil servants, whose generations of labor for the Prussian state were rewarded with a patent of nobility granted by the emperor to the ambassador's father, Willibald, in 1887. Willibald Dirksen was a typical parvenu aristocrat of the Wilhelmian era. He passed through the classic school in which the sons of prominent burghers acquired Junker values: the reserve cavalry. Through his marriage to a wealthy banker's daughter, he acquired the funds to purchase a vast, "representative" holding in Silesia. After his retirement from the Foreign Office, he stood for the *Reichstag* on the ticket of the conservative, nationalist, and rather anti-Semitic *Reichspartei*. He was a fanatical admirer of Kaiser Wilhelm II, whom he loyally visited at Doorn after the abdication.[1]

Like many another Junkerized bourgeois, Dirksen's father, psychologically insecure on his newly-reached social pinnacle, tried to force his children into the role of perfect aristocrats. From an early age their free development was stifled in a strict regimen designed to produce "exem-

---

[1] *Genealogisches Taschenbuch der briefadeligen Häuser, 1908* (Gotha, 1908), p. 215; Herbert von Dirksen, *Moskau, Tokio, London. Erinnerungen und Betrachtungen zu 20 Jahren deutscher Aussenpolitik, 1919-1939* (Stuttgart, 1950), pp. 9-10.

plary bearing." Herbert, who wished to prepare himself for a diplomatic career, was forced by his father into the domestic civil service in order that the son might, after the father's death, be technically qualified to manage the great estate to which he would fall heir. After completing his education at Heidelberg, where he had joined the most aristocratic fraternity, Herbert was enrolled in the fashionable Third Guard Ulan regiment at Potsdam.[2]

In all externals, Herbert von Dirksen became what his father wished him to be: a correct and proper aristocrat with all the right connections. But, unlike the true aristocrat, he had an uncommon respect for and fear of those who held authority and wielded power in the modern world. It was this characteristic, so relentlessly hammered into him by his father in another era, which separated Dirksen from the aristocrats of more ancient lineage such as Schulenburg and Welczek. It was this too which made him more than a loyal civil servant to the Nazis—a true if not ardent believer in Hitler. Finally, it was this quality which made it morally impossible for Dirksen, even after his disillusionment, to join in the resistance against Hitler in which his Moscow colleague met his death.

The attention of Ribbentrop was first drawn to Dirksen when the latter was ambassador to Japan. During the years 1935 to 1937, German policy in the Far East was one of the major issues over which the unseen struggle between the Nazi party and the older Foreign Office and military bureaucracy was fought out. The Foreign Office had traditionally based its Far Eastern policy on China, with which Germany had close commercial and military ties. The development of antagonism between Germany and Russia in the first years of the Nazi regime made it seem doubly important to keep good relations with China lest that country be driven by Japanese aggression into the arms of the Russians. To that end Germany established a group of military advisors with the Chinese government in 1934 and shipped it substantial quantities of arms. The German Foreign Office frowned on Japanese expansion in China, not merely because of its effect on Russo-Chinese relations, but also because it might mire the anti-Soviet potential of Japan in the quicksands of China. The Nazi party, on the other hand, early developed a policy of giving Japan a free hand in China in order to win the Far East's most powerful state as an ally of Germany. Ribbentrop was the architect of this policy long before he emerged from his paradiplomatic *Dienststelle* in the regalia of a Foreign Minister. Its visible expression—a great

[2] Dirksen, *Moskau, Tokio, London*, pp. 10-12.

personal triumph for Ribbentrop over the Foreign Office—was the Anti-Comintern Pact of November 1936.

During the development of this internecine feud, Dirksen maintained an ambivalent position. Out of a deeply felt affinity for the moderate expansionists of Japan, and with an ambassador's natural penchant for promoting good relations with the country of his accreditation, Dirksen favored the substance of Ribbentrop's policy. But he favored the Foreign Office in form; the Foreign Office alone should be the executor of foreign policy. When Dirksen learned (from a Japanese source) of the negotiations for the Anti-Comintern Pact, he went home to Germany, interviewed Ribbentrop, and transmitted his information to the ill-informed Foreign Minister, von Neurath.[3]

With the outbreak of the "China incident" in July 1937, the conflict between party and Foreign Office over Far Eastern policy reached a new fury. The Foreign Office enjoined strict neutrality in the conflict,[4] but maintained its military aid to China; while the party wheels—Goering, Ribbentrop, and Goebbels—all pressed for a pro-Japanese policy.[5] Dirksen took the Nazi line, urging that "the surest way of avoiding . . . conflicts with Japan would be to recall our military advisors from Nanking." Well aware that this suggestion would be unacceptable to the Foreign Office and army, however, he suggested further that his superiors consider German mediation in the Sino-Japanese conflict as a means to "extricate us from the difficulties of neutrality."[6] The difficulties, be it noted, were not merely international, but also domestic. Dirksen, occupying a position halfway between the Nazis and the old bureaucracy, was proposing to solve on the international plane a domestic struggle for control over foreign policy.

Thanks to the decision of the Western Powers to try to settle the conflict through the Brussels Conference, the German leaders accepted Dirksen's proposal. From October 1937, to January 1938, the negotiations dragged on, only to end in failure.[7] With the collapse of the mediation effort Dirksen drafted a dispatch in which he recommended a basic reorientation of Germany's Far Eastern policy toward Japan: the cessation of arms shipments to China, the withdrawal of military advisors, and the recognition of Manchukuo.[8] By the time this policy memorandum reached Berlin, Ribbentrop had become Foreign Minister (February 4, 1938). The new incumbent placed Dirksen's recommendations before

---

[3] Dirksen, *Moskau, Tokio, London*, pp. 184-185. See also Chapter 13, §IV above.
[4] *German Documents*, series D, I, 733-734.   [5] *ibid.*, pp. 752-754, 767-769, 772.
[6] *ibid.*, pp. 754-755.   [7] *ibid.*, pp. 771-825, *passim.*
[8] *ibid.*, pp. 826-831.

Hitler.[9] On February 20, the Fuehrer announced Germany's recognition of Manchukuo.

While Dirksen was en route home for a holiday in Germany, news reached him of his appointment to London. In the great February overturn of Foreign Office and army, Dirksen had emerged with the signal honor of succeeding the Nazi Foreign Minister in Germany's most important diplomatic post. Ribbentrop's selection is easy to understand: Dirksen had supported his pro-Japanese line throughout. He had gotten on well with the principal agent of the *Dienststelle Ribbentrop* in Japan.[10] He had joined the party in 1936 and was genuinely impressed with its economic and political achievements.[11] All these factors would have recommended Dirksen to Ribbentrop. True, Dirksen was a career foreign servant, and for this reason Ribbentrop could never wholly trust him. During neither his Japanese nor his British assignments was Dirksen made privy to the party's plans in foreign affairs. Yet the very fact that Dirksen was on good terms with the old school professionals might have its uses for the Nazi Foreign Minister as long as Dirksen remained loyal to the party line.

Dirksen too had some ambivalence about serving under a Foreign Minister whose unorthodox ways offended his bureaucratic sensibilities. "But as the poacher made forester often becomes quite a useful member of society, I thought, so Ribbentrop too, having attained the object of his vain desire, would be amenable to reason and good counsel. Besides, the competition between the Foreign Office and the Ribbentrop Bureau would now have to cease."[12] Yes, there would henceforth be but one authority over Germany's foreign policy. By that very fact the half-Nazi, half-aristocratic Dirksen was already obsolescent as a political person. Dirksen did not realize that the supremacy of the party in the Wilhelmstrasse would deprive him of the latitude which domestic rivalries had afforded him in Japan. Nor could he grasp the fact that his rigid bureaucratic ethic would prove a handicap in pursuing his own concept of the national interest when Ribbentrop's policies ran counter to it.

II

Dirksen prepared for his new mission in a mood of high optimism. His belief that Hitler desired good relations with Great Britain and wished to build further upon the foundations laid in the Anglo-German Naval Agreement of 1935 was confirmed by the somewhat vague in-

[9] *ibid.*, pp. 839-840.
[11] *ibid.*, pp. 182-187.
[10] Dirksen, *Moskau, Tokio, London*, p. 160.
[12] *ibid.*, p. 199.

structions of the Foreign Minister. Although Hitler angrily complained to Dirksen of Britain's lack of understanding for Germany's demands, the ambassador saw nothing permanent in the Fuehrer's negative attitude.[13]

On taking up his post in London on May 3, 1938, Dirksen at once sought to exploit to the utmost such powers as his ambassadorial position gave him to promote cordial relations between the two countries. At his initial call on Lord Halifax, a general conversation developed on the Sudeten question, just then emerging into dangerous prominence. Dirksen told the Foreign Secretary that the Germans "were very anxious to keep things quiet in Czechoslovakia"—a statement which could not have emanated from his home government, and which he did not report to it.[14] The ambassador quoted Halifax as entertaining the idea "that the Reich Government could perhaps make a contribution to the solution of the [Sudeten] question by formulating in writing their desires in this respect."[15] No mention of this suggestion appears in Halifax's record of the conversation. Thus in his first significant dispatch from London, Dirksen appears to have been trying to push his government toward negotiations on the Czech question faster than the British themselves wished to go. A few weeks later (June 8), in his effort to win the confidence of the British, Dirksen went so far as to be "frankly outspoken" with Halifax on the subject of Ribbentrop. He told the Foreign Secretary—frankly but falsely—that Ribbentrop recognized that his mission to England had been a failure because "he had always felt obliged to keep one eye so much on the German end. . . . None the less, he [Ribbentrop] still wished to establish closer relations between our two countries."[16] From some rather general remarks of Halifax on improving Anglo-German relations, the ambassador extrapolated for Wilhelmstrasse consumption the Foreign Secretary's "clearly discernible . . . intention of making an approach to the German Government again, with a view to resuming within measurable time the negotiations" interrupted by the rape of Austria.[17] By a little exaggeration of the will to improved relations in both capitals, Dirksen sought to pave the way for a *détente*.

The first month of Dirksen's mission was not an easy one. The so-called "week-end crisis" of May 21, when the Czechs mobilized in the mistaken

---

[13] Dirksen, *Moskau, Tokio, London*, pp. 209-210.

[14] *British Documents*, 3rd series, I, 240; cf. *German Documents*, series D, II, 255-256.

[15] *German Documents*, series D, II, 255.

[16] *British Documents*, 3rd series I, 455; cf. Dirksen, *Moskau, Tokio, London*, p. 209, where he states that Ribbentrop avoided any discussion of the failure of his London mission.

[17] *German Documents*, series D, II, 398; cf. *British Documents*, 3rd series, I, 454-455.

belief that the Germans were massing troops on their borders, provided a poor atmosphere for inaugurating a new phase in Anglo-German relations. In that crisis, Dirksen formed the impressions of both the Chamberlain government and of British public opinion which governed his thinking until the end of his mission. He was convinced that the ruling circles in Great Britain would do anything to avoid war, but would fight if Germany should resort to force. "Most brutal, but also most characteristic [wrote Dirksen in his report on the May crisis], is the advice given to a German acquaintance by an influential Englishman: 'Don't shoot Czechoslovakia, strangle her.' Or in other words: Anything which can be got without a shot being fired can count upon the agreement of the British."[18] Chamberlain, because he realizes clearly "that the social structure of Britain, even the conception of the British Empire, would not survive the chaos of even a victorious war . . . is committed to the idea of European settlement with all the obstinacy which is characteristic of his family. He knows very well that Anglo-German agreement is the keystone of such a European settlement."[19] Chamberlain's was "the first postwar Cabinet which has made agreement with Germany one of the major points of its program." It displayed maximum understanding of German demands, not only in the Czech question, but also "with respect to excluding the Soviet Union from the decision of the destinies of Europe, the League of Nations likewise, and the advisability of bilateral treaties and negotiations."[20]

While Dirksen stressed British willingness to accommodate to Germany's demands, he also pointed out the limits of British tolerance. British public opinion, he felt, had been revolutionized by the German action in Austria. In the May crisis, Dirksen wrote on June 8, "the feeling . . . of being made a fool of in that affair, grew up again, together with the determination not to allow unchallenged further alterations in the balance of power in Europe. . . . The attitude of the British people to the possibility of war has changed entirely since 1936. They are ready to fight should their government show them that this is necessary in order to put an end to a state of subjectively experienced threats and uncertainty. . . ."[21] The Chamberlain-Halifax government could well be unseated by a "psychotic" public opinion aroused by another German *fait accompli*. "To regard the excitement of the last weeks as mere bluff might

[18] *German Documents*, series D, II, 393.
[19] *ibid.*, 473.
[20] *Dirksen Papers*, p. 34; for Dirksen's reports on the British attitude toward the USSR, see also *German Documents*, series D, II, 434, 486.
[21] *German Documents*, series D, II, 323, 394-395.

turn out to be a fatal error." Alternatively, the Chamberlain government itself would, "without the slightest doubt," go to war if Germany resorts to war to achieve its ends. The willingness of the British government to make sacrifices to meet Germany's demands was limited by "the *one* condition, that Germany would endeavor to achieve these ends by peaceful means."[22]

Dirksen's evaluation of the British situation was realistic and his advice to the Wilhelmstrasse, within the framework of the German aim of hegemony in Eastern Europe, thoroughly sound: Chamberlain's government, he said in effect, is Germany's greatest political asset. But to realize its value, you must go slow, you must proceed by diplomatic blackmail, not by overt military force. As in the early days of his mission to Tokyo, Dirksen differed not with the stated aims of the Nazis but with their pace and method.

Did Dirksen's policy recommendations have any influence in Berlin? Certainly not at the level of grand strategy. On May 30, Hitler had issued his new directive for Operation Green, with its "unalterable decision to smash Czechoslovakia by military action in the near future." No mention was made of British intervention in this document. In a supplementary directive, dated July 7, French and British intervention during the execution of Operation Green was stated, in flat contradiction of Dirksen's expressed judgment, to be "contrary to our expectations."[23]

In the Wilhelmstrasse, opinion seems to have been divided. Weizsäcker, in early June, felt that the avoidance of Franco-British intervention must be "the first care" of German policy toward Czechoslovakia. "Germany is not free to choose the moment when this fruit may be plucked without too great a risk. She is only in a position to organize the desired development around the slogan emanating at this moment from Britain, 'Self-determination for the Sudetenland.' "[24] As opposed to the use of force, Weizsäcker advocated a "chemical process of disruption" which would take into account the kind of dangers pointed out by Dirksen. Ribbentrop seems to have largely ignored the question as to whether Britain's ultimate attitude should be taken into account. In his diplomacy from May to July his primary concern was to elicit, in the bluntest conceivable way, a British denial that the United Kingdom would support Franco-Czech military resistance if war should break out. He wished the British to make this denial in public form if possible, in order to weaken

[22] *ibid.*, p. 395; *Dirksen Papers*, p. 34.
[23] Royal Institute of International Affairs, *Survey of International Affairs, 1938* (London, 1951), II, 140-146; *German Documents*, series D, II, 475.
[24] *German Documents*, series D, II, 420-422.

Czech resistance to the "chemical process."[25] What the Foreign Minister must have thought of Dirksen's warnings of Britain's willingness to fight may be inferred from a marginal notation he wrote in English on a similar warning from another source: "Secret Service Propaganda!"[26] But even if the Western Powers would intervene, so be it. On July 21, Ribbentrop told Weizsäcker that Germany was prepared to fight on the Czech question and to win—to which Weizsäcker replied that "even if it was our business to fool foreign countries, it was nevertheless our duty not to dupe one another."[27]

Of Hitler's and Ribbentrop's full intentions Ambassador Dirksen knew nothing during the spring and early summer of 1938. Where Britain was fooled, Dirksen was duped. Both pinned their hopes not so much on Ribbentrop as on Hitler's good sense and the power of the restraining elements in his entourage.

When the sky grew darkest, there always seemed to be a ray of hope at hand. In July 1938, the Sudeten issue was seething again. Suddenly Captain Wiedemann, Hitler's personal adjutant, appeared in London on a highly secret mission to extend the olive branch to Britain. Of course Dirksen warmly welcomed Wiedemann, whose task was to sound out the British government on the possibility of a visit by Goering to Britain to discuss the improvement of Anglo-German relations. Wiedemann's purpose was entirely congenial to Dirksen. But the form of this approach created difficulties for the ambassador, difficulties which revealed the deliberate ambiguity in the line of responsibility in Hitler's administrative system. Wiedemann's mission had been undertaken under Goering's auspices and with Hitler's consent, but without the knowledge of Foreign Minister von Ribbentrop.[28] Although Wiedemann wished to keep Ribbentrop in the dark concerning his visit, Dirksen persuaded him to report to the Foreign Minister on the content of his conversation.[29] Dirksen was still trying, as in Tokyo, to keep the lines clear. But where in Tokyo he had to maneuver between the party and the old bureaucracy, he now had to contend with two wings of the party. The more aggressive of these, with whose aims he no longer sympathized, firmly controlled the Foreign Office to which he felt a primary bureaucratic allegiance. Throughout, Hitler seems to have given both groups some latitude—either because he had not made up his mind or because

[25] Cf. e.g., *German Documents*, series D, II, 377, 409-411; also Royal Institute of International Affairs, *Survey, 1938*, II, 137, note 1.

[26] *German Documents*, series D, II, 440.   [27] *ibid.*, p. 504.

[28] *British Documents*, 3rd series, I, 587.

[29] Dirksen, *Moskau, Tokio, London*, pp. 216-217.

he wished to confuse his potential adversaries with the open-ended character of his policies.

The Wiedemann mission greatly encouraged Dirksen. When he made his farewell call on Sir Horace Wilson before taking home leave (July 22), Sir Horace quite unexpectedly ushered him in to the Prime Minister, who expressed his gratification at Wiedemann's message and asked Dirksen to convey his views to Hitler if he saw fit. Dirksen was delighted with Wiedemann's assurance to Chamberlain that Hitler "would wish to get negotiations [between the Sudeten German party and the Czech government] resumed" if they should break down.[30]

How impossible it was to place any reliance on gestures of friendship from Ribbentrop's rivals was clearly shown in the ill-fated attempt of Halifax and Dirksen to win the support of Germany for the Runciman mission. Ribbentrop brusquely rejected Halifax's first request for support of the Runciman mission (July 26) as a "purely British affair."[31] On July 28, Halifax wrote a personal letter to Ribbentrop deploring the indifference of the German government to the mediation effort and again urgently requesting its support. Fearing that "in his present temper there was a real danger" that Ribbentrop "might not show it [Halifax's letter] to Hitler at all," the British took two further steps to reach "the sole arbiter of Germany's fate."[32] Chamberlain wrote a private letter to Dirksen in Germany, asking him to request Hitler "to give full consideration to the contents of the personal letter that Lord Halifax recently addressed to Herr von Ribbentrop in regard to Lord Runciman's Mission."[33] Correct as ever in his bureaucratic procedure, Dirksen submitted Chamberlain's letter and a draft reply to the Under-Secretary of State. The Under-Secretary, also taking account of von Ribbentrop's "present temper," excised from Dirksen's draft reply both a reference to German public sympathy for Runciman's mission and a promise to mention the Halifax letter to Hitler.[34]

Dirksen's chances of an interview with Hitler, slim at best, were surely not improved by submitting the Chamberlain letter to the Foreign Office. They became still weaker when Lord Halifax took a second step to circumvent Ribbentrop and to communicate directly with the Fuehrer. With Ribbentrop thoroughly outraged and with Hitler resolved neither

---

[30] *British Documents*, 3rd series, I, 618-620; *German Documents*, series D, II, 509-510.
[31] *German Documents*, series D, II, 517; *British Documents*, 3rd series, II, 13.
[32] *British Documents*, 3rd series, II, 41, note 1; I, 603.
[33] *ibid.*, II, 41.
[34] Cf. *German Documents*, series D, II, 542-543, with *British Documents*, 3rd series, II, 60.

to support the Runciman mission nor to retard his plan to force a military showdown,[35] Dirksen's hopes of laying Chamberlain's position before the Fuehrer evaporated. His application for an audience through the Foreign Office brought no results. He visited several high Nazis (Bohle and Hess) who might carry his message to Hitler indirectly. He tried again to get an interview with Hitler through an influential friend in the Fuehrer's Berchtesgaden entourage—to no avail. Not until the Nuremberg Congress in the second week of September was Dirksen finally granted an audience with his chief of state. The conversation lasted only seven minutes, during which Hitler maintained a completely closed attitude toward Chamberlain's plea and rejected any consideration of support for that "rabid democrat" Lord Runciman.[36]

With this interview ended the first phase of Dirksen's illusory efforts to achieve an Anglo-German *détente*. At Nuremberg, the ambassador was told that, in view of the acuteness of Anglo-German tension, he should not for the present return to his post. In the Munich crisis, Dirksen played no direct part. But his work in London had helped to prepare the ground for Hitler's most successful blackmail operation. Incapable of understanding the connection between the Nazi aims with which he sympathized and the Nazi methods which he disliked, he had, by his sympathetic discharge of his London mission, done his best to help encourage in the British statesmen the belief that moderate, conservative Germany still participated in the formulation of Hitler's policies.

After five months of labor, Dirksen had become little more than a voice of the British appeasers in the Nazi Foreign Office. In this respect, his position was not unlike that of his British opposite number, Sir Nevile Henderson—with the unfortunate exception that Henderson's voice was listened to in London, while Dirksen's was ignored in Berlin.

III

During the years of Dirksen's labors to further Nazi aims in the Far East and to mitigate the effects of Nazi policy in pre-Munich London, Count Werner Friedrich von der Schulenburg represented Germany in Moscow. A cool, somewhat skeptical nobleman of ancient family, Schulenburg showed none of the emotional instability or personal *Geltungsdrang* of his parvenu-aristocratic colleague. Where Dirksen was always

---

[35] *German Documents*, series D, II, 576-577, 593. Cf. also Ribbentrop's answer, August 21, to Halifax's personal message of July 28, *ibid.*, 599-600.
[36] Dirksen, *Moskau, Tokio, London*, pp. 229-231; *Dirksen Papers*, pp. 157-158.

on the lookout for opportunities to act or to make policy recommendations, Schulenburg was the patient, impersonal, and disengaged spectator of the passing show. His reports from Moscow contain policy suggestions only on the rarest occasions; and if, like all western diplomats in the Soviet capital, he perforce engaged in speculation, he did so less frequently and more soberly than most.

Schulenburg began his mission to Moscow in October 1936. His predecessor, Nadolny, a man of unalterable Eastern orientation, had resigned his post in protest against Hitler's total rejection of the Rapallo policy. Schulenburg was by temperament admirably suited to head an embassy which, with Russo-German relations at their nadir, could be little more than a highly important listening post during the next three years. His published dispatches for the years from 1936 to 1938 reveal nothing of that Eastern orientation for which he became famous through the pact negotiations and the later resistance movement against Hitler.

Schulenburg's political analysis was clearheaded and somewhat old-fashioned. In his evaluation of the USSR, he consistently played down the Marxist revolutionary component in the Soviet leaders' policies. The idea of *Staatsräson* dominated his thinking about Russia as about Germany.[37] At the root of all political activity in the Soviet Union, he said in November 1937, were two convictions: The first was "that Imperial Russia owed her defeat in the World War to the *lack of an adequate war industry*"; the second, "born partly of respect, partly of fear . . . that of the *fearful strength of the German people*." The second conviction had gained impetus through the rise of Hitler and German rearmament, which "led to the Soviet-French and Soviet-Czech mutual assistance pacts," to "the enormous increase in Soviet armament expenditures," and to the cultivation of Soviet patriotism, "a measure to strengthen the defensive spirit of the nation."[38] On the relationship of the purges then in progress to the basic convictions which he believed to motivate Soviet policy, Schulenburg felt unclear. He inclined to the current view that the purges were connected with Soviet isolationism, and was certain that the wave of persecution had "gravely shaken the organism of the Soviet State. . . . But [he added] it would be unwise to assume that this downward development *must* be permanent. . . . As for what may come tomorrow, we must wait and see."[39]

During the development of the Czech crisis, Schulenburg seems not

[37] Cf. Peter Kleist, *Zwischen Stalin und Hitler* (Bonn, 1950), pp. 34-35.
[38] From an address before the German Wehrmacht Academy, November 25, 1937. *German Documents*, series D, I, 899.
[39] *ibid.*, 899-900.

to have been fearful of a rapprochement between the Soviet Union and the West. Internal instability and fear of war on two fronts would, he thought, militate against any serious Russian intervention on behalf of Czechoslovakia, although minimum aid was not to be excluded. "The Soviet Union will intervene [Schulenburg wrote after the May crisis] only if she herself is attacked, or if it becomes manifest that the outcome will be favorable to the side hostile to Germany."[40] The core of Russia's policy, he insisted, was isolationist: to build up military strength and hold aloof from any potential conflict. How was this evaluation to be squared with Russia's repeated declarations of support for collective security in general and Czechoslovakia in particular? Schulenburg believed that it was Litvinov's basic aim to stiffen the resistance of the Western Powers to Germany by every means, whether promises or taunts. In this framework, Schulenburg interpreted a suggestion of a Soviet approach to Germany in June 1938. Not to be taken at face value, it merely gave the USSR "the opportunity once more to hold up before the French ally the specter of a German-Soviet understanding."[41]

With his premise that Russian policy was based on *Realpolitik*-from-weakness, Schulenburg was of course alert to any changes in the Soviet line which might offer opportunities for Germany. Reporting on a speech of Litvinov after the May crisis (June 23), he took seriously Litvinov's disappointment with the democracies' "compliant attitude" toward the aggressors. "Litvinov indicates that Soviet policy, whose aim it was only a few years ago to collaborate as closely as possible with the democratic great powers and to be admitted to the circle of these states itself, will henceforth—without abandoning the principle of collective security—break with the policy of the western powers and decide in each case whether its own interests require cooperation with England and France."[42]

A point of particular importance to Schulenburg was Litvinov's clear indication that the Soviet Union was no defender of Versailles. "If the Soviet Union has sided with the democracies and the League of Nations during the last few years, it has done so because Germany aims not merely at the restoration of her pre-war boundaries and the rights denied her by Versailles, but also pursues an open and 'mad' anti-Soviet policy and a policy of unlimited aggression."[43]

---

[40] *German Documents*, series D, II, 363-364, 423-426. Schulenburg's military attaché, General Köstring, freely communicated his estimates of Soviet military weakness and isolationism to his British opposite number. See *British Documents*, 3rd series, I, 418-424.
[41] *German Documents*, series D, I, 921.   [42] *German Documents*, series D, I, 929.
[43] *ibid.*, 928.

The ambassador drew no explicit conclusions for German policy from Litvinov's address. He merely pointed out that Russia was again reserving freedom of action, and that "the attempt to arrive at an objective attitude toward the Third Reich is striking."[44] Yet from his dispatch two implications emerge for the German Foreign Office: (1) that the Western orientation of the USSR was artificially induced by Hitler's "mad" anti-Soviet policy; and (2) that the USSR, if Germany were to assume a more friendly attitude, might well lend diplomatic support for the recovery of Germany's pre-world war I boundaries. Like Dirksen in London at the same time (June 1938), Schulenburg was informing his superiors that, in the government to which he was accredited, there was understanding for Germany's aims but not for Hitler's methods.

On the whole, Schulenburg's reports during the first nine months of 1938 could only reassure Hitler that he need have no immediate fears of Russia as long as he made no direct assault upon her. "Whereas the Soviet Union is attempting to force France and Great Britain to take the initiative against Germany, she herself will hold back." On August 26, 1938, when the Czech crisis was approaching its climax, Schulenburg stuck resolutely to this line, in the face of Litvinov's explicit statement to him that "the Soviet Union had promised Czechoslovakia her support; she would keep her word and do her best." He noted that Litvinov repeatedly attacked British policy, and that he avoided answering the question as to the form which Soviet help to Czechoslovakia would take. The German embassy estimated that Soviet aid would probably be confined to the shipment of war materials. "The sending of troops is . . . not in the interests of the Soviet Union."[45]

Such were Schulenburg's honest evaluations of Soviet intentions and capabilities, and they could only have heartened Hitler on his road to war with Czechoslovakia and the West. Yet the ambassador was not happy to provide this encouragement to the framers of Germany's adventurous policies, and did what he could to offset his professional analysis of Soviet policy. During August and September 1938, he reported fully and frequently opinions of the Moscow diplomatic corps to the effect that France and Britain would fight.[46] He cited the universal opinion that the Soviet Union would be "the only one to gain" from a European war. In two dispatches he quoted the words spoken to him by M. Coulondre, the French ambassador, words which doubtless expressed his own feelings: "I hope with all my heart that it will not

[44] *ibid.*, 923-924. [45] *German Documents*, series D, II, 630-631.
[46] *ibid.*, 602, 605, 631, 655-657, 666-667.

come to a French-German conflict. You know as well as I do for whom we are working if we come to blows."[47]

With his reporting on Western intentions, Schulenburg joined his warning voice to that of Dirksen. There is evidence to suggest that he took a more drastic step to avoid the catastrophe: a *sub rosa* approach to the British. On August 22, Herwarth von Bittenfeld, a member of the German embassy staff who was close to Schulenburg, appealed to the third secretary of the British embassy for a clearer declaration by his government of its willingness to fight. Herwarth showed himself familiar with the substance of Dirksen's warnings and informed his interlocutor that "little attention was paid in Berlin to Dircksen's [*sic*] reports, or, for that matter, to those from other missions abroad."[48]

He went on to reveal that the dispatches and instructions from the Wilhelmstrasse reflected Hitler's and Ribbentrop's confidence ". . . that Germany would be able to invade Czechoslovakia with impunity. This, our informant said, was very disturbing to professional diplomats like his ambassador, who saw their country about to involve herself in a war in which the odds would in their opinion be heavily against her. . . . The blame, they felt, would lie to a certain extent with His Majesty's Government, who, as in 1914, had failed to make their position sufficiently clear. *The only* hope in their opinion would be for a representative of His Majesty's Government to inform the Führer himself quite categorically that in certain circumstances Great Britain would quite certainly go to war in defence of Czechoslovakia."[49]

It cannot be proved that Schulenburg prompted Herwarth's appeal against British appeasement, but the secretary's references to his chief's views suggest that the ambassador stood behind him on his bold mission. Schulenburg's initiative in the affair would have been quite consistent with the strength of character he revealed in the later conspiracy against Hitler.

None of the foregoing evidence of Schulenburg's attitudes should be construed as indications of a Western orientation on his part. If he did what little he could to avoid a struggle with the West, it was out of cool consideration for his country's interest. If in his published dispatches of the pre-Munich years he showed no disposition to advocate an Eastern orientation, it was because the policies of his government were hopelessly unreceptive to any rapprochement with the Soviet

[47] *ibid.*, 602, 631.
[48] *British Documents*, 3rd series, II, 141.
[49] *ibid.*

Union.[50] A *Realpolitiker* of the old school, Schulenburg reported what he saw, acted when he could in his country's interest as he construed it, and bided his time.

IV

The Munich Pact sent a feeling of triumphant relief through the German Diplomatic Service. The Moscow mission was no exception. "At the Embassy [wrote the Counselor of Embassy] there prevails great jubilation over the enormous, unimaginable success which the Führer has won for Germany. . . . That the policy of Litvinov has suffered a complete fiasco, that the war, from which chaos and the weakening of Germany was expected, has not broken out, that the policy of pacts and alliances has failed, that the collective idea has collapsed, and that the League of Nations has disappointed the hopes reposed in it, can in my opinion not remain without consequences for Soviet policy. . . . As regards ourselves, a more positive attitude on the part of the Soviet Union might be possible."[51] Dirksen records the "great joy" he felt at the signature of the Anglo-German protocol, which he hoped "would open a new and happier chapter in the relations of the two countries."[52]

Both ambassadors assumed that Hitler, having achieved his aim in disrupting Czechoslovakia and the post-Versailles security system, must be ready to normalize relations with the capitals to which they were accredited. They now entered into a kind of unwitting competition with each other which culminated ten months later in a technical victory for Schulenburg with the conclusion of the Nazi-Soviet Pact.

Dirksen was well aware of the riven condition of British official and governmental opinion, but he was rightly convinced that Chamberlain and his closest followers were determined to do everything in their power to develop the cordial Anglo-German relations promised by the Munich protocol.[53] The important thing now, as Dirksen saw it, was for the German government to avoid all provocative utterance which might feed ammunition to the Conservative and Labor opposition. Thus the way could be smoothed for constructive diplomatic work.

Hitler at once crossed Dirksen's suggestions by a sharp public attack on the British opposition and British rearmament (Saarbrücken speech, October 9). In response to an inquiry by Lord Halifax concerning the

---

[50] The British ambassador Viscount Chilston was aware of Schulenburg's dilemma. Cf. *ibid.*, 141, note 1.

[51] *German Documents*, series D, IV, 602. See also Chapter II, §III above.

[52] Dirksen, *Moskau, Tokio, London*, p. 235.

[53] *German Documents*, series D, IV, 310.

treatment of non-Nazi Sudeten Germans, Hitler answered in his speech: "We cannot any longer tolerate the tutelage of British governesses. Inquiries of British politicians concerning the fate of Germans within the frontiers of the Reich—or of others belonging to the Reich—are not in place."[54] Dirksen wrote personally to Weizsäcker to persuade him that such outbursts could only give a new lease on life to the Churchill-Eden group.[55] This was but the first of a series of efforts by Dirksen to instruct Hitler and Ribbentrop on the best way to strengthen the hand of Germany's friend, Chamberlain. He advised that they avoid attacks on Churchill's group and on British rearmament; that they emphasize the line of the Anglo-German protocol: "Never again war between Britain and Germany"; and that they take the initiative in launching disarmament talks and respond with positive proposals to British feelers for a *détente*.[56] Dirksen urged bilateral disarmament discussions, which he felt, would strengthen Chamberlain's position to the point where a colonial settlement could be approached with every prospect of success. Dirksen's recommendations were not products of his imagination, but based on conversations with British Cabinet ministers and other intimates of the Prime Minister.

It soon became clear that Berlin was firmly resolved to ignore Dirksen's "do's" and "don'ts." Weizsäcker informed the ambassador that the German press campaign against British rearmament "was instigated on the direct instructions of the Foreign Minister." He advised Dirksen against forwarding to Ribbentrop a report by Dr. Hesse, head of Ribbentrop's own London *Dienststelle*, because Hesse's arguments "tend too strongly in a direction which, as things are now, is not the same as that taken here." It was only three weeks after Munich when the Secretary of State wrote to Dirksen: "Things here are moving rapidly but not in the direction of a German-British rapprochement at present."[57] Which way they were moving, the ambassador was of course not told. It is striking that Dirksen's October recommendations for future negotiations referred only to those questions which the British wished to discuss—disarmament and colonies—while the issues on which Hitler was preparing to act—rump Czechoslovakia, Memel, Danzig, and Poland—were almost wholly ignored.

With the shock of November pogroms, Dirksen had to suspend his efforts to prepare the ground for a *détente*. When in mid-December

[54] *ibid.*, 302-303.   [55] *ibid.*, 303-305.

[56] *German Documents*, series D, IV, 305-311, 319-323; also *Dirksen Papers*, pp. 160-161.

[57] *German Documents*, series D, IV, 311-312; cf. also p. 327.

he resumed them, he went to work on a more modest plane: that of economic relations. A new sense of urgency informed the ambassador's recommendation for pursuing an accord in the economic field. On December 16, 1938 he wrote to Weizsäcker: "How long Chamberlain can keep his place . . . is a question about which I am by no means so confident as I was a month or two ago. If therefore there should be any wish on our side for a certain degree of *rapprochement*, I should be in favor of not waiting too long."[58]

During January and February Dirksen had some grounds for optimism. Negotiations of an Anglo-German coal agreement were proceeding smoothly, and other industry conferences between the two countries were successfully initiated. Hitler himself made an unusually conciliatory speech on January 30. Although Dirksen failed to win his government's assent to a British request that Funk, the German Minister of Economics, pay a visit to England, he arranged for the issuance of an invitation to visit Germany to Sir Oliver Stanley, President of the Board of Trade.[59] Perhaps most encouraging to the ambassador was the fact that, at the end of February, Ribbentrop commissioned Dr. Hesse to approach Chamberlain through his personal press secretary with a view to a really broad rapprochement, to be crowned by an Anglo-German nonaggression treaty. Ribbentrop indicated his willingness to come to London to sign such a treaty.[60]

These promising beginnings of improved Anglo-German relations were once more crushed by the march into Prague. Germany's gestures of accommodation during the preceding two months were revealed as a mere decoy to distract the attention of the British from Hitler's next undertaking. The Hesse mission performed the same function in the second Czech crisis as the Wiedemann mission had in the first. Dirksen, with his unlimited will to believe in Hitler's good intentions, was equally fooled by both, and participated with innocent eagerness in the work of building decoys for the British.

If most of Dirksen's labors, during the period from October 1938 to March 1939, were conducted in ignorance of Hitler's precise intentions, he was privately informed of the impending march on Prague a week or more before the event when in Berlin on a short leave.[61]

---

[58] *German Documents*, series D, IV, 354.

[59] *German Documents*, series D, IV, 389ff.; cf. also *British Documents*, 3rd series, IV, 138, note 1. The Stanley visit was called off by the British after the march into Prague.

[60] *Dirksen Papers*, pp. 165-166; Dirksen, *Moskau, Tokio, London*, pp. 238-239.

[61] Dirksen, *Moskau, Tokio, London*, p. 240; cf. *Dirksen Papers*, p. 166.

Returning to England on March 9, Dirksen found "the same optimistic mood as had prevailed in February. Stanley's visit to Berlin was to take place soon—on March 17—and it was obvious that the British Government attached great importance to it."[62] The ambassador, loyal as ever to his government, did nothing to disturb the optimistic mood of the British, breathed no word of the impending coup in Prague. Before his recall to Berlin on March 18, Dirksen had two stormy conversations with the irate Lord Halifax. Despite the ambassador's attempt at a bold front, in which he drew once more upon his own hatred of Versailles, Halifax observed that "his demeanour was one that suggested that he felt considerable difficulty himself in defending the action taken by his government."[63] Dirksen's house of cards had collapsed no less than Halifax's. But Dirksen still drew no personal consequences from the fact. To justify his government's policy may have been difficult for Dirksen; to cease to serve that policy was still unthinkable. With Ribbentrop unwilling to receive or hear him on his return to Germany, Dirksen sulkily withdrew to his beloved Gröditzberg to wait for two months until his master should give the signal for his next jump through the hoop.

V

With the signing of the Munich Pact, Germany incidentally achieved one of the major aims of its foreign policy: the exclusion of the Soviet Union from the European international community. The German embassy in Moscow, on the morrow of Munich, expected the early dismissal of Litvinov, whose efforts to bolster the European security system had proved a "complete fiasco."[64] Although this event did not take place with the anticipated speed, the embassy felt that circumstances were favorable for an approach toward normalizing relations with the USSR. Schulenburg abandoned his previous reserve. Believing that the Soviets, in their isolation, would feel an increased need for foreign goods to support accelerated war production, Schulenburg authorized a proposal to the Foreign Office that it seize the occasion to negotiate a new economic agreement with the Soviet Union (October 10, 1938).[65] Little more than a fortnight later, Schulenburg was turning over a broader program in his mind: "It is my intention in the immediate future to approach

---

[62] *Dirksen Papers*, pp. 166-167; cf. L. B. Namier, *Diplomatic Prelude* (London, 1948), pp. 65-66.

[63] *German Documents*, series D, IV, 281-282; *British Documents*, 3rd series, IV, 270-272.

[64] *German Documents*, series D, IV, 602-603.   [65] *ibid.*, 603.

Molotov, the Chairman of the Council of People's Commissars, in an attempt to reach a favorable settlement of the questions disturbing German-Soviet relations. The most favorable opportunity for this step would be the beginning of the negotiations on the 1939 German-Soviet agreement on trade and payments and the larger credit on goods to the Soviet Union." This agreement would provide the basis for discussions of a long list of issues outstanding between the two countries: disputes arising out of the transport of German goods through the USSR to Iran, unfavorable treatment of applications for entry permits for German businessmen, failure to release from Soviet citizenship wives of German citizens who had left or been expelled from the USSR, etc.[66] It is striking that Schulenburg should have contemplated so complete a circumvention of Litvinov in favor of a direct approach to Molotov. There is, however, no indication that he carried out this plan.

This program of diplomatic action, broad as it was compared to anything which might have been contemplated before Munich, manifests no intention to produce a diplomatic revolution. In his sober fashion, Schulenburg drew—at least for his government—none of the radical conclusions entertained by his French colleague, Coulondre: that Munich would throw the Soviet Union into the arms of Germany.[67] The Polish question—the traditional hinge of Russo-German relations—is scarcely touched upon in the published diplomatic dispatches for the six months after Munich. The Soviet warning to Poland that the USSR would denounce the Soviet-Polish nonaggression pact if Poland marched on Czechoslovakia was interpreted by the German embassy as a "meaningless action," a wordy gesture born of Soviet weakness and isolation.[68] By November 18, Schulenburg had reached the conclusion that Soviet policy had undergone no major change since Munich. The Soviets had not given up "the hope that yesterday's methods (League of Nations, Popular Front) may once more be put to use."[69] Meanwhile, oppressed by the danger of encirclement, the Soviet government would do everything possible to strengthen its armed forces and their industrial base.[70] Herein Schulenburg saw Germany's opportunity for a short-run *détente* based on an economic accord.

Where Dirksen presented his short-range diplomatic proposals in terms of his grandiose objective of a reorganization of international

---

[66] *German Documents*, series D, IV, 607-608. It is not certain that Schulenburg forwarded this memorandum to Berlin at the time.

[67] Robert Coulondre, *De Staline à Hitler* (Paris, 1950), pp. 160-171.

[68] *German Documents*, series D, IV, 606.   [69] *ibid.*, 612.

[70] *ibid.*, 610-611, 613.

relations on the basis of an Anglo-German bloc, Schulenburg contented himself with exploiting an unexpected opportunity to strive for a modest *détente* of uncertain duration. Both ambassadors, at the turn of the year, concentrated their diplomatic efforts at the level of economic agreements, the bedrock of international relations. Dirksen had been pushed down to this level as a result of the deterioration of Anglo-German relations in October and November 1938. Schulenburg had climbed up to it out of the poisonous calm of the pre-Munich years.

Schulenburg's modest proposal for economic negotiations met with a reasonably warm response in Berlin. No broad political considerations were involved here. A memorandum by the Director of the Economic Policy Department of the Foreign Office explains the motivation for the discussions, in which Goering's hand is plain to see: "Germany's raw materials situation . . . is such that the emphatic demand has been raised by Field Marshal Göring's office and other interested agencies at least to try to reactivate our Russian trade especially insofar as imports of Russian raw materials are concerned."[71]

In December, preparations for negotiations were begun in Berlin with the deputy Soviet trade representative. The Soviets asked Germany to send a full trade delegation to Moscow for the talks. The Soviet ambassador explained that the invitation was an expression of his country's desire "to begin a new era in German-Soviet economic relations."[72] In the Wilhelmstrasse, counsels were divided. The Director of the Economic Policy Department recommended acceptance of the Soviet invitation. He recognized that "the Soviet government would like to demonstrate to the outside world the value placed . . . by the Third Reich on the continuance of economic relations," and that Germany had no political interest in such a demonstration. But, he advised the Foreign Minister, Germany's need for Soviet raw materials was so great "that it does not appear expedient to frustrate the negotiations in any way."[73]

It was difficult for Ribbentrop to oppose any policy connected with the strengthening of Germany's war economy, but he found the whole prospect of Soviet-German talks uncongenial and untimely. During the month of January, Hitler's and Ribbentrop's East European political interest centered on Poland. Hitler had made his proposals on the questions of Danzig and the Polish corridor to M. Beck on January 5. Ribbentrop was pursuing a scheme for attaining simultaneously Polish

---

[71] *German Documents*, series D, IV, 608; cf. also a later statement on the origin of the negotiations "on instructions from Field Marshal Goering," *ibid.*, 624.
[72] *ibid.*, 620.   [73] *ibid.*, 621.

acceptance of Hitler's proposals and Polish adherence to the Anti-Comintern Pact. He calculated that Polish national feeling over the loss of Danzig could find outlet in a firm anti-Russian combination with Germany.[74]

At the very time when Goering and the Ministry of Economics were urgently pressing for a Soviet-German economic agreement, Ribbentrop was preparing for a state visit to Warsaw to put the capstone on his anti-Soviet Polish-German combination. Eager to preserve all appearances of Soviet-German antagonism, he refused the Russian request to dispatch a trade mission to the Russian capital. It must have been with great reluctance that Ribbentrop approved, as a compromise arrangement, a visit to Moscow by Julius Schnurre, head of the East European section of the Foreign Office's Economic Policy Department.[75]

To quiet any possible Polish suspicions, Schnurre was to proceed first to Warsaw for economic talks, and to leave for Moscow only on January 30 after Ribbentrop's visit.[76]

On the 26th, Ribbentrop arrived in the Polish capital, where his reception was noticeably cool. Before he had begun serious talks with the Polish leaders, the *Daily Mail* and several French papers published the sensational news that Schnurre was en route to Moscow with a delegation of more than thirty prominent German economic leaders to develop a comprehensive plan for Russo-German economic collaboration.[77] Ribbentrop exploded in a fashion worthy of his Fuehrer. "At the moment when I want to achieve basic collaboration between Germany and Poland against the Soviet Union, they knife me in the back with this scandalous, disruptive report. Schnurre should return to Berlin at once!"[78]

Schnurre did return to Berlin at once and a monkey wrench was thrown into Schulenburg's machinery. So furious was the Foreign Minister over the failure of his Polish plan that he seriously contemplated a rupture of diplomatic relations with the USSR.[79] For once Schulenburg too lost his reserve and gave vent to his irritation at the recall of Schnurre. In a letter to Weizsäcker, he castigated those "to whom the maintenance of Russo-German antagonism is a matter of interest and

[74] Kleist, *Zwischen Hitler und Stalin*, pp. 17-18. As early as August 1937, Ribbentrop had tried to enlist Japanese support to win Polish adherence to the Anti-Comintern Pact. Cf. *German Documents*, series D, I, 750-752.

[75] *German Documents*, series D, I, 621.

[76] *ibid.*, 621-622.

[77] Kleist, *Zwischen Hitler und Stalin*, p. 20.

[78] *ibid.*, pp. 21-22. Cf. also *German Documents*, series D, IV, 622.

[79] Cf. *German Documents*, series D, I, 624-625.

who see something 'suspicious' if we import so much as a little timber, manganese and petroleum from the Soviet Union."[80] He suggested that the Poles were at the bottom of the business—a natural suspicion for a German concerned with Russo-German relations.

Despite the Schnurre incident and Ribbentrop's basically negative attitude toward a *détente* with the USSR, Schulenburg was permitted to pursue economic talks in Moscow until the eve of the march on Prague. The failure of Germany to win Polish assent to its plans no doubt contributed toward keeping the door to Russia ajar, but the decisive factor would seem to have been the insistence of Goering and other economic officials on the need for Russia's raw materials. It was only when the latter withdrew their support that Schulenburg's work was suspended.

On March 8, Schulenburg learned that Berlin was no longer willing to continue serious negotiations. This time it was the Ministry of Economics which spoke the decisive word:

"The pending negotiations . . . must be brought to a stand-still in a suitable way because [the] German economy, on account of its preoccupation with certain domestic tasks, is not in a position to make the necessary deliveries. . . . This deterioration of the production situation arose only recently as a result of newly issued instructions.

"It is generally agreed that the rupture of credit negotiations is regrettable in view of Germany's raw materials position. . . ."[81]

The "domestic tasks" with which the German economy was to be preoccupied can only refer to a vast increase in armaments production. As the needs of Germany's war economy had motivated the economic overtures to the Soviet Union, the acceleration of its production of direct armaments items on the eve of the second Czech crisis brought the negotiations to a halt. Whatever Schulenburg's personal attitudes, the German government had been motivated primarily by military-economic, not by political, considerations, and these no longer demanded a Russo-German economic accord. *Mutatis mutandis*, Schulenburg's situation was not dissimilar to Dirksen's in March 1939. The "constructive" diplomatic labors of both ambassadors after Munich had been disrupted by their government which, for the time being, had lost all interest in diplomacy as an instrument of international policy.

VI

Not until May 1939 was Dirksen informed that he should return to his London post. This time he refused to go unless Ribbentrop would

---

[80] *ibid.*, 623.   [81] *German Documents*, series D, IV, 630-631.

receive him first.[82] A strange Foreign Office, where an ambassador could gain access to his minister only by threatening to withhold his service.

Ribbentrop's instructions were clear and scarcely promising: ". . . We did not want war with Britain, but . . . were prepared for all eventualities. If Poland started anything with Germany, she would be smashed. We were prepared for a ten years', even for a twenty years' war. The British should stop supporting Poland."[83]

Given the nature of these instructions, and the concentration of British policy on somehow reconstructing the shattered security system against Germany, Dirksen decided to make no formal contact with the British until some approach should be forthcoming from their side. He felt he had to avoid any further weakening of his position in Berlin, and hence abandoned his pre-Prague "eager beaver" style for one of correctness and cautious informal probing.[84]

We have little documentary evidence for Dirksen's activity during May and June of 1939. His later account of his conception of his assignment at that time is consistent with what we know of his behavior. He saw his task as a threefold one: to warn his superiors of the determination of Great Britain to resist further aggression; to warn the British of the consequences of their "encirclement policy"; and to be alert to any possibilities for a *détente*.[85]

The execution of the second of these tasks was not uncongenial to Dirksen. He firmly believed in the justice of Hitler's anti-Polish policy. Like most German nationalists, he held the Poles in complete contempt, a contempt fortified in his case by service in Warsaw and Danzig in younger years. "Britain, by her guarantee to Poland, had placed the peace of the world in the hands of minor Polish officials and military men," Dirksen argued. In informal conversations, he regaled Halifax and others with examples of Polish adventurism and turpitude.[86] He wanted, he tells us in his final report, "to enlighten the English, who are unsophisticated in continental, and especially in East European, affairs, on the nature of the Polish State, and on our claims to Danzig and the Corridor."[87] He likewise left his British interlocutors in no doubt that the German people "were unanimously determined to parry this danger of encirclement and not to tolerate a repetition of 1914."[88] Tirelessly as ever, Dirksen labored to create understanding of Germany's stated aims.

[82] *Dirksen Papers*, p. 172.   [83] *ibid.*
[84] Dirksen, *Moskau, Tokio, London*, p. 247; *Dirksen Papers*, pp. 173-177.
[85] Dirksen, *Moskau, Tokio, London*, p. 247.   [86] *ibid.*, pp. 247-248.
[87] *Dirksen Papers*, p. 177.   [88] *ibid.*

Dirksen's will to believe in the power of the British appeasers was as unshakable as his faith in the ultimate reasonableness of Hitler, and both added up to the conviction that war could still be avoided. After the great wave of British indignation over Danzig in early July, Dirksen reported soberly that the British people would "not tolerate any more nonsense," were ready to fight, and had "taken over the initiative from the Government," and were "spurring the Cabinet on." Yet he closed his dispatch with a cheerful note: "The wave of excitement will ebb just as it rose, as soon as the proper conditions exist. The most important condition is a quieter atmosphere in England which would permit a more unprejudiced assessment of the German viewpoint. The germs of this already exist. Within the Cabinet and a small but influential group of politicians, a desire is manifested to pass from the negativity of the encirclement front to a constructive policy toward Germany. And however strong the counter-forces trying to stifle this tender plant may be—Chamberlain's personality is a certain guarantee that British policy will not be placed in the hands of unscrupulous adventurers [i.e., Churchill, Eden, etc.]."[89]

Was Dirksen too starry-eyed in his belief that something might yet be gained from the appeasers? He saw the "growing disillusionment" with Poland and Russia during the early summer. He knew well the reluctance of the Cabinet to enter the partnership with Bolshevism which public and Parliament were forcing upon it. In Chamberlain's and Halifax's speeches he read signs of a "dual policy": "England wants by means of armament and the acquisition of allies to make herself strong and equal to the Axis, but at the same time she wants by means of negotiations to seek an adjustment with Germany, and is prepared to make sacrifices for it: on the questions of the colonies, raw materials supplies, *Lebensraum*, and spheres of economic influence."[90]

How should Dirksen exploit this weakness in the encirclement front? Through Ribbentrop there was of course no hope. His mind turned to the selection of some Britisher who could talk directly to Hitler—"a person whom the Fuehrer would find congenial, that is, a straightforward, blunt and soldierly fellow who at the same time spoke German."[91] Dirksen's faith in Hitler is revealed in his explanation of the motivation of this approach to a *détente*: it was a remembered remark of Hitler, that "it would be easier to remove all difficulties with England

[89] *Dirksen Papers*, pp. 65-66.   [90] *ibid.*, p. 176.
[91] *ibid.*, p. 178.

if he could converse in German for two hours with a reasonable Englishman."[92]

Before the ambassador and his British friends had hit upon the proper person to approach the source of all power, Chamberlain and his good man Friday, Sir Horace Wilson, took the matter into their own hands. In mid-July, even as the British negotiations in Moscow were approaching the critical stage, the government made its final effort to make those broad concessions to Hitler which might enable the Cabinet to restore its foreign policy to a German axis. Before examining the content of the Wilson-Wohltat conversations in which the British made their final offer, we must briefly review the activities of Count Schulenburg in Moscow; for upon them the last efforts of Dirksen and the British to rebuild the collapsed structure of Munich were about to founder.

Ambassador Schulenburg's situation in the two months following the seizure of Prague could hardly have seemed to him more promising than Anglo-German relations did to Dirksen. His own government had called off the economic negotiations which had finally been inaugurated after so many difficulties. If the deterioration of Polish-German relations and Britain's extension of a guarantee to Poland created the objective basis for a Soviet-German accord, neither the Germans nor the Russians were in any hurry to reconstruct their policies on this foundation. Though the documentary evidence is sparse, there seems little evidence to support the contention, based on the testimony of Ribbentrop and Molotov in August and September 1939, that Stalin's speech to the Eighteenth Communist Party Congress "brought about the reversal in political relations" between the two countries.[93] By mid-April, Britain, France, and Russia had resumed their tentative exchanges looking toward the formation of a united front against the aggressor.

It must have been amply clear to the ambassador that, with the collapse of the Locarno-Munich system at Prague, the USSR controlled the balance of power in Europe, and that his task, even as Dirksen's, must be to forestall the encirclement of Germany by every means at his command. But there is no evidence that his superiors gave him any specific instructions to pursue this objective. Nor did Russia go beyond the hint of Ambassador Merekalov to Weizsäcker (April 17, 1939) that

[92] Dirksen, *Moskau, Tokio, London*, p. 249.
[93] A. Rossi, *The Russo-German Alliance* (London, 1950), pp. 7-10; for a sounder analysis, see Royal Institute of International Affairs, *Survey of International Affairs, 1939-1946: The World in March 1939* (London, New York, Toronto, 1952), pp. 530-531.

"there was no reason why she should not live with us [Germans] on a normal footing."[94]

Even Molotov's appointment as Foreign Commissar was not heralded by the German mission as the dawn of a new era, although Tippelskirch, Schulenburg's counselor of embassy, cautiously observed that the appointment was apparently connected with "differences of opinion in the Kremlin on Litvinov's negotiations" and Stalin's "caution lest the Soviet Union be drawn into conflicts."[95] In the succeeding weeks, however, the Soviet chargé in Berlin indicated in several quarters that his government desired better relations with Germany.[96] For a month, there had been discussions in Berlin about a political approach to the USSR.[97] This time Ribbentrop decided to put out a feeler in his turn, and instructed Schulenburg to suggest to Molotov the resumption of economic negotiations. These would be carried on in Moscow by the same Herr Schnurre whose visit had been so abruptly canceled in January.

In Schulenburg's conversation with Molotov on May 20, the Foreign Commissar was friendly, but scarcely open. He stated that the Soviet government had got the impression from the course of the previous economic discussions that the Germans "had only played at negotiating for political reasons. . . . The Soviet Government could only agree to a resumption of negotiations if the necessary 'political basis' for them had been constructed."[98] Schulenburg pressed Molotov in vain for a definition of his idea of the "necessary political basis." In reporting to Weizsäcker, the ambassador interpreted Molotov's position as an invitation to "more extensive proposals of a political nature" from the German side, which it certainly was. Schulenburg, more than usually bearish, offered no suggestions as to what Germany might propose. Just as Molotov feared that the Germans might use new talks merely to impede the Anglo-Russian negotiations, Schulenburg urged "extreme caution" in advancing political proposals "as long as it is not certain that . . . they will not be used by the Kremlin only to exert pressure on England and France. On the other hand, if we want to accomplish something here, it

[94] *Nazi-Soviet Relations*, p. 2. According to Peter Kleist (*Zwischen Hitler und Stalin*, pp. 26-29), the Soviet chargé informally expressed to him Russia's willingness for such a far-reaching agreement with Germany but Hitler and Ribbentrop were "frightened off" by it.

[95] *Nazi-Soviet Relations*, pp. 2-3. For an excellent statement of the significance of Molotov's appointment for Soviet policy, see W. L. Langer and S. E. Gleason, *The Challenge to Isolation, 1937-1940* (New York, 1952), pp. 105-107.

[96] *Nazi-Soviet Relations*, pp. 3-5.

[97] Kleist, *Zwischen Hitler und Stalin*, pp. 30-38.

[98] *Nazi-Soviet Relations*, pp. 5-7.

is unavoidable that we sooner or later take some action."⁹⁹ The ambassador saw the dilemma, but offered no way out of it. On May 21, Weizsäcker informed Schulenburg that Germany "would now sit tight and wait to see if the Russians would speak more openly," and "to see how deeply Moscow on the one hand and Paris-London on the other are willing to commit themselves."¹⁰⁰

Scarcely had the order to sit tight been given when two new factors suddenly increased the importance of Russia to Germany, both positively and negatively. On May 23, Hitler announced to his intimate advisers his intention "to attack Poland at the first opportunity." On May 24, Chamberlain reported to the House of Commons that the Anglo-Russian conversations had produced agreement on essentials.¹⁰¹ On May 30, Schulenburg was informed by Weizsäcker of a change in line: "Contrary to the policy previously planned, we have now decided to undertake definite negotiations with Moscow."¹⁰²

During June and July, most of the initiative was on the German side, but the negotiations proceeded slowly. The Russians took every advantage of the fact that they were being wooed by both the Western Powers and the Reich, and maintained a frigid reserve. To both sides, to be sure, they gave occasional encouragement. Thus on June 14, the Soviet chargé in Berlin told the Bulgarian minister—clearly for Wilhelmstrasse consumption: "If Germany would declare that she would not attack the Soviet Union or that she would conclude a non-aggression pact with her, the Soviet Union would probably refrain from concluding a treaty with England."¹⁰³

While the Germans kept hinting at possible areas of mutual interest— Poland, the Baltic states, the Berlin Treaty—the Russians responded by raising doubts as to Germany's intentions. Mikoyan, Commissar of Foreign Trade, proved a particularly sticky negotiator in the economic talks.¹⁰⁴

By the end of June, Berlin was getting distinctly fed up, and Schulenburg knew it. He tried to describe progress where little was to be recorded.¹⁰⁵ On June 29, Hitler very nearly called off the entire negotiations,¹⁰⁶ while Ribbentrop decided that Schulenburg should say nothing more in the political field until further notice.¹⁰⁷ In the first weeks of

---

⁹⁹ *ibid.*, pp. 8-9.   ¹⁰⁰ *ibid.*, pp. 7, 9.
¹⁰¹ E. H. Carr, *German-Soviet Relations between the Two World Wars* (Baltimore, 1951), pp. 130-131.
¹⁰² *Nazi-Soviet Relations*, p. 15.   ¹⁰³ *ibid.*, p. 21.
¹⁰⁴ Cf. e.g. *Nazi-Soviet Relations*, pp. 21-25.
¹⁰⁵ Cf. his interpretation of his interview with Molotov on June 29, *ibid.*, p. 27.
¹⁰⁶ *ibid.*, pp. 25-26.   ¹⁰⁷ *ibid.*, pp. 27-28.

July, Schulenburg seems to have feared that he would be reassigned, and asked his counselor of embassy to intercede with the personnel division to keep him at his post.[108] Tippelskirch tried to reassure the Foreign Office that "the Embassy and particularly . . . [Schulenburg] had done everything possible, but he could not drag Molotov and Mikoyan through the Brandenburger Tor."[109]

From June 29 to July 21, the economic negotiations seem to have been deadlocked. Then on July 22, the Soviets suddenly announced their resumption.[110] It seems to have been the Russians who broke the deadlock with a concession: to resume the economic negotiations, previously conducted in Moscow, in Berlin. Schulenburg had suggested such a course to the Wilhelmstrasse as a way of circumventing the thorny Mr. Mikoyan.[111] Just when the Germans proposed this solution to the Soviets does not emerge from the documents; on the basis of previous Russian sensitivity concerning the site of the discussions, however, one can only assume that the Russians finally accepted the German proposal in order to get the negotiations resumed. On July 24, only two days after the Russian overture to the Germans, Molotov made a concession to the West to break a deadlock of several weeks duration in the negotiations with Britain and France.[112] The Russian game of pitting its suitors against each other began to be played in earnest.

In the meantime, Prime Minister Chamberlain, who had been forced into the talks with the Soviet Union against all his instincts, developed a double game of his own. On or about July 20—two days before the Russian overture to Germany and four before Molotov's to Britain—Chamberlain tried to return to his appeasement policy with an offer of a "world-political partnership" between Britain and Germany. The recipient of this proposal was Goering's special assistant, Dr. Wohltat, who was attending the International Whaling Conference in London. Secretary Hudson of the British Ministry of Overseas Trade approached Wohltat on July 20 with plans for joint Anglo-German exploitation of world markets, notably those of the British Empire, China, and the USSR. Like a voice from the 1890's, Hudson spoke of delineating spheres of economic interest between the two Powers in order to avoid competi-

---

[108] *ibid.*, p. 31.   [109] *ibid.*

[110] *ibid.*, p. 25. The month-long deadlock is deduced from the absence of any documents in the collection.

[111] *ibid.*, p. 27.

[112] The full story of these negotiations has yet to be told. The most comprehensive, though often conflicting, accounts are to be found in Namier, *Diplomatic Prelude*, pp. 143-210 and Langer and Gleason, *Challenge to Isolation*, pp. 115-121.

tion.[113] Sir Horace Wilson supplemented Hudson's proposals in two conversations with Wohltat, in which he set forth in broad outline an agreement on political, military, and economic matters.[114] Wilson spoke from a prepared paper, and invited Wohltat to confirm Chamberlain's support of its contents by a personal interview with the Prime Minister, which the German declined. The conclusion of a nonaggression pact was the heart of Wilson's program—not "the customary pacts of nonaggression which Germany had concluded with other powers," but one which would involve "renunciation of aggression in principle."[115] According to Dirksen's memorandum on the second conversation, "Sir Horace Wilson definitely told Herr Wohltat that the conclusion of a nonaggression pact would enable Britain to rid herself of her commitments vis-à-vis Poland." The two nations were also to conclude a pact of nonintervention which was to embrace a "delimitation of spheres (*Grossräume*) of the Great Powers, in particular as between Britain and Germany." Some kind of international scheme for the governance of Africa was adumbrated to meet Germany's colonial demands. Finally, Sir Horace added that the British government would agree to the Germans adding any other questions to the agenda: "The Fuehrer had only to take a sheet of paper and jot down his points; the British Government would be prepared to discuss them." The decisive thing, Sir Horace said, was that the Fuehrer designate someone to discuss the program. Once this step were taken, "it was immaterial to the British how the further negotiations were conducted." Dr. Wohltat agreed to try to find out "whether the Fuehrer considered that the moment had now come to start such discussions."

Ambassador Dirksen was, of course, only on the periphery of these discussions. Nevertheless, he leapt at them as a proof of his earlier contention (June 24) that the British government was moving away from encirclement and toward a more "constructive" policy. Moreover, the strange amalgam of fin-de-siècle imperialism and Kellogg-Briand utopianism reflected in the proposals, if most ill-suited to Hitler's temperament, was quite congenial to Dirksen's. While the primary responsibility for reporting them lay with Wohltat, Dirksen, in a dispatch of July 24, outlined the principal points of Wilson's proposals, and emphasized that Germany must make the next move—and that soon—if "Churchill and the other incendiaries" were to be thwarted.[116]

[113] *Dirksen Papers*, pp. 67-68. See also *Documenti Italiani*, 8th series, XII, 511-512.
[114] *Dirksen Papers*, pp. 67-68.   [115] *ibid.*, pp. 68-72.
[116] *ibid.*, pp. 73-76.

We do not know when the pouch bearing Dirksen's significant dispatch of July 24 reached Berlin. By the 31st, neither Ribbentrop nor Weizsäcker had seen it.[117] Their first knowledge of the full scope of the British proposals came in the form of Wohltat's written report which was transmitted to the Foreign Minister by Field Marshal Goering.[118] On July 31, Ribbentrop sent Dirksen a heated telegram requesting an immediate report on Wohltat's negotiations—"especially a report on Wohltat's conversations with you, since he states that the political negotiations were conducted in agreement with the Ambassador."[119]

Goering had, no doubt, sent a copy of Wohltat's report to the Fuehrer. But more was at stake now than the rivalry between two high Nazi courtiers. On July 25, it became known that France and Britain were sending military missions to Moscow. Ribbentrop decided to press the Russian negotiations on the broadest possible basis and "at an unheard-of tempo."[120] On July 26, on Ribbentrop's instructions, Schnurre had really put the German cards on the table in an informal evening of conversation with the Soviet chargé and the chief of the trade mission. He had proposed the establishment of really good relations in a series of stages, of which the last would remove all conflicts of interest from the Baltic to the Black Sea. German policy, said Schnurre, was aimed primarily against England. "What could England offer Russia? At best, participation in a European war and the hostility of Germany, but not a single desirable end for Russia. What could we offer on the other hand? Neutrality and staying out of a European conflict and, if Moscow wished, a German-Russian understanding which, just as in former times, would work out to the interests of both countries."[121] But, he argued against the Russians, agreement must be reached quickly. If Russia should come to an accord with Britain, it would be too late.

On July 29, Weizsäcker drafted instructions to Schulenburg to sound out Molotov for his reaction to Schnurre's overtures. If Molotov abandoned his previous reserve, Schulenburg was to "advance another step": to introduce the Polish question and to express Germany's readiness for an understanding with the Soviets on Poland against the possibility of war.[122] Thus when Wohltat's report of the British overture reached the Wilhelmstrasse, Germany was sailing full steam ahead toward the east.

---

[117] *Dirksen Papers*, pp. 88, 91-92. [118] *ibid.*, p. 91.
[119] *ibid.*, p. 88.
[120] Kleist, *Zwischen Hitler und Stalin*, p. 46.
[121] *Nazi-Soviet Relations*, p. 34; for the entire discussion, see pp. 32-36.
[122] *ibid.*, p. 36.

The Chamberlain-Wilson offer must have thrown open once more the whole question of Germany's foreign policy, if only for a moment. Germany had been competing with Britain for the favor of Russia on the assumption that she could not realize her aims in Eastern Europe without Britain resorting to arms. Now Germany, the aggressor, was herself being courted by Britain with an offer which would "enable Britain to rid herself of her commitments *vis-à-vis* Poland." In the extraordinary triangle of European power politics, Germany was now the wooed. How should she choose?

In working out an answer, Weizsäcker called on Dirksen. Nine hours after Ribbentrop had dispatched his peremptory telegram, Weizsäcker sent another, asking the ambassador "whether these British overtures presume at the same time the abandonment of the encirclement policy negotiations, in particular with Moscow."[123] Dirksen answered with a vigorous affirmative: "leading persons" in London regarded an adjustment with Germany as obviously incompatible with the prosecution of the encirclement policy. "The continuation of the negotiations for a pact with Russia, in spite of—or rather, just because of—the dispatch of a military mission is regarded here with skepticism. This is borne out by the composition of the British military mission: the admiral, until now Commandant of Portsmouth, is practically in retirement, and was never on the staff of the Admiralty; the general is likewise purely a combatant officer; the air general is an outstanding aviator and air instructor, but not a strategist. This indicates that the object of the military mission is more to ascertain the fighting value of the Soviet Army than to make operational arrangements."[124]

Poor Dirksen! He thought that this information could only heighten the Foreign Minister's receptivity to the British overtures. Instead it had the opposite effect. The ambassador confirmed what was implied by Chamberlain's overtures: that the Anglo-Russian military negotiations would come to naught, for, whatever the Soviet attitude, the British were not really interested. Dirksen's belief that his masters would under these circumstances be interested in an adjustment with Britain that would "chemically dissolve the Danzig problem" was superannuated, to say the least.

On the evening of August 2, the day when Dirksen's answer to

---

[123] *Dirksen Papers*, pp. 91-92.
[124] *Dirksen Papers*, p. 103. This statement throws some incidental light on the veracity of Weizsäcker, who tells us in his *Erinnerungen* (Munich, 1950), (p. 246) that he was certain from the reports of the ambassador in London of the successful prosecution of Russo-French-British negotiations.

Weizsäcker had probably arrived in Berlin,[125] Ribbentrop summoned the Russian chargé. He resumed the line taken by Schnurre on July 26, but with a new air of assurance. There was no longer any talk of speedy solutions. Ribbentrop stated that "our policy was a direct and long-range one; we were in no hurry. . . . We were making no fuss about it; the choice lay . . . in Moscow."[126] The Foreign Minister, with a new sense of security, was enjoying his work. On August 3 he reversed previous instructions for Schulenburg to carry on the conversations in Moscow: "We are anxious to continue . . . the clarification . . . *in Berlin.*"[127]

The tragi-comedy of the two ambassadors was nearing its end. Neither Dirksen nor Schulenburg were quite irrational enough to be realistic in evaluating the strange diplomatic world of August 1939. Dirksen pursued the will-o'-the-wisp of an Anglo-German world-political partnership which would solve the Danzig problem without war. In a two-hour conversation with Sir Horace Wilson on August 3, Dirksen convinced himself that a German reply to the British feeler could save the day.[128] He resolved to go to Berlin to throw his weight behind earnest consideration of the British proposition—"perhaps in collaboration with Wohltat." Arriving on August 14 after a departure oddly leisurely, Dirksen found the city alive with rumors of the impending blow against Poland. When he asked Weizsäcker how his reports on the British proposals had been received, the Secretary of State "shrugged his shoulders and made a gesture as though he were brushing something off the table." Dirksen learned that his reports of the Wilson conversations had been interpreted as a further sign of British weakness.[129] He learned too that Germany's masters did not believe that the British would intervene in the German-Polish war. The ambassador who had come home to preach one illusion now had to devote himself to dispelling another. But he could find no audience for his warnings. Ribbentrop scolded him from afar for his defeatist utterances, but would not receive him.

Dirksen's experience in the last weeks before the war reads like that of the protagonist of Kafka's *The Castle*: the same hopeless attempt to reach the masters who neither wanted nor released him, the same incapacity to grasp the nonrational rules by which the Castle operated, the same ambiguous treatment by the lower officials, and the same blind effort to serve rather than merely to obey. It was a fitting if psychologi-

---

[125] Dirksen's briefer telegram of July 31 had certainly been received by that time. Cf. *Dirksen Papers*, pp. 89-90.
[126] *Nazi-Soviet Relations*, p. 38. [127] *ibid.*, p. 37. Italics mine.
[128] *Dirksen Papers*, pp. 117-125.
[129] Dirksen, *Moskau, Tokio, London*, pp. 255-256.

cally gruesome climax to Dirksen's career under the Nazis. Equally fitting was the fact that he neither resigned nor was fired. He simply withdrew to his Gröditzberg estates on indefinite leave, to remain there until the Russians drove him out.

Was Count Schulenburg better able to understand the world of August 1939 than his London colleague? His task was easier, he was riding the wave. But down to the last ten days of the Russo-German negotiations, his analyses would hardly have justified confidence in the early conclusion of the pact. His belief in Soviet mistrust of Germany was too well grounded by his long experience. On August 4, he wrote after an interview with Molotov: "My overall impression is that the Soviet Government is at present determined to sign with England and France if they fulfill all Soviet wishes. I believe that my statements made an impression on M.; it will nevertheless take considerable effort on our part to cause the Soviet Government to swing about."[130] Perhaps Schulenburg was right in principle; what he lacked was the knowledge which Ribbentrop had just received from Dirksen: that England had no intention whatever of "fulfilling all Soviet wishes." On August 10, the Soviet chargé in Berlin, while indicating that Russia's negotiations with England "had been entered upon without much enthusiasm," felt that his government, even though the conversations with Germany were well under way, still could not "break off something which had been begun after mature consideration."[131] A few days later, Schulenburg wrote to Weizsäcker: "I am still of the opinion that any hasty measure in the matter of our relations with the Soviet Union should be avoided; it will almost always be harmful. . . . The British and French military missions have been in Moscow for three days now. . . . I assume that the negotiations will last a long time."[132] While Schulenburg was committing these restrained notions to paper (August 14), Ribbentrop was drafting his dramatic proposal for a personal visit to Stalin to "clear up jointly the territorial problems of Eastern Europe." Less than ten days later, the Nazi-Soviet Pact was signed, the diplomatic revolution accomplished.

However responsible Schulenburg may have been for the groundwork of the Russo-German alliance, he neither advised Ribbentrop's lightning courtship of Stalin nor anticipated its astonishing success. Like Dirksen, Schulenburg moved in a political world he could not fully understand. But where Dirksen erred on the plus side in his evaluation of diplomatic possibilities, Schulenburg erred on the minus side. The Moscow ambassa-

---

[130] *Nazi-Soviet Relations*, p. 41.   [131] *ibid.*, p. 46.
[132] *ibid.*, p. 41.

dor shared few of the illusions about Nazi Germany which captured the imagination of Dirksen and his idol, Neville Chamberlain. For all his sustained skeptical realism, Schulenburg permitted himself to overestimate the rationality of the Nazis on one fateful point: that they would not jettison an achievement of such obvious value to the German national interest as the Russo-German Pact in favor of a suicidal two-front war. Less than two years after the victory of the eastern orientation which ended Dirksen's career, Schulenburg found himself recapitulating Dirksen's experience of August 1939, vainly trying to dissuade his superiors from launching an unnecessary war on false political assumptions. Thus for all their differences in temperament and character, Schulenburg and Dirksen saw their intertwined but polaric diplomatic achievements united in destruction. Both had to learn the hard way that the time-honored principles of *Realpolitik* could not be made to govern the political behavior of Nazi Germany.

Though their diplomatic labors met a common fate, the two men drew different consequences from it, each according to his character and social tradition. Dirksen, who could not contemplate a revolt against constituted authority, whatever its nature, withdrew from politics into the spurious but satisfyingly aristocratic isolation of a Silesian *Rittergutsbesitzer*. It was the role his father had cut out for him many years before. Schulenburg, heritor of an older and more autonomous aristocratic tradition, stayed in the civil service but entered the resistance movement. In doing so, he was motivated still by his loyalty to the German state. The same allegiance to an abstraction which had enabled him to justify his service to the Nazis for a decade led to him to rebel against them. For his conception of *Staatsräson* permitted him, however belatedly, to distinguish, in Germany as in Russia, between the state and those who held power in it. His realism told him when to break from the latter in the interest of the former. Had the plot against Hitler succeeded, Schulenburg might have become the Foreign Minister of the state he hoped to save from destruction. Instead, with other aristocrats of the old school, he met his death in the attempt.

16

Ciano and his Ambassadors

BY FELIX GILBERT

"IN ITALY, the most Fascist ministry is that of Foreign Affairs," Galeazzo Ciano said proudly to a German visitor in October 1937.[1] The Fascist penetration of the Italian Foreign Office appeared to him a remarkable achievement, the result of a slow and difficult process; it is clear, moreover, that he believed that he deserved the credit for having accomplished it. "In Italy," he confided to his Diary, "fifteen years were needed to conquer the Palazzo Chigi."[2] The time span mentioned is significant. Ciano himself had become Foreign Minister in 1936, just as the fifteenth year of the Fascist regime was dawning; and there is no doubt that he believed that his arrival at the Palazzo Chigi was the decisive event through which Italian foreign policy became fully Fascist.

Ciano's Diary is full of sudden ideas without practical consequences, of fleeting thoughts which disappeared as soon as they had been put down in black and white. As a source for the history of Italian diplomacy, the Diary must be used with caution.[3] But Ciano returned so frequently and insistently to the claim that, under his direction, Italian foreign policy had become a malleable instrument of the regime, that this view must be accepted as a true expression of his mind, as one of his basic ideas.

But what does Ciano actually mean by the assertion that he had imposed a Fascist pattern on Italian foreign policy? Did his arrival in the Palazzo Chigi imply a change in Italian diplomacy? Was a tradition— the tradition of professional diplomacy which worked within the rules of the game and on the foundation of historically tested experience— thrown overboard and replaced by a new Fascist diplomacy with different methods and new aims? Was there any reality behind Ciano's airy claim of having introduced a truly Fascist diplomacy?

[1] Galeazzo Ciano, *1937-1938 Diario* (Bologna, 1948), p. 40.

[2] *ibid.*, p. 55.

[3] On the authenticity of Ciano's Diary and on the value of its various editions, see Mario Toscano, "Fonti documentarie e memorialistiche per la storia diplomatica della seconda guerra mondiale," *Rivista Storica Italiana*, LX (1948), 106-108.

The most obvious explanation is that Ciano believed he was the first real Fascist installed at the head of the Palazzo Chigi. A closer examination of this statement is interesting because of the light it sheds on the view which Ciano held about his own role in the Fascist regime. Insofar as it testifies to the influence which diplomatic tradition and professional diplomats had exerted in the first decade of the Fascist regime, the statement contains an element of truth. As it was shown in a previous chapter,[4] even the appointment of such a zealous Fascist as Dino Grandi had not broken the strength of this tradition. On the contrary the professionals had tamed the young radical and made him an advocate, among the party hierarchy, for the maintenance of the traditional course. Grandi's dismissal in 1932 was the result of Mussolini's dissatisfaction with the docility with which his Foreign Minister had absorbed the atmosphere of professional diplomacy. According to Mussolini, Grandi "had permitted himself to become prisoner of the League of Nations, had conducted a pacific and internationalist policy, had acted the ultra-democrat and League of Nations man; he had made Italian policy deviate from the straight course of egoism and realism and compromised the aspirations of a new generation."[5]

But when, after Grandi's departure, Mussolini took over the Foreign Ministry, changes were less radical and thorough than one would have expected. For this there were various reasons. Being not only Foreign Minister but also head of the government, Mussolini was unable to exert a detailed control and supervision over the Palazzo Chigi from the Palazzo Venezia. The new situation created by the rise of Nazism demanded experience and caution. Because of the widening gap between the Western Powers and Germany, and because of the Nazi pressure on Austria, Italian foreign policy was not only offered new opportunities but it was also faced with new dangers. There was no fundamental conflict between Mussolini and the professionals about the evaluation of this new situation. The career diplomats shared Mussolini's view that the rift among the Great Powers offered a unique chance for the realization of Italy's African aspirations, and the Palazzo Chigi took an active part in preparing the developments which led to the Abyssinian War.[6] In the course of the Abyssinian crisis, however, a divergence of views emerged. The professionals were concerned with making the Abyssinian enterprise

---

[4] See Chapter 7, §III above.

[5] Roberto Cantalupo, *Fu la Spagna. Ambasciata presso Franco Febbraio-Aprile 1937* (Verona, 1948), p. 42.

[6] See Raffaele Guariglia, *Ricordi 1922-1946* (Napoli, 1949), pp. 212ff.

an episode rather than a new departure and with preventing a development which would constitute a definite and final break with the traditional system of Italian foreign policy. They looked with skepticism upon the Fascist claim that through the conquest of the African empire, Italy had been raised to the status of a Great Power of the first rank; thereby they laid themselves open to the accusation of diplomatic pusillanimity and betrayal of the heroic spirit of the regime. A press campaign making such charges was promoted by the Ministry of Press and Propaganda over which Ciano then presided, and this served to prepare his entry into the Palazzo Chigi.[7] Thus Ciano took over as the representative of the Fascist outlook.

Even if there is some basis for the claim that, before 1936, the Italian Foreign Office had not been much affected by party enthusiasm and had preserved a traditional outlook in foreign affairs, few people in Italy would have considered Galeazzo Ciano as particularly suited for the task of accomplishing the Fascization of the Palazzo Chigi, for he was far from being a typical representative of the Fascist party. Ciano's unique position in the Fascist hierarchy is sharply outlined in a story told by Gafencu.[8] The Rumanian statesman was present when an official delegation arrived for a reception with the Italian king. The Duce was marching at the head, clad in his black shirt; his glance was imperious, his gait exaggerated, the dignitaries followed in serried ranks; in front of them, but behind the Duce, walked Count Ciano, sprightly and carefree, waving joyously whenever he saw an acquaintance.

Ciano stood out from the bulk of Fascist hierarchs. In party circles he was a most unpopular figure. The older leaders of the party—men like De Bono and Volpi who had been well known when they had joined Mussolini's movement after the first world war—considered Ciano as a spoiled child of fortune, raised to prominence because he was the son of one of Mussolini's chief assistants and the Duce's son-in-law. Ciano fully reciprocated these feelings; his Diary indicates that he considered these older leaders as unbearably dull and loquacious fools;[9] it seems most unlikely that in his behavior he succeeded entirely in concealing the contempt he felt for them. The widely held belief that Ciano was groomed by Mussolini to become his successor must have been resented by the men of the middle generation like Grandi and Balbo whose chances for succession were ruined by the arrival of this youngster. The glee with

---

[7] *ibid.*, pp. 213, 328.
[8] Grigore Gafencu, *The Last Days of Europe* (London, 1947), p. 136.
[9] For instance, Ciano, *1937-1938 Diario*, pp. 34, 125.

which, in his Diary, Ciano sets down every unfriendly thing he hears about them reflects the feelings of rivalry and competition which existed between Ciano and these men. Even before foreigners he gave free vent to such feelings; Grandi, he said to Serrano Suñer, was not worth knowing: "He is quite uninteresting and has the intelligence of a mosquito."[10]

Born in 1903, Ciano was a schoolboy at the time of the march on Rome. While most of the others who had reached prominent positions in the 1930's could claim to have joined the Fascist party when this action involved risks or commitments, Ciano had arrived, after the battle was over, to enjoy the victory and to participate in the loot. His claims to this privilege were supported by good looks and a nimble mind, but certainly more by the influence of a father who had been a national hero of the first world war and subsequently one of Mussolini's most valued collaborators.[11] His alliance by marriage with the family of the Duce was doubtless also useful. In any event, he had no difficulty in advancing rapidly from one interesting job to another—diplomat in Argentina and China, Under-Secretary and Minister of Press and Propaganda—until, at the age of thirty-two, he had become Italy's Foreign Minister and the most important political figure after the Duce. The party hierarchs must have resented the preferment of a man who came to reap the fruits of work performed by others.

It is characteristic of Ciano that he seems to have been quite unconcerned about these chinks in his Fascist armor. He was proud of his youth and gloried in being the representative of a new generation. Institutional questions, like the corporate state—central issues of Fascist belief to a man like Bottai[12]—did not interest Ciano. One is tempted to conclude that he regarded concern over questions of political organization and political principles as something obsolete, as a sign that those who bothered about them had not yet freed themselves from the egg-shells of the pre-Fascist period. Ciano had no doubt that he was a true representative and embodiment of Fascism, but the precise ideas which he associated with this concept are difficult to discover. Perhaps one comes closest to an explanation if one says that Ciano considered Fascism chiefly as a new "style of life"; he regarded himself as a perfect Fascist specimen because only the new generation which had grown up in an atmosphere entirely unencumbered by the heritage of the past could

[10] Ramon Serrano Suñer, *Entre Hendaya y Gibraltar* (Mexico, 1947), p. 325.

[11] It should perhaps be noted that, while Ciano's noble title was not of Fascist creation, its origins were very recent. His father had been made Count as a reward for his naval exploits in the war.

[12] Giuseppe Bottai, *Vent'Anni e un Giorno* (Editore Garzanti, 1949).

fully "live" the new attitude. In a passage of his Diary, Ciano gave expression to his admiration for D'Annunzio;[13] it seems likely that in Ciano's rather immature mind Fascism had become identified with the amoral belief in living life to its fullest that one finds in the hero of a D'Annunzio novel. Certainly there is a D'Annunzian flavor to his confession to Serrano Suñer: "Life is always good and pleasant. When I am eighty I shall stroll along here swinging my cane and enjoying the lovely sun. I want to die here in Leghorn after I have seen all my enemies passing before me on their way to death."[14]

But the doubts which could be raised against Ciano from the point of view of Fascist orthodoxy cannot have given much reassurance to the professional diplomats; they had every reason to regard the advent, at the Palazzo Chigi, of this self-styled leader of the young Fascist generation with suspicion and displeasure.

When Ciano spoke of the Fascist outlook which Italian diplomacy acquired in the 1930's was he thinking principally of his influence on foreign policy or could he point also to changes in personnel and organization? In the years preceding Ciano's assumption of office, Fascism had made hardly any inroads in the Diplomatic Service. It is true that in 1928, in order to permeate diplomacy with a new spirit, a number of Fascist party members without special professional training had been taken into the Diplomatic Service, but the power of the professional diplomats had been strong enough to restrict sharply the number of new admissions and to keep the "men of '28," the "*ventottisti*" as they were called by the career diplomats, in subordinate positions.[15] At the first glance it would seem that in Ciano's time also the diplomatic bureaucracy was able to continue its successful resistance against the penetration of outsiders and to preserve its professional and career character.[16] At least during the years before the war, all the great embassies were headed by career diplomats. The key position in Berlin was held by Bernardo Attolico. He had been a member of the Italian delegation at the Paris Peace Conference and, for five years, from 1922 to 1927, had directed the Communications Section in the League of Nations Secretariat at Geneva; he had also served as ambassador in Rio de Janeiro and Moscow before he came to Berlin in 1935. When Ciano became Foreign Minister,

---

[13] Ciano, *1937-1938 Diario*, p. 221, also p. 124.

[14] Serrano Suñer, *Entre Hendaya y Gibraltar*, p. 316.

[15] Mario Donosti, *Mussolini e l'Europa* (Roma, 1945), p. 15.

[16] For a list of the Italian diplomatic corps as of January 23, 1939 and the officials of the Italian Foreign Office as of October 12, 1938, see *Documenti Italiani*, 8th series, XII, 633-645.

Vittorio Cerruti, who had started his diplomatic career at the Italian embassy in the Vienna of the Emperor Francis Joseph, was ambassador in Paris; in 1938 he was replaced by Raffaele Guariglia whose "professionalism" is perhaps best attested by the fact that he became Italian Foreign Minister in 1943 when, after the fall of Mussolini, Badoglio formed his cabinet of technical experts. Also Augusto Rosso, the ambassador in Moscow, had started his service in Italian diplomacy in the prewar era. The only prominent Fascist who directed one of the great European embassies was Dino Grandi, who was in London from 1932 to 1939, but since Mussolini had moved him from Rome to London for being too much inclined to adopt the Foreign Office point of view, Grandi can hardly have been regarded as an alien and hostile element by the professionals.

Representatives abroad had no policy-making function: the policy makers were at Rome, in the Palazzo Chigi. But here too, career diplomats were in charge. Work at the Italian Foreign Office was distributed among three political divisions, that of General Affairs, of European and Mediterranean Affairs, and of Overseas Affairs. Each of these divisions was headed by a director and throughout the 1930's these positions were held by professionals: Leonardo Vitetti, Gino Buti and Emanuele Grazzi. Thus from the point of view of personnel there seems to be little substance to Ciano's claim of having conquered the Palazzo Chigi for Fascism.

But the impression of a continued dominance of the professional tradition in Italian diplomacy is deceiving. A report by Roberto Cantalupo gives insight into the strange situation at the Palazzo Chigi soon after Ciano had taken over.[17] Cantalupo, who was Italian ambassador in Brazil, had returned to Rome after several years of absence from Italy. He found at the same desks the same faces he had known before, but something had changed in the atmosphere. Cantalupo says he felt that "the clockwork was broken." The functionaries were like shadows, moving around in the usual way but without purpose. He was told that the officials did not know what was going on because all important work was done by the Gabinetto. And so he heard for the first time of the growth of that organization which became Ciano's chief instrument for directing the course of Italian foreign policy, and which, in relatively short time, reduced the traditional apparatus to an empty shell.

In the past the Gabinetto had been nothing more than the personal

[17] Cantalupo, *Fu la Spagna*, pp. 67-68.

secretariat of the Foreign Minister. Under Ciano it grew rapidly.[18] He filled it with young men who shared his general attitude towards life and looked up to him admiringly as future leader. "The officials of the Gabinetto 'spoke seldom, but all their words were tuneful sweet,' like those of the great souls banned by Dante into the Limbo, and they treated their colleagues in the other offices with an icy, smiling and contemptuous politeness, typical of a great lord who has dealings with people who don't belong to his class."[19] Among the officials of the Gabinetto, the most influential and probably the most intelligent was Ciano's contemporary and long-standing friend, Filippo Anfuso, who in the later years of Ciano's foreign ministry became head of the Gabinetto.[20] A chief function assumed by the Gabinetto—and the function about which the professional diplomats complained most bitterly—was control over the distribution of incoming information. The officials of the Gabinetto determined whether reports should be handed over to the political desks of the Palazzo Chigi or whether they would be kept in the Gabinetto for the use of the Minister. Thus the Gabinetto developed into a center where all the most important information and reports of special significance were handled.

The memoirs of Italian career diplomats are filled with stories describing the confusion and errors caused by the arbitrary proceedings of the functionaries in the Gabinetto. Newly appointed ambassadors who wanted to read the relevant diplomatic correspondence before leaving for their posts were told by division heads that the most important interchanges were kept in the Gabinetto, that they had not seen them, and that complete files did not exist. A serious mistake occurred in the critical summer of 1939, when the Italian ambassador in Moscow received detailed information about the progress of the German-Russian negotiations from his German colleague in Moscow and forwarded it to Rome. Since Soviet Russia seemed only on the periphery of decisive events, the Gabinetto simply handed the reports from Moscow on to the political desks as of no particular significance. Thus, when the news of the German-Russian agreement arrived, Mussolini and Ciano were more surprised than they should have been, in view of the fact that the Palazzo Chigi was in pos-

[18] On the role of the Gabinetto, see—aside from Cantalupo—Emanuele Grazzi, *Il Principio della Fine* (Roma, 1945), pp. 8-11, and in general, Donosti, *Mussolini e l'Europa*, pp. 12-20. See also the introduction to *Documenti Italiani*, 8th series, XII, ix-x.

[19] Grazzi, *Il Principio della Fine*, p. 10.

[20] He has written very revealing memoirs: Filippo Anfuso, *Roma Berlino Salò (1936-1945)* (Editore Garzanti, 1950). He remained loyal to Mussolini till the end.

session of the most relevant facts.[21] This lack of coordination was characteristic of Ciano's reformed Foreign Office and was the result of a development which was of central importance for the conduct of Italian diplomacy: the decline in the importance of the regular political divisions and of the professional diplomats who staffed them.

The key importance which the Gabinetto gained in Ciano's time explains the apparent contrast between his claim to have achieved a Fascization of Italian diplomacy on the one hand and his continued irritation against his professional diplomats and his complaints about their cautiousness, timidity, and lack of true dignity in the face of foreigners on the other.[22] When Ciano spoke of a Fascization of Italian diplomacy he did not mean that he had transformed diplomacy by infiltrating new men, Fascists, into the existing diplomatic bureaucracy. What he could rightly claim was that he had restricted the sphere of action of the professional diplomats. The diplomats were not asked to give advice or make recommendations. Decisions were made from above, perhaps prepared and discussed by the young men whom Ciano had assembled in the Gabinetto. In Ciano's time, Cantalupo remarks, "the Ministry existed only to obey."[23]

The low estimation of the role of professional diplomacy permeated the routine business of diplomacy. There was a kind of silent war, between Ciano and his young men on the one side and the professional diplomats on the other. Ciano wanted to keep all the threads in his own hands, perhaps because he was afraid that the professionals might take concerted action against him. He discouraged direct contacts and exchange of information among the Italian ambassadors. Neither information about the general political situation nor news of developments with which they were specifically concerned were regularly transmitted to the Italian representatives abroad.[24] Ambassadors had to leave for new destinations without thorough briefing; when they wanted to see Ciano before their departure he had nothing to say to them and often no time to receive them.[25] This happened so frequently that it cannot have been entirely by accident, although occasionally Ciano's lack of time may have been caused by his passionate devotion to the pleasures of Roman society.

[21] Mario Toscano, *L'Italia e gli Accordi Tedesco-Sovietici dell' Agosto 1939* (Firenze, 1952), p. 38.

[22] Ciano, *1937-1938 Diario*, pp. 75-76, or *Diario* (Milano, 1948), I, 17.

[23] Cantalupo, *Fu la Spagna*, p. 67.

[24] Guariglia, *Ricordi*, pp. 357-358; Grazzi, *Il Principio della Fine*, p. 123.

[25] Guariglia, *Ricordi*, p. 357; Grazzi, *Il Principio della Fine*, p. 18; Dino Alfieri, *Due Dittatori di fronte* (Milano, 1948), p. 23.

Because of the distrust with which the Gabinetto regarded the professional diplomats, its young men placed little reliance on the heads of missions for collection and evaluation of information, but tried to develop an information service of their own, sometimes with grotesque results. When, after the outbreak of the second world war, the Italian ambassador in Athens maintained that the British had no intentions of landing in Greece, the Gabinetto refused to accept this view and turned directly to the various Italian consuls. It is reported that even Ciano's young men were startled when in reply they received from one of the consuls the following telegram: "The hairdresser of my wife told her this morning that a British landing is expected within a week."[26]

Quite in accordance with this contempt for professional diplomats, Ciano liked to work outside the regular diplomatic channels. At important embassies he had confidants, through whom he acted behind the back of the ambassador. Particularly important contacts were established and maintained through special emissaries. One of them was Anfuso; he was sent to Franco in the early months of the Spanish civil war, and, in a secret mission to Hitler in 1936, it was he who prepared the terrain for Ciano's visit of October of that year, which marked the beginning of the close cooperation between Italy and Germany.[27] Ciano cultivated the method of direct meetings with foreign statesmen; he was frequently away from Rome, traveling to Germany and to the capitals of Eastern and Southern Europe.

As Ciano was quite uninhibited by the traditions of the diplomatic profession, the range of his activities went far beyond what is customarily considered to be the sphere of action of a Foreign Minister. He himself established contact with revolutionary forces of other countries when they could be used in favor of Fascist Italy, and he extended his interference into the military sphere when the aims of his foreign policy could be promoted by direct military action.[28] Cantalupo had a typical experience of the subordinate role which the professional diplomat held in Ciano's strategy of foreign policy.[29] Ciano had appointed him in 1936 to be the first Italian ambassador in Franco Spain. Cantalupo was most anxious to hear the views of the newly appointed Foreign Minister on the Spanish problem, the first great political issue with which Ciano was concerned. When the civil war broke out the Western Powers were trying to bury the sanctions issue and to build golden bridges for Italy's

[26] Grazzi, *Il Principio della Fine*, p. 104.   [27] Anfuso, *Roma Berlino Salò*, pp. 20-26.
[28] See below, note 43.
[29] For the following see Cantalupo, *Fu la Spagna*, pp. 62-67, 75-78, 244-250.

return to Geneva. Thus, the handling of the Spanish crisis would reveal whether the Abyssinian Affair was intended to become a soon forgotten episode, permitting Italy to return to its traditional system and friendships, or whether the masters of Italy would try to embark on an entirely new course. Cantalupo found the manner in which Ciano explained the Spanish issue to him most reassuring and satisfactory. Ciano indicated that Mussolini had only very hesitantly agreed to lend Franco military support. Italy had no territorial ambitions in Spain. Aside from the fact that the establishment of Bolshevism there must be prevented, Italy was not concerned with ideological issues, and had no special interest in promoting a totalitarian regime in Spain; Franco should be advised to take a reconciliatory attitude towards other parties. Thus the Spanish conflict should not widen the gap between Italy and the Western Powers and, as soon as the Spanish affair was composed, Ciano added, he hoped to make a visit to Paris.

As satisfactory as Ciano's exposition of the Spanish situation sounded to Cantalupo, he noticed some things which disquieted him. Before he left Ciano's office, Ciano explained to him the military situation in Spain. A big map was spread out on the table, with little flags indicating the position of the various military units, and soon Ciano and Anfuso began to move them around, like enthusiastic schoolboys, becoming engrossed in planning Franco's campaign. Furthermore, Cantalupo soon learned that Ciano had established at the Palazzo Chigi a special office for Spanish affairs which was concerned with the military aspects of the enterprise. Finally, when, immediately before his departure, Cantalupo saw Ciano again for a farewell visit, the Foreign Minister told him that the Italian Fascist party was exerting strong pressure on him to take a radical ideological line in the Spanish issue, and that he was forced to make some concession; Farinacci, the old party wheelhorse, would therefore go to Spain on a special mission as representative of the party. Ciano assured Cantalupo that he did not need to worry about this. Actually Farinacci's presence in Spain ruined any chances Cantalupo's embassy may have had. He refused to have any contact with Cantalupo; he himself soon came to be considered as the true mouthpiece of the Italian leader in Spain; and Cantalupo could make no headway with his more conciliatory recommendations. Moreover, after he returned to Rome, Farinacci began a systematic campaign against Cantalupo's "defeatism," and the ambassador was recalled after two months. Upon his return he soon realized that he had fallen into disgrace; people studiously avoided him, and the police kept checking on all his movements and contacts. When he was finally admitted to Ciano, he found a different man, cool and distant; Ciano was unwilling to permit Cantalupo to present his views to Mussolini and showed himself entirely uninterested in what Cantalupo had to report. Cantalupo's diplomatic career had ended.

It is possible that when Cantalupo was appointed ambassador to Franco the course to be followed by Italy in the Spanish civil war had not yet been definitely set. The Italian-Spanish Agreement of November 28, 1936,[30] which preceded Cantalupo's mission, guaranteed the inviolability of Spanish territorial possessions and provided for close cooperation between the two countries. The common outlook between the Fascist regime and the Spanish Nationalist government was emphasized though the wording of the treaty was not incompatible with what Ciano had told Cantalupo about Italian policy in the Mediterranean. After the defeat of the Italians in the battle of Guadalajara, which took place while Cantalupo was in Spain, an intransigent and radical line may have seemed necessary in order to restore Italian prestige. But it is equally possible that, from the outset, Ciano had higher aims than gaining a friend for Italy in the Western Mediterranean and that he was working for the establishment of a regime identified with Fascist Italy also in internal structure. If this is the case, he used Cantalupo's mission as a cover behind which he hid his true intentions and simultaneously kept open a line of retreat in case his maximum aims could not be obtained. In any case Cantalupo's mission to Franco is a striking example of the variety of instruments on which Ciano relied in the conduct of foreign policy. Among these instruments, the professional diplomat was only a very minor and not a very highly esteemed factor.

II

As has been noted, the Spanish civil war was the first great issue with which Ciano had to deal as Foreign Minister. In referring to this event we have touched upon the central problem of our study. To what extent did Ciano's diplomatic methods, his Fascization of diplomacy, change Italy's attitude to the outside Powers and vary or deviate from the traditional course of Italian foreign policy?

Ciano indicated frequently that the traditional diplomats had failed to give foreigners the right impression of Italy's newly acquired strength. Now the diplomats were supposed to show a stern and imperious face to the outside world, they were expected to employ a *tono fascista*.[31] In

---

[30] For the text see Galeazzo Ciano, *L'Europa verso la Catastrofe* (Verona, 1948), pp. 120-121.

[31] Guariglia, *Ricordi*, p. 193.

his Diary, Ciano notes with evident contempt occasions when foreign statesmen or diplomats showed signs of emotion when they were worried or perturbed, or became pale or had tears in their eyes. He evidently expected that Italy's representatives would show none of these weaknesses, and his diplomats were well aware of how they were supposed to behave. The reports which they sent home sound frequently more like the descriptions of military encounters than the résumés of polite diplomatic interviews.[32] It is reported that Grandi during the Abyssinian crisis delivered a conciliatory speech in England. The conciliatory passages were carefully deleted from the text which he sent to the Palazzo Chigi.[33] When Guariglia was appointed ambassador in Paris, he showed Ciano the draft of a speech which he wanted to deliver in presenting his credentials to the President of the French Republic. This draft contained the customary allusions to the common European heritage and the historical bonds between the Italian and French people, but when Ciano returned the draft these innocuous expressions of diplomatic politeness had been cut out.[34] Ciano modeled his own conduct upon the precepts he gave to his ambassadors. When a report had arrived that the Greek military attaché in Budapest had made some disparaging remarks about the military qualities of the Italian army, Ciano threatened to break off diplomatic relations between Italy and Greece, and serious consequences were avoided only because the Greek government agreed to retire the talkative officer.[35]

The same brutal disregard of custom was shown also in the use of intercepted messages.[36] The Italian government had a particularly well-functioning secret service which provided the Palazzo Chigi with complete information about the interchanges between the British ambassador in Rome and the London Foreign Office, and also with the diplomatic correspondence of many other countries. Ciano was not satisfied with

[32] As an example see Grandi's report on his interview with Chamberlain and Eden in February 1938, shortly before Eden's dismissal, in Ciano, *L'Europa verso la Catastrofe*, pp. 249-278. For further examples of the approved *tono fascista*, see *Documenti Italiani*, 8th series, XII, 82-83, 120-125, 157-158, 507, 610.

[33] Guariglia, *Ricordi*, p. 743.

[34] *ibid.*, pp. 355-357, where Guariglia's original draft and Ciano's revised text are both printed.

[35] Grazzi, *Il Principio della Fine*, pp. 12-13.

[36] "The brazen and extensive use made of material thus acquired" is discussed by Namier in his review of "Ciano's Early Diary," printed in L. B. Namier, *Europe in Decay* (London, 1950), pp. 112-115, where most of the facts mentioned above are discussed. The article by Mario Toscano, "Problemi Particolari della Storia della Seconda Guerra Mondiale," *Rivista di Studi Politici Internazionali*, XVII (1950), 388-398, deals with the interesting question of the influence which these interceptions had on the course of Italian foreign policy.

using the secret information for the planning of his diplomatic moves; he was eager to impress other statesmen with Italian omniscience and he used the material as a means of increasing tension. On a famous occasion, a dossier of English reports about Germany was prepared and shown to Hitler with the desired effect of inciting him against the British; on another, Schuschnigg of Austria was harassed with some incautious remarks which the Austrian Foreign Minister had uttered when he was dining at Geneva with Vansittart.

The *tono fascista* of Italian diplomacy in itself did not represent a new course of action but it was important in determining and restricting the framework within which Italian policy could and would take action. Slow proceedings and cautious legal formulas were considered as contradictory to the emphasis on decisive action which was supposed to be characteristic of Fascism and to animate its diplomacy. Collective agreements and multilateral treaties were condemned;[37] preference was given to those countries where an individual had the full power of decision, where concern for parliamentary bodies was unnecessary, and where agreements could be reached in personal meetings. Ciano was much influenced by his personal impressions of foreign statesmen; he preferred to deal with those who corresponded to the "new fascist type." The development of the relations between Yugoslavia and Italy offers a characteristic example. In March 1937, an agreement was signed between these two countries who had been bitter opponents. From the Italian point of view the agreement represented an attempt to undermine the Little Entente and thereby to weaken the French influence in the Balkans; at the same time, it was meant to block the expansion of Germany which was beginning to draw Austria more and more into her orbit. Ciano was particularly proud of this agreement, in which he saw a first fruit of his own activities as Foreign Minister, but his "new course" was based entirely upon his estimate of the personality of the Yugoslav Premier Stojadinovic, whom he regarded as a man of the new type. When in 1939, the future Yugoslav dictator was thrown out of power like any weak parliamentary Prime Minister, Ciano took this almost as a personal affront and immediately resumed plotting with the Croatian opposition against the existence of the Yugoslav state.[38]

The contempt for the usual procedures and customs of diplomacy and the disregard of the rules which had been developed in international

[37] Ciano, *L'Europa verso la Catastrofe*, pp. 286, 338: "contrario allo nostro stile diplomatico per il suo carattere di Patto collettivo."
[38] Ciano, *Diario*, I, 34, 52, 61.

relations aggravated the difficulties of cooperation with those nations which placed emphasis on these rules and tried to reinforce them. Though Mussolini's Italy had never been friendly to the League of Nations, a working relationship had existed in the 1920's.[39] The completely negative and aggressively hostile attitude towards the League which had developed in the Abyssinian crisis and was maintained and accentuated by Ciano's foreign policy, rigidified the Italian position. By hardening the contrast between Italy and the West into a conflict between two opposite ways of life, it placed formidable obstacles in the way of eventual resumption of cooperation.

With increasing emphasis on the contrast between the democratic and the Fascist concept of foreign policy, Italy was naturally drawn to emphasize similarities with the other great anti-Western Power, Germany. Even in the earlier years of his regime, Mussolini had expressed the idea that a new world war was inevitable, and he had pointed to the 1940's as critical years. At that time, he regarded England and Russia as the great antagonists and believed that the conflict should be used by Italy to cut out an empire of her own.[40] With Italy moving close to Germany, the idea of an inevitable new world war persisted, but the perspective changed. The war became a war between totalitarian and democratic Powers; together with Germany, Italy would be one of the main protagonists, Germany destined to rule in the north, Italy in the south of Europe. One can see in Ciano's Diary how, in his discussions with Mussolini, the decadence of the democracies and the inevitability of war became recurrent themes.[41] It is true that the time of this war remained vague and in a not clearly defined future; but the feeling that the world would soon assume an entirely new aspect could only strengthen the tendency towards an irresponsible freedom of action in foreign policy.

It is hard to imagine Ciano achieving prominence in any other situation. In his pride of being the representative of a new, ruthless generation, he fitted perfectly into a *fin de siècle* atmosphere where everything that served to improve Italy's position for the future decisive clash seemed justifiable, and in which, under the threat of a coming world war, he could carry out actions which, in less critical times, would have been impossible for him. Ciano was not concerned with the slow and gradual strengthening and widening of the foundations which had been laid

[39] See Chapter 7, §v above.
[40] See the report about a conversation with Mussolini in Cantalupo, *Fu la Spagna*, pp. 42 ff.
[41] Ciano, *Diario*, I, 12; Ciano, *L'Europa verso la Catastrofe*, p. 375.

in the past. Instead, he groped in all directions where opportunity for gain or prestige and expansion of power seemed to beckon, becoming deeply involved in the military aspects of the Spanish civil war, and after Stojadinovic's fall, promoting plans to partition Yugoslavia and to bring Croatia under Italian control. But in Spain and Yugoslavia Ciano was dealing with situations which had arisen before he took office; the enterprises into which he put his whole energy were those which he conceived and planned personally: the actions against Albania and Greece.

Although the operation against Greece was probably conceived before 1939,[42] it was executed only after the European war had started, and it need not be considered here. In any case, the military action which led to the incorporation of Albania into the Italian empire is sufficiently typical of Ciano's methods.[43] There was no pretense, as in the case of Greece, of military or strategic considerations; and despite Ciano's later pride over having acquired Albania for the Italian crown, it still seems to have been a superfluous acquisition. Absorption of Albania by a more gradual procedure would have been entirely possible although even this seems unnecessary in view of the protectorate which Italy had acquired in the 1920's. Yet, when Ciano represented the Italian government at the marriage of King Zogu in May 1938, he decided that Italian policy should be directed toward complete and outright acquisition of Albania; and he obtained Mussolini's agreement and stuck to what he called the "integral solution." Ciano kept all the threads of this *coup* in his own hands; in the diplomatic sphere he agreed with Stojadinovic on compensating Yugoslavia by a strip of territory in northern Albania, but abandoned the idea of such a grant after Stojadinovic's fall. He prepared an internal revolt against Zogu's regime by organizing the distribution of money to the Albanian opposition leaders, and he supervised the military preparations for the enterprise. Finally, when the military action started, on Good Friday of 1939 (a day which to many people seemed hardly fitted for an action of this kind), Ciano himself flew to Albania to watch over his private experiment in empire building.

The Albanian annexation was achieved without raising more serious repercussions than paper protests. The Italian leaders regarded this enterprise as a sign of the freedom of action which Italy had achieved in the Mediterranean area. But actually this was an illusion and shows only

---

[42] Ciano, *1937-1938 Diario*, p. 44; *Diario*, I, 99.
[43] Ciano, *1937-1938 Diario*, pp. 118, 140, 150, 165, 170, 267; *Diario*, I, 24, 34, 35, 55, 64; *L'Europa verso la Catastrofe*, pp. 305-316, 409-412.

how little Ciano was able to conceive of Italian foreign policy as an integrated and coherent whole. Ciano once made a remark which shows how precarious the Italian position actually was. He said that one of the desirable consequences of the establishment of Italian power in the Balkan peninsula would be that it would create a balance against the growth of German influence there.[44] This was almost an admission that by conducting an expansionist policy which pointed towards the east, the south, and the west of the Mediterranean, and threatened the *status quo*, Italy had thoroughly disturbed her neighbors and greatly increased the possibility of interference by outside Powers in this area. By replacing a policy of clearly limited aims with a policy of unrestricted use of power within the whole of the Mediterranean area, Italy was in fact more deeply drawn into the vortex of European power politics and lost much of her freedom of action in her relations with the Great European Powers.

The advantages gained in the Mediterranean necessarily remained insecure because the fate of Italy depended on Italy's alignment in the constellation of the Great European Powers. The central issue of Italian foreign policy in the three years before the second world war was the relation of Italy to Germany and to Britain. As we have said before, in the summer of 1936, when Ciano took over the direction of Italian foreign policy, Italy had to decide whether she wanted to reestablish the traditional cooperation with Britain, disturbed by the Abyssinian war and to resume in the European state system the balancing role which she had played in former years.[45] When Ciano became Foreign Minister, not more than 15 months had passed since the Stresa Conference, at which Italy had aligned herself with France and Great Britain against Germany, and the increase in power which Nazi Germany had gained in the intervening period through the reoccupation of the Rhineland gave special urgency and importance to the decision which Italy would now have to make. The Western Powers tried to terminate whatever actions they had undertaken against Italian aggression, and efforts were begun to relieve the Anglo-Italian tension. The progress of negotiations was slow, cumbersome, and interrupted, however. A first positive result was obtained in January 1937 when the two governments published a dec-

[44] Ciano, *L'Europa verso la Catastrofe*, p. 311.
[45] For a discussion of the situation at the end of the Abyssinian war, see Maxwell H. H. Macartney and Paul Cremona, *Italy's Foreign and Colonial Policy 1914-1937* (London, 1938), chapter xv, and Donosti, *Mussolini e l'Europa*, p. 42. For the historical roots of the contrast between a rational and emotional-aggressive Italian foreign policy, see Federico Chabod, *Storia della Politica Estera Italiana dal 1870 al 1896*, 1: *Le premesse* (Bari, 1951).

laration usually called the Anglo-Italian "Gentleman's Agreement," a reciprocal agreement to preserve the *status quo* in the Mediterranean.[46] But in the face of Italy's increasing military commitments in the Spanish civil war the value of such an assurance became questionable; and a bitter anti-British press campaign reduced relations to the previous state of tension. Even an exchange of messages between Mussolini and Chamberlain in the summer of 1937 did not revive the Anglo-Italian talks. It was only after Eden's dismissal in February 1938 that negotiations were resumed, resulting in the conclusion of a British-Italian Accord on April 16. This treaty reaffirmed the agreement of 1937 and regulated a number of issues in the Mediterranean and Near Eastern area connected with Italy's conquest of Abyssinia, but its real point was Britain's recognition of Italy's African empire and Italy's agreement to withdraw a substantial number of volunteers from Spain.[47] Once again, however, the Accord seemed to remain a piece of paper because Italy did not carry out the latter condition.[48] Nevertheless, after Munich, Chamberlain considered himself satisfied with a token withdrawal of volunteers, and the Accord finally came into force in November 1938. This was immediately followed, however, by violent anti-French demonstrations in the Italian Chamber and in the press; and Ciano showed little interest in the British attempts to improve Franco-Italian relations.[49] Nevertheless Chamberlain and Halifax carried out a visit to Rome in January 1939 to put the seal on the normalization of Anglo-Italian relations; but, as Ciano wrote, from the Italian point of view it was a visit "on a minor scale."[50]

In contrast to the hesitant course along which Anglo-Italian negotiations proceeded, Italy's advance towards friendship with Germany seemed smooth and steady.[51] Germany had been quick in recognizing Italy's African empire; and in October 1936 Ciano visited Germany and

[46] For the text, see Royal Institute of International Affairs, *Documents on International Affairs, 1937* (London, 1939), pp. 87-89.

[47] For the text see *Documents on International Affairs, 1938*, pp. 141-156.

[48] For a summary of the British complaints see the "Extracts from Foreign Office Memorandum on Anglo-Italian Relations" in *British Documents*, 3rd series, III, 812-815.

[49] *ibid.*, 478ff.; IV, chapter 4.

[50] Ciano, *Diario*, I, 20; see also the somewhat reticent tone of Mussolini's and Ciano's telegrams at the end of the visit: *British Documents*, 3rd series, III, 540.

[51] The basic work on the relations between Italy and Germany remains Elizabeth Wiskemann, *The Rome-Berlin Axis* (New York, 1949), but material which has come out since the publication of this book has now to be taken into account. Mario Toscano, *Le Origini del Patto d'Acciaio* (Firenze, 1948), is based on the Italian Foreign Office documents and gives an admirable presentation of the details of the diplomatic negotiations. The most recent survey is given by M. Magistrati, "Berlino 1939: da Praga al Patto d'Acciaio," *Rivista di Studi Politici Internazionali*, XIX (1952), 597-652.

saw Hitler. A few days later in a speech in Milan on November 1, Mussolini, in evaluating the importance of this visit, coined the famous phrase that the Berlin-Rome line represented "an Axis." Both countries, Germany and Italy, were quick in recognizing Franco and acted in concert in the London Non-Intervention Committee. Visits of Nazi hierarchs to Italy emphasized the maintainance of close contacts and Mussolini's visit to Germany in September of 1937 became an imposing demonstration of the closeness of Italian-German relations. By signing the Anti-Comintern Pact and by abandoning the League of Nations Italy increased the impression of Italo-German solidarity. On Hitler's visit to Rome in May of 1938 drafts for an alliance treaty were exchanged. These negotiations were interrupted by the Czech crisis, and, after their revival in October, were further slowed down by the attempt to include Japan in the treaty, but on May 6, 1939, after a meeting of Ciano and Ribbentrop in Milan, an announcement was made that a German-Italian alliance was concluded and on May 22 the Pact of Steel—a military alliance which did not even contain the usual escape clause restricting the obligations for assistance to the case of an enemy attack—was solemnly signed in Berlin.

During the tense years preceding the outbreak of the second world war, many people believed that an alliance had existed between Germany and Italy ever since 1936 and that they had conducted a concerted policy in which every move was carefully planned and agreed upon. This theory assumed that the leaders of the two countries denied the existence of an alliance treaty and pretended to act independently and on their own in order to obtain greater concessions from the Western Powers; that they did not want to lose the advantages to be gained by holding out as a bait the possibility of an alignment with the West; and that by maintaining contacts with Britain and France they were better able to prevent common action against aggression or at least to delay such action till the dictatorship had acquired enough strength to resist.

The documents which have been published since the war prove irrefutably the erroneousness of this interpretation. The Italian leaders were surprised by Germany's occupation of Austria, they were left guessing about Germany's true intentions in the Czech crisis, they had no previous knowledge of Germany's move into Prague. On the other hand, Germany was not previously informed about the Italian action against Albania. Both countries—Germany and Italy—did not feel sure that the other might not be willing to make a deal with Britain. Ciano prepared his famous dossier to incite Hitler against Britain; when the British-Italian agreement came into force Ribbentrop appeared in Rome with offers of an alliance. Behind the façade of public proclamations of German-Italian solidarity there appears lack of frankness and hidden doubts of the reliability of the partner.

Since the days when the myth of German-Italian solidarity was widely accepted, opinion has shifted and currently the view is often expressed that it would have been possible for the Western Powers to win Italy away from Germany and to prevent the conclusion of the German-Italian alliance. According to this view, Britain acted slowly and hesitantly; the Quai d'Orsay was haughty and prejudiced especially after the bitter Italian attacks against France in the winter of 1938-1939; feelers which one group in the French government put out were counteracted by another[52] so that the Italians could not be convinced of the seriousness of the French intentions; and these mistakes of the Western Powers drove Italy into German arms.

Ciano's Diary has been adduced as proof of the contention that Italy was not given a full chance to disentangle herself from the German embrace or at least to keep Germany at a respectable distance. The Diary shows irritation against the Germans after the *Anschluss* and particularly after the coup of Prague;[53] and it makes clear that the question of the South Tyrol and that of the Brenner frontier remained sore spots in Italy despite Hitler's solemn renunciations. Italy was deeply upset by the extension of German influence into the Balkans; after the occupation of Austria as well as after Munich, Ciano toyed with the idea of supplementing the horizontal Rome-Berlin axis with a vertical Rome-Belgrade-Budapest-Warsaw axis which was to form a barrier against further German penetration into Southeastern Europe.[54] Furthermore, various moves undertaken by the Italian leaders in 1938 are regarded as symptoms of Italian hesitancy. Despite the official assurances that the Anglo-Italian negotiations were not directed against Germany, Italy began to show serious interest in their progress at the very moment in February 1938 when Germany resumed an aggressive policy against Austria.[55] On Ribbentrop's visit to Rome in October 1938 Mussolini, despite an emphatically stated enthusiasm for a German-Italian alliance, mainly elaborated on the necessity of delay and of cautious procedure.[56] The quickness and willingness with which Mussolini

[52] See Chapter 12, §III above.   [53] Ciano, *Diario*, I, 55-58.
[54] Ciano, *1937-1938 Diario*, pp. 114, 263.
[55] See Ciano's instructions to Grandi in Ciano, *L'Europa verso la Catastrofe*, pp. 245-246.
[56] Toscano, *Patto D'Acciaio*, pp. 30-35.

grasped at the offer to act as mediator in the Czech crisis has been taken as a sign that he was glad to retreat from the exposed position into which Italy had advanced.[57] When Hitler had come to power in 1933, Mussolini had proposed a Four Power Pact and—it is said—this remained the true aim of his policy throughout.

Finally, the dramatic clash between Ribbentrop and Ciano in August 1939 is often regarded as decisive proof of the reluctance with which Italy had tied herself to Germany and of the divided mind of the Italian leaders.[58] If, then, we are to judge the strength of the thesis that Italy could have been detached by the Western Powers and the validity of the evidence which seems to support this, it might be well, first, to recapitulate briefly the circumstances of the Ribbentrop-Ciano meeting and the effect it had on Ciano's subsequent conduct in August 1939.

Attolico, the Italian ambassador in Berlin, had for some time been sending alarming reports to Rome, stating that the Germans had decided to take military action against Poland and were willing to risk a general war.[59] The ambassador suggested a meeting between Hitler and Mussolini at which Hitler would be forced to define his plans and at which Mussolini should, if necessary, exert a moderating influence. Ciano was displeased at being pushed into the background, and there seems to have been some suspicion in Rome that Hitler might persuade Mussolini to rash commitments, instead of Mussolini restraining Hitler. Thus, after some hesitation and delays, it was decided that Ciano should go to Germany. When he arrived in Salzburg on August 11, he seems to have considered Attolico's fears as exaggerated and to have felt reasonably sure that a common line leading to a conference of the Great Powers and to a peaceful international settlement could be worked out by Italy and Germany. After his first talk with Ribbentrop, however, Ciano's mood was grim. "We have come to blows," was his résumé of the interview and it is clear that Ribbentrop had admitted that Germany now in-

---

[57] The bellicose speeches which Mussolini made in September are explained as a means to maintain contact with Hitler so that Hitler would accept Mussolini's mediation.

[58] The most recent treatment is contained in Toscano, *L'Italia e gli Accordi Tedesco-Sovietici*. Ciano's reports are contained in *L'Europa verso la Catastrofe*, pp. 449-459, and in *Diario*, I, 140-141. Magistrati, Ciano's brother-in-law, who was a member of the Italian embassy in Berlin and present in Salzburg, has written two articles "Salisburgo 1939," and "Le Settimane Decisive," *Rivista di Studi Politici Internazionali*, XVI (1949), 479-509, and XVII (1950), 187-232, while Attolico's views are given in Leonardo Simoni, *Berlino Ambasciata d' Italia 1939-1943* (Roma, 1946), pp. 11-18. Important information is also contained in Donosti, *Mussolini e l'Europa*, pp. 198-201.

[59] See, for instance, *Documenti Italiani*, 8th series, XII, 263-264, 291, 378-381, 559-562.

tended to push things to the utmost. The luncheon following took place in an icy atmosphere; hardly a word was exchanged between guest and host. In further talks with Ribbentrop Ciano emphasized his conviction that Britain and France would support Poland if she were attacked and that the military outlook for the Axis Powers would be doubtful. Italy in any case would not be ready to participate in such an adventure. Ciano had the courage to maintain this position even against the prophetic assuredness of the Fuehrer.

Back in Rome Ciano began his fight to keep Italy out of the war which he now considered inevitable. The Duce was deeply disturbed by the idea that Fascist Italy—like the parliamentary Italy of 1914—should renege her word and become again a "traitor nation." One of the most violent discussions, wrote Ciano, took place on August 21: "Today I have spoken clearly, I have used up all my ammunition. When I entered the room Mussolini confirmed his decision to go along with the Germans. 'You, Duce, cannot and must not do it. The loyalty with which I have served you in carrying out the policy of the Axis warrants my speaking clearly to you now. I went to Salzburg in order to adopt a common line of action. I found myself face to face with a *Diktat*. The Germans, not ourselves, have betrayed the alliance in which we were to have been partners, and not servants.' "[60]

In his efforts to persuade Mussolini Ciano had the loyal and enthusiastic support of the professional diplomats, especially Attolico who traveled back and forth between Rome and Berlin and who worked hand-in-hand with him. Ciano had at long last become the protagonist of the traditional line of Italian foreign policy. But he was handicapped now by the carelessness of his own new diplomacy. In negotiating the alliance with Germany, the initiative was left to the Germans, and drafts which they submitted formed the basis of the treaty; a decisive weakness of the Italian position was the lack of written German assurances that the alliance had been signed with the understanding that action which might lead to war should be avoided for the next few years.[61] Because he had neglected to weigh carefully the reports about the German-Russian negotiations,[62] Ciano was surprised when the news of the Nazi-Soviet Agreement arrived; the situation seemed again transformed and the fight for Italy's neutrality had to be resumed. In the end Ciano

[60] Ciano, *Diario*, I, 146.

[61] This point had been made by Ciano to Ribbentrop in Milan and had again been stressed in the so-called *Memoriale Cavallero* of May 30. See Toscano, *Patto d'Acciaio*, pp. 186-191.

[62] See note 21 above.

succeeded in gaining Mussolini's agreement to Italy's neutrality. A professional diplomat put the final seal on this decision. On August 26 Attolico had been instructed to transmit to the German government a long list of military material which Italy needed to enter the war and which Germany was asked to provide. When the German officials wanted to know when the delivery was expected Attolico replied on his own initiative and without instructions "immediately before the beginning of hostilities," barring all possibility of further negotiations on the topic.[63]

There can be no doubt that, from the moment when Ciano met Ribbentrop at Salzburg, he was a changed man, thoroughly upset by the recklessness with which the Germans had violated the clause of the alliance providing for reciprocal consultation, and by the lightheartedness with which they embarked on a general war. And there is no question that, from this time on, he remained suspicious of the Nazi leaders and hostile to them. But, granted all this, what bearing does it have on the argument that Italy might have been won from Germany's side if only the Western Powers had been more intelligent in their diplomacy?

The answer to this question depends on our understanding of Mussolini's own position and upon an appreciation of the relations between Mussolini and his son-in-law.

The bulk of available evidence indicates that Mussolini was irrevocably set on a pro-German course of Italian foreign policy. He too may have had moments of doubt—particularly because he must have been continuously aware of Italy's economic deficiencies—but if so, he overcame his doubts quickly under the sway of Hitler's persuasive personality or under the impact of demonstrations of German strength. Ciano's Diary makes it quite clear that Mussolini's outbursts of irritation about German arbitrariness were short-lived—shorter than Ciano's; Mussolini always returned quickly to his pro-German course.[64] After Munich he scotched Ciano's plan of insisting on a common Polish-Hungarian frontier, in order to permit the formation of a vertical Axis.[65] Mussolini may have been utterly sincere when in October 1938 he justified to Ribbentrop his hesitation to conclude an alliance by citing the unprepared state of public opinion.[66] Soon after the meeting with Ribbentrop,

---

[63] Simoni, *Berlino Ambasciata d'Italia*, p. 17.
[64] Ciano, *1937-1938 Diario*, p. 134; *Diario*, I, 57, 60, 62.
[65] Ciano, *1937-1938 Diario*, p. 269.
[66] This differs from the interpretation given by Toscano, *Patto d'Acciaio*, pp. 33-34.

however, the Italian claims against France were announced and a bitter press campaign was unchained; and this widened the rift between France and Italy and served to demonstrate the usefulness of German support to the Italian public.[67] In comparison with the overwhelming amount of material which shows Mussolini's steady determination to arrive at a complete identification of German and Italian policy the few indications of doubt and hesitation can have no weight.

But could not Ciano himself, if given proper encouragement by the Western Powers, have prevented the full consummation of the German-Italian rapprochement? This would, in view of Mussolini's attitude, have involved an assertion of independence on his part. Was he capable of such a gesture? There is every reason to doubt it. The tone of his Diary in the years before the outbreak of the second world war was one of unreserved admiration for the Leader of Fascism.[68] The pervading theme is that "the Duce is always right." Doubts and criticism appear only later; it is possible that some resentment had already developed in earlier years and was then suppressed. The close family relationship may have had its drawbacks; Mussolini disapproved of his son-in-law's personal conduct quite as much as Ciano of his father-in-law's.[69] But if Ciano began to have some reservations they lay almost certainly in the purely personal sphere. There is no indication that before the summer of 1939 they extended into serious doubts about the Duce's political wisdom.

Moreover, in reshaping Italian diplomacy Ciano had been a true follower of the Duce. It has been shown[70] that Mussolini took over power full of contempt for the international system established at Paris and anxious to inaugurate an active foreign policy based on force, but he had been restrained by the adverse constellation in the European state system and by the impossibility of overcoming the resistance of the diplomatic bureaucracy. Ciano was the docile pupil who carried out the intentions of his master at a time when their realization was possible. The Italian diplomacy of the last three years before the war can be called Ciano's diplomacy less because the ideas of the new course were his own than because Ciano carried them out with an uninhibited and thoughtless energy, peculiar to this figure of a second-generation Fascism.

The transformation of the Italian diplomacy is an interesting example of the manner in which a revolutionary regime established complete

---

[67] Ciano, *Diario*, I, 104.
[68] Such expressions are collected by Namier, *Europe in Decay*, pp. 108-110.
[69] See Ciano's remark to Serrano Suñer, *Entre Hendaya y Gibraltar*, p. 317.
[70] See Chapter 7, §11 above.

control over a bureaucracy and reduced the professionals to powerlessness. But the reorganization to which Ciano subjected Italian diplomacy is also a decisive reason for rejecting the thesis that Italy's alliance with Germany could have been prevented, or that Ciano's views on this issue differed fundamentally from those of Mussolini. Ciano had fashioned an instrument to carry out a new course in foreign policy; it would have been a denial of what he had done if he had used the new instrument for carrying out the old, traditional foreign policy. Ciano loved to imagine himself as a free agent who could shape the world according to his will, and he liked to toy with plans and with projects. In moments of doubt and annoyance he may have played with the idea of siding with the French and English but actually he could not escape the momentum and weight of the movement to which he had turned the instrument of diplomacy. A time for reflection and choice arose only when the outbreak of the second world war created an entirely new situation.

Ciano's conversion at Salzburg in August 1939 was, then, not the result of a long evolutionary process in which he had nurtured growing doubts about the wisdom of the Duce's policy or during which he had seriously considered the advisability of returning to the traditional bases of Italian diplomacy. The important thing about the conversion was that it was sudden and, as such, in complete accordance with Ciano's characteristic approach to diplomacy. As we have seen, Ciano was little inclined to base his policy on considerations of permanent and underlying forces and interests. He approached policy in terms of personality, relying heavily upon his judgment of the leading figures of other countries. Thus, Ribbentrop's arrogant announcement of Germany's approaching military action against Poland, which revealed that the Italians had been trapped and overplayed, was a blow to Ciano's pride. He must have regarded it as quite a personal failure of his diplomacy, and turned now with vehemence against those whom he had misjudged.

III

There is irony in the fact that in September 1939, Fascist Italy with her proudly advertised first-rank-Power foreign policy ended up roughly in the same position in which parliamentary Italy had found herself at the beginning of the first world war. Likewise there is irony in the fact that from the summer of 1939 on Ciano developed into a practitioner of the policy of *combinazioni*—i.e. of trying to reap advantages from maintaining an undecided balancing position in the struggles of stronger Powers—a policy which in earlier years Ciano had regarded as characteristic of the weakness of democratic Italy and condemned as un-dignified and unfitting to the reborn strength of Fascist Italy.[71]

But Ciano never learned to discern the real and concrete factors of power behind the surface of appearances and his inability to see things as they are played a role in his final fate. When he left the Palazzo Chigi in 1943 he took over the embassy at the Vatican in the hope of establishing contacts with the victorious Western Powers—strangely unaware how little qualified he must have appeared to the democracies for this task. Ciano also seems to have failed to realize that he was the last who would reap benefits from taking an active part in Mussolini's overthrow. And when he was in custody in Germany he moved heaven and earth to be returned to Italy[72] where he seems to have hoped that activity would again become possible for him; actually he gave himself into the hands of his most implacable enemies.

When the ultra-Fascists who ruled Mussolini's Republic of Salò condemned him to death in Verona, Mussolini did not interfere. He decided that "sentiment" should not prevail over "reason of state"; he was nevertheless profoundly moved by the events in Verona and, in-deed, regarded them "as the most dramatic chapter in his restless life."[73] Perhaps he felt that responsibility for this wasted life belonged also to those who had raised Ciano into power without making him aware of the limits of its possibilities and its uses. The German ambassador at the Republic of Salò had great difficulty in restraining Mussolini from pub-lishing the next day in his newspaper an encomium on the Conte Galeaz-zo Ciano.[74]

[71] Ciano, *1937-1938 Diario*, p. 52.
[72] Anfuso, *Roma Berlino Salò*, pp. 392, 451.
[73] Quotations from his letter to Serrano Suñer about Ciano's death, published in Serrano Suñer, *Entre Hendaya y Gibraltar*, p. 323.
[74] Rudolf Rahn, *Ruheloses Leben* (Düsseldorf, 1949), p. 251.

17

....

Two British Ambassadors: Perth and Henderson

BY FELIX GILBERT

IN DEMOCRATIC STATES, it is generally considered that the making of policy is the responsibility of the Cabinet. In foreign policy, however, Cabinet decisions are necessarily influenced by the reports received from members of the diplomatic corps serving in foreign capitals, and the importance of such reports increases in times of emergency. In the years when Neville Chamberlain's appeasement policy was being inaugurated, the two most important posts in the British Diplomatic Service were Berlin and Rome. An appraisal of the work of the two ambassadors who represented Great Britain in those capitals—Sir Nevile Henderson and the Earl of Perth—is, therefore, of some importance if we are to understand the relationship of diplomacy and policy-making in times of crisis.

I

In the prologue of his book of memoirs, Henderson gives a brief definition of the principal functions of a diplomat. "The first commandment of a diplomatist," he writes, "is faithfully to interpret the views of his own government to the government to which he is accredited; and the second is like unto it: namely, to explain no less accurately the views and standpoint of the government of the country in which he is stationed to the government of his own country."[1]

It cannot be said that, during the years when Henderson had reached the high point of his professional career as British ambassador to Nazi Germany, he lived up to this formulation. Henderson was in Berlin from April 1937 till the outbreak of the second world war. During the first year of his mission, he was chiefly concerned with creating an improvement in the atmosphere of German-British relations; during the

[1] Nevile Henderson, *Failure of a Mission* (New York, 1940), p. viii.

last six months, after the German march into Prague, the British government had decided to take a firm line against the expansionism of Nazi Germany. Thus, the decisive year of Henderson's activities in Berlin, when his personal diplomacy came into its own, was the year 1938, which was dominated first by Hitler's annexation of Austria and then by the Czech crisis, ending in Hitler's triumph at Munich in September. It is precisely in this period that Henderson's conduct as diplomat is at variance with his own definition of the diplomat's duties.

Certainly, a reading of the British documents gives the impression of a tug-of-war between Henderson and his own Foreign Office rather than a picture of a diplomat anxious to act as "faithful interpreter" of the instructions received from London. On the one hand, we find examples of open censure, directed by the Foreign Office against the ambassador; on the other hand, and more frequently, we discover remonstrances on Henderson's part against the contents of his instructions, coupled with intimations of reluctance to execute them in the form in which they are presented to him.

Many illustrations of this kind of friction can be given. A direct clash between Henderson and the Foreign Office occurred immediately after Hitler's invasion of Austria. The ambassador was instructed to protest to Goering against this German action. In talking with the Field Marshal, however, Henderson agreed with Goering "that Doctor Schuschnigg had acted with precipitate folly"—a remark which led Lord Halifax to write subsequently that, by this admission, "you cannot have but diminished the force of the protest you were instructed to make."[2]

When the spotlight had shifted to Czechoslovakia, Henderson immediately took the line that the place where pressure would have to be applied was Prague: "I should be very loath to speak even unofficially to [the] German Government on the subject unless it was certain that [the] Czechoslovak Government meant to work on the basis of nationalities rather than on that of [a] national centralized state."[3] Consequently, Henderson was unhappy about the decision which the British and French governments had reached in their conference in London at the end of April,[4] namely, to make representations both at Prague and Berlin. As Hitler and Ribbentrop were in Italy at the time, Henderson was instructed to initiate the allied action by seeking an interview with Field Marshal Goering.[5] Henderson answered that he "had been gravely

---

[2] *British Documents*, 3rd series, I, 24, 29; see also L. B. Namier, *Europe in Decay* (London, 1950), pp. 210-212.

[3] *British Documents*, 3rd series, I, 115, also 110.

[4] *ibid.*, pp. 198-233, 243-245.   [5] *ibid.*, pp. 245-246.

exercised" in his mind "as to the expediency of making the communication in question to Goering rather than to Ministry of Foreign Affairs which would be more normal and recognized procedure"; and he succeeded in getting his instructions changed, so that his first discussion of the issue was with the Political Director of the German Foreign Ministry.[6] When, after Ribbentrop's return, the formal *démarche* was about to take place, Henderson asked for permission to have "a certain latitude in expression of personal opinion" in discussing the Sudeten matter with the German Foreign Minister. This time, however, the Foreign Office did not agree with Henderson's suggestion,[7] probably fearing that, if Henderson talked at greater length with Ribbentrop about the possibilities of a solution of the Sudeten crisis, he might, in accordance with his previously expressed views, suggest that the British government was in favor of a radical solution and thereby encourage the Germans to raise their demands.[8] For this apprehension there was some reason. It is evident that Henderson's concern about the manner in which the instructions for a *démarche* in Berlin should be carried out was inspired less by those reasons of formal correctness to which he alluded in his dispatches than by the wish to minimize the elements of urgency and pressure and to soft-pedal British opposition to German aims.

The inclination of the ambassador to accept the German point of view led to another implied censure later in the summer. In answer to a report from Henderson to the effect that the Germans declined any responsibility for the actions of the Sudeten party in Czechoslovakia, Sir Orme Sargent told him that "we do not really help ourselves if we allow the Germans to get away with these statements which we find hard to credit."[9]

Despite warnings of this nature, Henderson revolted again against instructions which he had received when the Sudeten crisis reached its climax in September. The ambassador was attending the Nazi Party Congress at Nuremberg, and Lord Halifax asked him to demand an interview with Hitler, in which he should leave no doubt that a world war was likely to start if Germany used force against Czechoslovakia. Against this instruction Henderson conducted an almost passionate campaign, in which he used the services of Chamberlain's confidential ad-

---

[6] *ibid.*, pp. 252, 256-257, 260.   [7] *ibid.*, pp. 273, 281.

[8] The suspicion of the Foreign Office had been aroused by Henderson's interview with the Political Director in the German Foreign Office; Henderson had indicated that Britain was urging a comprehensive settlement such as a state of nationalities. See *ibid.*, p. 260.

[9] *ibid.*, p. 592.

viser, Sir Horace Wilson; and in the end, he succeeded in getting the instruction rescinded.[10]

When Henderson returned to London in October for a leave of several months, he was indignant to learn that certain people in London believed that, by his behavior during the Sudeten crisis, he "had completely failed to impress upon the Germans the gravity of the position and the seriousness of Britain's determination."[11] Yet the charges of Henderson's critics seem to be corroborated by the documents that have been published since the end of the war. So far, in describing the ambassador's differences with the Foreign Office, we have cited only the British diplomatic papers. But the impression gained from these is strengthened by the abundant material on Henderson in the German Foreign Office files. This indicates all too clearly that, in his conversations with German statesmen, Henderson frequently made use of the diplomatic technique of "expressing a purely personal opinion"; and that, on the occasions when he indulged himself this way, he went very far in accepting the German point of view on Central European questions. In view of this, the Germans had every reason to question the "seriousness of Britain's determination."

Here again, a few examples may illustrate the point. In the summer of 1937, more than six months before the *Anschluss*, Henderson discussed the Austrian question with Franz von Papen and said that "he was convinced that England fully understood the historical need for a solution of this question in the Reich German sense."[12] Likewise, throughout the entire development of the Czech crisis, he was wholly uninhibited in expressing views which could only encourage the Nazi leaders in their plans. He was fond of expressing the opinion that Britain had not the slightest interest in fighting a war for Czechoslovakia and was often outspoken in his condemnation of the policy of the Czech government. After the May crisis of 1938, he accused the Czechs of spreading rumors of German troop concentrations "for the express purpose of serving as a pretext for planned partial Czech mobilization."[13] In August of the same year, he repeatedly emphasized in private conversation that "Great Britain would not think of risking even one sailor or airman for Czechoslovakia."[14]

Perhaps the greatest indiscretion of this kind was committed by Henderson at the Nuremberg Party Congress in 1938. Here, at a time when

---

[10] *ibid.*, II, 647-650.   [11] *ibid.*, IV, 590.
[12] *German Documents*, series D, I, 504. See also Namier, *Europe in Decay*, pp. 210ff.
[13] *German Documents*, series D, II, 449.   [14] *ibid.*, p. 536.

he was arguing in his reports to London that a special warning to Hitler was unnecessary since the German government must be fully aware of Britain's determination to stand with France and Czechoslovakia, he told a German S.S. leader that "he personally had no sympathy at all with the Czechs and moreover considered the placing of Sudeten Germans under Czech domination to be a grave mistake. He expressed his aversion to the Czechs in very strong terms."[15]

Such utterances cannot be justified by the fact that Henderson's views reflected more truly the attitude of leading men in the British government than did his official instructions. Although it may be said that the policy which Britain followed during the summer of 1938 was a policy of bluff, it was a conscious policy carefully worked out together with the French. Pressure was to be brought to bear simultaneously upon the two critical spots: Prague was to be threatened with withdrawal of support by the West; and Germany was to be warned that France and Britain would side with Prague in case of a military conflict. The Germans were not supposed to be encouraged to assume that the guns would not go off.[16] It was hoped that this double-barreled action would bring Germany and Czechoslovakia together on a middle line. In view of Hitler's decision to go the whole way, this policy probably never had a real chance of success; but it was not the function of the diplomat who was charged with the execution of this policy to counteract and undermine it by bandying around so freely his very different personal opinions.[17]

According to Henderson, the second commandment of a diplomat is to explain "accurately the views and standpoint of the government of the country in which he is stationed." The faults of the diplomatic technique which we have just discussed would weigh less heavily if they were not combined with a complete misinterpretation of the policy of Nazi Germany, of its general aims as well as its functional structure. Henderson's general conception of the objectives of German foreign policy was relatively simple; he thought about them in terms of nineteenth century nationalism. Henderson accepted the Nazi attacks against the Treaty of Versailles at their face value and regarded Nazism as a revolt against the Peace Treaty and as an attempt to right the injustices which had been done to Germany.[18] He believed that Nazi Germany

[15] *ibid.*, p. 768.
[16] *British Documents*, 3rd series, II, 56.
[17] In general, see *Survey of International Affairs, 1938*, II: *The Crisis over Czechoslovakia.*
[18] *British Documents*, 3rd series, II, 648.

was still struggling for the fulfillment of traditional national aspirations. He did not realize that the Nazi emphasis on race was a means rather than an end; instead he was convinced that an absorption of the German minorities into the Reich was the final goal of German foreign policy, that, after the achievement of this aim, Germany would become a saturated Power, and that the revolutionary fermentation would gradually disappear.[19] Henderson was not unaware, of course, that this development might imply a shift in the balance of power, through which Germany would become the dominant factor in Eastern and Southeastern Europe; but he regarded this as a natural development which could take place without changing the foundations of the European state system and without reducing the Western Powers to the status of German satellites.

It must be admitted that this misconception of German policy and of the dynamism of German expansion was shared by many influential people in Britain and elsewhere. "Doctrinaires" and "idealists," who base their conceptions of the policy of a country on an analysis of its economic policy or who conclude, from evidence of complete lack of morality in domestic policy, that cooperation in foreign policy is impossible, have always been regarded as "unsound" by the "realists" in governments and Foreign Offices; and Henderson was only one of many self-declared realists in positions of influence at this time. But, granted this, a more serious failure of Henderson as a political observer lies in his complete misjudgment of the mechanism by which decisions were made in Nazi Germany.

In Henderson's view, a continuous struggle was going on in Nazi Germany between moderates and extremists. He had little contact with those whom he considered to be extremists. His views about men like Himmler and Goebbels seem rather vague and shadowy. The only representative of the radicals whom he saw frequently, and whom he disliked intensely, was Ribbentrop. Henderson's main contacts in Germany were among the moderates, high officials of the German bureaucracy, and especially of the Foreign Office, like Neurath and Weizsäcker. The leader of this group and its most important and influential figure was, in Henderson's opinion, Hermann Goering. Henderson cultivated contacts with Goering; even after the war had broken out, he was still able to say that he found Goering "by far the most sympathetic among the big Nazi leaders" and that he had a "real personal liking for him."[20]

As for Hitler, in Henderson's view he could not be definitely as-

<hr>

[19] *ibid.*, I, 108-112, 286-287.   [20] Henderson, *Failure*, p. 76.

signed to either of the two groups but rather wavered between the moderates and the extremists. In Henderson's eyes, the Fuehrer was a psychopath and a visionary, subject to bursts of rage and swayed by sudden intuitions.[21] We know now that the real Hitler was very different from Henderson's conception of him, that his vacillations were more apparent than real and that, in fact, he followed a carefully worked out plan in which the *Anschluss* and the annexation of Czechoslovakia were only the first steps on the way to German domination over Europe. Henderson, however, believed that the decision to realize the *Anschluss* was taken suddenly, as a result of anger over Schuschnigg's precipitate action of calling a plebiscite. "I do not believe," he wrote to Halifax, "that on the 11th March Hitler himself envisaged the complete assimilation of Austria to the German Reich."[22] This concept of Hitler determined the line which Henderson advocated during the summer of the Czech crisis. Fundamentally, the ambassador did not believe that Germany planned military action or wanted war. At the height of the Czech crisis in August and September, he was still saying that it was untrue that "Hitler has already decided on aggressive action against Czechoslovakia this autumn,"[23] and was still capable of writing about "Hitler's own love for peace, dislike of dead Germans and hesitation of risking his regime on a gambler's throw."[24] Henderson felt, however, that the catastrophe of a war might happen if "Hitler were pushed over the edge."[25] He reverted continually to the *démarche* which Britain and France had made on May 21 on the basis of rumors about the mobilization of the German army against Czechoslovakia; he believed that this action had had a most unfortunate effect on the Fuehrer, and had made him much more intransigent than he had been before. At all costs, the ambassador wanted to avoid a repetition of this performance, and he was most unwilling to undertake any step that might infuriate Hitler again.

Henderson became deeply involved in a complicated game designed to support the moderates in Nazi Germany. Because he hoped to strengthen their position and influence, he was inclined to recommend concessions which, the moderates told him, were necessary to restrain Hitler. And

[21] See Henderson's characterization of Hitler in *British Documents*, 3rd series, I, 97-100.

[22] *ibid.*, p. 99. Even the march into Prague a year later was not, in Henderson's view, premeditated, but again a reaction to sudden developments. *Ibid.*, IV, 595.

[23] *ibid.*, II, 133.

[24] *ibid.*, pp. 243, 245.

[25] In particular, see Henderson's letters from Nuremberg, September 1938, *ibid.*, pp. 649-654.

this was a view to which the ambassador held to the bitter end, arguing always that "everything depends on the psychology of one abnormal individual."[26] Even in his final report, he insisted that, if only unfortunate accidents had not upset Hitler and driven him to extreme measures, things might have worked out all right, a striking proof of his lack of comprehension of German realities. Henderson never for a moment suspected that he was wrong or that his failure to appreciate the purpose and the definiteness of Hitler's policy was really promoting the Fuehrer's aims. Yet his repeated argument that the moderates had a real chance of dominating German policy not only made it possible for Hitler to win major concessions from London but gave British policy-makers a fallacious basis on which to plan their German course.

Analysis of Sir Nevile Henderson's activities in Berlin, then, shows that he can hardly claim to have carried out satisfactorily those fundamental tasks which he himself describes as the first two commandments of a good diplomat. Henderson may not—as *The Times* said after his death[27]—have been in the first rank of British diplomats; but, even so, it is strange that the man who had filled in a long and varied career a number of diplomatic positions[28] should have gone astray in what are, or are recognized by him to be, the most elementary duties of his profession. This is a problem which demands closer investigation, and the explanation of this paradox will be one of the chief purposes of this study.

II

In analyzing the reasons for Henderson's "failure," we have to acknowledge that he had to work on a particularly treacherous terrain: he was the ambassador of a democratic country to a totalitarian state. For this reason, a comparison of Henderson's diplomatic activity with that of the British ambassador in Rome has particular relevance. For the British ambassador in Rome had a very similar task, namely, that of improving the relations between the Western democracies and Fascist Italy.

Throughout the 1930's, the British ambassador in Rome was Sir Eric Drummond, who, in 1938, became the sixteenth Earl of Perth. Drummond had received his early political training under the most favorable auspices; he was private secretary to the most brilliant British states-

[26] *ibid.*, p. 296.   [27] *The Times* (London), January 4, 1943.
[28] After serving in Constantinople and Egypt, Henderson had been for one year at the British embassy in Paris. In 1928, he became minister in Yugoslavia, in 1935 ambassador in Argentina.

men of the early years of the twentieth century—to Grey, Asquith, Balfour, and Curzon—and he became their close friend. When, after the first world war, the League of Nations was founded, he was chosen as its first Secretary General and in this position he played a leading role in all the political crises and decisions of the postwar years, for fourteen years, until 1933.[29] It was he who was responsible for the important decision that the League Secretariat should not be staffed by officials in the service of the various member nations but should have its own international civil service; and it is chiefly due to him that this first experiment in an international bureaucracy was successful and was later followed when the United Nations was established. His handling of the political tasks of the League has been criticized as overcautious, but he did not lack courage for decisive action when such action was necessary for the maintenance of the authority of the League.[30] His slow and somewhat hesitant approach was useful in avoiding disappointments and setbacks and contributed to the League's steady gain in prestige.

Thus, the man who was appointed as ambassador to Italy in 1933 and who served in Rome until the eve of the war was one of Britain's most successful and experienced diplomats. For this reason, it is interesting to note that some of the features of Henderson's correspondence with London appear also in the reports of the Earl of Perth. His reports show the same concern with the mood of the dictator as Nevile Henderson's. He too argues that it is difficult to get close to Mussolini and that he has to be treated with great caution when he is in "a highly sensitive condition."[31] Frequently, Perth too seems to have had the feeling that the instructions sent him from London do not fit the special circumstances of the totalitarian country to which he is accredited, and he doubts that they may "produce any effect beyond irritation."[32] From Ciano's Diary, we know that Perth frequently gave to the Italian Foreign Minister his "personal views," which were apt to be sympathetic to Italian claims. In particular, Perth was inclined to agree with the Italian view that the French attitude toward Italy was unreasonable.[33] When, in the spring of 1938, Italian intransigence put obstacles in the way of the execution of the Anglo-Italian agreement of April 1938,[34]

---

[29] For Drummond's activities as Secretary General see F. P. Walters, *A History of the League of Nations* (2 vols., London, 1952), especially I, 75-80; II, 556-560.

[30] *ibid.*, I, 393 for his action in the conflict between Bolivia and Paraguay.

[31] *British Documents*, 3rd series, III, 319, 329, 358.

[32] *ibid.*, IV, 349.

[33] Ciano, *1937-1938 Diario* (Bologna, 1948), pp. 307, 313. *L'Europa verso la Catastrofe* (Verona, 1948), pp. 327, 355.

[34] See Chapter 16, § II.

Perth tried to keep the door open;[35] and, after the Munich conference, he pressed his government hard to put the agreement into force.[36] During these years, Perth seemed continuously concerned with demonstrating to the Italians that London was in a conciliatory mood.

In his reports to London, moreover, Perth frequently defended Italian policy. Ciano, who, because of the efficiency of the Italian secret service, was able to read many of Perth's reports, states in his Diary that the British ambassador, although opposed to the Fascist regime when he came to Rome, had developed into a "sincere convert" who "understood and even loved Fascism."[37] Though caution must always be employed when using Ciano's statements, Perth's reports suggest that there was a certain amount of truth in this remark. When, in November 1938, the Italians raised their claims against France, Perth certainly attempted to minimize the importance of the anti-French demonstrations.[38] His explanations of Italian aspirations in the Mediterranean suggest, indeed, that he was not immune to the historical arguments for revision pounded out by official Italian propaganda agencies. He considers the "grievances felt by Italy over the Peace Treaties" as "the crux of the matter"; "the feeling has grown in Italy that if the injustices inflicted upon the vanquished by the Peace Treaties are in process of swift revision, how much more ought the injustices suffered by one of the victors at the hands of her own allies to be repaired."[39] A consequence of this tendency to explain Fascist foreign policy as a result of Italian national aspirations was that Perth misjudged the decisive trend in Italian foreign policy: he underestimated Mussolini's eagerness to conclude an alliance with Germany[40]—an eagerness determined less by historical aspirations than by Fascist ideology.

These common elements in the diplomatic activities of Henderson and Perth, in Berlin and Rome, cannot have been accidental. They clearly derived from the difficulties of the situation in which democratic ambassadors found themselves in totalitarian countries. Since political decisions in these countries were exclusively in the hands of one man, and since this man was difficult to reach, the prognostication of political developments degenerated into a kind of psychological guessing game. Moreover, the methods in which diplomats had been trained to evaluate political trends in the country where they were stationed were of little use

---

[35] Ciano, *L'Europa verso la Catastrofe*, pp. 318-321, 327.
[36] *British Documents*, 3rd series, III, 322.
[37] Ciano, *1937-1938 Diario*, p. 309.
[38] *British Documents*, 3rd series, III, 463, 464, 466.
[39] *ibid.*, pp. 499, 506.   [40] *ibid.*, p. 322.

in totalitarian countries. Diplomats are not schooled to base their opinions and recommendations on an intensive study and expert knowledge of economic developments and military budgets; they gauge the trend of future policy from an analysis of public opinion as it is expressed in newspapers, in political meetings, and in conversations with the various political personalities with whom they must keep in contact. In a country where there is a strictly controlled press which publishes only what the government wants it to publish, and where there are no political parties or people who express their opinions freely to the foreigner, this kind of analysis of political opinions is hardly possible. The slogans which government propaganda presents are, therefore, easily overestimated and regarded as an expression and reflection of long-lasting and deeply rooted national aspirations. Neither Perth nor Henderson was impervious to this kind of influence.

On the other hand, because the situation in totalitarian countries is so different from that in democratic countries the diplomat finds it necessary to emphasize and explicate the point of view of the totalitarian regime. The person who explains glides easily into the role of the person who justifies and advocates. It is an inherent danger of the diplomatic profession that representatives abroad tend inevitably to associate themselves with the government to which they are accredited, and to defend its policies; and this tendency grows in direct proportion to the resistance of the home office to such persuasion.

It should not be said that Perth succumbed to these dangers to the same extent as Henderson. Although Perth's reports show something of Henderson's eagerness to understand, and to make understood, the dictator's policy, he never displayed the enthusiasm which Henderson showed in this endeavor. Perth's reports to the Foreign Office were always marked by certain reservations, and he was always aware of the limitations set by circumstances upon Italian aspirations. His negotiations with the Italian government for an Anglo-Italian agreement had clearly defined and limited objectives. Italy was a much less powerful country than Germany, and there was not the same reason to pay for Italian friendship. Moreover, because the leaders of Italian policy had to act from a much more restricted power basis, their moves remained on a much more calculable basis. Perth may have misjudged Mussolini's attitude to Germany but, in the last analysis, even here he was not far wrong, for the limitations of Italian power made it impossible for Mussolini, in 1939, to carry out his intention of siding with Germany in the war.

Moreover, Perth had come to Rome with a sound basis of skepticism. In his post at Geneva, he must have felt little sympathy for the Italian leaders, who had been less than enthusiastic about the League of Nations. Soon after his arrival in Rome, he became involved in the Abyssinian crisis; and, perhaps still under the influence of the Geneva experience, believed that the Italians were bluffing and seems to have taken a rather strong line against them.[41] It is only natural that, when the League policy in the Abyssinian affair had proved to be a failure, and when the course in London had been changed, he should have been concerned with ending his diplomatic career with success and should have become a supporter of Chamberlain's "new course." Even so, the skepticism and the reserve remained; whereas, in contrast, Henderson—appointed to Berlin at a moment when the policy of London demanded the abandonment of all possible reservations and probably by nature the least skeptical man alive—had had no previous experience with the Nazis which could influence, or guide, his judgment and was rather proud of his "freedom from prejudice."

III

For both Perth and Henderson the decisive period of their embassies in Rome and Berlin were the years when British foreign policy was set on a new course, that of Chamberlain's appeasement policy. It is striking to read the word appeasement in the diplomatic reports of the time. The word is used in a matter-of-fact way which shows that it had a much more general meaning, and a much less invidious one, than it has now. Today appeasement has been entirely identified with the idea of buying peace by making concessions to aggression, whereas, in its original meaning, concession was merely one of several means which might be employed to attain a general easing of European tension. The truth of the matter is that Chamberlain's appeasement policy had a more comprehensive character than is now assumed.[42] It was directed towards the reestablishment of a concert of Europe which should be directed by the four Great Powers: Britain, France, Italy, and Germany. In a sense, it was an attempt to reestablish the Locarno policy, which had been destroyed by the Nazi rise to power and by the break between Italy and the League of Nations.

But the situation was now very different from that of the 1920's,

---

[41] Raffaele Guariglia, *Ricordi 1922-1946* (Napoli, 1949), pp. 236, 243, 248.
[42] For Chamberlain's concept of foreign policy see Keith Feiling, *The Life of Neville Chamberlain* (London, 1946), particularly chapters 23-24.

when Locarno had been concluded; and great difficulties now stood in the way of realizing Four Power cooperation. First of all, Germany and Italy had to be persuaded, by concessions of some kind, to cooperate once more with the Western Powers. At the same time, Russia, who had moved closer to the West, had once more to be excluded from Europe. Most of all, the whole concept of collective security and the League of Nations had to be abandoned. This policy would be a deviation from the line which Britain had followed since the end of the first world war. Despite the fact that certain aspects of League activity had been criticized by the Dominions, the League of Nations had become a useful instrument for harmonizing the policy of Great Britain with that of the Commonwealth, and the shift to a more exclusively European policy might place the relation between the mother-country and the Dominions under a severe strain. Although the United States was not in the League of Nations, the abandonment of collective security and of the idea of the League would certainly increase the difficulties of cooperation with that great Atlantic Power. In addition, the concessions which would have to be made to Germany would mean the break-up of the French alliance system and the weakening of the French position.

Finally, in addition to these considerations of power politics, there were certain moral issues. The abandonment of collective security and of the League of Nations would eliminate whatever progress had been made in the development of a peaceful system of international relations. It might bring war nearer because it would restore what has been called the period of "international anarchy." Considerations of morality and power politics could not be entirely separated. If Germany and Italy were promoted to full participation in the hegemony of Europe, would it not mean that ruthlessness and immorality were being rewarded? And could one not say that, if the violations of international law by Germany and Italy were condoned, it would be useless to expect permanent cooperation between the Four Powers?

Thus, Chamberlain's appeasement policy was an adventure and, as such, it met strong resistance in the Foreign Office. Against this, Chamberlain reacted sharply. In previous chapters, reference has been made to the interference of the Prime Minister in Foreign Office business, especially in the time of Lloyd George and Ramsay MacDonald. Neville Chamberlain carried this interference much further. His struggle with the Foreign Office falls roughly into two periods. The first one stretches from his coming to 10 Downing Street until February 1938, when Anthony Eden, who was, and remained, opposed to Chamberlain's concepts, was dismissed. During this time, Chamberlain constantly employed special emissaries who established contact outside the official channels of the Foreign Office. His confidants maintained close relations with the German and Italian ambassadors in London,[43] and their activities were coordinated by Sir Horace Wilson of the Department of the Treasury upon whom Chamberlain fully relied for the carrying out of his new policy. Chamberlain tried to break the resistance of the Foreign Office at the same time by establishing a more personal relationship with the dictators than had existed in the past. On the German side, his chief effort of this kind was the mission of Lord Halifax to Hitler in November 1937. A somewhat parallel development—the more sinister because less official—was the use which Chamberlain made of his sister-in-law, Lady Austen Chamberlain, to establish contact with Mussolini and revive the long-stalled Anglo-Italian negotiations for a Mediterranean settlement.[44] Through Lady Chamberlain, the Prime Minister assured Mussolini that he would recognize the Italian empire in Abyssinia, at a time when the Foreign Office was insisting that no such assurance should be made before the beginning of negotiations.

After Eden's dismissal, the situation was changed. Halifax, the new Foreign Secretary, was fully in Chamberlain's confidence, and the policy of appeasement now dominated the Foreign Office. Even so, Chamberlain and his friends remained distrustful of the permanent officials of that organization. As one of the members of Chamberlain's group said, the Foreign Office was dominated by a pro-French group, whose influence could be broken only slowly and gradually.[45] Chamberlain and Sir Horace Wilson, therefore, continued to interfere with the details of policy execution; and the lack of coordination in British foreign affairs administration went on.

It is clear that this development placed the two ambassadors at Berlin and Rome in a difficult position. Just as German diplomats under the Nazis were faced with the necessity of choosing between the Foreign Office line and the party line, so were Henderson and Perth forced to identify themselves either with the views of the Foreign Office or the policy of the Prime Minister. The decision was not difficult for Perth. He had been in Rome before Chamberlain came to power; he had been in close contact with the entire policy of the Foreign Office in the previous period; and, in any case, the mission of Lady Chamberlain showed that

---

[43] Ciano, *L'Europa*• *verso la Catastrofe*, p. 251, where Sir Joseph Ball appears as Chamberlain's liaison man.

[44] Ciano, *1937-1938 Diario*, p. 87, 103.

[45] *German Documents*, series D, I, 223-225.

he did not belong to the group that Chamberlain fully trusted. Naturally, when the course was set on an understanding with Italy, he was pleased to assume this more responsible activity; but there was never any question of his failing to remain strictly within the functions assigned to him by the Foreign Office.

The position of Nevile Henderson was quite different, for his appointment had been intended to indicate and underline the inauguration of Chamberlain's new approach to policy. His predecessor, Sir Eric Phipps, had been a typical representative of the Foreign Office tradition and had aroused criticism and opposition among the Nazi leaders.[46] Although it must be denied that Henderson was appointed at the request of the Nazis, his selection had certainly been influenced by the fact that he was clearly untinged by anti-German or pro-French bias.[47] When he was in London before departing for Berlin, he had had a long talk with Chamberlain, who explained the principles of his new policy.[48] From that time on, Henderson considered himself less as a subordinate of the Foreign Office than as a personal agent of the Prime Minister, whose policy he was charged to carry out. Thus, he remained in constant touch with Sir Horace Wilson and directed appeals to him whenever he disapproved of the instructions which he received from the Foreign Office.[49]

The result was that Henderson was deeply involved in the planning of Britain's policy toward Germany. He felt entitled to give advice, and he was heard. In the various stages of the Czech crisis, he recommended definite policies and played an active role in all the decisive steps. The idea of the Four Power Conference appears first in his reports.[50] Although it is not clear to what extent the idea of Chamberlain's visit to Hitler was Chamberlain's own, or suggested to him by Henderson, he was one of the few who were informed of this plan in its early stages.[51] And Henderson insisted on the absolute necessity of agreeing to the separation of the Sudeten area from Czechoslovakia, once this idea had been launched.[52]

But it is also evident that the fact that Henderson played a policy-making role influenced and colored his views on Germany. He had gone

[46] See Chapter 16 above.

[47] Because he had spent much time in the Near East and the Balkans and hardly any in the great European capitals. See note 28.

[48] Henderson, *Failure*, pp. 6-8.

[49] *British Documents*, 3rd series, II, 647-650.

[50] *Survey of International Affairs*, 1938, II, 427-428.

[51] Feiling, *Chamberlain*, p. 357.

[52] *Survey of International Affairs*, 1938, II, 342.

there with a mission, namely, that of carrying through Chamberlain's policy, and he had a burning desire to win, not merely success, but what might later be described as a triumph. It is characteristic that one of Henderson's first thoughts upon being appointed to Berlin was of "the Latin tag about failure and success which ominously observes that the Tarpeian rock, from which failures were thrown to their doom, is next to the Capitol, where the triumph of success is celebrated."[53] But triumph depended upon finding in Germany a basis for cooperation; and Henderson himself admits that he set out to see the "good side" of Nazi Germany.[54] A critical or objective approach would have made the reasons for his appointment futile; his mission would have been even less than the fulfilment of a routine function and would, indeed, have destroyed the foundations of the Chamberlain policy to which he was fully committed.

IV

There remains a psychological question, namely, the question why Henderson felt he had to play this kind of historical role; why he was not content with the honorable but rather restricted role which a diplomat plays in the twentieth century; why he aimed at being a "great ambassador" in the style of the eighteenth or nineteenth century. It is sometimes said in explanation of Chamberlain's policy that the Prime Minister had a totally insular outlook and that this accounts for the shortcomings of his theory of foreign affairs. However this may be, it seems clear that Henderson had an insular outlook in reverse. He himself says that after he entered the Foreign Service he never spent more than three or four continuous months in England. The result was not that he became alienated from England but, rather, that he became more English than the English. Certainly the Germans saw in him the typical Englishman.[55] In the excitement and turmoil of the Munich Conference, he walked about unperturbed, immaculately dressed, with a red carnation in his buttonhole—always "the man with the flower," as Hitler called him.[56] But there was more to this attitude of studied calm than this. It was an external sign of the extent to which Henderson felt that, in contrast to the restlessness and vulgarity of his era, he had

---

[53] Henderson, *Failure*, p. 3.
[54] *ibid.*, p. viii.
[55] Paul Schmidt, *Statist auf diplomatischer Bühne* (Bonn, 1949), p. 390.
[56] Jacques Davignon, *Berlin 1936-1940* (Paris, Bruxelles, 1951), p. 88 and Filippo Anfuso, *Roma Berlino Salò* (Editore Garzanti, 1950), p. 79.

to represent the attitude of an older and better world.[57] From this perspective, he looked down on foreigners and was little inclined to become excited about special degrees of ruthlessness and cruelty in other countries.

But he felt separated not only from the non-English world; he began to feel out of step with developments in his own country as well. In England too, the world in which Henderson had grown up had begun to disappear.[58] He saw only the negative side of this process and had no understanding of the new forces which were coming into the foreground. The family from which he sprang had risen in the prosperity of the Victorian and Edwardian age, but, in Henderson's lifetime, this progress was halted. The estate which his father had bought, and on which Nevile had grown up, was sold; decline had set in before the family had been firmly established as part of the hereditary ruling group. These circumstances made Henderson something of a snob.[59] Because he was strongly attached to the values of a disappearing order, he felt uprooted in the 1920's, the time of the rise of the Labor party and of internationalism in foreign policy. Unintellectual, and traditional in his thinking, clinging to the values of the past—like many men of a conformist character in times of changing values—he grasped after a faith, an absolute. When he heard of his appointment to Berlin, he felt that God had granted him a special mission; he saw himself making a contribution to the salvation of society; in fulfilling this mission, his life would gain meaning.

For these reasons, it can perhaps be said that Henderson is more than merely a diplomat who failed. He is, rather, typical of the helplessness with which members of a declining ruling class faced the social transformation of the 1920's and 1930's.

V

Henderson's colleague in Rome did not have to face the bitter feelings of failure and futility in which Henderson's life ended.[60] The Earl of

[57] See Henderson's interesting remarks on aristocracy in *German Documents*, series D, II, 769ff.

[58] See, in general, Nevile Henderson, *Water under the Bridges* (London, 1945), a book of more personal reminiscences in contrast to his political memoirs, *Failure of a Mission*.

[59] It is characteristic of Henderson that, in *Water under the Bridges*, he recounts that, when he became nearly involved in a car accident while driving with Princess Olga of Yugoslavia, his "only thought was that, if one had to die, one might die in worse company than that of a Royal Princess." P. 18.

[60] In his last years, Henderson himself said that it was a mistake to have sent him to Nazi Germany, and he doubted his fitness for a diplomatic career.

Perth returned to Britain before the outbreak of the second world war. He could claim to have steered Anglo-Italian relations through a period of stormy weather into calmer waters, and the success of his diplomatic mission seemed confirmed by Italy's remaining neutral when the war broke out. His position in the highest ranks of the British aristocracy led him immediately into new activities. During the war, he performed useful services in the Ministry of Information, and he became deputy leader of the Liberal party in the House of Lords. In the upper chamber, he was an ardent defender of the diplomatic corps against criticisms made of it. Thus, he repudiated the accusation that the British "missions abroad . . . failed on occasion to inform the Government fully of the general trend of political movements in the countries to which they were accredited."[61] He denied sharply that "the members of the diplomatic and consular service can be held responsible for such failures, if failures they have been."[62] He insisted that "they surely must rather be attributed to our foreign policy, and foreign policy is primarily the concern of the Secretary of State for Foreign Affairs, though it ultimately must and should be the responsibility of His Majesty's Government as a whole."[63] There was, of course, a good deal of truth in these statements; but the special emphasis which Lord Perth placed upon them probably indicates some misgivings on his part concerning the role of Britain's representatives in the most important European capitals in the last years before the debacle.

[61] Parliamentary Debates: Lords, 5th series, CXIX, 610.
[62] *ibid.*
[63] *ibid.*

18

The Voice in the Wilderness:
Robert Coulondre

BY FRANKLIN L. FORD AND CARL E. SCHORSKE

IN A WORLD of bewildered and myopic makers of foreign policy in the last prewar years, Robert Coulondre stands out as a determined and clear-headed diplomat. History has given him stature by confirming the wisdom of his political judgment. To this it may be objected that history has as often sanctioned the prejudice of a fool as the judgment of a wise man; but this formulation would do less than justice to a remarkable observer. In Coulondre's political outlook, prejudice unquestionably played its part. During the critical years of his missions to Moscow (1936-1938) and Berlin (1938-1939), this Huguenot diplomat clung with dogged consistency to two simple ideas: first, that Germany must be stopped; second, that only a tight military alliance between the Western Powers and the Soviet Union could stop her. If he drew these conceptions from a well-established French tradition of foreign policy,[1] he tested and confirmed them by careful analysis of the modern international scene. If the course he advocated was not adopted by his government, it was not—insofar as we can judge from the sparse materials available—because of Coulondre's lack of skill in presenting his ideas. He exploited to the utmost the limited sphere of action open to the modern diplomat to make his policies prevail.

I

Coulondre was appointed to Moscow in the autumn of 1936 under the first Popular Front government of Léon Blum. With the government theoretically committed to an anti-Fascist foreign policy, the atmosphere might be thought favorable for the development of Franco-Russian relations. But the Popular Front was already suffering from internal tension

[1] Robert Coulondre, *De Staline à Hitler. Souvenirs de deux ambassades, 1936-1939* (Paris, 1950), p. 22.

and external pressure. The Communists, who had refused to enter the government, supported it in Parliament but kept their hands free for exercising pressure upon it from without. They participated actively in the intense labor struggles of 1936, which evoked fear in the Center and on the Right. In broad sectors of centrist and rightist opinion, the Soviet Union was held responsible both for France's domestic and social tensions and for the "red" civil war in Spain. Republican Spain was widely regarded as a beachhead for a revolutionary invasion of France. During the late summer of 1936, a strong resolution against Soviet intervention in French affairs was adopted by the Radical Socialist party congress. The red scare and the concomitant hostility to the USSR thus reached into the heart of the Popular Front itself.

In this atmosphere Coulondre prepared for his difficult mission. He was surprised to find the Foreign Office singularly lacking in information on Russia. The skimpy files showed him "that relations with the USSR, reestablished in 1924, had been neither very close nor very well cultivated since then, notwithstanding the pacts."[2] The political and governmental leaders whom Coulondre consulted were tinged by the prevailing mood of bitterness toward the USSR. Foreign Minister Yvon Delbos in particular was deeply suspicious of Soviet intentions. He suggested that the Soviets might be trying to drive the French into a preventive war against Germany. And if war should come, he asked, what aid would the Russians give France? By what routes could military assistance be provided? Concerning the value of the Franco-Soviet Mutual Assistance Pact of 1935, Delbos manifested the greatest skepticism. The Russians, he felt, were merely using it as a cover for their revolutionary propaganda in France and out. If this should continue, French public opinion "would force the hand of the government" into a thoroughly negative attitude toward the USSR. The fate of the Franco-Soviet agreement, he felt, "lies much more in their hands than in ours."[3] Thus the Foreign Minister, along with most of the leading politicians with whom Coulondre spoke, viewed Franco-Soviet relations primarily in terms of French domestic struggles rather than in terms of the European security problem. Only Blum, Reynaud, and Herriot assigned real importance to the strengthening of ties with the USSR.[4]

Whatever the prevailing sentiment in Paris, Coulondre was convinced that his primary objective must be the achievement of a tight military-political association between France and the Soviet Union to contain German aggression. If the attempt should fail, he felt, the only alterna-

[2] *ibid.*, p. 12.   [3] *ibid.*, p. 13.   [4] *ibid.*, pp. 14, 16-18.

tive would be a victory for those who sought the security of France on the dangerous road of collaboration with Germany.[5] What could he, a mere diplomat, do to create a more receptive attitude in his own government for a Soviet alliance? As he saw it from Paris, his mission was to make the Soviet government understand that it must cease its intervention in French affairs, that it must, in effect, choose between the promotion of French Communism and the protection of its vital security interests through a military alliance with France. Surely Coulondre's perspective was somewhat narrow. His unspoken assumption was that the French Right and Center would be adequately anti-German if only the Soviet Union would call off its Communist dogs. Was not social conflict in France too deep-rooted to be suppressed by the Soviet Union, even if the Soviets had had the will fully to curb their French following? There was something unreal about Coulondre's attempt to create the domestic basis for a Franco-Soviet military accord by diplomatic means. But the attitudes prevailing in official circles were those with which the ambassador had to work, and his only means were diplomatic. The alternative to the course he set for himself would have been inactive resignation.

In his initial interview with Foreign Commissar Litvinov, Coulondre ignored the customary diplomatic formalities to lay his cards directly on the table: "I have come here without prejudice for or against the Russia of the Soviets. I am, however, a convinced partisan of the assistance pact because I believe it to be one of the elements necessary to safeguarding the peace to which both nations are equally attached. . . . Well then, I come to tell you [that], if things continue as they're now going, there will soon be no more assistance pact. French public opinion is sick and tired of Comintern meddling in the domestic affairs of France —meddling which, we know . . . is inspired if not directly operated by the Soviet Government itself. . . ." Soviet interference, Coulondre continued, threatened not only to ruin the Popular Front, but also to swallow up the pact itself. "Either it shall cease, or the pact will become . . . a dead letter."[6]

Litvinov assured the ambassador that he would repeat previous orders to the Soviet embassy in Paris to stay out of French affairs. With respect to the Comintern, he could only make the customary specious denial that it had anything to do with Soviet foreign policy.[7]

The Soviet view of the problem Coulondre was to hear from President Kalinin. In accepting Coulondre's credentials, the President aired the Soviet grievances against France quite as bluntly as Coulondre had

---

[5] *ibid.*, pp. 22-23.   [6] *ibid.*, pp. 31-32.   [7] *ibid.*, p. 33.

spoken his to Litvinov. If intentions must be judged by acts, and the value of an agreement by its results, said Kalinin, then the French could not set much store by the assistance pact. Soviet efforts to acquire military supplies in France had met with resistance everywhere. Germany had offered to deliver the supplies on credit—even arms, Litvinov added. The Soviets had rejected these offers. But France had signed a pact of assistance with the USSR; it must also apply it.[8]

Coulondre had been aware of the reluctance of the French military authorities to supply the Soviets with equipment, but not of the depth of Soviet resentment against the treatment they had received. Kalinin's counteroffensive convinced the ambassador that his effort to win Soviet cooperation in the matter of noninterference in French domestic affairs must be paralleled by an attempt to make his government see the necessity of acquiescing in Soviet requests for military supplies. If the pact of 1935 were to be transformed into an effective military alliance, the deadlock would have to be broken more or less simultaneously in both capitals. The difficulty was that neither side was prepared to make the initial concession which might encourage a more accommodating attitude in the other.

How to extract a vital concession from either Moscow or Paris?—that was the problem which dominated Coulondre's diplomatic activity for almost two years. In the absence of any French documentary publications for the pre-Munich period, we can discover no more than the bare outlines of Coulondre's activity. We shall merely touch here on a few examples which illustrate the ambassador's situation and the methods by which he sought to break out of it.

On the Russian side, Coulondre quickly became convinced that Litvinov and his Foreign Commissariat had no power to produce any changes in Comintern behavior. Somehow, he must get the ear of Stalin. With neither instructions from his government nor any *quid pro quo* to offer the Communist dictator, the ambassador could not make a direct approach. He therefore utilized a GPU agent—one of the many who, with one or another official function, infested the diplomatic colony—to carry to Stalin his message on the Comintern. Stalin asked Coulondre, through the same intermediary, what he would propose. Coulondre replied that the Comintern should be, if not dissolved, then transferred out of Russia. Stalin answered that he could not accept this suggestion for the present. He made the unusual admission that the Comintern was a factor in the USSR's defense system; in view of the German situation,

[8] *ibid.*, pp. 33-34.

he could not let the control of it out of his hands. He stated that all he wanted of France was to be "strong and resolute in the face of Germany." As for internal affairs, Stalin cited the case of Turkey, with which he enjoyed excellent relations although its government was scarcely "soft" [*tendre*] with the Communists.[9]

Stalin's answer, though frank, was on the whole negative. Coulondre concluded from it that any French government, however rightist, would be an acceptable partner to the USSR if, as Litvinov said a few weeks later, it followed the "patriotic" policy of Poincaré and Clemenceau.[10] But the Comintern and the French Communists remained; as long as they did, and as long as they opposed any deviation by France from Soviet foreign policy, the French government would continue distrustful if not hostile. On the Soviet side, Stalin could not abandon the Comintern in the face of the Anti-Comintern Pact, concluded on November 17, 1936, only a few days after the delivery of his message to the French ambassador. Nor would he, as Coulondre realized, surrender his foothold in French domestic politics if it should ever become his policy deliberately to weaken France as a factor in European international life.

Having early struck bedrock in his efforts to effect a change in Soviet policy, Coulondre devoted most of his energy during the remainder of his mission to influencing his own government's attitude. In this shift in focus, he shared in a general tendency of diplomats who represented democratic powers in totalitarian countries. The monolithic structure of totalitarian government left a diplomat little room for maneuver. His only hope in influencing the omnipotent leadership abroad was through some change in his own government's policy. The divided counsels in the governing strata of the democracies strengthened the temptation for an ambassador who was frustrated in his host country to influence policy at home rather than merely to follow instructions.[11] In Coulondre's case, this natural penchant was reenforced by a conviction of the overriding importance of cementing the Franco-Russian alliance. The more conscious Coulondre became of the depth of Stalin's concern over the German menace and his fear of any internal challenge to his power, the more urgently he pressed the need for meeting Russia half way. Like his German colleague Schulenburg, Coulondre analyzed the purges in the context of the vast Soviet industrialization and militarization program. Although the internal upheaval might weaken Russia in the short run,

[9] *ibid.*, pp. 39-40.　　　　　[10] *ibid.*, pp. 40-41.
[11] See above, Chapters 14 and 17, for instances in which ambassadors succumbed to this temptation.

it was nevertheless, in Coulondre's eyes, "a crisis of growth." Not, of course, growth toward democracy, but toward counterrevolutionary absolutism, nationalism, and—above all—industrial and military might.

Where the Western observers on the whole tended to interpret the era of the purges as reducing the importance of the Soviet Union in world affairs, Coulondre drew the opposite conclusion. Where many Westerners rejoiced in the increasing isolationism of Russia, Coulondre was frightened by it. He did not believe that the USSR would withdraw from Europe in fact, even if it could not find a *modus vivendi* with the democracies. The essential question for France to ask itself about Russia, Coulondre insisted, was not "Will Russia be with us or not?" but "With whom will Russia go?"[12] France was the first string to the Soviet bow, but if France should prove recalcitrant, the Soviets would not hesitate to try a German string.

Since 1935, the Russians had repeatedly made overtures for closer military ties with France, but had met, in the words of Blum, with responses of "a generally dilatory character."[13] In February 1937, Blum requested and received of Soviet ambassador Potemkin a Russian general staff estimate of the aid which the USSR could render in the event of a German attack on France or Czechoslovakia. General Gamelin, according to his own account, was not asked by Daladier, Minister of War, to comment on this memorandum until April 9, 1937.[14] In the Soviet memorandum, the difficult question of transit for Soviet troops through Poland and Rumania was already adumbrated. The French general staff commented that "the state of the conversations which France has had with these states does not permit an answer to the question." But the staff scarcely encouraged the search for an answer when it stated that, in any case, Poland and Rumania would need their railways for their own troop concentrations and could not spare them to transport Russian soldiers.[15]

Coulondre was in Paris during these April discussions, but there is no evidence that he was given an active part in them.[16] Although a program for a "military pre-accord" was drafted on April 15, it never reached the negotiating stage. General Gamelin's view that, because of the Polish-

---

[12] Coulondre, *De Staline à Hitler*, p. 44. For his views on the changes in the USSR during the era of the purges, cf. *ibid.*, pp. 43-45, 58-59, 72-125.

[13] *Commission d'Enquête parlementaire, Les événements survenus en France de 1933 à 1945, Témoignages et documents*, I, 90, 128-129, 272-273; Paul Reynaud, *La France a sauvé l'Europe* (Paris, 1947), I, 115-117.

[14] Général Gamelin, *Servir* (Paris, 1946), II, 285-286.

[15] *ibid.*, II, 287.

[16] Coulondre, *De Staline à Hitler*, p. 48.

Rumanian problem, a precise military accord could only lead France up a blind alley presumably prevailed.[17] Another attempt to inaugurate Franco-Russian staff conversations, made by Litvinov on a visit to Paris in May 1937, likewise came to nothing.[18] During the succeeding nine months, Coulondre was condemned to the role of an impotent observer while the ice gathered on the skeletal structure of the Franco-Russian alliance.

The rape of Austria and the threat posed by this event to the existence of Czechoslovakia infused a new vitality into the issue of France's relations with the Soviet Union. From March until May 1938, the international situation and the concomitant fluidity in French policy gave Coulondre both room for maneuver and grounds for hope that his project of an Anglo-French-Russian security bloc might be realized.

When Czechoslovakia became the nerve center of the European crisis, Coulondre advised his government that the Russian factor had now acquired its maximum importance for preserving the peace or, if war should come, for winning an armed conflict. Poland offered no comparable platform for joint resistance. If Hitler were to attack Poland, the Soviet Union could hardly be counted on as a reliable ally of France. The Czechs, unlike the Poles, were firmly committed to the European *status quo*. Above all, Czechoslovakia was "the only country on which the action of the three great peaceful Powers could be conjoined."[19]

We have no explicit evidence on the reception given to this advice in Paris, but the governmental atmosphere was certainly favorable to it in mid-March 1938. With the formation of the second Blum cabinet during the Austrian crisis, the weary and indecisive Yvon Delbos was replaced as Foreign Minister by Joseph Paul-Boncour. The first public diplomatic act of the new government was a demonstrative reception of the Czech ambassador by Blum and Paul-Boncour to assure him that "France would uphold its obligations to Czechoslovakia . . . effectively, promptly and completely."[20] To be sure, a meeting of the Permanent Committee of National Defense, summoned to consider what France might do militarily in the event of aggression against Czechoslovakia, revealed the usual pessimism on the part of the military authorities concerning French, Czech, and Soviet powers of resistance.[21] But the very bleakness of the

[17] Gamelin, *Servir*, II, 287.
[18] Vice Commissar Potemkin told Coulondre that the French ministries of air and navy favored the discussions, but that the ministry of war gave no answer. Coulondre, *De Staline à Hitler*, p. 127.
[19] *ibid.*, pp. 137-138.
[20] *British Documents*, 3rd series, I, 53-54; *German Documents*, series D, II, 217.
[21] Gamelin, *Servir*, II, 322-328.

military outlook confirmed Blum and Paul-Boncour in the conviction that the construction of an international resistance front was the more urgent. The Foreign Minister indicated unequivocally to the German ambassador that aggression against Czechoslovakia "meant war" with France.[22] He tried without success to induce the British government to take a similarly strong stand.[23] The British Foreign Secretary, Lord Halifax, replied that the British would honor their commitments to France under Locarno, but could not "see their way clear to adding to them."[24] Where Paul-Boncour urged a firm, overt stand against the Germans, Halifax counseled pressure on the Czechs. Halifax indicated, however, that Great Britain would not really let France succumb to Germany, and Paul-Boncour was prepared to take the risk that, if France took a firm position, Britain could ultimately be brought into line.[25] Meanwhile, however, it would be necessary for France to take the lead in Eastern Europe to reconstruct its disintegrating security system.

At the end of March, Paul-Boncour summoned the French ambassadors to the principal Central and Eastern European capitals for a conference to determine a consistent policy for the defense of Czechoslovakia. Very little is known about the course or outcome of this conference (April 5), except that there was sharp protest against the previous policy of drift and of shallow reliance on Geneva, and a general determination to place France's policy in Eastern Europe on a more realistic basis by applying all possible pressure to eliminate the conflicts of policy among France's eastern allies.[26] The Quai d'Orsay tried to enlist British support for this program.[27] The German ambassador in Paris described the projected French campaign in the Eastern European capitals as "a tendency which merits our most serious attention."[28]

Coulondre's role in the formulation of the new policy is impossible to determine from the sparse and contradictory evidence available.[29] On his

[22] *German Documents*, series D, II, 214.

[23] *British Documents*, 3rd series, I, 50-54.

[24] *ibid.*, I, 84.

[25] *ibid.*, I, 85; J. Paul-Boncour, *Entre deux guerres. Souvenirs sur la III République* (Paris, 1946), III, 83-84, 97-98.

[26] Léon Noël, *L'agression allemande contre la Pologne* (Paris, 1946), pp. 196-197; Paul-Boncour, *Entre deux guerres*, III, 93-94, 98-99; *German Documents*, series D, II, 215-217.

[27] In the aide-mémoire to London (April 9), the help of Britain was solicited in securing the cooperation of "the other countries of Central Europe and Danubian Europe" —a formulation which excluded the USSR. *British Documents*, 3rd series, I, 146.

[28] *German Documents*, series D, II, 222.

[29] Six weeks after the ambassadors' conference, Coulondre told the British chargé d'affaires in Moscow that "when he was in Paris last M. Blum was in power, and that he had felt constrained on that occasion to tender very moderate and guarded advice, of a

return to Moscow, however, he set to work to mobilize diplomatic opinion in support of an eastern containment front. Coulondre and his Czech colleague simultaneously advised their governments to launch an action in Bucharest and Moscow to solve the troop transit question. The Rumanians were to receive assurances concerning their continued possession of Bessarabia, which the Soviet Union had never recognized, in exchange for transit rights for Soviet troops to Czechoslovakia.[30] The French and Czech military attachés spoke to their British opposite as if Soviet intervention on behalf of Czechoslovakia were a foregone conclusion—a view which the British embassy hardly shared. On April 18 Colonel Pallace, the French attaché, told his British colleague that France would have "to speak very strongly to Poland and force her back to the side of France. For this purpose it was essential that M. Beck should be removed. Poland must be forced to allow Soviet troops to pass through their country."[31] Coulondre felt, "in that vague and intuitive manner in which one senses such things in Soviet Russia," that the new determination of his own government was paralleled by an increasingly earnest attitude on the part of the USSR. He was struck with Litvinov's change in manner, from sarcasm and skepticism to "the seriousness and moderation of one who has a sense of new responsibilities, who knew that the Kremlin would play its part in a European conflict."[32] A more tangible factor which led Coulondre to the same conclusion was the changed situation in the Far East. With stiffening Chinese resistance and Japanese military energies deflected into Central China, the Soviet government was relieved of anxiety in that part of the world, and could make "a correspondingly greater effort in the West."[33] Coulondre felt that the moment was extremely favorable for concluding the long-postponed military convention between France and the USSR. In early May, when he had just resolved on his own initiative to go to Paris to press his case, Coulondre was sum-

---

distinctly pessimistic nature moreover, in regard to Soviet affairs and the chances of the Soviet government taking a more positive part in counteracting German machinations . . ." (*British Documents*, 3rd series, I, 304). Coulondre states in his memoirs that, on his visit to Paris, he had stressed that the initiative and interest shown by the Soviets in the Czech question was a sign that they meant business; he had advised his government that it was "more useful and more urgent than ever to open military conversations with the USSR." (*De Staline à Hitler*, p. 135.) Coulondre's memoirs seem unreliable for this period: he states that he reported the above to Yvon Delbos, but the Foreign Minister at the time was Paul-Boncour, whom he does not mention.

[30] Coulondre, *De Staline à Hitler*, p. 137.
[31] *British Documents*, 3rd series, I, 172-173.
[32] *ibid.*, I, 304; Coulondre, *De Staline à Hitler*, p. 304.
[33] *British Documents*, 3rd series, I, 305. Cf. also Coulondre, *De Staline à Hitler*, pp. 139-140.

moned home by the new Foreign Minister in the Daladier cabinet, Georges Bonnet.

On the day of his departure from Moscow (May 16, 1938), Coulondre took an unusual step. He laid before the British chargé d'affaires and his military attaché an evaluation of the Soviet political and military position.[34] Coulondre was then under the erroneous impression that the British government had notified Berlin that it would regard a German attack upon Czechoslovakia as a *quasi casus belli,* and undoubtedly wished to associate his British colleague in his attempt to strengthen Soviet participation in safeguarding Czech independence.[35] His effort was a total failure. The British chargé, Mr. Vereker, expressed himself as "slightly mystified as to the motives underlying M. Coulondre's invitation, for I have always understood that he is usually reserved and uncommunicative." Vereker concluded that Coulondre's main object was "simply to clear his mind and be able to go to Paris fortified by an independent and unbiased third party opinion."[36] Vereker rejected out of hand Coulondre's contention that "one could in fact place some reliance on the Soviet government both in a political and military sense at this juncture." There was no reason for the Frenchman to feel "more optimistic of possible Russian intervention on the side of Czechoslovakia at the present moment than he had been heretofore."[37] The British chargé gave his "independent and unbiased" opinion "that the Russians were Asiatics . . . and that with the present Byzantine regime in the Kremlin anything might happen." But "there was no good hoping vainly that the Russians might be of some value as a counterpoise to the Germans when the balance of probability lay on the other side."[38] The conversation provided an accurate foretaste of the British attitude which was to play so large a role in the failure of Coulondre's Moscow mission.

During the interval between Coulondre's two visits to Paris in the spring of 1938, France had suffered another cabinet overturn. Rightist criticism of Paul-Boncour's energetic foreign policy had played no small part in the collapse of the short-lived Blum government, and the new premier, Edouard Daladier, decided to jettison Paul-Boncour in favor of the more flexible Georges Bonnet.[39]

The foreign policy which took shape under the new government deserves brief examination here, since it was to provide the background for Coulondre's activity. With Paul-Boncour out of the way,[40] Lord Halifax

[34] *British Documents,* 3rd series, I, 301-307. [35] *ibid.,* 301.
[36] *ibid.,* 307.   [37] *ibid.,* 305.   [38] *ibid.,* 307.
[39] Paul-Boncour, *Entre deux guerres,* III, 93-94, 100-101.
[40] The British Foreign Office opinion of Paul-Boncour was perhaps characteristically

returned to the assault to dissuade the French from their drastic stand on Czechoslovakia, and warned the French government against persisting in too optimistic an interpretation of Chamberlain's hint that Great Britain might go beyond her legal commitments in defense of France.[41] In the Anglo-French conversations at the end of April, the French, unable to extract a commitment from Great Britain on Czechoslovakia, began the process of surrender to the British lead by agreeing to put pressure on the Czechs to make the "maximum concessions."[42]

Bonnet was not yet, however, prepared to shift the focus of French diplomatic activity from the reconstruction of a containment front to the mitigation of Czech-German tension *à l'anglaise*. In early May, he held conversations with Litvinov in Geneva. Litvinov again seems to have suggested staff talks in order to determine with precision the action to be taken by the allies in the event of hostilities.[43] Bonnet also sounded out Petresco-Comnène, the Rumanian Foreign Minister, on the ticklish issue of troop transit, although he did not go beyond mere inquiry to the exercise of anything like pressure on the Rumanians.[44] Bonnet later said that his policy at this date was first "to bring about a rapprochement between England and the USSR, then to conclude a military accord with Russia, finally to settle the question of passage for Russian troops through the [eastern] border countries."[45] The British documents supply no evidence that Bonnet pursued the first of these aims. His policy in May 1938 might better be described as according primacy to accommodation with Britain while exploring possibilities for a firmer foothold in Eastern Europe. Reduced to its simplest terms, French policy was teetering on the brink between appeasement and resistance.

On May 20, Ambassador Coulondre was received by his Foreign Minister. Bonnet detailed his conversation with Litvinov and expressed his readiness to inaugurate staff conversations with the Russians to deter-

---

expressed by Alexander Cadogan to Czech ambassador Masaryk (April 4, 1938): "Paul-Boncour was not a Foreign Minister who at so serious a moment could be a worthy partner in a discussion of the European crisis." *Documents and Materials*, p. 103.

[41] *British Documents*, 3rd series, I, 141.

[42] Royal Institute of International Affairs, *Survey of International Affairs, 1938* (London, New York, Toronto, 1951), II, 101-108.

[43] *ibid.*, II, 132; Coulondre, *De Staline à Hitler*, p. 142. Bonnet makes no mention of Litvinov's request for staff talks; cf. Georges Bonnet, *Défense de la paix* (Paris, 1946), I, 125.

[44] Bonnet, *Défense*, I, 126-127; cf. N. Petresco-Comnène, *Preludi del grande dramma* (Rome, 1947), pp. 37-40, where the Rumanian answer, though hardly encouraging, appears less absolutely negative than in Bonnet's account.

[45] Bonnet, *Défense*, I, 123.

mine the scale and modalities of Soviet aid. Coulondre was instructed to draft plans for the conduct of negotiations in Moscow.[46]

During the next two days, while Coulondre was preparing his memorandum, the Czech issue erupted into a major crisis. It was thought in the Allied capitals that Germany was about to invade Czechoslovakia. On May 21, Bonnet reaffirmed in a press conference that France would stick by Czechoslovakia.[47] Halifax instructed the British ambassador in Paris to dispel at once any illusions on the part of Bonnet: "If . . . the French Government were to assume that His Majesty's Government would at once take joint military action with them to preserve Czechoslovakia against German aggression, it is only fair to warn them that our statements do not warrant any such assumption."[48]

The military situation was such that the conquest of Czechoslovakia could not be prevented, "even," Halifax added pointedly for Paris, "with such assistance as might be expected from Russia."[49] By the night of May 22, after hearing Halifax's message, Bonnet was a chastened man. He told the British ambassador that "he would not dream of taking action . . . without ample consultation" with Great Britain. If Czechoslovakia were unreasonable, France "might well declare . . . herself released from her bond."[50] Daladier, on the same evening, was weeping on the shoulders of the German ambassador, begging the Reich not to compel him to go to war for an alliance which he "had not made . . . and was certainly not happy about. . . ."[51]

On the next morning, Coulondre returned to present to the Foreign Minister his draft plan for Franco-Russian-Czech military talks. Coulondre was astonished at Bonnet's change in attitude. Bonnet was hesitant; he feared, he told his ambassador, that the prospect of Soviet military support might "incite certain French elements to appear bellicose." "What had happened since May 20?" Coulondre asks in all innocence in his memoirs.[52] Despite his hesitation, Bonnet authorized Coulondre to submit his plan to Daladier. The Premier too was cautious, urging that the negotiations be conducted in the greatest secrecy in order to avoid any reaction on Hitler's part. Daladier felt that his doubts about the value of the Soviet army must be tested in staff talks, and gave his consent. Again Coulondre saw Bonnet, who expressed further doubts: the military unpreparedness of Britain and France, the attitude of Poland, the ambiguity of Soviet policy. Coulondre brought forth his battery

[46] Coulondre, *De Staline à Hitler*, p. 142.   [47] *British Documents*, 3rd series, I, 340.
[48] *ibid.*, I, 345-346   [49] *ibid.*, I, 346.   [50] *ibid.*, I, 357.
[51] *German Documents*, series D, II, 327.   [52] Coulondre, *De Staline à Hitler*, p. 143.

of arguments once more: Soviet policy was least ambiguous in Czechoslovakia; France could not maintain indefinitely two contradictory alliances in the east, and must choose the USSR over Poland as the Power
constituting the greater bar to Hitler's progress, etc. Bonnet agreed and
finally approved the opening of military talks.[53]

Coulondre departed for Moscow with a real sense of achievement.
It appeared as if his hopes were at last on the way to realization. He was
soon disabused. During the last days of May, Bonnet tried in vain to
persuade Poland to declare her support for Czechoslovakia in the event
of a conflict. When Litvinov asked what France would do if Poland attacked Czechoslovakia and Russia in turn attacked Poland, Coulondre
answered that France would stand by Czechoslovakia; Bonnet told the
Soviet chargé in answer to the same question posed in Paris that the
matter would have to be studied.[54] Understandably enough, Bonnet
found it difficult to give up the Polish alliance in favor of a doubtful
partnership with the USSR. But his equivocation did not help the cause
of Czechoslovakia. With respect to that hapless power, French policy
turned, after the May crisis, into a mere auxiliary of British policy. By
May 29, Bonnet, under British exhortations, was already applying that
pressure upon the Czechs which was to continue in a straight line until
the "resolution" of the Czech question at Munich.[55] The corollary to that
policy, in fact if not out of necessity, was the decision to stay with the
Polish alliance rather than to strengthen the ties with Russia. Coulondre
was not informed by Bonnet of these decisions. It dawned on him only
slowly that the plans approved, however hesitantly, on May 23 were
being abandoned. On July 1 he learned the full story—not from his own
government, but from a dispatch of the Czech ambassador in Paris which
his Moscow colleague Fierlinger gave him to read: "The French Government will not follow up Franco-Soviet military conversations for the
present, in order not to offend the susceptibilities of the English conservatives."[56] An oversimplified analysis, but not without truth.

With French policy veering into other channels, Coulondre could do
nothing but sit out the dog days in Moscow in frustrating inactivity. He
smarted at French policy, which, rather unjustly, he held primarily
responsible for reducing history in the summer of 1938 to "a kind of
tragic tournament between two men, one of whom carried an olive
branch, the other a knife."[57]

---

[53] *ibid.*, pp. 145-146. Bonnet's *Défense* contains no reference to the Coulondre visit or
the contemplated action.

[54] Coulondre, *De Staline à Hitler*, pp. 152-153.   [55] Bonnet, *Défense*, I, 155ff.

[56] Coulondre, *De Staline à Hitler*, p. 153.   [57] *ibid.*, p. 154.

When the Czech crisis entered its final phase at the end of August, there was again a brief flurry of activity in Paris and Moscow. On both sides, however, suspicions ran too deep to be allayed by anything short of a dramatic gesture which neither side wished to take for fear of offending the Germans.

On October 4, it was Coulondre's unpleasant duty to inform the Vice-Commissar for Foreign Affairs officially of the content of the Munich agreement. Potemkin received the ambassador coldly and let him speak his piece. " 'I simply wish to state,' he said to me [Coulondre] when I had finished, 'that the Western Powers have deliberately kept the USSR out of the negotiations.' The silence weighed on us. Then his emotions gained the upper hand and, though a Slav and a diplomat, he spoke his thoughts freely to me: 'My poor fellow, what have you done? For us, I see no other consequence but a fourth partition of Poland.' "[58]

Potemkin's words provided Coulondre with the text for a brilliant dispatch in which he analyzed the consequences of Munich for Soviet policy. His analysis was not unlike that of his German colleague Schulenburg,[59] stressing the fact that the Soviet Union had now lost all confidence in collective security and would have to rethink her policy. As a Frenchman, however, Coulondre could go further than Schulenburg in pointing out that Russia, rejected by the West, and uninhibited by any ideological sentiments, had no choice but to try "to return to the policy of understanding with Germany which she had abandoned in 1931."[60] Less than two weeks after this last Cassandra cry, Coulondre received the news of his transfer to Berlin.

Coulondre's mission to Moscow could only be reckoned a political failure. The brief promise of the spring of 1938 was cut off by the May crisis and the shift in French policy which followed it; and the ground once lost could never be regained. Was Coulondre overoptimistic concerning the possibility of cooperation between Russia and the West? Did he rely too much on Litvinov, failing to realize the strength of other tendencies in Moscow or to see that Litvinov's position was already weakened by the failure of collective security in Abyssinia and Spain? Did he underestimate the costs of France's taking the diplomatic initiative out of British hands? Did he underrate the risks of placing too much pressure on Poland and Rumania, perilously receptive as they were to German blandishments and threats? There is no evidence to justify an affirmative answer to these questions. As far as we know, Coulondre never advocated rash or foolish commitments to Moscow. Even though

---

[58] Coulondre, *De Staline à Hitler*, p. 165.   [59] See above, Chapter 15, § v.
[60] Coulondre, *De Staline à Hitler*, pp. 165-168.

a firm alliance with the Soviet Union was his primary objective, his diplomatic methods were sober and cautious. He worked to keep the lines open between Paris and Moscow, and urged upon his government nothing more than to explore possibilities which could have been pursued if profitable but closed off again if too costly. Even such modest diplomacy toward Russia was too much for the timorous and prejudiced framers of French foreign policy after May 1938. Whatever one may think of Coulondre's positive aims, one must grant that he had the rare political virtue of asking the right question, which he permitted no sentimental considerations to obscure: "Not, 'Will Russia be with us?' but, 'With whom will Russia go?'" His superiors paid no attention to the question. As a result, Coulondre in Berlin was to have the bitter experience of seeing it answered at the expense of his country's vital interest.

II

Coulondre arrived in the German capital to take up his new duties on November 19, 1938. Even if there were not major gaps in the sources, it would be pointless here to recount all the details of what was in many respects no more than an epilogue to the ambassador's period in Moscow. What can, and should, be done with the materials we do have is to organize them around certain critical points between the autumn of 1938 and the outbreak of the second world war. The resulting discussion will call attention to some aspects of Coulondre's record as an observer and spokesman of France within the Reich, but it will place greater emphasis on his role as proponent of a definite line of action—a line which he would presumably have advocated regardless of his particular assignment. For dramatic as were the events of his nine and a half months in Germany, his personal importance consists much more in the continuation of his arguments with Paris over the general European power situation than in his specific functions as envoy to Hitler's government. This second ambassadorship was a continuation of the first, in that Coulondre brought to it, and never abandoned, the basic convictions he had formed while in Russia. Its special character arises from the fact that he had, while in Berlin, to restate those convictions in a constantly changing context of diplomatic developments.

For obvious reasons, Coulondre felt the lurch of suddenly shifted gears as he began his new mission. From 1920 until 1936, at the Quai d'Orsay, he had followed German affairs closely; and in 1931, he had been along on Laval's state visit to Berlin.[61] Between those experiences

[61] André François-Poncet, *Souvenirs d'une ambassade à Berlin* (Paris, 1946), p. 26.

and the autumn of 1938, however, had intervened the two years in Russia. "After having gone to Moscow to work for an entente against Hitler, I was now to go to Berlin to work for an entente with Hitler."[62] Despite his lack of enthusiasm for the latter prospect, he insists that he loved his craft too well to be completely pessimistic or cynical. "M. Coulondre told me," recorded Ribbentrop of their initial interview, "that, on taking up his appointment, he intended to do all he could to improve Franco-German relations. . . . He personally was not biased in any particular direction and was open to all suggestions."[63] The new ambassador's first statement to his own staff, as he recalls it, included the following: "Munich is our point of departure. Each of us is free to judge as he sees it the policy which led there. The fact remains that, to safeguard the peace, the Western Powers went there. The question, the only question now before us, is whether peace can actually be found by this route."[64]

The possibility of a negative answer is clearly left open, as it had to be, given Coulondre's sentiments. His whole position while in the Soviet Union had been predicated on distrust of any deal with the Nazis, and he considered it quite possible that efforts at conciliation would only increase Hitler's appetite. "Policies of weakness, like others," he said later, "entail risks, generally the most dangerous."[65] Nevertheless, immersed as he was in day-to-day negotiations, he could not claim that Olympian perspective which would have justified his condemning appeasement without giving it a chance. Hence, throughout his dispatches of those winter months of 1938-1939 run conflicting tendencies. An official policy which he feared had to be tried. A stiffer line which he favored could not as yet be espoused save by indirection.

This opening period began when Coulondre presented his credentials to Hitler on November 22, 1938. The ambassador expressed his hope, based on a rereading of the Fuehrer's speeches, that France and Germany might reach a solid understanding. He alluded specifically to François-Poncet, whom Hitler had mentioned in flattering terms, and stressed the desirability of an early manifestation of mutual good will, as foreshadowed in the former ambassador's farewell visit to Berchtesgaden the previous month. Hitler showed himself receptive, citing his exserviceman's horror of war and his belief that no change in the Franco-German boundary would justify the sacrifices it would entail.[66] Coulondre had

---

[62] Coulondre, *De Staline à Hitler*, p. 189. [63] *German Documents*, series D, IV, 456.
[64] Coulondre, *De Staline à Hitler*, p. 204. [65] *ibid.*, p. 195.
[66] *French Yellow Book*, pp. 29-31.

left Paris already in possession of a draft friendship pact which had been handed him at the Ministry of Foreign Affairs, and three days after his talk with the Fuehrer he was notified by Bonnet that this text had been approved by the Germans.[67] The Ribbentrop-Bonnet declaration, solemnly repudiating all cause for hostility between France and the Reich, was signed at Paris on December 6.[68]

Thus far Coulondre had figured as little more than an agent carrying out functions bequeathed by his predecessor. He appears as an observer in his own right only with the dispatch which he sent on December 15 as a summary of first impressions in Berlin. The German people, he stated, were genuinely opposed to war and relieved by the rapprochement with France. He added, however, that the Nazi party's aim was not general peace but rather enough security in the West to permit eastward expansion toward the Ukraine. "The integration of *Deutschtum* into the Reich has been carried out more or less completely," he pointed out. "Now the hour of *Lebensraum* has come."[69]

This apprehensive tone was intensified after Coulondre spent an hour with Ribbentrop early in February. In the course of a long monologue, the dependably arrogant Foreign Minister described German foreign policy as aimed at combatting Bolshevism and eventually regaining the lost colonies. In addition, however, he blustered about the Allies' alleged refusal to recognize vital German interests in terms which seemed to have little to do with either the Soviet Union or Southwest Africa. Concerning the Reich's eastern neighbors, Coulondre could only reply that "France had no intention of giving up her friendships or her interests in any part of the continent."[70]

What put the French ambassador in a particularly weak position at this time was the remarkable maneuver which his own government had just embarked upon, in an effort to divert Italy's territorial demands. This, it will be remembered, was the winter when shouts of "Tunisia! Corsica! Nice!" had erupted in the Italian Chamber of Deputies. While François-Poncet in Rome was seeking to convert Mussolini to four-Power friendship, Coulondre in Berlin had obeyed instructions to advise the Wilhelmstrasse of French concern over the Duce's impatience and the threatening presence of Italian troops in Spain.[71] Meanwhile, Paul Baudouin, President of the Banque de l'Indochine, had been sent to Rome and on February 2 had confidentially offered Ciano concessions in

[67] *ibid.*, p. 32.   [68] *ibid.*, p. 35.
[69] *ibid.*, pp. 41-45.   [70] *ibid.*, pp. 57-59.
[71] *German Documents*, series D, IV, 490-491, 492.

Tunis and Djibuti and the directorate of the Suez Canal.[72] Ribbentrop, who learned of these overtures through Ambassador Mackensen, immediately saw to it that they were made public; but Coulondre, operating in the dark so far as the Quai d'Orsay's gambit was concerned, obediently issued a formal denial to the press, on orders from Bonnet. Simultaneously, Count Fernand de Brinon arrived in Germany, introduced himself to the ambassador as merely a tourist, then went straight to Ribbentrop as a secret spokesman for the French government and "in a discreet manner suggested mediation between France and Italy."[73] The German Foreign Minister was certainly not interested in seeing France freed of Italian pressure, but in the process of defeating the move he had the malicious pleasure of asking Coulondre how he had brought himself to deny the true reports concerning Baudouin. The ambassador was understandably furious over Bonnet's deviousness and went to Paris on February 10 demanding hotly that in the future he be kept as well informed as the German Foreign Office appeared to be.[74]

If the Baudouin-Brinon incident underscored the difficulty and ambiguity of Coulondre's position in Berlin, the extinction of rump Czechoslovakia changed his whole definition of his task. As early as the preceding December he had pressed the Wilhelmstrasse for the joint guarantee envisaged at Munich for the revised Czech boundaries,[75] and in the *French Yellow Book* one may trace his futile efforts along this line during the ensuing weeks. When, in March, the Reich swallowed Bohemia and Moravia, Coulondre advised Paris that "the Munich agreements no longer exist," and that, although Hitler was still oriented eastward, the Allies should not overlook the danger that he might attack in the West at some future date if his lead in armaments seemed to be shrinking. France must rebuild her strength "to the limit of our capacity," but with as little publicity as possible.[76] To Weizsäcker, who became appropriately indignant, Coulondre spoke on his own initiative of "the contravention of the Munich Agreement, in contradiction to the relationship of confidence which he had expected to find here and to the aims

[72] Galeazzo Ciano, *Diario* (Milano, 1948), I, 32-33, 35, 61.

[73] *German Documents*, series D, IV, 495.

[74] The final editors of the *French Yellow Book* discreetly omitted any reference to this episode, and Coulondre himself treats it only briefly in his *De Staline à Hitler*, p. 233. It is discussed, however, by John W. Wheeler-Bennett, *Munich: Prologue to Tragedy* (New York, 1948), pp. 312-313; by André Simone, *J'accuse* (New York, 1940), p. 298; and by "Pertinax" (André Guéraud), *The Gravediggers of France* (New York, 1944), pp. 234-235.

[75] *German Documents*, series D, IV, 483.

[76] *French Yellow Book*, pp. 102-106.

which he himself had set for his mission."[77] His assignment, he privately concluded, had now lost its positive aspects; henceforth he would remain in Berlin as a scout in an advance observation post.[78]

In this capacity he watched the Polish crisis begin to take shape in April, with Hitler's denunciation of the 1934 nonaggression pact, and reported each measure in the uneven crescendo of that spring and summer. He was sure that the critical test had come: to yield on Danzig would be to expose another nation to Czechoslovakia's fate, destruction in two stages. "It is not only the fate of the Free City," he wrote after the Reichstag meeting of April 28, "it is the enslavement or liberty of Europe which is at stake in the issue now joined."[79] Yet he was not enthusiastic over the Allies' sudden veering from appeasement to unconditional support of Beck. At the very least, he felt, Poland, "after its odious conduct toward Czechoslovakia," should now be required to seek an understanding with the Soviet Union, as its contribution to a general system of defense against Hitler.[80]

Throughout all his dispatches covering the first flareup over Danzig and the Corridor in April, the relative easing of overt German pressure in May and June, the tense, sultry atmosphere of July, up to the final outburst beginning in mid-August, Coulondre reiterated tirelessly his belief that the Allies must push their own rearmament swiftly but quietly and take a clear line with Berlin. In his eyes, the danger of war ultimately centered about three possible Nazi calculations: that the West might yet abandon Warsaw, that Danzig might be taken through a "spontaneous" rising within the Free City, and that if war did come Poland might be defeated before any help reached her. The Allies had the responsibility of disabusing Berlin on all three counts.

Concerning their readiness to resist direct aggression and their refusal in advance to be duped by a local *Putsch* in Danzig, Paris and London could, of course, clarify their position by their own statements and actions. Concerning the third point, the ultimate fate of the Polish army, however, they could scarcely impress Berlin unless the system of guarantees included some major Power east of the Rhine. This could only mean Russia. For Coulondre, there was no point in discussing resistance unless Hitler could be placed *between* formidable opponents.

At the same time, recalling the Soviet reaction to Munich, he was painfully sensitive to the threat of a Berlin-Moscow agreement. He noted with foreboding that Hitler had not attacked Russia in his *Reichstag*

[77] *German Documents*, series D, IV, 273.   [78] Coulondre, *De Staline à Hitler*, p. 274.
[79] *French Yellow Book*, pp. 134-135.   [80] Coulondre, *De Staline à Hitler*, p. 264.

address of April 28, though he believed the Fuehrer would await the outcome of negotiations for a military alliance with Japan before deciding on a future policy vis-à-vis the USSR.[81] A few days after that speech came the frightening announcement from the Kremlin that Litvinov was no longer Foreign Commissar. On May 7, the ambassador passed along the view of a well-placed German informant (it was Air General Boden-schatz) that "something is doing in the East" and that a fourth partition of Poland was not out of the question.[82] "The Reich would do its best," he wrote in late May, "to take advantage, to the detriment of France and Great Britain, of any failure, however veiled, in the [Allied] conversations now taking place with Moscow."[83]

So it went all spring and summer, the ambassador relaying each new evidence of an impending diplomatic revolution and adding to his admonitions his pleas for decisive counteraction. He was sometimes in despair over the resistance of the British government and his own superiors, including Lebrun; he was sometimes encouraged, as when Political Director Rochat assured him while he was in Paris in April that a way would be found to bring London and Moscow together.[84] Down to the last possible moment he was still urging the Quai d'Orsay, on its own and through pressure on Chamberlain, "to expedite to the very utmost the conclusion of the agreement with the Soviets. I can never repeat too often how important a psychological factor this is for the Reich."[85] The preceding statement was written only a week before Ribbentrop's departure for Moscow on August 22, 1939. Coulondre's series of dispatches on the Soviet issue ends with a laconic sentence in a message sent that day to Paris: "The announcement of the non-aggression pact with Russia has contributed powerfully to the strengthening of the Army's confidence in the success of German arms."[86]

The preceding night he had signaled the beginning of the final act: a German concentration of forces on the Polish frontier was underway.[87] The details of the next fortnight have already been published many times. So far as Coulondre's official activities during the war crisis are concerned, they can be summarized in a few words. He remained throughout in close touch with Sir Nevile Henderson and with the Polish ambassador,

---

[81] *ibid.*, pp. 267-269.

[82] *French Yellow Book*, pp. 145-149. Also, Coulondre, *De Staline à Hitler*, pp. 270-271.

[83] *French Yellow Book*, p. 164.

[84] Coulondre, *De Staline à Hitler*, p. 265. Coulondre later said (page 281) that this effort had in fact been made "with an intelligence and a tenacity worthy of a better fate."

[85] *French Yellow Book*, p. 269.   [86] *ibid.*, p. 287.

[87] *ibid.*, pp. 282-283.

Lipski. On August 25 he saw Hitler and received the latter's personal message to Daladier that France had no cause for war and should recognize that Polish behavior was intolerable for Germany—his own reply was that if war came the only winner would be "M. Trotsky."[88] The next day he was back at the Chancellery with Daladier's response, stressing Poland's willingness to negotiate and deploring the threat of another Franco-German conflict.[89] Coulondre reported late that night that Hitler had not reacted as hoped either to the Premier's letter or to the ambassador's own forty-minute plea: "Perhaps I moved him; but I did not prevail. His mind was made up."[90] On the 27th, however, Coulondre added that the *démarche* had been necessary and might yet bear fruit.[91] The same afternoon Ribbentrop gave him a copy of Hitler's formal reply and embellished its negative tone regarding Poland with his own comment that "we shall strike at the first incident."[92]

Not until the night of August 31 was Coulondre back at the Foreign Office, to receive from Weizsäcker a copy of Hitler's cunningly delayed "alibi" offer to Poland, communicated to the British and French ambassadors as though it had been ignored by Warsaw and had already expired.[93] Word of the German invasion reached the French embassy early on the morning of September 1, while Coulondre was in the garden with his staff, at work on air raid trenches. He went at once to hear Hitler's speech to the *Reichstag*. At 10 o'clock that evening he delivered to Ribbentrop the French government's affirmation of its intention to carry out its obligations to Poland unless German military operations were suspended.[94] Thirty-six hours later, on the morning of the 3rd, he was ordered by Paris to notify the Minister of Foreign Affairs that if the German response to the *démarche* had to be taken as negative, France would fulfill her engagements to Poland as of 5 p.m. that day.[95] Shortly after noon the ambassador carried out these instructions, delivering the French declaration as soon as he had been assured that the German government had no intention of halting its military forces. "Well," Ribbentrop remarked, "it will be France who is the aggressor." Coulondre replied that "history would judge of that."[96] Next morning he and his mission left Berlin aboard the diplomatic exchange train.

Coulondre's recommendations to his own superiors during those final days had been consistent with his views as stated for months past. With respect to Poland, his personal hope lay in a population exchange.[97] He

[88] *ibid.*, pp. 302-305.   [89] *ibid.*, pp. 311-312.   [90] *ibid.*, p. 317.
[91] *ibid.*, p. 319.   [92] *ibid.*, p. 320.   [93] *ibid.*, pp. 356-357, 366-367.
[94] *ibid.*, pp. 376-377.   [95] *ibid.*, p. 399.   [96] *ibid.*, pp. 400-401.
[97] *ibid.*, pp. 307, 331. Also Coulondre, *De Staline à Hitler*, p. 296.

was, nonetheless, insistent that the Polish attitude should be firm and dignified, that no conversations should be entered upon until all threat of force had been withdrawn, that Beck should not come abjectly to Berlin, and that Warsaw's plenipotentiary, whether Lipski or someone else, should not open negotiations by merely receiving Germany's terms but should present the Polish viewpoint in a manner calculated to safeguard some balance in the talks.[98]

As for France herself, she must not repeat the Czech fiasco by accepting any settlement based on "vague undertakings and hypothetical promises in further matters."[99] "We cannot . . . expect a happy result . . . unless we are careful not to give the impression that we are on the watch for every possible compromise, whatever the cost may be."[100] Finally, in a personal letter which he wrote to Daladier on August 30 and which the Premier read to the Cabinet the next day in Paris, he opined that Hitler was weakening after having met resistance and that France must continue to call his bluff while avoiding any move which might push him to an act of despair.[101]

In order to comprehend this consistent hostility to appeasement, one must bear in mind two crucial factors in the ambassador's own conceptual scheme: the essential nature of Nazi foreign policy and the potential role of Soviet Russia. Coulondre's assessment of either or both could and still can be disputed. It cannot, however, be lightly dismissed, especially since it set him clearly apart from numerous other figures discussed in this book.

His analysis of German aims rested on his certainty that Nazi dynamism could not be accommodated or diverted, that it could only be checked by greater force opposing it. The Russian dictatorship, he believed, because of the geographical and social characteristics of the nation it controlled, might maintain a prewar economy indefinitely without being impelled toward actual conflict. The German dictatorship, he was equally sure, could do no such thing.[102] He conceded that there were differing degrees of impatience represented among the leading Nazis; but he could not, given his emphasis on the underlying

---

[98] *French Yellow Book*, pp. 308-309, 341-342, 354-355.

[99] *ibid.*, pp. 308-309.   [100] *ibid.*, p. 319.

[101] The text of this letter is given in Coulondre, *De Staline à Hitler*, p. 299, note 2. Paul Reynaud has written that the message "exercised a profound influence on Daladier." *La France a sauvé l'Europe*, I, 597. Coulondre, however, insists that it was delivered to the Premier while the Cabinet was in session, that the personal notes of Champetier de Ribes show that the decision to stand firm had already been taken and that hence his letter did nothing more than to confirm the ministers' resolve. *De Staline à Hitler*, pp. 304-305, note 2.

[102] *ibid.*, p. 247.

forces at work, interest himself as much as did most other foreign diplomats in the distinctions among various party chiefs or between the Nazi
leadership corps as a group and the Foreign Office. He viewed Hitler's
perfidy and rapacity as constants which would operate to the limit fixed
by circumstances.[103] He considered Goering "at once ridiculous and
formidable," even when espousing relative moderation. He found Hess
uninteresting, Ribbentrop contemptible, Rosenberg pontifical, Goebbels
—"ce petit diable boiteux"—not unimpressive in his amoral acuteness.
Old acquaintances at the *Auswärtiges Amt*, such as Woermann, Ritter,
and Gaus, proved incapable of talking candidly any longer, captives of
the regime they served.[104] He was inclined to believe that Weizsäcker
did not want war with France;[105] but his feeling for the Secretary of
State never went beyond that to real cordiality or confidence, and nothing in the German documents suggests that it should have.

Coulondre's argument that Hitler would not stop of his own volition
was matched by his claim that the Fuehrer could and would stop if
faced by sufficiently great odds. One of the ambassador's more surprising
statements, suggestive of a perhaps unavoidable degree of wishful thinking, was in a dispatch of June 1939 to the effect that Hitler "has never
up till now undertaken any move which was not sure of success."[106] This
judgment strained the history of the mid-1930's, but it was consistent
with the view that Coulondre was still expounding in his August 30
letter to Daladier: Hitler might be bluffing and might yet be halted
short of war if the Allies left no doubt in his mind concerning their determination to resist any further aggression.

This gamble Coulondre had been especially willing to accept while
the Soviet Union could still be thought of as a possible ally against Germany. His belief that, even after Munich, Russia's self-interest would
have made it cooperate with the Western Powers, had they been willing
to talk business in Moscow, will doubtless always be a subject of disagreement. Whether or not he was deluded, however, this conviction,
abandoned only with the coming of the Nazi-Soviet Pact, takes its place
beside his view of Nazi dynamism as the second of his basic premises.
Future historians will have to judge his position in the light of what-

[103] *ibid.*, p. 229.
[104] *ibid.*, pp. 217-221.
[105] *ibid.*, p. 314. Weizsäcker himself later complained of Coulondre that "he seemed
not to realize—or perhaps he did not trust his own feelings—that in me he could have
had an ally for the achievement of the higher interests we both had at heart." Ernst von
Weizsäcker, *Erinnerungen* (Munich, 1950), pp. 210-211.
[106] *French Yellow Book*, p. 181.

ever further evidence may turn up concerning the Third Reich and the USSR, to sustain or to refute those premises.

The question will still remain: how did Coulondre's policy recommendations relate to his underlying sentiments? How can his insisting to the end that peace might be saved by calling Germany's bluff be reconciled with his view of the internal thrust behind Nazi expansionism and his characterization of Hitler as power-corrupted, increasingly irrational, "the monstrous specimen of a debased humanity?"[107] There are two alternative answers. One would be that Coulondre was sure that war was coming and could only hope that France would meet the test firmly, with a clear public awareness of the issues and without conceding the Nazis any further preparatory conquests. Calling Berlin's putative bluff would at the worst mean the Allies would be facing the issue. This explanation, framed in less sympathetic terms, is suggested by Weizsäcker's remark that "Coulondre spoke as if his words were to appear right away . . . in a Yellow Book."[108]

The other possible key to the ambassador's performance would relate less to a calculated campaign and more to the mind's ability to cushion terrible conclusions. Coulondre was unusually clearheaded in his assessment of the Nazi threat and the diplomatic flexibility required to meet it. He did not delude himself about Hitler's personality. He did not insist on patching up a Western European balance, regardless of cost, for the sake of the social *status quo*. But he would have had to possess an almost inhuman coldness of intellect not to seek an escape from his own prognosis. Might not a clear stand by the West force Berlin to count the risks and draw back from the fatal decision? The answer proved to be no. It would, nevertheless, be unjust to Coulondre not to consider carefully his reasons for posing the question.

[107] Coulondre, *De Staline à Hitler*, p. 326.
[108] Weizsäcker, *Erinnerungen*, p. 210.

19

....

The Diplomacy of Colonel Beck

BY HENRY L. ROBERTS

AMONG the public figures of countries overrun by Nazi Germany, Colonel Jozef Beck, Poland's Foreign Minister from 1932 to 1939, has probably received the least sympathy. Despite his determined resistance to Hitler's threats in the crisis leading to the outbreak of the second world war, he has been remembered as one of the Pilsudskian *epigoni*, as the man who refused to work with the Little Entente or the League of Nations, who pursued, in substance, a pro-German policy after 1934, who joined in the dismembering of Czechoslovakia, and, finally, as the man whose stubborn refusal to enter any combination with the Russians contributed to the failure of the Anglo-French-Soviet negotiations of the spring and summer of 1939.

After Poland's defeat and Beck's internment in Rumania the world heard little of him. He died in obscurity, of tuberculosis, on June 5, 1944. Less than a year after his death the war of which his country was first victim came to an end, but Poland soon fell under the domination of the Power that Beck always felt to be the ultimate enemy. This retrospective vindication of his Russian policy, the postwar publication of Polish, French, German, and British evidence bearing on his activities, and the recent appearance of Beck's own diplomatic memoirs[1] suggest a reappraisal of this controversial and rather elusive figure.

I

Although it has been said that Beck lacked diplomatic training,[2]

[1] Colonel Joseph Beck, *Dernier rapport: Politique polonaise 1926-1939* (Neuchâtel, 1951). Although these memoirs, three memoranda dictated between 1939 and 1943, are fragmentary and were intended as preliminary drafts, they are sufficiently complete to provide many insights into Beck's own view of his diplomatic role. Supplementing these, and of considerably greater value as a record of Polish foreign policy, is the journal of the Under-Secretary of State for Foreign Affairs: Comte Jean Szembek, *Journal, 1933-1939*, trans. by J. Rzewuska and T. Zaleski (Paris, 1952). This was published too late to be utilized fully here.

[2] L. B. Namier, *Diplomatic Prelude, 1938-1939* (London, 1948), p. 438.

it is doubtful whether his shortcomings as a statesman can be attributed to amateurishness. He did not, it is true, come to the Foreign Ministry from a career in the Diplomatic Service, but he was not lacking in experience. At the time of his fall, he was dean of European Foreign Ministers in terms of uninterrupted occupation of his post. Born in Warsaw in 1894, educated at the polytechnic school in Lwów and the *Exportakademie* in Vienna, he participated in the first world war as one of Pilsudski's legionnaires. During the period of confused fighting following the Russian revolution and the collapse of Germany he seems increasingly to have been chosen for diplomatic missions, official and clandestine. In 1922 Pilsudski sent him as military attaché to the Polish legation in Paris. After a year he was abruptly recalled under unpleasant but somewhat obscure circumstances with, perhaps, a permanent feeling of rancor for certain French circles.[3]

Following his return from France he entered the Polish War College and appeared to be moving toward a military career. As an active participant in the *coup d'état* of 1926, however, he entered the circle of Pilsudski's close collaborators and was the Marshal's *chef de cabinet* between 1926 and 1930. Some time before 1930 Pilsudski is reported to have said to an official of the war ministry: "Do not count on Beck; you will never have him. M. Beck is not going to make his career in the army. M. Beck will go to Foreign Affairs, to be charged with responsibilities of high importance."[4] In December 1930 he became Under-Secretary of State in the Foreign Office and in November 1932 Minister of Foreign Affairs, replacing August Zaleski. For the next seven years he directed Poland's foreign policy, as Pilsudski's agent until the latter's death in 1935, then largely on his own.

On the other hand, the French ambassador, Léon Noël, who found Beck "one of the most unusual, in certain respects one of the most mysterious, and above all one of the most interesting persons it has fallen to me to be associated with," was probably correct in his observation that Beck showed many of the characteristics of the young man who had climbed the ladder too rapidly and easily.[5] He was unduly confident in his own opinions and decisions. Moreover, he was of the generation of those who were twenty in 1914, a generation inclined to be self-consciously proud of its own "realism." Certainly, this tall, elegant,

---

[3] Léon Noël, *L'Agression allemande contre la Pologne* (Paris, 1946), pp. 106-107. Noël, French ambassador in Poland from 1935 to 1939, adds, however, that "it is not necessary to have recourse to this explanation to have the key to his policy in general and to his policy toward France in particular."

[4] Beck, *Dernier rapport*, p. xix.   [5] Noël, *L'Agression allemande*, p. 20.

and rather Mephistophelean figure conveyed an impression of hardness without depth.

Noël also felt that while Beck had a talent for diplomacy, his experience in military intelligence accentuated a tendency to employ *deuxième bureau* techniques in his conduct of foreign policy. All his fellow diplomats found him evasive, uncommunicative, and tortuous in his methods. One of Noël's colleagues remarked that when Beck had occasion to speak the truth, one noticed it at once.[6] His own memoirs, however, do not wholly support this impression of elaborate deviousness. Indeed, he seemed to operate on surprisingly simple premises, and was irritable rather than conspiratorial in his reluctance to explain or discuss his actions. Many of his more round-about maneuvers were made largely because they seemed to represent correct diplomatic form.

For, curiously enough, Poland, a new or at least resurrected state, displayed a distinctly old-fashioned diplomatic wardrobe. While the interwar diplomacy of the Western Powers exhibits the powerful impact of political and public pressures, and while the diplomacy of Poland's two great neighbors, Germany and the Soviet Union, was but one branch of the foreign activities of an ideologically imbued totalitarian order, Beck's diplomacy had Metternichean overtones.[7]

To a degree, of course, this continuation of cabinet diplomacy was a reflection of Polish society and government. Poland's rather hectic experience with untempered parliamentarianism was brought to an end with Pilsudski's return to power in May 1926. The constitutional structure remained for a time, and even some parliamentary activity, but under the stern supervision of the old Marshal. The new constitution which came into effect in 1935 was distinctly authoritarian. Following Pilsudski's death, his associates, the "Colonels," governed in a quasi-dictatorial fashion. The regime was not fascist or totalitarian but, as one Pole said, merely carried on the spirit of the former gentry, "We are Poland."[8] In the confused circumstances of Polish domestic politics after Pilsudski's death, it would be difficult to say what might have been the eventual outcome of this system. In any event, it is clear that the government was not responsible to the Diet, the *Sejm*, and that Beck was able

[6] *ibid.*, p. 22, note 1.

[7] Beck, for example, thoroughly admired the "meticulous British protocol" surrounding the coronation of King George VI, as the ideal atmosphere for diplomatic contacts and conversations. *Dernier rapport*, p. 128.

[8] Wladyslaw Grabski, *Idea Polski* (Warsaw, 1936), quoted in Raymond Leslie Buell, *Poland: Key to Europe* (3rd ed., New York, 1939), p. 99.

to retain his post, as were President Moscicki and Marshal Smigly-Rydz, throughout successive changes in the Cabinet.

The setting in which important decisions on policy were reached is described in a passage in Beck's memoirs: "Marshal Pilsudski, in the spring of 1934, suggested to the President of the Republic of Poland that he convoke a conference on foreign policy, chaired by the President himself, and at which all the public figures who, since 1926, had performed the functions of Prime Minister should take part. The conference was held in the Belvedere Palace. . . . By the wish of the President it was the Marshal who opened the conference; he declared that this form of conference, bringing together the men who had assumed the responsibility for all the affairs of the country, appeared to him to be very useful at moments of great decisions or important events. Comparing this sort of conference with analogous and permanent institutions of other countries, in particular with the privy council of the King of England, of which the members were designated and convoked by the King himself, he vigorously urged the President to institute the custom."[9]

Beck, who thoroughly approved of this procedure, continued the practice of calling together the inner circle from time to time to discuss the foreign situation and the action to be taken. Apart from these conferences and infrequent statements to the Diet, Beck directed his foreign policy as he saw fit. The outcries of the opposition seem to have carried little weight in determining or altering his line of action. To be sure, as in all such situations, there were tensions and conflicts within the ruling oligarchy: Beck had been a rival of his predecessor Zaleski; no love was lost between the Foreign Minister and the inspector general of the army Smigly-Rydz, upon whom the greater part of Pilsudski's mantle had fallen and who seemed much more aware of the German military threat; friction between Beck and his subordinates was not infrequent. Even these intramural clashes, however, do not appear to have influenced Polish foreign policy markedly in the years after 1932.

It would seem, then, that the rather perverse course of Polish diplomacy under Beck is not to be explained by the fumblings of the inexperienced or by the vagaries of public opinion and party politics. For an understanding of Beck's policy it is necessary to go further: to examine the extremely difficult and complex foreign problems which Poland faced in the second decade of its independence and to follow the line of Beck's reasoning in his effort to resolve or contain them.

[9] Beck, *Dernier rapport*, p. 61.

II

Without question, geography has set the most difficult problems for Polish foreign policy. While the term "natural frontiers" has been badly misused—after all, the Rhine was singularly unsuccessful in delimiting French and German territory, and the ridge of the Carpathians failed to bring agreement between Rumanians and Hungarians—it is true that, except for the comparatively limited stretches of the Baltic Sea and the Carpathians, Poland lacked any striking geographical boundaries. More important than the topography, however, were the confused historical background of Poland's political frontiers and the intermingling of nationalities and languages. It is simply not clear where Poland begins and ends.

Rendering perilous the confusion over frontiers was the fact that Poland was wedged between Germany and Russia, both much more powerful and populous states, both with a record of partitioning Poland, and both, in the interwar period, with open or suspected designs on territory Poland had acquired from them. It cannot be overlooked that Poland's existence as an independent state resulted from a coincidence which could not have been anticipated in 1914: the collapse through defeat and revolution of both Russia and Germany. In consequence, Poland's security was inevitably endangered by the recovery and growth of either or both of these Powers; if they should regain their strength and pursue a policy of close cooperation, Poland was, in all likelihood, doomed. In the last analysis, Poland's security as a state depended upon Russia and Germany being comparatively weak, as they were in the 1920's, or having hostile relations, as they did in the mid-1930's.

Poland, unfortunately, was not in a position to create or to maintain either of these conditions, which were determined by factors largely beyond its control. Hence, the task of Polish diplomacy was twofold: first, to seek where it could a means of counterbalancing the potential menace of its two powerful neighbors; and second, to render as secure as possible its position within the unstable framework of German-Polish-Soviet relations. The great question was whether these two lines of policy could be harmonized or whether the pursuit of one would threaten the attainment of the other.

In theory, protection against German and/or Soviet pressure might be obtained through an international order collectively securing the integrity of nations, through the creation of an intermediate bloc of states lying between Germany and Russia and similarly threatened by their recovery or rapprochement, or through alliances with other Great Powers. In theory likewise, Poland's relations vis-à-vis Germany and Russia might be best served by judicious balancing between the two, or by drawing closer to one or the other, depending on the circumstances. These possibilities and the position taken by Beck and the Polish regime toward them will be considered in the following pages.

III

Inasmuch as Poland's reappearance as an independent state was intimately associated with Wilson's Fourteen Points and the Versailles treaties, it might seem axiomatic that Poland should have been an ardent upholder of the Versailles system and of the League of Nations, which was to be the basis for a new international order. Such was not Beck's attitude, however. He regarded Wilson as an opinionated reformer who had contributed to the unfortunate practice of incorporating *exposés de motifs* in the treaties at the end of the first world war. An admirer of the "old diplomacy," he felt that a treaty should deal only with concrete issues: if a nation lost a war, it should be forced to make certain concessions, but without argument or justification. The Versailles treaties, however, which he saw as the work of parliamentarians, not diplomats, were filled with explanatory clauses open to rebuttal and debate. In Beck's view this weakness in the formulation of the treaties was important in paving the way to war in 1939.[10] While it can be argued that the Versailles phraseology dealing with such items as disarmament, "war guilt," and so on, did provide a convenient wedge for the German revisionist counterattack, this argument is not without danger to a state such as Poland, which had been dismembered by the old diplomacy and was brought back into existence, in part at least, because of a widespread revulsion against this method of carrying on international relations.

Beck's second major criticism of the treaty was "the complete absence of a well established hierarchy defining the degree of importance of the different clauses of the treaty."[11] Citing Pilsudski as his mentor, as he usually did, he contended that the territorial settlement was of the highest importance, limitation of German armaments next, and then, of much less significance, all the other clauses. Sanctions and collective measures should have been designed and reserved for the protection of the vital clauses; instead there had been a fruitless expenditure of energy on issues of secondary importance, and the indispensable portions of

[10] Beck, *Dernier rapport*, pp. 48, 251-252.
[11] *ibid.*, p. 252.

the treaty were gradually undermined. In retrospect this criticism appears largely justified.[12]

While Beck was critical of the Versailles treaties, he was definitely hostile to the League of Nations, to the "spirit of Geneva," and to the statesmen who rested their hopes in that organization, particularly the representatives of other successor states active in the League, Benes of Czechoslovakia and Titulescu of Rumania. The absence of the United States, he argued after his fall, had effectively deprived the League of its universalism and nullified its claim to represent a new international order. One may suspect, however, that this contention was a rationalization for the real basis of his dislike of the League: the pretensions of that body to concern itself with the internal affairs of the middle and small states, especially through such agencies as the ILO and the minority treaties. This meddling had the effect of disorganizing their internal stability and rendering them vulnerable to the propaganda of the aggressive Powers: "It is enough to study the political campaign and propaganda undertaken by the Third Reich while preparing the invasion of Eastern Europe to realize the support which it constantly found in the debates of Geneva and in the interpretations of the treaties on the protection of minorities."[13] Moreover, Beck felt that the League put the small and middle Power in a particularly difficult situation. It was forced by the Great Powers "to make unforeseen friends and enemies in connection with questions which had nothing in common with their own interests."[14]

It is not possible here to go into Poland's internal affairs, but there is little doubt that much of Beck's touchiness concerning the League stems from Poland's minority question, which was a source of continual friction with its neighbors and of domestic discord. About 30 percent of Poland's population was made up of non-Polish minorities, a large number of whom were Ukrainians. With the Soviet Union's entry into the League in 1934, Beck "deemed that the moment had come to finish with the question of the treaty on minorities. It was, in effect, inadmissible that the representative of the Soviet Union could discuss and decide the internal affairs of Poland."[15] With evident pleasure at causing a stir, Beck, in September 1934, announced to the Assembly of the League of Nations that, "pending the introduction of a general and uniform system for the protection of minorities, my Government is com-

[12] For a recent discussion of this point see R. F. Harrod, *The Life of John Maynard Keynes* (London, 1951), pp. 269-270.
[13] Beck, *Dernier rapport*, p. 256.   [14] *ibid.*, p. 266.
[15] *ibid.*, p. 71.

pelled to refuse, as from today, all cooperation with the international organizations in the matter of the supervision of the application by Poland of the system of minority protection."[16] Since he neither expected nor desired the minority treaties to be converted into a general system applicable to all countries, he was, by this unilateral act of denouncing an international obligation, flatly rejecting the competence of the League to concern itself with Poland's minorities.

Beck also resented another function of the League which intimately concerned Poland: its supervision of the Free City of Danzig, which the Treaty of Versailles had taken from Germany but had not given to Poland. The real danger to Poland here was, of course, Germany. Nevertheless, Beck was pleased with the difficulties the League High Commissioners were having with the growing Nazi domination of Danzig and proud of his ability to straighten out affairs by direct negotiation with the Third Reich. In reflecting on a minor crisis in 1936 Beck later commented: "The roles were thus reversed: It was no longer the League of Nations which protected Poland at Danzig, it was Poland which had to defend the League of Nations in the Free City. This corresponded, moreover, to the reality of things which Geneva, up to then, had so obstinately refused to see."[17]

By this policy on the minorities question and Danzig, Beck was, in effect, removing them from the sphere of international concern to that of direct German-Polish relations. In 1939 this transfer had dire consequences when Hitler began his assault on Poland with precisely these issues. Still, Beck could reply, "And what would the League have done to protect Poland in 1939?"

On the one occasion when the League undertook collective measures against aggression—its imposition of sanctions against Italy—Beck was lukewarm about the whole affair: the dispute was far from Poland; he approved of Laval's efforts to avoid a break in French-Italian relations; he wanted to maintain Poland's coal exports to Italy; he mistrusted the ideological overtones of collective security;[18] and he was bored and irritated by the tenor of Titulescu's anti-Italian tirades in the "little world" of Geneva. Indeed, Poland was the first Power to drop sanctions. In a letter to the President of the Council of the League, on June 26,

---

[16] League of Nations, *Official Journal, Special Supplement No. 125. Records of the Fifteenth Ordinary Session of the Assembly* (Geneva, 1934), p. 43.

[17] Beck, *Dernier rapport*, p. 123.

[18] In a conversation with Anthony Eden on October 9, 1935, Beck remarked that "sanctions should not lead to a reinforcement of the action of the Second International, which was patronized by the Third." *Ibid.*, p. 290.

1936, Beck, after emphasizing that the adoption of economic sanctions was a "sovereign decision" for each state to make, declared that since further measures were useless Poland was terminating its application of sanctions. In his memoirs he said that this action was not intended to hasten recognition of the Italian annexation, but was simply a response to the fact that "unfortunate Abyssinia had already ceased, *de facto*, to exist as an independent country."[19]

In retrospect the sanctions episode was a sorry one, which failed to check Italian aggression and contributed to driving Mussolini toward Hitler. It is painful, though, to hear a Polish statesman employ the "ceasing to exist" argument, when the soul of Poland's survival has been its obstinate refusal to admit the loss of national existence.

It is clear that the realist Beck placed very little confidence in the League of Nations as a defense for Poland. In considering the unhappy fate of those smaller states which did embrace the "spirit of Geneva" with such ardor, one may admit he had reason for his skepticism. After all, the League was not an independent, supranational authority, nor could it enforce the peace unless the Great Powers, France and Great Britain—not to speak of the absent United States—exerted their power on its behalf. This they did not do; a far greater responsibility for the failure of the League attaches to them than to Colonel Beck's scornful attitude. It cannot be said, however, that his activities in this field were of any positive value in the preservation of the peace or of international responsibility in those darkening years.

IV

In the absence of an international body, the maintenance of peace, in the century preceding 1914, had come to be regarded as a function of the "Concert of Europe," the Great Powers of the continent. During the interwar years one can follow a thread of attempts to reconstruct this concert, from the Locarno treaties of 1925, through the Four Power Pact of 1933, to the Munich Conference in 1938, attempts to settle major problems by consultation and agreement among Great Britain, France, Italy, and Germany (the Soviet Union was not included).

Beck's attitude toward this approach to international security is not difficult to guess. If he was scornful of the League, he saw these efforts as a positive menace in their aim of settling affairs to the satisfaction of the Great Powers, but in disregard of the middle and small states. He quoted with approval Pilsudski's blunt comment on Locarno that "every

[19] *ibid.*, pp. 107-108.

good Pole spits with disgust at the name." By the Locarno agreements, two categories of frontiers in Europe had been created, and in Beck's opinion Germany was thereby solemnly invited to attack to the East for the price of gaining peace in the West.

The Four Power Pact, while eventually reduced to a rather vague and innocuous statement,[20] aroused great indignation in Poland. Other middle and small states of Eastern Europe were equally alarmed, but upon learning of the eventual terms of the agreement, were willing to accept it. This compliance on the part of the Little Entente enraged Beck, who said that Europe had three categories of states: Great Powers, middle and small Powers with a will to pursue their own policy, and client states. Putting Poland in the second category—he always denied that Poland was a Great Power in the sense of having world wide interests—he was intent on maintaining an independent course against the infringements of the Great Powers and the submissiveness of the client states.

Since the Little Entente Powers had dropped their opposition to the revised pact, the Polish government felt obliged to show its displeasure alone; and Pilsudski and Beck consequently arranged that the newly appointed Polish ambassador to Italy should announce his resignation on the ground that Italian policy in pressing the Four-Power agreement was contrary to the international interests of his country.

This particular technique of taking abrupt action to indicate disapproval of some international move potentially affecting Poland became characteristic of the Beckian diplomacy and greatly contributed to his reputation for deviousness. In fact, Beck had a rather simple pride in this "style" of Polish diplomacy, fast ripening into a tradition. The sudden harshness of his last moves against Czechoslovakia in September 1938 were in part occasioned by this same intention to register a protest against the Four-Power decisions at Munich.

Unquestionably Beck had every reason to be suspicious of the "Concert of Europe." It was a danger to the independence of the smaller states. Nevertheless, to assume this attitude was to raise a difficult problem, for if both the old principles of the Concert and the new principles of the League were rejected, as they were by Beck, what alternatives remained for a state which was neither so situated nor so powerful as to be able to stand in splendid isolation?

Beck did not provide any satisfactory answer to this question. He insisted that states should mind their own affairs, and he spoke of the

---

[20] See above Chapter 4, §IV.

advantages of bilateral agreements between nations to settle mutual problems without infringing upon the rights of others. But quite evidently, such principles are only desiderata, which a professed realist like Beck could not find sufficient in a world of contending Powers, and on occasion he quite flagrantly contradicted his maxims. In practical terms, of course, the refusal to rely on the League or to admit the benefits of Great Power paternalism meant that Poland must acquire allies, either among the states of Eastern Europe or in the West.

V

That the states of Eastern Europe had much to gain from a policy of cooperation and mutual assistance against the German and Soviet dangers seems more than obvious. Unfortunately, throughout most of the inter-war period, Poland's relations with two of its immediate neighbors, Lithuania and Czechoslovakia, were far from cordial, and this condition made it impossible for Poland either to create a solid Baltic bloc or to cooperate with the Little Entente.

The conflict between Poland and Lithuania arose from the Polish seizure of Vilna after the first world war. Although its population was largely non-Lithuanian, Vilna had been the capital of the medieval duchy. Its loss was not recognized by the Lithuanian regime, which refused to establish diplomatic or economic relations with Poland. Despite occasional feelers, this anomalous relationship between two states once intimately connected continued up to March 1938.

The reestablishment of diplomatic relations with Lithuania is one of the oddest examples of Beck's diplomatic technique. While anticipating and accepting the German-Austrian *Anschluss*, Beck felt, nonetheless, that it would be "dangerous to remain entirely passive in face of the German expansion."[21] It was necessary to give proof that Poland was alert and able to react swiftly. At the same time, since the action in Austria did not directly affect Polish interests, "our response should be very prudent."

While mulling over these thoughts, he received word that, in a frontier incident, Lithuanian guards had killed a Polish soldier. He

[21] Beck, *Dernier rapport*, p. 149. In December 1936, in a conversation with Szembek, Beck said he was expecting a crisis to develop in central Europe. In such a situation, Poland had five choices, of which two were unacceptable: passivity or an alliance with Czechoslovakia against Germany. The other three were: (1) to occupy Teschen, permit Hungary to take Ruthenia, and gain a common frontier with the Magyars; (2) to take Kaunas; (3) to occupy Danzig. Szembek, *Journal*, p. 220. Apparently Beck felt he would have to do something, no matter in what direction.

grasped this occasion and, on March 17, 1938, arguing that in such tense times it was dangerous for Lithuania to refuse diplomatic recognition to Poland, sent a forty-eight hour ultimatum demanding, mildly enough, resumption of normal relations. Certain sectors of Polish opinion urged more extreme measures against Lithuania and the abrupt action raised further doubts about Beck as a responsible diplomat, but it appears that his real intent was the symbolic gesture of demonstrating that Poland, too, could issue ultimata. In actual fact, the action did not lead to further trouble, and Polish-Lithuanian relations showed signs of improvement. But by 1938 it was very late.

Much more serious was Poland's conflict with Czechoslovakia, arising out of the rival claims for Teschen. The Poles felt that the Czechs had obtained, in 1920, an unfairly large part of this district at a time when Poland had been fighting the Bolsheviks. While the Teschen issue was the focus of irritation, Beck had more far-reaching reasons for disliking the Czech state. He objected to Czechoslovakia's alliance in 1935 with the Soviet Union and claimed that the Comintern was using Prague as a headquarters for anti-Polish activities. Benes' work at the League aroused his scorn, and he held that the Czechoslovak regime's much advertised "liberalism" was but a façade for a classic "police state"[22] governed by an innately brutal nationality.[23]

Moreover, the existence of the Czech state as such did not appeal to Beck. Marshal Pilsudski was accustomed to say that there were two states which would not survive, Austria and Czechoslovakia; the only important point was to know which would disappear first. Beck obviously subscribed to this analysis. In December 1931, before he was Foreign Minister, he and Pilsudski decided to increase the aid sent the Polish minority in Czechoslovakia and to be more energetic in educating and organizing it.[24] There is little use in seeking consistency between Beck's own highly sensitive attitude toward external interference with Poland's minorities and this policy of aiding and propagandizing the Polish minority in Czechoslovakia. The divine right of one's own nationality is rarely a principle admitting of reciprocity.

When the Four Power Pact was under negotiation in 1933, Pilsudski did approve of some confidential negotiations with the Czechs, but this brief attempt at rapprochement collapsed with Czechoslovakia's willingness to accept the pact as finally drafted. In the following year he ordered practice maneuvers for Polish military operations to assure the

---

[22] Beck, *Dernier rapport*, p. 52. [23] *ibid.*, p. 171.
[24] *ibid.*, pp. 9-10.

acquisition of Teschen in the event Czechoslovakia should disintegrate or capitulate in face of Germany.[25] The Polish regime was not interested in the maintenance of Czechoslovakia, regarded it as a doomed state, and was solely concerned with seeing to it that Poland gained its appropriate share of the remains.

With such an attitude toward Czechoslovakia, Poland was not likely to enter the Little Entente. Beck, however, had further objections to this bloc. He observed quite correctly that each of the Little Entente members was potentially threatened by a Great Power—Czechoslovakia by Germany, Rumania by Russia, and Yugoslavia by Italy—yet the Entente was, in fact, directed solely against Hungary, which was militarily weaker than any of its three neighbors. Consequently, the Entente provided for no united defense against aggression by a Great Power; and Beck had no desire to join an anti-Hungarian combination, since an improvement of Polish-Hungarian relations was a major aim of his foreign policy. He concluded that Poland had no reason to concern itself more intimately with the affairs of the small Powers south of the Carpathians. The 1921 Polish-Rumanian alliance, directed against the Soviet Union, was the one Eastern connection which seemed to him to meet a real problem.

His attitude toward Czechoslovakia also influenced Beck in rejecting the French effort to create an Eastern bloc in 1934. While his major objection to this project, as will be seen presently, lay in his ambition to maintain a balance between Germany and Russia, he did not wish to enter any agreement which would oblige Poland "to guaruntee the Czechoslovakian frontiers."[26]

Beck was not lacking in plans, however, for an organization of the Eastern European states. In the first place, he had hopes for a Baltic-Scandinavian bloc. Poland as a Baltic Sea Power should develop its ties with the advanced and more enlightened Scandinavian states: "The bridge which united Poland with the Occident and our western friends passed, for me, by way of the Baltic and the solid Scandinavian nations rather than by the artificial combinations of the Little Entente south of the Carpathians."[27] In pursuit of this project, he made several goodwill tours, including one in the critical summer of 1938. The basic difficulty in the way of this bloc was, of course, that the Scandinavian states, for all their stability, were on the sidelines of the European power conflict and still pursued a policy of neutrality and non-involvement.

[25] *ibid.*, p. 83. [26] *ibid.*, p. 73.
[27] *ibid.*, p. 154.

A second project, which Beck worked on when the expansion of Germany began to appear alarming, was the creation of a Rome-Belgrade-Budapest-Bucharest-Warsaw connection. In March 1938, on the eve of the *Anschluss*, he had several conversations in Rome with Mussolini and Ciano. After assertions on both sides that they did not intend to pull chestnuts from the fire for other Powers—a common figure of speech that passed for diplomatic sophistication in those years—there was mutual agreement that while an understanding with Germany was a necessary part of Italian and Polish foreign policy, the effort should be made to strengthen ties with Hungary, Yugoslavia, and Rumania, presumably as a check to overly great German domination.[28]

In support of this program Beck became increasingly anxious to establish a common frontier with Hungary. Just as the eastern prolongation of Czechoslovakia was, in part, strategically designed to give that country and Rumania common frontiers, so in the late 1930's, especially after Czechoslovakia's future seemed problematic, Beck's advocacy of Hungary's claims in Slovakia and Ruthenia was aimed at providing a geographical basis for increased cooperation between Poland and its "best neighbor."

A serious obstacle, of course, to Beck's rather jejune project was the fact that Hungary and Poland's ally, Rumania, were bitterly antagonistic. Beck did his best to patch up relations between these two states but without success. In mid-October 1938, after Munich, he proposed to the Rumanian ambassador that, in the event of Czechoslovakia's further disintegration, Hungary and Rumania should divide Ruthenia between them. A few days later, in a visit to King Carol, he elaborated on this proposal. While not overlooking Rumania's old ties with Czechoslovakia, he urged that, if Hungary and Rumania took such an action in concert, their mutual relations would improve, Rumania would gain an additional rail connection with Poland, and, incidentally, Poland and Rumania would be rid of a center of Ukrainian agitation unsettling to their minorities. Carol, however, declined the offer, and Beck was subsequently outraged to learn that the Rumanian Foreign Minister, Petresco-Comnène, had spread the story that Poland was attempting to lure Rumania into aggression against Czechoslovakia.[29]

[28] *ibid.*, pp. 145-148. See also Galeazzo Ciano, *1937-1938 Diario* (Bologna, 1948), pp. 127-129. While Beck found Ciano, underneath his theatrics, a precise and accurate agent for his father-in-law, Ciano felt that Beck was not very strong, rather rambling and imprecise.
[29] For Beck's account of this episode, see *Dernier rapport*, pp. 172-175; for the views of the Rumanian Foreign Minister, whom Beck called a perfect imbecile and who

Apart from such complications, Beck's scheme for an Italian-Eastern Europe bloc had two fatal drawbacks. In the first place, by basing his plans on Italy and Hungary rather than on the Little Entente, he was fostering the forces making for territorial revision of the Versailles system and weakening those defending the *status quo*. In so doing, he was undermining the very arrangement which had enabled Poland to make its reappearance as the largest state in eastern central Europe. In the second place, Germany was the most powerful and active of the revisionist nations. It is therefore difficult to see just how a Rome-Budapest-Warsaw axis—Belgrade and Bucharest in this connection merely represented the wreckage of the Little Entente—could be the instrument to check German ambitions.[30] By 1938 Germany was in a position to overshadow and outmaneuver any such combination, as was made clear by the absolute worthlessness of the common Polish-Hungarian frontier which was achieved by the Hungarian absorption of Ruthenia in March 1939.

But, if Beck's program may be dismissed, it must be admitted that in all probability no arrangement by the Eastern European states could have assured the security of the area, even had their statesmen been far wiser and more self-restrained. Apart from the internecine quarrels, which were perhaps an inescapable by-product of the same spirit of national self-determination which created these states from the destruction of the old multinational empires, this unhappy area, by its history, its geography, and its low economic and industrial level, was scarcely in a position to maintain itself against external aggression or internal strain. Beck may certainly be criticized for his contribution to the disastrous confusion which afflicted this area in the 1930's, but the fact remains that the responsibility for Eastern Europe ultimately rested with the victorious powers of the first world war.

VI

If Poland's defense against Germany and Russia was not to be obtained through association with other states in Eastern Europe, the remaining alternative was the support of other Great Powers. The United States in the interwar period was of little value. Great Britain's position until the spring of 1939 was summarized by Sir Austen Chamberlain's

---

suspected Beck of secret aggressive agreements with Germany, see N. Petresco-Comnène, *Preludi del grande dramma* (Rome, 1947), pp. 276, 283-294.

[30] See Chapter 16, § 11 above.

private remark in 1925, that, "for the Polish corridor, no British Government ever will or ever can risk the bones of a British grenadier."[81]

There remained France, upon which had been placed far too great a burden for the preservation of the Versailles system. A Franco-Polish alliance was, at the end of the first world war, an obvious development. France favored a strong state on Germany's east and had worked for a large Poland at the Peace Conference. France mistrusted the revolutionary intentions of the new Soviet regime and supported Pilsudski in repulsing the Red army from the gates of Warsaw in 1920. The two nations, in February 1921, signed an accord which included a provision for mutual assistance and contained a secret military convention covering a German attack against either signatory or a Polish-Soviet conflict.[82] When the Locarno treaties created a distinction between Germany's Eastern and Western frontiers, France attempted to compensate for this shortcoming by signing a further treaty of guarantee with Poland on October 16, 1925.

Poland, however, profoundly mistrusted the trend toward Franco-German cooperation during the Stresemann-Briand era and was not enthusiastic about France's support of the Little Entente. France, for its part, found the Pilsudski regime after 1926 a trying and truculent ally. These strains were greatly sharpened after Hitler came to power. Each state seemed to the other to be inclined to come independently to terms with the Third Reich, France through the Four Power Pact and Poland through its 1934 agreement with Germany.[83]

In April 1934 the French Foreign Minister, Louis Barthou, visited Pilsudski. The conversation turned to Germany:

"I have had enough of these concessions; the Germans must be made to feel that we will no longer yield an inch," M. Barthou declared.

"You will yield, Messieurs, you will yield," the Marshal answered; "You would not be what you are if you did not yield."

"How can you suspect us of such a thing, M. the Marshal?"

"Perhaps you yourself do not wish to yield, but then either it will be necessary to dismiss you, or parliament will vote against you and defeat you."[84]

Commenting on this visit Beck later wrote: "It was always the

[81] From a letter cited in F. P. Walters, *A History of the League of Nations* (2 vols., London, 1952), I, 284.

[82] General Gamelin, *Servir* (3 vols., Paris, 1946-1947), II, 225, 466.

[83] For a discussion of Poland's motives in signing the agreement with Germany see below, §VII.

[84] Beck, *Dernier rapport*, p. 59; Szembek, *Journal*, p. 5.

same thing: the Marshal wished to intensify the purely military cooperation in face of the German menace, whereas the French sought to drag
us into their own combinations in South-East Europe, combinations
which had scarcely any connection with the German problem, the only
decisive problem in the event of war."[35]

From the Polish point of view, then, the French were failing to stand
up to the Germans but at the same time were busy building elaborate
diplomatic constructions in Eastern Europe which the Poles could not
welcome and in which they refused to participate.

From 1934 on, as France sought to include Russia in its security
arrangements, this situation grew worse. Beck regarded Russia's admission to the League of Nations as a great mistake, since Russia lacked
practically all the qualities which were demanded of League members.[36]
The project for an "Eastern Locarno," which was in theory to be an
extensive pact of guarantee and mutual assistance organized by France
and Russia but open to Germany, was seen by Beck as merely a means
of pushing the states of Eastern Europe into the arms of Russia and
then to tie this group to French policy.

It is rather strange that, after criticizing the Locarno treaties for
creating a disequilibrium in Europe, Beck should have opposed a similar
system of guarantees for the East. His position, however, was expounded
at some length in a memorandum to the French government, drafted
in September 1934. In the first place, Poland had finally succeeded in
signing pacts with Germany and Russia; these, he hoped, would relieve
the *malaise* troubling Eastern Europe. The main point, however, was
that an Eastern Locarno required the presence of Germany: "Our principal thesis was that the participation of Germany in this pact represented
for us a condition *sine qua non* for the maintenance of our policy of
equilibrium between the two great powers which we had for neighbors."[37]
Since Germany refused to join, Beck was not going to endanger his new
pact by taking part in a combination that would have an anti-German
bias.

While Beck respected Barthou as the last of the French statesmen who
vigorously defended France's interests, he was somewhat relieved, after
the latter's assassination, to find that Laval put far less pressure on
Poland for an eastern pact. In Beck's view the real trouble-maker in
France was the "all powerful influence of the bureaucracy of the Quai
d'Orsay" for which he repeatedly indicated his dislike.

[35] Beck, *Dernier rapport*, p. 60.   [36] *ibid.*, p. 68.
[37] *ibid.*, p. 74.

After the project for an Eastern Locarno collapsed, France pursued the more restricted objective of a mutual assistance agreement with the Soviet Union, with which was associated a Soviet-Czech pact. When Laval passed through Warsaw in May 1935 on his way to Moscow to sign this agreement, Pilsudski was unable to see him; the old Marshal was dying. From that point on, Beck's and France's ways tended to part: France attempted in a rather halfhearted fashion to build up a defense system with Russia and Czechoslovakia, Beck relied upon the security given him by his pact with Germany.

The melancholy story of French-Polish relations during the next three years has been told at some length and with much feeling by the French ambassador in Warsaw, Léon Noël. In his view, Pilsudski, while having no respect for French democracy, was firmly attached to the principle of the French alliance. Beck, on the other hand, was definitely anti-French in his policy. He restricted the Franco-Polish alliance to the narrow terms of common action in the event of an actual attack by Germany but did not seek to concert with the French in the more general area of foreign policy.[38]

French criticism of Beck loses some of its point, however, if one considers the crisis of March 7, 1936, when Germany denounced the Locarno agreement and sent its forces into the demilitarized Rhineland. Seeing this move as a definite test of force by Hitler and also as a test of the value of the Franco-Polish alliance, Beck, without waiting for any word from Paris, summoned the French ambassador and requested him to inform his government that Poland intended to live up to her treaty obligations. So at this decisive moment, which was probably the dividing line between possible peace and eventual war or German hegemony, the Polish response was prompt and apparently unequivocal. Some French diplomats were of the opinion that Beck made this proposal because he anticipated no French action. This supposition, while quite possibly correct, is not wholly relevant.[39] France's failure—for which Great Britain bears her share of responsibility—to act on this fatal occasion gives a certain plausibility to Beck's subsequent actions. If France was unable to take measures to prevent the remilitarization of the Rhineland,

[38] Noël, *L'Agression allemande*, pp. 104, 115-116.

[39] Szembek, who saw Beck after the meeting with the French ambassador, recorded in his journal: "Beck then expressed the opinion that the violation by Germany of the demilitarized zone did not constitute for us a *casus foederis*. . . . He does not think that war will result. France, without the support of England, will surely not move, and Great Britain is neither sufficiently prepared nor sufficiently armed to risk a conflict with Germany." Szembek, *Journal*, p. 167.

a step which inevitably meant that Germany would eventually be free to strike in the East without fear of immediate invasion from the West, the states in Eastern Europe were unavoidably driven to an attitude of *sauve qui peut*. It must be added, however, that in his memoirs Beck says that it was difficult to believe that the Germans could be prevented, in the long run, from militarizing the Rhineland. He felt, though, that since Germany was taking a serious gamble, Hitler "was ready to accord significant political concessions to assure the success of his action."[40] In other words, Beck was less concerned with the strategic import of the act, which he felt the French could have accepted if given an adequate compensation, than with the diplomatic method employed. He feared that an unchallenged *fait accompli* would give Hitler inflated ideas.

The immediate consequence of the events of March 1936 was increased French-Polish mistrust. By the autumn of that year Noël was suggesting that Smigly-Rydz, who was to visit France to conclude a military and financial agreement, be told quite frankly: "The French Government is wholly disposed to aid you, but you know, rightly or wrongly, the French have no confidence in M. Beck; the Chambers and French opinion will refuse, we fear, to permit the grant of an important loan to Poland so long as he retains the foreign affairs portfolio."[41] Noël had reason to believe that Smigly-Rydz did not care for Beck's diplomatic policy, and the French government, apparently, was inclined to accept his suggestion. As it turned out, however, the French government did not press for Beck's removal, primarily, it seems, because of reluctance to make what would be construed as an anti-German gesture. This mood of rather irresolute hostility on the part of France served only to confirm Beck in the course he was following.

By the time of the Czechoslovakian crisis in 1938 France was in the unhappy situation of seeing one of its alliance partners, Czechoslovakia, increasingly threatened by another, Poland. Nevertheless, while the French were properly indignant over Beck's actions, France itself was guilty of forcing Czechoslovakia to yield to Hitler. Indeed, an extremely vicious circle had developed. A common Polish-Czech front of resistance to Germany in 1938 might have driven France to a support of its commitments; on the other hand, Beck's belief that France was not going to oppose Germany helped keep him on his anti-Czech course. Noël states that Beck had said to him several times during the first days of his stay in Warsaw: "We have no illusions, we know very well that our alliance

[40] Beck, *Dernier rapport*, pp. 113-114.
[41] Noël, *L'Agression allemande*, p. 140.

with you is unilateral; if you were attacked by Germany Poland would march to your aid, because it would be in its interest; but the reverse is not true; we do not forget the press campaigns in France on the theme: we shall not fight for the Corridor."[42] In May 1938, when the French government proposed that Poland join the French and British ambassadors in warning Berlin against the use of force, Beck, while refusing to associate himself with this move, referred to the Polish attitude of March 7, 1936 and declared that Poland "was ready to honor its obligations as an ally of France."[43] As the crisis became more acute, Beck, in a conference with other Polish leaders, gave the following analysis of the situation: 1) the Czechs would not fight; 2) the Western Powers were not prepared, either morally or materially, to come to their rescue. He went on to say, however, that "if my basic hypothesis was contradicted by the facts, it would be necessary, within a period of twenty-four hours, to modify completely the policy of Poland, for, in the event of a real European war against Germany, we could not be on the side of the latter, even indirectly."[44] As it turned out, both of Beck's premises were correct.

More fateful than this deterioration of the Franco-Polish alliance was the fact that the alliance itself, by the late 1930's, no longer had the strategic significance it possessed in the 1920's, when Russia was recovering from revolution and civil war, when Germany was disarmed and when France had the most powerful army on the continent. France alone was no longer able to counterbalance the growing power of Germany, nor, as it later proved, were France and Britain together. Consequently, Poland's security was more and more coming to depend upon the marginal influence it had in balancing itself between Germany and Russia.

VII

In a conversation with Pierre Laval, in January 1935, Beck explained the basic premises of Polish foreign policy by saying: "Polish policy rests on the following elements: it follows from our geographical position as well as from the experiences of our history that the problems to which we must attach decisive importance are those posed by the relations with our two great neighbors, Germany and Russia. It is therefore to these problems that we must devote the greatest part of our political activity

---

[42] *ibid.*, p. 252. On the other hand, in January 1935, Beck told Szembek that he did not think there was any chance that France might denounce her alliance with Poland, since such an action would amount to suicide on the part of France. Szembek, *Journal*, p. 32.

[43] Beck, *Dernier rapport*, p. 319.   [44] *ibid.*, pp. 162-163.

and of our modest means of action. History teaches us: 1) that the greatest catastrophe of which our nation has ever been victim has been the result of concerted action by these two Powers, and 2) that in this desperate situation there was not to be found any Power in the world to bring us assistance. . . . Another conclusion which imposes itself is that the policy of Warsaw should never be dependent upon Moscow or Berlin."[45]

To meet this difficult situation Beck, in theory at least, tried to pursue a policy of even balance between the two states. For example, in 1934 he timed a visit to Moscow to match the signing of the German-Polish pact. He insisted that his policy was clear and unequivocal and that having closer relations with one of the Powers than with the other "would fatally drag us into a political activity or even into armed conflict which would not be justified by any vital interest of Poland and the only result of which would be to transform our territory into a battlefield for foreign interests."[46]

While one may accept Beck's view that this was a reasonable position for Poland to take, the policy of balance leaves certain questions unresolved. It did not in itself prevent Germany and Russia from working together at Poland's expense. Moreover, while Beck contended that his diplomacy was based on "extremely simple" principles, it is not surprising that other nations found it increasingly complicated. The simple intention of riding two horses at once can lead to some exceptionally strenuous acrobatics. The real difficulty with Beck's desire to remain midway between Moscow and Berlin was its failure to indicate what should be done in the event one state was moving off on a clearly aggressive and revisionist tangent, whereas the other, for the time being at least, was not. In classical balance of power theory, a state trying to maintain itself between two more powerful states should move toward the less aggressive. In Beck's hands, however, the idea of preserving a balance seemed to mean that, if Germany took an aggressive action, Poland should respond by an act perhaps half as aggressive. There are several reasons for this rather peculiar behavior, which inevitably brought Beck closer to the Germans and farther from the Russians.

A number of authorities have said that in 1933, upon Hitler's coming to power, Pilsudski offered to join the French in an action against Germany and that, only after being rebuffed and after witnessing the conclusion of the Four Power Pact, was he impelled to turn to Germany for the nonaggression pact of January 1934. The evidence for this offer,

<hr>

[45] *ibid.*, p. 283.   [46] *ibid.*, pp. 37-38.

reports of which began to circulate as early as the summer of 1933, is elusive, however, and the present author is doubtful of its authenticity.[47] A proposal for preventive war is not mentioned in Beck's own memoirs, nor does it correspond to his retrospective interpretation of Polish views at the time.

According to Beck, Pilsudski had attentively examined the "pros and cons and all the odds of a preventive war before taking the decision to negotiate with Germany. There were obviously many elements to consider in this connection. In the military field the Marshal estimated that the weakest point in our army was the high command. The weakness of our eventual allies at this period made us abandon the idea of a preventive war, and what happened later, at the time of the occupation of the demilitarized zone of the Rhine by German troops, amply confirmed the estimate of the situation."[48]

Apart from these negative considerations, it is unlikely that Beck or Pilsudski felt Hitler to be an immediate menace. Beck records that Pilsudski did not think Hitler's coming to power meant the pursuit of a more violent anti-Polish policy, and he advised Beck, in making a speech before the Polish Diet, not to attach importance to the excitement of the European press but to be calm, firm, and moderate.[49] In his speech of February 15, 1933, Beck confined himself to saying: "Our attitude with regard to Germany will be exactly the same as Germany's attitude toward Poland. Speaking practically, more depends on Berlin in this respect than on Warsaw."[50]

At the same time, however, the victory of the Nazis had increased tension in Danzig, the "barometer" of Polish-German relations. Pilsudski felt a vigorous step was needed and quickly moved to reinforce the Polish garrison at the Westerplatte. But, as Beck put it, the warning of this abrupt measure "was perfectly understood in Danzig and Berlin," which adopted a conciliatory attitude. The question then arose whether Poland was in a position "to profit from the internal revolution of the Reich to ameliorate our neighborly relations with that country."

The reasons for Polish optimism on this point appear in a memorandum Beck prepared in the autumn of 1933. His conclusions were as follows: (1) the National Socialist movement has a truly revolutionary

---

[47] For a further discussion of this point see the Note at the end of the chapter.
[48] Beck, *Dernier rapport*, p. 66.   [49] *ibid.*, p. 24.
[50] Jozef Beck, *Przemowienia, Deklaracje, Wywiady, 1931-1937* (Warsaw, 1938), pp. 58-59. The German translation, *Beiträge zur europäischen Politik, Reden, Erklärungen, Interviews, 1932-1939* (Essen, 1939) includes Beck's speeches up to January 1939.

character; (2) at all times reformers have wanted to reinvestigate old problems; (3) all reformers are primarily concerned with internal changes, and for that they need a period of external calm; (4) Hitler is more or less an Austrian, in any case not a Prussian; no Prussian figures among his direct collaborators; and this fact creates a new situation, since the old Prussian traditions were chiefly responsible for the anti-Polish feeling in Germany; and (5) the Hitlerian movement is the last act of the national unification of the German people. The conclusion drawn was that "we found ourselves before a unique occasion for redressing our situation in the European balance."[51]

In the spring and summer of 1933, Hitler, publicly and privately, gave reassurances to the Poles that he had no intention of violating existing treaties or stirring up trouble in Danzig. In November, the Polish government explained to Hitler that Poland's security was founded on direct relations with other states and on collaboration through the League of Nations. Since Germany had now withdrawn from the League, the Polish government wished to know whether there was any chance "of compensating for the loss of this element of security, in direct Polish-German relations."[52] From this opening, the path led directly to the signing of the nonaggression agreement of January 26, 1934; and there is no indication in Beck's memoirs that, after getting a favorable German response, Pilsudski turned once more to France before signing the agreement.

Without doubt, Beck himself was much pleased with the German pact, which he regarded as the greatest and most valuable achievement of Polish foreign policy.[53] After Pilsudski's death, he paid a cordial visit to Berlin and was able to reassure the Nazi leaders that Polish policy would not change with the Marshal's passing. Commenting on that visit, he wrote later: "It will doubtless be very interesting one day to study to what degree the complete reversal of German policy several years later

---

[51] Beck, *Dernier rapport*, p. 29. The same line of thought appears in the introduction to the Polish White Book: "There seemed a possibility that the National Socialist revolution might force German opinion to accept the idea of a rapprochement with Poland, though this had been impossible under the Weimar Republic. The Hitler regime transferred the power in Germany to men who had not come from Prussia, the land of traditional hatred for Poland." *Polish White Book*, p. 3.

[52] *Polish White Book*, p. 17. On October 1, 1933, Pilsudski called a conference to discuss the situation created by Germany's departure from the League. He ordered a report on the state of German rearmament. He also wanted to ask the French what information they had on the subject, and added: "It is necessary to draw the attention of the French to the fact that this work is secret, that we are not journalists nor in the service of journalists, and that we are not sounding the alarm." He concluded by saying that he had not yet formed an opinion with regard to German rearmament. Szembek, *Journal*, p. 2.

[53] *ibid.*, p. 41.

can or should be attributed to Hitler himself, in what measure eventually it was owing to the overly great ease with which his imperialist policy went from success to success, or, finally, if and to what point it had its origin in a reaction of the old Prussian spirit in the interior of Germany itself."[54]

Here seems to be the real clue to Beck's policy vis-à-vis Germany. While no pro-German, he was definitely attracted by, and had confidence in, what he thought to be the Hitlerian foreign policy.[55] He had no illusions that it was a static policy, but he thought it was based on nationalist principles. Consequently, he expected an attempt to take over Austria and, subsequently, action against Czechoslovakia; but he was quite willing to accept these developments as not imperiling Poland.

Beck never felt that he was becoming a German satellite or compromising the independence of Poland's foreign policy.[56] He did not join Germany in an anti-Bolshevik or anti-Russian crusade, although he was gratified whenever the Nazis told him of their dislike, not merely of Communism, but of any Russian state whatever its complexion. As early as the autumn of 1934, Göring had thrown out some hints that Poland might well join Germany in an anti-Russian agreement, but Pilsudski "cut short this conversation by declaring that Poland, a country bordering Russia, had to adopt toward that Power a moderate and calm policy and could not adhere to any combination of the sort to revive tension on our eastern frontiers."[57] Beck appears to have held to this view in face of subsequent hints and offers.[58]

[54] Beck, *Dernier rapport*, p. 101.

[55] In a conversation with Anthony Eden on April 2, 1935, Szembek remarked: "In any event, for the Poles there is no doubt that of all the possible regimes in Germany the present Hitlerian regime is the most satisfactory; the proof is that we have arrived at an understanding with it. A socialist or communist regime would inevitably entail a return to the Rapallo policy; the German Nationalists, . . . quite apart from their Russophile tendency, would, if they came to power, be most hostile to Poland. Hitler is the only German statesman who has wished, and known how to reach, an understanding with us. For these reasons, it is impossible for us, or at least very difficult, to join any action whatsoever which is directed against Hitler and the policy which he represents." Szembek, *Journal*, pp. 55-56.

[56] The difficulty, however, of maintaining this independence in practice is shown by a remark of Szembek to the Polish ambassador to Russia in December 1938: "It is exceedingly hard for us to maintain a balance between Russia and Germany. Our relations with the latter are entirely grounded on the belief of the leading personalities of the Third Reich that, in the future conflict between Germany and Russia, Poland would be the natural ally of Germany. In these conditions, the good-neighbor policy, which has its origin in the 1934 accord, could easily appear to be but a pure and simple fiction." Szembek, *Journal*, p. 386.

[57] Beck, *Dernier rapport*, p. 34.

[58] For example, in his conversations with Ribbentrop in January 1939, Beck explained the impossibility of Poland's joining the Anti-Comintern Pact. At the same time, he was

Some authors, Polish and of other nationalities, have gone so far as to argue that the chief fault of Beck's diplomacy was not the German connection, which was actually Pilsudski's responsibility, but the fact that, having achieved it, he did not then ride it for all it was worth. It is difficult to guess how such a venture might have turned out. In the short run, gains in the east might have compensated for the loss of Danzig and control over the Corridor. But, at the end of this road lay Machiavelli's warning: "A prince ought to take care never to make an alliance with one more powerful than himself for the purpose of attacking others, unless necessity compels him . . . because if he conquers, you are at his discretion."

Even Beck's unpleasant performance at the time of the Munich crisis was not planned in concert with the Germans. Western diplomats as well as many Poles felt, in the summer of 1938, that Poland's rapprochement with Germany was "degenerating into an undignified imitation of the small fish that seek their meat in the wake of the shark."[59] Nevertheless, Beck insisted he was pursuing an independent policy. As he later expressed it, "I formulated on the part of Poland a simple and at the same time very supple demand. I declared we demanded simply that, if the government of Prague decided to make concessions to other countries, our interests should be treated in exactly the same fashion. When the diplomats asked me to define our demands or claims, I categorically refused to do so and affirmed that Poland did not have the intention of dismembering the Czechoslovak state or of taking the initiative in an attack against this country, and that, consequently, it did not feel called upon to give a rigid precision to its claims. That if, however, the Czechoslovak state, a veritable mosaic of nationalities hitherto governed by methods of brutal centralisation, had the intention of revising its policy or its regime in order to take better account of the interests of a particular national group, we could not admit that the Polish minority, which was grouped in a very compact manner in a region situated on our frontier, should be less well treated than any other ethnic group."[60]

Having taken this "most favored nation" attitude, Beck was bound to be evasive when queried by the French or British ambassadors. The

---

on sufficiently close terms with the Germans to discuss with them the problems which might arise if internal pressures in Russia should lead to a war or if the Soviet Union should break up into national states. He did not, however, think that either eventuality was likely in the near future. Szembek, *Journal*, p. 413. On Ribbentrop's interest in Polish adhesion to the Anti-Comintern Pact, see Chapter 15, §v above.

[59] *British Documents*, 3rd series, I, 431.
[60] Beck, *Dernier rapport*, p. 159.

Germans, however, were equally uncertain of his intentions. On July 1, the German ambassador, Moltke, reported on a conversation with Beck: "As usual, when he wishes to avoid definite statements, M. Beck said a great deal without saying anything of importance." Moltke doubted that Poland would side with France if it intervened, but he would not assume that Poland would be on Germany's side: "Poland will . . . always act exclusively according to her own interests."[61] In September, Moltke denied rumors that he had been trying to influence Poland. "Practical cooperation already exists and great emphasis on this point would not be advisable in view of M. Beck's disposition. . . . It is correct to say that Beck attached great importance to achieving Polish aims as far as possible independently and that he is trying particularly to avoid giving the outside world any impression of dependence on Germany."[62]

The basic danger in Beck's "supple" policy was that the more Germany raised its claims, the more he was obliged to raise his. As the dispute moved beyond autonomy for the Sudeten Germans to the right of self-determination and plebiscites, Beck came to demand equivalent treatment for the Polish minority.[63] When the decision was reached to cede certain Sudeten territories without a plebiscite, the Poles in turn demanded frontier revision without plebiscite.[64] By September 21, the Polish government was pressing hard on the Czechs, denouncing the 1925 Polish-Czech convention dealing with minorities and demanding rapid action. To the Czech appeal for negotiation, the Poles responded even more peremptorily, in part because of a belief that the Soviet note of September 23, threatening to cancel the Polish-Soviet nonaggression pact, was somehow related to the Czech notes.[65]

Then came the Munich Conference at which the dispute was suddenly taken over by that old enemy of Polish diplomacy, the Four Powers. Germany gained its demands; Poland was not even invited to the meeting. Beck decided that an immediate reaction was in order and asked for a march on Teschen as a "protest against the Munich proceedings." On September 30, he sent a twelve-hour ultimatum to the Czechs, the text of which, as Benes subsequently remarked, was "almost identical with the ultimatum which Hitler sent to Beck himself a year later with respect

[61] *German Documents*, series D, II, 449-452.
[62] *ibid.*, pp. 973-974.
[63] *ibid.*, p. 811.
[64] *ibid.*, p. 849.
[65] Beck, *Dernier rapport*, pp. 163-164. It was agreed by British and German observers alike that the one thing likely to push the Poles explicitly into the German camp was the appearance of Russian interference.

to the solution of the question of Danzig."[66] This was not Colonel Beck's finest hour.

The first inkling that Polish-German relations were up for review came shortly after Munich when, on October 24, Ribbentrop proposed to the Polish ambassador a general settlement of issues between Poland and Germany. This settlement included the reunion of Danzig with the Reich, an extraterritorial road and railway across Pomorze, a guarantee of frontiers, joint action in colonial matters, and a common policy toward Russia on the basis of the Anti-Comintern Pact.[67] Beck's response was conciliatory but held that "any attempt to incorporate the Free City into the Reich must inevitably lead to conflict."

According to Beck, writing in October 1939, the turning point in his own mind concerning relations with Germany was his interview with Hitler on January 4 of that year. To his alarm he noted "new accents" in Hitler's remarks. The Chancellor, while continuing to propose German-Polish cooperation, now "treated with levity the ideas which he and German propaganda had hitherto elevated almost to the level of a religion."[68] Still unwilling to revise his estimate of Hitler, Beck thought that perhaps the Fuehrer was still inclined to be cautious but that Ribbentrop, "a dangerous personality," was urging a reckless course. Upon his return to Warsaw, Beck felt sufficiently alarmed to tell Moscicki and Smigly-Rydz that these shifts in the German mood might presage war. Ribbentrop visited Warsaw later in the month, but the conversations were not fruitful. Beck refused to give way on Danzig or Pomorze despite suggested compensation in Slovakia and even mention of the Black Sea.[69]

With the German occupation of Prague and Memel in March, the situation deteriorated rapidly. If Poland's Ukrainian problem had been relieved by Hungary's taking over Ruthenia, this gain was far outweighed by Germany's annexation of Bohemia and Moravia and its virtual military control over Slovakia, which, as General Jodl said, now made it possible to "consider the Polish problem on the basis of more or less favorable strategic premises."[70] By March 28 the German ambassa-

---

[66] Letter from Benes to L. B. Namier, April 20, 1944, in Namier, *Europe in Decay* (London, 1950), p. 285.

[67] *Polish White Book*, p. 47.

[68] Beck, *Dernier rapport*, p. 182. See also Szembek, *Journal*, p. 407.

[69] Beck, *Dernier rapport*, p. 186; *Polish White Book*, pp. 54-58.

[70] Cited in Royal Institute of International Affairs, *Survey of International Affairs, 1939-1946: The World in March 1939* (London, New York, Toronto, 1952), p. 291.

dor was accusing Beck of wanting "to negotiate at the point of a bayonet." To which Beck replied, "That is your own method."[71]

Thus, Beck's efforts to maintain good yet independent relations with Germany had come to failure. His basic error was a misreading of the Nazi movement and of Hitler's personality. That he was deeply chagrined by this turn of events, which undid his whole diplomatic strategy, is not surprising.[72] It was reported that, after his highly popular speech of May 5, in which he courageously stood up against the German menaces, "in a fit of rage, [he] had thrown a whole pile of congratulatory telegrams into a corner."[73]

Whatever Beck's personal feelings, it was clear that if he was to resist Germany he had to look abroad. Britain, and secondarily France, were the Powers to which he necessarily turned. But, as has been observed above, by the spring of 1939 it was far from certain that Britain and France were capable of rescuing Poland. Polish-Soviet relations now assumed decisive importance.

VIII

Although Pilsudski and Beck declared that their policy was to keep Poland evenly balanced between Germany and the Soviet Union, Polish diplomacy was in practice perceptibly off-center. Pilsudski brought with him the deep anti-Russian feelings of his revolutionary and wartime career. To these were added a justifiable suspicion of Bolshevik intentions and a concern about the large Ukrainian and White Russian minorities in Poland's eastern provinces. As in many states bordering on Russia, the outcome was a conviction on the part of the government, so pervasive as to be almost unspoken and undebated, that no positive and fruitful relationship with the Soviet Union was possible.[74] In the 1920's, a Polish

---

[71] *Polish White Book*, p. 69.

[72] For an illuminating picture of Beck's mood and outlook at this time, see the account of a train journey with him by the former Rumanian Foreign Minister, Grigore Gafencu. *Last Days of Europe* (New Haven, 1948), pp. 26-53.

[73] According to the Polish Under-Secretary of State, Miroslaw Arciszewski, who is reported to have given this information to the German ambassador, Beck was not happy about the Anglo-Polish declaration of mutual assistance, was forced to make his address of May 5 because of the Fuehrer's speech of April 28, and was exasperated by the Polish public's enthusiastic reception of it. "M. Beck even now basically favors the previous policy." *Vorgeschichte*, p. 253. It is difficult to tell whether this statement actually represented Beck's views, since it was designed for German ears. Moreover, on several occasions Arciszewski seems to have gone beyond his instructions and acted on his own.

[74] The government's view was not identical with that of Polish opinion in general. In March 1936, Szembek remarked, "Polish opinion is thoroughly hostile to Germany and, in contrast, is favorable to France and even Sovietophile. I consider that it is indispensable to make the principles of our foreign policy popular." Szembek, *Journal*, p. 172.

ambassador returning from Moscow reported to Pilsudski that he had not tried to settle conflicts of little importance but had rather sought to ameliorate general relations between the two countries. The Marshal interrupted him to say, "Now, that is curious. I should have done exactly the opposite."[75] While Beck always stressed the importance of an independent Polish policy and the value of bilateral negotiations, he was not enthusiastic about dealing bilaterally with the Soviet Union. When discussing in his memoirs the negotiations leading to the Polish-Soviet pact of 1932, he observed that Poland's traditional policy demanded "solidarity with all the western neighbors of Russia."[76] There was no equivalent sense of a need for solidarity with Germany's eastern neighbors when it came to negotiating with that Power.

Certain steps were taken, however. Poland (along with Estonia, Latvia, and Rumania) signed the Litvinov protocol on February 9, 1929, the Polish-Soviet pact of nonaggression of July 25, 1932, and—with Russia's other neighbors—the London convention for the definition of aggression of July 3, 1933; and, in 1934, Beck made his trip to Moscow to balance the signing of the German-Polish pact.

Within the next two years, however, Polish-Soviet relations fell off greatly. In July 1936 the new Polish ambassador in Moscow, Grzybowski, was received by Krestinsky, Litvinov's deputy, with blunt words: "The political relations between us could not be worse. We are working to increase the prestige of the League of Nations, and for collective security; we are combatting all forms of aggression and all forms of fascism. At the present time we are pursuing an anti-German, anti-Italian and anti-Japanese policy. Poland is pursuing a diametrically contrary policy, tending to weaken the League of Nations, combatting attempts to realize collective security, supporting Italy and sympathizing with Japan. Poland is within the orbit of German policy."[77]

Grzybowski, of course, denied this interpretation and his rather rueful comment on this meeting must sound familiar to those who have had occasion to deal with the Soviet Union: "Irrespective of Polish policy, the Soviets constantly interpreted it so as to contrapose it to their own policy."[78] Nevertheless, it is true that Beck disapproved of the Soviet entry into the League of Nations, regarded collective security as a Communist device, and was highly critical of France and Czechoslovakia for signing

[75] Beck, *Dernier rapport*, p. 6. [76] *ibid.*, pp. 10-11.
[77] *Polish White Book*, p. 195.
[78] Grzybowski himself, however, was not pleased with Poland's Soviet policy, which he regarded as uselessly hostile. See his remarks in December 1938, Szembek, *Journal*, pp. 386-387.

treaties of mutual assistance with the USSR. Indeed, the more one considers the course of Polish diplomacy the more this deep-rooted and altogether natural mistrust of Russia seems to give a distinct flavor to Polish attitudes on almost all issues. Beck said at the end of his career, "In the course of the twenty years of my political activity in the field of foreign affairs, I acquired the conviction that the essential element which created divergences between Polish policy and French policy was not the German question but, invariably, the manner of viewing the Russian problem."[79]

Beck not only regarded the Soviet Union as a dangerous power but he denied that it could serve as a counterweight to Germany, notwithstanding the mutual hostility of these two powers in the 1930's. In 1937 he and Winston Churchill informally discussed this issue while relaxing at Cannes but were unable to agree. "I could not avoid the impression," Beck later wrote, "that this eminent statesman lived too much on his memories of the preceding war and that he was too inclined to consider Russia as a relatively important counterweight to German dynamism. I tried to make him understand that Europe could not have the least confidence in Soviet Russia and that we, its neighbors, had more evidence than anyone for judging the Russian phenomenon with skepticism."[80]

When Beck went to London in April 1939 to negotiate the British-Polish mutual assistance pact, he felt he should state Poland's position on having Russia as an alliance partner. Poland, he said, had no confidence in Russia or in the ends it pursued. It had had experience with Tsarist imperialism and with Communist imperialism, and they came to the same thing. However, in face of the German menace, there was no point in rebuffing Russia; one should at least be assured of its neutrality. Though doubtful of its achievement, he would not oppose an English-French-Soviet entente, but such an accord could not impose new obligations on Poland. He would be satisfied if an arrangement were made whereby, in case of war with Germany, arms could be sent to Poland via Russia and Russia could provide raw materials.[81]

The involved story of the unsuccessful efforts by the British and French to reconcile this position with the mounting demands of the Russians in the abortive negotiations of the spring and summer of 1939 cannot be told here. There is no question, however, that the Polish refusal to agree to the presence of Soviet troops on Polish soil was, as a

[79] Beck, *Dernier rapport*, p. 193.   [80] *ibid.*, p. 127.
[81] *ibid.*, p. 193. See also British comments on Polish attitude toward military cooperation with Russia, in *British Documents*, 3rd series, IV, 428, 453.

debating point at least, an important factor in the breakdown of the negotiations. The reluctance of the Poles to make this concession is certainly understandable, nor is it by any means certain that a greater show of cooperation on their part would have deflected the Soviet Union from its pact of August 23 with Germany. Nevertheless, the utterly negative quality of Polish-Soviet relations appears very clearly in a set of conditions laid down by the Polish ambassador in a conversation with Molotov in May 1939: "We could not accept a one-sided Soviet guarantee. Nor could we accept a mutual guarantee, because in the event of a conflict with Germany our forces would be completely engaged, and so we would not be in any position to give help to the Soviets. Also we could not accept collective negotiations, and made our adoption of a definite attitude conditional on the result of the Anglo-Franco-Soviet negotiations. We rejected all discussion of matters affecting us other than by the bilateral method. . . . I indicated our favorable attitude to the Anglo-Franco-Soviet negotiations, and once more emphasized our entire loyalty in relation to the Soviets. In the event of conflict we by no means rejected specified forms of Soviet aid, but considered it premature to determine them definitely. We considered it premature to open bilateral negotiations with the Soviets before the Anglo-Franco-Soviet negotiations had achieved a result." The ambassador continued, "M. Molotov made no objection whatever."[82] Indeed, there seemed to be very little to say.

Interestingly enough, Beck was quite pleased that Molotov had replaced Litvinov, whom he regarded as the "notorious enemy of our country." "It was possible to suppose that the anti-Polish complex peculiar to this man, who was by origin a *litwak*, had disappeared with him."[83] Just as Hitler, an Austrian, was to alter the anti-Polish bias of the Prussian tradition, so, presumably, Molotov was to rid Soviet policy of the anti-Polish prejudices of the *litwak* Litvinov.[84] Here again Beck's own nationalism was misleading him. By reducing foreign policy to such motives he was unable to grasp the basic drives of either the Nazi or the Soviet dictatorship.

For a brief period, it is true, Molotov adopted toward the Poles an attitude of "the greatest courtesy." The Soviet government offered to supply them with war materials; the Soviet press urged resistance to German demands. In retrospect, of course, this amiability, which con-

---

[82] *Polish White Book*, p. 208.

[83] Beck, *Dernier Rapport*, p. 200.

[84] Beck described the *litwak* as the "worst of the Jewish types, deported from Russia to the Polish provinces and who, at Vilna or at Bialystok, offended Polish ears with his Russian jabber." (*Ibid.*, p. 139).

tinued until the German attack, appears altogether sinister: intended at first to conceal the German-Soviet rapprochement and then, perhaps, to prolong Polish resistance in the event France and Great Britain failed to declare war on Germany.

In this instance, however, Beck's position did not change. To the last he refused to have Soviet troops on Polish territory;[85] and the most he would concede was that, after hostilities had started, he might agree to reexamine the question with a view to possible Soviet-Polish cooperation.

IX

Beck's diplomatic career ended in complete disaster. All his policies turned against him. The nonaggression pact with Hitler did not prevent a German assault; the disintegration of Czechoslovakia weakened rather then strengthened his southern frontier; his refusal to admit Russian soldiers to Polish soil did not keep them from overrunning eastern Poland in September 1939. Nor was this just bad luck. His views on the art of diplomacy, his estimate of the international situation, and his analysis of political motives were filled with inconsistencies that inevitably led to self-defeating policies.

He was not just an opportunist, though the charge of unprincipled opportunism has been laid against him. He adhered, rather arrogantly and purblindly, to a set of axioms which he took to be Pilsudskian heritage and which made up in their obvious preoccupation with the Polish national interest what they lacked in coherence and universality. But, unlike Churchill, who was fighting against the current and whose speeches of the 1930's have the real mark of prophetic insight, Beck was engulfed in the currents of his time, and his prophecies tended to be self-fulfilling ones which his own activities and outlook helped bring to pass.

Still, when all this has been said, an appraisal of Beck cannot be wholly negative. For all the errors of his policy, he was not one of the really malignant creatures of the decade. Contrary to widespread contemporary belief, he was not in league with Hitler, even though the two often appeared to be working in collaboration. Even in the case of his least defensible action, the ultimatum to Czechoslovakia, he was, to a large degree, the victim of his own "most favored nation" formula; the movement of events which drove him to such an unfortunate action came from the interaction of German aggressiveness and the wobbling retreat of the

[85] In mid-August 1939, Beck said to Noël, "Nothing assures us that, once they are installed in the eastern parts of our country, the Russians will participate effectively in the war." Noël, *L'Agression allemande*, p. 423.

Western Powers, France and Great Britain. He did not like Czechoslovakia, but he did not plot its destruction.

Nor can one say that he contributed greatly to the disaster that overtook Europe, except in the sense that his actions fed into a vicious circle which intensified and compounded the weaknesses of the existing international order. The League of Nations was indeed a weak reed, though attitudes such as Beck's helped make it so. Russia was indeed a dangerous and unpredictable Power, though Beck's policy toward Russia did nothing to make it less dangerous or unpredictable and seemed to provide a rationale for Soviet actions in 1939. In this respect, he is highly symptomatic of the 1930's. The feeling, so apparent in his memoirs, that there were no feasible alternatives, was characteristic of a general European mood which was creating, and being created by, the approaching catastrophe.

In one regard, however, Beck definitely deserves respect. When the final test came, he did not yield. In a desperate situation, partly of his own making, he took an unprovocative but courageous stand. The result, to be sure, was a horrible war, the outcome of which was not real peace and which had tragic consequences for Poland during and after the hostilities. For this reason there have been some to criticize him for not allying himself with Hitler, just as there have been those to rebuke Great Britain for not having been shrewd enough to let Poland fall as it had let Czechoslovakia fall. Whatever the results of such policies, one thing would have been missing in the future: the will to defy. Even in the painful situation of the world today, it is heartening to know that this value was not permitted to drain out of the life of nations as it threatened to for a time in the 1930's.

These considerations, however, extend beyond the horizon of Beck's career, which stopped in September 1939. By the end of his life he was far removed from politics and diplomacy. In August 1943, only ten months before his death, he wrote to his daughter-in-law: "Reading what you report to me, I have had the impression of a kind of doubling of my personality. Here am I, taking care of my lungs, which are in a pitiable state, and, there, a phantom moves about the world, another Jozef Beck with whom I have had no relations for four years. He goes this way and that, engages in conflicts, is attacked, is spoken of in books. He is a solid enough type, since he has moved about so long without my aiding him in anything. What a strange spectacle! I ask myself if someday I shall have the possibility and the desire to meet him again in this world or whether I shall abandon him to his own devices."[86]

NOTE ON POLISH PROPOSALS FOR PREVENTIVE ACTION AGAINST GERMANY

A number of writers and diplomats have referred to a proposal, or proposals, for preventive action against Germany which Marshal Pilsudski is said to have made to the French shortly after Hitler came to power. There seems to be no authoritative contemporary evidence, however, and the stories are not altogether consistent.

The Communist journalist "André Simone" stated that, in March 1933, Pilsudski informed the Daladier government of the alarming progress of German rearmament and proposed to France that the Hitler regime be crushed by a "preventive war." Daladier demurred, then refused. The offer was repeated in April, but there was no response. (*J'Accuse: The Men Who Betrayed France*, New York, 1940, p. 53). This account seems to be the source of substantially the same story which appears in J. W. Wheeler-Bennett, *Munich, Prologue to Tragedy* (London, New York, 1948), pp. 283-284. The emphasis here upon Pilsudski's concern over Germany's rapid arming is in conflict with Ambassador Noël's statement that Pilsudski believed Germany would require a generation before being ready to make war (*L'Agression allemande contre la Pologne*, pp. 67-68).

Pertinax stated that in April 1933 Poland proposed a preventive war, knowing that it would not be taken up, as a preliminary to its move toward Germany (*Les Fossoyeurs*, New York, 1943, II, 83).

The Polish journalist Stanislaw Mackiewicz wrote that in March 1933 Pilsudski deliberately tried to start a war with Germany. While granting that no evidence had been found in Poland of a memorandum addressed by Pilsudski to Daladier, he contended that Pilsudski's reinforcement of the Polish garrison on the Westerplatte was intended as a provocative act. (*Colonel Beck and His Policy*, London, 1944, p. 15) Beck, in his memoirs, interpreted this move as a warning to Germany of Poland's alertness, not as a provocation (*Dernier rapport*, pp. 25-27).

L. B. Namier has written that on three occasions, in March and November 1933 and again in March 1936, the Poles suggested to France armed action against Germany; he adds that Pilsudski's initiative in 1933, though authentic, cannot be easily documented (*Diplomatic Prelude*,

---

[86] Beck, *Dernier rapport*, p. xxiii.

1938-1939, London, 1948, p. 97, note 3). With regard to the November effort: "Pilsudski was sounding Paris once more about common action against Hitler. The talks were confined to military channels—the first approach was made through General d'Arbonneau, French Military Attaché in Warsaw. The result was negative . . ." (*ibid.*, p. 15). Apparently the source for this statement was Jozef Lipski, Polish ambassador in Berlin, who wrote to Namier: "After the German Ambassador, von Moltke, had on November 27 presented to Marshal Pilsudski the German draft of a non-aggression pact, I was instructed by Colonel Beck to keep the matter strictly secret, and that also towards the *corps diplomatique*. Pilsudski, who personally dealt with the problem, would not sign a pact with the Germans before sounding Paris once more about jointly taking decisive action against Hitler, which was a further reason for his instructing me to preserve absolute silence." (L. B. Namier, *Europe in Decay*, London, 1950, p. 282, note 1). Lipski elsewhere makes the same point: "Pilsudski se rendait clairement compte des possibilités militaires de l'Allemagne. La preuve en est qu'il me chargea d'employer devant le dictateur du Reich l'argument de la force. Hitler le comprit et proposa à Pilsudski un pacte de non-agression. Étant en possession de l'offre allemande, le Maréchal fit encore une fois des ouvertures à la France, suspendit les pourparlers avec Berlin, et partit pour Wilno. Cette fois encore Paris ne manifesta aucune volonté d'action." (J. Lipski, *Sprawy Miedzynarodowe*, No. 2-3, 1947, p. 15, quoted in Beck, *Dernier rapport*, p. 32, note 1).

Against this rather scattered evidence is the fact that there appears to be no mention of any Pilsudskian proposals in 1933 in the documents the Germans captured in Warsaw, in Léon Noël's memoirs, in the volumes thus far published by the French parliamentary commission of enquiry (*Les Événements survenus en France de 1933 à 1945*), or in Beck's three memoranda written between 1939 and 1943 (*Dernier rapport*). If Beck's interpretation of Pilsudski's point of view is to be trusted, the Marshal, in 1933, did not regard the Hitler regime as a serious threat, though he seems to have given some theoretical consideration to the advisability of preventive action. Apparently, military intelligence studies made in 1933 and 1934 (see note 52 above) led the Polish regime to believe that neither Germany nor Russia was in a condition to undertake any immediate military action. Beck, however, felt that of the two Russia was the more likely to risk an adventurous undertaking (*Dernier rapport*, pp. 65-66). His view was shared by Under-Secretary of State Szembek, who said to Eden in April 1935: "We have, however, arrived at the conclusion that the policy of Soviet Russia is to a certain degree hysterical, in any event less logical, and consequently less calculated than the policy of the Third Reich; it is for that reason that we consider we are threatened by surprises more from the side of Russia than from the side of Germany." (Szembek, *Journal*, p. 55.) If such was the case it would be both unnecessary and dangerous to move against Germany.

20

Yosuke Matsuoka and the Japanese-German Alliance

BY JOHN HUIZENGA

ON July 22, 1940, Yosuke Matsuoka, who had been absent from the international stage since his dramatic performance of Japan's withdrawal from the League of Nations in 1933, suddenly reappeared in the role of Foreign Minister. With few exceptions Japanese Foreign Ministers had, since the inauguration of a professional diplomatic service in 1893, come from the ranks of career officials. It was symptomatic of the change in the control of Japanese foreign policy midway between the wars that Matsuoka, who had left the Diplomatic Service in 1921 after a successful career of almost two decades, should have found an entirely different route to the top of the Kasumigaseki.

The civilian career diplomacy, like the brief promise of genuine parliamentary government which developed in Japan after the first world war, fell victim to the increasing domination of political life by the military after 1931. It became the instrument rather than the maker of policy. Whereas in other countries party governments sometimes imposed handicaps on professional diplomacy, in Japan professional diplomats could have retained control of foreign policy only if parliamentary government had succeeded. The reason was, of course, that in Japan the alternative to disciplined party cabinets was government by bureaucracy. In a contest of bureaucratic factions the active military services, with their unique prerogative in Japan of providing or withdrawing Ministers of War and Navy, held the key position. By the simple expedient of withdrawing a service minister they could upset a cabinet if the Foreign Minister attempted to follow a line of policy disapproved by them. They could commit the government's policy by local action, as they did in the Manchurian incident in 1931, in the certain knowledge that Japanese nationalist pride would not permit a civilian government to retreat. They could hamper negotiations with other Powers by staging local incidents prejudicial to negotiations, as was done frequently after 1937 when the invasion of China led to the violation of rights of third Powers there. They could conduct domestic propaganda, as the army did through controlled newspapers, especially the chauvinist organ, *Kokumin*. They could, if necessary, covertly sponsor and protect young officer fanatics in the employment of terror and assassination against opponents of extremist policies, as they did in the episode of February 26, 1936.

In March 1936, after the Okada Cabinet had been brought down by assassination in the February 26 Incident, the Cabinet of Koki Hirota, ironically enough a professional diplomat himself, set the pattern of military control.[1] It was not overt control, for an open military dictatorship was less desirable in the eyes of the military than effective control behind a façade of civilian government. Moreover, in view of the code of honor customary in Japanese public life it was dangerous, in the event that serious reverses of policy occurred, to be placed in the position of having to "assume the responsibility." With respect to foreign policy, military control did not become absolute, mainly because of factional differences within the services themselves. Nevertheless, no policy could be pursued by the Foreign Ministry without military approval, and in the end career diplomats were reduced to playing the game of faction and intrigue themselves.

On June 30, 1936, the Japanese War and Navy Ministers in the new Hirota Cabinet agreed on a "Basis of National Policy" which was "to consist in advancing toward and developing the South Seas as well as obtaining a firm position in the East Asiatic Continent." In detail it was stated that "Japan intends to get rid of the menace of the USSR, to prepare against Britain and the United States, and to bring about close collaboration between Japan, Manchukuo and China." Further, it was agreed that "in the execution of this continental policy, Japan must pay due attention to friendly relations with other powers."[2] Presumably the authors had in mind here the courting of Germany which had been carried on assiduously for some time by the military attaché in Berlin, Col. Hiroshi

---

[1] G. B. Sansom, *Japan in World History* (New York, 1951), p. 89; Royal Institute, *Survey of International Affairs, 1936* (London, 1937), pp. 894-895.

[2] *International Military Tribunal for the Far East* (hereafter cited as IMTFE), Exhibit No. 216. Most of the German and Japanese documents used in this study were introduced in the 1946-1948 Tokyo trial and may be found under exhibit numbers in the trial record.

Oshima, and was to result in November 1936 in the Anti-Comintern Pact between the two countries.

This outline of policy, which in broad terms charted Japan's course in the ensuing years, was then, on August 11, 1936, adopted by the Five Ministers Conference in which the two service ministers were joined by the Prime Minister, Foreign Minister, and Finance Minister. The procedure followed illustrated graphically that in Japan foreign policy, in consequence of the decisive role assumed by the military, had become inseparable from military policy. This fact was to condition profoundly Matsuoka's brief and stormy tenure at the *Gaimushō*.

I

Matsuoka had identified himself early with the military's foreign policy views. The South Manchurian Railway, of which he became Vice President in 1927, had been deeply involved in the Manchurian incident and had profited from the establishment of the puppet state of Manchukuo.[3] His associates in Manchukuo included members of what later became known as "the Manchuria gang," men like Tojo, who became Prime Minister of the war cabinet, Ohashi, who was to serve under Matsuoka as Vice Minister of Foreign Affairs, and Hoshino, who was later to occupy the key post of Chief of the Cabinet Planning Office. Matsuoka's role at Geneva in 1933 won him wide popular acclaim at a time when the military, who did not then exercise the control of public opinion which they later acquired, could only have welcomed a civilian hero personifying Japan's defiance of world opinion. "His fellow-countrymen looked upon him as a modern Horatius defending his people against the onslaughts of the world," Ambassador Grew reported. "His arrival home was the occasion for a public patriotic demonstration of a size seldom seen in Japan."[4] The significance of what Matsuoka had done at Geneva could not have been lost upon the military proponents of what in Japan was called a "positive" foreign policy. For by her withdrawal from the League Japan had declared her intention to repudiate the peace settlement for the Far East embodied in the Washington Treaties of 1922. In these treaties, according to the advocates of a "positive" policy, weak civilian diplomacy had betrayed Japan's victory in the first world war and her vital interests.

Not long after his return from Geneva in 1933 Matsuoka identified

---

[3] Report of Ambassador Grew to the Department of State, March 24, 1933, in *Foreign Relations, 1933*, III, 247-251.

[4] Report of Ambassador Grew to the Department of State, Dec. 14, 1933, *ibid.*, pp. 713-715.

himself publicly with another favorite theme of the military party. Although he had been elected to the Imperial Diet in 1930 and again in 1932 as a member of the Seiyukai party, he appealed for the abandonment of party government. "Western style party government," he declared, "does not conform to the conditions of our country nor the character of our people. . . . The time has come when the Japanese race must carry out its important mission in the interests of peace. . . . As a first step I advocate the dissolution of parties."[5] It was said in Japan at the time that his ambition had been fired by the public acclaim he had received, and that he repudiated his reputation as a political liberal because he expected a reactionary cabinet and hoped to be a member of it. He was correct in his judgment as to where the path to future power would lie, even if it was to be some time before he could set foot upon it. At least, in 1935, he was rewarded with the presidency of the South Manchurian Railway Company.

When in November 1936 the Anti-Comintern Pact with Germany was announced, "most of the comment on the Government's action was definitely critical."[6] The *Tokyo Asahi* wrote on December 2, 1936, that Japan "would not derive much benefit" from the association with Germany and warned that "if Japan should make an enemy of England, which holds much latent power in the Far East, it is not difficult to imagine that England, France, America, and Russia would cooperate."[7]

The Japanese Foreign Ministry itself accepted the Pact reluctantly. In a statement accompanying release of the Pact it was at pains to make it clear that Japan was not entering upon a relationship of alliance with Germany, but was "desirous of cooperating with as many Powers as possible for the purpose of perfecting their defensive measures against the Comintern menace, but for that purpose alone."[8]

The truth was that the military party had forced the Pact through against the better judgment of the Foreign Ministry. As the newspaper *Nichi Nichi* put it, "Foreign Office circles received the rapprochement

---

[5] *ibid.*, p. 714.

[6] *Survey of International Affairs, 1936*, p. 927. See also the comments of the German ambassador on the opposition of court circles and industrialists in Herbert von Dirksen, *Moskau, Tokio, London* (Stuttgart, 1949), p. 188. See also Chapter 13, § IV and Chapter 15, § I above.

[7] Quoted from a longer extract of the *Asahi* editorial in David H. James, *The Rise and Fall of the Japanese Empire* (London, 1951), p. 185.

[8] The English text of the statement is published in *Foreign Relations: Japan 1931-1941* (Washington, 1943), II, 155-157. Foreign Minister Arita promised the Privy Council in obtaining its approval of the Pact that the announcement would make it clear that the Pact did not mean that Japan would thereafter "act in concert" with Germany. IMTFE, Exhibit No. 484.

with Germany with much hesitation, but the enthusiasm of the Army was so strongly expressed that the Cabinet was obliged to conclude the agreement as national policy."[9]

It was characteristic of statements of public policy in Japan that they were so vaguely or loosely phrased that contending factions were allowed to preserve face. Opponents of the Pact had been allowed a statement which seemed to minimize the Pact's significance, particularly in terms of alliance with Germany. On the other hand, the military party had the Pact itself, including a secret protocol which amounted to a military arrangement with Germany against the Soviet Union.[10] It would be left to events or the efforts of the contending factions to resolve contradictions or ambiguities.

The military party began at once a campaign to win support for the Pact and at the same time to interpret it as an alliance with Germany. It was Matsuoka who now appeared as a principal advocate. In a speech delivered in Dairen on December 23, 1936, he attacked the lukewarm and apologetic attitude shown toward the Pact by the government and the press. He said that the meaning of the Pact was not to be found only in cooperation against the Comintern. "The historical significance of the Pact can be understood," he declared, "only if it is regarded as an alliance by which Japan, for the first time since 1922, entered upon an active foreign policy. And this alliance cannot be close enough; it must mean going together through thick and thin, and it must be based on complete loyalty and mutual self-sacrifice, as these find expression in Japanese *shinjū*."[11] Matsuoka was said sometimes to be quite carried away by his own impassioned oratory and on this occasion seems to have reached heights of true prophecy, for the Japanese-German alliance did indeed come to have something of the character of a suicide pact.

A formal alliance with Germany was to be long in coming, however. In 1937 when the Japanese began their invasion of China, the Germans resisted attempts to represent them as supporting the Japanese action, since the German Foreign Ministry and German army did not wish to sacrifice the considerable German interest in China.[12] Ribbentrop, then

[9] Quoted by Hugh Byas in his dispatch to the *New York Times* printed on November 26, 1936.

[10] The text of the protocol remained secret until after the second world war when it was found among documents captured by the Allies. It is printed in *German Documents*, series D, I, 734.

[11] The speech was printed in pamphlet form under the title "The Significance of the Japanese-German Anti-Comintern Pact" (*Nichi-doku Bōkyō Kyōtei no Igi*, Dairen, 1937).

[12] *German Documents*, series D, I, 742-744; Dirksen, *Moskau, Tokio, London*, pp. 185, 190-191.

the coming man in German foreign policy, felt no such hesitations, however. In January 1938, shortly before becoming Foreign Minister, he recommended to Hitler that an alliance with Japan be sought,[13] and discussed it with Oshima in the summer of that year.[14] In October he disclosed the plan to Mussolini, who gave his consent on January 3, 1939, to the signing of a triple alliance which it was then thought could take place within a few weeks.[15] In Japan, however, the army advocates of the plan met with resistance they could not overcome, for the opponents of the alliance now included the navy, which was willing to accept an obligation against Russia but was not willing to be committed against Britain as well, the only terms on which Germany would conclude.[16] The Japanese Cabinet remained in a state of virtual paralysis over this issue until Germany's surprise announcement of the nonaggression pact with Soviet Russia in August 1939. "This wholly unexpected turn of events, which the greatly embarrassed Hiranuma Cabinet described as 'intricate and baffling' . . . immediately brought to an end the life of the Cabinet itself as well as the whole scheme of an alliance against Russia."[17]

Marquis Kido, who became Lord Privy Seal in 1940, wrote in his diary on August 22, 1939 that he "was astonished at this extremely treacherous act, considering the existence of the Anti-Comintern Pact and the Secret Pact."[18] The really devoted adherents of the tie with Germany were only briefly shaken, however. In Berlin, Oshima, who at the army's insistence had been named ambassador, accepted Secretary of State von Weizsäcker's advice that "it was not legal technicalities that were of consequence, but realities as they were understood between men and soldiers," and withheld the formal protest his government had ordered him to present. He even informed Tokyo falsely that he had carried out these instructions. After the conclusion of the Polish campaign when, as he explained to Weizsäcker, "the step was no longer of so much consequence," he presented a version of the protest diluted on his own authority with the suggestion that it "be allowed to disappear in the archives."[19]

---

[13] *ibid.*, pp. 162-168.   [14] Oshima Interrogation, IMTFE, Exhibit No. 776.
[15] *German Documents*, series D, IV, 515-520, 543-545.
[16] An account of this episode based on the Tokyo trial exhibits is given in Herbert Feis, *The Road to Pearl Harbor* (Princeton, 1950), pp. 28-32. See also *Documents on International Affairs, 1939-1946*, I (London, New York, 1951), pp. 145-159, which prints English translations of relevant Italian documents.
[17] Memorandum by Prince Fumimaro Konoye, "On the Tripartite Alliance," IMTFE, Exhibit No. 2735A.
[18] Extract from Kido Diary, IMTFE, Exhibit No. 775.
[19] Weizsäcker's memoranda of conversations with Oshima on August 26 and September 18, 1939, are printed in *Department of State Bulletin*, June 16, 1946, pp. 1038-1039.

Despite a statement of the Japanese army expressing "disappointment" over the Nazi-Soviet Pact, activist elements were saying in the columns of *Kokumin* that the military alliance with Germany was still needed because Britain was the real enemy of "Japan's new order" in Asia. It appeared that what disturbed the army supporters of the alliance with Germany was not so much the fact that Germany had made a pact with. the Soviet Union, but that they had not been informed of it in advance. There was no little loss of face—and in Japan "face" was an ingredient of power—in being thus cavalierly treated by the partner with whom they had proposed to enter into a brotherhood of arms.

Matsuoka was not officially involved in these events, although he moved closer to the center of the political stage during the period in which the alliance with Germany was under consideration. He was named member for foreign affairs of the Cabinet Advisory Council during Prince Konoye's 1937-1939 Cabinet, and in 1939 he resigned the presidency of the South Manchurian Railway Company to give his full time to political activity. A busy backstage pleader, he never wavered in his support of a German alliance on the army's terms during the 1939 deadlock, a fact which doubtless had much to do with his rise to power the following year.

The period of phony war in Europe was reflected in a period of phony truce in Japanese internal politics, with the active partisans of the Axis alliance obliged to efface themselves because of their "disgrace." The German attack in the West, the collapse of France and the Low Countries, and the peril of Britain threw the Japanese domestic scene into confusion once more, however. The prospects opened up by the sudden reversal of the balance of power in Europe led the military activists to raise a new clamor for the control of Japanese foreign policy. Not only did their earlier demand for closer ties with Germany seem to represent prescient wisdom, but the ambitious programs of expansion so long advocated by them seemed at last to be attainable. "The German military machine and system and their brilliant successes have gone to the Japanese head like strong wine," Ambassador Grew noted in his diary.[20]

The moderate Cabinet of Admiral Yonai made desperate efforts to save itself. On June 29 Foreign Minister Arita scheduled a radio address in which he proposed to announce his government's intention to consolidate its friendship with the Axis. The army, however, insisted on the revision of his speech, protesting that a "policy of sympathy for the Axis is not compatible with the policies hitherto pursued by the Cabinet," and

[20] Joseph C. Grew, *Ten Years in Japan* (New York, 1944), p. 325.

declaring that it would not allow the Cabinet to use "a sudden stress on friendship with the Axis as a maneuver to take the wind out of the sails of the opposition . . . and to save its own existence." The military police arrested the press officer of the Foreign Ministry who had revealed the army's action on Arita's speech to the newspaper *Asahi*.[21]

On July 5 the Chief of the Metropolitan Police in Tokyo uncovered an assassination plot, the victims of which were to have been Prime Minister Yonai and other government leaders.[22] The "plot" may have been serious or it may have been only the ritual by which the military party indicated that it meant to have its way by extreme measures if necessary. In any case, three days later the Vice Minister of War, General Anami, called on the Lord Privy Seal, the official who would be responsible for initiating a Cabinet change, and laid down the army's terms. He said that "the character of the Yonai Cabinet is not at all suitable for making negotiations with Germany and Italy and it might even cause a fatal delay." The army wanted Prince Konoye and would leave the choice of a Foreign Minister up to him.[23] On July 16 War Minister Hata resigned and the army refused to nominate a successor, thus forcing the Yonai Cabinet out of office. There followed the usual ceremonial consultations with elder statesmen, a title now assigned to former Prime Ministers, but it was noteworthy that no names other than Prince Konoye's were mentioned.[24] It seemed to be clearly understood that the army would not be denied.

Konoye's choice of Matsuoka as Foreign Minister was a natural one. He was an experienced professional diplomat and there were few if any diplomats who would have had the army's confidence at that moment. Only a man who had not opposed the Axis alliance in 1938-1939 would have been acceptable. In addition, Matsuoka, with his American education and experience of diplomatic service in Washington, may have seemed to Konoye the right man to handle Japan's difficult relations with the United States, relations likely to become more difficult as Japan drew closer to the Axis. The shifty vagueness of Japanese political language always left a great deal unclarified, and it is most unlikely that Konoye could have anticipated his later difficulties with Matsuoka on relations with America.

The government which took office on July 22, 1940, was perhaps as

[21] Telegram, Ambassador Ott to German Foreign Ministry, July 3, 1940, IMTFE, Exhibit No. 531.
[22] Kido Diary Extract, July 5, 1940, IMTFE, Exhibit No. 532.
[23] *ibid.*, July 8, 1940.
[24] *ibid.*, July 17, 1940.

unified in its foreign policy aims as any which Japan had had in some years. It had taken a radical realignment of the balance of power in Europe to accomplish this result. The reason was clear. The inherent limitations of Japan's power had always greatly restricted her freedom of action. Her whole forward progress as a Power had been based on association with a dominant Power or Powers in Europe. Her one serious humiliation and reverse, the Triple Intervention of 1895, resulted from her error in exposing herself in isolation to the united front of a combination of European Powers. The great debate in Japanese policy after the challenge of Nazi Germany had developed in Europe was between those who wished to link Japan's fortunes to this new Power, and those who preferred her traditional association with the Western Powers, or who at least did not regard Germany as a sufficient counterweight against Anglo-American naval power. During the Hiranuma Cabinet of 1939, the demand of the army for the former course had been staved off by a narrow margin. Now events seemed to have terminated the debate. And Matsuoka, long active in the shadow world of intrigue behind the façade of Japanese public life, qualified by his associations and his publicly expressed views, gained the opportunity to play the role which his ambition had so long coveted.

II

In the view of the new Cabinet the most urgent task which confronted it, a task in which delay might be fatal, as General Anami had said, was that of clarifying its relations with Nazi Germany, now suddenly by virtue of its dramatic victory the dominant Power in Europe. The impact of the German victory seems to have been, if anything, greater in Japan than elsewhere. "The world is now on the threshold of a stupendous historic change," were the opening words of a Cabinet policy statement approved on July 26, 1940.[25] Matsuoka later told an imperial conference that the defeat of Britain had seemed likely within the first ten days of the new Cabinet's existence.[26]

The gratification in Japan over the prospects opened up by a British defeat was mixed with genuine alarm and uncertainty as to the view which a victorious Germany might take of the new situation in the Far East. Would Germany acknowledge Japan as the inheritor of the remnants of Western empire in Asia or would she put forward successor claims of her own based on her military successes?

[25] IMTFE, Exhibit No. 540.
[26] On Sept. 26, 1940. IMTFE, Exhibit No. 550.

Foreign Minister Arita had already made some effort to deal with this problem as it emerged. On April 15, 1940, he issued a statement that "the Japanese Government cannot but be deeply concerned over any development accompanying an aggravation of the war in Europe that may affect the *status quo* in the Netherlands East Indies."[27] A German reaction was disconcertingly slow in coming and was obtained by specific request only after other Powers had at once acknowledged their support for the *status quo* in the Indies. At length on May 20 German Ambassador Ott was authorized to make an oral declaration to Arita of Germany's "disinterestedness in the Netherlands East Indies question."[28]

On June 19 Ambassador Kurusu received instructions in Berlin to suggest "a German declaration to the effect that Japan would have a free hand in Indochina."[29] No immediate reply was forthcoming and ex-Foreign Minister Sato, who was on a special mission to Italy, was sent to Berlin where he had a talk with Ribbentrop on July 8. He found the German Foreign Minister "non-committal" on the subject of the Dutch East Indies and Indochina. Sato said in his report to Arita that he was not prepared to conclude that Germany harbored "an ambition on the Southern colonies" but it must be recognized that German thinking had undergone a change in consequence of the great victory that had been won.[30]

The reserve shown by Ribbentrop, it is now evident, resulted from his confidence that the Yonai-Arita Cabinet was in its last days of life and that there was no need to assist its survival. There would soon be a government in Japan more to his liking, one dominated by men with whom he had dealt covertly for years in the expectation that they would one day rule Japan. Ott had reported on June 24 that "leading personalities of the Konoye circle are obviously trying to make contact with me" and that a new government under Konoye was indicated.[31]

Even the new government, however, was not entirely confident that the German attitude toward Japanese aspirations would be all that might be desired. Matsuoka himself said later, though perhaps in part to reflect credit on his diplomatic skill, that "German enthusiasm for cooperation

---

[27] *Foreign Relations, Japan*, II, 281.

[28] Telegram, Ribbentrop to Ott, May 20, 1940, IMTFE, Exhibit No. 517.

[29] Telegram, Ott to German Foreign Ministry, June 19, 1940, in *Department of State Bulletin*, June 16, 1946, pp. 1039-1040. Kurusu had replaced Oshima as ambassador in Berlin in 1939 and was replaced by him again in the winter of 1940-1941.

[30] Exchange of telegrams, Sato-Arita, July 13 and 15, 1940, IMTFE, Exhibits Nos. 525, 526.

[31] Telegram, Ott to German Foreign Ministry, June 24, 1940, IMTFE, Exhibit No. 523.

with Japan was generally at a very low ebb."[32] He was therefore careful not to show excessive eagerness. Already on July 18, before taking office, he had conveyed "confidentially" to Ambassador Ott his intention to accept the post of Foreign Minister and his request for "friendly co-operation."[33] He waited until August 1, however, before inviting Ott for their first political conversation. The delay may have seemed the more justified since on July 22 Lord Halifax rejected Hitler's peace offer of three days earlier and the collapse of Britain seemed, if not less certain, at least less imminent.

The German ambassador appeared on August 1 armed with a bundle of outstanding complaints. The Japanese had been insufficiently helpful in facilitating shipments via Manchukuo of raw materials purchased in Asia. Damage claims arising from Japanese operations in China had gone unremedied. The English language press in Japan had carried on anti-German propaganda. Japanese officials had impeded the repatriation via Japan of German nationals stranded in the Americas. Ott "left the Foreign Minister with no doubt that Japan had much to make up for to bring about even a state of benevolent neutrality toward Germany."[34]

Matsuoka was "most cordial" and promised to look into all these matters. Then, indicating his distaste for diplomatic language and indirection, a formula he employed often by way of showing his honesty and candor, he plunged into the business at hand. As the ambassador had no doubt heard, there was a disposition in Japan to strengthen relations with the Axis. The Cabinet had decided nothing, but he, Matsuoka, an old advocate of closer relations with Germany, wished to explore the German attitude with a view to urging such a course on his colleagues if possible. What view would Germany take of Japan's proposed new order for Asia, including the South Seas? What were Germany's expectations with regard to relations with America and with the Soviet Union? How did Germany anticipate that Japan's relations with these two countries should develop?

The German ambassador wanted to know first what area was meant by Matsuoka's reference to the South Seas. Matsuoka cautiously gave it as his personal opinion that Japanese aspirations for the present extended as far as Siam but might be enlarged if circumstances indicated. Ott raised no objections to this and went on to say that Germany's views on the

---

[32] IMTFE, Exhibit No. 550.

[33] Telegram, Ott to German Foreign Ministry, July 18, 1940, IMTFE, Exhibit No. 535.

[34] Telegram, Ott to Weizsäcker, August 2, 1940, IMTFE, Exhibit No. 622.

South Seas region would, of course, depend on the further course of her war against Britain, and particularly on whether the struggle against Britain was prolonged into an effort to destroy the British empire. In this case, he implied, a Japanese contribution in some form might be expected. In the light of these perspectives he answered Matsuoka's other questions. Germany's relations with Russia were stable, and particularly since the German victory in the West, involved no danger. He thought Japan would be well advised to negotiate for improved relations with Russia and proposed German good offices. As for America, Germany did not expect her participation in the war. The tide of American opinion had turned against Roosevelt's efforts to involve the country. Germany had no intention of courting any future disputes with the United States and hoped for an eventual improvement of relations. He called particular attention to this point as it was important that a similar attitude be held in Germany and Japan toward the United States. Matsuoka agreed that Japan also hoped for peaceful relations with the United States.[85]

It was clear from this conversation that a meeting of minds was nearer than might have been hoped. The dispatch with which concrete negotiations were taken up confirmed this impression. Within a month a special negotiator had arrived in Tokyo. He was Heinrich Stahmer, in charge of Far Eastern questions in the *Dienststelle Ribbentrop*, and named minister for this assignment. For those familiar with Ribbentrop's working methods and his preference for circumventing his own Foreign Ministry in important negotiations, this was another sign of the seriousness of German intentions. When Konoye, Matsuoka, War Minister Tojo, and Navy Minister Yoshida on September 4 laid down the guiding principles for the negotiations, they noted that the sending of Stahmer indicated that the mission was likely to be more than exploratory.[86]

The four agreed that the principal object remained to obtain a recognition of the Japanese *Lebensraum* in East Asia, a convenient application of a German concept which showed that the Japanese had not lost their talent for appropriating Western ideas to their own uses.[87] The area of Japanese hegemony was to embrace India on the West and Australia and New Zealand in the South. The Germans were to be told for the present, however, that the outer limits were to be Burma and New Cale-

---

[85] Matsuoka's Memorandum of Conversation, August 2, 1940, IMTFE, Exhibit No. 545.
[86] IMTFE, Exhibit No. 541.
[87] Ambassador Grew noted in his affidavit presented at the Tokyo trial (IMTFE, Exhibit No. 1105) that the expression "Japan's New Order in East Asia" began to be employed in 1938. The German successes in that year obviously led the Japanese to believe that with similar slogans the walls of Jericho might fall for them, too.

donia, India being left to the Soviet sphere if necessary. It was recognized that German claims on the Dutch East Indies might be encountered and it was hoped at least to negotiate a "predominant position" there by "preferential supply to Japan of natural and material resources" while guaranteeing existing German undertakings.

It was further agreed that peace should be maintained with the Soviet Union and that the partners should join in "inducing the Soviet Union to bring her policy into line" with theirs. There should be cooperation in preventing the United States from interfering in regions outside the Western Hemisphere and United States possessions, and mutual assistance in the event that one of the partners became involved in war with the United States.

While it was recognized that "unless we are resolved on the employment of armed force, it will be impossible for us to carry on any useful talks with Germany" a request for military cooperation against Britain was to be met for the present only with an agreement in principle. It would be explained that, pending settlement of the China Incident, Japan felt obliged to confine herself to actions short of war, unless conditions took a decidedly favorable turn. Japan would, however, continue her political and propagandistic harassment of the British in Asia as a contribution to the German-Italian war against the Empire.

Matsuoka, still thinking it best not to show too much eagerness, allowed Stahmer to cool his heels in Tokyo for some days. When he finally saw Stahmer and Ott on September 9 the business proceeded with remarkable ease. After meetings on three successive days they were near to agreement on a draft. The Germans "did not ask any detailed questions" about the territorial limits of "Greater East Asia" and only asked that Germany's economic needs in that area be accommodated.[38] Further, Germany did not "look for Japan's military assistance at this juncture in connection with her war with England." The German attention was focused almost exclusively on the United States. "What she [Germany] wishes of Japan," Stahmer said, "is to have Japan play the role of restraining and preventing the United States from entering the war." This was an immediate and pressing objective for, barring American entry, the war might soon be terminated. Then there was the "long view," for even after the defeat of England there would be a "stupendous struggle against the British Empire, not to say the Anglo-Saxondom including America" and this struggle would "go on for tens

[38] Matsuoka Statement to Imperial Conference, Sept. 26, 1940, IMTFE, Exhibit No. 550.

of years yet, in one form or another." By declaring herself at once Japan would assist the immediate aim of keeping the United States out of the war, and would assume in the longer view the posture which was in accordance with her interests, for "war between Japan and the United States cannot eventually be avoided."[39]

On September 19 Ribbentrop arrived in Rome to give his Italian allies their first information on the alliance which they would be expected to sign within a few days. No more than his spokesmen in Tokyo did he speak of the territorial limits of *Lebensraum* or haggle over the terms of Japanese hegemony in East Asia. He discussed the proposed pact entirely in terms of completing the victory over Britain. The invasion was prepared, he said, and would be undertaken after eight or ten days of good weather for air operations. The fact that the British in their desperate circumstances continued to be "particularly impudent" was, in the Fuehrer's view, due partly to "lack of comprehension" but also to the hope of outside intervention by Russia and America. "It is in order to meet this eventuality," the Italian record of the conversation continues, "and above all to paralyze America, that Herr von Ribbentrop has prepared, and now submits for the Duce's approval, the project of a tripartite alliance with Japan. . . . In German opinion, the formation of an alliance of that nature should have the advantage of reinforcing the isolationist reaction against Roosevelt's interventionist policy."[40]

This was the Duce's opinion, too. "One must bear in mind," he said, "that the Americans are very much afraid of Japan and of her fleet in particular, since the American fleet, while being quantitatively large, must be considered an amateur organization like the English army."[41]

Meanwhile in Tokyo the laborious machinery of Japanese policy making moved with unaccustomed speed. On the night of September 14 Marquis Kido sat with War Minister Tojo at the death watch for Prince Kitashirakawa and Tojo related to him secretly that the army and navy had that day given approval to the Axis alliance.[42] The Privy Council, which, as its history showed, could be extraordinarily obstructive and which surely still contained many opponents of the pro-Axis course, gave its consent on September 26. The great range of questions asked of Cabinet ministers suggested that a number of its members were more

---

[39] Japanese Foreign Ministry Memorandum: "Salient Points in the Informal Conversations Between Matsuoka and Stahmer," September 9-10, 1940, IMTFE, Exhibit No. 549.

[40] Galeazzo Ciano, *L'Europa verso la catastrofe* (Verona, 1948), p. 587.

[41] *ibid.*, p. 590.

[42] Kido Diary Extract, September 14, 1940, IMTFE, Exhibit No. 627.

cowed than convinced.[43] Matsuoka had glib answers for everything. Would the alliance drive the United States and Soviet Russia into each other's arms? There were no signs of it and he intended to take up Soviet-Japanese problems at once with German assistance. Was it not true that German-American relations were susceptible of improvement while Japanese-American relations were not, and hence was there "no fear of Japan alone drinking from the bitter cup?" Matsuoka replied that everything would be done to avoid war with America and to this end the German alliance would be helpful since there were 20 million Americans of German descent. Ribbentrop sometimes used this argument to discount the American danger but Matsuoka could hardly have been ignorant of its falsity.

The old Viscount Ishii, who had negotiated Japan's adherence to the Allied side in the first world war, and had written of the "shiftiness" of German policy under the Kaiser,[44] was full of warnings. Allies of Germany in the past had suffered only disaster; Hitler was a Machiavellian who had publicly stated that one should not hesitate to break alliances when convenient; he was known to have held anti-Japanese views in the past. Ishii would not oppose the pact because he believed that in terms merely of the balance of power the national interests of the three countries were parallel and Japan needed allies. But, he warned, "the national character of Germany is such as would suck the blood of others" and he hoped that after the pact was signed the government would not "neglect to take exhaustive and scrupulous care so that we need have no future regrets."[45]

If the men who now governed Japan were little inclined to heed this cautious voice of an older generation of statesmanship, they were still Japanese enough to hedge carefully the commitment they were undertaking. Article 3 of the Pact stated that the three Powers "undertake to assist one another with all political, economic, and military means when one of the three Contracting Parties is attacked by a power at present not involved in the European War or in the Sino-Japanese Conflict."[46] This seemed straightforward enough, but Matsuoka had obliged Ribbentrop to withdraw his original phraseology which required

---

[43] Protocol of Privy Council Investigation Committee on Tripartite Pact, Sept. 26, 1940, IMTFE, Exhibit No. 552.

[44] Kikujiro Ishii, *Diplomatic Commentaries* (Baltimore, 1936), p. 42.

[45] Record of Privy Council Meeting in Imperial Presence, September 26, 1940, IMTFE, Exhibit No. 553.

[46] The full text of the Tripartite Pact, signed at Berlin on September 27, 1940, is published in *Foreign Relations, Japan*, II, 165-166.

that aid take effect if one of the partners was attacked "directly or indirectly."[47] Moreover, he had obtained from Ott a letter which included the statement: "It is needless to say that whether or not a Contracting Party has been attacked within the meaning of Article 3 of the Pact shall be determined upon consultation among the three Contracting Parties."[48] He also assured the Privy Council that "in the event of the worst situation" Japan would "be able to choose the time and place to let the Japanese Navy participate in the war." The Japanese had shown great agility in the willful interpretation of written agreements; it could scarcely be doubted that in the fulfillment of this Pact, too, they would find ways to consult their own interests if necessary.

Despite the long period in which a German-Japanese alliance had been promoted in the two countries, the Pact which was actually made in 1940 had something hasty and impromptu about it, and it is doubtful that the participants looked very far down the long dark vistas which it opened up. As has been seen, in the minds of Ribbentrop and Hitler the Pact was prompted largely by the immediate concern to restrain the United States and Russia from intervening to defraud them of their anticipated early victory over Britain. It was a characteristic maneuver of Nazi diplomacy in the sense that its value was reckoned primarily in terms of immediate propaganda impact. For Matsuoka and his colleagues the first concern had been to accommodate themselves as quickly as possible to the prospects of a British defeat. This meant to obtain insurance that the vacuum which would be left by the collapse of British power in the Far East would be filled by Japan and that other potential aspirants would be excluded, among them Germany herself. The implications of the Pact, if it should prove necessary to implement it against the United States, were faced only reluctantly in the discussions which took place in the Privy Council. And the calculation on which both parties agreed, that the Pact would cause the United States to stand aside because it would strengthen those in America who opposed intervention, was in error. On the contrary, the interventionist case in the struggle to win American opinion was strengthened, for the danger to the United States, once given the shape of a worldwide conspiracy of aggressors, seemed more real and intervention to forestall it more imperative. It was to this theme, that the United States faced a conspiracy of Powers which entertained unlimited aggressive aims, that the Roosevelt administration appealed in opening the campaign a few

[47] IMTFE, Exhibit No. 550.   [48] IMTFE, Exhibit No. 555b.

months later for Lend-Lease.[49] Far from deterring, the Pact accelerated the process of American involvement and widened the area of the contest, so that in the American mind the problem of peace or war with Japan became inseparable from the problem of peace or war with Germany. On November 1, 1940, Ambassador Grew noted in his diary: "Now that the Tripartite Alliance has been concluded, we can no longer regard and treat with Japan as an individual nation. She has become a member of a team, and our attitude toward Japan must be our attitude toward the team as a whole."[50]

III

As the Japanese leaders had agreed in laying down the terms of negotiation on September 4, the alliance with Germany and Italy was not conceived as an isolated maneuver but was linked with the intention to solve the problems presented by Russia and China. If attention was to be focused on an advance into South Asia and the South Seas in the wake of the collapse of the Western empires, it would be necessary to free Japanese forces from their commitment in China and to insure that Russia would not menace Japan from the rear.

Every Japanese Cabinet since 1937 took office with promises that first attention would be given to solving the China Incident, a festering sore which for the Japanese people was as psychologically disturbing as it was economically taxing. The new Konoye Cabinet was no exception. In its policy statement of July 26 it promised that its foreign policy would "be directed, first of all, toward a complete settlement of the China Affair."

Matsuoka, when he assumed Office, appeared confident of his ability to liquidate the China problem. He told the German ambassador on August 1 that Japan would be able to deal with it alone, and rather pointedly rejected a hint that German mediation could be of assistance. Obviously he was aware that a Japan which continued to flounder in the morass of China would be a less desirable ally in German eyes. Ott, who had long believed that Japan's value as a partner for Germany depended on disengagement of her forces from China,[51] pressed for an explanation of Matsuoka's plans and indicated that in his view negotiation with Chiang Kai-shek should not be excluded. Matsuoka replied that Japanese policy was committed to the position that Chiang had to be crushed en-

[49] See President Roosevelt's "arsenal of democracy" speech of December 29, 1940, printed in *Foreign Relations, Japan*, II, 173-181.
[50] *Ten Years in Japan*, p. 349.
[51] See his report of November 1, 1938 in *German Documents*, series D, IV, 685-689.

tirely. He did not believe that a military solution was the only possible one, however, and would not absolutely refuse to negotiate with Chiang.[52]

There was some suggestion in this conversation and in later statements he made to the Germans that Matsuoka would have liked to introduce somewhat more flexibility into Japan's China policy. He indicated during his Berlin conversations in the spring of 1941 that he was in personal touch with Chiang Kai-shek, and that the latter "knew him and trusted him."[53] Whatever the nature of these efforts may have been, Matsuoka did not succeed in altering the essential line of Japanese policy. During the first months of the Konoye Cabinet it was obviously hoped that the impact of British reverses, which had forced the British on July 18 to halt military shipments to China via Hong Kong and Burma, together with the threat imposed by Japan's incursion into Indo-China effected on September 22, would shake Chungking's resolution. In addition, there was Japan's alliance with the victorious Axis, which in the prestige-conscious Orient might set off a flight from the camp of national resistance. The only way held open to the Chinese, however, was by way of reconciliation with, or in effect submission to, the Wang Ching-wei regime at Nanking. Wang, who had departed Chungking at the end of 1938 to sponsor a peace movement, had been installed in Nanking on March 30, 1940, as head of a new "Central Government." This step, perhaps undertaken more as a maneuver of the weak Yonai-Arita Cabinet to improve its domestic position than as a well-considered measure of China policy, had only rendered a settlement in China more difficult. The Japanese, however, had refrained from giving full recognition to the Nanking regime, and Matsuoka, when he spoke of not refusing entirely to negotiate with Chiang, apparently thought that there was still room for maneuver. The reopening by the British of the Burma supply route on October 18, however, required a new gesture to document Japan's implacable determination in China, and on October 25 it was decided to give formal recognition to the Nanking regime. Before taking this step, however, resort would be had to German intervention. The German Foreign Minister was to be asked to give the Chinese ambassador in Berlin a final warning that the recognition move was imminent and to suggest that Chungking should "discontinue the useless war against Japan as soon as possible" if it did not wish to be "left behind in the advance of the new world situation."[54] Ribbentrop did oblige,

---

[52] IMTFE, Exhibit No. 545.   [53] *Nazi-Soviet Relations*, p. 305.
[54] Japanese Foreign Ministry Memorandum, October 25, 1940, IMTFE, Exhibit No. 628.

though in somewhat more moderate language and with protestations that he had not been prompted by the Japanese.[55] The Chinese found Ribbentrop a no more plausible advocate for submission than the Japanese themselves, and on November 30 Japan was obliged to proceed with the recognition of the Nanking regime.

It is evident that Matsuoka, whatever hints he may have passed about secret negotiations with Chiang Kai-shek, either had no fresh ideas to overcome the stagnation of Japan's China policy, or was not in a position to bring them forward. Certainly the latter was likely to have been true in any case, for the views of the Japanese army on China were fixed. The prestige of the Japanese army, and therewith its claim to a dominant role in Japanese domestic politics, depended on the attainment of its announced objectives in China. The army well remembered the cloud under which it had fallen in consequence of the fiasco of the Siberian expedition. The result had been a loss of face which had much to do with the movement toward civilian control and even party government in Japan in the decade before 1931. There had been demands for cuts in military budgets and—as the military zealots put it—a traitorous abandonment of the Empire's sacred mission. The army's views on China policy had been fixed since 1937. At the end of that year an attempted German mediation had provided an opportunity to negotiate a settlement with Chiang Kai-shek, but pressure on Tokyo from the army command in China had led to the drafting of terms wholly unacceptable to the Chinese. The German ambassador learned that even the General Staff was deterred from an inclination to seek peace "in view of the radical opposition and the striving on the part of some Army groups to eliminate Chiang Kai-shek completely."[56] By the end of 1938, after the fall of Hankow and Canton, it had become the official determination of the Japanese Government, "to carry on the military operations for the complete extermination of the anti-Japanese Kuomintang Government."[57] The military had thus forced Japanese policy on China into complete rigidity. Matsuoka's formal recognition of the Wang Ching-wei regime was a further abdication of diplomacy to military policy. This was a bankrupt policy which insisted on ignoring the force of modern Chinese nationalism and proposed to subdue China by methods reminiscent of both the Mongol invasion and nineteenth century Western imperialism. Even if Matsuoka would' have preferred

[55] *Nazi-Soviet Relations*, p. 224.
[56] *German Documents*, series D, I, 789-790, 799, 802-804.
[57] Statement of Prime Minister Konoye, December 22, 1938, printed in *Foreign Relations, Japan*, I, 482-483.

to preserve a more fluid situation in China, he had no real choice. It was precisely on this issue of no retreat from the positions staked out in China that in October 1941 Tojo broke with Konoye, and declared that war with the United States was preferable to repudiating the sacrifices of the Japanese army in China.[58]

IV

The alternative to negotiating with Chungking was, short of the total victory which the military wanted but could not produce, an attempt to further isolate it and to constrict its sources of outside aid. This, quite aside from the desire for a secure rear for the "Southward advance," was a principal motivation for the approach to Russia which it was agreed should follow in the wake of the Tripartite Pact. It was calculated not only that the Soviet Union might be induced to withdraw its support from Chungking but also that it would then take the Chinese Communist party out of the anti-Japanese front, and thus remove "the greatest obstacle to the rise of the influence of the advocates of peace in Chiang Kai-shek's camp."[59]

When Matsuoka presented the draft of the Tripartite Pact to the Privy Council he thus made it clear that an attempt to reach an understanding with the Soviet Union was an integral part of his foreign policy program. He held out no certain promise of success in the attempt, however. He put the chances at "fifty-fifty" and indicated that the outcome would depend entirely on the assistance that might be obtained from Germany.[60]

Ribbentrop had, in fact, ever since Germany's own pact with Russia, urged the Japanese to follow in his footsteps to Moscow. He saw Oshima in the opening days of the Polish campaign and told him that Germany was "quite capable and if desired also ready to mediate for a settlement between Japan and Russia."[61] In Rome on March 11, 1940, the German Foreign Minister solicited Mussolini's support. He asked the Duce to give his ambassadors in Moscow and Tokyo instructions to work for a Russo-Japanese settlement. He had found Stalin "very reasonable" on this subject, and pointed out: "The greater liberty Japan has vis-à-vis Russia, the better she will be able to exercise her useful function as a means of putting pressure on England and America."[62]

[58] Konoye Memorandum, "Facts Pertaining to the Resignation of the Third Konoye Cabinet," IMTFE, Exhibit No. 1148.
[59] IMTFE, Exhibit No. 628.　　　　[60] IMTFE, Exhibit No. 552.
[61] Telegram, Ribbentrop to Ott, September 9, 1939, IMTFE, Exhibit No. 507.
[62] Ciano, L'Europa verso la catastrofe, p. 538.

The Abe Cabinet which assumed power at the outbreak of the war did succeed in terminating the Nomonhan incident which saw Soviet and Japanese troops engaged in full-scale battle on the Mongolian border in the summer of 1939. The Russian willingness to liquidate this affair, which was accomplished by Molotov and the Japanese ambassador in Moscow on September 16, 1939, was doubtless related to the activation of Russian policy in the West. On the morrow of the agreement Russian troops entered Poland in execution of the partition agreed upon with Germany. By the end of the year, however, the German ambassador in Tokyo was reporting that no further progress in Soviet-Japanese relations was to be observed. There had been desultory negotiations on border questions and on fisheries but the important political issue, the question of Soviet support for Chiang Kai-shek, had not been touched.[63] Like its predecessor, the Yonai Cabinet which followed in January 1940 was principally preoccupied with the problem of improving relations with the United States. It was perhaps also recognized that even if a political agreement with Russia could be obtained it would be likely to hinder rather than help a solution of the American problem.

On conclusion of the Tripartite Pact, however, the attempt to come to terms with the Soviet Union entered on a new phase. Ribbentrop now undertook to provide more active assistance, and it was this which was the principal reliance of Matsuoka's policy with respect to Russia. Molotov's visit to Berlin in November 1940 provided Ribbentrop the occasion to press the Japanese suit.

Already in his letter to Stalin of October 13, 1940, in which the invitation for Molotov to visit Berlin was extended, Ribbentrop raised the question of Russo-Japanese relations, arguing that "friendly relations between Germany and Soviet Russia as well as friendly relations between Soviet Russia and Japan, together with the friendship between the Axis Powers and Japan, are logical elements of a natural political coalition which, if intelligently managed, will work out to the best advantage of all the powers concerned."[64]

The character of this "natural political coalition" in which Russia would associate herself with the signatories of the Tripartite Pact was spelled out for Molotov in Berlin on November 12 and 13, 1940. The four Powers were to agree on a delimitation of their spheres of interest and were to aggrandize themselves jointly at the expense of the "Brit-

[63] Telegram, Ott to German Foreign Ministry, December 31, 1939, IMTFE, Exhibit No. 3503.
[64] *Nazi-Soviet Relations*, p. 213.

ish bankrupt estate," the defeat of Britain being, according to Ribbentrop, already an accomplished fact. They would all agree that their natural areas of expansion lay to the South, and Ribbentrop assured Molotov that in Japan, too, "*Lebensraum* policy . . . now was oriented not toward the East and North, but toward the South." Therefore, "just as it had been possible to delimit the mutual spheres of interest between Soviet Russia and Germany, a delimitation of interests could also be achieved between Japan and Russia."[65]

Molotov showed himself little interested in these grand perspectives. Far from dividing up remote regions of the British Empire, the talks became a near wrangle over "spheres of interest" in the immediate area of Soviet-German contact, particularly in Finland and the Balkans. Concerning a delimitation of areas of interest between Japan and Russia Molotov would only say that he found "quite vague" the idea of the "Greater East Asian Sphere" which had been assigned to Japan in the Tripartite Pact. He would have to obtain a "more accurate definition of this concept." Moreover, "Russia wanted to come to an understanding with Germany, and only then with Japan and Italy, after she had previously obtained precise information regarding the significance, the nature, and the aim of the Tripartite Pact."[66]

In one of his two talks with Hitler, Molotov made one other remark which would hardly have cheered Matsuoka, for it showed that Russia would not be likely to assist, as Matsuoka had planned it, in bringing Chiang Kai-shek to reason. Molotov said that "an honorable solution would have to be assured for China, all the more since Japan now stood a chance of getting Indonesia."[67] This was surely a plain enough hint that the inclusion of China in the "Greater East Asian Sphere" would be disputed. Matsuoka's conception had been that Russia, intimidated by the encirclement of the Tripartite Pact, despite the formal assurances given to her in its Article V, would withdraw support from Chiang Kai-shek and assist Japan to settle the China Incident. Molotov was far from intimidated at Berlin, either on Far Eastern or on other issues. German assistance to bring Russian policy into line proved to be an illusion. Matsuoka was wrong in supposing it might be possible to approach Moscow by way of Berlin.

It was in recognition of this error that, a little more than a month later, Matsuoka resolved to proceed to both these capitals in person. On December 19 he apprised Ott of his desire to accept an invitation to Berlin which the German Foreign Minister had extended at an earlier

[65] *ibid.*, p. 220.   [66] *ibid.*, p. 225.   [67] *ibid.*, p. 247.

date. Ott reported that Matsuoka emphasized "his need to make a strong gesture in favor of the Tripartite Pact and if possible to personally overcome the deadlock in the negotiations with Russia and China."[68] This was an acknowledgment, in effect, that the Pact had thus far failed in one of its main objects. Conceived as a gesture which, under the impact of the apparent German triumph over Britain, would cause Russia and China to fall in with Japanese plans for Greater East Asia, it now in turn required a new "gesture" to sustain its effect. There was a further revealing note in Ott's account of his conversation with Matsuoka on the proposed Berlin visit. He had the impression, he said, that Matsuoka "would like to enhance the weight of his policy and himself." Evidently Matsuoka felt the need for a "gesture" on his own behalf as well.

V

By the time Matsuoka reached Berlin, toward the end of March 1941, there was much more involved than a ceremonial visit for purposes of prestige. On December 27, 1940, the German naval command pressed on Hitler the importance of operations against British sea power before the invasion of Russia, already in preparation, was carried out. It was suggested that the Japanese might be encouraged to undertake an assault on Singapore.[69] By the end of January Ott reported from Tokyo that there was some sentiment in favor of such a move in certain activist circles but he thought that the Japanese would probably agree to the attack only if it could be made simultaneously with a German invasion of Britain.[70] On February 23 Ribbentrop took up the matter with Oshima, who had just returned as ambassador to replace Kurusu. The attack on Singapore, to be made "with lightning speed, if at all possible without a declaration of war," would be a decisive blow which would force Britain to sue for an early peace, he said. He hoped that Matsuoka would bring with him "a final decision to attack Singapore soon."[71]

The conversations in Berlin which opened on March 27 brought together in Hitler, Ribbentrop, and Matsuoka the three foremost practitioners of the art of the statesman's monologue, that characteristic form of diplomatic intercourse among the Tripartite leaders.[72] In all their

---

[68] Telegram, Ott to Ribbentrop, December 19, 1940, IMTFE, Exhibit No. 567.

[69] "Fuehrer Conferences on Naval Affairs, 1939-1945" in *Brassey's Naval Annual, 1948*, p. 161.

[70] Telegram, Ott to Ribbentrop, January 31, 1941, IMTFE, Exhibit No. 562.

[71] Telegram, Ribbentrop to Ott, February 28, 1941, IMTFE, Exhibit No. 571.

[72] Five lengthy memoranda on the Berlin talks are printed in *Nazi-Soviet Relations*, pp. 281-316.

discursive speeches, however, Hitler and Ribbentrop returned to the same theme: Britain was tottering on the brink of defeat and only a final push was needed to bring all the Tripartite partners into their inheritance; the time had come for Japan to act and what Germany wanted was an attack on Singapore.

Considering that six months earlier, at the conclusion of the Tripartite Pact, it had been stated that no Japanese help against Britain would be expected, a Japanese statesman might have been given pause by the new line. Not so Matsuoka; he declared himself fully in accord with the German suggestion. He hastened to add, however, that he was not in a position to commit his government. "According to his idea," he said, "the attack should come as soon as possible. Unfortunately he did not control Japan . . . at the present moment he could under these circumstances make no pledge on behalf of the Japanese Empire that it would take action."[73]

It was typical of the indecisive ways of Japanese diplomacy that Matsuoka had undertaken his long and arduous mission without any clear authority to commit his government on the principal issue which concerned his German ally. In a memorandum written while en route to the Berlin talks Ambassador Ott set down the views of the Japanese military on the question of attacking Singapore. Both the army and navy were rushing preparations, but the Chief of the Navy's General Staff expressed "misgivings" because of possible British and American countermeasures. The Chief of the Army's General Staff was equally uncommitted although for a different reason. The army demanded that it be freed first from the danger of Russian intervention.[74]

The accomplishment of the latter object by diplomatic means was in fact the only concrete objective of Matsuoka's mission.[75] It was the issue of relations with Russia which made of the Berlin talks a comedy of double duplicity. Hitler and Ribbentrop did not tell Matsuoka that planning for a German attack on Russia had been going on for months, but he was given the broadest hints that relations were not cordial between Berlin and Moscow, and that anything was possible. "The Russians," according to Ribbentrop, "had for some time demonstrated their unfriendliness to Germany wherever they could." He did not think that Stalin "was inclined toward adventure, but it was impossible to be sure. The German armies in the East were prepared at any time. Should

---

[73] *ibid.*, p. 295.
[74] Ott Memorandum of March 25, 1941, IMTFE, Exhibit No. 576.
[75] This is confirmed by Toshikazu Kase who was a member of Matsuoka's delegation. See his *Journey to the Missouri* (New Haven, 1950), p. 156.

Russia some day take a stand that could be interpreted as a threat to Germany, the Führer would crush Russia."[76]

There cannot be any doubt that Matsuoka understood the significance of this startling intelligence well enough, but he did not press too closely for an explanation. He said that his talks with Stalin and Molotov en route to Berlin had been the result of Russian initiative.[77] He added that he would probably have to take up the matter of a nonaggression treaty and other pending questions on his return trip to Moscow and asked "whether he should go very deeply into these questions or treat them only superficially."

Ribbentrop replied that "in his opinion only a purely formal, superficial handling of these points was advisable."[78]

When on his return visit to Moscow Matsuoka did sign a Neutrality Pact with the Soviet Union, the Germans were surprised and annoyed. This annoyance was not decreased by Matsuoka's bland assertion to the German ambassador in Moscow that he had explained in Berlin that "he would be compelled to do something in case the Russians were willing to agree to Japanese wishes" and that Ribbentrop "had agreed in this point of view."[79]

While Ribbentrop may have been entitled to some pique for a certain lack of candor on Matsuoka's part, the Germans had in no way indicated that the deterioration of Russo-German relations at which they so broadly hinted would lead to a request for Japanese assistance against the Soviets. On the contrary, Ribbentrop had said that "if the Russians should pursue a foolish policy and force Germany to strike, he would—knowing the sentiments of the Japanese Army in China—consider it proper if that army were prevented from attacking Russia. Japan would best help the common cause if she did not allow herself to be diverted by anything from the attack on Singapore."[80] In another connection he had said that "one thing was certain: if Russia should ever attack Japan, Germany would strike immediately. He could give this firm assurance to Matsuoka, so that Japan could push southward toward Singapore without fear of any complications with Russia."[81]

All this was in strict accord with German military plans of that date, which specifically excluded any expectations of Japanese assistance in the attack on Russia. A Hitler directive on military cooperation with Japan, which called for technical assistance to the Japanese in encouraging operations by them against British forces in Asia, stated that "Bar-

[76] *Nazi-Soviet Relations*, p. 285. [77] *ibid.*, pp. 296-297. [78] *ibid.*, p. 309.
[79] *ibid.*, pp. 322-323. [80] *ibid.*, p. 309. [81] *ibid.*, p. 303.

barossa," the planned German attack on Russia, would itself provide "militarily and politically a favorable basis" for a Japanese attack on Britain in the Far East. It also stated: "No intimation of any sort is to be given the Japanese concerning the Barbarossa operation."[82]

If, as has been indicated, the principal object of his mission was to secure Japan's rear for the anticipated "Southward advance," Matsuoka had succeeded magnificently. Not only did he obtain a guarantee in the form of the Neutrality Treaty at practically no cost,[83] but he also obtained verbal assurances in Berlin that Germany would vouch for Japan's security vis-à-vis the Soviet Union. Actually these gains, so favorable to the military plans then being made in Tokyo, fell into his outstretched hands without very much effort on his part. The Germans were eager to guarantee Japan against all dangers if she could be persuaded to attack Britain in the Far East. Stalin, alerted to the German danger by Berlin's silence following the ominous note struck during Molotov's visit there, as well as by specific warnings received from the United States and Britain, was only too glad to enter into the neutrality arrangement. While he surely would not have placed much confidence in the paper guarantee of neutrality, he could not have been unaware at that critical moment of the advantage of setting the Japanese in motion to the South.

It is impossible not to have some sympathy with Matsuoka in the difficult position in which he found himself on his European visit. His German ally was hinting broadly that there might be trouble between Germany and Russia, but being at the same time most vague as to the time when such a contingency might develop, and also telling him that Japan must ignore this possible development and proceed with her assigned task, which was to assault Singapore. On the other hand, his Russian hosts had adopted a cordiality most strange indeed considering the belligerent tone which had been customary with them for some years past, particularly since Japan's invasion of China. A pact with the Soviets would constitute a personal triumph of a kind most important to Matsuoka's prestige in the shifting sands of Japanese internal politics. In the circumstances Matsuoka reached out and took what the Soviets offered him, and trusted that his explanations to his German friends would not be found wanting. It is hard to say whose was the shabbier role in this low

[82] OKW Directive of March 5, 1941, printed as document 075-C in *Trial of the Major War Criminals*, XXXIV, 302-305.

[83] Matsuoka told the German ambassador in Moscow that he refused to pay Stalin's price—abandonment of Japanese concessions in North Sakhalin—and Stalin gave in. *Nazi-Soviet Relations*, pp. 322-323.

comedy, but it must be conceded that if Matsuoka was less than candid with his allies they had hardly deserved better of him.

VI

During his European visit Matsuoka had seen his stated policies threatened with confusion, but his homecoming was to bring him new troubles in another quarter. While the Germans in Berlin were threatening a reversal of Tripartite policy toward Russia, some of Matsuoka's colleagues were exploring a possible change in the Pact policy toward America. On April 16, attempts which had been made for some time by private persons to initiate negotiations between Japan and the United States bore fruit in the presentation of a proposal by the American government.[84] Despite the Axis alliance and the far-reaching and officially approved plans for expansion in Asia at the expense of the Western Powers, there remained influential elements which hesitated to execute these plans at the risk of a clash with the United States. Court circles, certain business interests, some leaders of the navy still welcomed an attempt to reach an agreement with the United States.

In present perspective it is clear enough that these negotiations never had any prospect of success, both because the gap between the positions from which the two sides proceeded was too wide to be bridged by any verbal formula, and because those men in the Japanese government who really desired an agreement did not have control of that government. Matsuoka at once sensed the danger of such negotiations to his personal position, recognizing that what they implied was an attempt to detach Japan from the Axis. In this he was correct, for as the American record states: "This Government was impressed . . . by the consideration that the hope of defeating Hitlerism in Europe would be greatly enhanced if the more conservative elements in Japan should succeed in what was represented as their effort to divert Japan from courses of conquest and to cause Japan to withdraw—even though gradually—from the Axis camp and align itself with the United States."[85]

Matsuoka resorted first to tactics of delay, and gained two weeks by a convenient illness with which he came down in consequence of the exertions of his European trip. When he saw the German ambassador on May 5 he said that he was using the interval to arouse activist groups

[84] A full record of the Japanese-American negotiations thus launched is printed in *Foreign Relations, Japan*, II, 325ff.
[85] *ibid.*, p. 335.

of younger officers against the proposals for an understanding with the United States.[86]

His next step was to attempt to prejudice the negotiations in advance by sending a preliminary reply to Secretary of State Hull in which he stressed that Japan could undertake nothing which might adversely affect the position of Germany and Italy, to whom her honor was engaged as their ally in the Tripartite Pact. He reported the full confidence of his Axis allies in victory and their conviction that American entry, although it might prolong the war, could not alter its outcome. In a second message he proposed a Pacific nonaggression pact.[87]

The first of these messages Ambassador Nomura made only a half-hearted attempt to deliver, and after indicating his disagreement with its contents, readily accepted Mr. Hull's suggestion that he exercise his "discretionary authority" to withhold it. The nonaggression pact Mr. Hull simply "brushed aside" as incompatible with the basis of negotiations on which the talks had begun.[88]

As a result of the American negotiations Matsuoka was soon menaced by the mistrust both of his own colleagues and of his allies. He could not refuse altogether to pursue the negotiations with the United States, and on May 12 he was obliged by the Cabinet to send off a reply to Washington without awaiting the German comment which he had requested.[89] Oshima warned from Berlin that the Germans were strongly suspicious that they were being betrayed and he himself protested against what he called "two-faced diplomacy."[90]

The negotiations which Admiral Nomura now proceeded to carry on in Washington were to drag on in an endless exchange of drafts and counterdrafts, and they did not therefore force an immediate choice between a settlement with America and loyalty to the Axis. But there was no doubt where Matsuoka stood. He may have been sincere enough in his often-expressed desire to avoid war with the United States, but he had no policy for dealing with the American problem beyond that laid down in the Tripartite Pact: the United States was to be neutralized by the threat of that alliance and was to withdraw its interest from all those extensive regions which the Tripartite partners claimed for their own. This was a policy of bluff, and the diplomacy by gesture which

[86] Telegram, Ott to Ribbentrop, May 6, 1941, IMTFE, Exhibit No. 1068.
[87] "Konoye Memoirs" printed in *The Investigation of the Pearl Harbor Attack*, Senate Document 244, 79th Congress, Pt. 20.
[88] *Foreign Relations, Japan*, II, 412.
[89] "Konoye Memoirs," *Pearl Harbor Attack*.
[90] Telegrams, Oshima to Matsuoka, May 20, 1941, IMTFE, Exhibit No. 1075.

Matsuoka preferred to coming to grips with the realities of Japan's situation.

While he was engaged in these maneuvers to prevent loss of control over Japanese policy to those who wished to negotiate with America, and at the same time to prevent the Germans from discerning his weakness, Matsuoka was evidently increasingly uneasy about the development of Russo-German relations. In one of his first conversations with the German ambassador after his return he gave Ott an opportunity to enlighten him. He ventured the opinion that the possibility of American intervention and a long war "could induce the Fuehrer to resolve upon a solution of the Russian question by violent means in order firmly to secure areas of supply." He also added: "In this case, Japan would be driven by the force of necessity to attack Russia at Germany's side." Ott did not rise to this bait, but continued to stress the importance of the Singapore action.[91]

In the end the Germans did not give Matsuoka much time to accommodate himself to the drastic turn of events signalized by their attack on Russia. On June 6 a telegram from Oshima reported an interview with Hitler in which the latter announced the German decision, although he did not yet specify the date.[92] Matsuoka represented to Marquis Kido, however, that in his opinion "the conclusion of an agreement was 60 percent possible and the outbreak of war 40 percent in spite of Ambassador Oshima's observations."[93] On June 21, however, he repeated to Ott his earlier promise to join in a Soviet-German war but expressed the hope that this development might come in such a manner as to "ease his own position."[94] His position was now deteriorating rapidly, for Konoye, Kido, and the powerful Interior Minister, Hiranuma, were on that day discussing ways to be rid of him. These three had no intention of allowing Japan to be dragged in the wake of Germany into an unplanned war against Russia, clearly now Matsuoka's purpose.[95]

As always, the decision really lay with the Japanese army. When on June 28 War Minister Tojo told Kido that the army's policy toward the German-Soviet war was that they should be "calm and prudent,"[96] Matsuoka had lost the argument. On the same date Ribbentrop appealed for the first time for Japanese aid against the Soviets, arguing

[91] Telegram, Ott to Ribbentrop, May 6, 1941, IMTFE, Exhibit No. 1068.
[92] Kase, *Journey to the Missouri*, p. 160.
[93] Kido Diary Extract, June 6, 1941, IMTFE, Exhibit No. 1084.
[94] Telegram, Ott to Ribbentrop, June 21, 1941, IMTFE, Exhibit No. 635.
[95] Kido Diary Extract, June 21, 1941, IMTFE, Exhibit No. 781.
[96] *ibid.*, June 28, 1941, IMTFE, Exhibit No. 1098.

that an opportunity for a "total solution" of the Russian problem was offered and promising a quick victory which, by making available oil and raw materials, would also insure the subsequent defeat of Britain.[97] This argument changed nothing and the decision of the Imperial Conference of July 2 was to stand aside and await the progress of events, with a reservation that intervention might be undertaken "should the conditions of the German-Soviet war progress favorably to Japan."[98] Meantime Japan would continue its effort to dispose of the China Incident and would pursue the "Southward advance." Matsuoka was obliged to confess to Ott that, although he himself shared entirely the German view that Japan should attack Russia at once, he was unable to prevail on the Cabinet.[99]

Matsuoka now found himself almost completely isolated within the government, but instead of accommodating himself to the views of his colleagues he adopted an increasingly provocative course which virtually invited his ejection from power. In addition to advocating war with Russia he sought to impose conditions on the continuation of negotiations with the United States which all other members of the Cabinet, including the military, believed would cause a breakdown of the talks. When he went so far as to send instructions to Ambassador Nomura without getting Cabinet approval, the Konoye Cabinet, on July 16, resigned for the specific purpose of jettisoning the Foreign Minister.[100]

It seems evident that Matsuoka would not have invited his expulsion from power without good reason. There is every indication that he calculated that he would soon be able to return. On June 23, in his first conversation with the German ambassador after the German attack, he had asked to have an inquiry made in Berlin as to whether an early collapse of the Stalin regime was to be expected.[101] In a personal message on July 1 Ribbentrop replied that German armed forces had succeeded in eight days in "breaking the backbone of the Russian Army." He promised further: "The coming operations of the German Army will, I have no doubt, destroy the remaining forces of the enemy in the same manner and it can be counted on that perhaps even in only a few weeks Russian resistance over the whole European area of the Soviet Union

---

[97] Telegram, Ribbentrop to Ott, June 28, 1941, IMTFE, Exhibit No. 1096.
[98] IMTFE, Exhibit No. 588.
[99] Telegram, Ott to Ribbentrop, July 3, 1941, IMTFE, Exhibit No. 796.
[100] Kido Diary Extract, July 15, 1941, IMTFE, Exhibit No. 1115.
[101] Telegram, Ott to Ribbentrop, June 23, 1941, IMTFE, Exhibit No. 795.

will be broken. It is very likely ... that this in turn will result shortly in the total collapse of the Bolshevist regime."[102]

When Matsuoka defied his Cabinet colleagues he was gambling that this forecast would prove correct, that Japan would surely then take the course he was urging, and that his faithful advocacy of unwavering collaboration with Germany would be vindicated. Matsuoka was both very ambitious and convinced that world power relations were undergoing revolutionary change. "I think the days of small things are now definitely over," he told the America-Japan Society in a speech on December 19, 1940. "We must think big and act big. It is no time to deal in small change."[103] And at Berlin in congratulating Hitler on the "decisiveness and power" with which he was leading the German people in "this great period of upheaval, a period without parallel in previous history" he added significantly: "The Japanese people [have] not yet found their Führer. He [will], however, certainly appear in time of need and with determination take over the leadership of the people."[104] It is not excluded that Matsuoka saw himself in this role. It is certain at least that he was opposed by conservative politicians of the type of Hiranuma, Kido, and Konoye for reasons in addition to his foreign policy views. They mistrusted his brazen disregard of the conventions of Cabinet politics in attempting to by-pass the Prime Minister and influence the Emperor directly, and beyond this they mistrusted in him his talent for frenzied demagogic oratory and his pretensions to popular leadership.

VII

These qualities of opportunism and ambition are likely to figure as largely in any historical evaluation of Matsuoka as they did in the mistrustful appraisal of his contemporaries. In terms of the history of modern and Japanese diplomacy, however, he deserves notice for other reasons.

In his methods he was above all representative of the school of totalitarian diplomacy as it flourished in the years before the second world war. The leading characteristic of that school was its application of the techniques and apparatus of propaganda to the purposes of diplomacy, its reliance upon the immediate impact of the dramatic or seemingly dramatic gesture to bring opponents to terms. Matsuoka himself was

---

[102] Telegram, Ribbentrop to Ott, July 1, 1941, printed in *Department of State Bulletin*, June 16, 1946, p. 1040.

[103] Full text in *Foreign Relations, Japan*, II, 123-128.

[104] *Nazi-Soviet Relations*, p. 298.

much more practiced in public statements, usually carrying vague over-tones of menace, than he was in the private art of negotiation.

It was true, of course, that Japanese foreign policy, committed as it was to upsetting the whole order of power in the Far East, had little use for the art of negotiation, for to negotiate seriously would have meant a willingness to reach agreements on the basis of existing treaty relationships. Matsuoka was more acute than his Cabinet colleagues in recognizing the futility of negotiations with the United States, given the objectives which Japan had set for herself. On the other hand, he did not appear to discern that these objectives exceeded the limits of Japanese power, or if he did, he blandly accepted a policy of despera-tion. In this he was representative of almost the whole of his genera-tion of Japanese leaders, men who, perhaps because they were dazzled by what they conceived to be the breakup of the European system of Great Powers and its hegemony in the Far East, launched Japan in pursuit of undefined goals beyond her capacity to attain. They showed themselves to be mere technicians of power, men who were deficient in those qualities of imaginative statesmanship which had enabled the leaders of the Meiji Restoration, by a nice balance of daring and caution, to bring Japan into the circle of the Great Powers in less than a half century.

It would be too much to say, however, that Matsuoka for all his opportunism and heedless pursuit of power, both for himself and for Japan, was entirely without any systematic conceptions of foreign policy for Japan. One idea to which he held fanatically was that Japan must not allow herself to be isolated, that her aims could not be fulfilled ex-cept in alliance with a European Great Power. In his Dairen speech of December 1936, cited above, he rebuked those in Japan who had taken pride in the "honorable isolation" which had followed the Manchurian Incident and the withdrawal from Geneva. He said that for twenty years prior to the Washington Conference Japan's entire diplomacy had been based upon the Anglo-Japanese alliance, that with its termination Japan had become a rudderless vessel, and in the Manchurian affair had therefore "struck a reef." "The vessel of Japan," he added, "has now obtained a new rudder in the form of the agreement with Ger-many, and so this agreement must be made the basis of the Empire's future diplomacy." To this conception he was absolutely faithful and it doubtless explains his readiness to follow the Germans when in June 1941 they changed course without, as was their way with their allies, the courtesy of an advance warning.

Matsuoka not only believed in a policy of alliance for Japan, but specifically in a German-Japanese alliance, and in a German-Russian-Japanese bloc if that should prove feasible. As a young man Matsuoka had been a protégé of Count Shimpei Goto, Japan's Foreign Minister for a time in 1918 when Matsuoka was serving in the Foreign Office and as secretary to the Prime Minister. The South Manchurian Railway Company had been organized under Count Goto as its first president in 1907, and it was under his sponsorship that Matsuoka became a director of the company in 1921, at which time he also left the Diplomatic Service. As Foreign Minister in 1918 Count Goto had been an active proponent of the Siberian expedition, but in the early 1920's he became an equally active supporter of Soviet-Japanese friendship, and played a part in launching the negotiations which led to the resumption of relations between the two countries in 1925. At the same time, however, he was a friend of Germany. He had studied medicine there as a young man and after his return had founded the Japanese-German Cultural Institute in Tokyo. He was regarded in Japan as the author of the conception of a Japanese-German-Russian bloc. The formulation of this theory commonly attributed to him was that "Germany, Russia, and Japan are a three-horse team, but the Russian horse must proceed in the middle so that it cannot break lose and upset everything." To the extent that Matsuoka was able to plot a course in terms of systematic ideas, these were derived from Count Goto.

It was consistent with these ideas that the system of the Tripartite Pact anticipated an adjustment of Soviet-Japanese relations. Russia was to be a passive participant in that system, assigned to proceed quietly between German-Japanese traces. When Molotov visited Berlin in November 1940 he made it clear that the Soviets would not accept this role. "The participation of Russia in the Tripartite Pact appeared to him entirely acceptable in principle," he said, "provided that Russia was to cooperate as a partner and not be merely an object."[105] Hitler was not accustomed to dealing with others as partners and chose to regard the Russian behavior as dangerous and unruly. When he then decided to attack the Soviet Union, Matsuoka was confronted with an awkward situation, but not one which was basically inconsistent with his conceptions. It may be that he thought of his nonaggression pact in Moscow as an attempt to check a too headlong shift of the German course, but in the end he was willing to accommodate himself to it. He was doubtless the more willing since he believed that the Communist danger

[105] *ibid.*, p. 233.

would have to be dealt with sooner or later. In Berlin he had suggested to Ribbentrop that the Anti-Comintern Pact, due to expire in 1941, be renewed.[106] Even before the Tripartite Pact was signed, when there was no hint of any break in Soviet-German friendship, he told the Privy Council in his justification of the Pact on September 26, 1940, that he regarded any settlement which might be reached with Russia as only temporary. "Even though the Russo-Japanese relation may be readjusted it will hardly last for three years. After two years, it will be necessary to reconsider the relations among Japan, Germany, and Russia." And on the same occasion he stated flatly: "Japan will aid Germany in the event of a Soviet-German war, and Germany will assist Japan in the event of a Russo-Japanese war."[107] These were the conceptions to which he held firm in the divided councils of the Japanese government in June-July 1941, and for which he allowed himself to be expelled from power in the conviction that his vindication would not be long in coming.

No Foreign Minister was the master of Japanese foreign policy in the years before Pearl Harbor. The plague of faction was endemic in Japanese political life and, persuasive as he was said to be, it was quite beyond Matsuoka's powers to win consent and unified support for his policies. Above all, however, it was his error to place himself at odds with the military. Early in his tenure of power Matsuoka told Ambassador Grew that it "had been a *sine qua non* of his taking office that he was to direct Japan's foreign relations," and that he would not allow the military to "dictate to him."[108] This remark was at the time tailored to Grew's special pre-occupation with the military's violation of American rights in China, but Matsuoka doubtless meant it in his own sense. If so, it was a presumption which no Foreign Minister in prewar Japan could allow himself, and because of it, Matsuoka passed from the scene as suddenly as he had appeared a year earlier.

[106] *ibid.*, p. 305.
[107] IMTFE, Exhibit No. 552.
[108] Grew, *Ten Years in Japan*, p. 345.

··

Two American Ambassadors:
Bullitt and Kennedy

BY WILLIAM W. KAUFMANN

Winston Churchill has characterized the recent international conflict as the unnecessary war. By this, presumably, he means that if the Powers threatened by Germany, Italy, and Japan had acted together early enough and boldly enough they could have thwarted the aggressor states without the fearful costs and consequences of a second world war. Whatever one may think of Mr. Churchill's hypothesis, it is certainly true that the effort to test it was not forthcoming largely because of the policy of isolation followed by the United States in the interwar period.

That policy had never won complete acceptance in the public mind. Ever since 1919 powerful groups had advocated American participation in the work of the League of Nations and the World Court, but it was not until 1938 that the basic premises of isolation were called into question and a broad discussion started about the role of the United States in European affairs. The debate that followed was in many respects partisan and uninformed; for two years it proved inconclusive. That was to be expected: the problem was new and complex. What seems more surprising in retrospect is the discovery that at the same time a similar situation prevailed within the administration itself. Despite far-flung information services, an elaborate bureaucracy in Washington, and expert consideration of the problem, the American government lay virtually paralyzed in the realm of foreign affairs. It is true, of course, that the President and Secretary Hull eventually progressed to all-out aid for Britain and a firm stand against Japan; but these decisions matured very painfully over a period of three years, and the final act of war against the Axis resulted, not from some tortured and secret plot, but from the attack on Pearl Harbor.

No doubt the reasons for this funereal pace are many and complex; probably not all of them have as yet been divined. Certainly the role and responsibility of American diplomats remains to be assessed. In this connection two men—William Christian Bullitt and Joseph Patrick Kennedy —present particularly intriguing problems for the student of history. They occupied the key diplomatic posts of Paris and London, they witnessed the unfolding of the Czechoslovak crisis with all its sinister overtones, and they remained on duty until after the fall of France. Finally, as a result of these experiences, they came to urge utterly divergent points of view on the President and Secretary of State. What, one wonders, was their influence during this difficult period, how did they exercise it, and what explanations can be found for the positions that they took?

Neither man fits comfortably into the category of professional diplomat, although Bullitt probably comes closer to it than does Kennedy. Born in Philadelphia of a wealthy and socially prominent family, he inherited all the qualifications considered appropriate to the American foreign service. These he improved upon by spending four years at Yale and one at the Harvard Law School. After serving as foreign correspondent and associate editor of the Philadelphia *Public Ledger*, and making the acquaintance of Colonel House, he became a special assistant to the Secretary of State during the Wilson administration, went to Paris as a member of the American peace delegation in 1919, and from there paid his celebrated visit to Lenin and Chicherin as an emissary of the President. The mission was to have a fateful influence on his career. It convinced him of the necessity of reaching an early agreement with the Bolsheviks, and he returned to Paris with this recommendation. When the Big Four ignored his advice he resigned his post and later, before the Senate Foreign Relations Committee, denounced the whole peace structure of Versailles.[1] For that act, and for what was regarded as his disloyalty to Wilson, the Democratic Party virtually ostracized him. During the next fourteen years Bullitt occupied himself with an interest in the motion picture business, a novel, marriage to the widow of the American communist, John Reed, and a good deal of travel.

The election of Roosevelt in 1932 brought him back into the government service, where he was to remain for twelve exciting years. Once more he started as special assistant to the Secretary of State, and again he participated in negotiations concerning the Soviet Union. This time, however, his efforts, combined with those of the administration, resulted

[1] Bullitt's testimony before the Senate Foreign Relations Committee is conveniently available in *The Bullitt Mission to Russia* (New York, 1919).

in American recognition of that country, and his own appointment as the first postwar ambassador of the United States to Moscow. It was with this varied and unorthodox experience that Bullitt reached the Place de la Concorde in the autumn of 1936, thoroughly disillusioned with the Soviet Union, to take up his duties as the American envoy to France.

Kennedy's interests and career had proceeded along somewhat different lines. A Bostonian, educated at Harvard, like Bullitt a lifelong Democrat, he quickly involved himself in the world of business and finance. His experience ranged from shipbuilding and investment banking to the motion picture business and the intricacies of corporate finance. It also included the accumulation of a large fortune and the rearing of nine children.

Kennedy's interest in Franklin Roosevelt began early. He was a supporter of the President and a contributor to his campaign before the Democratic convention in 1932, and at Chicago is reported to have used his influence with William Randolph Hearst to bring the California delegation into the Roosevelt camp.[2] His rewards followed rapidly. In 1934 he became the chairman of the newly created Securities Exchange Commission; in 1937 he received the chairmanship of the Maritime Commission; and early in 1938, following hard upon the rumor that he would succeed Henry Morgenthau, Jr., at the Treasury, he replaced the ailing Robert Bingham as American ambassador to the Court of St. James.[3]

II

The scene that greeted Bullitt and Kennedy in the Europe of 1938 was a turbulent one. The precarious equilibrium so casually constructed at Versailles was teetering on the verge of collapse. Not only had Germany regained a goodly portion of her armed strength; she had won the Saar by plebiscite and the Rhineland by a skillful *coup de main*. Civil war was flaming in Spain, Austria was about to fall, and Czechoslovakia was coming under the guns of the Wehrmacht. France, the principal guardian of the latest statute of Europe, meanwhile appeared to be slipping into a permanent decline, while Britain, still outwardly powerful, contented herself with the role of the impartial spectator. All of Wilson's early schemes had been tried, however ineptly, and had failed; the ideas and

[2] For this, and other sidelights on Kennedy's relations with Roosevelt, see James A. Farley, *Jim Farley's Story* (New York, 1948); Edward J. Flynn, *You're the Boss* (New York, 1947); and Raymond Moley, *After Seven Years* (New York, 1939).

[3] For indications of Roosevelt's attitude on the Treasury, see *Jim Farley's Story*, pp. 115, 126.

mechanisms of the League of Nations lay discredited. Europe was not the idyl of contented, democratic, and cooperative nations envisaged at Versailles, but the very cockpit of competing states which the peacemakers of 1919 had hoped to banish forever from the earth. The problem no longer was one of adopting measures to enhance the contentment of Europe; it had resolved itself into one of determining at what point, and by which means, the competition for power launched by Germany was to be resolved. For the nations in the Western camp two major alternatives lay open: the classic policy of the balance of power so recently disguised under the anomalous heading of collective security, and the equally ancient though less venerated policy of concession and appeasement. To the statesmen in Paris and London each had its drawbacks. Appeasement, with all its indubitable attractions, might lead to aggrandizement without a corresponding change in attitudes. A policy predicated on the balance of power was both difficult and dangerous to operate; and, without the cooperation of the United States and the Soviet Union, it might not suffice to deter or subdue the aggressor states.

Although this, essentially, was the dilemma plaguing Paris and London in the spring of 1938, its outlines had not yet become wholly clear either to the statesmen of the two capitals or to Bullitt and Kennedy. In part the obscurity resulted from the traditional difficulties in Anglo-French relations. But the dilemma also found concealment in a variety of other issues. Powerful groups both in France and in England sympathized with many aspects of the Nazi and Fascist regimes, and this sympathy, combined with an intense dislike of the Soviet Union, led them to underestimate the consequences of a further increase in the power of Hitler and Mussolini. Moreover, parties of both the Left and Right questioned the propriety of the Versailles settlement. Doubting the nature and expression of the values embodied in the treaty of 1919, they found it difficult to oppose the ideals advanced by Germany and Italy, however brutally these might be stated. Leading public figures such as Flandin, Bonnet, Baldwin, Simon, and Chamberlain had thus reduced their credos to a single value: peace—peace at almost any price. And they were encouraged in the search for peace by their own military weaknesses, by the comparative remoteness of the objects that Hitler was seeking (why fight for Danzig?), and by their unwillingness or inability to appreciate the true character of the Nazi regime.

Nevertheless there were occasions on which this fantastic structure of complacency and delusion was suspected of containing fatal defects. Although governing circles in France and Britain leaned toward appeasement, they often peered over their shoulders and yearned after the promise of collective security. The trend was by no means irremediably in the direction of wholesale surrender. Chamberlain might reject the tentative overtures of President Roosevelt in the winter before Munich; the French might speak, quite justifiably, of the American capacity for words rather than deeds; but both London and Paris were, for the most part, more than anxious to obtain the good will of the United States.

In these circumstances the position of the American ambassador in either capital was one of great potential importance. Whoever the individual, he was bound to be sought after and consulted. As the official representative of the United States his words, however informally spoken, could not help but carry great weight. He was also bound to be well informed. The Foreign Offices of both countries, in their efforts to win the support of the United States, were willing to reveal to the American envoys much of their most highly classified information. Leaders of contending parties, diplomats from other countries, refugees, businessmen, all were anxious to provide a fact or discuss a point of view. The data were inexhaustible. The gregariousness, ambition, and interest of Bullitt and Kennedy were such that they took full advantage of the opportunities open to them. Bullitt established extremely confidential relations with French political and military leaders of all stripes; Kennedy, who had won a special place in British hearts by shooting a hole-in-one at Stoke Poges shortly after his arrival in England, frequented the great country houses of the Cliveden Set and became an intimate of Prime Minister Chamberlain. Both men entertained lavishly and reported back their impressions to Washington with an equally free hand.

Their position in relation to the Roosevelt administration was similar in many respects to the one that they occupied in France and Britain. For in Washington as well as in Paris and London there was debate and confusion in the realm of foreign policy. The choices open to the Executive admittedly were limited at this stage by isolationist sentiment, the intransigence of the Congress, and the neutrality legislation. The military establishment, moreover, was in a deplorable state. Had it not been for the existence of the Navy, the United States would surely have ranked as a third-rate Power in its ability to influence contemporary events. Nevertheless, even with these constraints, there remained much that the President and State Department could do. The work of clarifying their own views, educating Congress and the public, bolstering national defense, and organizing bold and forthright leadership presented great opportunities for action despite the complacency of the country. And

Bullitt and Kennedy could play a significant role in persuading the Executive to grasp them.

This was so for a number of reasons. Although the President was becoming increasingly preoccupied with problems of foreign policy, his views on the subject had by no means matured. His love of analogy, his tendency to think in Wilsonian terms, until recently his concern with the domestic program of the New Deal, and, above all, the overwhelming mass of business that crossed his desk, prevented him from obtaining a very profound understanding of international relations.

The thinking of Cordell Hull and Sumner Welles was of a similarly fluid character. The idea that the United States might formulate a comprehensive program of action and then bring influence to bear in order to implement it was quite alien to the principal inhabitants of the State Department. Intimates of high officials have in fact expressed perfectly their philosophy during this period by saying that policy was the product of cables received from abroad rather than of a dynamic conception of American interests. In part, such thinking was due to the tradition of isolation and a lack of experience on the part of the professional diplomats. They had had so little to do for so many years. But it was also a consequence of inadequate political analysis. The Secretary, and many of his advisers, tended to depict other nations in their own image. Being satisfied with the existing degree and scope of American influence, and having economic problems uppermost in their minds, they found it difficult to believe that the states of Europe could be discontented for other than economic reasons. Their world was static, rigidly divided by oceans, yet peopled largely by foreign-speaking Americans. The result was that prior to Munich their thinking ran to trade agreements, lectures on international morality, and efforts to bring together the heads of the great European states in order to resolve around a table the differences that divided them.

Despite these preconceptions, the President at least was open to argument. Those who suspect him of having engaged in some vast and complicated plot to drag the United States into war overlook completely the uncertainties that beset him between 1938 and 1941. He knew that the situation in Europe was deteriorating rapidly, but before and even after Munich, what this condition portended for the United States, and what action he should take, were still matters of intense personal debate. The consequence was that American emissaries in key posts abroad could exert a considerable influence on the development of his thought. This was particularly true of men like Bullitt and Kennedy, for the President distrusted foreign service officers as a class. He referred to them sarcastically as the profession of perfection, and on one occasion he wrote to Cordell Hull: "I am reminded of a remark made to me by an old career service man—'You can get to be a Minister if (a) you are loyal to the service (b) you do nothing to offend people (c) if you are not intoxicated at public functions.' " In the same memorandum he remarked that there was "a lot of dead wood in the top three grades that should never have got there."[4]

All of his ambassadors were authorized to communicate with him directly, but, in view of this feeling about professional diplomats, it seems likely that he gave the closest scrutiny to the reports of his personal appointees. To a man of Roosevelt's temperament, Bullitt and Kennedy were bound to inspire more confidence than the supposedly apolitical foreign service officer. Both men were avowed Democrats; they had contributed liberally to the party's campaign chest; and they had participated wholeheartedly in the implementation of the New Deal's domestic program. Their ideological credentials thus were very much in order.

Bullitt maintained a particularly close relationship with the President. He advised him on foreign service matters generally and exercised considerable influence in the determination of diplomatic appointments. His embassy in Paris became the channel through which a great deal of the information from Europe passed on to Washington; and Bullitt himself was something more than the American ambassador to France. He acted as both a roving emissary, reporting on his experiences in Britain, Germany, and Poland, and the informal inspector-general of the Diplomatic Service. He was in constant communication with the President by letter, cable, and telephone. The two men had even worked out a special code for their transatlantic conversations, and talked cryptically about Yale-Harvard baseball scores and the ages of the President's elderly relatives.[5]

Although Bullitt and Kennedy were nominally subject to the control of the State Department, their status in the Democratic party and their relations with the President gave them a freedom of action not ordinarily accorded to professional diplomats. These considerations, together with the uncertainty that reigned in high official circles, endowed them with

---

[4] Elliott Roosevelt, ed., assisted by Joseph P. Lash, *F. D. R., His Personal Letters, 1928-1945* (2 vols., New York, 1950), II, 913-14.

[5] Bullitt's connections with the President are discussed briefly in Joseph Alsop and Robert Kintner, *American White Paper* (New York, 1940); *Jim Farley's Story*; Bertram D. Hulen, *Inside the State Department* (New York, 1939); and William L. Langer and S. Everett Gleason, *The Challenge to Isolation, 1937-1940* (New York, 1952).

the opportunity to affect policy in Washington as well as in Paris and London. How then did they employ this opportunity?

III

Until after Munich they allowed themselves to be swept along by the current of thought then prevalent in France and Britain. A great deal of information about German intentions had already become available by this time. There was not only the evidence of *Mein Kampf*, the statements of leading Nazis, and the record of internal persecution, rearmament, the Rhineland, Spain, and Austria. There was also the whispering gallery of Europe—composed largely of the aristocracy and prominent refugees, and supplied with data by such prominent German officials as Weizsäcker in Berlin and Schulenburg in Moscow—which gave forth an extraordinary amount of accurate information about Nazi intentions. Unlike the Soviet Union of today, the Germany of 1938 was a comparatively open society. Colonel Lindbergh and General Vuillemain were treated to intimate and detailed views of the growing might of the Luftwaffe. In June 1938, Mr. Churchill was able to ascertain that the Wehrmacht had at its disposal at least thirty-six infantry and four armored divisions; estimates that M. Daladier in Paris confirmed.[6] There was, in other words, a large volume of concrete evidence about the Nazi threat awaiting employment, yet neither Bullitt nor Kennedy appears to have assimilated or evaluated it.

To the extent that Bullitt had formulated a consistent and harmonious view about the situation in Europe, he permitted it to be dominated by his distrust of the Soviet Union. He had gone to Moscow full of enthusiasm and hope; he left for Paris, three years later, disgusted and disillusioned. Like all but one of his successors he had become convinced that "the aim of the Soviet Government is, and will remain, to produce world revolution. The leaders of the Soviet Union believe that the first step toward this revolution must be to strengthen the defensive and offensive power of the Soviet Union. They believe that within ten years the defense position of the Soviet Union will be absolutely impregnable and that within 15 years the offensive power of the Soviet Union will be sufficient to enable it to consolidate by its assistance any communist government which may be set up in Europe. To maintain peace for the present, to keep the nations of Europe divided, to foster enmity between

[6] For this and other items of intelligence about Germany collected by Mr. Churchill, see Winston S. Churchill, *The Gathering Storm* (Boston, 1948), pp. 118-119, 121, 123, 144, 145, 189, 236-237, 338.

Japan and the United States, and to gain the blind devotion and obedience of the communists of all countries so that they will act against their own governments at the behest of the Communist Pope in the Kremlin, is the sum of Stalin's policy."[7] In order to counteract such a policy, the United States should instruct its "diplomatic representatives in Europe to use all opportunities in personal conversations to point out the danger to Europe of the continuation of Franco-German enmity and to encourage reconciliation between France and Germany." Above all, Bullitt concluded, "we should guard the reputation of Americans for businesslike efficiency, sincerity, and straightforwardness. We should never send a spy to the Soviet Union. There is no weapon at once so disarming and effective in relation with the communists as sheer honesty. They know very little about it."[8]

After a year and a half in Paris Bullitt remained more or less constant to this view. His reception in France was precisely what he must have hoped for, and failed to obtain, in Russia. Whereas polo equipment for the Red army, baseball games and zoo parties for Bolshevik functionaries had failed to soothe the Soviet beast, elaborate fetes and a superb chef at the Place de la Concorde brought him the most intimate confidences of high French society. Lord Chilston, the British ambassador to the Soviet Union, is reported to have said, "It is not what an ambassador can do in Moscow but what he can stand." Bullitt, who undoubtedly nourished similar sentiments, found Paris and all her celebrities a glittering and bewitching contrast. So great was his popularity, especially in governmental circles, that the wits dubbed him minister without portfolio in the kaleidoscope of French cabinets. And in this atmosphere Bullitt responded with affection, devotion, and trust. Just as the Soviet Union was the implacable enemy, so France became the cherished friend. It followed from this, first, that the Franco-Soviet alliance should not develop beyond the innocuous limits set by the treaty of 1935; and, secondly, that the French position should be strengthened by a rapprochement with Germany. What Bullitt had advocated in the spring of 1936 he continued to favor until after the debacle of Munich.

Ambassador Dodd in Berlin suspected him of pro-Nazi inclinations, although precisely on what grounds it is difficult to say. In his reports to the President and State Department Bullitt took pleasure in mocking Goering's "German tenor" proportions and repulsive mannerisms. On

---

[7] Bullitt to Hull, Moscow, July 19, 1935, *Foreign Relations: The Soviet Union, 1933-1939* (Washington, 1952), p. 227.
[8] Bullitt to Hull, Moscow, April 20, 1936, *ibid.*, pp. 294, 296.

one occasion he even informed the Reichsmarshal that in the event of trouble there were enough trees in the United States on which to hang the five million German-speaking Americans, if that should prove necessary; and by 1937 he was calling the atmosphere of the Wilhelmstrasse "as cocky as before the war."[9] Nevertheless, despite these appraisals, or perhaps because of them (for they were not particularly profound), he remained an advocate of improved Franco-German relations and even suggested to Bonnet that "such a reconciliation would have the full benediction of the United States."[10]

That such an accord might involve a heavy sacrifice for France did not seem to occur to him, and he became intensely annoyed with the English when they began to show some awareness on this score. He confided to Dodd that he cared "not a damn" for Britain, and, after a conversation with Sir Eric Phipps in Paris, he concluded that the British ambassador had instructions "to prevent the French from having any tête-à-tête conversations with Germany; that the policy of Great Britain is still to keep the Continent of Europe divided . . . and that little or nothing is to be expected from Great Britain in the way of support of the policy of reduction of barriers to international commerce and restoration of the economic life of the world."[11]

If the *bête noire* of Bullitt was the Soviet Union, with Great Britain playing the role of minor villain, the ghost that haunted Kennedy was war. As befitted a former chairman of the Securities Exchange and Maritime Commissions, his primary interest lay in economic matters, and the problem of promoting business recovery in the United States governed all his thinking. As he looked out on the world from Grosvenor Square it was only natural, therefore, that he should have established a direct correlation between peace and prosperity. At times he also linked up the survival of free institutions with the existence of these two conditions. Thus, if peace could be preserved, prosperity would follow, and only in a setting of peace and prosperity would free institutions flourish. However, if war should break out in Europe, with all its accompanying costs and uncertainties, economic recovery would be wrecked and free institutions stifled. The obvious inference from this line of thought was, first, that the avoidance of war was worth almost any sacrifice, and secondly, that whatever might happen in other parts of the world, the United

[9] *F.D.R., His Personal Letters, 1928-1945*, I, 489; *Trial of the Major War Criminals*, XXXVII, 594-601; Charles Callan Tansill, *Back Door to War* (Chicago, 1952), p. 361.
[10] Tansill, *Back Door to War*, p. 321.
[11] William E. Dodd, Jr., and Martha Dodd, eds., *Ambassador Dodd's Diary, 1933-1938* (New York, 1941), p. 309; Tansill, *Back Door to War*, p. 330.

States must strive to remain aloof from conflict. If she did not, her economy would crumble and bring down with it all of her democratic traditions. Kennedy thus started his mission in London with the conviction that peace in Europe was necessary and therefore possible. This preconception inevitably colored all his analyses of the continental scene.

The revolutionary character of the Nazi regime was not a phenomenon that he could easily grasp in these circumstances. It was far simpler, and more in accord with his own premises, to explain German aggressiveness in economic terms. The Third Reich was dissatisfied, authoritarian, and expansive largely because her economy was unsound. Let her gain dominion in southeastern Europe and she would either achieve prosperity and shed her dictatorial mannerisms, or become crippled and helpless with indigestion. Kennedy was not sure which would be the likelier eventuality, but either was preferable to an effort to block the expansion.[12]

There may have been other reasons for Kennedy's unwillingness to interpose obstacles in the way of German ambitions. It is difficult to say. The German ambassador in London, Herbert von Dirksen, held a number of conversations with him during the summer and autumn of 1938. He reported to the Wilhelmstrasse that Kennedy was not only sympathetic to a great many of Hitler's policies, but also anxious to visit Berlin and discuss with the Fuehrer measures for improving German-American relations. Among other things, he had learned that the Nazis were doing "great things for Germany and that the Germans were satisfied and enjoyed good living conditions." He "repeatedly expressed his conviction that in economic matters Germany had to have a free hand in the East as well as in the Southeast. He took a very pessimistic view of the situation in the Soviet Union."[13] An effort by Kennedy to be tactful and conciliatory may have been mistaken by Dirksen for a genuine expression of his views. But, whatever the case, the American saw in Nazi Germany not something to be frustrated by all available means, but rather a force to be satisfied and tamed.

Bullitt had become interested in sponsoring a Franco-German rapprochement as a way of thwarting Soviet ambitions. Kennedy, for his part, favored an Anglo-German entente, partly as a means of preserving peace, and partly as a means of preserving England. He liked the British; he enjoyed particularly the relations he had established with Chamberlain and Halifax; he sympathized with the view that they and

[12] For one expression of Kennedy's reasoning on this subject, see *British Documents*, 3rd series, II, 213.
[13] *German Documents*, series D, II, 368-369; I, 714-718.

their associates took of European affairs. Although his principal duty lay in sparing the United States from the rigors of war, he came increasingly to include the England governed by these friendly people within the circle of his goodwill. So solicitous of their welfare did he in fact become that at the height of the Czechoslovak crisis Roosevelt reportedly exclaimed: "Who would have thought that the English [the Cliveden Set] could take into camp a redheaded Irishman?"[14]

With preconceptions such as these it was only natural that Bullitt and Kennedy should have had difficulty in providing the President and State Department with comprehensive and accurate reports of prevailing trends in Europe. They were not looking for the data that mattered, as, for example, was Churchill. But then, Churchill had started with some hypotheses about the nature of international politics which bore considerable relation to existing reality. Bullitt and Kennedy did not have this advantage. To a very large extent their dispatches were in the classic diplomatic tradition. That is to say, they consisted, more often than not, of gossip, accounts of conversations with prominent officials in Paris and London, scraps of unassimilated information, rumors, horseback opinions written at the gallop, and predictions. In many respects the two men were reporters rather than analysts, and so much of their data came from official sources that they tended to adopt the interpretations of the governments to which they were accredited. The influence at their disposal in Paris and London they therefore employed largely to confirm and reinforce the views already held by Daladier and Chamberlain.

The tendency to become subject to the prevailing trend of French and British thought was particularly evident throughout the Czechoslovak crisis. In May 1938, Bullitt expressed the opinion that eventually the existing conflict of ideologies would seem as idiotic as the old wars of religion were now considered to be. Americans, he said, could not accept the idea that war was inevitable; reason and understanding might yet prevail.[15] As the German pressure on Czechoslovakia increased he became more pessimistic, as did Daladier, and estimated that the chances of war and peace were about evenly balanced. Nevertheless he told the British ambassador on September 2 that "Hitler had invited M. Herriot and M. Piétri to Nuremberg and that he gathered they were accepting the invitation. This seemed to be a slightly more hopeful sign." What he feared almost more than Hitler's fanaticism was some desperate action

---

[14] Henry Morgenthau, Jr., "The Morgenthau Diaries," *Collier's*, October 18, 1947, p. 16.
[15] *New York Times*, May 30, 1938, p. 4.

by German or Russian "agents provocateurs." Meanwhile he held to the optimistic belief that "the last word lies with Lord Runciman, against whose summing up Germany will hardly dare to act."[16] He still toyed with the possibility of bringing France and Germany together, and only excised the suggestion from a speech he was to give early in September when the French Foreign Minister informed him that this was not the appropriate moment for such a proposal. As the tension reached its pitch in the last week of September, his fear of war came to match that of Bonnet and Daladier; and after the signature of the agreement at Munich he rushed to Bonnet's apartment, with tears in his eyes and his arms full of flowers, to convey "le salut fraternel et joyeux de l'Amérique."[17]

Kennedy's emotions followed a similar course. The ambassador was at the Foreign Office almost daily during the heat of the crisis, and consulted frequently with Chamberlain. Until the end of August he was unable to see any dispute or controversy in the world that might warrant the sacrifice of his or anybody else's sons. When the Prime Minister informed him that Germany might actually invade Czechoslovakia he seemed surprised, but loyally agreed that Britain was in no position to stop Hitler and that, in the circumstances, it would be unwise to utter threats. He thought that the consequence of any German action would be absolute hell, and asked whether there was anything that the President could do to avert the catastrophe. For example, should Roosevelt make another speech? When the Prime Minister said he thought that would be unnecessary, Kennedy seemed relieved and expressed the conviction that the President had decided "to go in with Chamberlain; whatever course Chamberlain desires to adopt he would think right."[18]

By September 10, when the nature of German intentions had become fully apparent, and the Prime Minister was reluctantly assuming a belligerent posture, Kennedy articulated the view "that it was essential to take every possible step to avoid misunderstanding in Herr Hitler's mind and that only overwhelming argument" should suffice to prevent the British from giving the Wilhelmstrasse a final warning against aggression. He thought that the alerting of the Royal Navy had been fully justified and even wondered "whether over the weekend it might not be possible for the Soviet Government to make some movement that would compel attention, such as concentration of aeroplanes near the

[16] *British Documents*, 3rd series, II, 218-219.
[17] Georges Bonnet, *Défense de la paix* (2 vols., Geneva, 1946-1948), I, 294.
[18] *British Documents*, 3rd series, II, 213.

frontier."[19] By the 29th, however, all the fight had gone out of him. Chamberlain was in Munich, and Kennedy told Halifax that "he himself was entirely in sympathy with, and a warm admirer of, everything the Prime Minister had done." While hoping for the best from the negotiations he recognized "all the dangers and difficulties that still had to be surmounted. The situation, in his view, was one that had to be faced in a spirit of realism by those on whom the responsibility rested, although . . . there was nothing easier or more attractive than to pursue ideals with small regard to hard realities when no responsibility [was] attached to doing so."[20]

The role that the two men envisaged for the United States during the Czechoslovak crisis was the product of a variety of factors. Kennedy, because he wanted peace, Bullitt, because he feared the Soviet Union, consistently underestimated the nature and imminence of the German threat during the summer of 1938. Kennedy, admiring Chamberlain yet isolationist, Bullitt, following faithfully in Daladier's footsteps and probably confused by this latest turn of events, therefore pictured the United States as the disinterested peacemaker who would bring together the contending factions in Europe. On this score they were in virtual accord. Where they differed was on the concrete steps by which the President and the State Department should act out the mediatory part. Kennedy was by far the less forward of the two. He had a tendency to see in Europe a kind of Miltonian Hell, inhabited by selfish politicians, fighting eternally for petty objects. Starting with such a view, he could hardly understand why the United States should become involved in the competition, however much he might sympathize with men like Chamberlain. He was not convinced that a common interest existed between the American people and any other nation, and he opposed any kind of alliance with a foreign state, even though such an arrangement might be temporary and designed to prevent war. The only activities that he regarded as legitimate on the part of the President were the tendering of advice and the emission of ambiguous statements about the intentions of the United States in the event of a European war.

He himself was willing, as he told Lord Halifax, to encourage Roosevelt to make another speech, to pay an ostentatious call on Chamberlain at the height of the crisis, even to think of manufacturing publicity out of the arrival of several American cruisers in British waters. But he was also willing—perhaps without appreciating the significance of what he was

[19] *ibid.*, pp. 284-285.   [20] *ibid.*, p. 625.

doing—to tell the counselor of the German embassy in London that he intended using all his influence to keep the United States out of war.[22] Such an indiscretion, however well-intentioned, was bound to negate the admittedly small effect of his other actions. Whatever else he might say or do, however the State Department might instruct him, Kennedy was irresistibly tempted to reduce American influence abroad to the sum of zero. He might desire peace, but faced with the complexities of the Czechoslovak crisis he could not see how or why the United States might contribute to that end. The paradox was, and remains, startling.

Bullitt, by contrast, ended up by urging a fairly active role upon the President. Already in July he was castigating certain nations for resorting to the "murder of defenseless men, women and children"; he also asserted that without "international morality as without national morality, there can be no human life worth living."[22] But by early September he had grown cautious again. His opinion was that the anti-German sentiment in the United States not only did not imply an early American entry into some future war, "but that it did not even imply any alteration of the Neutrality Act favorable to the Powers fighting Germany, at the very earliest, till after the meeting of Congress in January." As he reminded his listener, against the anti-German feeling "must be set a very definite objection on the part of the American people to be involved again in hostilities in Europe only twenty years after the last war, with the likelihood that they would again get more kicks than ha'pence for their help." He had already explained himself on this score to the French government and felt that they were not laboring under any illusions.[23]

Only two days later, however, Bullitt coupled the timeworn American nostrums for peace (trade and disarmament) with the statement that if war should break out in Europe no one could predict whether or not the United States might become involved.[24] As the crisis over Czechoslovakia deepened, his interest in an active American policy underwent a corresponding growth. On September 13 he advised Hull that Chamberlain and Daladier were considering a three-Power conference with Hitler and that they might like to have other states join them at the table. However muted the hint, it sufficed to send the Secretary off on an evening of croquet and anxious thought.[25]

More revolutionary suggestions were yet to come. On the 24th, Bullitt

[21] *British Documents*, 3rd series, II, 213, 296; *German Documents*, series D, II, 744.
[22] *New York Times*, July 9, 1938, p. 4.
[23] *British Documents*, 3rd series, II, 218-219.
[24] Bonnet, *Défense de la paix*, I, 207.
[25] Alsop and Kintner, *American White Paper*, pp. 7-8.

became bolder and actually urged the President to make a concerted effort to preserve the peace. Admittedly, his thoughts as to how the President should proceed were of a conventional order, and possibly inspired by Daladier and Bonnet. At first he wanted the President to summon a meeting of the Great Powers at the Hague, and send an American delegation to the conference. Shortly thereafter, he recommended that Roosevelt offer himself as arbitrator of the dispute and issue a warning against the dispatch of troops across any European frontier.[26] But this was overly strong medicine for the State Department, and the net result of Bullitt's efforts was a series of Presidential appeals to the heads of the Powers immediately involved in the crisis. These had no effect on the summoning of the Munich conference; and, as Chamberlain departed for his particular Canossa, the best that Roosevelt could muster by way of advice was a terse "Good man!"[27]

Nevertheless, Bullitt had at last stepped down from that pedestal of righteous aloofness occupied by so many American diplomats during the 1920's and 1930's. Not only had he pushed the threat of the Soviet Union temporarily into a corner of his mind; he had actually begun to cast about for measures by which the President could shape the European situation according to the requirements of American interests. The change reflected itself in a rapid revision of his sentiments about the Munich settlement. Already on October 3 he was reporting that "Daladier sees the situation entirely, clearly, realizes fully that the meeting in Munich was an immense diplomatic defeat for France and England, and recognizes that unless France can recover a united national spirit to confront the future, a fatal situation will arise within a year."[28] Ten days later he was in Washington to urge upon the President himself the desperate nature of the French and British positions.

Kennedy reacted more gradually. He quoted Chamberlain as saying that Hitler was "uncouth and certainly not the kind of fellow one would like to go around the world with on a two-wheeled bicycle."[29] But, in a speech delivered at a Trafalgar Day dinner, he still proclaimed as a theory of his "that it is unproductive for both democratic and dictator countries to widen the division now existing between them by emphasizing their differences which are self-apparent. . . . After all, we have to

[26] Cordell Hull, *The Memoirs of Cordell Hull* (2 vols., New York, 1948), I, 590; Langer and Gleason, *The Challenge to Isolation*, pp. 33, 34.

[27] Langer and Gleason, *The Challenge to Isolation*, p. 34.

[28] *ibid.*, p. 37.

[29] Tansill, *Back Door to War*, p. 432.

live together in the same world, whether we like it or not."[30] Only in December did he acknowledge publicly that things were in bad shape and that the situation was changing every day, "and not for the better." Indeed, so pessimistic had he become at this point that he even informed reporters of his retirement from the field of prophecy, despite a record of accurate forecasts about the prospects of peace and the stock market.[31]

By December, then, both men had given full marks to the German menace. Where they still differed was on the extent to which American interests were endangered, and on the kind of action that the United States should take. The problem, admittedly, was a difficult one, raising as it did the costs of alternative types of policy. It was particularly difficult to resolve when threats to the established order were emanating from so many sides—from Japan and possibly the Soviet Union as well as from Germany and Italy. Indeed, the situation was almost out of hand from the standpoint of making rational and calculated decisions. There were so many imponderables to evaluate and equate, including the relative power of the democracies and Germany, the full extent of Hitler's ambitions, and the costs of continued appeasement as compared with the risks of war. Such are the problems which, despite the daydreams of experts, make politicians necessary.

Rules of thumb in such circumstances are always dangerous. Nevertheless, history appears to indicate that, where alternatives cannot be carefully weighed for relative merit, the statesman can do worse than to define broadly the interests of his country and act boldly for their protection. That at least gives him a share in the government of events. The alternative of withdrawal involves surrendering the shape of an unknown future to other and perhaps unfriendly hands. Yet this was the course that Kennedy now advocated for the United States.

It was comparatively easy for him to fall into a position of extreme isolation. Throughout the Czechoslovak crisis he had remained steadfast in his belief that wars solve nothing and that whatever ailed Germany could be cured by infusions of peace and prosperity. Therefore, while regretfully acknowledging the Nazi threat, he strove manfully to fit it in with his preconceptions. Between Munich and the outbreak of the war his efforts on this score took several different forms. One conception which greatly interested him involved the creation of four or five great spheres of influence dominated by Britain and France, Germany, Japan, the

[30] Royal Institute of International Affairs, *Documents on International Affairs, 1938* (2 vols., London, 1942), I, 421.
[31] *New York Times*, December 16, 1938, p. 13.

United States, and possibly Russia. Each sphere would be more or less self-sufficient economically. Each would achieve military security at relatively low cost. And each could obtain what it needed in goods and services from the outside either by barter or by free trade. Such a system might bring about the conditions in which free institutions would develop once more. It would involve, admittedly, the surrender of most of Europe to Germany, and all of the Far East to Japan, but that was a condition that was long overdue anyway. Another conception, which Kennedy regarded less enthusiastically, was predicated on the outbreak of war in Europe and the defeat of Britain and France. Given this situation, he was willing to have the United States expand its sphere of influence to include a number of British and French possessions. Such a move, while hardly desirable, would be necessary in order to counteract the increase in power of Germany that the collapse of Britain and France would entail.[82] Still a third conception, and one to which Kennedy became increasingly addicted, required Britain and the United States to stand with arms folded while Hitler obligingly marched eastward and collided with the Soviet Union. The mutual destruction of the two great totalitarian Powers would then resolve once and for all the problems of the democratic world.[83]

In this search for a rational justification of his deepest convictions there was one point of consistency: all three conceptions permitted the United States to stay out of war. Each argument in effect demonstrated that American interests either would not be affected by what was occurring in Europe, or could be maintained successfully without resort to violence. This conclusion did not imply, however, that Americans should remain idle spectators of the approaching storm. The experience of the Czechoslovak crisis had convinced Kennedy that, whatever the outcome of Germany's struggle for power, the United States must rearm. However much he might desire American isolation from Europe, and the creation of an island of peace and prosperity in the Western Hemisphere, however much he might worry about the stock market and the stability of America's financial structure, he acknowledged the need of the United States to prepare militarily against any contingency. He had a similar admonition for the British. As long as Chamberlain remained in Downing Street he could apply many of his prescriptions to England as well as to the United States. Not only did he wish the British well from a dis-

[82] Franklin D. Roosevelt Library, Hyde Park, N. Y., President's Secretary's File, 1938, Box 39.
[83] Langer and Gleason, *The Challenge to Isolation*, pp. 122-123.

tance; he actually encouraged the President to consider repeal of the Neutrality Act and became the advocate of limited financial aid to Britain. With Chamberlain in power, England was worth helping, provided that the cost was nominal and the effort did not include American military action.

For the most part, however, Kennedy's attitude was akin to that of the weather prophet. He saw clouds on the horizon and he correctly predicted rain; but he hoped that the storm would either dissipate itself or blow off in another direction. It never seems to have occurred to him that politics, unlike the weather, are man-made, the product of multiple influences and subject to a measure of control. He was content to watch, pray, keep his distance, and urge the purchase of umbrellas. His credo forbade him to advise a more active course for the United States even though bold and firm measures might possibly have forestalled the very war which he so greatly and understandably dreaded.

The consequence of this outlook was that in the last dreary months before the war Kennedy's reports had something of the frantic incon-sistency that one associates with accounts of mysterious natural phe-nomena. The omens were uniformly ominous, yet he hoped that events would take a turn for the better, and he grasped at every straw in the wind. In his blacker moments he thought that the British and French were "putting coal into an engine that is not going any place, but they are just keeping it up because there doesn't seem to be anything else to do."[34] After the signature of the Nazi-Soviet Pact he found Chamberlain similarly discouraged. Kennedy reported that, according to the Prime Minister, "the futility of it all is the thing that is frightful; after all they cannot save the Poles; they can merely carry on a war of revenge that will mean the destruction of the whole of Europe. . . ." He himself felt that the Poles should be encouraged to make a deal with the Nazis so that Hitler could continue uninterrupted his eastward march.[35]

On other occasions, however, his mood was bullish. In February 1939 he relayed the opinion that England was on her way and that Germany would not attack. A month later, after a visit to Italy, he expressed the belief that the United States could "accomplish much more by sending a dozen beautiful chorus girls to Rome than a flock of diplomats and a fleet of airplanes. . . . Every time the President says anything, nobody in the Cabinet or Government in Rome is fit to talk with for the rest

[34] Arthur Krock, "How War Came: Extracts from the Hull Files," *New York Times Magazine*, July 18, 1943, p. 34.
[35] Langer and Gleason, *The Challenge to Isolation*, pp. 196, 76.

of the day."[36] This, he apparently regarded as a hopeful sign. There were other good omens as well. Hitler might yet attack the Soviet Union instead of Poland; the thought buoyed him up even through the agonies of the Anglo-Russian negotiations. As he told Joseph E. Davies, "Russia would have to fight for Poland and Rumania anyway, and regardless of whether there was a formal agreement with France and Britain or not, because it was vital to Russia's self-interest."[37] Even after Stalin had discredited this analysis by signing a nonaggression pact with Hitler, Kennedy clung to shreds of hope. On August 29 he reported that the door to Berlin still was open and that the Fuehrer was merely trying "through blackmail . . . to squeeze the last drop of possible advantage out of Poland without war." The next day his news was even better. The British Cabinet felt it had "Hitler on the run," and Halifax had found it advisable to soften a note to the Wilhelmstrasse for fear of provoking Hitlerian ire and Polish stubbornness.[38]

When, on September 1, Germany invaded Poland, the reaction set in and Kennedy crashed into the darkest kind of foreboding. All was over, the party was on, it was the end of the world, the end of everything. So bleak was his despair that the President, burdened as he was with new responsibilities, felt obliged to comfort him a little.[39]

Henceforward, Kennedy was to be a prophet of unrelieved gloom, even though this attitude would cost him his position with the administration. As long as Roosevelt had remained of two minds about foreign policy, Kennedy's reports had probably left their mark. But now that the President was groping toward an active policy for the United States, he began to ignore and by-pass his ambassador. Missions went abroad to observe and report independently of Grosvenor Square. Negotiations between Britain and the United States had their locus in Washington more frequently than in London, or, after Churchill's accession to power, took place directly between Prime Minister and President. The policy of isolation that Kennedy had advocated for America was to be applied with increasing rigor to himself.

Nevertheless he continued to perform his duties to the best of his abilities for yet another year. Britain, he persuaded himself during this time, was going to lose the war. Already in September 1939 he had announced that she did not have a Chinaman's chance. "England and

---

[36] Tansill, *Back Door to War*, pp. 449, 517.

[37] Joseph E. Davies, *Mission to Moscow* (New York, 1943), p. 440.

[38] Arthur Krock, *New York Times Magazine*, July 18, 1943, p. 37; Langer and Gleason, *The Challenge to Isolation*, p. 198.

[39] Alsop and Kintner, *American White Paper*, pp. 59, 68.

France can't quit, whether they would like to or not and I am convinced, because I live here, that England will go down fighting. Unfortunately, I am one who does not believe that it is going to do the slightest bit of good in this case."[40] Later in the year he declared that morale in England and France was low, economic conditions wretched, and that the people yearned for an early peace.[41] Communism was just around the corner. He had very little idea what the war was being fought for, he told one British journalist, and nobody else seemed much more enlightened in this respect.[42]

His thoughts seemed to turn rather frequently to the past. The British people did not adequately appreciate Chamberlain; they should erect a bust to him for the services he had rendered at Munich. After all, the time won by the sacrifice of Czechoslovakia had given Britain the opportunity to rearm. Still, he doubted whether enough could be done to turn the tide. The Nazis were too clever, British industry too inefficient, the air raids too disruptive. In each phase of the war he predicted the direst consequences for England. In 1939 he discovered that the Germans were building submarines faster than the Royal Navy could sink them; the Luftwaffe, for its part, was outstripping the RAF both in quality and in quantity.[43] During the Norwegian campaign he discanted at length on the lack of preparedness in the military establishment and the inefficiency of the government. On the eve of Dunkirk he announced that only a miracle could save the British expeditionary forces from being wiped out.[44] When the miracle occurred he began to evoke the nemesis of the Luftwaffe. So heavy did the gloom become that the President felt impelled to write him: "when the real world forces come into conflict, the final result is never as dark as we mortals guess it in very difficult days."[45]

But Kennedy was beyond the reach of comforting words. Hitler's progress merely deepened his conviction that American interests would be most effectively served by a policy of neutrality and isolation. He became increasingly vocal on this score as the war unfolded and Allied fortunes deteriorated. Only by making the Western Hemisphere an isolated fortress, set off from the madness of Europe and Asia, was there

---

[40] Langer and Gleason, *The Challenge to Isolation*, pp. 251-252.
[41] *ibid.*, p. 345.
[42] George Bilainkin, *Diary of a Diplomatic Correspondent* (London, 1942), pp. 58-60.
[43] Langer and Gleason, *The Challenge to Isolation*, p. 345.
[44] *Memoirs of Cordell Hull*, I, 763; Langer and Gleason, *The Challenge to Isolation*, p. 466.
[45] *F. D. R., His Personal Letters, 1928-1945*, II, 1020.

any hope of preserving the values to which he was so deeply attached. The idea permeated his dispatches, speeches, and conversations; but only later did it come to dominate him wholly. In 1939 and 1940 Britain was still more important than Iceland. He had stayed too long in England not to be affected by the struggle; the thought of abandoning so many friends must have tormented him often. His relations with Chamberlain remained excellent; one of his last acts before retiring from the embassy was to call on the dying statesman.[46] Even Churchill, that "raconteur of history," so different in temperament and outlook from his predecessor, could occasionally arouse Kennedy's sympathy and enthusiasm. The ambassador admitted that the United States must show consideration for its friends; and, although not much consulted, he found it in himself to advocate measures of aid to Britain from time to time. Rifles and ammunition after Dunkirk, and fifty destroyers, were not too much to give, and principle might be abated in favor of limited lend-lease.[47]

For the most part, however, his heart was not in the fight. Peace remained his goal, even if it meant the domination of Europe by the Nazis. Just as he had proposed isolation for the United States, so he favored a compromise peace between Britain and Germany. Only eleven days after the beginning of the war he opined that "this situation may crystallize to a point where the President can be the savior of the world. The British Government as such certainly cannot accept any agreement with Hitler, but there may be a point when the President himself may work out plans for world peace."[48] The German attack in the West only increased his interest in the subject; but now he feared that opinion in England had so hardened against Hitler that the populace would gleefully reject any German offer of compromise. An even more horrifying thought struck him. The British, buoyed up by aid from the United States, might go on rejecting a settlement in anticipation of eventual American intervention. With this in mind he repeatedly warned Washington: "Don't let anybody make any mistake; this war, from Great Britain's point of view, is being conducted from now on with their eyes only on one place and that is the United States. Unless there is a miracle, they realize that they haven't a chance in the long run."[49] His warnings went unheeded. By July 1940 the great swing in American sentiment and policy had already occurred. The Destroyer Deal was

---

[46] Bilainkin, *Diary of a Diplomatic Correspondent*, p. 214.
[47] Langer and Gleason, *The Challenge to Isolation*, p. 493.
[48] *ibid.*, p. 249.   [49] *ibid.*, pp. 491, 711-712.

about to be consummated and Lend-Lease lay just over the horizon. Kennedy had lost his battle and he appeared sick and disillusioned. In October he relinquished his post and returned to the United States, there to observe and protest. By the time that Winant replaced him in London a new era in Anglo-American relations had opened. To Kennedy's dismay and disappointment the United States was becoming far more than merely considerate of its friends.

Bullitt, too, ultimately joined the ranks of the dissenters from Roosevelt's foreign policy. But his loss of faith and influence was to occur much later on and for wholly different reasons. From the autumn of 1938 until well after his retirement from the French embassy in the summer of 1940, he acted as one of the most enthusiastic supporters— and, on occasion, initiators—of the administration's policy. In retrospect this is hardly surprising for it is clear that where Bullitt differed from Kennedy was in the character of his perspectives. They were more cosmopolitan.

It is probably true that Bullitt lacked any studied and reasoned conception of international politics; he therefore had difficulty in evaluating the trend of events before the crisis over Czechoslovakia: there were too many conflicting strains to disentangle and comprehend by intuitive means. But intuition, intelligence, and wide experience enabled him to see clearly after the rude shock of Munich. The situation had suddenly simplified itself; Hitler's excursions assumed an orderly if ugly pattern. The threat to his beloved France now stood forth in stark and ominous outline; a great many of his most influential acquaintances were turning their backs on appeasement; the days of illusion had passed. In fact, Bullitt saw the new dispensation so clearly that he fell prey to every rumor about German intentions and sent clouds of excited dispatches to Washington. His perturbation was understandable. The time left to practice the arts of diplomacy was uncommonly short.

Although Bullitt still nourished the hope that a peace with honor might yet prevail, he now appreciated that its realization would depend, not on the kind of mediatory gestures that he had advocated before Munich, but on the organization of a strong front against Germany. He was also becoming aware of the shortage of materials with which to accomplish the task. French ties with Britain needed strengthening; the British themselves required prodding, particularly in the matter of conscription; and the Anglo-French coalition cried out for accretions of strength, even if that involved an approach to the Soviet Union. He doubted that one could rely much on treaties with the Russians but agreed with Daladier that no stone should be left unturned, "even though one might expect to find vermin under it." His personal feeling was that if Herriot went to negotiate a treaty in Moscow he should be accompanied by someone as unscrupulous as the Bolsheviks.[50]

Bullitt combined this interest in the foreign relations of France with a growing concern about her military capabilities. During the Czechoslovak crisis he had believed that, despite the quality of the German air arm, the French army was the finest in the world.[51] Now he was no longer so sure: the disparities in aerial strength disturbed him. He had begun to delve into the problem of French plane production as early as the spring of 1938. After Munich he attacked it with all his great vitality. The French obviously could not mobilize sufficient resources to match the Luftwaffe at an early date, and the British would be unable to fill the gap by themselves. The Spitfires and Hurricanes were only beginning to come off the assembly lines in quantity and the RAF had gaping holes in its own organization. The only other source of supply lay in the factories of the United States. Bullitt plunged into the business of making these resources available as quickly as possible. He saw the President in Washington on October 13 and presented the case for expanded plane production by the United States. Roosevelt immediately endorsed his view, and in December a French purchasing mission slipped into New York, the first of what was soon to become a plethora of such agencies.[52]

The effort to overcome French deficiencies in the air may well have suggested to Bullitt a conception of the role that the United States could play in relation to Europe. He told the President that Britain and France constituted the first line of American defenses. Since the policy of appeasing Germany no longer offered any possibility of success, it would therefore be to the interest of the United States, not only to denounce Nazi aggression and rearm, but also to act as a military arsenal for the democracies. Roosevelt, who was becoming increasingly impatient with the passive role envisaged by the State Department, happily accepted Bullitt's reasoning and indicated to Congress, in his message of January 4, 1939, that, in the event of war, he would throw America's material support to the side of Britain and France.[53]

The German occupation of Prague and Memel, and the Italian seizure of Albania, left Bullitt feeling that even this position might not suffice

[50] ibid., p. 70.
[51] British Documents, 3rd series, II, 218-219.
[52] Langer and Gleason, The Challenge to Isolation, pp. 37-38.
[53] ibid., p. 58.

to protect American interests. He had tired of the moral strictures with which Roosevelt, Hull, and Welles were raking the enemy and wanted action of a more concrete order. Here, however, he was on uncertain ground. He knew, as he continually told the French, that the likelihood of American participation in a war against Germany was very small. It is not clear, in fact, whether he yet saw the need for the United States to throw all its power and energy into the balance. As late as March 1939, he still seemed to think of the problem of deterring Hitler primarily in European terms. The task of actually standing up to Germany lay with Britain, France, and the Soviet Union.[54] But the consequences of their not doing so, he realized, would be serious for the United States. He therefore begged the President to denounce the latest Nazi aggression and ask Congress for repeal of the neutrality laws.[55] After Mussolini's occupation of Albania he urged that Italian funds in the United States be frozen; he also warned that the time for words had passed. The only response of the administration was the Haydnesque "Saturday surprise" message of April 15, a symphony of words in which the President asked Hitler and Mussolini to guarantee the independence of certain European states believed to be in immediate danger.[56]

It was a discouraging prospect for Bullitt, who had at last realized that for Americans "the acceptance of war is a less horrible alternative than the acceptance of enslavement."[57] But what was there left for him to do? He turned his energies to the improvement of Anglo-French and Anglo-Soviet relations and to the prognostication of impending catastrophe. In the final crisis of August 1939, he contented himself with getting the last-minute Presidential messages to the various heads of states phrased in such a manner that the onus for starting the war would fall squarely on Hitler.[58] Although occasionally, even at this late date, he may have slipped back into the contemporary delusion that diplomatic gestures would somehow alter Hitler's purpose, for the most part he stuck to the position that the contest had resolved itself into a struggle between the big battalions, of which France and England had too few. But since Washington refused to look this fact directly in the face, he could do no more than await the arrival of a new set of events to prove his contention.

[54] H. L. Trefousse, *Germany and American Neutrality, 1939-1941* (New York, 1951), p. 20.
[55] Langer and Gleason, *The Challenge to Isolation*, pp. 66-67.
[56] *ibid.*, pp. 81-82, 84.
[57] Louis Fischer, *Men and Politics* (New York, 1941), p. 592.
[58] *Memoirs of Cordell Hull*, I, 662.

Once the war had started these were not long in forthcoming. The pace of the Nazi blitzkrieg, the Soviet occupation of eastern Poland, and the massing of the victorious German armies on the western frontiers of the Reich were ominous enough. Even worse was the showing of the French forces when they took the field. Their mobilization and deployment, combined with a winter of stagnation, showed how far the finest army in Europe had deteriorated since the first world war. General Gamelin remained serene and confident but Bullitt could not share his optimism. The havoc wrought by the German panzers in Poland, a tour of the Maginot Line, and the confused state of the French services of supply left him more than ever persuaded that the Allied cause would fail without large-scale assistance from the United States. At one point he even expressed the fear that Britain and France might collapse before American production could be brought into play.[59] Unlike Kennedy, however, he did not permit this conclusion to cool his enthusiasm for a bold American policy. He encouraged the French to follow more aggressive purchasing policies in the American market; at the same time he was in the forefront of those advising repeal of the arms embargo. The matter of plane production remained a source of continued interest to him. So did the awakening of his countrymen to the dangers that surrounded them. On his return to the United States late in 1939 he complained that Americans were "still in the state of mind of England before Munich."[60] Although he may have hoped that American material aid, however late in arriving, might yet shift the balance of power in favor of Britain and France, and that American military intervention would not be necessary, he no longer doubted that the United States should be ready and willing to act outside its own backyard. Even if the British and French managed to make their way alone, it would be a close-run thing.

An awareness of this delicacy of balance, and of the odds working against the Allies, did not prevent him from reviving his bitter hostility to the Soviet Union. Although the policies of the Kremlin had done much to precipitate the German invasion of Poland, it is not clear, even in retrospect, that any hostile act short of an attack on Russia itself would have brought the Soviet Union into the war. In 1939 and 1940, however, it seemed that Stalin might yet choose sides, and many well informed and experienced people therefore believed that it would be well to act with discretion toward Moscow. Bullitt did not share this view.

[59] Langer and Gleason, *The Challenge to Isolation*, p. 219.
[60] Davis and Lindley, *How War Came*, p. 51.

When the Red army invaded Finland he sprang into action. Despite his knowledge that Germany by herself was almost more than a match for Britain and France, he was instrumental behind the scenes in having the Finnish case brought before Geneva; and he urged the United States to participate in the act of expelling the Soviet Union from the League.[61] The expulsion, in which Hull refused to share, left no apparent mark on the armor of the Soviet mind; but it was a daring step to advocate at a time when another weight on the Nazi side of the scale might have proved fatal to the cause in which Bullitt was now inextricably involved.

On the subject of Italy he adopted a more calculated attitude. Although Mussolini was bedazzled by Hitler's success, and far more likely to support him than was Stalin, Bullitt continually harped on the desirability of keeping the Italians out of the war. His own ideas as to how this should be done took shape in a wide variety of proposals. At first he thought that measures such as repeal of the arms embargo might suffice to deter the Duce.[62] But after the German attack in the West he moved into bolder spheres. "It occurs to me," he cabled in May, "that nothing would have a greater restraining influence on Mussolini than a genuine fear that the Pope might leave Rome and take refuge in a neutral country."[63] Another thought was that the Pope might be persuaded to threaten the Duce with excommunication.[64] His interest, at a more mundane level, centered on the American fleet in the Atlantic. At various times he suggested sending it on courtesy calls to Greece, Lisbon, and Tangier. On May 29, with the French position growing desperate, he pleaded directly with the President: "Al Capone will enter war about fourth of June, unless you can throw the fear of the U.S.A. into him. About U.S. opinion I know nothing, but the only hope in my opinion is for the rest of the Atlantic Fleet to follow" the three ships which had already gone to Lisbon. "There are United States interests in Tangier, after all. If, as I believe, Al Capone is going to try to get to Tangier, why not get there before him with something good?" Unfortunately, Mussolini had no intention of going to Tangier and the President was unwilling to spare the Atlantic Fleet.[65] On June 10, when Italy declared war on France, Reynaud commented to Bullitt: "What really distinguished, noble and admirable persons the Italians are, to stab us in the

---

[61] Langer and Gleason, *The Challenge to Isolation,* p. 333.
[62] *Memoirs of Cordell Hull,* I, 693.
[63] Langer and Gleason, *The Challenge to Isolation,* p. 459.
[64] *Memoirs of Cordell Hull,* I, 781.
[65] Langer and Gleason, *The Challenge to Isolation,* p. 462.

back at this moment." Beyond promising all material aid to the Allies, and a rapid increase in the pace of American rearmament, Roosevelt could do no more than turn this phrase into his celebrated denunciation of Mussolini's act.[66]

American assistance to France herself was of a similarly limited character. The German breakthrough at Sedan on May 14 had exposed those weaknesses in the French military machine which Bullitt had so accurately foreseen. In a frantic effort to stave off disaster the ambassador pleaded once more for planes, ships, and denunciations. But everything was in short supply except words, and they proved useless against Rundstedt's armored spearheads. Sumner Welles complained that the flood of suggestions from Paris was "something fantastic."[67] And so it must have seemed to one not so closely identified with the struggle as Bullitt. To him the collapse of France was more than a catastrophic loss to the Allied cause; it was a personal tragedy. Even so, once it became clear that defeat was certain, the ambassador acted with remarkable energy to salvage what he could from the wreckage. He succeeded in getting a portion of France's gold reserve out of the country; he also obtained pledges from Reynaud, Pétain, Darlan, and others that the French would not surrender their fleet intact to the Nazis. And, despite the pain that such a duty must have caused him, he obeyed his instructions from the State Department to inform Reynaud that a declaration of war by the United States, or even the clouds of planes that the Premier had demanded, were out of the question.

The last days of free France must have proved especially agonizing. The surrender of the Belgian army under King Leopold, the British evacuation at Dunkirk, and the final collapse of French resistance followed one another in quick succession while Bullitt stood helplessly by. In angry frustration he lashed out at the British. Their refusal to send more planes to France was more reprehensible than the defection of Leopold. To Roosevelt and Hull he even communicated the suspicion that the British were conserving their air force and fleet as bargaining counters for future negotiations with Hitler.[68]

One last gallant gesture nevertheless remained. Over Hull's protests he stayed on in Paris, after the French government had fled, in order to receive the conquerors and prevent the sack of the city. After two weeks of Prussian correctness, he went down to Clermont-Ferrand, ob-

---

[66] *ibid.*, p. 515.   [67] *ibid.*, p. 489.
[68] William L. Langer, *Our Vichy Gamble* (New York, 1947), p. 18; *Memoirs of Cordell Hull*, I, 774.

served the beginnings of the Vichy regime, and then departed for home. He arrived in time to find Frank Knox appointed Secretary of the Navy in his stead, to help formulate the American policy toward Pétain, and to support wholeheartedly the measures by which the United States began to project its weight into the tottering European balance.

IV

Although the views and recommendations of Bullitt and Kennedy thus came to diverge sharply, it is the similarity between them rather than the differences separating them which is most interesting for the historian. This, of course, is particularly true for the period before Munich. Both men had difficulty in evaluating the German threat; both found it hard to believe that the traditional methods of diplomacy might fail of results. And, although they both placed a high value on peace, neither envisaged a role for the United States in its preservation. By the time that they had become fully cognizant of the gravity of the European situation, the chances of deterring Hitler had declined radically. Yet even so, Kennedy never, and Bullitt only tardily, acknowledged the need for an active and forceful policy by the United States. With the contacts that they had, the incomparable sources of information at their disposal, and positions of influence in Paris, London, and Washington, they had many opportunities to accelerate American appreciation of and adjustment to the increasing responsibilities of the United States. It is not unfair to say that they did not make the most of their opportunities. To make such a judgment, however, is to say very little. More important, and more interesting, are the reasons why their perceptions were so tardy, their points of view eventually so divergent, and their recommendations often so little related to what, in retrospect, appear to have been the exigencies of the situation. Here, of course, we can only speculate.

No doubt the personalities, temperaments, and previous experiences of the two men played their part. Kennedy, coming from the specialized atmosphere of the business world, found it particularly difficult to adapt his thinking to the complex discourse of international politics. His tendency, naturally, was to apply to the new game the rules and techniques he had learned in another arena, however impracticable in the long run they might prove to be. But even Bullitt, with a wider range of interests and the advantage of greater experience in the field, encountered similar difficulties of adjustment. He has been variously described as a *Childe Harold*, a romantic revolutionary, a lover of causes:

impatient and inclined to be governed by his emotions.[69] Perhaps these characteristics prevented him, as a business background may have prevented Kennedy, from appreciating the nature and extent of Europe's danger.

Their location in London and Paris, and the volume of business which confronted them in their embassies, surely must have contributed to their confusion. They moved, for the most part, in a society that thought in terms similar to their own, and they both tended to assume the coloration of their environment. Churchill might describe Chamberlain as a town clerk looking at the situation in Europe through the wrong end of a municipal drain pipe, but Kennedy found in him a congenial and sympathetic personality. Bullitt seems to have thought equally well of Daladier until the disasters of 1940. Instead of influencing they were influenced, took their cues from the heads of the governments to which they were accredited, and issued reports and recommendations in much the same style as did Whitehall and the Quai d'Orsay. There is, in fact, an extraordinary similarity between their views in 1938 and 1939 and the views of the British and French governments. The failures of vision on the part of Chamberlain and Daladier almost seemed to transmit themselves through Kennedy and Bullitt to act as a serious constraint on the President.

The reliance of Kennedy and Bullitt on these sources is understandable. They were both executives, accustomed to rapid decision—men of action rather than contemplative students of affairs. Their duties were diverse, imposing, and never-ending. In the constant stream of reports, speeches, social calls, and receptions there was little opportunity for reflection and analysis. The demands upon their time were already enormous. Moreover, the situation which they had to evaluate was extremely complex. The problem of Germany, while the most urgent, was not the only one that confronted them. Italy barked at their heels; the Soviet Union loomed menacingly across at them; and, in the distance, Japan stretched out a grasping hand. By contrast, Britain and France were weak; they suffered from internal differences, confused leadership, and doubts about the justice of their cause. The United States was aloof, disarmed, and preoccupied with domestic problems. So disorderly was the perspective, particularly before Munich, that even a simple and stable personality like Lord Halifax suffered from nightmares reminiscent of Kafka. As Kennedy lamented, there were no perfect plans, no

[69] See, for example, Alsop and Kintner, *American White Paper*, p. 13; and Martha Dodd, *Through Embassy Eyes* (New York, 1939), pp. 178-180.

simple solutions. To every course of action there was attached the possibility of an undesirable consequence. Bullitt and Kennedy had both breathed the political atmosphere long enough to be conscious of the pitfalls inherent in long-range planning and unpopular policies. It was only natural, therefore, that they should have eschewed such modes of thought. The short-run, the tentative, and the popular were bound to attract men who had risen by political preference, particularly if they aspired to rise still higher.

But these were not the only factors. The American tradition of isolation hung over them like a cloud; it obscured their vision and shackled their thought. Kennedy never was able to break with the tradition, and even Bullitt, with all his sensitiveness and quick intuition, found it difficult to do so. Europe, the eternal battleground with its interminable quarrels, seemed so remote and so incomprehensible. Why should America intervene, and what could she accomplish if she did? The answers, in 1938, were neither simple nor obvious and the question died hard.

The State Department did little to kill it. The men in the upper reaches of the departmental hierarchy were for the most part intelligent and able public servants. But during this period they had become the prisoners of a doctrine that had little sense and less utility. This doctrine, repeated as an article of faith by all good foreign service officers, proclaimed that the State Department made policy, but that policy was a function of the reports coming in from abroad.[70] The idea had theoretical merits: it defined areas of responsibility, gave the State Department ultimate control over policy formation, and at the same time assigned a key role to the foreign service officer. In practice, however, the doctrine produced two unfortunate consequences. The first was that the State Department and President awaited events from abroad to formulate their policy. They rarely initiated a strategy dictated by some conception of American interests; rather were they the pawns of situations created by others. Foresight, the definition of objectives, planning, all were impossible as long as American foreign policy was a tail wagged by a European or Asiatic dog.

This meant, inevitably, that the diplomat abroad, as the principal source of information for the State Department, was in a position actually to shape policy; for what he said, and how he said it, would influence the nature and orientation of departmental thought. Yet doctrine ex-

[70] Typical expressions of the doctrine may be found in Alsop and Kintner, *American White Paper*, pp. 3-4; and James Rives Child, *American Foreign Service* (New York, 1948), pp. 35-36.

pressly forbade him to make policy; his duty was to report and perhaps to evaluate the information that he purveyed. Here, then, was the doctrine's second consequence. Since policy was made on the basis of the cables, no criteria existed by which the diplomat could determine what was relevant to put into the cables. In an immense sea of fact and supposition, without a sense of direction, without any indication of what they ought to look for—with the admonition merely to observe and report—is it any wonder that Kennedy and Bullitt should have had difficulty in orienting themselves to their respective situations? They could obtain little or no guidance from the State Department, except in matters of detail, because for the most part the Department did not know where it was going. The result was the interlocking confusion and paralysis that characterized American foreign policy in the period of Munich. Lacking in direction from above, Bullitt and Kennedy could only rely on their own sense and intuition to report back what might prove useful. And the State Department, depending on the cables to give it impulse, found itself beset with chitchat, rumor, and irresponsible prediction. These were hardly propitious circumstances in which to cope with the dynamism of Germany and Japan.

In default of guidance from above, Bullitt and Kennedy might have expected to receive competent advice from below. Both were served by staffs of professional diplomats presumably skilled in observation, analysis, recommendation, and tactics. Could they not find here a fund of knowledge and experience that would compensate for their own shortcomings and the deficiencies of the State Department? The answer, generally, is no. With the exception of a few skilled professionals like Henderson, Grew, and Messersmith, the foreign service officer had remarkably little to offer in the way of useful advice and assistance. Indeed, most of the faults attributable to Bullitt and Kennedy derive from the sterility which characterized the thought of the professional diplomat during the interwar period. No doubt his exclusion from a significant role in the events of the 1920's and early 1930's had prevented him from refining his craft. But his problem was more complicated than that. One of the great tragedies of both Europe and Asia, as well as of the United States, during this period was that the professional diplomat had lost contact with the world in which he lived. His universe was that of the eighteenth and nineteenth centuries, and it bore little relation to the revolutionary cosmos of which Nazi Germany, Fascist Italy, Soviet Russia, and Imperial Japan were parts.

The failure for so long to grasp the true nature of Hitler Germany, the tragic voyages of Chamberlain to Godesberg and Munich, the unworldly belief of Sumner Welles that a conference on norms of international behavior might alter the trend of events, the suggestion that the President and Prince Konoye might resolve Japanese-American differences by meeting somewhere in the Pacific, the frantic search for peace by Kennedy, Bullitt's recommendation that the Pope should be brought to the United States as a means of preventing Mussolini from entering the war—all this was symptomatic of something more than stupidity, wrongheadedness, or ideological blindness. In more instances than not, the good intentions were present; what was lacking was the boldness of vision and conception to convert these intentions into effective policy. Professional diplomats, despite the many rebuffs that they suffered in the interwar period, were in positions everywhere to provide the political leaders with effective advice on this score. That they did not do so is ample testimony to the low estate into which their art had fallen.

In view of the factors militating against a rapid and vivid appreciation of the situation in Europe, what is surprising about Bullitt and Kennedy is not that they performed so badly, but that they did not do worse. Although theoretically they were in positions to exert great influence on the State Department and the President—if not in shaping basic trends, at least in clarifying issues and indicating directions in which it would be desirable to move—in practice this was too much to ask or expect of them. The obstacles raised by personality and background, the complexity of the situation, the milieu in which they moved, and the American tradition of isolation: these might have been overcome, as Bullitt eventually overcome them, if only the theory of statecraft and diplomacy had kept pace with the times. Without such a theory, without a tested device by which Americans could measure and protect their interests, without even a tradition such as the one that lifted Churchill to such brilliant heights, the United States could only grope and fumble, first as a spectator, then as a cautious partisan, until Pearl Harbor projected her into the fray.

List of Contributors

··

ELIZABETH R. CAMERON is a former teacher of European history at Bryn Mawr College. She has been given a Fulbright Travel Grant to enable her to pursue her studies on recent French diplomatic history. She is author of *Prologue to Appeasement*.

RICHARD D. CHALLENER is Assistant Professor of History at Princeton University. He is author of "The Military Defeat of 1940 in Retrospect" in E. M. Earle (ed.), *Modern France: Problems of the Third and Fourth Republics*.

GORDON A. CRAIG is Professor of History at Princeton University. He was collaborating editor of and contributor to *Makers of Modern Strategy: Military Thought from Machiavelli to Hitler* and is author of articles on military and diplomatic subjects.

RODERIC H. DAVISON is Associate Professor of European History at the George Washington University. He is author of articles on the history of the Near East.

FRANKLIN L. FORD is a member of the Faculty, European history, Bennington College. He has been given a Fulbright Travel Grant to enable him to pursue his studies on French history. He is author of *Robe and Sword: The Re-Grouping of the French Aristocracy after Louis XIV*.

FELIX GILBERT is Professor of History at Bryn Mawr College. He was collaborating editor of and contributor to *Makers of Modern Strategy* and editor of *Hitler Directs His War*.

HAJO HOLBORN is Townsend Professor of History at Yale University. He is the author of numerous historical books, the most recent being *The Political Collapse of Europe*.

H. STUART HUGHES is Associate Professor of History at Stanford University. He is author of *An Essay for our Time* and *Spengler*.

JOHN HUIZENGA was, until recently, when he transferred to another department of the government, a member of the Board of Editors of *Documents on German Foreign Policy, 1918-1945*.

WILLIAM W. KAUFMANN is a research associate in the Center of International Studies at Princeton University. He is author of *British Policy and the Independence of Latin America, 1804-1828*.

[682]

THEODORE H. VON LAUE is Lecturer in European History at Bryn Mawr and Swarthmore Colleges. He is author of *Leopold Ranke: The Formative Years.*

ERIK LÖNNROTH is Professor of History at the University of Uppsala, Sweden. In 1951, he was Visiting Professor at Princeton University.

DEXTER PERKINS, Watson Professor of History at the University of Rochester, is author of numerous works on American diplomatic history, including four volumes on the Monroe Doctrine and a series of essays on the American Approach to Foreign Policy.

HENRY L. ROBERTS is Assistant Professor of History at Columbia University. He is author of *Rumania: The Political Problems of an Agrarian State.*

CARL E. SCHORSKE is Associate Professor of History at Wesleyan University, Middletown, Conn. He is author (with Hoyt Price) of *The Problem of Germany.*

HENRY R. WINKLER is Associate Professor of History at Rutgers University. He is author of *The League of Nations Movement in Great Britain, 1914-1919.*

PAUL E. ZINNER is a fellow at the Russian Research Center, Harvard University, and author of articles on eastern European problems.

Index

Printed in the United States
22191LVS00002B/215

9 780691 036601